BY MITCHELL LEASKA

The Novels of Virginia Woolf:
From Beginning to End

Virginia Woolf's Lighthouse:
A Study in Critical Method

The Voice of Tragedy

AS EDITOR

The Pargiters:
The Essay-Novel Portion of *The Years*

Pointz Hall:
The Earlier and Later Typescripts of *Between the Acts*

The Virginia Woolf Reader

A Passionate Apprentice:
The Early Journals of Virginia Woolf
1897–1909

AS CO-EDITOR

The Letters of Vita Sackville-West to Virginia Woolf

Violet to Vita:
The Letters of Violet Trefusis to Vita Sackville-West

GRANITE AND RAINBOW

GRANITE AND RAINBOW

THE HIDDEN LIFE OF VIRGINIA WOOLF

MITCHELL LEASKA

PICADOR

First published 1998 by Farrar, Straus and Giroux, New York

First published in Great Britain 1998 by Picador
an imprint of Macmillan Publishers Ltd
25 Eccleston Place, London SW1W 9NF
and Basingstoke

Associated companies throughout the world

ISBN 0 330 35436 1

Permissions Acknowledgements

Excerpts from *The Diary of Virginia Woolf*, Volumes I–V edited by Anne Olivier Bell, copyright © 1977, 1978, 1980, 1982, 1984 by Quentin Bell and Angelica Garnett; *The Letters of Virginia Woolf*, Volumes I–VI edited by Nigel Nicolson and Joanne Trautmann, copyright © 1975, 1976, 1977, 1978, 1979, 1980 by Quentin Bell and Angelica Garnett; *The Letters of Leonard Woolf* edited by Frederic Spotts, copyright © 1989 by the Estate of Leonard Woolf; *Moments of Being* by Virginia Woolf, copyright © 1976 by Quentin Bell and Angelica Garnett; *A Passionate Apprentice: The Early Journals of Virginia Woolf*, edited by Mitchell A. Leaska, copyright © 1990 by Quentin Bell and Angelica Garnett; *To the Lighthouse* by Virginia Woolf, copyright 1927 by Harcourt Brace and Company and renewed 1954 by Leonard Woolf; *Virginia Woolf: A Biography*, copyright © 1972 by Quentin Bell, all reprinted by permission of Harcourt Brace & Company. Every effort has been made to contact copyright holders of material reproduced in this book. If any have been inadvertently overlooked, the publishers will be pleased to make restitution at the earliest opportunity.

1 3 5 7 9 8 6 4 2

A CIP catalogue record for this book is available from
the British Library.

Printed and bound in Great Britain by
Mackays of Chatham plc, Chatham, Kent

Frontispiece: Viginia upstairs in sitting room at Monks House

ACKNOWLEDGMENTS

First I should like to thank the authors and publishers from whose works brief quotations or references appear in this text as specifically acknowledged in the endnotes. I also record here my debt to the editors of the *Diary* (1977–84), Anne Olivier Bell and Andrew McNeillie; and of the *Letters* (1975–80), Nigel Nicolson and Joanne Trautmann Banks. This debt extends to the late Quentin Bell for his *Virginia Woolf: A Biography* (1972); Leonard Woolf for his five-volume *Autobiography* (1960–69); Nigel Nicolson for *Portrait of a Marriage* (1973); and Angelica Garnett for *Deceived with Kindness* (1983).

Thanks are also extended to the Society of Authors and to the Executors of the Virginia Woolf Estate for permission to quote from a wide range of previously published and unpublished works; to Anne Olivier Bell and the Hogarth Press for permission to use the Family Tree designed for the *Diary*; to the British Library for permission to quote from extracts of the letters of Julia Duckworth; to Marvin Taylor, Curator of the Fales Library, at New York University, for making available material about Octavia Wilberforce; to Rodney Phillips, Curator, and Steven Crook of the Henry W. and Albert A. Berg Collection of American and English Literature of The New York Public Library, Astor, Lenox and Tilden Foundations, for access to the letters of Leslie Stephen; and to John W. Bicknell for furnishing me with transcripts of a portion of those letters. Harcourt Brace and Company, Virginia Woolf's American publishers, also kindly granted me permission to quote from her published works.

During my graduate study at New York University many years ago, Louise Rosenblatt taught me to pay close attention to readers of literature in the process of meaning-making, and Leon Edel did much to de-mystify that strange dynamic by which certain men and women create novels and poems and plays; this book is a very small token of appreciation to them both for those valuable early lessons.

While this work was in progress, I had the benefit of two sabbatical leaves of absence, and I want to document here my thanks to Dean Ann Marcus and Associate Dean W. Gabriel Carras for making both possible. I have had the good fortune to work with Jonathan Galassi, Aoibheann Sweeney, and Ethan Nosowsky of Farrar, Straus and Giroux; whatever thanks I may offer for their generous advice and unfailing goodwill must remain inadequate to the full measure they are due. As always, John Hochmann, my agent, who first suggested that I write this biography, has been everything an author could wish, so that my thanks to him must likewise remain fragmentary. And, finally, I doff my cap to the students at New York University who never once gave me the benefit of the doubt.

M.L.
New York
March 1997

For Leon Edel and Louise Rosenblatt

CONTENTS

Consider one's own life; pass under review a few years that one has actually lived. Conceive how Lord Morley would have expounded them; how Sir Sidney Lee would have documented them; how strangely all that has been most real in them would have slipped through their fingers. Nor can we name the biographer whose art is subtle and bold enough to present that queer amalgamation of dream and reality, that perpetual marriage of granite and rainbow.

Virginia Woolf
October 30, 1927

INTRODUCTION

In the opening pages of her "Sketch of the Past," begun in April 1939, Virginia Woolf described herself as a child of about six standing on tiptoe to look at herself in a looking glass, which she did only if she was alone. It was something she was ashamed of. The reason or reasons for that shame were not made clear, but "the looking-glass shame has lasted all my life . . . I cannot powder my nose in public. Everything to do with dress . . . still frightens me; at least makes me shy, self-conscious, uncomfortable." Many years earlier, however, on February 24, 1905, to be exact, she had installed a great mirror in the most important spot in her room. The purchase is recorded in her journal: "Out and bought fire irons . . . to match my fender, which is a source of great joy to me. Also I bought that great looking glass, which will just fill the space over my writing table."

There is a reason for recalling this inconsistency. A decade or so after her death, Clive Bell predicted that Virginia Woolf's letters and diaries would eventually be published; and "fascinating" as they might be, her accounts of what people did and said, he warned, "may be flights of her airy imagination" and ought to be read in that spirit. Her documents, in other words, were not entirely trustworthy. One evening long after her death, he recalls Leonard Woolf's reading passages from her diary to a group of close friends. In the course of the reading, Leonard suddenly stopped in mid-sentence. Clive guessed, accurately as it turned out, that Leonard had come upon a passage that would mortify some of the people present. Yes, that was the reason for stopping, said Leonard. But he was going to skip ahead in the diary because he saw that the pages he was reading didn't have "a word of truth in them." Clive Bell thus felt moved to warn "a vast posterity of enchanted readers to be on their guard."

There are already seven or eight biographies of Virginia Woolf in existence and an even greater number of critical studies. The moment we ask which of these is the "real" life, which the "correct" interpretation, we are forced to confront the question of how one makes sense, makes meaning, in a limitless world of data. If the surviving facts of Shakespeare's life and the total body of his plays and poems had one and only one meaning, then we should have one enduring biography and one and only one complete body of critical readings of the plays. But even a cursory glance at the sagging shelves in public libraries reveals more than a hundred biographies and an even greater number of volumes of criticism. The same is true of Dickens and Austen and Henry James and a great many other writers. Interpretations of identical source material differ as widely as reviews of the same novel differ in literary journalism. Meaning, one inevitably concludes, ultimately does not reside in the text alone: a substantial part of the sense one makes of *any* artifact derives in part from the epistemological history of the particular reader, at a particular time and place, under a particular set of circumstances.

The same holds true for biographers. They interpret the lives they are reconstructing largely under the influence of their own private repertoire of experience and history and values and assumptions about the world. Try to imagine a biography of Adolf Hitler written by Oskar Schindler and the point becomes clearer. Biographers have always brought to the lives they are re-creating their own preoccupations and "shoulds" and notions of right and wrong. It is the natural thing to do. That is to say, just as there is no such thing as a generic reader, so there is no such thing as "objective" reporting so long as the process involves human perception—a perceiving "I."

"Who was I then?" Virginia Woolf asked herself toward the end of her life. "Adeline Virginia Stephen, the second daughter of Leslie and Julia Prinsep Stephen, born on 25th January 1882, descended from a great many people, some famous, others obscure; born into a large connection, born not of rich parents, but of well-to-do parents, born into a very communicative, literate, letter writing, visiting, articulate, late nineteenth century world." By which she meant, Virginia Stephen was brought up in the very sober, Victorian atmosphere of 22 Hyde Park Gate, as the daughter of an elderly man who was wholly committed to the social rules and regulations of his age and class.

Whether she recorded accurately or haphazardly in her journals the details of her life has not been deemed as significant as the way she conveyed her perception of people and places and events. For that experience was *her* truth, the only truth, so far as we are concerned, that mattered. For many reasons which the following pages will show, Virginia Woolf saw the world as polarized and divided. Despite the happiness and wonder in the stumblings of her childhood, it was a world of discord and dissonance. That perception, again, was *her* reality, and therefore the only one of significance.

When her mother died in 1895, Virginia plunged into a depression serious enough to require medical attention. From the few stray remarks Sir Leslie made in his memoir, her condition appears to have been characterized by severe mood fluctuations, alternating between intense nervous irritability and paralyzing melancholy. Her physician at the time diagnosed the condition as neurasthenia, a vague catch-all label applied to a whole range of mental and emotional disorders. It was Leonard Woolf who later described Virginia's illness as fulfilling all the criteria of manic-depressive psychosis, and once satisfied that he was accurate in his diagnosis, he watched over her scrupulously throughout their married life. He realized after living through the nightmare of her 1913 madness and suicide attempt that her condition did not alter the basic core of her personality.

When Virginia was well, Leonard said in his autobiography, "she would discuss her illness; she would recognize that she had been mad, that she had had delusions, heard voices which did not exist, lived for weeks or months in a nightmare world of frenzy, despair, violence." Before marrying him in 1912, apart from her depression of 1895–96 Virginia suffered two other psychotic episodes: one after her father's death in 1904 and another in 1910. After their marriage she collapsed in 1913 and again in 1915, the last of her major periods of madness. Virginia's brother Adrian and his wife Karin Costelloe were both qualified psychoanalysts; and from the early 1920s the Woolfs were Sigmund Freud's publishers. But Virginia never sought help from that quarter of the medical profession. Instead she consulted "nerve specialists."

Many years later, in describing the composition of her autobiographical novel *To the Lighthouse*, she said, when the novel was finished: "I ceased to be obsessed by my mother. I no longer hear her voice; I do not see her. I suppose I did for myself what psycho-analysts do for their patients. I expressed some very long and deeply felt emotion. And in expressing it I explained it and then laid it to rest. But what is the meaning of 'explained' it?" She had no answer to that. Nor, it seems to this day, has anyone else.

Not until 1969 was it known that manic-depressive psychosis was *not* a neurotic process but a genetically transmitted affective disorder that profoundly modifies cognition, sleep patterns, and metabolism. Neuroscientists have since learned that psychotic episodes are associated with a complicated hormonal imbalance which further involves chemicals in all brain functions. A stressful life event, such as the death of a loved one or a parent, for instance, may trigger a manic-depressive episode, without in itself being the primary cause. Equally important was the finding that anyone suffering from the disorder would not respond to any form of psychoanalysis or psychotherapy. Such treatment might be helpful in learning how to live with the condition, but the various therapies do not affect the disease process itself.

The question we're left with is: Does this genetically transmitted disorder account for—indeed "explain"—Virginia Woolf's extraordinary powers as a novelist and essayist? Can we attribute her gift for writing some of the best letters of the century to her illness? Probably not. The manic periods may have accelerated her productivity; they may have helped her to see more intensely, but it seems unlikely that her illness was responsible for the quality of her writing. Many poets have smoked opium, but only one wrote "Kubla Khan."

Virginia set off for Italy in 1908 with Clive and Vanessa, now Mr. and Mrs. Bell, and on the afternoon of September 3 she went to the Collegio del Cambio in Perugia to look at the frescoes by Perugino. In fact she studied them closely. "Each part has a dependence upon the others," she wrote in her journal; "they compose one idea in his mind. That idea has nothing to do with anything to be put into words. A group stands without relation to the figure of God. They have come together then because their lines and colours are related, and express some view of beauty in his brain."

This remarkable observation is worth noting, for Virginia was paying attention to the formal relations of composition; and her remark came close to what Roger Fry, still unknown to her, would articulate later. It was only when an object exists for no other purpose than to be seen, he wrote, that the beholder really begins to look at it. "Those who indulge in this vision," he went on, "are entirely absorbed in apprehending the relation of forms and colour to one another, as they cohere within the object . . . [and] there comes to us, I think, a feeling of purpose; we feel that all these sensually logical conformities are the outcome of a particular feeling, or of what, for want of a better word, we call an idea . . . the expression of an idea in the artist's mind."

But for Virginia in Perugia in September 1908 the relationship of Perugino's form and colors expressed "some view of beauty in his brain." That to her was the important idea; and as a fledgling novelist she too would express beauty, but of another sort: "I attain a different kind of beauty, achieve a symmetry by means of infinite discords, showing all the traces of the mind's passage through the world; and achieve in the end, some kind of whole made of shivering fragments." If her perception of the world consisted of infinite discords and shivering fragments, then her work as a novelist would consist of transforming fragments and discord into wholeness and harmony, of making poetry and song out of prose and parody.

At about this same time, she began to question the capacity of fiction for reflecting the various forms and curvatures of life. What was the truth of fiction? What indeed did such a phrase mean? What was plot? Or narrative line, or visual depiction, or character description? Whatever they were, they were not satisfying. Or real. Somehow they didn't tell the truth. "I should like," she said, "to write not only with the eye, but with the mind; and *discover real things beneath the show**—an almost verbatim restatement of what she was to say thirty years later in her memoir about needing to discover "some *real thing behind appearances.*" Once again, an echo of what Roger Fry would say of Cézanne's "desperate search for the *reality hidden beneath the veil of appearance.*" This aim, when she learned how to achieve it, would become her way of revealing the granite of reality behind her rainbow of words. Only when she got the relations of those "shivering fragments" and "infinite discords" right would she have achieved the thing she set out to do—to create through her art the shimmering, evanescent quality of life itself. "I make it real by putting it into words," she said toward the end of her life. "It is only by putting it into words that I make it whole; this wholeness means that it has lost its power to hurt me; it gives me, perhaps because by doing so I take away the pain, a great delight to put the severed parts together."

The art of fiction thus provided Virginia Woolf with the means of reuniting and reconciling those warring factions she felt so acutely within. Writing also provided her with an open line of communication with the world outside, which threatened increasingly to become entirely private and frighteningly unreal. Fiction became in the end her only connection between the inner and outer worlds. Writing novels permitted her to externalize much of what, locked within, might have remained dissonant, fragmentary, and devastating. It might also be said that Virginia turned instinctively to fiction because there were satisfactions in fantasy that she couldn't find in the real world.

There were many family secrets, paralyzing vulnerabilities, and emotional phantoms in the Stephen ledgers that could only be talked about in hushed voices and darkened rooms. In Virginia Woolf's world, the world of the mind, there was no place for godlike statement, for omniscient narration, which explained motives and indulged in moral digressions. The stories she

---

* All emphases throughout this section have been added.

had to tell permitted no such luxury. Hers must be dramatized; thoughts and feelings must be communicated to the reader without authorial mediation. The reader must make sense of it, deduce character and motive, make meaning of all that has been left unsaid. The finer the perceptions of the fictional people, the harder the reader must work in drawing inferences from the gauzy webs of nuance.

All the novels were created from the past, from family history, augmented and enriched with fertile layers of fantasy; Rachel Vinrace (*The Voyage Out*), motherless, and doomed to a mysterious death when marriage raised its head and lowered Rachel's; Katharine Hilbery (*Night and Day*), trying to work out a life of solitude without loneliness; Jacob Flanders (*Jacob's Room*), fatherless, and emotionally crippled by an adoring and overprotective mother; Clarissa Dalloway and Septimus Warren Smith (*Mrs. Dalloway*), both grappling with socially unsanctioned love and guilt. And it was always to that ancient world of the past and its silent population that she returned throughout her writing life—for "I prefer, where truth is concerned, to write fiction." To make wholeness and harmony out of ancient "fragments" and discords," she learned the delicate art of sublimation—the art of purifying and making socially agreeable something otherwise base and offensive; of conveying not only what people said, but of insinuating the volumes they left unsaid. In this way only could she reach "the real things beneath the show." What, for instance, was the "real thing" behind Clarissa Dalloway and Septimus Warren Smith—the sane Clarissa, the insane Septimus—the polar characters who never meet? To get at the real thing, Virginia Woolf had to work out an exact design of their formal and emotional relations, a design better illustrated than explained.

She found it necessary to assemble two separate sets of images and ideas, one of them belonging to the Clarissa Dalloway story, and the other to that of Septimus Warren Smith. In the novel's first pages, a seemingly random thought crosses Clarissa's mind as she is walking down Bond Street: "She remembered once throwing a shilling into the Serpentine." Her thought has no connection to anything before or after it. But some 268 pages later, when she learns of Septimus's suicide, she returns to her earlier thought, but now with a significant addition: "She had once *thrown a shilling into the Serpentine*, never anything more. But he had thrown it away." In another part of the book, Clarissa recalls her youthful passion for Sally Seton: "But this question of love . . . this falling in love with women. Take Sally Seton . . . Had that not, after all, been love?" The question links up with another thought of Sally— Sally Seton was "beneath this roof!" Clarissa remembered "going cold with excitement . . . going downstairs and feeling as she crossed the hall 'If it were now to die 'twere now to be most happy.' That was her feeling—Othello's feeling, and she felt it . . . as strongly as Shakespeare meant Othello to feel it, all because she was coming down to dinner in a white frock to meet Sally Seton."

Clarissa then turns to Septimus's suicide: "But this young man who killed himself—had he plunged holding his treasure? 'If it were now to die, 'twere now to be most happy,' she had said that to herself once, coming down in white." From these carefully juxtaposed (but seemingly random) memories, we infer that as her love for Sally Seton was her "treasure," so with Septimus there must be a similar love object, his treasure.

The Septimus story is thus introduced. His narrative thread is slighter, subtler, harder to follow. But with the lightness of a poet, Virginia Woolf scatters a separate set of "shivering fragments," a syncopated antiphony of "infinite discords," throughout the text—all connecting with Evans, the officer Septimus loved, who died in Greece by his side. And here Woolf inserts only splinters of memory for the reader to follow: memories of trees; of birds singing in Greek; of Evans singing; of love, universal love; of dogs busy at railings; of dogs "busy with each other." She then finally brings them all together: In the trenches, Septimus "developed manliness; he was promoted; he drew the attention, indeed the affection of his officer, Evans by name. *It was a case of two dogs* playing on a hearth-rug . . . snarling, snapping, giving a pinch now and then at the old dog's ear . . . They had to be together, share with each other, fight with each other." When Evans was killed, Septimus, "far from showing any emotion or recognising that here was the end of a friendship, congratulated himself upon feeling very little and very reasonably."

Thus, through this complex of strategically positioned images, we infer the significance of those relations, which suggest the "real thing behind appearances"—that just as Clarissa has maintained her sanity by bringing to consciousness her socially unacceptable passion for another woman, so Septimus succumbs to madness and suicide because his *un*lawful love for Evans has had to remain buried and unacknowledged. His confession in the doctor's office has been interrupted and his communication failed.

"Communication is health; communication is happiness, communication—" Septimus had muttered these words earlier. But to discover how Virginia Woolf intended that thought to end, we must turn to another text—to Woolf's essay on Montaigne in the first *Common Reader*, published three weeks earlier than *Mrs. Dalloway*: "Communication is truth; communication is happiness," she wrote. "To share is our duty; to go down boldly and bring to light those *hidden thoughts which are the most diseased*." Unable to confess, to bring to full consciousness, his "diseased" love for another man, Septimus cannot escape his tormentors, clamoring, "Kill yourself, kill yourself."

And should the reader have overlooked these details, Virginia Woolf inserts one more item in this mosaic of innuendo. She puts a copy of Dante's *Inferno* into Septimus's hands. Not *Hamlet*, not *Oedipus Rex* or some other classic. Why? Because in the Seventh Circle—the Septimus Circle—punishment is meted out to soldiers (Septimus and Evans), suicides (Septimus), and sodomites (Septimus and Evans). Here then was the novelist juxtaposing ideas and images for the mind to mix, just as Roger Fry saw the French Impressionists juxtaposing shapes and colors for the eye to mix, to convey the deeper, truer, often harsher *reality* behind the chromatic mists of *appearance*. And, ultimately, the worlds of Clarissa and Septimus are joined by the image of Clarissa's shilling thrown into the Serpentine.

The world that mattered to Virginia Woolf was the world of emotional and sensory experience eddying endlessly in atmospheres of the mind, in twilit regions of memory where past and present merge and blur. It was a world where houses and rooms are furnished not with carpets and curtains but with reminiscence and feeling. This alone was real. It was not concerned with what life was like, but more with what the actual experience of living felt like.

William James, in his *Principles of Psychology* (1890), had described the nature of human thought with the "stream of consciousness" metaphor. Consciousness, he said, was not "chopped up in bits. Such words as 'chain' or 'train' do not describe it fitly . . . It is nothing jointed; it flows. A 'river' or a 'stream' are the metaphors by which it is most naturally described." Thought was the center and pulse of experience and was yet surrounded by a band of haze—a "halo or fringe"— of other thoughts. The "stream of consciousness" metaphor was meant to convey the continuous, ever-changing movement of the mind with its constantly shifting focuses of attention. Some nine years later, in Vienna, Sigmund Freud published *The Interpretation of Dreams*. With the idea of dream "condensation," "displacement," and "symbolization" came the notion that dreamers have the capacity to disguise their dreams, a process which conceals a dream's real (its *latent*) meaning from the dream's *manifest* content—an earlier and slightly different phrasing of Virginia Woolf's need to "discover real things beneath the show."

. . .

In France, Marcel Proust had completed the first two volumes of his monumental *A la recherche du temps perdu* in 1913 and in England James Joyce's *A Portrait of the Artist as a Young Man* had been serialized in 1914–15. Both were products of a romanticism whose heroes were emotional and self-obsessed; the earlier rationalism and restraint had yielded to feeling and introspection. The locus of attention had shifted from the head to the heart. Soon another shift would refocus on the head *and* the heart: the mind would attempt to divine those unquiet flutters of feeling. Storytelling was moving from the externality of Balzac and Dickens to the interior realities of Proust and Joyce, who wrote in an atmosphere that valued the inwardness of human life, with its strange, fleeting moments of experience. If Joyce succeeded in catching the flux of the mind in dense verbal circuits, Proust was successful in trapping the treasures of involuntary memory, a method indebted in part to the work of Henri Bergson. Both novelists were achieving a new kind of realism by unburdening themselves of the barriers that blocked the free-flowing quality of human experience, just as the Impressionists were shedding earlier methods of photographic documentation. The old realism, it was beginning to appear, was no realism at all.

In April 1919, Virginia Woolf published an essay in the *Times Literary Supplement* called "Modern Novels"; it was later revised for inclusion in the first *Common Reader* under the title "Modern Fiction." Her argument focused on the preoccupations of novelists who saw only the material shell of life and nothing of its mysterious interior. One needed only to look at an ordinary mind on an ordinary day to realize how that mind was bombarded with thousands of impressions—some trivial, some opaque, some fantastic. From all sides these impressions would fall like "an incessant shower of innumerable atoms; and as they fall, as they shape themselves . . . the accent falls differently from of old." Realists wrote from convention, not from what they felt and saw; and because they were thus guided, new horizons were closed to them. Everything was prescribed, predictable, imposed. Life appeared to them "a series of gig lamps symmetrically arranged." And that was the mistake, for life was not like that at all. It was a "luminous halo, a semi-transparent envelope surrounding us from the beginning of consciousness to the end." It was the novelist's duty to "convey this varying, this unknown and uncircumscribed spirit, whatever aberration or complexity it may display." It was the novelist's duty to capture and concretize these subjective, interior states, to "record the atoms as they fall upon the mind in the order in which they fall." This was what James Joyce had done in *A Portrait of the Artist* and was doing with greater finesse in *Ulysses*.

In contrast to the exterior novelists—Arnold Bennett, H. G. Wells, John Galsworthy—Joyce was trying to lay bare the "flickerings of that innermost flame which flashes its messages through the brain." He was disregarding entirely those conventions which in the past had helped readers imagine the world beyond its material plane to places they could neither touch nor see. Joyce, like the French Impressionists, was recording only what he saw, not what convention had taught him was there. Modern fiction brought readers closer to life itself because it had its genesis in a truer, more direct rendering of human perception. It was trying to liberate the more substantial reality that forever lurked *behind* appearance.

In 1924 Virginia Woolf read a paper to the Society for Heretics in Cambridge called "Character in Fiction," which was later published as the now-famous *Mr. Bennett and Mrs. Brown*. It was written originally in December 1923 as a response to Arnold Bennett's statement that the "foundation of good fiction is character-creating and nothing else." In that essay she made what must have come at the time as a startling announcement that "on or about December, 1910, human character changed." She was referring, of course, to London's first Post-Impressionist exhibition, held from November 1910 to January 1911. To Virginia Woolf the paintings hung in this exhibit represented a shift in human perception and consciousness. The English who came to see the new works, men and women accustomed to the documentary realism of painters like John Singer Sargent, roared with laughter or shouted abuse at the canvases of Cézanne, Manet, Van Gogh, and Picasso. The "nonsense" they saw before them was anarchy, madness, the scrawls of children. It was inexcusable and disgusting.

What they failed to see was that the realist painters they so vigorously supported were as unfaithful in representing reality as the Edwardian writers Virginia Woolf was repudiating. The so-called realists, whether writers or painters, produced like a camera mechanical likenesses, not human impressions. And like the camera, they reflected pre-existing structures. They imitated. They borrowed. They copied. What they could not do was create those fleeting impressions which characterized the ever-changing impressions of real-life experience. Try to imagine Arnold Bennett writing *Mrs. Dalloway*.

William James had objected to words like "train" and "chain" to describe the constantly moving, continuously changing "stream" of human thought.

So too did Virginia Woolf. Characters in fiction "feel" and "think" and "hope" and "fear" and "brood." And they do so with their minds. To express that mental movement in "formal railway line" sentences as the Edwardian novelists did was unrealistic and false. For people, she insisted, "don't and never did feel or think or dream for a second in that way; but all over the place."

But here the writer faced a problem. The novelist had words alone to work with; and words could only be written one at a time. That fact was inescapable. Writing was sequential. Writing was therefore temporal. Writing (and reading) happened in Time. Therefore, as a novelist, she had to design her story *in time*. The painter could create images with "splashes" in space. *Simultaneous* splashes. The novelist could not. Virginia Woolf could only hope to simulate, to convey certain moments of reality by creating certain carefully thought-out *temporal* relations—recall Clarissa's shilling in the Serpentine given at two crucial positions in the novel.

In writing *To the Lighthouse*, Woolf made the painter Lily Briscoe, her artistic deputy, and Lily's problems with space parallel the novelist's problems with time. There is evidence to suggest that Virginia Woolf was slowly becoming influenced by Roger Fry's preoccupation with expressive structural relations in painting. "Structure is still the primary consideration . . . over the 'impression,'" he would write in *Cézanne*; "but those accents which clamp the structure together no longer need to be so heavily insisted on, the atmosphere becomes freer, lighter and more exhilarating." In the novel Lily Briscoe begins to solve her problem of space when she realizes the need for a similar structural sturdiness: "Beautiful and bright it should be on the surface, feathery and evanescent . . . but beneath the fabric must be clamped together with bolts of iron."

In describing Cézanne's achievement of architectural balance, Fry pointed to a landscape, *Maisons au bord de la Marne*, and noted that a "grassy bank is almost uniform and featureless. Behind, a tree divides the composition in half with the rigid vertical of its trunk." And this is exactly what Lily Briscoe decides to do: "I must move the tree to the middle; that matters—nothing else." Virginia acknowledged to Roger himself his influence on her formal integration of the novel. Soon after its début, he wrote to tell her it was the "best thing" she'd written to date. Better even than *Mrs. Dalloway*. "You're no longer bothered by the simultaneity of things and go backwards and forwards in time with an extraordinary enrichment of each moment of consciousness"; but he wasn't quite sure what the lighthouse meant.

"I meant *nothing* by the Lighthouse," she replied. "One has to have a central line down the middle of the book to hold the design together. I saw that all sorts of feelings would accrue to this, but I refused to think them out, and trusted that people would make it the deposit for their own emotions—which they have done, one thinking it means one thing, another another."

The ambiguity was calculated, deliberate. This was the closest one could get to reality. Through all her writing, even in her adolescence, the stylistic feature that stands out most prominently is that elegant turn of phrase that is poetic, undetermined, and suggestive. She, the writer, *suggested*, and we, the readers, *supplied*. When she spoke of the poetic aspect in writing, she invariably meant the degree of semantic density and the range of semantic resonance—the possible stretch of meanings a word or phrase might generate. The writer's task, she wrote, is "to take one thing and let it stand for twenty: a task of danger and difficulty; but only so is the reader relieved of the swarm and confusion of life and branded . . . with the particular aspect which the writer wishes him to see."

Fry's comment on her movement in time enriching moments of consciousness brings us finally to that feature of Virginia Woolf's fiction which marks it as characteristically her own, and she describes it best in a passage about herself as a young woman setting out to become a novelist. At the start she was an "ignorant girl who used to sit scribbling reviews" but someone who also spent a lot of time just mooning. "She mooned and mooned. Sometimes perhaps she wrote a sentence; sometimes she looked out of the window. But what did she see? Nothing real. What did she think? I doubt that she thought at all. Did she not construct a plot? No never. What she was doing was letting her mind—if we like to grant her one—feed unfettered upon every atom and crumb of her experience; to let her imagination sweep round every angle and rock and cranny of the world as it lies in the depths of her subconsciousness."

Here was the free, questing mind pulling the past into the present, making time and memory the core of fictional exploration, just as Proust had done in his remembrance of things past. Memory was also at the center of Henri Bergson's concept of time—*durée*, the real measure of the experience of living. As Bergson wrote in *Matter and Memory*, the present is always and only that "invisible progress of the past, which gnaws into the future." Consciousness thus lights up, at any moment in time, "that immediate part of the past which, impending over the future, seeks to realize and associate with it." That is to say, the present moment, although it appears to have an independence of its own, is in reality "the shadow of the past projecting itself into the future." It was out of this concept that time and consciousness became fused.

"It took me a year's groping to discover what I call my tunnelling process, by which I tell the past by instalments," Virginia wrote in her diary on October 15, 1923, when she had completed about a hundred pages of *Mrs. Dalloway*. It was finally clear to her that when she dug tunnels behind a character to reveal some memory or recall some past experience, she had to stop the tick-tocking of the mechanical clock governing the novel's external narrative and move vertically instead in psychological time, time linked to memory. Time on the wall clock and time in the mind were two very different dimensions, and were experienced in very different ways. Five hours spent in pleasure, for instance, seemed like five minutes, whereas five minutes of pain felt like five hours.

In human consciousness, past and present were constantly merging with one another. What William James called "halo" or "fringe" and Virginia Woolf designated "luminous halo" were ultimately phases of a human psychic process which signaled the merging of the past with the present and the disappearance of the present into the future. This was what Virginia Woolf was referring to when she challenged writers to record "the atoms as they fall upon the mind in the order in which they fall . . . however disconnected and incoherent in appearance, which each sight or incident scores upon the consciousness." In practice this meant that when a memory was recalled from a chronologically distant past, that memory would become instantly alive and *re-experienced* during the moment of recall. So that when Woolf tunneled into a character's past, the memory was experienced in the *present* (by the character and the reader) and *not* as an event of the past.

Clive Bell, in his book on Proust, called this province of memory the spawning place of monsters. But Proust at last learned to bring "these monsters up from the deep by the simplest of devices. A surprise, the taste of a madeleine soaked in tea, the phrase of a sonata by Vinteuil . . . such were the jolts that for him provoked explosion." *A la recherche du temps perdu* was indeed a series of explosions by means of which the past was brought into the present, "the deep-sea monsters of memory to the surface." He could pull these from the deep "by an appropriate shock. Proust's first gift that conditioned his method, was his capacity for giving himself shocks."

It may not be irrelevant that Virginia Woolf in her 1939–40 "Sketch of the Past" used a similar "shock" image. In an effort to overcome—both as a child and often as an adult—her sense of being "powerless" and "passive," she had to learn to "explain" the "sledge-hammer" blows of experience. "I think that is true, because though I still have the peculiarity that I receive these sudden shocks . . . they are particularly valuable." This "shock-receiving capacity is what makes me a writer. I hazard the explanation that a shock is at once in my case followed by the desire to explain it. I feel that I have had a blow; but it is not, as I thought as a child, simply a blow from an enemy . . . it is or will become a revelation . . . a token of some real thing behind appearances; and I make it real by putting it into words." Words, writing— these would become the means by which Virginia Woolf preserved her identity from slipping into nothingness.

The shocks would become revelations. That was the key. There was the private story and the public. The familiar separation of life and work upon which most literary biography depends does not apply to Virginia Woolf. Her life and her work were inseparable, and part of that life was inscribed in every novel she wrote. For as she said in her 1928 introduction to the Modern Library edition of *Mrs. Dalloway*, there was nothing "more fascinating than to be shown the truth which lies behind those immense façades of fiction . . . Slowly and cautiously one would have to go to work, uncovering, laying bare, and even so when everything had been brought to the surface, it would still be for the reader to decide what was relevant and what was not." And so the novels of Virginia Woolf would always be in essence double stories: the story *told* and the story *deduced*. The real thing behind appearances. There would always be granite behind the rainbow.

DEAREST LESLIE / DARLING JULIA

❉ 1877-1895 ❉

In the late afternoon of September 23, 1903, a few days after the family returned from their summer holiday, Virginia read in the evening newspaper the story of a woman who had drowned herself in the Serpentine. At the mortuary nothing could be found to identify her, and no one could discover who her relatives were. She had ended her life in complete anonymity. Pinned inside her dress was a scrap of paper upon which was written her last, barely legible message to the world: "No father, no mother, no work. May God forgive me for what I have done tonight."

So deep was the impression that "I could not get the words out of my head," wrote Virginia, aged twenty-one. " 'No father, no mother, no work,' and so she killed herself." Had this been the report of a young girl it would have been sad enough; but that this was a woman of about forty-five made it all the more tragic. For if she was a wife or a mother, it clearly counted for nothing. It was for her father and mother that the drowned woman yearned—"a father and mother, maybe who died when she was a child."

Then suddenly, without warning, Virginia momentarily slipped into the character of this middle-aged woman: "Without husband or children, I yet had parents. If they were alive now I should not be alone. Whatever my sin my father and mother would have given me protection and comfort. For the first time in her life perhaps she weeps for her parents and . . . her loneliness without them." The loss was bitter enough in youth with all the world before one, "but in middle age that loss is one that nothing can heal and no fresh tie renew. Your husband may die and you can marry another—your child may die and others may be born to you, but if your father and mother die you have lost something that the longest life can never bring again."

Virginia had lost her mother eight years earlier, and downstairs at 22 Hyde Park Gate her father was dying of cancer. Like the woman she had just re-created, Virginia too had no work, no identifiable self as the writer she longed to be. Within a year, she too would attempt to take her life. In the uncertainties of this troubled autumn, the journal entry Virginia had just written would become her first requiem for her father, as well as a chilling prophecy. For, indeed, "No father, no mother, no work" would soon become the trinity holding her in its dim center for the remainder of her life.

Virginia's father, Leslie Stephen, was born on November 28, 1832, the fourth of five children—the first, Herbert, having died in adolescence and the second, a girl (unnamed), in infancy. So that he grew up with an older dominating brother, James Fitzjames (Fitzy), and an adoring younger sister, Caroline Emelia (Milly). His father, Sir James Stephen, Permanent Under-Secretary for the Colonies and later Regius Professor of History at Cambridge, was a man with a "natural inclination to gloom and to self-mortification." Sir James and his youngest son were "not at ease in each other's company . . . they were too much alike: they were both extremely sensitive." There was a certain affection between them, but there it ended. Each was more comfortable when the other was not present.

Sir James married the daughter of John Venn, the Rector of Clapham, who stood at the very center of the Evangelical movement in the Church of England. Jane Venn, a woman of sanguine temperament and common sense, became Leslie's first unofficial biographer. Until he was about five, she carefully chronicled everything the little boy said and did and felt. By the age of two, he was a "most independent-spirited little fellow, very bold and very persevering . . . and seems to have no fear at all when he is trying to do anything . . . He is rather violent in his temper, and, if displeased, will cry out most loudly." Lady Stephen found her little boy very impetuous and, indeed, "very turbulent and self-willed and rather passionate . . . A word or even a look of blame puts him into an agony of distress . . . A hasty word will make him burst into fits of crying."

In 1835, the vigilant mother continued: "Leslie is of all the children I ever saw the most sensitive of a balk . . . A sort of nervous feeling seems to come over him . . . It seems as if every kind of encouragement was good for him, and every notice that is taken of him seems to draw him out and do him good." At age four: when Leslie "is naughty it seems more like nervous irritability than real naughtiness." At five: "He is the most sensitive child I ever saw . . . In telling a story he cannot endure to hear of the boys being naughty or even the animals in a make-believe story. He always begs me to make them good instead." Little Leslie, it seems, could not even bear Biblical stories; when he heard the account of the Saviour's betrayal, "he pressed his hands to his head with a look of the greatest distress and suffering." And even a half hour of lessons made him pale and languid.

This same little boy, however, who hid his face at the picture of the Crucifixion, who trembled when poetry was read to him—this same delicate child, it was rumored, had once, to everyone's astonishment, hurled a flowerpot at his mother in an explosion of temper. She must have reasoned that it was his sensitivity that made him so irritable; but the outbursts went uncontrolled and unexplained.*

When Leslie was ten, Sir James Stephen moved the family to Windsor and enrolled his sons at Eton. Both Leslie and Fitzjames were bullied from the start, though Leslie got the worst of it. They had entered the school as day-boys, and day-boys at Eton were despised; the day-boy, wrote Noel Annan, was "suspect because he might be the son of a Windsor grocer or footman at the Royal Household who was attempting to break into the upper classes by insisting that his sons be educated in their home town."

Leslie rose at six every morning, read the Bible with his mother, and, after a day of misery at school, returned each evening to prepare the following day's lessons. There was no break in this schedule, and until he finished at Eton he would remain friendless, fragile, and defenseless. The only person he could turn to was his tough, brave brother Fitzy to defend him from the almost certain beatings his size and vulnerability excited in the bigger, rougher boys.

One such incident in October 1842 is recorded in Lady Stephen's journal. "One day this week Fitzjames went to his room at Dodd's and found the door locked. When it was opened, he found there a great boy who had been 'licking' Leslie, as they called it. Leslie was crying in the corner of the room. F. immediately began to lick the great boy and, according to his own account, did it so thoroughly that there is no fear of his attacking Leslie again." Many years later, when writing the *Life* of his brother, Leslie described the difference between himself and his sibling as "the difference between the willow and the oak."

Until the Christmas term of 1850, when he went up to Cambridge, Leslie studied with private tutors and was matriculated for several terms at King's College, London. His health was still precarious, and he was very lonely; and so the bond between mother and son grew stronger than ever. His father was still unapproachable and his brother still overpowering; the willow would

---

* It has been suggested that Leslie Stephen's unpredictable mood swings, in childhood and throughout his life, were due to cyclothymia, a mild form of manic-depressive disorder. See Caramagno, 103.

not grow in the shade of the oak. Sir James Stephen, having suffered three nervous breakdowns himself, had the good sense to realize that the competition of Trinity College, where Fitzjames was enrolled, was more than Leslie's health and morale could tolerate, and so enrolled his younger son in his own college, Trinity Hall, where Leslie, thin and pale and shy, took up residence at the end of 1850.

At some point during this interval, Leslie took an inventory and found himself wanting. No matter how hard he tried, he was always at the bottom rung of the ladder; and when he looked around him, he found that compared to his contemporaries he was pretty much a zero. All the combinations and permutations of effort had been played out, and still he couldn't shine. Surely he had a right to feel angry and resentful at being pushed and shoved and bullied. And just as surely he had the right to lighten his burden with self-righteous indignation and a certain measure of self-indulgence. He felt puniest when comparing himself with his brother. He was inept: Fitzy was efficient; he was weak: Fitz was strong; he was passive: his brother was aggressive. Something more complicated, however, was brewing during these formative years. In the tangles of childhood and adolescence, Leslie translated the pains of growing up into acts of deliberate punishment. And the more he suffered, the more he felt superior to his tormenters: better, more exalted, in fact than most of the boys around him. More than that, he soon realized that however much humiliation he had been forced to bear from the male half of the world's population during this painful stretch of growing up, he had his mother to turn to—the dependable woman and comforter who dispensed her bounty without reservation or condition.

As the years passed, then, Leslie began to feel it his privilege to indulge in fits of peevishness, his right to demand pity and sympathy. Indeed, his mother had been so morbidly preoccupied with the state of his health that he learned from her to take himself with the same deadly seriousness, which in time would become excessive, extravagant, even tyrannical. He was "thin-skinned" and demanded the world treat him with kid gloves. What began as a wish would soon become, as in most interpersonal disturbances, an incontrovertible claim.

At Cambridge, Leslie's health, much to the surprise of his family, improved and, during his bachelorhood at least, would trouble him no longer. Still, ashamed of his nervous irritability and childhood weakness, he joined the rowing team; and though he was not a good oarsman, he gave the impression of being an athlete, an athlete who despised anything resembling frailty. He found a working schedule that suited him physically and temperamentally, settled down to his books, and, at the end of his first year at Trinity Hall, won a scholarship.

During his undergraduate years, Leslie remained the "tall, gaunt, and shy man who read mathematics, and hovered on the edge of a conversation without boldly taking his part." Perhaps his one real disappointment was in not being invited to join the Apostles, the secret intellectual society to which his brother belonged. At the end of his fourth year, however, in December 1854, Leslie Stephen's name was put forward for a fellowship that had recently fallen vacant. Recipients of the award were required to take Holy Orders, and this he did the following year, being ordained deacon in 1855 and made junior tutor in 1856. The Reverend Leslie Stephen, B.A., aged twenty-three, had turned from a delicate, sickly youth to a fanatical athlete with powerful lungs and long, indefatigable legs—first as coach for the rowing team, then later as walker and cross-country runner, and by 1859 as a devout mountain climber. That is to say, the bony weakling of old, the real Leslie, had transformed himself into a glorified ideal, prepared to face the world now on a more confident, but still fragile, footing.

During these Cambridge years, Leslie Stephen's reading of Mill, Comte, Hobbes, and the British empiricists led him to abandon Christianity and write a series of articles on agnosticism. (Julia Duckworth later read these pieces during her widowhood; they not only reinforced her own views but made Leslie appear inordinately attractive as well.) The more he read, the more seductive became the premises of scientific humanism, the more judicious the idea of human reason controlling the social environment. Ethics began to triumph over theology. In 1862, the young reverend found himself unable to perform his priestly duties in Trinity Hall's chapel. Within two years, convinced of his agnosticism, he left Cambridge permanently and shed whatever there remained of Christian dogma. He discovered not that its creed was false but that he had "never really believed." "I now believe in nothing, to put it shortly; but I do not the less believe in morality, &c. &c.," he wrote at the beginning of 1865. "I mean to live and die like a gentleman if possible." He was at last relieved of a "cumbrous burden."

He moved back to London to live with his mother and sister in 19 Portchester Terrace. Upon his father's death he received a small private income, but to supplement that money he needed to get work of some kind. Once again his brother stepped in to help. Some ten years earlier, Fitzjames had married Mary Cunningham, daughter of the Evangelical Vicar of Harrow, and was not only a successful barrister but also one of London's leading journalists. With Fitzjames's influence Leslie, before long, was writing prolifically for the distinguished *Saturday Review*, the newly founded *Pall Mall Gazette*, and *The Cornhill Magazine*, whose editor he would become in a few years' time. He was a facile journalist and during these early years often produced four articles a week. When he felt the need to ventilate his agnosticism, he turned to the pages of *Fraser's Magazine*. Also as a journalist, Leslie's sympathy with the Union led to a visit to the United States and to friendships with James Russell Lowell, Charles Eliot Norton, and Oliver Wendell Holmes.

Shortly after coming to London, Leslie Stephen wrote James Russell Lowell that he had just torn himself "up by the roots" from Cambridge. The business of a parson had become "odious" to him and now they "won't let me teach mathematics any longer, or, to speak more truly, it does not answer to wait . . . unless you accept the prize of a college living." It wasn't a simple matter giving up "a warm, easy place like Cambridge, where I had been vegetating for near fifteen years in comfort." He had a luxurious set of rooms. He walked about in a handsome cap and gown, and everyone he met doffed their hats to him. Here in London no one noticed him. "I can walk down the Strand without causing any visible sensation . . . I was fond of the university. But it is also a lazy sort of place for men who, like me, had no share in the teaching, and therefore I have come to a more stimulating atmosphere."

On November 28, 1866, Leslie made the following entry in his journal: "This is my thirty-fourth birthday. I put down a note or two as to my position . . . As to my employments, I am still writing regularly for the *Saturday* [*Review*], but with less interest, and, I fear, less power than previously." He had given up the *Pall Mall Gazette*: the articles he had written for it on Philistines had been turned down as being unsuitable. Now, "I am writing fortnightly letters for the *Nation* . . . My writing is unsatisfactory, chiefly because I want an object—at least I think so . . . I am going on languidly in everything, and doubt much whether I shall come to much good." He trusted his fortune would soon change. "If I don't take a turn for the better, I shall take one for the worse, that is pretty clear . . . If it were not for my mother and [sister] I sometimes think that I would leave England. But it is too late at thirty-four to be still at a loose end . . . I must get enthusiastic about something. I have got enthusiasm in me, but it won't come out."

At about this time, Leslie met the two daughters of William Makepeace Thackeray, Anne Isabella (Anny) and Harriet Marian (Minny), living at 16 Onslow Gardens; and before he knew it, his "enthusiasm" burst forth in the shape of Minny, the younger of the sisters, with whom Leslie Stephen fell head over heels in love. On December 7, 1866, he wrote to another of his American friends—his "Beloved" Oliver Wendell Holmes—to announce that he was engaged to Miss Minny Thackeray. He loved Miss Thackeray with all his "heart and soul." They would be married in early summer of the following year. That same evening, he wrote to his betrothed on the back of a menu from the Political Economy Club dinner: "My dearest Minny, I am suffering the torments of the damned for that God-forgotten [economist] Thorton, who is boring on about supply and demand, when I would give anything to be with you. He is not a bad fellow, but just now I hate him like poison."

Leslie's fear that if he didn't marry soon he'd dry up into a "hopeless mummy" came to an end on June 19, 1867. His mother noted the event in her journal: "This day Leslie married to M. Thackeray—a most original wedding—at 8 o'clock in the morning . . . nobody invited, but a large number of friends and acquaintances assembled . . . As soon as it was over L. and M. set out for Paris."

For a few short years, Leslie Stephen was a supremely happy man. Minny was a gentle and affectionate soul who was judged neither beautiful nor clever; but her curiosity and childlike innocence were endearing. She was extremely young for her age. At twenty-one, she still enjoyed "playing with children and kittens and hated reading." But this seems to have suited Stephen perfectly. The only person to ruffle the equanimity of their eight and a half years of married life was Leslie's sister-in-law Anny. Minny loved her sister deeply, thought her a genius, and often, to Leslie's exasperation, deferred to her. He might have been more tolerant of the woman had she kept her distance. But Anny did not keep her distance. She lived with them at Onslow Gardens, and her cheerful impetuosity and inexhaustible vivacity sometimes fanned Leslie into flames of fury.

Anny Thackeray has been described as a novelist whose stories were "tenuous, charming productions in which the narrative tended to get lost and in which something of her own vague, erratic, engaging personality is preserved." Leslie and his high-spirited sister-in-law were exact opposites: "he loved silence and she was for ever talking; he loved order, and she rejoiced in chaos; he prided himself in realism, she was unashamedly sentimental; he worried about money, she was recklessly extravagant; he prized facts, she was hardly aware of them." Behind the endless confusions and exploding tempers, however, it appeared that both Leslie and Anny were competing for Minny's love; and it was perhaps the openness of Leslie's need for Minny that made her choose in the end her husband over her sister.

Minny gave birth to a baby girl on December 7, 1870. They named her Laura but called her "Meemee." "I have never felt so happy," wrote the proud father to Lowell in America, "and never seen a sight that pleased me so much as when I am sitting by these two ladies and watching my wife's eyes gloating over her poor little baby." Domestic happiness, however, was not destined to last long. Before Laura reached her fifth birthday, she would be motherless.

On the evening of November 27, 1875, Minny fell ill and retired to a separate room where Anny's maid could keep an eye on her. During the night, Leslie was called. "I found my darling in a convulsion. I fetched the doctor. I remember only too clearly the details of what followed; but I will not set them down. My darling never regained consciousness. She died about the middle of the day, 28 November, my forty-third birthday."

Earlier in the year, Leslie's mother had died. Now Minny too was gone. And before long he would discover that his sweet little Meemee was mentally deficient. It was almost more than one could endure. With nowhere to turn, he sank into a deep and stony grief. His forty-third birthday was the saddest day he had ever known.

 Living next door was Julia Prinsep Jackson, the beautiful young widow of Herbert Duckworth. She had been a friend of the Thackeray sisters, and just the night before Minny's death had come to visit. Little could anyone guess that before long, Julia, with three children of her own, would become the second Mrs. Stephen and the mother of four more, one of them, the future Virginia Woolf.

The few facts we have of Julia's life come from Leslie Stephen's memoir. She was born in India on February 7, 1846, the third daughter of Dr. John Jackson and the beautiful Maria Pattle, fourteen years his junior. Jackson was educated at Catherine Hall, Cambridge, in the 1820s and from there went to Calcutta where he prospered as a physician. At the age of two Julia came to England with her mother; her two elder sisters, Adeline (Vaughan) and Mary (Fisher), had come over earlier and were living in London with Maria Jackson's sister, Sara, and her husband, Henry Thoby Prinsep. Dr. Jackson joined them in England in 1855, when Julia was nine. From that time the Jackson family lived at Brent Lodge, Hendon, and regularly visited the Prinseps at Little Holland House, the well-known gathering place for artists and writers.

It was not long before the exquisite young Julia was discovered. The sculptor Thomas Woolner, struck by her beauty, proposed to her, as did Holman Hunt, the Pre-Raphaelite painter. "Both proposals," Virginia was later to write, "were made and refused when she was scarcely out of the nursery." She posed for Edward Burne-Jones. G. F. Watts made chalk sketches of her. And at fourteen or fifteen she was Carlo Marochetti's model. Sir Henry Taylor had written a poem to her beauty, and of course her aunt Julia Cameron snapped her in countless photographs. Several years earlier Leslie Stephen remembered her "as I might have seen and remembered the Sistine Madonna or any other presentation of superlative beauty." Uncle Thoby, whom Julia worshiped, made a great fuss over his exquisite niece.

Maria Jackson was uncomfortably aware of how much attention Julia attracted and had a " 'superstition' that every man who met her in a railway carriage fell in love with her." But Julia was presumably free of vanity. "Her mother's judicious care no doubt helped to protect her simplicity. She knew, of course, she was a beauty . . . and there was clearly no want of admirers . . . But nobody could have been more absolutely unspoilt and untouched by the slightest weakness of self-complacency."

Maria Jackson, however, may have had another good reason for protecting her daughter from ravenous eyes and worshiping men. She had begun to suffer from rheumatism shortly after her husband returned from India, when Julia was just ten or eleven; and with Adeline already married to Henry Halford Vaughan, and Mary about to become the wife of Herbert Fisher, only her youngest darling and pet, Julia, remained. So it was Julia who would become her mother's principal care-giver and traveling companion as they scoured the Continent in search of "cures."

The idea of being her mother's nurse evidently had great appeal to the young girl and filled her with a precocious sense of importance. For during the next ten years, just before the Jacksons moved in 1866 to a country house called Saxonbury in Frant, near Tunbridge Wells, Julia was scarcely ever more than a few feet from her mother's side, and curiously almost never by her father's.

As Leslie Stephen described him, Dr. Jackson "had had a life of almost unbroken health." He was a well-built man, sensible, good, and kind. Despite these enviable qualities, however, Jackson was "not a man of any great mark." He was, according to his son-in-law, the parent who didn't seem to count "as fathers generally count in their families." Mrs. Jackson may have been a good wife, but there was nothing "romantic" in her attachment to the old man. He was "respected or esteemed rather than ardently loved." Of all Julia's relations her father was the one whom she looked upon "with the calmest affection." Perhaps this was due to Dr. Jackson's robustness. He had never had a day's illness in his life. So that Julia's "instincts, so often excited by suffering, had not, in his case, been called into activity."

At any rate, while in Venice visiting her sister Mary Fisher and her new husband, Julia met their friend, the handsome, carefree barrister Herbert Duckworth, who was there on holiday. Julia was just sixteen at the time. Duckworth was not professionally inclined and, according to Leslie Stephen, scarcely "devoted himself to his work in the spirit of a man who has his living to make by it." He had once said to Julia, in the first days of their marriage, that he was "inclined to be penitent for caring so little for his profession, being quite content with having such a wife."

It was natural, after Minny's death, for Leslie to turn to a woman for help. The devoted Anny tried for eighteen months to keep house for him, but the arrangement was doomed from the start. Then the lovely, melancholy Julia stepped into Leslie's broken world and tried to ease him out of his desolation. Although she knew Leslie Stephen only slightly, she held him in a kind of intellectual awe. Since her husband's death she had suffered a loss of faith, and it was perhaps Leslie's agnosticism that made him now seem approachable.

The Stephen clan were of a class grounded in tradition and dedicated to facts and commonsense notions of the world. They were inclined for the most part to theology, law, education, and politics. Almost all of them were intellectuals and writers with "plenty of moral, physical and mental audacity." When Leslie Stephen gave up the secure, quiet life of Cambridge, he became a towering literary journalist with all the capacity for work so characteristic of the great Victorians. In the last two decades of the century, there was no one, according to Noel Annan, "who could match both the enormous range of his reading and the intellectual power under perfect control which expressed itself in a fluent, sinewy style." As editor of the *Cornhill*, he worked shoulder to shoulder with many of the foremost writers of the day, while maintaining his own prodigious output. With his impressive *History of English Thought in the Eighteenth Century*, published in 1876, he climbed to the top of English literary life; and among his comrades in the world of letters were George Meredith, Thomas Hardy, Henry James, and John Addington Symonds.

Julia's side of the family, with its aristocratic connections, lived in a world that was decidedly more open-minded than that of the Stephens'. Maria Pattle, Julia's mother, was one of seven sisters—six of them known for their beauty, the seventh, Julia Margaret (Cameron), famous for her photography. The Prinseps, the Camerons, and the Duckworths, a long-established Somerset family of inherited wealth, were people of influence. When Julia's aunt Sara (Mrs. Thoby) Prinsep said in 1850 that she needed a place large enough to set up an informal "salon," Little Holland House, enclosed by an ancient wall, was suggested. An old farm dwelling shaded by poplars and elms, with a bucolic atmosphere, it was in actuality only a couple of miles from Hyde Park Corner and just a short distance from Kensington High Street.

The summer Sunday afternoon "at homes" were distinctly cosmopolitan in spirit. The Prinseps entertained many of the leading poets and artists of the day—Tennyson, Browning, Rossetti, Ruskin, Burne-Jones, G. F. Watts; and it was here that the young, exquisite Julia caught the eye (and heart) of more than one aristocrat of the art world. It is "not hard to find labels for the paternal and maternal sides: sense and sensibility, prose and poetry . . . or more simply, masculine and feminine."

Julia Duckworth began to make a place for herself in the troubled Stephen household. Certainly little Laura needed to be looked after. Anny had attempted to take charge of the child, but Leslie had sabotaged her efforts by instructing the nurse to disregard Anny's orders. More than once Julia had had to intervene. Then came the shocking love affair between Anny and young Richmond Ritchie, her godson and junior by seventeen years. This was more than Leslie could stomach. How could the silly woman so offend propriety? On one unfortunate occasion Leslie walked in on them kissing in the drawing room, and his Puritan blood curdled. They must either marry at once or separate. That was an order. Anny packed her trunks and departed from the Stephen household, leaving her brother-in-law with frayed nerves and a thorny housekeeper.

Milly, Leslie's sister Caroline Emelia, stepped in to take Anny's place but she too failed. Leslie found his sister a "most depressing companion" and her worthy and clever friends "intolerably dull." So that if Anny was too "exciting a companion, Milly was much at fault on the other side, and would have been a permanent strain upon spirits already low." Such was Leslie's estimate of the situation. The plan was given a chance, nevertheless. Milly stayed with him for three weeks. Then her health broke down, and her nurse and doctor carried her off to her own house in Chelsea. She begged Julia "to give an eye" to Leslie's household concerns.

Julia complied. Soon her presence was felt at the Stephen hearth. Leslie began bringing his troubles to her and gradually came to depend upon her judgment and good sense, in addition to the comfort he found in her company. And if Julia found Leslie alarming, as she claimed, nothing in her behavior betrayed her alarm. Nor was there much evidence that Leslie was, as he said, the most "skinless" of men. Not many weeks passed before a friendship blossomed between them; and this soon developed into a courtship of sorts.

One of the greatest disappointments in Leslie Stephen's life was Laura Makepeace Stephen, the mentally defective child of his first marriage. It was several years before anyone was aware that something was wrong with her. Surely by 1877 Leslie must have seen something odd in her behavior. His daily letters to Julia began in that year, and he was reporting Laura's activities with increasing frequency and mounting frustration.

In these letters one senses the full effect of Laura's deficiency—the crushed hopes of a man who placed so much value on mental agility. That he did not understand his little girl's predicament is clear from the start. In some of them, one reads his confusion and shame; in others, his pity and anger. In all of them the struggles of someone trying to deal reasonably with a situation in which reason had no legitimate place.

"I came home," he wrote to Julia from their Brighton holiday, "and found little Meemee who had been at the Cockerells. Louise [nurse] pleased me by saying that the Cockerells of her age are actually smaller than she. I did not dare ask whether they were as backward in other ways." A day or two later: "I had another argument with Laura today; but I am so far pleased that she really tried to be good. That is a great change, for I was beginning to doubt that she had any moral sense at all."

During their summer holiday, now with Caroline Emelia to accompany them, Leslie wrote from Coniston: "The chief sufferer is my poor little Laura. She seems indeed to be unconscious of her misfortunes and is very happy and (sometimes) very naughty—just now, for example, over her letters (Lord! how I hate those letters!) but she amuses herself with 'benting' as she calls it, meaning painting." Milly, he said, had taken charge of Laura with some success; "but it is silly to be too sanguine and I have no doubt that Laura will be a worry to me as long as she and I both live."

Soon after returning from a climbing expedition in the Swiss Alps in January 1877, something strange and wonderful happened to Leslie Stephen. He was ambling along a London street one day when he heard himself say, "I am in love with Julia!" He lost no time communicating this "flash of revelation" to Julia herself. "It was revealed to me a little while ago that I loved you—as a man loves the woman he would marry," he wrote to Julia on February 5. "I am convinced," he went on, "that even if you loved me, I could hardly make you happy as my wife . . . I write to put you on your guard against me for your own sake; to beg you to help me to be a friend without being a lover . . . Whatever happens I shall love you (in one sense) as long as I live."

On the following day, Julia wrote back: "I hope that it does not make life harder to you to hear that you are very dear to me, but I cannot bear to have given you pain . . . Do not put a strain on yourself with the idea that you may pain me by your words—that can never be. I must always care to hear all that you feel and think." And with this ambiguous reply an epistolary court-ship began that would soon have exhausted the most strenuous of lovers. Marriage, she said, was out of the question: they were for the future to be "on terms of the closest friendship: but never upon closer terms."

In the months following, they were frequently separated for short periods of time. Most of Julia's letters preserve something of the fuzzy redundancies she employed to keep herself free and inaccessible and ascendant. Leslie's pursuit of his object, however, was relentless; and the two or three letters he wrote daily to Julia (as well as her replies) sound the peculiar dissonance their divergent personalities were capable of producing. At the end of March 1877, for example, Julia wrote from Saxonbury, where she was staying with her mother, to say she had been dreaming of him and wished she could hold his hand, for she knew and understood all he felt. "As for myself," she went on, "I have had so many years of pain and struggle that it never seems to me as if what happened to me now mattered much . . . I feel as if I ought to tell you that with this love I am still so tired of going on living . . ."

A few days later, Leslie admitted that neither of them could start a "fresh life"; they were both of them "too much crushed." But he couldn't help wishing "the world was civilized enough to let us meet just as we pleased without insisting on all this hypocrisy." What he had in mind was that they should, in fact, legally marry so that he could be with her as much as he liked. Julia rejected the suggestion outright. She loved Leslie "too well" to agree to such a thing. This startling proposition, however, gave her the open-ing once more for insisting that she was disturbing his life, that she was wounding rather than healing him. "Things are quite different to a woman. We expect less and are more or less slaves I suppose. What I do care for most of all is for you and I can't bear to be a fret and a worry . . . I have had a horrid feeling sometimes that I could only hurt you. Don't let me hurt you."

The peculiar thought that she had the extraordinary power to hurt people who loved her was one of Julia's favorite fantasies and she returned to it the following day: "I am doing just what I have been telling you I feared I might do. I have been making your life more restless . . . I may be called away to nurse people for weeks or have invalids in my house for weeks and be so tied as to be unable to see you . . . Don't let me be a thorn in your flesh . . . I can't have your life worried and vexed and tormented."

Leslie was now beginning to notice the odd angles in Julia's logic. He was also beginning to see how easily she could trap him with that one particular argument. It was a comfort, he told her, to know that some of her thoughts were purely fanciful—especially "your ingenious notion that you do harm to everyone." This remark of course simply fueled Julia's sense of her own deadly powers: "I have felt before this that I had more power to wound than to heal, but it has never come home to me as it does now. However that is caused by my fault and I would bear anything if I could save you . . . What will and must [hurt] will be if I see your heart getting worn out and your life fevered and destroyed . . . I feel sore all over today and feel I have done you a harm I can never repair . . . I can go right away and if it be better for you, I will . . . I should like to come now and put my arms around you and tell you how dear you are to me . . . In the impulse to go to you and tell you how much I cared for you I acted selfishly . . . I should have waited and remembered that I might be only laying up pain for you."

There is no sign that Leslie saw from this letter how deeply troubled and divided Julia was, but he did see clearly enough now that she had him running in circles. "Let me say one or two things," he began, ". . . not about my feelings but about my utter incapacity to affect your opinions about anything in the slightest degree. You treat me like a baby: 'don't cry, dear; or I shall take your toy away altogether and that will be much worse won't it?' Well, I am or have been a baby and you were perfectly right and a very kind nurse, though you have not been able to make your medicine altogether sweet . . . Do for once lay aside your pigheadedness and believe me." He was not a person to whine for what he couldn't get, and he most assuredly did not expect her to change one iota. All he wanted was Julia in his life—and her love. "If you cut me off from you, because you will be making my life restless, it would be just as sensible as to cut off a person's bread and water because he sometimes wanted cake and wine." His only refuge, he threatened, would be in hard work regardless of how ruinous to his health. "So there—cut me off if you dare." Here was a little blackmail at its best. He had a few tricks of his own up his sleeve and was almost as good at Julia's game as Julia herself.

Summer came and they were both still at it. Leslie was again off on a holiday—Laura and Milly in tow—at Coniston in the Lake District, and Julia was once more trumpeting her deadly powers of doom and desolation: "I like to think that you feel me about you and that it is some good to you— not very much, I fear, but you may feel that I love you and must get all the good and as little of harm as you can out of it. I wish I could think there were no harm, but I can't."

Leslie entreated her on the following day never again to tell him in a letter that her affection was harmful. She could tell him when she was with him, for then he could contradict her and have done with it. Or she could tell him as often as she pleased she could never be his wife. "But that other thing which you will say to me affects me as if you had given me your hand and had hidden a pin in it to prick me. It is like putting a little drop of poison into the one cup I like to drink from . . . That is the only thing you ever say which is really and unmixedly painful." To which Julia characteristically re- plied: "I don't know that it will be any comfort to know that whatever pain you get, it goes through me first. I will try not to give you any more."

3 As it happens, almost all of Leslie Stephen's letters to Julia and a good many abstracts of hers to him have been pre- served. He turned to them soon after Julia's death, to write a memoir he would leave for his children which became known as the *Mausoleum Book*. The letters themselves re- veal much about the man who played so large a part in the tense and thunderous atmosphere of 22 Hyde Park Gate.

To begin with, Leslie Stephen was an extraordinarily greedy and self- centered man. Again and again in his letters to Julia, how naturally he per- ceived himself the repository of all her benevolence. And Julia's equally obvious need for self-sacrifice made her a natural target. So that almost from the start, we discover Leslie "rewarding" Julia with promises to stay in good health, with childish avowals that his well-being would give her cause to rejoice. His perception of their relations was decidedly one-sided: "My com- fort depends upon you so entirely." "I have learned to love you, because you harmonize so fully with all my feelings . . . You are so . . . curiously adapted to me." "Trust me and believe that you can be the greatest of blessings to me." "I wish that you could come in [to my study] sometimes and sit opposite me, that I might have something to look at." "Love me, dear . . . I feel it to be good for me in every fibre."

It is amusing to think how Julia privately responded to these lopsided manifestations of love. She probably saw from the beginning that with each successive letter he sank deeper and deeper into the quagmire of dependency, more and more under her spell. And she did nothing whatever to discourage it. One of the earliest signs of Julia's grip over Leslie was his surrendering to her his financial responsibilities. "I shall lay before you a financial statement and do what you bid me (if you will benevolently take that responsibility) in regard to my affairs. The more responsibility you take the better pleased I shall be. My main object in life has always been to shuffle my duties . . . upon other people and I mean to burden you with some of my cares." This happened in early February 1877, a full year before their marriage.

With his money management safely off his shoulders, he had then to think of what to do about Laura. In July 1877, he wrote to his brother about his will and directed him to make Julia Duckworth Laura's guardian with the same authority she would have as the child's mother. "My own," he wrote to Julia in December, "I have so much confidence in you . . . I am entirely your own and you can do with me just what you like." And this was precisely what Julia did.

He wrote to her from the Lake District in July that he had done something "for which I hope that you will forgive me. I know that it was very wrong and disobedient," he went on elaborately. It turns out that Leslie's naughtiness consisted of walking up a tiny hill with a companion. "Now, though I perhaps ought not to have gone after what you had said, it has certainly done me a deal of good." He slept better; he felt better; his neuralgia didn't hurt him, no sniffles threatened; and besides that, how many husbands could his darling name who refused to go out in the rain?

He was pleased with himself for having found someone upon whom he could lean so freely; and no matter how busy he was on his holiday: "I shall find time to tell you that I have had a good sleep and am all the better for my walk." A day or two later, Leslie again made his boyish appeal: "Dearest, are you angry with me for having this walk? . . . I am twice the man I was and some of your fresh air at Frant will pick me up and make me saucy and mischievous." He was always careful, however, not ever to appear too healthy, for good health made Julia feel redundant.

In all his confessions and admissions and indulgences, Leslie had made claims on Julia she could never be free from; and that, evidently, was exactly what he was working toward. His motto might have been: If I bare my soul to this extent, you must promise never to leave me and always to love me—no matter how much I abuse your goodwill or ignore your own needs or rights. In encouraging me to tell you all I think and feel—you are agreeing to this contract. He said as much, very succinctly, in a tactless and overly confident letter: "Nothing cheers me up like a good grumble at things in general. I have somehow put my burden upon your shoulders and am again in a tolerably elastic state."

Leslie had made himself clear from the very beginning. He was childish, helpless, reckless, and outrageously blunt. But malice and deceit were foreign to him. Julia had had fair warning. One of Leslie's favorite tricks was to do or say something that would rouse her anxiety. He saw no moral violation in what he was doing. For his most coveted alibi was that he was "skinless" and "sensitive" and therefore "irritable." He had a right to behave this way. There were times when he was boastful of his little maneuvers: "I can fancy myself . . . sitting alone with you; and seeing you look affectionately at me . . . and threatening you to overexert myself in order that you may show your anxiety about me . . . and affecting to be ill and tired that you may caress me. You did not know, perhaps, that I was so Jesuitical and full of stratagems in my behavior to you. But, dearest, it does not want many stratagems to make you treat me as I like to be treated . . . I do not really play tricks upon you; if only because you are much too simple minded . . . Only it is quite true that you are so tender to me . . . that I do feel slightly disposed at times to exaggerate my discomforts. It is worth a little lying to be taken care of by you."

To the very end of Julia's life, Stephen went on playing his little games. Being babied and petted was to his mind the same as being loved—something his little Virginia would learn from him and carry into her own adult and married life. Even after eight years of marriage he could still say to Julia: "I feel with my irritable skin . . . that I cannot get on comfortably unless I have a good set of buffers round me to protect me against the world." Later still: "You look worn, my darling . . . I will try not to bother you, beloved. It is a horrid trick of mine to tease you in order to comfort myself." Surely, anyone with eyes must have seen how thoroughly he had worn down his already overburdened Julia; yet just a year before her death, he still felt justified in complaining: "You know how I hate to see you slaving—for other people."

Julia was a perfect foil for Leslie. He might be demanding, obstinate, disagreeable. But so was she. If he saw a snow cloud, she expected a blizzard; if he was vague, she was inscrutable; if he was depressed, she was suicidal. Julia could match her husband, trick for trick, and was very far from the saintly portrait Leslie painted of her in the *Mausoleum Book*. From the very first of Julia's preserved letters, one detects the premise upon which she built her relationship with Leslie Stephen and the position of dominance it implied. "I hope it does not make life harder to you to hear that you are very dear to me, but I cannot bear to have given you pain." From the start, then the message was clear: Leslie's love made him vulnerable and gave Julia certain liberties; but she was impervious to whatever power he thought he had over her.

When he handed over his financial accounts, Julia knew her plans were materializing. But their relations were moving ahead too quickly. She must somehow slow matters down. Perhaps she might lapse into a little self-denigrating. That would certainly impede progress—and test his love as well. Was he really capable of caring for one as disappointed in life and pessimistic as she was? "You do not know how inferior I am to what you think I am, how much lower my standard is than yours and how short I fall of that even," she wrote him shortly.

It isn't likely that Julia thought this for a moment. Even her phrasing suggests this, for she was careful not to say she *was* inferior to him, but inferior to what *he thought she was*—a very different matter. And when she was certain of her conquest, she kept herself reachable but not entirely accessible. She must somehow remain solicitous of his cares while simultaneously devaluing the love: "My poor dear, I know all that you feel . . . I have known and felt for you all the sadness and all the dreariness." So exhausting was the business of living, "I always feel as if Death would be the greatest boon I could have bestowed on me."

With this fantastic statement Julia had played her trump card. Leslie's love must have seemed trivial indeed compared to Julia's suicidal melancholy. At any rate, it is safe to assume that by March 31, 1877, Julia had made her position clear. She would control future events (Fräulein Klappert, Laura's new caretaker, was the one exception), and Leslie would have little choice but to follow.

Where Leslie was concerned, Julia was very confident of herself. She was rocklike, steadfast, immutable. She could also be silent and reproachful. As her mother had said, she could be "a very icy creature." The sooner Leslie realized he was in Julia's thrall, the sooner and better matters could proceed. He had come a long way from his initial declaration of love, but Julia had turned the tables on him. There were times when he felt he was talking to her through a "convent grating," so inaccessible could she make herself. Despite the self-denigration and self-sacrifice, she was a stern, impatient woman who could be very harsh with the people she cared for. "The better I know you," Leslie confessed, "the more I dislike the thought of offending you. I fancy you looking at me, as I have seen you look at some people and feel that I should sink into the earth . . . I don't think there is anybody who could frighten me more—if you chose." To which Julia replied with some stridency: "Who are the people—and what are the looks, and when have you seen them and why if they exist should I ever give them to you? I shall expect a proper answer to these questions. I can't conceive when or at whom I have looked in this awful way, but I shall be very glad to look at you again and if you don't like my looks, you can tell me."

At a later date, Leslie made the mistake of referring to some "loathesome tourists," to which Julia, not one to let an unsubstantiated judgment slip her by, was quick to remind him that as a tourist himself, his remark was illogical. "I don't think it illogical," countered Leslie in his don's tone. "In the first place I never said that I was not loathesome; next it does not follow that all tourists are loathesome because I met some that were loathesome . . . but, in fact, the tourists here are almost universally loathesome . . . So you see, dear, that I consider myself an exceptional case and entitled to abuse everybody without abusing myself."

Julia by this time knew most of Leslie's weak spots and seems to have learned how to maneuver effortlessly from one to another; and if she made the point of being bad for Leslie as often as she did, it was probably to convince him that when the time came to marry him it would be out of sheer self-sacrifice. Her marriage would be the act of a martyr. But she would also have to dramatize her unworthiness a little, her own culpability, deficiency, weakness, and all the rest of it. This became a second motif she would now develop.

In a letter of July 31, Julia wrote: "I feel as if I had so often told you why I feel as if I could never marry . . . When I am near you I feel peaceful and sheltered: but even then, when we are nearest I don't feel as if I had any courage for life left in me—this is what I really feel, that if I could be quite close to you and feel you holding me I should be so content to die. Knowing what I am it is no temptation to me to marry you from the thought that I should make your life happier or brighter—I don't think I should . . . But it seems to me from what you said that you feel this uncertainty to be trying—and that is my fault. At first I loved you less, I suppose and it was easier to meet and to part. Perhaps now it would be easier at least, I mean wholesomer for you that we should be less near . . . All this sounds cold and horrid—but you know I do love you with my whole heart—only it seems to me such a poor dead heart . . . If there is wrong or difficulty it is I only who have caused it."

Five days later, she continued her lugubrious message: "If you really knew me you would know what a poor creature I am compared to you. I feel as if I were altogether in a lower atmosphere than yours...I feel as if I had some illness of which there was little hope of cure and you wanted to marry me...I think and think and picture what the future might be with you and though I cling instead of shrinking to the idea of being as close to you as can be, I cannot ever realize or face the idea of a fresh life and fresh interests... but now I have said all that it is in my heart to say and if you think it wiser and better that our relations should be different I shall understand and agree, my own darling, to whatever you do."

It was up to Leslie now to cast the deciding vote. But this he refused to do. "I did not mean for one moment," he replied, "to propose that you should marry me in hopes of a subsequent change." He, too, was "scarcely fit for a new life." They had their "common sorrow and sadness; we are both cripples and can help to bear each other's burdens." He then said, "If you did not exactly encourage your sadness, you still did not consciously try to get the better of it." It seemed as if Julia "had a kind of morbid shrinking from happiness." He ended his letter with a note he would sound again and again years later in his memory of her. He felt for her, he confessed, "reverence as well as love. *Think* me silly, if you please...You see, I have not got any saints and you must not be angry if I put you in the place where my saints ought to be." He knew that Julia was still wavering. But she must take her time. There was no rush. She could think of him as he thought of his dog—"a nice kind loving animal who will take what I give and be thankful."

When Leslie, with Laura and his sister Caroline Emelia, returned to London at the end of September, the problem of a caretaker for Laura had to be dealt with at once. His sister had tried and failed. So when Leslie made inquiries and a Fräulein Klappert was recommended, he moved quickly and informed Julia of his intention to take her on. The news threw her off balance. She suddenly realized that the presence of a governess assuming the responsibilities of the Stephen household would make her own position precarious. More than that, Fräulein Klappert would become a wedge between her and Leslie. It occurred to her, probably for the first time, that she *needed* Leslie's *needing* her far more than she needed her own self-imposed exile into melancholy.

Leslie, of course, immediately sensed Julia's confusion; and his record of the situation reveals how skillfully he nudged his "saint" into matrimony. "I spoke of the final decision to Julia with a sadness resulting...from my feeling that this would be a definitive arrangement, setting the seal, as it were, upon our separation. Then the thought came to her whether, after all, she could not make the effort to come to life again." With matters in this state of suspension, Leslie went to Brighton for Christmas with Laura, and Julia went to her mother in Saxonbury.

From Julia's letters during this holiday, Leslie sensed a change come over her. "The Klappert scheme brought the difficulty home to us. My Julia was in a state of painful indecision. She recognized now the existence of a 'possibility' [of marriage]: yet she could not find courage to make it a reality." All the old doubts came back. Wasn't she to blame for confessing her feelings to him? Wasn't she bound to keep herself for her children? On and on went the questions. But Leslie remained steadfast and planned his next move. This one would carry a certain amount of risk: If, he wrote her two days after Christmas, she ever felt that she might marry him, then "well and good. If not, you won't; and feelings can only grow; they won't be argued into . . . Whether you marry me or not I will love you with all my heart."

On the following day he fired off another letter to drive his point home: "Be my wife or not my wife; you can't help being my help and comfort." Their letters crossed in the mail: "I know that things would not be all smooth . . . ," Julia wrote, "but these are things which could all be met and dealt with as they occur and if I were sure of myself—not of my love for you but of my own self, I think I could face all else and only think of the happiness." Julia was on the verge of yielding. Leslie was almost certain of his triumph. He knew Julia would not willingly surrender her position of dominance to a governess. He had shown himself over the past few months as infantile, vulnerable, clutching, unwilling to assume responsibility. He had a hunch that to Julia's mind, he, Leslie, could become an ideal long-term project: someone she could nurse and cradle and manage—the beautiful young widow with her great old bearded intellectual under her wing. What a colossal sacrifice, people would say! Was there anyone more charitable, more suited to the task? All this, of course, meant control. It meant power. And Julia loved both.

 The question of matrimony remained unresolved at the time Leslie Stephen returned to London; but he had gotten into the habit of seeing Julia in the evenings. And so, on January 5, 1878, he went next door to sit with her as usual. "We talked the matter over once more," he recalled, "and I rose to go. She was sitting in her arm-chair by the fire-

place—I can see her now!—when suddenly she looked up and said 'I will be your wife and will do my best to be a good wife to you.'" (The word "love" was not used in Julia's acceptance.) They kept the engagement a secret for a brief period; and within a day or two, Julia went off to Freshwater in the Isle of Wight to nurse her beloved uncle, Thoby Prinsep, until his death a month later.

Leslie, in the meantime, was anxious to announce his good fortune. There is a lady, he wrote to Oliver Wendell Holmes, who is "good and beautiful." She is a person to whom everyone comes "in trouble or illness . . . We are to be married before very long . . . and if I am not happy again, it will be my own fault." To James Russell Lowell he wrote on January 9: "I am engaged to be married to Mrs. Herbert Duckworth . . . [She] has passed through seven years of widowhood in retirement from the world and entire devotion to her children and her sick or troubled relations . . . She has been so noble, so patient and unselfish." No one would be surprised that he should have fallen in love with her. A similar letter was sent to his friend Charles Eliot Norton.

On March 26, 1878, they were married at Kensington Church. Leslie gave his bride as a wedding present the portrait G. F. Watts had painted of him. With their marriage two very large, different, and not altogether harmonious families were united.

Like Maria Jackson, who was fourteen years younger than her husband, all three daughters married men considerably their senior. Herbert Duckworth, thirteen years older than Julia, was the perfect example of the public school man. Neither inclined to athletics nor predisposed to intellectual pursuits, he was a man whose "sweetness of temper" made him fit to "take his place in any society, without being the least of a dandy or a fop." George Duckworth, Julia's favorite, bore a striking resemblance to his father, though Herbert "was a little heavier of build and slower of mind." Leslie had read through all of Julia's letters to Herbert and half grudgingly felt bound to admit that she "owed her purest happiness" to him. If she brought to the union her youth and beauty, Herbert brought his complete and utter devotion. Julia was all he wanted in life, and so long as he lived, his happiness was complete.

Julia claimed, so Virginia said later, that in her marriage to Herbert she was "as happy as anyone can be." It was not easy to measure the happiness of a young woman who was pregnant throughout her married life, bearing three children in about as many years; and as Virginia wrote, "like all very handsome men who die tragically, he left not so much a character behind him as a legend." But on Julia's side, their love was like something out of a fairy tale, to which Julia's beauty belonged and where the prince never died.

But in this fairy tale the prince did die. He died suddenly, unexpectedly, shockingly; and the young bride, in her grief, abandoned her God, slipped into a deep and lasting depression, and in time married another man—a scholar and hypochondriac, an egotistical, demanding, utterly dependent man—with whom every day now became filled with tension and discord. This is the life which many years later Virginia would recover in *To the Lighthouse*. In the novel she would re-create the summer of 1894, the last holiday the entire family was to spend at St. Ives. From the child's perspective, it was a world of freedom and excitement. But behind the sound of children playing and waves breaking, one could also just barely hear traces of sorrow and secrecy.

Mrs. Ramsay—let us think of her as Julia Stephen—the most elusive figure (both in life and in fiction), is portrayed as a brooding woman, with "her hair grey, her cheek sunk, at fifty . . . now formidable to behold"—with her "strange severity, her extreme courtesy." There is something large and forceful about her. Indeed she had the whole of the male sex "under her protection"; men were "trustful, childlike, reverential." But there is some deep mystery behind these surface impressions. There is someone always hovering at her side, someone unnamed, an unspecified presence. As she went on her errands of mercy, holding her black parasol erect, she moved with an "air of expectation, as if she were going to meet someone round the corner." Tansley noticed it; so did Lily. She remembered Mrs. Ramsay "walking rather fast in front, as if she expected to meet some one round the corner." But who is this "someone"? A stranger? Her phantom lover perhaps? Herbert Duckworth perhaps?

Mrs. Ramsay was beautiful still and could never quite shake herself free of the sense of it. She carried the "torch of her beauty" into any room she entered; and "veil it as she might . . . her beauty was apparent. She had been admired. She had been loved." Men had confessed their secrets to her; tears had been shed in her presence. Indeed, she was "like some queen who, finding her people gathered . . . acknowledges their tributes silently, and accepts their devotion . . . their tribute to her beauty."

Henry James acknowledged Julia's beautiful face and head, but confessed that to the "outside world" that was her "main interest." He had often wondered why such a beauty should have "consented to become, matrimonially, the receptacle" of Leslie Stephen's "ineffable and impossible taciturnity and dreariness." But Leslie Stephen was not "taciturn." From the start he was at

Julia's elbow, plucking like a child, begging for sympathy, imploring her to reassure him he was not a failure, that his books would be read, that he too "lived in the heart of life; was needed." And so she reassured him "by her laugh, her poise, her competence . . . that it was real; the house was full . . . If he put implicit faith in her, nothing should hurt him . . . not for a second should he find himself without her."

How exhausted he left her though; how much she lavished on him; and in her weariness, there often crept "some faintly disagreeable sensation with another origin"—the "sensation" of feeling superior, of feeling better than he was. That bothered her, made deep fissures in their relations, diminished what little harmony they made together. He acted so often like a petulant child with his demands, his petty annoyances, his chronic whimpering—"if his little finger ached the whole world must come to an end."

What the world must know, however, was that Mr. Ramsay—like Leslie Stephen—was an intellectual. Had this not been his first powerful attraction? Had she not in the beginning admired him precisely for his mind? She often "made herself out even more ignorant than she was, because he liked telling her she was a fool." He liked thinking "she was not clever, not book-learned at all."

And, as if this were not enough to ask, he wanted always something else— "wanted the thing she always found it so difficult to give him; wanted her to tell him that she loved him." She knew that he was thinking, "You are more beautiful than ever. And she felt herself very beautiful. Will you not tell me just once that you love me? . . . But she could not do it; she could not say it." And the reason was simple, at least in their daughter's perception— Mrs. Ramsay, like Julia Stephen, did not love her husband. Nurse and protect him, yes. Bear his children, yes. Love him, no. And Virginia Woolf, the novelist, knew that pity and vanity and self-sacrifice, when mixed in the right doses, could be made very much to resemble love.

Indeed there were times when Julia (speaking through Mrs. Ramsay) "could not understand how she had ever felt any emotion or affection for him." During their courtship Julia had uttered countless declarations of love, but she was too proud of her integrity and altogether too direct to speak a deliberate lie. She might not tell the *whole* truth, but conscious deception to her mind was a sign of weakness, and weak she was most assuredly not. Nor was it any perversity that stopped her from giving her husband this small satisfaction. What she felt for him was *pity*, not love. And pity was all Julia had to give. She was full of pity. Sometimes her own weariness came from "pitying people." The truth was that Mrs. Ramsay (like Julia) "pitied men always as if they lacked something." And so, after their marriage Julia would never again say she loved Leslie. She might wear herself out in his behalf; she might die of exhaustion for him, but words of love she could not speak. It had nothing to do with obstinacy or pride. It had to do with secrecy. And the secret was that Julia still loved Herbert Duckworth—she was still *in love* with Herbert Duckworth.

Herbert Duckworth had become her phantom lover and one day she would join him again. This is what Virginia was hinting at when three times she described Mrs. Ramsay as "walking as if she expected to meet someone round the corner." This is what she was hinting at in the lyrical passage describing Mrs. Ramsay's melancholy: "Never did anybody look so sad. Bitter and black, half-way down, in the darkness ... perhaps a tear formed; a tear fell; the waters swayed this way and that, received it, and were at rest. Never did anybody look so sad. But was it nothing but looks, people said? What was there behind it—her beauty and splendour? Had he blown his brains out, they asked, had he died the week before they were married—some other, some earlier lover ..." This train of feeling slowly builds throughout the novel, image by image, until a scene materializes with Mrs. Ramsay sitting alone with James; somehow the lighthouse moves into the foreground; time and place begin to lose their boundaries in a succession of incantations and images—" 'It will end, it will end,' she said. It will come, it will come ... There rose ... there curled up off the floor of the mind, rose from the lake of one's being, a mist, a bride to meet her lover."

This is what the narrative has been leading to—"the bride to meet her lover"—Julia, her eyes on the searching beams of the lighthouse, waiting to be reunited with her lover—at peace, in solitude, in silence, away from the clamor of children, away from the demanding husband, alone to await Herbert. Death meant reunion. This was the dream no one could share, no one must know. Watching the lighthouse in this calm, she felt its silver beams of light were stroking "some sealed vessel in her brain whose bursting would flood her with delight, she had known happiness, exquisite happiness, intense happiness." And all of it owing to her handsome, carefree, pleasure-loving Herbert. As Julia's sister once said, when Herbert Duckworth smiled, it was like "a beam of light."

There is a short, seemingly straightforward passage in the novel where Mr. and Mrs. Ramsay are out for a stroll before dinner. It runs as follows: Ramsay wanted to tell his wife

> ... that when he was walking on the terrace just now—here he became uncomfortable, as if he were breaking into that solitude, that aloofness, that remoteness of hers ... But she pressed him.

What had he wanted to tell her, she asked, thinking it was about going to the Lighthouse; and that he was sorry he had said "Damn you". But no. He did not like to see her look so sad, he said. Only wool gathering, she protested, flushing a little. They both felt uncomfortable . . .

They had reached the gap between the two clumps of red-hot pokers, and there was the Lighthouse again, but she would not let herself look at it. Had she known that he was looking at her, she thought, she would not have let herself sit there, thinking. She disliked anything that reminded her that she had been seen sitting thinking. So she looked over her shoulder, at the town.

Neutral as this passage reads, it raises several questions, because Mr. and Mrs. Ramsay's fluctuating emotions are left entirely without explicit motive. What, for example, is behind Ramsay's initial awkwardness and Mrs. Ramsay's remoteness? Why is she "flushing"? Why does she dislike being seen watching the lighthouse? And what is she "thinking" of? Virginia Woolf has omitted a great deal of information the reader needs to supply if the passage is to make any sense. If we "read into" the passage the *added* bracketed words as deletions the reader is meant to infer, we get a better idea of how Woolf went about achieving her effects:

Ramsay wanted to tell his wife that as he was pacing

the terrace just now—here he became uncomfortable, as if he were breaking into that solitude, that aloofness, that remoteness of hers . . . But she pressed him. What had he wanted to tell her, she asked, thinking it was about going to the Lighthouse . . . But no. He did not like to see her look so sad, he said. [He did not like her so preoccupied, still, with Herbert.] Only wool gathering, she protested, flushing a little. [She flushed in embarrassment; her husband had seen her longing, had guessed her fantasy.] They both felt uncomfortable . . . They reached the gap between the two clumps of red-hot pokers, and there was the Lighthouse again, but she would not let herself look at it. [There was too much of the earlier happiness and passion she could no longer speak of.] Had she known that he was looking at her [earlier, in her private moment gazing at the lighthouse in all her intensity], she would not have let herself sit there, thinking. She disliked anything that reminded her that she had been seen sitting thinking [about her phantom lover. That was too sacred, too private, too much her own.] So she looked over her shoulder, at the town.

Julia's sorrow, like Mrs. Ramsay's, was attached to her absent lover, but that sorrow was always waiting nearby for her "to dip into privately." It was also the absent lover who made Mrs. Ramsay shun the mirror; for she was resentful "that she had grown old, perhaps, by her own fault." For the fantasy must stop in old age; with her beauty vanished, she might even seek to hasten her own death. The young Virginia must have felt this in some mysterious way, for had she not, as a child of thirteen, seen a man sitting on her mother's deathbed? Had her mother not lain on Herbert's grave, alone with him for hours? Had he not been the only man she had ever loved? And was this not all part of the fairy-tale world of Julia Duckworth's marriage and widowhood? Virginia Woolf, the mature novelist, must have been very sure it was. But apart from this, there was still another, earlier, and more difficult world grounded in self-doubt.

Julia Jackson had been born into a world of beauty and vanity. In this world what was good was beautiful, Sappho had said. Physical beauty was a sign of interior goodness. Throughout the ages, the civilized world had perceived beauty as being equal to moral superiority, as being exalted in spirit and in deed. And if you were lovely, you were loved. This, or something like it, was the creed of those who inhabited Julia's world.

But did Julia herself believe this? Probably. Or at least a good part of it. After all, while she was still a child, artists had proposed to her, had painted and sculpted and photographed her. As a young woman, men and women had fawned on her, confided in her. So if she was treated like a beauty, she behaved like a beauty. If she was the best, she must behave like the best. Something of the self-fulfilling energy must have drifted into her personal field almost from childhood.

But there was a problem here. It must have occurred to her almost from the start that she, Julia, was "loved" for *how she looked* and not necessarily for *what she was*. This realization brought with it the troublesome afterthought that people accepted her on the outside alone, never questioning or doubting what lay beneath. Further, without ever having experienced rejection, she also had no experience in dealing with it; she had, in effect, no immunity to refusal and disillusionment. Most important, Julia's self-esteem depended entirely on the estimate of others; and so she grew up having very little notion of her own worth. If her beauty came first, then self-doubt must have followed closely on its heels.

Maria Jackson's life centered on her three beautiful daughters. She loved them all, but Julia principally—Julia was "so unhappy"; Julia devoted so much of herself to her mother. She was Maria's "dearest child." But being the "dearest" *anyone* to Maria Jackson, whose multifarious ailments overshadowed everything else in her life, meant being her mother's full-time nurse. For Maria Jackson was as susceptible to bodily torment as her husband was immune to it. The extraordinary bond between mother and daughter seemed, therefore, to have developed in the special relationship which grew up between the grateful patient and the adoring nurse. In these early years spent in the presence of pain and suffering, Julia seemed to have begun seeing herself chiefly as a healer and giver and doer of good; and with that perception came a more solid sense of self-worth. She was loved now for what she *did*, not for how she *looked*. If Julia felt self-doubt, it could now be quelled by simply reminding herself that as a healer, she was on her surest footing. In the dispensation of care, she was on safe ground.

Most important was the realization that her extraordinary beauty was of no consequence in the sickroom. The homeliest of nurses was needed and sought out. So that if her looks were a source of self-doubt, she would, for the rest of her life, rely upon the sick and the needy to reverse that forever-threatening sense of unworthiness and irrelevance. Her identity as a valued human being would thus always be in a constant state of renewal and ratification; and so it would remain as long as she practiced public welfare and private sacrifice.

Julia once said to Leslie that her mother always indulged in the "pleasing delusion" that any man who saw her in a railway carriage immediately fell in love with her. We mark her phrase, "pleasing delusion," for that to Julia is exactly what it was. On another occasion she herself suggested that her benevolence was a little misleading: "One is always being called upon to sympathize in trouble . . . So I am grateful when any one gets through it and then I *cease to think about them*, which sounds brutal and perhaps it is rather . . . I at once put people away on a sort of mental shelf when they are bright again."* Nowhere does she speak more directly of her attitude toward the sick. This admission also explains Julia's coolness toward her father, whose good health did nothing to bolster her forever-flagging sense of self; and so long as he lived, he would remain "put . . . away" on that "mental shelf."

"I have often wondered," Julia Stephen began her *Notes from Sick Rooms*,

* Emphasis added.

"why it is considered a proof of virtue in anyone to become a nurse. The ordinary relations between the sick and the well are far easier and pleasanter than between the well and the well." Such a remark must have come as a surprise to those who knew her, for one did not usually associate pleasant relations with sickrooms. There are passages in Leslie's memoir which also hint at the deeper motive in Julia's benevolence. "My darling was always making her rounds—" he wrote, "more alas! than her strength justified— among people whom she could help." He had often found her devising some way to bring comfort to someone who needed it. "She kept in mind all manner of anniversaries which justified such acts . . . I used to laugh at her for her multitudinous recollections of birthdays of nephews, nieces and cous- ins . . . I confess that I grudged a little this incessant round of kindly services." They were laborious and exhausting and were not what one would call im- promptu acts of kindness. Indeed, they were "part of a system, carried out in the forethought . . . She was constantly preparing them: anxious (a little too anxious I used to think at times) to conceal herself or find some excuse which would make the bestowal of a present look like the payment of a debt." Rarely did she meet anyone she "liked or pitied without asking herself what little thing can I do to give them pleasure?" Julia—of necessity, perhaps— thought suffering so common that she lost no opportunity in trying to relieve it whenever she could. She had so thoroughly set herself apart to relieve pain and sorrow that when "no special object offered itself for her sympathy, where there was no patient to be nursed . . . she had a stream of overflowing goodwill which forced her to look out for some channel of discharge."

In *To the Lighthouse*, Carmichael's refusing Mrs. Ramsay's offer to buy him tobacco makes her uncomfortable. "It injured her that he should shrink. It hurt her . . . that she was suspected; and that all this desire of hers to give, to help, was vanity. For her own self-satisfaction was it that she wished so instinctively to help, to give, that people might say of her, 'O Mrs. Ramsay! dear Mrs. Ramsay . . .' and need her and send for her and admire her? Was it not secretly this that she wanted . . ."

From its earliest stages, Julia and Leslie's relationship was freighted with discord. Both were very determined, self-willed, fractious people. "Milly is alarming from her silences . . . ," Julia complained, "but she is not alarming in her speech as you are—that is the difference. You scorn and shrivel one up after having sat in judgement silently." Leslie's complaint was far more serious. Of all the weapons in Julia's armamentarium, the deadliest was the silent threat of withdrawal, of moving beyond his reach. "You want me to tell you all I feel and so I do; but how can I do it openly with such a threat hanging over me?"

What tended most to confuse him was the contradictory, double-faced way she alternately appeared to him. At one moment she was the exalted, proud, defiant woman who saw the whole of life as a challenge. At another moment she was downtrodden, exhausted, depressed, harboring a certain vague self-contempt: "I am only unhappy because I deserve to be so," said Julia. "It is always so difficult for me to realize that any one can have an intense feeling for me." Or "I get so puzzled about your caring for me . . . I always have the uneasy feeling that you would not like the real me a bit!" Or again: "I don't know whether as you say I am reviving from drowning; sometimes I feel as if I could not make the effort and . . . only wished to come to an end."

Such persistent devaluation might have struck the ordinary spouse dumb, but Leslie had too much invested in Julia to remain silent. "You speak in some of your letters," he said, "as if you had a kind of superstitious feeling that you ought not to be happy." Reasonable though he seemed at the time, what Leslie did not understand was that people like Julia felt satisfied only when they were suffering, for only then did they feel special. Julia had the knack for engineering scenes in such a way that almost *anything* Leslie said had the potential to hurt her; and by this strategy she maintained her exalted position. There was a further advantage to being "permanently" unhappy and gloomy and discontented: when she agreed, finally, to whatever it might be, her submission was a serious matter, not unlike some heaven-sent miracle; and this, one assumes, was precisely the effect she wished to produce. So that if Leslie thought matrimony would change matters in the least, he was sadly mistaken. In marriage, Julia promised him, he would find her "a bothering old thing . . . I shall stick to you like a burr and interfere with all your pleasures." And as Virginia Woolf noted in *To the Lighthouse*, the Ramsay marriage was "no monotony of bliss."

Julia's first five years as Mrs. Leslie Stephen were almost entirely consumed in pregnancy. Between May 1879 and October 1883, she bore Leslie four children in addition to looking after her own three from her Duckworth marriage, and Laura.* She took charge of Laura after marrying Leslie, but when her own four children were born, Laura was kept in a separate part

---

* Vanessa: May 30, 1879; Julian Thoby: September 8, 1880; Adeline Virginia: January 25, 1882; Adrian Leslie: October 27, 1883. And there were from the Duckworth marriage: George Herbert: March 5, 1868; Stella: May 30, 1869; and Gerald de l'Etang: October 29, 1870.

of the house. When Julia was away, Leslie continued to mention her in his letters. "I wish she could make other people fond of her—though nobody will be so silly as to love her like her papa." He knew that Julia was impatient with the children and advised her, where Laura was concerned, to move slowly, not to press too hard. But Laura's refusal to read made him despair: "She may not be idiotic but she can never be really like other people, I fear."

While he was away negotiating the lease on Talland House, he slipped into his letter to Julia a little note for Laura: "My darling Laura," it began, "I am in a beautiful place called St. Ives. We shall come in the summer I hope. There is a beautiful beach for the little ones. You will bathe there and learn to swim ... It is a very nice house, with a garden and a fountain and grapes and strawberries and peaches. I hope that you have been good. It makes me very unhappy if mother tells me you have been naughty. Your loving father." She was eleven at the time of this letter.

Laura's "obstinacy" floored him. "I long to shake the little wretch ... It poisons even the pleasure of hearing about the little ones." Her "mulishness and perversity" were dreadful. She needed discipline; she needed punishment; she was hopeless. "I tremble when I think of her alone with you. It gives me a shudder when I think how I am forced to treat her. Those dreadful fits of passion are heartbreaking." "Laura's howls ... ring in my ears. If she could only know how she tortures me!"

But the torture continued. "I cannot see how Laura could get on at a school with other girls, not of her own kind," he wrote in 1884. In October of the same year: "She—Laura—told me when I asked her if she had been good, that she had been choking all dinner-time. What a struggle it is, for what a little! ... I shall still try to arrange for her living somewhere with some one to manage her." In July 1885: "Laura was in one of her tempers just before I came away ... It is all very painful, but I suppose that I shall get hardened to it in time!"

In November of that year: "When she is good, it is as pathetic to me as it is painful when she is naughty—I can't help thinking that there are gleams of something that might have been charming." And so the letters and the years accumulated. By age thirteen or fourteen, Laura was reading, minimally, *Robinson Crusoe*, and at sixteen she appears to have read aloud parts of *Alice in Wonderland* to Thoby. Between June and August 1889, she was committed to the Earlswood Asylum for the Imbecile and Weak-minded in Red Hill, Surrey, established by Dr. Langdon-Down, where she remained until January 1897, at which time she was transferred to Brook House, Southgate.

"My poor Laura," wrote Leslie in his memoir, "was settled with Dr. Corner at Brook House, Southgate, on 14th January. We had heard some complaints of Red Hill, where he had been physician, and upon his setting up this establishment thought it best to place her there . . . when I saw her the other day, I was pained by her looks and ways. She is unable apparently to recognize any of us clearly."* During her interval of childbearing, Julia wrote nine stories for children, several adult essays, and her small book called *Notes from Sick Rooms*. And in 1882 Leslie undertook the massive project of editing the *Dictionary of National Biography*. Between the *Dictionary* and Julia's pregnancies and a household of children and servants to be managed, there was a good deal of tension at No. 22 and frequent explosions of temper.

In late 1881, Leslie purchased the lease of Talland House in St. Ives, Cornwall, where the family would spend their summers until Julia's death in 1895. St. Ives was to become one of Virginia's most cherished spots, the source of her happiest memories and the setting for *To the Lighthouse*. Talland House was a large square white structure set on the high ground above the bay of St. Ives. It was for the children a rich playground of sensations and excitement. There was the endless joy of tree climbing, bathing, cricket, and bug hunting—butterflies by day and moths by night. By day, too, they watched the passing ships and by night the pulsing beams of the Godrevy lighthouse.

> On Saturday morning Master Hilary Hunt and Master Basil Smith came up to Talland House and asked Master Thoby and Miss Virginia Stephen to accompany them to the light-house as Freeman the boatman said that there was a perfect tide and wind for going there. Master Adrian Stephen was much disappointed at not being allowed to go.

Thus wrote Virginia Stephen, aged ten, for the September 12, 1892, issue of *Hyde Park Gate News*, the Stephen children's family bulletin. The thirteen summer holidays at St. Ives made for "the best beginning to life conceivable," wrote Virginia many years later.

Talland House, always untidy and sandy and swarming with guests, had large bay windows and balconies with a splendid view of the sea. It was surrounded by a fragrant escallonia hedge. Situated on a steep slope was a large expanse of lawn divided by hedges into a series of smaller gardens, named by the children the "coffee" garden, the "love" (loo) corner, the foun-

---

* According to her death certificate, Laura Stephen died of cancer on February 9, 1945, at Priory, a psychiatric facility at Roehampton. She was seventy-five.

tain, the kitchen garden, the cricket lawn, and the strawberry bed. Most enchanting of all, however, was the sound of the sea, which could be heard in every room of the house.

In July of 1893, Leslie took the children with him alone to St. Ives, while Julia remained in London to nurse Stella through the mumps. His letter home gives some idea of the freedom and fun they had with all the Cornish enchantments. "Here is another beautiful day... Yesterday we went to Trencrom. The children had their inevitable nets; for they are quite mad about bugs. When we got to the top of the hill, a high wind was blowing and several butterflies hovering about just on the rocky slope. A tremendous chase took place... I at last called them off; but luckily they caught one at the end and so came home in triumph. They are all very well..."

Leslie loved his children not only for themselves but in the more private way as evidence of his manhood and vitality. He was, after all, almost fifty when he began his second family with Julia. In the bright and boisterous family circle, it was the baby Virginia he loved most. In October 1883, when Julia was away nursing her mother, Leslie wrote her his daily bulletin. He looked forward each evening to coming home to see the "brats." 'Ginia, as he called her, was the most affectionate. "She sat on my knee to look at Bewick and every now and then said Kiss and put her cheek against mine." A few months later came a longer report: "Little 'Ginia is already an accomplished flirt. I said today that I must go down to my work. She nestled herself down on the sofa by me; squeezed her little self tightly up against me and then gazed up with her bright eyes through her shock of hair and said 'Don't go, Papa!' She looked full of mischief all the time. I never saw such a little rogue."

There were many periods of domestic contentment in the early years of their marriage, but they were brief and separated by long intervals of tension. Leslie's general irascibility and chronic faultfinding coupled with Julia's continuing melancholy over her beloved Herbert kept the atmosphere at No. 22 cheerless and charged.* Clouding the atmosphere further was Leslie himself, who could not understand love as a union based on open-

---

* There is a surviving letter from Julia to Virginia about a woman who kills her baby by squeezing the air out of its body while dancing it around the room. Virginia must remember never to "waltz children round the rooms," Julia admonishes in this bizarre communication to her extraordinarily sensitive young daughter (Berg Collection, New York Public Library; undated).

ness and equality. That basic concept eluded him. His notion of a good wife and a happy marriage required Julia's being entirely at his service, assuring him that no one deserved more to be pitied. Something close to morbid dependency, to Leslie's mind, was indisputable proof of connubial love. So that the unending demands he made on Julia were, to his way of thinking, not demands at all: they were merely the symptoms of a wholesome devotion. And Julia, more often than not, urged him on in these endless claims and childish sentiments.

Financial worries, whether real or imagined, plagued Leslie Stephen all his life. Although Julia had an income from Herbert Duckworth's estate and assumed the financial responsibility of supporting George, Stella, and Gerald, with St. Ives there were now two large houses to maintain and a household of servants. Leslie handed over to Julia the task of managing the household expenses and then subjected her to weekly scenes of self-pity when he inspected the accounts. This practice continued after Julia's death, first with Stella and later with Vanessa.

From the time of his father's death, Leslie had a private income and throughout his life, although never pressed for money, often imagined himself at the point of bankruptcy. The whole family would end up on the streets begging for coins, he moaned with unnerving regularity. His preoccupation with money in the family was the result, partly, of his determination to make clear that "those dependent on him were really dependent and partly from his desire for gratitude and appreciation," wrote his biographer, Noel Annan. "The subconscious process runs: if I can impress upon them that but for me they would be in the workhouse they will love me and appreciate my talents all the more." Judging from his letters, however, one questions how "subconscious" that process really was.

The pressure of work was a constant source of tension in Leslie Stephen's life. He was a prodigious worker and brought his colossal energy and intelligence to the worlds of literary journalism, philosophy, and biography. He was always afraid that he might be just a bit too facile, however. "Victor Marshall," he said to Julia, "has an unlucky way of telling me everything unpleasant that has been said about me and mentions that a person had called me a 'notorious penny-a-liner'. There is a horrible plausibility about the name which makes it disagreeable." Julia, true to form, replied: "V. Marshall is very stupid to repeat such things, but not ½ so stupid as you are to mind them. Good night, Dearest."

Apart from his journalism and editorial duties, Leslie Stephen published books which he hoped would advance his name as a philosopher. *The History of English Thought in the Eighteenth Century* was more highly regarded than the book he most cared for, *The Science of Ethics*. The toll such work exacted on his peace of mind, however, caused endless anxieties. Family responsibilities and imaginary fears of financial ruin motivated his decision to take on the editorship of the *Dictionary of National Biography* in 1882. Although he fulfilled his position efficiently, the torments of so exacting a job suited him neither intellectually nor temperamentally. He took great pride in his philosophical writings, and the *DNB* could not provide that kind of satisfaction. It became, consequently, an ever-increasing source of frustration. His office on 15 Waterloo Place was his "place of drudgery"; he woke in the middle of the night with "attacks of horrors"; his work on the *Dictionary* was perpetual "bondage."

He tended naturally to exaggerate his woes to Julia, but occasionally he was willing to admit that "it is hard work, but not altogether uninteresting and it is pleasant to be employed on a really solid job." Once, in fact, he felt sufficiently expansive to confess that "Dictionary bothers are really superficial. They ruffle my temper but they don't disturb me below the surface much."

After nine years as its editor, Stephen retired from the *Dictionary*. But those nine years provided him with perfect justification for so channeling his energies. His children needed never to doubt his worth or apologize for the contributions he made to the world of letters. "Certainly I will admit that I am not a 'failure' pure and simple," he wrote toward the end of his life, "and if my books have not sold largely, I admit that reasons may be given, not all uncomplimentary, and that in any case failure to win such popularity would not justify whining." There was one sense, however, in which he had failed. "I have scattered myself too much. I think that I had it in me to make something like a real contribution to philosophical or ethical thought. Unluckily, what with journalism and dictionary making, I have been a jack of all trades." Had he concentrated his efforts, he might have made a better job of it. As it was, his contribution to the history of English thought in the nineteenth century would "only be mentioned in small type and footnotes." When the time came, Virginia would portray her father's frustrated ambitions in Mr. Ramsay's final realization that as a philosopher—on the metaphysical spectrum of A to Z—he was stuck at "Q" and would never proceed beyond that point.

Throughout her life as Mrs. Leslie Stephen, Julia never took a moment's rest. Though there were eight children to think of, they were a minor affair against what she saw as her responsibility. She seems to have had an unrealistic sense of her physical capacities, together with a deep-seated belief that she was unvanquishable. Whether she labored across London visiting the indigent and the sick or spent the summer in St. Ives looking after the penniless and the dying, she saw this work as her mission. There were clothes and provisions to be furnished and sickbeds to see to. She was a nurse. This was her duty. The thoroughness of her slender volume *Notes from Sick Rooms* eloquently testifies to the care and seriousness with which she practiced the art of healing.

And at the close of each day, exhausted but determined, Julia sat at her desk answering endless letters from people who wanted her help, her advice, her comfort. There was a letter from a woman out of work, from a mother whose daughter was in trouble, from people whose poverty was heartbreaking. All of these Julia answered. In addition a large part of every overcrowded day had to be sacrificed to the demands of her husband and the equally endless needs of the children.

It must have come as a relief to Julia when it was time for Leslie to go off on one of his "rest" holidays. Some of them, in fact, were instigated by Julia herself; and he never failed to write at length, complaining how bored and lonely he was away from her. Mixed into the sulking were daily reports of the meals he ate, the state of his "insides," the hours of sleep he managed, the distances he walked, the regularity of his bowels, and all the other crucial information his beloved Julia longed to know. As Virginia was to say, her father's health was her mother's "fetish."

Leslie was aware of Julia's preoccupation and knew with this one card in his deck he could always be certain of getting his way. Exactly what was wrong with him, especially when he overworked, has never been made clear; but it appears that most of his troubles came from nervous tension and prolonged periods of stress. A day or two away from work and his symptoms invariably subsided, no matter how close he was to "physical collapse."

One such instance occurred shortly after he finished the *Life of Henry Fawcett*. "I undertook to write this [biography] almost immediately after his death, and the work involved a good deal of labour in 1885. It is one of my weaknesses that I cannot work slowly; I must, if I work at all, work under high pressure." The strain of the biography, coupled with his labor on the

Dictionary, wore him down. On January 19, 1887, therefore, he went off to Switzerland and remained there, briefly in the company of Lucy Clifford, the novelist, her daughters, and the writer Olive Schreiner. By the twenty-first, he was "feeling stronger every day." But Miss Schreiner grated on his nerves: "She seems to be one of the small literary people who call other people Philistines and are full of conceit ... I cannot hear Miss S. very well as she sits on my deaf side and I wish I could not hear her at all." Even Lucy Clifford's literary "twaddle" irritated him. By the twenty-fourth, all the bother about his health was "damned nonsense." "I am *quite well* and I walked my 25 miles in the snow today without effort." On the twenty-ninth, although he professed hating to be away, he decided to stay on a few days longer. He would do some Alpine climbing with his friend and guide Melchior Anderegg. Midway through his letter, however, the grumbling began: "I rather grudge the money I'm spending ... I am not an invalid now and I begin to have questions about the dictionary." Then on the thirtieth: "I shall be a day longer than I said yesterday." By January 31, he began to write as though he were being detained against his will: "If I am ever forced to do anything of this kind again, we must arrange for my not doing it in solitude." If he stayed any longer, he was sure to "get into the tantarums." When he did return, the family would go on holiday to Brighton. That was the plan. "It will ... please your mother, I hope. But what about the money?"

Leslie returned to London from his "exile" and within days Julia was off to Brighton alone. Her father, now eighty-three years old, was fatally ill and her mother desperately needed her. He stayed behind with Stella and the children and did his best to be magnanimous, but, after all, his own well-being did come first.

Dr. Jackson did not linger: he died on March 31, 1887. Leslie wrote, assuring Julia that she need think of nothing but herself and her mother. "It is good that it is all over," he wrote on April 1. "I hope that you will come when the funeral is over and bring your mother ... it would be a comfort to me to think that we were of some use to her." Later that day he wrote a second letter: "I need not say again how glad I shall be to have her here ... Dearest, sweetest of darlings, I want you back ... we have been apart a terribly long time this year." Didn't marriage confer certain privileges?

Five days passed and there was no sign of Julia. Mrs. Jackson was evidently taking more time to recover from her grief than he thought necessary. Now he grew impatient: "I do not feel that it is right that such a sacrifice of you should be asked or made." In his second letter, on April 5, Mrs. Jackson's claim on Julia became a moral issue: "It is really not right ... I hope your mother will see it and see that it is also for her own good to move." On the following day the hectoring continued: "Nobody seems to see that you are sacrificing yourself by staying away from me and the children for weeks." His mother-in-law should be aware of the harm she was doing. "If I acted on my own opinion, I should tell her distinctly . . . that she was unintentionally cruel to you and acting injudiciously . . . It is all I can bear to see you—worn and bothered as you are—calmly submitting to be tormented."

Leslie went to Brighton himself to make his case. They had been separated some six weeks by this time. But he returned to London alone. Julia must remain behind to help her mother sort through her father's papers. And so the abandoned husband continued to whine, to badger, even to threaten: "Tell your mother that till she comes I shall do nothing but work." The longer she delayed the more likely she would return to find him a mere "bag of bones." He needed soothing, comforting. His loneliness and his health were not doing the trick.

Perhaps some domestic news would move his coldhearted wife. His favorite, the precious and precocious little Virginia, was always an item of interest: " 'Ginia tells me a 'story' every night—it does not change much but she seems to enjoy it. She wrote to Miss Vincent [governess] today in a most lovely hand." Two days later: " 'Ginia said she would make a speech tonight. She stood in the window and declaimed a long rigmarole about a crow and a book till her hearers coughed her down. She would have gone on till now." But where was the mother of this lonely household? He needed her. They needed her. If she had again to postpone returning home, he said, "I shall tear all my hair off."

Leslie had trouble, now and always, concealing his resentment toward anyone who interfered with his possessions—and Julia belonged to him. Not once, however, did it occur to him what Julia herself might need. It never crossed his mind that she wanted and needed to stay on in Brighton at this time. Finally she told him so, and his response was one of utter astonishment. "I thought, my darling, that you were worn and tired out; but I did not understand that you were so worn out as to feel that staying away was good for you . . . I really feel bewildered—I don't know what you do wish."

Julia's mother died at 22 Hyde Park Gate on April 2, 1892, with Julia by her side. As one of the beautiful Pattle sisters, Maria Jackson was a vaguely benevolent, silly, gushing, sentimental woman—the one person Julia loved unconditionally; and she was the most cherished daughter. Mrs. Jackson wrote to Julia "sometimes three times a day and often there would be an additional telegram to her 'dear heart,' her 'lamb.' " Her main topic of interest was illness. When, after Herbert Duckworth's death, Julia became "a kind of unofficial nurse, she reported symptoms to her mother who, with great assurance, diagnosed and recommended treatment." When Mrs. Jackson had no sick relations to report, she fell back on her own long scroll of bodily torments. Her second topic of importance was "the question of beauty, and here too she was full of excellent advice." Reading the voluminous correspondence between mother and daughter, wrote Quentin Bell, one felt as though one were "struggling through a wilderness of treacle." Maria Jackson's death left Leslie now the principal contender for his "noble" wife's cares and ministrations.

One of the curious features of their marriage was Leslie's perception of himself as Julia's savior and consoler. He was convinced of this despite the fact that it was he who clamored for comforting and cradling. In October 1881, while Julia was pregnant with Virginia, Leslie wrote: "Dearest love, the more I think, the more I feel that you are overworked in every way. You ought not to have so many burdens on your shoulders . . . If you became an invalid, life would be black for me . . . If I felt that your health had broken down because of my selfish indifference, it would go near to destroy all my happiness." A year of two later, from St. Ives "Dearest, as to our little argument, you must see that I had not the least thought of blaming you! or of complaining of anyone for not making me happier . . . What I did and must think of is that you seem so often over burdened . . . and then it seems as if I could do nothing to help." "I wish," he wrote at a still later date, "I could see my way to getting some of your burdens lightened—I *can* see a way of not adding to them."

But he did add to them. He added to them greatly, blindly, from the most selfish of motives. Several times when the family was moving from London to St. Ives for the summer holiday, for instance, he decided he would walk part of the way to Cornwall. The exercise, he insisted, would do him good. On those occasions he left Julia with the entire responsibility and confusion of moving eight children, servants, endless crates and pieces of luggage and household provisions on this long and difficult train journey. "I ought really to take more of your household worries on my shoulders," he conceded. "It is not so much that I am incompetent—though I am rather—as that I get into such tantarums."

Leslie hated to see his beloved Julia "slaving—for other people." This was to be his refrain to the very end. Julia had told him once she felt like a person drowning, that she no longer had the strength to go on and only "wished to come to an end." Her wish came true. After seventeen years of marriage. The exhausted swimmer gave up. At the age of forty-nine, the sacrificial Julia Stephen went under, used up and worn out. She fell ill. Doctors came. Whispers of rheumatic fever sounded throughout the house. And on May 5, 1895, the unthinkable happened: Julia died. She was not unvanquishable after all.

While he was alive, Herbert Duckworth nourished Julia's youth and beauty; and as Virginia observed, her mother's "treasuring" her first love "changed it perhaps to something far fairer than it could have been, had life allowed it to endure." Her marriage to Leslie Stephen, however, aroused the full spectrum of energies "set apart to relieve pain." Naturally her beauty flattered Leslie and bolstered his sometimes anxious manhood. During their courtship, he enumerated for Julia the full menu of his needs, and Julia responded to them fully and beautifully. She was genuinely interested in his difficulties. She was a superb listener. She encouraged him to pour out everything he felt. She spoke always in his terms. She made him feel the center of her universe. She shone her beauty upon him alone. And last but not least, she bore him four beautiful children. What more could he ask for? If Julia's marriage to Herbert was founded on passion, her union with Leslie was grounded in sacrifice. Now and to the end of her life, her power must come from serving others. And, not infrequently, she gave her service where no service was needed.

Julia, like Mrs. Ramsay, feared exposure; and with the onset of middle age and the fading of beauty came the companion fear of inconsequence. These twin fears made intimacy with others difficult, often impossible. So that Julia, despite all appearances to the contrary, was essentially friendless. She confided in no one. She depended on no one. She turned to no one. It is no surprise, then, that Julia found "ordinary relations between the sick and the well . . . far easier and pleasanter than between the well and the well."

All of Julia's caregiving was open and visible. It was in a sense a public performance. She flourished in the sickroom, imposed her will, and took control. Nursing furnished her with a perfect setting for the exercise of power, and no one could accuse her of being domineering or suspect her of being petty or mean. As a nurse, Julia was privileged to dictate what was "right" for her patient. Whatever she did was always for the "good" of the patient. So that in enforcing that "good" she might even perhaps ignore her patient's wishes. Why else would Virginia have called Mrs. Ramsay's beneficiaries her "victims"?

The power motive carried over into all of Julia's relations, and explains

why Mrs. Ramsay, like Julia, preferred babies to grown-ups; why she preferred "boobies" to clever men who wrote dissertations; how she dared to
preside "with immutable calm over destinies which she completely failed to
understand." There is a little scene in *To the Lighthouse* which reveals just
how strong Virginia thought her mother's will to power was. At the dinner
table Mrs. Ramsay was reminded of old acquaintances she had long since
forgotten: "For it was extraordinary to think that they had been capable of
going on living all these years when she had not thought of them more than
once all that time."

This trait of omnipotence cropped up repeatedly in Julia's letters to Leslie.
How often she thought herself capable of doing him harm. What Leslie failed
to understand was that Julia's assumptions about the world were fundamentally primitive. In her mind, life was an arena where might made right, the
world a place of conflict and hostility where power counted. He simply did
not understand her demand for obedience, for deference; how desperately she
needed to believe that people could not survive without her.

Virginia Stephen understood her mother far better than Leslie understood
his wife. She sensed her mother's need to control in a world governed by
jungle ethics. It was Mrs. Ramsay—and Julia—against the world: "she was
always trying to get the better of it . . . she must admit that she felt this thing
that she called life terrible, hostile, and quick to pounce on you if you gave
it a chance." And so long as Julia could relieve "suffering, death, the poor,"
no one could accuse her of counterfeit motives.

This was not altruism, however. It was ultimately the need to dominate,
to put people under obligation. Her performance required gratitude for services rendered. It was exploitation at its subtlest. Leslie profited most from
Julia. He offered himself as a needy, clutching child. She accepted him as he
was and kept him that way throughout the seventeen years of their marriage.
But in the end her generosity and sacrifice were life-denying. In her efforts
to rule, Julia gradually ceased to lead a life of her own. So long as she needed
outside affirmation, she had to live through the ills and hardships of others.
Eventually, love and hate and victory and defeat slipped into insignificance.
A lifetime of struggle and uncertainty left Julia just the shell of a woman,
grown old before her time, her shoulders stooped, her beauty ravaged. She
could never give Leslie what she had once given Herbert Duckworth. Instead
she became his savior. And just as Jane Venn had saved the pale, delicate,
"skinless" boy, so too would Julia—as wife, mother, and nurse. But the price
was high. After several weeks of illness, the elusive Julia gave up the struggle
and like the "exhausted swimmer" sank into death. At last she would rejoin
her lover—or so Virginia seemed to imagine.

PICKPOCKETS AND SURROGATES

✖ 1895-1904 ✖

6 It was late in the evening of May 4, 1895, that Virginia was taken to see her mother. This might be the last time she would see her alive. Julia was lying on her side in that large bed where she had brought the four Stephen children into the world. After kissing her goodbye, as she crept out of the room, she heard her mother's voice: "Hold yourself straight, my little goat." Those were her last words to Virginia.

A little before dawn the children, wrapped in towels and given warm milk with a thimble of brandy in it, were led by George to their mother, who had just died quietly and effortlessly. Their father staggered from the room as they approached. Virginia stretched her arms out to him, but he brushed past her, crying something unintelligible. Inside the darkened room candles were burning; a sliver of morning sunlight was just breaking through the heavy drawn curtains. Somewhere in the shadows a nurse was sobbing, and Virginia remembered thinking as she stooped and touched her mother's cheek with her lips: "I feel nothing whatever." Her face was still warm. She had stopped breathing only a few minutes earlier. Everything in the room was blurred, dark, and silent. At about six in the morning, leaning out the nursery window, Virginia saw Dr. Seton walking away up the street "with his head bent and his hands clasped behind his back . . . I got a feeling of calm, sadness, and finality." It was a clear, still spring morning. But her father had ignored her outstretched arms, had brushed her aside. If Julia had been a rival in life, the rivalry would increase after her death. Her father's terrible grief made that unequivocal.

In the evening, Stella took Virginia into the room again to kiss her mother for the last time. Now Julia was lying straight in the middle of her pillows, looking remote and austere. When Virginia kissed her this time, "it was like kissing cold iron"—the face had become cool and granulated. Virginia started back. Stella saw her shock but said nothing. When they returned to the nursery later, Stella said, "Forgive me. I saw you were afraid." Virginia then began to cry. "When I see mother," she said, "I see a man sitting with her." Stella looked up, surprised, perhaps frightened. "Did I say that in order to attract attention to myself? Or was it true? I cannot be sure . . . But certainly it was true that when she said: 'Forgive me,' and thus made me visualize my mother, I seemed to see a man sitting bent on the edge of the bed. 'It's nice that she shouldn't be alone,' Stella said after a moment's pause." With this little scene the world that Virginia had known her first thirteen years—a world busy with family life and crowded with people, and Julia at its center—that world came to an end. Virginia was left stranded somewhere between childhood and adolescence. And the father she worshiped had brushed her aside, excluded her. Virginia's only assurance, protection, defense—whatever we are to call it—in safeguarding her father for herself was to reunite her mother with Herbert Duckworth, the only man she ever loved.

Number 22 Hyde Park Gate and all its inhabitants were plunged in gloom. Through its front door marched an army of aunts and cousins and various other relations, prepared to shed copious tears, clutch their bosoms, and offer condolences to the tragic widower and his bewildered children. With the heavy scent of flowers everywhere, the darkened house grew daily more suffocating and unreal. Leslie was the chief mourner and the noisiest. Most of the day he was cloistered with some sister-in-law or niece or cousin pouring out his sorrows, soaking up their sympathy, repeating over and over again his grief, his loss. He had been a widower once before. How could he be expected to endure this again? What was there left for him now—deaf, bereft, isolated, his few remaining friends either dying or dead? Even his notepaper now had a border of black so wide there was scarcely room enough to copy in his lamentations.

The three or four days before the funeral were jumbled, histrionic, almost hallucinatory. The children all sat in the drawing room around Leslie's chair sobbing. He had set the stage, and now they were expected to act out emotions which neither their age nor their experience made it possible for them to understand. All of them were dressed in black, shrouded in smothering silence, their mouths shut tight. Now they must think whether what one was about to say was the correct thing to say. What one said must be a help of some kind. But how could one help? Leslie had sunk into such despair he was unapproachable. If he could be made to talk—and that was their duty—it must be about the past, the "old days."

So he talked and he groaned and he talked some more. The deafer he grew, the louder his groans. Indoors he paced the floor, "gesticulating, crying that he had never told mother how he loved her." Such scenes were frequent. "We were his only hope, his only comfort, he would say. And there kneeling on the floor one would try—perhaps to cry." The days became veiled and cautious and hushed. The tragedy of Julia's death, however, was not that she was gone but that Leslie's grief "made her unreal." And the children were made to play parts that were "immeshed in the conventions of sorrow."

Sixteen days after Julia's death, Stephen began writing for his children the *Mausoleum Book*, an intimate journal of his two marriages. In it he "sought to assuage his terrible grief" and less consciously, perhaps, to purge himself of whatever guilt he may have felt about Julia's shocking death at the age of forty-nine. Leslie was sixty-three at the time and had every reason to believe that his life would end in her loving arms. There was nothing to console him now, except perhaps the memoir. His solemnities, however, transformed the beautiful Julia, on paper at least, from wife and mother into a full-blown saint; for the children she became someone artificial and remote. To Virginia she turned into "an unlovable phantom."

There were minatory, erotic airs nosing round the nursery and bedrooms at Hyde Park Gate, Virginia claimed, and she was the first to confront them in the shape of George Duckworth. Georgie, as he was called in the family, resembled Herbert Duckworth and was Julia's special love, a living reminder of her first husband. He was an emotional young man of twenty-seven at the time of Julia's death. Like his father he was extraordinarily handsome, generous, fashionable, and very social. To the friends and relatives who now kept a watchful eye on the Stephen household, he was a model brother. Certainly the time and trouble he took with his two half sisters was exceptional. He arranged excursions for them, gave them presents, took them to parties, and introduced them to London society.

But George Herbert Duckworth was not a man who could give quietly. He was by nature demonstrative. In one needlessly lavish scene after another, he offered his shoulder to Virginia and Vanessa, threw his arms open for their comfort, gave the unhappy sisters long, unwelcomed embraces, and often wept at the slightest provocation. Vanessa, having a strong and natural reserve, seems to have resisted these endearments. But Virginia, who craved the embraces and petting of approving adults, was by far the more vulnerable of the two; and it became daily more difficult to determine just exactly where the fraternal hugs crossed the line to become a "nasty erotic skirmish."

George continued to live at 22 Hyde Park Gate for the next nine years "in the thickest emotional haze" and in "complete chastity," apart from an occasional lingering embrace with some elderly society hostess. Perhaps the most damaging part of this unfortunate "fondling" was Virginia's enforced reticence. There was no one to whom she could voice her objections, no way of knowing precisely where the limits were, and she was never sure that what she confessed about George's behavior wouldn't flare up into "a painful and embarrassing scandal." Her father, Stella, Aunt Mary, Aunt Minna "all would have been bewildered, horrified, indignant and incredulous." This was not how a Duckworth behaved. Such ingratitude for so much attention and generosity. Years later, in a letter to Vanessa, Virginia recounted the reactions of her Greek teacher Janet Case to George Duckworth. Miss Case, it seems, had a strong dislike for him "and used to say 'Whew—you nasty creature', when he came in and began fondling me over my Greek. When I got to the bedroom scenes, she dropped her lace, and gasped like a benevolent gudgeon."

The story of both half brothers' "malefactions," as Virginia called them, had a much earlier history. One memory she was to describe many years later took place when she was about six years old. It was Gerald Duckworth this time who lifted her on to a ledge outside the dining-room door and explored her body. "I can remember the feel of his hand going under my clothes . . . I remember how I hoped he would stop; how I stiffened and wriggled as his hand approached my private parts. But it did not stop. His hand explored my private parts too. I remember resenting, disliking it—what is the word for so dumb and mixed a feeling? It must have been strong, since I still [in 1939] recall it."

George's later intrusions, whatever form they took, after their mother's death generated a great many confused emotions that lasted throughout Virginia's life. The motherless girl, always hungry for affection, turned to the maternal Vanessa when she wanted to be stroked and soothed. But George's embraces aroused in her some forbidden or ambivalent or, as she said, "mixed" feelings. Whatever the truth was, it was George she later blamed for the sexual "cowardice" of her adulthood. Still, it was George she tried so pathetically to please in her adolescence.

After Julia's death, then, the Stephen and Duckworth families were cooped up in mourning. Virginia and Vanessa were closer than ever before; and it was to Vanessa alone, Virginia's second mother from nursery days, that Virginia confided her half brother's violation. Vanessa was evidently troubled sufficiently by George's behavior to approach Dr. Savage on the matter after Virginia's breakdown in 1904. When Savage raised the subject, George is said to have explained, and excused, himself. He was merely trying to comfort Virginia during her father's illness, he said. This appears to have satisfied the doctor.

"I do not know enough about Virginia's illnesses," wrote Quentin Bell, "to say whether this adolescent trauma was in any way connected with them . . .

The first 'breakdown' or whatever we are to call it, must have come very soon after her mother's death. And here we come to a great interval of nothingness." That is to say, there is almost no record of 1895 or 1896 which describes the trouble Virginia was in. But one thing is certain: from 1895 on, Virginia "knew that she had been mad and might be mad again." To live with that knowledge from the age of thirteen must have been just barely endurable; it was like living with "a cancer of the mind." In her journal of this period, Bell continues, Virginia scarcely mentioned her trouble, and when she did, it was mainly the physical symptoms—racing pulse, nervous irritability, excruciating headaches, insomnia. "She became terrified of people, blushed scarlet if spoken to and was unable to face a stranger in the street." The family doctor ordered all lessons to stop and recommended plenty of outdoor exercise; and "it was one of Stella's self-imposed duties to take her for walks or for rides." The *Hyde Park Gate News*, run first by Thoby and then principally by Virginia, came to a halt; and because the lease on Talland House was sold, there would no longer be summers at St. Ives. In 1895 the family went to Freshwater in the Isle of Wight. "That was their blackest period of mourning."

Stella kept an abbreviated diary for 1896 which provides a few concrete details of life at 22 Hyde Park Gate. On January 25, Virginia's birthday, her visit to Dr. Seton was canceled. On January 28, Virginia did errands with Stella. On February 3, with Virginia by her side, Stella put flowers on the grave of her cousin James Kenneth Stephen, something Julia had always done on the anniversary of his death. In fact, from these diary entries, one gets the impression that Virginia spent most of her time with Stella.

James Kenneth Stephen, Virginia's first cousin, was another member of the Stephen family who suffered from a mental affliction. In 1892 he died in a lunatic asylum. He was Leslie's (and Julia's) favorite nephew, a large, handsome, gifted man whose mental disorder was presumably the result of a head injury sustained in 1886, which at the time appeared negligible. At Eton he was a brilliant scholar and athlete, later a Fellow of King's College, Cambridge, then private tutor to Prince Eddy, son of the Prince of Wales. Jem, as he was called, was author of *Lapsus Calami*, a collection of "dazzling parodies which were the talk of London."

His father, James Fitzjames, was enormously proud of him. When his behavior became too eccentric to be ignored, however, his family, refusing to acknowledge what appears today to have been manic-depressive psychosis, asked that the door to 22 Hyde Park Gate be closed to him. This Julia refused to do. She adored the young man. "I cannot shut my door upon Jem," she repeated whenever the manic stage was full-blown and Jem was pounding to be let in. It soon became clear, however, that something had to be done, for young Stephen was becoming increasingly ungovernable and even dangerous.

Once, in a state of terrifying excitement, he stormed into the nursery at No. 22 at tea time, whipped a blade out of its sheath, and stabbed it into a loaf of bread. At another time, he carried little Virginia off (with Julia at his heels) to his room in the family home in De Vere Gardens to paint her portrait. He was a great painter, he'd suddenly decided, and in a state of frenzy smeared a piece of board with paint. Then there was the morning that Leslie and Julia would never forget. Jem burst into the dining room as they were eating breakfast and announced with glistening eyes that Dr. Savage had just told him he faced either death or madness. He roared with laughter at this.

One of the saddest things about his illness was his passion for Stella. He loved her madly and pursued her with violence. Matters finally got to the point where the children were instructed to say that Stella was not at home, that she was away in the country, whenever their cousin appeared. Eventually his behavior became so bizarre and so offensive that he was expelled from his club. On November 21, 1891, Dr. Savage committed him to St. Andrew's Hospital, Northampton, where he died on February 3, 1892, at the age of thirty-three. His death certificate gives the cause of death as: "Mania, 2½ months. Persistent refusal of food 20 days. Exhaustion." James Fitzjames Stephen, who refused, still, to admit his son's madness, died two years later, on March 11, 1894, brokenhearted and broken in spirit.*

Jack Waller Hills, who had been courting Stella, was also much in attendance during this interval. He had proposed to her on March 5, 1896, and been refused. How could she think of marrying with the children and her stepfather to look after? Leslie had "laid a claim on her conscience." To abandon her stepfather now, to desert the children who depended so much on her, would be heartless, unpardonable. But there were other considerations too.

---

* Leslie's father, Sir James Stephen, claimed he "had the power of going mad at will" (Annan, 117). There were mental problems on Julia's side of the family too. Leslie Stephen recorded in the *Mausoleum Book* (109) in April 1901 that Hervey Fisher had "gone off his head entirely" and, against his mother's wishes, was finally installed in the Hospital of St. Mary of Bethlehem, an asylum in Lambeth. His brother, Arthur Fisher, was also "off his head" and had to be placed in an institution where he died not long afterward.

Stella was now twenty-seven and had to think of children of her own. She was not old, but certainly she should not sacrifice her future attending an old man who might easily live for many more years.

There was Vanessa, after all. She was seventeen now and the only Stephen not dependent on Stella. From childhood, Vanessa had assumed a maternal role in the nursery. She had always been calm, judicious, and practical. It was Vanessa who should now rightly assume the responsibility of her father, who should take over the running of the household. She, after all, was the natural daughter and sister.

After the March 5 refusal, Stella and Jack apparently broke off relations, but by the middle of June, she began to reconsider the proposal. For on August 22 at Hindhead, Jack and Stella were finally engaged; and it was just a few weeks after the announcement that Virginia again needed medical attention. Stella noted in her diary on October 13: "Took Ginia to [Dr.] Seton. He says she must do less and be very careful not to excite herself: her pulse is 146. Father in a great state. We are to see Seton again in a week." Then on October 21: "To Seton with Ginia. He says she must give up lessons entirely till January and must be out 4 hours a day—I to go see him again in 4 weeks time."

Leslie Stephen noted in his memoir on September 23, 1896: "We have just returned from a holiday spent at Hindhead House, Haslemere . . . The great event of the holidays, the greatest that has happened since our calamity, was my darling Stella's engagement to J[ack]. W[aller]. H[ills]. on 22 August . . . My Julia had constantly talked of the affair to me: she would have been more delighted than any of us; the thought of her approval would have reconciled me if reconciliation had been needed . . . If anything could make me happy, this ought to: but my happiness is a matter of rapidly diminishing importance."

Before Julia had settled into the ground at Highgate Cemetery, Stella found herself in charge of the Stephen household. She accepted her mother's place without question or complaint. From the day of Julia's death, Leslie had abandoned himself to self-indulgence. If anyone could help him through life's brambles, surely his gentle, loving Stella would. But Virginia must have seen this as a second act of exclusion. Instead of turning to her for comfort, her father had turned to Stella. It was like brushing past her outstretched arms for a second time. Virginia had lost again, now to a surrogate mother.

Meanwhile the grieving father played out the old refrain—he was lonely and unloved, he groaned. He was full of remorse. What would become of him now, an old man, deaf and friendless? Who would look after him in his hour of need? He had been "over-sensitive and nervously irritable"; he had caused his darling Julia so much worry, so many sleepless nights. "Oh dear! it grieves me to think of it . . . All this comes back to me—trifles which were not quite trifles—and prevents me from saying, as I would so gladly have said, that I never gave her anxiety or caused her needless annoyance . . . I used to be a little worried without sufficient cause when I made up our balance-sheet and some of my worry was reflected upon her . . . I used some-times to complain to her that she would not say to me in so many words, 'I love you'. (She had said it often enough in her letters before, when there was a reason for saying it!) My complaint was only in play for I loved even her reticence."

Would his children believe that? Did Stella believe that? Did she under-stand how deeply her mother had loved him? These confessions had to be made. He needed absolution and had no scruples in laying before his step-daughter his suffering. "I was not as bad as Carlyle, was I?" Surely he would die in shame if anyone thought he had treated Julia as badly as Carlyle had treated Jane!

But Stella did not know how Carlyle had treated Jane. She was not a reader; she seldom opened a book. All she knew was that among her mother's bequests was Leslie Stephen, a formidable man she had only previously known "with respect and formal affection." She knew also that he needed to be soothed and comforted. Here she was, closeted with this irritable old man who had made endless demands on her mother, who probably more than anyone else was responsible for her premature death. How should she feel toward him? She didn't know. For as Virginia was later to say, Stella was "not clever." Living so closely to her quick, sharp, imperious mother, she "exaggerated her own deficiency . . . was always contrasting their differences." Stella felt an almost "canine devotion" to Julia; it was a "passive, suffering affection . . . a complete unquestioning dependence." She lived in her mother's shade, fatherless from infancy, generous to a fault, "conscious that she had not the best of all to give." And Julia, where Stella was concerned, was ruthless, for she saw her daughter as "part of herself"—and because her daughter was a "slower and less efficient part," Julia did not hesitate to treat her with some severity.

Stella was the reflecting moon to Julia's blinding sun. And so with a sense of her inferiority, beautiful, gentle Stella accepted her role as surrogate mother to the Stephen children and surrendered herself as the Julia substitute—

indeed she was the pallid image of her mother—to Leslie's urgent need of attention, affection, and companionship. With her customary reticence she dried her tears, put aside her loneliness, and took up the task that Julia had left unfinished. And with patient, infinite consideration for others, she assumed the care of the children; but principally she devoted herself to Virginia, whose mood swings from wild excitability to profound depression were at times "urgent, heartbreaking and terrible."

Virginia recalled the suitors Stella attracted. At that time, there were "many young men ... sitting round her." Vaguely they knew that Arthur Studd, the painter, was in love with her, and another young man called Ted Sanderson, and Charles Eliot Norton's son, Richard. James Kenneth Stephen—Jem—too, was in love with her. But the one suitor who stood out among the others was Jack Hills. He had been to Eton with George and later to Balliol College, Oxford.

He was an unremarkable but determined young man, the English country-gentleman type. His father was "a commonplace little round man—Judge [Herbert Augustus] Hills—'Buzzy' he was called in the family ... short, jocular, in knickerbockers ... Buzzy had once written a sonnet that had been taken for Shakespeare's" and liked making little jokes with young women. As Judge of the Court of Appeals, Cairo, "Buzzy lived chiefly in Egypt, and Mrs. Hills—Anna, her name was—lived mostly alone at Corby [Castle in Cumberland]." Anna Hills was a "hard, worldly woman, tightly dressed in black satin in London; up at Corby, a county lady, collecting Chelsea enamel snuff boxes ... the friend of intellectual men. She detested women." She liked getting up little gatherings of slightly well known literary males "in the snobbish Victorian manner." She had two other sons, Edmund and Eustace; but Jack was, for some reason, her least favored; and so it was no coincidence when he lived alone on Ebury Street, working very hard to succeed as a solicitor in the firm of Roper and Whately, very hard up and lonely, that once as a dinner guest of George Duckworth's, Jack was immediately drawn to Julia Stephen and came to her regularly after that first evening for her mothering and sympathy.

Jack Hills was honest, affectionate, and a perfect gentleman—who stuttered. He was also a "passionate countryman." He rode well; he fished well, and there was in him "a vein of poetry." Jack was intellectually "nothing out of the way," Virginia had heard her mother once say. Nor were his looks anything special, but he had "beautiful brown eyes," was scrupulously clean—he "washed all over ever so many times a day"—and, of course, he loved animals, dogs especially. He brought the country into the Stephens' "distinguished literary, book-loving world." He taught the children all about bug hunting: how to "sugar" trees with rum and molasses, how to catch moths and how to mount their catches. In fact, he gave them his own copies of Francis Morris's *British Butterflies* and *British Moths* in four volumes over which Virginia spent many hours of her childhood in her post as "Name Finder" in the family Entomological Society.

A few years later, Jack would be the first man ever to speak to Virginia openly and deliberately about sex. "He opened my eyes . . . to the part played by sex in the life of an ordinary man. He shocked me a little, wholesomely." Women and sex, Jack explained, were subjects men constantly talked about— men "had" women all the time; it was a common boast. But was that "honourable"? Virginia wanted to know. Wasn't "having" a woman something one should be ashamed of? Not at all, Jack said. "Sex relations had nothing to do with honour. Having women was a mere trifle in a man's life." Virginia knew nothing about men's lives and thought all men, "like my father, loved one woman only, and were 'dishonourable' if unchaste, as much as women." This was the part of Jack Virginia admired most: he was honest in a clean and open way. There was no hint of smut in what he said.

And so, that night of August 22, 1896, at Hindhead House, after being out with Jack in the garden for a long time, and with the children in their rooms holding their breath, Stella accepted his proposal. Blushing and radiant the next morning, Stella made her announcement: she and Jack were to be married and she was very happy. Virginia looked on, confused. Adrian started to cry and Jack kissed him. He would be losing a mother for the second time. Leslie gently reprimanded Adrian: "We must all be happy, because Stella is happy." And besides, his Julia had always wished it; of that he was sure.

But the announcement came as a blow to Leslie. He was angry. He'd been deserted. Jack had picked his pocket. "How could Stella marry such a man?" Even the name "Jack" sounded to him like the "smack of a whip." He had been betrayed and could be pacified only if Stella promised not to leave 22 Hyde Park Gate. And to this she evidently agreed. The exact terms of the arrangement are not known, but it is possible that Leslie exacted that promise as "the condition of his blessing."

Jack, however, was not to be so easily manipulated. He had won Stella; now he must win her freedom from the Stephen household, from Leslie's clutches. What would Jack's position be if Stella were still under Leslie's control? The young couple may at first have agreed to stay on with the Stephens, but when they began to consider "rooms, and habits, conveniences and rights," it soon became clear that the plan would not succeed. They must have a house of their own. A great deal of discussion followed and emotions ran high. Finally, a compromise was reached. Leslie would not die of desertion if Stella promised to take a house nearby. She must live within easy access. Upon this, he insisted. Stella conceded, and Jack apparently did too, for they agreed to live just across the street. Number 24 Hyde Park Gate would soon be available; the Hills would settle there. Leslie's equanimity was almost restored; but still the idea of losing Stella made him despondent. He groaned whenever the wedding was mentioned. He was jealous of Jack Hills, and blinding himself, Leslie did his best to make the engagement "incredibly involved, frustrated, and impeded."

Many bristly questions still needed resolution, but on the whole, there was a future in sight again and Stella gradually quickened to life. Her "eyes shone, her pale cheeks glowed constantly with a faint rose. She laughed and had her tender jokes." Fears returned at times, but there was Jack to comfort her out of them, "to show her a sane future." He was never very far from her side. In fact, he began spending so many evenings with Stella that George found it necessary to intervene and invoke the time-honored proprieties.

By 1897, Virginia, now passing into young womanhood, was still cloistered within the walls of 22 Hyde Park Gate. Her days were spent reading, writing, doing (very briefly) her lessons. So that anything which altered life at Hyde Park Gate directly altered Virginia's life. Stella's engagement and impending marriage were, needless to say, creating something of a stir. It was in this tense, unsettled, and constantly changing atmosphere that Virginia began in January 1897 to keep a diary, which she ended on January 2, 1898, with: "Here is a volume of fairly acute life (the first really *lived* year of my life) ended, locked and put away."

It was much in the character of an amateur diarist that Virginia wrote in her book regularly for the first seven months and sporadically for the remaining five. Against the crowded canvas of the people recorded in its pages and the events she thought worthy of documentation—visits to art galleries and museums, theater performances, Queen Victoria's Diamond Jubilee, preparations for Vanessa's "coming out" and, even more important, for Stella's wedding—Virginia, in the role of family historian, provided a lively record of daily life at 22 Hyde Park Gate: what happened during the morning hours; who came to lunch, to tea, to dinner; how the afternoons were passed, and the evening hours. There is often a sense of compulsion in the entries: "This is written just before father calls for me to go out, and I can think of no sentence to fill the blank."

Life was indeed lively in 1897. Everyone, it seems, was doing something all the time. The schedule of a representative day, for instance, ran something like this: In the morning, after breakfast, George Duckworth went off to his job as unpaid secretary to Charles Booth, who was at the time preparing his massive sociological study *Life and Labour of the People in London*, and Gerald set off for his office at Dent's, the publishers. On Mondays, Wednesdays, and Fridays, Vanessa went to her drawing classes at Arthur Cope's School of Art in South Kensington in preparation for the Royal Academy. And Adrian, now fourteen, departed for Westminster School, with half his belongings left behind. Sometimes the morning post brought a letter from Thoby, who was now at Clifton College in Bristol. Stella, as mistress of the house, descended to the basement to arrange the day's meals with Sophie Farrell, the Stephens' long-time cook; and Virginia, with her father, began the regimen of daily exercise, prescribed by Dr. Seton, in Kensington Gardens for about an hour or so, after which Leslie retired to his study at the top of the house and Virginia to the back room or the nursery to translate German or Greek or to read history. (On February 15, Dr. Seton permitted her to resume her lessons, though she was still in a very precarious state.)

After lunch there was more outdoor exercise—the prescription was for four hours a day. With Stella, Virginia went out to shops or to see Dr. Seton. (Stella, ill since Christmas 1896 with her "gastric chill," went from time to time to consult Dr. Elizabeth Garrett Anderson.) In the late afternoon there was another walk through the gardens, now with Vanessa just back from her drawing classes. Then tea, usually with a crowd of Fisher or Stephen relations, followed by more reading. And finally dinner, with a guest or two, followed by a theater party or an evening at home with Leslie reading aloud from a novel or a volume of poetry.

Apart from the medical schedule set down for Virginia, however, the family routine was not particularly rigid, for the house seemed always swarming with visitors—the Milmans, the Stillmans, the Fishers, the Stephens, Cousin Mia (MacNamara), Aunt Minna (Duckworth), Aunt Anny (Ritchie), General Beadle, Susan Lushington, Kitty Maxse. It was a busy and congested household. Sometimes Virginia seemed amused by the Victorian upper-middle classes trooping through the drawing room. But there were times when everything was cause for irritation and anxiety. Sometimes the neighboring streets seemed alive with danger and casualty: runaway horses, overturned carts, injured bicyclists. It was almost as if she were trapped in a battle zone whenever she ventured out into the streets of London. There were also days when she was rigid with frustration and fury.

In February, visiting the Stillmans, for instance, "poor Miss Jan [Virginia herself] utterly lost her wits, talked nonsense, and grew as red as a turkey cock." In April: "To bed very furious and tantrumical." Later, "I regret to say that various circumstances conspiring to irritate me, I broke my umbrella in half." (Only once did Leslie make a note of her condition—on April 10, 1897: "Virginia has been out of sorts, nervous and overgrown . . . I hope that a rest will bring her round.") And, as in her later years, so too during this period, books became a refuge—"the greatest help and comfort."

The number of books—forty to fifty hefty volumes at least—Virginia read during this interval was extraordinary. Volume after volume of history and biography, of diary and essay, as well as many volumes of fiction and poetry. From Virginia's earliest years, Leslie had noted her sharp mind and hoped she would one day become his literary successor and intellectual heir. In an 1893 letter to Julia, when Virginia was eleven, he said that writing articles "I suppose will be 'Ginia's line unless she marries at 17." Two days later: "Yesterday I discussed George II with 'Ginia. She takes in a great deal and will really be an author in time; though I cannot make up my mind in what line. History will be a good thing for her to take up as I can give her some hints." For as he noted on her ninth birthday, "She is certainly very like me."

But even Leslie Stephen at times found his 'Ginia "devouring books, almost faster than I like." During the first half of 1897, she had read the two volumes of Janet Ross's *Three Generations of English Women*, James Anthony Froude's two-volume *Life and Times of Thomas Carlyle*, Mandell Creighton's *Queen Elizabeth*, ten small volumes of John Lockhart's *Memoirs of the Life of Sir Walter Scott*, Carlyle's *Reminiscences*, James Dykes Campbell's *The Life of Coleridge*, her grandfather Sir James Stephen's *Essays in Ecclesiastical Biography*, Carlyle's *French Revolution* and *Life of Sterling*, Thomas Arnold's *History of Rome*, Macaulay's five-volume *History of England*; then there were essays by her godfather, James Russell Lowell, and novels by Dickens, Thackeray, Trollope, Henry James—the list goes on and on.

Virginia knew she could gain her father's favor by reading, and this, more than anything, she craved. Leslie may have failed in teaching his daughter mathematics, but he was matchless when it came to history and literature: Virginia must learn to read "with discrimination, to make unaffected judgments, never admiring because the world admires or blaming at the order of the critics."

Apart from her pieces in the family chronicle, *Hyde Park Gate News*, and possibly an essay or two, Leslie saw nothing of Virginia's first serious attempts at writing, though there was quite a lot to see. Even before she turned thirteen she was attempting to imitate Nathaniel Hawthorne's prose style. Then one day her father brought her Hakluyt's *Voyages* from the London Library. Thereafter "she modelled herself upon the Elizabethans, wrote a long essay entitled *Religio Laici* and another, seemingly more characteristic effort, *A History of Women*. Of these early manuscripts nothing remains."

On her fifteenth birthday, Jack Hills gave Virginia a pair of ice skates (Stella had bought Vanessa a pair) and naturally the question of whether it was safe to skate came under heated debate. "Walked in the morning with father," wrote Virginia in her journal on Friday, January 29. "Went round the Pond as usual. No one skating and we heard that 40 of yesterday's crowd had fallen in . . . It was just freezing . . . We are to go with our new skates to Wimbledon Park tomorrow if it freezes tonight." On Saturday, the thirtieth: "Woke to find it thawing hard. Everything dripping, and skating out of the question." As Virginia was making this entry, Leslie, upstairs in this study, was writing to Thoby: "It is a regular thaw, though Stella wants to take Vanessa and Virginia to the skating place in the Botanical Gardens. I said that it was not safe as a lot of people fell into the pond on Friday and the thaw will have made the ice worse. *She* said that Jack said it was safe. I said that Jack was a _____ no, I did not say that because I have been told that she is to marry him on the 1st of April: a very proper day, I think."

This letter says something of Leslie's feeling for Jack and the approaching wedding. As it happened, Jack had to be operated on Saturday morning, January 23. It was nothing serious, but still it required his remaining in bed for three weeks, after which he and Stella planned to go to Bognor for his convalescence. They suggested having Virginia as chaperone. "A terrible idea started that Stella and I should take lodgings at Eastbourne [Bognor] . . . where Jack is going next week—Impossible to be alone with those creatures, yet if I don't go, Stella will not, and Jack particularly wishes her to—The question is, whether Nessa will be allowed to come too." On the following day, Virginia went with Vanessa to see Jack and "told him with great plainness that I *could not* go with him and Stella alone." After some gentle pressure from Stella, it was settled that they would go to Bognor—"Stella, Jack, Nessa and I, father perhaps coming down for two days . . . the whole thing most horrible."

It was indeed "most horrible." The lodging was damp and dismal, the weather gray and cold. Jack slept at a hotel nearby, and joined them at meals. One afternoon they tried going for a walk but it drizzled and then rained; and so they splashed back to their lodging "in mud and wet, umbrellaless, most dismally." Spending more time in this "stupid Bognor (the name suits it) would have driven me to the end of the pier and into the dirty yellow sea beneath." That Leslie should be prepared to detest Bognor or, for that matter, any place or plan connected with Jack Hills is understandable. Jack had stolen his precious Stella. But Virginia's behavior at this time could not be so easily explained.

The wedding was now only five weeks off and there was still much to be done. In early March Gerald gave Stella "a wonderful opal and diamond necklace as a sort of first wedding present." On the thirteenth, Madge Vaughan's wedding present arrived, an old looking glass. A few days later, Stella went with her cousin Adeline Fisher to be fitted for her wedding dress. On the morning of the nineteenth, Virginia and Stella went to Liberty's to change a screen their cousin, Florence Maitland, had given her as a wedding present.

On Wednesday Stella went with Virginia to Madame Dubois, the court dressmaker in South Kensington, to be fitted for her "going away dress," and on Sunday, March 28, they went finally to St. Mary Abbotts. This was the last Sunday Jack and Stella's banns would be read. Two days later, Stella took Vanessa and Virginia to see about their dresses and after lunch took Adrian to Hyams to buy him a suit. On Saturday, April 3, "The whole morning was spent in arranging the presents"; and after countless visits about Vanessa and Virginia's dresses, Saturday, April 10, the momentous day, at last arrived.

The morning was "rather a hurly-burly." Eustace, Jack's brother, came often to consult with Stella. Huge boxes of flowers arrived throughout the morning and had to be arranged. At noon, the Fishers came, and Stella went up to dress. "Goodness knows how we got through it all. Certainly it was half a dream, or a nightmare. Stella was almost dreaming I think." They went to church at two. Jack had already arrived and was looking happy. Then at "about 2.15 or 30, Stella and father came in—Stella walking in her sleep—her eyes fixed straight in front of her—very white and beautiful." The long service was soon over. "We went up and saw her change her dress—and said goodbye to her. So they went—Mr and Mrs Hills!"

Leslie was not bearing up quite as well under his "loss." He confided only to his journal: "Today Stella was married in Kensington Church to J. W.

Hills. I will not put down even here the thoughts which have agitated me
... The last seven or eight months of the engagement have brought me a
good many selfish pangs: but—well, I should be a brute if I really complained." Later that evening he wrote a letter to Stella herself: "I am tired
and excited and don't precisely know whether I am standing on my head or
my heels ... I know that we love each other and shall continue to love each
other. I know that you will do all you can for me ... I said to her [Julia] that
I not only loved but reverenced her ... Now one cannot exactly reverence a
daughter but I have the feeling which corresponds to it—you may find a
name for it—but I mean that my love for you is something more than affection ... Love me still and tell me sometimes that you love me."

The following morning, a Sunday, George, Gerald, and the four Stephen
children took Stella's wedding flowers to their mother's grave in Highgate
cemetery; and on Wednesday at 2:45 in the afternoon, April 14, the Stephen
family started for Victoria Station. They were to spend their Easter holiday
in Brighton, near the Fishers, in a roomy and comfortable house rented from
Roden Noel's widow. Virginia had her stock of books with her. Everything
was there to make the holiday a pleasant one. But not for Virginia. She was
restless and irritable. By the second day she was longing to be back in London
"with a nice quiet morning ... in front of me." The weather was bad: one
day was windy and dusty; the next day it rained. Everything was "diabolical"
or "dismal," or "gruesome." The Sunday boardwalkers were a hideous spectacle. All the "third rate actresses" were out on parade, with huge hats and
"dreadful young men to escort them." Virginia became so fidgety that even
watching Mrs. Amelia Dyer, the baby-farmer and murderer, hang in a penny
slot machine on the West Pier commemorating her execution was a welcome
relief.

But the days passed and soon letters came from Stella in Italy. There was
not much left of the holiday. When the family returned to London on the
Wednesday afternoon of April 28, George was at Victoria Station to meet
them, with bad news. The Hills had returned early from their honeymoon.
Stella was ill. She was "in bed with a bad chill."

This was to have been a period of change. Things were going to be happier.
Vanessa would be coming out that summer; and with Stella now married
life at home would be broadened to include the newlyweds. Thoby was turning into a fine young man. Adrian was becoming less awkward. Soon Leslie
would begin training Virginia for the profession of letters for which she was

clearly destined. There would be the excitement of watching the Hills begin their new life together. And Stella was going to have a baby. The summer of 1897 was going to mark the beginning of a better, more normal life.

When the family reached Hyde Park Gate, however, they found themselves in the "midst of serious illness, nurses, consultations, interviews and whispers." In this whirlpool of emotion, Virginia's nervous irritability moved steadily into the danger zone. She turned to her books to narcotize the pain she was beginning to experience. "Read Mr [Henry] James to quiet me, and my beloved Macaulay." "Finished the 5th and last v. of my beloved Macaulay!" "Finished the 3rd and last vol. of Cromwell." "Finished 1st vol of Arnold's Rome."

From late April to the middle of July, Stella's illness lingered unpredictably, alternately improving and worsening. During its course, Virginia began to show a curious change of mood. By the end of April, for instance, at the onset of Stella's illness: "I slept with Nessa, as I was unhappy. News that she is better at about 11 o'clock—What shall I write tomorrow?" The next day: "Slept with Nessa again." On May 4, Stella briefly rallied. To Virginia this was "most satisfactory—but I am unreasonable enough to be irritated." Five days later: "I was examined by Dr. Seton. No lessons—milk and some medicine which I forget." On May 21 Aunt Minna's gossip with Stella "made me so angry that I turned my back and made myself generally unpleasant."

The meaning of Stella's illness to Virginia was much more complicated than the simple concern for the well-being of a family member. Throughout its course Virginia assumed a certain critical attitude toward Stella which put a great emotional distance between them. There was, for example, her response to Stella's rallying for the second time on May 9: "Now that old cow is most ridiculously well and cheerful—hopping about out of bed etc: Thank goodness, nevertheless." That "nevertheless," as Quentin Bell pointed out, "certainly gives one cause for speculation." But the illness, with all its fluctuation, progressed relentlessly. Stella, it is true, was not getting well and as that fact became daily more apparent, Virginia's "health deteriorated, her psychological illness was accompanied by physical symptoms." On Sunday, July 11: "I was very miserable and achey with rheumatism?" On the twelfth: "I spent the whole day with Stella, as she would not let me go out because of my aches." On the thirteenth: "In the morning Nessa and I went over to Stella. I was rather worse." Dr. Seton came that afternoon and ordered Virginia to bed. She was too ill even to be moved across the street to her own room. On Wednesday, July 14: "I hardly saw her all the morning . . . At night I had the fidgets very badly, and she sat with me till 11:30—stroking me till they went. I slept in Jack's dressing room, just opposite their bedroom." On Thursday, the fifteenth: "She did not come to me all day long, and I guessed that she was ill."

By Saturday, July 17, Virginia was recovered enough to be moved to her own bed. George carried her across the street, and Stella called out "Goodbye" as they passed her door. On Sunday afternoon Dr. Broadbent and another surgeon examined Stella and decided to operate at seven o'clock that evening. The operation was said to be successful and everything appeared satisfactory. On Monday, July 19, however, once more the unspeakable happened: "At 3 this morning, Georgie and Nessa came to me, and told me that Stella was dead—That is all we have thought of since; and it is impossible to write of."

 "My mother's death," Virginia was to write many years later, "had been a latent sorrow—at thirteen one could not . . . deal with it." Stella's death two years later, however, was a different matter. "Even if I were not fully conscious of what my mother's death meant, I had been for two years unconsciously absorbing it through Stella's silent grief; through my father's demonstrative grief; again through all the things that changed and stopped . . . the black clothes; the suppressions, the locked door of her bedroom. All this had toned my mind . . . made it I suppose unnaturally responsive to Stella's happiness." Then came the second blow of death which "struck on me; tremulous . . . with my wings still creased, sitting there on the edge of my chrysalis."

Perhaps the saddest recollection in Virginia's memoir was her first vision of love between a man and a woman. If Stella was "passively" in love with Jack, he was "passionately" in love with her. "It gave me a conception of love; a standard of love; a sense that nothing in the whole world is so lyrical . . . as a young man and a young woman in their first love for each other." One day Virginia came by chance upon a letter from Jack that Stella— discovered reading, perhaps—had slipped under the blotting paper; Virginia read it. "There is nothing sweeter in the whole world, than our love," Jack had written. Virginia put the letter down with a feeling of ecstasy. Their love had been a revelation. Many people were in love as they were, said Stella, gently kissing her. "You and Nessa will be one day." But Stella was dead and now, on July 19, only one thing seemed vaguely threatening to Virginia:

that the year 1897 marked the beginning of something that would only become clear to her four decades later, when she began to assemble her life in
a final accounting.

When Stella took over Julia's role as mistress of 22 Hyde Park Gate, she
became Leslie's nearest crutch. He reached for her with his customary self-
indulgence. Like her mother, she was meticulous over her stepfather's health,
and like her mother, she was very beautiful. Was it not natural that the
observant Virginia in 1897 should note the delicacy of Stella's ministrations
and see the danger of her father's position? Was it not also natural that
Virginia should perceive, however dimly, Stella not only as a new rival but
also as an intruder, trespassing on territory upon which she had no claim?
As widower, Leslie took for granted his stepdaughter's servile observances.
For in manhood, as in childhood, he depended upon the sympathy of a
woman, and would not have seen Stella's concern as anything out of the
ordinary. And certainly he was too puritanical by temperament and training
to see how his behavior might be construed as being perhaps just a little too
intimate. Stella had become a second mother to Virginia in 1895. She had
become a rival too, or so it must have seemed. It is easier in this light to
understand Virginia's confusion when Stella herself died in July of 1897. More
than that, Stella's love and marriage to Jack now appeared as chimeric and
spectral as all the other catastrophes Virginia had so scrupulously preserved
in the pages of her journal.

Stella had died at three in the morning on Monday, July 19. On Wednesday
she was buried next to her mother in Highgate. None of the family went to
the cemetery. It is unlikely that Stella's burial was accompanied by a service
of any kind; and even if there had been, the Stephens, being godless, would
not have participated.
    The following Tuesday, Dr. Seton examined Virginia and found her nor-
mal. On Wednesday, the whole family moved for the summer holiday to the
Vicarage, a rented house in Painswick, Gloucestershire, two miles from Frederic Maitland's family's estate. The weather was perfect for walking, butterfly
hunting, and taking photographs with their new camera. There were visits
from the Vaughan and Fisher cousins, and Virginia brought along a large
store of books to see her through the holiday. Jack Hills came to them on
weekends, spending much of his time with Vanessa and Virginia, and writing
to them daily during the week. As the days passed, Virginia's journal dwin-

dled. The entries grew shorter and more telegraphic; often there were no entries at all. But the less she wrote, the more she read. It was risky to be without some occupation.

The family returned to London on Wednesday, September 22, and on Saturday, after much deliberation and some reluctance, Virginia and Vanessa accompanied Jack to Corby Castle, where his family awaited him. Their job was to "soothe the first shock of his home-coming." Gerald saw them off from Euston Station at 11:30 in the morning with newspapers and magazines for the journey. They had lunch and tea on the train and arrived at Carlisle at 5:30, then took another train on to Wetheral and got to Corby at about six in the evening. "Terrible long dinner," Virginia recorded in her journal. "Everything grand and strange. Jack unhappy. Old Hills silly. Mrs Hills talkative and rather unpleasant . . . V. S. and A. V. S. silent and miserable." And so the sisters returned home a week later, relieved that the dreadful visit was over. At least part of Virginia's misery came from the suspicion that Jack seemed not to recognize how much effort she and Vanessa had put into easing his sorrow.

Being the eldest of the Stephen children—she was now eighteen—and still acting the maternal figure of the nursery, Vanessa now faced the inevitability of assuming a position of responsibility. The full weight of family needs and expectations now lay upon her shoulders. "Everyone turned to her, and she moved, like some young Queen . . . mournful and uncertain of her way." She would replace Stella and become her father's next "victim." Everyone at 22 Hyde Park Gate needed something from Vanessa: George needed her devotion, Gerald her affection, Adrian her protection, and Virginia her motherly love and sisterly petting. But loudest of all in making his needs heard was Leslie. Increasingly cut off from company by his deafness, he felt isolated. Didn't anyone care what became of him? Didn't Vanessa care? Hadn't she seen how her mother had looked after him? Or Stella? Was Vanessa blind? When he was sad, he expected her to be sad; when he was angry, as he was whenever she asked for money, he expected her to weep. But no, Vanessa stood there silent, solid, like a pillar of stone. It took very little to trigger Leslie's temper. When Vanessa presented him weekly with the account books, Leslie felt particularly miserable and he insisted that his misery be "appreciated and shared"; so he made a scene which began with "groans and sighs, then expressions of rage, then really terrible outbursts of bellowing fury . . . he, a poor, broken, bereaved old man was being callously hounded to ruin."

But Vanessa would not tolerate such scenes, and an "uncompromising anger took possession of her," Virginia was later to write. "We made him the type of all that we hated in our lives; he was the tyrant of inconceivable selfishness." Stella, in all her docility, had been able to bring together so much that was incompatible; but Vanessa, for all her bewilderment, was too resolute and determined in character to make simple communion possible.

It was Jack Hills, more than anyone else, who had lost and suffered most in Stella's death. After the week with his family in Cumberland, he began coming regularly in the evening to Hyde Park Gate for solace and companionship. In the devastation of Stella's death, he turned increasingly to Vanessa for sympathy. When Virginia saw her sister getting so much of Jack's attention, she became jealous and resentful, first because that intimacy excluded her, but equally because with Stella's death Vanessa was becoming daily more a mother to her than a sister. Virginia's relations with Vanessa now bordered on obsession, and if Jack intervened—if he "picked her pocket" too—she would be denied the maternal figure she needed more than anything else now and for the remainder of her life. Nothing more frightening could happen than to be shut out of Vanessa's life. When Virginia protested that Jack did not appreciate all he was being given, Vanessa became reticent and withdrawn, a reaction that stung her into remembering how similar this was to Julia's moments of silent withdrawal. Virginia soon realized that Vanessa was falling in love with Jack and he, it seemed, was "not unwilling to be loved." This was betrayal. Her father had deserted her at thirteen for Stella. Now Vanessa was deserting her for Jack.

It was George Duckworth, finally, who approached Virginia. Vanessa, he said, was spending altogether too much time in Jack's company. People were beginning to talk; unpleasant rumors were circulating. Would Virginia talk to her? Try to use her influence? Surely this alliance must stop. What George also impressed upon the younger half sister was that under English law as it then stood, a man could not legally marry his deceased wife's sister. The love affair between Vanessa and Jack was, therefore, "of necessity something guilty."

If there were further ethical considerations, they were beyond George's understanding or articulation. As a slave to propriety, he cared only that "people were talking," and if his half sister continued to sneer at decorum, she would soon become a "social liability." Would Virginia therefore do everything in her power to bring the entanglement to a halt? When Virginia approached Vanessa, she got only the bitter reply: "So you take their side too."

Even Thoby sided with the rules. Vanessa should listen to George, be more conscious of the delicacy of her position. Like so many other matters in their lives, this one too was not open to discussion. Sex was not a subject one talked about. Nor was love. Nor were strong emotions. And so the matter remained a sore spot that would fester for a year or two more before relations between Jack and Vanessa finally broke off. A good many feelings were hurt in the process. But it was perhaps Virginia who felt most keenly Vanessa's treachery. Just as the elder sister had usurped Thoby's love in the nursery, so now she claimed Jack's.

In 1898 Adrian was still a day boy at Westminster School, Thoby a boarder at Clifton College in Bristol, and Vanessa a student at Cope's School of Art. Jack was in a solicitor's office, George at work for Charles Booth, and Gerald at his newly founded publishing house, Duckworth & Co. Leslie was writing his two-volume *Studies of a Biographer*. In November 1897 Virginia had been pronounced well enough to begin classes in Greek and history at King's College, Kensington, under the tuition of Dr. G. C. W. Warr; and in October of 1898, she took up intermediate Latin once a week with Clara Pater, the sister of Walter Pater. There were new friends too: her Vaughan cousins Emma (Toad) and Margaret (Marny) and their sister-in-law Madge Symonds on whom Virginia had once nourished a passionate childhood "crush." Madge had married Will Vaughan in July 1898.

The family spent August and September 1899 at the Rectory, Warboys, a Fenland village in Huntingdonshire (now Cambridgeshire). The few relics that survive of this period suggest that this holiday was probably the best Virginia had had since the summer of 1894 in Cornwall, when her mother and Stella were still alive. She now seemed more organized and her energy more focused. The slim Warboys journal was very different from the one she had kept in 1897. This 1899 production consisted largely of essays, and the writing here was more detached, more self-conscious in style and manner. She seemed to be practicing the art of the essay seriously for the first time. One called "A Chapter on Sunsets" was even dated and signed. Among the more accomplished pieces in the collection is one which she described as a "grim day of pleasure" in Godmanchester with her equally grim Stephen cousins. The following is a fragment of that memorable occasion:

> We reached Godmanchester at 2.15 and found the party on the verge of lunch ... R[osamund].—who loves the rich, is anxious to imitate their charms and flyaway manners ... She is remarkably

square, and short; with small vivacious eyes ... She was once described by her father as a "winsome frolic." This is a character that
she tries to deserve. She is, I think, tinged strongly with the usual
Stephen solidity and cumbersomeness; so that her attempts to be
winsome and frolicsome are oddly and ludicrously out of harmony
with her appearance ... They all bring with them the atmosphere
of the lecture room; they are severe, caustic and absolutely independent and immovable. An ordinary character would be ground
to pulp after a week's intercourse with them ... One remarkable
sign of character in this [Stephen] race is that they are able to sit
speechless without feeling the slightest discomfort while the whole
success of the party they have invited depends on them ... Picture
us uncomfortably seated on a towing path; half the party in a ditch,
the other half in long grass ... no glow in east or west—but a grey
melancholy vista of sky ... we slowly packed our baskets and
started back for Godmanchester.

Toward the end of their holiday Virginia was struck with the idea of
preserving her essays in some volume beautifully bound in "ancient tooled
calf." And so on one of her last drives into the nearby town, she found exactly
the book to serve her purpose in an old secondhand bookstore. It was a book
by Dr. Isaac Watts, D.D., on whose cover page was the full title

LOGICK:
OR, THE
Right Use of REASON
WITH
A Variety of RULES to Guard Against
ERROR in the AFFAIRS of RELIGION and
HUMAN LIFE as well as in the Sciences

published in London in 1786. Virginia performed a bit of surgery on this
ancient and venerable text and pasted in her essays. Any other book almost
would have been "too sacred to undergo the desecration that I planned; but
no one methought could bewail the loss of these pages."

The Warboys holiday was altogether satisfactory. As Virginia said to her
"Beloved Toad," Emma Vaughan, "I have never been in a house, garden, or
country that I liked half so well ... It is the only place for rest of mind and
body, and for contentment and creamy potatoes and all the joys of life." And
in that mood Virginia's year, and the century as well, drew to an end.

9 Just as Leslie Stephen represented the typical Victorian, so too was life at No. 22 "round about 1900 . . . a complete model of Victorian society." The day began with breakfast at 8:30. Vanessa, Virginia, Adrian, and Leslie were first at the table. (Thoby was now away at Trinity College, Cambridge.) Adrian, still at Westminster School, gulped down his food and dashed off as in childhood, leaving behind most of his gear. Leslie ate his breakfast slowly, "sighing and snorting." If there were no letters for him in the morning post, he would groan that everyone had forgotten him. Large business envelopes meant bills from the stores, and bills brought on explosions of temper. When George and Gerald came down, Vanessa would descend to the kitchen to Sophie to order dinner and then hurry off to catch the bus to her painting classes. Sometimes Gerald gave her a lift in the hired hansom he rode in daily to his office. George, having breakfasted more leisurely, would persuade Virginia to linger a bit in order to tell her about the previous night's party; then he too would button his frock coat and leave for his job at the Treasury.

With his departure, Virginia and her father were left alone with the servants for the remainder of the morning. The maids did the bedrooms, polished silver and brass, and dusted, while Sophie haggled over joints with the tradespeople in the basement, and Shag slept comfortably on his mat. After a strenuous walk in Kensington Garden with her father, Virginia went to the old nursery, now converted into a study at one end and a sleeping area at the other, and stood, with Liddell and Scott by her elbow, translating Sophocles or Euripides, while Leslie, settled in his study, wrote away at his book on biography.

From ten in the morning to one in the afternoon, the Victorian world was shut out to father and daughter and might also be kept at bay for an hour or two after lunch. But from 4:30 in the afternoon society began to assert itself. Virginia and Vanessa must be "in" to give their father his tea. They had to be dressed and tidy and prepared to receive guests, mostly their father's—Mr. F. W. Gibbs, Mrs. Humphry Ward, Mr. C. B. Clark, and, among the younger generation, perhaps the Misses Stillmans, Kitty Maxse, her sister Susan Lushington, and a long list of others. Whoever it might be, the Stephen sisters had to be "ready with small talk; ready to take father's [ear] trumpet and convey whatever was likely to help; ready to take part."

Special rules of conduct had to be observed during this tea ceremony. Vanessa and Virginia, with Julia's shining example before them, did their utmost to continue the ritual. There must be no awkward break in the conversation, and no one must say anything to upset their father. If anyone present was silly or unlucky enough to say that Leslie was looking remarkably well, down instantly plunged a curtain of icy disdain. It was sympathy he demanded. But there was always someone who came to the rescue and changed the conversational course. Some young man might ask Leslie if he remembered John Stuart Mill, and the deaf old man "would unbend . . . and say how he had met Mill with his father in Chelsea," and equilibrium was once more restored.

The sisters had also to be watchful that the guests' feelings were not bruised by their father's often disconcerting remarks. As he grew older and deafer, his discourteous comments to others increased in frequency and his groans of impatience in amplitude. Tea with Leslie Stephen was not a pleasant affair, especially for the Stephen sisters. The tea-table manner was not natural to Vanessa and Virginia, but they learned it thoroughly and remembered it. The manner had its disadvantages in writing, however, as Virginia was to remark later: "When I re-read my old *Common Reader* articles, I detect it there. I lay the blame for their . . . politeness, their sidelong approach, to my tea-table training."

It was in the evening, however, that Victorian society became most oppressive. At 7:30 the sisters went up to dress. Regardless of the weather, they took off their day clothes and, standing before their wash basins shivering with cold, scrubbed their arms and neck, "for we had to come into the drawing room at 8 o'clock in evening dress: arms and neck bare." Dress and hairstyle in the evening had far greater importance than sketch pads and Greek exercises. Try as she might to make herself presentable as she stood before George's Chippendale mirror, Virginia found it difficult on an allowance of fifty pounds a year to achieve the degree of sartorial splendor her half brother expected, indeed insisted upon. George inspected Virginia with the keen and pitiless eye of a customs officer examining a suspicious parcel. On one occasion she made the mistake of having a dress made of upholstery material bought at a furniture store because it was cheaper than dress fabric. Down she came in her new evening dress. All the lights were on in the drawing room, and George, in his evening jacket, sat by the fire. He studied her thoroughly from head to toe. Then a terrible look appeared, "a look in which one traced not merely aesthetic disapproval; but something that went deeper; morally, socially, he scented some kind of insurrection; a defiance of social standards." She stood before him, squirming with humiliation and despair. Go tear it up, he said. His voice was rasping, peevish. Virginia detected his profound disapproval at her violation of a code more important to him than he cared to admit.

In spite of the resistance George encountered, he was determined to launch his half sisters in society: he would open doors for them to the great London houses. Vanessa was the first to fall into his plan, and if George was determined, Vanessa was too. In the beginning, she rather enjoyed going out to dances, but soon the long, glittering evenings, the lovely clothes, the ever-changing tableaux of faces began to make her feel herself a sacrifice at some mysterious altar. She was shy; she was naturally reticent; she grew uneasy dancing and talking to young men she scarcely knew. She felt out of place and marooned in a ballroom of strangers, with no place to turn. And so she began to buck and rear. She began refusing her incredulous half brother.

Indeed, George could not believe his ears. How could a girl with an allowance of fifty pounds a year refuse the gifts, the flowers, the invitations, the dresses her proud half brother showered upon her? Was she confused? Was she ungrateful? Was she out of her mind? It was unthinkable that she should refuse his bounty; and the more vehement Vanessa's refusals, the more persistent were George's efforts. But Vanessa was firm. She stood before him, young, beautiful, motherless, in her white satin dress, wearing a flawless amethyst—gifts from George. The battle went on for over a year. With each new invitation, George would implore; Vanessa would resist. At last George surrendered himself to the idea that Vanessa was unappreciative, unwomanly, and downright stubborn. Virginia would surely be less troublesome. After all, she'd been with Vanessa to the Trinity Ball and met Thoby's friends; she'd enjoyed herself, found it amusing. He must take Virginia under his wing. She'd succeed where Vanessa had failed.

And so one morning while Virginia was translating some Greek, George presented her with a small jewel box. He was creased with bitterness and disappointment, and poured out to Virginia all the trouble Vanessa had caused him, implying even that she had come close to driving him into the arms of whores! But never again! Under no circumstances would he ask her to accompany him into London society. She'd had her chance. Her obstinacy was appalling. No one could accuse him of coercion or say he had forced his half sister to act against her wishes.

By the end of the interview, Virginia agreed to accompany him a few nights later to the Dowager Marchioness of Sligo's ball. And it was at Lady Sligo's that Virginia discovered exactly what it was that Vanessa had found so detestable. After being stranded for two hours on the edge of the dance floor waiting to be introduced to strange young men, she danced briefly— and badly—and was again stranded. Small talk was difficult; she felt awkward and tongue-tied, and at last found herself with a slice of iced cake to eat alone in a corner, scarlet with embarrassment. As she said at the time, she and Vanessa were failures. They just didn't shine at dances. "We ain't popular—we sit in corners and look like mutes who are longing for a funeral." On one occasion, she confessed, "Providence inscrutably decreed some other destiny for me. Adrian and I waltzed (to a Polka!)... I would give all my profound Greek to dance really well."

Worse was yet to come. Having assured Virginia that all she needed was a little practice, George next took her to dine with the Dowager Countess of Carnarvon, who was "simplicity itself," and her sister Mrs. Popham of Littlecote, "a lady also of distinction." With all of George's reassurances and hand-stroking, Virginia felt herself fortified for the grand event, and the two ladies themselves seemed harmless enough. If George had complained of Vanessa's brutal silences, Virginia was prepared to remedy that situation. After the assembly was seated at the dinner table, Virginia began. She would show them that she, Virginia Stephen, aged eighteen, could indeed talk, and off she went. "Heaven knows what devil prompted me... to discourse upon the need of expressing emotions!" That, she said, was the great lack of modern life. The ancients, she said, discussed everything in common. Had Lady Carnarvon read the Greeks? And once started, Virginia Stephen, aged eighteen, was too busy fueling her monologue to notice Lady Carnarvon and Mrs. Popham twitching or George in an agony of embarrassment. Only later could he whisper into Virginia's ear that the distinguished ladies were not accustomed to young women saying anything. Although Virginia realized she had failed, she was still alert enough to see George, as if to apologize for his half sister's impropriety, draw Lady Carnarvon behind a pillar in the hall for a passionate kiss, despite Mrs. Popham's valiant effort to deflect Virginia's attention.

The evening was not yet over. Next they went to the theater to see a French play. Virginia, still feeling snubbed for her faux pas, was not paying attention to what was happening onstage until she noticed the odd reaction of the ladies now "positively squirming" in their seats. Lady Carnarvon and Mrs. Popham were "both agitated by the same sort of convulsive twitching which had taken them at dinner." Virginia turned her attention to the play and saw what the matter was. The shrieking heroine, exhausted from being pursued by the love-starved hero, suddenly collapsed on the sofa and her grunting hero, visibly unbuttoning his clothes, threw himself on top of her. The curtain fell and George with the two ladies rose simultaneously and without a word filed out of the theater. Virginia Stephen, aged eighteen, had been taken by Lady Carnarvon and George Duckworth "to see the French actors copulate upon the stage." In the carriage taking them home, all the

Countess could say in a tremulous voice was that she hoped the evening hadn't tired Miss Stephen too much—which meant, Virginia added, that "she hoped I wouldn't lose my virginity or something like that."

Virginia's social education was prolonged that evening by one further stop in Melbury Road at the Holman Hunts', where the great painter himself, in a long Jaeger dressing gown, sipping cocoa and stroking his beard, was "discoursing to his admiring guests on the symbolism of *The Light of the World*." George made a deep bow to the man of genius, but Holman Hunt had not the foggiest notion who George Duckworth was, nor for that matter who anyone else was. Virginia felt as much an outsider here among artists as she felt earlier in the fashionable world of high society.

This scandalous evening in George's company ended with a bedroom scene which she read an account of some twenty years later to a group of friends, intending to shock and amuse them. Back in her room at Hyde Park Gate, she had taken off her satin dress and, stretched out on her bed, was still thinking of the Countess and Plato and *The Light of the World* and copulation, when quietly her bedroom door opened and she heard George's hushed voice—"Don't be frightened . . . And don't turn on the light, oh beloved. Beloved"—as he flung himself onto the bed and took Virginia in his arms. "Yes," she concluded, with a touch of mischief, "the old ladies of Kensington and Belgravia never knew that George Duckworth was not only father and mother, brother and sister to those poor Stephen girls; he was their lover also." Virginia could not resist a good story and no doubt exaggerated for effect; but still, did one laugh or shudder at such a report? "One felt like an unfortunate minnow shut up in the same tank with an unwieldly and turbulent whale."

George's conduct and the tea-table manner and the evening with the Countess were all part of Victorian hypocrisy—a veneer of propriety camouflaging sordid behavior. It disguised the real thing beneath the show; it was the very discrepancy that would cause Septimus Warren Smith, unable even to name his "crime" of loving officer Evans, to commit suicide. The social order of the nineteenth century would not acknowledge, much less condone, alternate forms of human love. It was this cleavage that made the move to Bloomsbury a few years later significant. For Bloomsbury was only meaningful against the background of 22 Hyde Park Gate, Kensington.

Early in 1902 Virginia took up bookbinding. She also began Greek lessons with Janet Case. Vanessa and George went off together for three weeks to Rome and Florence. And during the Easter holiday, Leslie learned that he had abdominal cancer. When the diagnosis was confirmed by Sir Frederick Treves, he wrote in his journal: "It is enough to say now that I consider this to be the equivalent to a warning that my journey is coming to an end. How long it will be does not seem to be foreseeable; but not very long, and all down-hill. At present I have only discomfort." He made this note in April 1902.

In November of the previous year, Leslie had received an honorary doctor of letters from Oxford, and now on June 26, 1902—during the Coronation Honours (Queen Victoria had died on January 22, 1901)—he was made a Knight Commander of the Bath (K.C.B.). He was at first inclined to refuse the honor, but the children, Thoby in particular, pressed him to accept. "My motives for refusing," he wrote, "were not pure—perverted vanity perhaps! Anyhow the thing has been pleasantly received. I am also elected a Vice President of the Royal Historical Society. I have as many honours as I deserve."

Although his illness forced him to remain close to home, Sir Leslie joined his family for the summer holiday at Fritham House, Lyndhurst. It was here that Virginia was to form a deep and loving attachment to Violet Dickinson, whom she had earlier known only casually. Violet had been a friend of the Duckworth family and was particularly close to Stella. Her family, like the Duckworths, came from Somerset. She was the daughter of a Somersetshire squire, her maternal grandfather having been the 3rd Lord Auckland. Violet had a London house in Manchester Street, but lived most of the time in Welwyn with her brother Oswald (Ozzie), a barrister and later Secretary to the Home Office Board of Control in Lunacy. Neither of them ever married. Violet was thirty-seven and Virginia just twenty during this summer of 1902 at Fritham House, when their intimacy began. The whole Stephen family, including Leslie, was fond of her. One of her outstanding features was her height. She was six feet two inches tall, a fact Virginia never tired of joking about; but every inch of her brimmed with sympathy, good humor, and intelligence. She had a kind of "breezy masculine assurance, a cheerful imperturbable balance" and was a "lofty and reassuring tower of strength."

Violet drew Virginia to her as a magnet draws metal shavings. Apart from the love Virginia received in generous measure, apart from the encouragement, there was one thing in particular that she loved in Violet—and that was her tendency to laugh at herself. Virginia was nicknamed Goat by her brothers and sister, and behind that silly and demeaning label were depths of feeling guessed by no one, even Vanessa. Behind Violet's carefree façade,

Virginia detected similar depths, traces of sadness, flickerings of wasted passion. Here was the source of that overpowering magnetism. Most of all Virginia felt safe with Violet, perhaps for the first time in many years. And there was no rivalry. Whatever she said, however twisted or peculiar or perverse, Violet would understand. In that understanding was safety. No one, except perhaps Vanessa, had ever given her that before. So if Virginia at this point in her life felt unprotected, newly broken from her chrysalis, Violet encouraged her to test her strength, try her wings; and Violet's offerings were received with an intensity verging on passion. Unlike Julia's "general presence," Violet was a solid and specific woman.

Also there was trust. For a long time Virginia had been writing pieces she had shown to no one. But now there was Violet. Surely she could read them. In just a few short months, Violet was receiving in the post essays Virginia had written before and during her summer holiday in Salisbury—"Stonehenge," "Salisbury Cathedral," "Thoughts on Social Success." She had written some thirty essays of varying length and quality during 1903, and shy as she was about her writing, she felt no hesitation in dispatching them to Violet for criticism.

 When the family returned to London in September of 1903, it was clear that Sir Leslie's death was not far off. As his cancer progressed, it was to the steadfast and immensely generous Violet that Virginia turned. Vanessa made no secret of her feelings for her father: he had been unkind to her and she had very limited sympathy for him. Virginia sensed this and gravitated increasingly to Violet in her sorrow. Leslie Stephen's death was not going to be easy for the younger sister. The earlier tyrant had once more become her ally in the world of books, her intellectual comrade and mentor. What would she do when he was gone? The future was uncharted, her prospects vague. Here and now, in the midst of this illness, Virginia had only pen and paper and postage stamps. With these, she would write herself through what was to become a long, wearisome trek toward young womanhood. But Violet would be there, and with Violet, reality and appearance were one and the same.

In her letters, Virginia scarcely concealed her craving for Violet's bony embraces. In fact, she began to demand "hot" letters, passionate letters: Do write "a good hot letter," Virginia begged; "I like them hot and affectionate." She also invented for herself a small menagerie of animals whose identities she could assume as the mood struck her. Most of the time her alias was the "sparroy" (sparrow plus monkey): "I weep tears of tenderness to think of that great heart of pity for Sparroy locked up in stone—never to throw her arms round me—as she would if she could." "Sparroy only flaps her warm blooded paw, and says she has tender memories of a long embrace, in a bedroom." Sometimes, though, it was a wallaby. "I feel myself curled up snugly in old mother wallaby's pouch. My little claws nestle round my furry cheeks." "It would draw tears from your stony eyes to see little Wallaby nosing around with her soft wet snout for a letter—and none comes . . . Write to me, and tell me that you love me, dearest. I wish no more. My food is affection."

Just how Violet Dickinson interpreted these endearments from the twenty-year-old Virginia we don't know. It was only clear that Virginia was in great need. Sir Leslie's health was a difficult subject, and "I would not write to you," said Virginia, "only writing is easier than talking." And two days later: "You are the only sympathetic person in the world. That's why everybody comes to you with their troubles."

Leslie Stephen took a long time in dying. He had a remarkable constitution, and the several physicians who saw him kept predicting terminal dates quite off the mark. Throughout the illness Virginia wrote Violet daily. In May, Sir Frederick Treves, once Surgeon Extraordinary to Queen Victoria, again saw Leslie: "He says that six months is the longest it can last." By autumn 1903, he was getting steadily weaker, less able to read or talk, more inclined to drowse the day away. Then suddenly, "Father has some inflammation—it came on 2 days ago . . . he may become unconscious at any moment . . . I think he wants to die . . . If he does die you are the only person who can help—and I will ask you to come." Almost at once Hyde Park Gate was crawling with aunts and cousins and friends, filling the house with funereal sounds. "Three mornings have I spent having my hand held, and my emotions pumped out of me."

While the physicians continued to miscalculate the end, the four Stephens, with Vanessa in charge, decided that as soon as their father was laid to rest, they would leave Hyde Park Gate and find a small house to settle in—probably in Bloomsbury, a world apart from Kensington. When consulted about the move, Gerald agreed. The Duckworth brothers were, after all, a generation older than the Stephens and it made sense for them to separate.

This was Gerald's view. George, however, was of another mind. He was going to stick to the family no matter what. He even agreed that Bloomsbury was a good place to settle. "George has been so extraordinarily understanding and feeling about all this," wrote Virginia, "that one forgets his irritating ways, and I believe we shall all get on very well together."

Sir Leslie was still able to work a little in October. He was trying to finish his book on Hobbes for the *English Men of Letters* series. He was also, occasionally, able to take a short walk up the street, but he was growing weaker every day. "He said he didn't mind dying for himself," Virginia confided to Violet, "but he should like to see a little more of the children. He feels, I think, that we are just grown up, and able to talk to him—and he wants to see what becomes of us."

On November 14, fourteen days before his seventy-first birthday, too weak to write himself, Leslie dictated to Virginia the final entry of his journal: "I shall write no more in this book," he said. "I just note that an operation was performed on me by Sir F. Treves on 12 December 1902. It was considered to be successful, and I improved in strength for two or three months afterwards . . . I have only to say to you, my children, that you have all been as good and tender to me as anyone could be during these last months and indeed years. It comforts me to think that you are all so fond of each other that when I am gone you will be the better able to do without me."

But still Leslie Stephen lived on, day after day, week after week. By December he was weak and depressed, and scarcely able to read. Then one of the physicians thought the growth might be spreading. Despite the unsteady course of the disease, however, the old man still had remarkable strength. One could only take each day as it came.

On Christmas, he was the same, but living had become very hard work. "He does want to have done with it all . . . If only it could be quicker!" It was a family custom on Christmas Eve for Leslie to recite Milton's "On the Morning of Christ's Nativity." This year he was too exhausted to say the words. On New Year's Eve, Adrian and Thoby sang the New Year in. "We should never get on without this kind of thing," she confessed to Violet.

On January 25, 1904, Virginia turned twenty-two. "Father gave me a ring—a really beautiful one, which I love—the first ring I have ever had . . . It amazes me how much I get out of my Father, still—and he says I am a very good daughter! . . . Lord knows how we shall ever get along alone." The time was drawing near. On the afternoon of February 21, Sir Leslie slipped into unconsciousness; he died at seven the next morning, with the family at his bedside. Vanessa breathed a sigh of relief. The tyranny was over. Virginia perhaps heard the sigh, sensed the relief. For the moment it did not matter.

. . .

The funeral was held two days later at Golders Green, and on the twenty-eighth the four Stephens, together with George Duckworth, set off for Manorbier, Pembrokeshire, on the south coast of Wales, a wild, desolate country, in many ways reminiscent of Cornwall. They needed a change of atmosphere. What they didn't need was an army of relatives flooding the house with tears.

Manorbier was cold and clear. There were few houses, an odd little church, and a great feudal castle. The only sounds were of wind and sea. It was a place swept clean of human debris, a perfect refuge for spiritual cleansing, for expiation. And almost at once Virginia began to suffer pangs of guilt. Her poor father. All the things she might have said and done and failed to do. He was so lonely; she had never comforted him as she might have done. Had she only known what his death would mean to her. It was too late, however. She had missed her chance. But the newspaper obituaries! The journalists—"Stupid fools!"—had misunderstood him, had distorted his image, had given the wrong impression of the man he really was. "All this stupid writing and reading about father seems to put him further away . . . and I have the curious feeling of living with him every day. I often wonder as we sit talking what it is I am waiting for, and then I know I want to hear what he thinks." By the middle of March she had sunk into a slough of despair. "I don't find the affairs of this world easy to realise. Much thinking would send me down bottomless pits . . . I can't believe that all our life with Father is over and he dead." If only she could tell him now how much she cared.

She couldn't talk of this to her brothers, and from Vanessa she could expect little sympathy. So she unburdened herself to Violet. "I find the country a good place to work in. I have really finished quite a lot."* Altogether, however, it was a bad time. "I keep thinking I shall find Father at home—and what I shall tell him—I wonder how we go on as we do, as merry as grigs all day long." She was irritated at the lighthearted manner she sensed in Adrian and Vanessa. Only in retrospect did she see that her own grief was so morbid it cut her off from them.

When the four weeks were up, the four Stephens agreed to accompany

---

* Many years later (on September 3, 1922) Virginia noted in her diary that for a long time she had wanted to begin writing a book but was never certain what the subject was to be. "That vision came to me more clearly at Manorbier aged 21 [22], walking the down on the edge of the sea." This writing, she also confessed, was really a test of her sanity: she was trying to prove that nothing was wrong with her, when in fact something was terribly wrong.

Gerald to Venice. Violet Dickinson was going to Florence. Why not all be in Italy together? Part of the motive for this additional expedition may have been Thoby and Vanessa's sensing Virginia's rapidly deteriorating condition and hoping that Venice might provide the necessary diversion, if that indeed was what their increasingly depressed sister was in need of. When they returned to London from Manorbier, Virginia found a letter of condolence waiting for her from Frederic Maitland, whom Sir Leslie had authorized to write his "Life." It was a beautiful letter, said Virginia, "almost the only one I have had worth keeping."

Her letters to Violet, however, began showing signs of desperation. Vanessa could simply not help her: "... you can't think what a relief it is to have someone—that is you, because there isn't anyone else to talk to." Thoughts of her father were haunting her. "I can't bear to think of his loneliness, and that I might have helped, and didn't ... I think he just knew how much I cared ... and now it's all over. That is what seems so cruel. If I could only tell him once ... My Violet—it is a help even to write this to you." This was Virginia's state of mind when on April 1 the party set off for Italy.

The trip was as picturesque as a travelogue. There were snowcapped mountains, lakes of the purest blue, and brilliant sunshine flooding the landscape. Upon their arrival, however, they discovered they had no place to stay. No one had troubled to reserve rooms; and so they tramped the streets of Venice past midnight hunting for somewhere to sleep. At last they found "three very dingy little rooms—sleeping together in a dirty little place off the Piazza S Mark." Gerald grew cranky and refused to join them in their explorations; but Adrian and Thoby were "rampant with excitement," and Vanessa was enchanted with her first sight of the place that had always fascinated painters. Virginia herself, in the beginning, marveled at the sights and wandered about "open mouthed." But before long Venice became "a place to die in beautifully: but to live in I never felt more depressed." She had had her fill of floating in gondolas, eating ices at Florian's, listening to the band in the Piazza San Marco, and watching honeymooners strolling by. The beautiful and the sublime were becoming sordid and ugly, and she felt trapped.

Violet Dickinson met them in Florence on April 13, and here too Virginia suffered countless petty irritations. Everywhere she turned she ran into someone she would rather have avoided—the Prinseps, the Humphry Wards, the Carnarvons, and, finally, even Aunt Minna and Edith Duckworth! Virginia began to hate Italy, its people, and its habits. One day when they were out sightseeing, they found themselves pursued by a throng of little boys and cripples. "We walked faster than the cripples," said Virginia, but not faster than the boys. One youngster promised to stop following them if they gave him money. When they refused, he cursed them roundly and slunk away. Never was there a "beastlier" country.

They went from Florence to Paris (without Violet) on May 1 and were entertained there by Clive Bell, whom Virginia and Vanessa had earlier met in Cambridge in Thoby's rooms. They were taken to dinner and introduced to Gerald Kelly (who would later become President of the Royal Academy). It was the sisters' first glimpse of a thoroughly bohemian party, where they all talked late into the night about music and painting and sculpture, smoking one cigarette after another. On the following day, they visited Rodin's studio. For Vanessa it was a sensual feast, and she was ravenous. Sir Leslie's death was like an escape from prison. Virginia saw this and felt betrayed—now for a second time.

Vanessa's scarcely concealed indifference to their father's death made Virginia feel more isolated than ever. The more exhilarating Paris became, the deeper Virginia descended into the pit that would soon swallow her up in madness. Everything was losing its color and tone, becoming gray and monotonous. The diversions of the French capital, the taste of freedom were not enough to intercept Virginia's rapid spiral into the pandemonium awaiting her. In the first week of May she wrote Violet a desperate letter. How cross and irritable she had been; how much she had forced Violet to put up with; how she wished she could repay all "the bad times with good times . . . Oh my Violet if you could only find me a great solid bit of work to do when I get back that will make me forget my own stupidity I should be so grateful. I *must* work."

They returned to Hyde Park Gate on May 9. On the tenth, what remained of Virginia's darkening world caved into blackness and nightmare. The irritability and depression she felt since February now grew to "frantic intensity." It was the most frightening she had ever experienced. Never before had she required nurses and sequestration, and with this second breakdown she needed both. The acute stage lasted from May through July—"all that summer she was mad." Then came a further three months of convalescence.

During the worst period of her illness, she was plagued with voices telling her to do "all kinds of wild things." She heard King Edward, lurking in the bushes, spewing out the vilest obscenities. She grew hostile to Vanessa, who had deserted her. The voices came from overeating, she must starve herself. At times she became so violent it required the strength of all her nurses—

those horrible "fiends"—to restrain her. She heard birds singing in Greek. Here was the nightmare world of Septimus Warren Smith she would re-create in *Mrs. Dalloway*.

Dr. Savage was called in. But it was Vanessa who assumed the main responsibility of care. She was helped enormously by Violet, who moved Virginia to her house in Burnham Wood, Welwyn, where she remained for almost three months. Nurse Traill, who had just recently cared for Sir Leslie, went with her. It was at Welwyn that Virginia made her first suicide attempt. Like Septimus Warren Smith, who leaped from a window to his death, so too did Virginia plunge. Luckily, the window was not high and she suffered no serious injury.

Her condition remained critical throughout the summer months. During the early part of September, with Nurse Traill in attendance, Virginia was transported to the Manor House, Teversal, in Nottinghamshire, where the Stephens went for their summer holiday. Here she was allowed to take short walks, do a little Latin with Thoby, go for country drives, and write brief letters. By the middle of the month, her health began to return: the blood was flowing into her brain again, she said. It was the oddest feeling, as though a dead part of her were coming to life again. "Oh my Violet, if there were a God I should bless him for having delivered me safe and sound from the miseries of the last six months! . . . Sorrow, such as I feel now for Father, is soothing and natural, and makes life more worth having, if sadder. I can never tell you what you have been to me all this time . . . if affection is worth anything, you have, and will always have, mine."

The Stephens' most important guest at Teversal was Violet, and Virginia's letter asking her to visit was pitiful. She felt diseased and unclean and contagious. But this would pass. And in her recovery during these late summer days, she felt her restlessness returning, and most of all the need to write: that was to become her principal restorative. "I am longing to begin work," she said to her friend. "I know I can write, and one of these days I mean to produce a good book."

Dr. Savage, however, who had known Virginia all her life, insisted upon peace and quiet. He was aware of her natural volubility and urged her to avoid excitement, to leave London for a while. This suggestion fell in favorably with Vanessa's plans, for she had undertaken the supervision of the move from Kensington in early October to their new home at 46 Gordon Square. Only the four Stephens would be living there. Gerald had decided to live on his own and took bachelor's rooms in a more fashionable quarter of London, and George—to everyone's relief, including probably his own—on September 10 had married Lady Margaret Herbert, daughter of the 4th Earl of

Carnarvon. He had lived, he said to Jack Hills, in complete chastity until his marriage.

And so, when the business of house moving began, it was agreed all round that it would be easier if Virginia stayed in Cambridge with their Quaker aunt, Caroline Emelia—"Nun," as she was known to the Stephen children. Caroline Emelia, or Milly, as Leslie had called her, led a life of "tranquil benevolence" in her small house, The Porch. Surely, there would be enough peace there for anyone's health. And nearby was Adrian, now a Cambridge undergraduate.

But how did Virginia feel, being packed off to a kind but exceedingly dull aunt? She was still not sleeping well and remained troubled by headaches and neuralgia; that much she would admit. It was Vanessa's managerial manner, shipping her off so conveniently, however, that most rankled. It was rumored, said Virginia peevishly, that Vanessa was very happy "in the arms of her Kitty," who came the minute her back was turned. Virginia was certainly not fond of Kitty Maxse, who had taken it upon herself to teach Vanessa the ways of London society while Virginia was locked away in Cambridge with the Nun.

There was something to be said for the Quaker aunt, however. The Porch was an ideal retreat. It was like living in a cathedral close and the Quaker's voice was like a tolling church bell. She was soporific and the restless niece wanted to "blow her up with gunpowder." But something better was about to happen that would make a great deal of difference in the weeks ahead. That something had nothing to do with Savage's enforced regimen or with Caroline Emelia's sleepy benignity. It was, rather, a request made by Frederic Maitland, now Downing Professor of History at Cambridge, who had already begun work on *The Life and Letters of Leslie Stephen*. Would Virginia read through her father's and mother's letters and copy out passages he might quote? The letters were much too personal for anyone outside the family to see. Would she also feel inclined to write a brief account of Sir Leslie's last years with his children to include in the biography? It would be a valuable contribution to the book.

Maitland had made a wise choice in appealing for this help, particularly at this time and place; for Caroline Emelia was the "great authority" on Leslie Stephen and would be invaluable assistance, even though she was reluctant to contribute her own recollections, which were not "altogether happy or characteristic." She did, however, possess a hoard of diaries, her own as well as her mother's; and her mother, Jane Venn Stephen, had kept a daily journal of everything her four children had said and done from the day of their birth until 1873, two years before her death.

For Virginia, it was not merely the busy work of reading and copying out letters or writing a reminiscence that mattered at this time. It was rather that Maitland's request restored her—if only symbolically—to the mother she had lost nine years earlier and especially to the father she now desperately longed for. More than that, the task made her feel useful and valued; and as she helped to preserve the memory of her father, her own life seemed to become revitalized. Some of the impotence and dependency would soon begin to recede into the background. "I am perfectly happy alone, so don't come out of charity," she wrote Violet on October 24. And as Vanessa was now engaged in settling 46 Gordon Square, Virginia added that Violet was to make her understand that she was on no account to make an effort to come if she was busy—"because, tho' I want her naturally, I can subsist without her . . . Don't let her come if she has other things to do," Virginia repeated. Such a statement a few months earlier would have been inconceivable. Here was Virginia putting off the two people she loved above all others. But work was giving her a sense of independence. She could stand on her own two feet, now that she had her Mother, her Father, her Work.

"I am getting through my copying," she wrote to Violet; now she must go through two volumes of extracts from Leslie and Julia's letters to each other. They were so private that Maitland wouldn't look at them himself. Virginia would have to decide what he ought to see and possibly publish, and she was anxious to do the work. At one point Violet was unable to make the trip to Cambridge, and Virginia swept it aside as if the visit were an interruption. "As a matter of fact," she wrote, "I ought to stick to my letter reading and copying so as to give Fred an important bundle before I leave." She seemed oblivious to what Violet might feel by this sudden indifference. For nothing now seemed to matter except the work at hand. She could manage any interference if it came.

And interference did come. It came from Jack Hills, who suddenly became a thorn in her side. In the middle of her work, she received a "solicitorial" letter: "Whatever you do, *don't* publish anything too intimate," it said. Virginia bristled and fired back her reply: she cared "10,000 times more for delicacy and reserve" where her father and mother were concerned than he possibly could, adding that whatever selection she made "was to be final." Jack, in her estimation, was nothing but a "poor little redtape parchment Solicitor!" She would not permit him to meddle. But Vanessa mustn't hear of this, she said to Violet, because she evidently still had embers kindling in her bosom and couldn't therefore stand up to "the authoritative Jack" and his "thickskulled" proprieties.

The greater Virginia's sense of purpose grew in helping Fred Maitland, the greater her sense of self, and the greater that sense of self, the more acutely she felt locked out of her own house. Imagine her reaction when Dr. Savage, at the end of October, informed her that she must continue to convalesce in peace and quiet *away* from Gordon Square. It was easy to harbor the suspicion that Vanessa wanted to be free of the burden of looking after her. Vanessa did in fact side with Dr. Savage and "took the exasperating view that doctor's orders were doctor's orders and must be obeyed." Virginia could not make Vanessa or Violet see how cruel it was to make her spend "two more months wandering about in other people's comfortless houses," when she had her own to go to. She longed for a room to herself, with pictures and music and books "where I can shut myself up, and see no one, and read myself into peace." Why couldn't Savage see that? And why couldn't Violet of all people understand that? She felt abandoned and unwanted. In fact Vanessa "contrived to say that it didn't much matter to anyone, her included, I suppose, whether I was here or in London . . . but then she has a genius for stating unpleasant truths in her matter of fact voice!"

But the doctor was firm. And so was Vanessa. There was still too much house arranging to be done at 46 Gordon Square; it would be better if Virginia were resting comfortably elsewhere, whether she liked it or not; and so Virginia was sent off to Yorkshire to stay with her cousins, the Vaughans; but before going she did have a chance—her first—to sleep in her own bed. During this ten-day interval in London, two events took place that were to have enormous significance in her life. The first was Violet's introducing Virginia to her friend Mrs. Arthur Lyttelton, editor of the Women's Supplement of *The Guardian*, a London Anglo-Catholic weekly; and the second was meeting Leonard Woolf on November 17. He was Thoby's dinner guest and would be sailing for Ceylon the following day, where he would remain for seven years.

On Saturday morning, November 18, Virginia was on her way to Giggleswick, in Yorkshire, where she would stay with Madge and Will Vaughan for almost two weeks. William Wyamar Vaughan, Virginia's cousin, was at the time headmaster at the Giggleswick School. Madge, the daughter of John Addington Symonds, had once spent a winter at Hyde Park Gate, and Virginia, aged seven, had been "in love" with her. Madge in those days was indeed a very romantic figure, a young woman writer growing up among the Swiss mountains, passionately devoted to the arts, and always a little melancholy. "Madge worshipped her father," wrote Leonard Woolf many years later, "as so many daughters have since the time of Electra, in a way which was not fully understood" until Freud explained the Electra Complex. She was the first woman "to capture [Virginia's] heart, to make it beat faster, indeed to make it almost stand still." Virginia was to confess later that at sixteen, she had stood in her room at the top of the house saying to herself, "Madge is here; at this moment she is actually under this roof"—almost the same words Clarissa Dalloway would use for Sally Seton.

While Virginia was in the Yorkshire country, Mrs. Lyttelton sent her two volumes to review for *The Guardian*, a book of essays called *Social England* and *The Son of Royal Langbrith*, a novel by William Dean Howells. She reviewed both books and sent Mrs. Lyttelton, in addition, an account of the Brontës she had written after visiting Haworth Parsonage. Virginia had absorbed a lot about the profession of letters from her father and knew there was a "knack" of writing for newspapers which had to be learned—and "quite independent of literary merits." So that when Violet said Mrs. Lyttelton would offer her candid criticism, Virginia replied: "I don't in the least want Mrs L's candid criticism! I want her cheque!"

It would be a relief to know she could earn a little money. Her illness had been an appalling expense. She needed cash. Beneath this pose of the crusty journalist, however, she felt a certain anxiety in these first attempts at professional journalism. She had worked hard and gone about her apprenticeship seriously and thoroughly. One may well imagine her triumph when the first three pieces ever to be published appeared in the newsstands—the *Social England* and the Howells reviews on December 7 and 14, and her essay on the Brontë parsonage on December 21. At last Virginia was earning a living by her pen. First would come independence—then freedom. With an income the possibilities were endless. And so, the end of 1904 brought to a close the "seven unhappy years" which had begun in 1897 with Stella's death.

In early December, after returning from Yorkshire, Virginia wrote Madge a letter showing just how carefully she thought of herself as a writer. "I do enjoy flattery!" she said. But Madge had used the word "genius" in her praise. And " 'genius' is not a word to be used rashly; it gives me enormous pleasure . . . that you should find anything of that kind in me. I am no judge; and honestly don't know from hour to hour whether my gifts are first—second or tenth rate . . . but when I am in my lowest depths I shall haul myself out of the water by reading your words of encouragement because, however extravagant, I know you mean them honestly."

Aunt Minna Duckworth had lent the Stephens her house in the New

Forest, and it was there that the four of them spent their Christmas. Virginia was a changed young woman, and when they returned to Gordon Square in January, Dr. Savage pronounced her well enough to resume a normal life. She had lost her mother; she had also lost her father; but she had at last found work.

THE VOYAGE OUT

1905-1912

Virginia began a new journal on Christmas Day 1904 which she would continue through May 1905. In its outward aspect, it resembled that of 1897. It was as though a record of life written down compulsively from day to day provided her once more, as in the earlier diary, with a grasp of reality she could find nowhere else. But the resemblance was a superficial one; for in substance and tone the entries were now professional: they were the record of a writer who kept track of events and times and places for future use. The entries of this journal were also more optimistic, and with good reason.

First of all, she was now a budding journalist—for *The Guardian* only at the moment—but in the early months of 1905 she would also be invited to write for *The Times Literary Supplement*, edited by Bruce Richmond, for the *National Review*, owned and edited by Kitty Maxse's husband, Leo, and on a more tentative basis also for the *Academy and Literature*. She was more than a merely competent writer to have been contributing to four publications in so short a time. Second, there was her work for Fred Maitland. His request went far beyond making her feel useful: it engaged her in the actual resurrection of her father for posterity, making of him and for him a permanent monument in words. Third, Dr. Savage's lifting the ban on her reading and writing made her in a sense "certifiably" sane. For, as much as she detested physicians and questioned their competence, she needed them to ratify her mental well-being. So when Savage pronounced her cured on January 14, 1905, she felt an enormous weight lifted from her shoulders. Not only could she read and write again, she was now also allowed to accept a teaching post at Morley College, an evening institute in South London for working people. Lastly, there was a kind of resurrection in leaving the dark, overcrowded rooms of Hyde Park Gate in Kensington and moving into the spacious, light-filled house in Gordon Square. "The gulf which we crossed between Kensington and Bloomsbury," Virginia would later write, "was the gulf between respectable mummified humbug and life crude and impertinent perhaps, but living." Paintings now hung against large, bare white surfaces; the "family idol of old, G. F. Watts . . . belonged to the dark Victorian past; the new generation wanted air, simplicity and light. The move to Bloomsbury was to be an escape from the past and all its horrors."

Virginia had now entered the professional ranks and was finally, like her father, earning a living by her pen. In her modest way, she had taken the right steps toward becoming Sir Leslie's literary successor. Whatever grumbles she may have had in early January about London's interminable roars and rattles and noisy wheels now ceased altogether. Beside her breakfast plate on January 10 lay her first installment of wages—"£2.7.6 for Guardian articles, which gave me great pleasure. Also a book . . . for review, so that means more work, and cheques ultimately."

In entering this new phase of her life, Virginia began to see herself in a new way; and she would soon become acquainted with matters to ruffle the artistic vanity. In the meantime, she would learn the pleasure of watching a commissioned piece expand under her shaping hand. She might clench her teeth when an editor tampered with her words, especially if those words were signed "Virginia Stephen," but she would also feel relief and pleasure when Mrs. Lyttelton or Bruce Richmond or Leo Maxse was "delighted to accept my article—which is a load off my mind." By late February, her diary became the calendar and record of a young professional.

Time was now a salable commodity. A strict working schedule was essential. When there was no essay in progress or book to review, and these times were few indeed, there was always some Greek to translate. Even the Sunday Afternoon Concerts at Queen's Hall became regularly scheduled entertainments, as, in March, were Thoby's Thursday Evenings "at home." With her writing, reviewing, and teaching, Virginia was feeling not merely recognized and valued but independent as well. On the evening of March 1, there was to be a housewarming party at 46 Gordon Square. Half the swells of Kensington and Bloomsbury were to be present. "Our suite of apartments is to be flung open for the occasion, and four superb objects of art—the 4 Stephens in fact—are to be on view." There would be lobster and champagne; the Fishers and Duckworths and Violet with her troop of ladies would be there along with other old notabilities "wearing scarlet plush, with amber beads." Even Will Vaughan, having made arrangements for evening prayers to be said in his absence, would attend the celebration. The party marked the beginning of a new era for the four Stephens.

. . .

Throughout most of January* Virginia worked at her Note for Fred Maitland. Vanessa read it approvingly, but Virginia had reservations about her
sister's opinion on the subject. She then gave it to Thoby and was more
assured by his appraisal. On Saturday, February 25, Maitland's verdict arrived. It was Virginia's day of triumph. Her recollection of her father, he
said, was "beautiful, and if this were the proper occasion I would write a
page of praise. But of course I know that this is not what you would like
and I can only say that what you write is just what your Father would have
wished you to write." Maitland could not have phrased his approval more
perfectly.

Virginia's teaching brought her in touch with the principal of Morley College,
Miss Mary Sheepshanks, a large, kind, capable woman and the daughter of
the Bishop of Norwich. "I am to start a girl's club at Morley and talk about
books &c!"—her object being to amuse and instruct simultaneously. She
found her "Morley College soirée" challenging and the women enthusiastic.
They seemed to love books and were indeed "refreshing after the educated."
Despite the cool, careless tone she adopted in her letters to Violet, Virginia
took the teaching seriously and put a great deal of time into preparing her
lectures; in fact, she wrote them out in some detail. During one class in late
January, she spent the session describing their journey to Italy in April 1904.
It was an odd session, she said, but the sort of thing the women liked—
anxious to know "whether there were fleas in the beds at Venice." Violet
would have to come and talk to them one week, Virginia insisted—"lots of
jokes is what they like—and then they blossom out—and say how they have
written poetry since the age of 11!" When it came to English history, Virginia's imagination caught fire. "Tomorrow . . . is my working women, for
whom I have been making out a vivid account of the battle of Hastings. I
hope to make their flesh creep!"

There was also essay-writing to be taught, and at some point Miss Sheepshanks decided she ought to see her novice in action. It was a Wednesday

* A journal entry was made on January 11, 1905, that is unrelated to anything that precedes
or follows. It runs: "A poor old woman, blind, trustfully quavering out her song by the roadside
in hope of coppers, while the traffic went thundering by." Readers will recognize it as a passage
that eventually found its way into *Mrs. Dalloway*: "this battered old woman with one hand
exposed for her coppers, the other clutching her side, would still be there in ten million years."

evening class she observed, a lesson in English composition. There were "10 people: 4 men, 6 women. It is I suppose the most useless class in the College," Virginia said to Violet. Sheepshanks "sat through the whole lesson last night; and almost stamped with impatience. But what can I do?" And then there was a Dutchman who at the end of the class thought she had been "teaching him Arithmetic."

No record remains to measure the success or failure of Virginia's sally into the world of pedagogy. We know only that she remained at Morley College until the end of 1907. During her tenure she persuaded Vanessa to give a class in drawing and Thoby a few lessons in Latin. Adrian and Clive Bell, at some point, also participated. But none of them was sufficiently stimulated by the work to continue for long. When Virginia left, she took with her a sense that these working men and women had certainly a healthy native intelligence—more indeed than she had anticipated; but they had been denied the privilege of an education by the social system. This was something she would remember when she came to write *A Room of One's Own* many years later.

In January 1905 Nelly Cecil, whom Vanessa and Virginia had met two years earlier, asked Vanessa to paint her portrait. Lady Robert Cecil was a woman of money and influence. Virginia described her after their first meeting in a lively essay called "An Afternoon with the Pagans." Lady Robert, she said, "sat lightly upright glancing round her like some bright bird. Her eyes, poor thing, have to do double work." She was profoundly deaf and heard nothing of what they were saying, but "her large eyes, seeing us laugh, laughed too. It was curiously pathetic."

Vanessa began the portrait in early March and completed it in about a week. It was an important landmark in her career, for it was the first of her paintings ever to be exhibited. It was hung at the 18th Summer Exhibition of Works by Living Artists at the New Gallery, a show that included the works of John Singer Sargent among other notables. Virginia, impatient with her sister's modesty, rushed down to the New Gallery to see if the portrait had in fact been hung. It was, and she dashed back home to "general rejoicing." In the afternoon Virginia went again, and this time Vanessa joined her "most unwillingly." Just as Virginia was launched as a journalist at the end of 1904, so was Vanessa as a painter in early 1905.

. . .

On March 29 Virginia and Adrian went on holiday to the Iberian peninsula. The voyage out to Portugal on the *Anselm* would, a few years hence, be fictionalized in the opening chapters of *The Voyage Out*. The early days of the voyage were a "paradise," marred only by a passenger who "strikes one full face, as a single nose. He is a typical Jew, and initiates everything, and is a friend of everyone." He was an intolerable bore and they went to considerable lengths to avoid him, but reading books was no protection. There were plenty of compensations however. "We had the loveliest sight of Cornwall," she wrote to Violet, "and the Land's End, passing so close that we saw the houses and the people." There was the fresh air too. "I am out of doors a good 8 hours a day, inhaling sea breezes enough to make the dead walk." She was enjoying herself, eating well, untroubled by headaches, getting plenty of sleep. There was even a change in temper toward her younger brother. "Adrian is very happy, and takes great care of me, and does my hair at night, and fastens my dress."

In Lisbon they visited Fielding's grave at the English Cemetery and freed a caged bird that was singing by his tomb. On April 9, in Seville, they began their morning's explorations by visiting the Cathedral, the largest in Spain; but Virginia did not "much care for such elephantine beauty." The next day they "did" the Alcazar, a splendid Moorish palace, but this too held no charm for her. In Granada something did catch her fancy: the tomb of the first Catholic monarchs of United Spain, Ferdinand and Isabella. They stayed at the Washington Irving Hotel, high up over the city, just across the road from the Alhambra; and here Virginia was as enchanted by the Moorish palace as by the fragrant inlaid terraces of the Generalife.

On the afternoon of April 20, they embarked on the SS *Madeirensa* at Lisbon and reached Liverpool on the evening of the twenty-third, Easter Sunday. It had been a satisfactory holiday, but both were glad to be home, with hot baths, clean beds that didn't rock, and Sophie's well-cooked English meals.

Bruce Richmond had returned a review Virginia had written before leaving of Edith Sichel's *Catherine de' Medici and the French Reformation*. *The Times Literary Supplement* needed, as Virginia reported to Violet, "a serious criticism from a historical point of view. I am really thankful to have the beastly thing in my waste paper basket." But a few days later Richmond sent her "3 fat books about Spain" to review. Virginia was an amateur traveler, but she was anxious to get back to work; for she needed money. The holiday had been a drain on her bank balance.

As a beginner, she was extremely sensitive to the editors and publishers who accepted her work. From the offhand remarks in her journals and letters, one gets the impression that earning money was her primary motive; but this was only partly true. What was equally important was being paid to make literary judgments and the importance this implied. Then there was the public approval and professional endorsement. One didn't feel quite so small or powerless when one wrote for *The Times Literary Supplement* on a regular basis. Influence was important to someone who saw herself as vulnerable.

12

Early in 1905 when Thoby, now reading for the bar, wanted to see his Cambridge friends, he announced that on Thursday evenings he would be "at home." On Thursday, February 16, Saxon Sydney-Turner, taciturnity itself, made an appearance. He, Thoby, and Gurth (the dog) spent the evening alone. How the time passed, what they talked about (if indeed they talked at all) is hard to imagine. Nevertheless, it was technically this date that marked the first "Thursday Evening—At Home." On Thursday, March 2, Virginia reported "Sydney Turner and Strachey after dinner, and we talked till 12." There is nothing for March 9. On the sixteenth, "Sydney Turner and Gerald after dinner—the first of our Thursday Evenings!" Clearly, she got her dates mixed. But what matters is that in the beginning Virginia found these young men a "great trial. They sit silent, absolutely silent, all the time; occasionally they escape to a corner and chuckle over a Latin joke." If they were falling in love with Vanessa, it would be "a silent and very learned process. However I don't think they are robust enough to feel very much."

This impression faded, however, and it soon dawned on her that Thoby's friends were not just unusual, they were special. She and Vanessa had met a few of them in Cambridge during May Week two years earlier, but for the most part, Virginia heard of them from Thoby himself, who tended to romanticize his friends. When home on school holidays, he talked to Virginia by the hour about Clive Bell, Lytton Strachey, Saxon Sydney-Turner, Leonard Woolf. Bell, for instance, the younger son of a rich coal-mine owner and Thoby's closest friend, was "a sort of mixture between Shelley and a sporting country squire"—a mixture of innocence and enthusiasm. He had never opened a book in his life before coming to Trinity; then one day he suddenly discovered Shelley and Keats and "nearly went mad with excitement."

And there was Lytton Strachey, "the Strache" as Thoby called the future biographer and essayist—cultured, hypochondriacal, witty, formidable, and homosexual. Leonard Woolf was another of Thoby's astonishing friends—"a man who trembled perpetually all over"—as special in his own way as Bell and Strachey were in theirs. What, Virginia wanted to know, caused his trembling? He was savage; he was violent, Thoby replied. Woolf was a misanthrope; he hated the human race; and for this Thoby thought him "sublime." Once Woolf dreamed he was strangling a man and he dreamed with such force that he pulled his thumb out of joint. "I was of course inspired with the deepest interest," wrote the future Virginia Woolf, "in this violent, trembling, misanthropic Jew" who abandoned the civilized world and fled to the jungles of Ceylon, where he would remain for seven years. He was a romantic figure. She remembered the terrifying man at their dinner table on November 17, 1904, the evening before his departure. And so he remained for her—distant, shrouded in mystery.

Saxon Sydney-Turner was one of those unearthly people, "an absolute prodigy of learning" who had the whole of classical literature within his grasp. This thin, silent creature was nocturnal in his habits and would creep out at three in the morning and tap on Thoby's window "like a moth." He hardly spoke, but when he did, it was to relieve a head full of ideas and facts. He was the most brilliant of his contemporaries, Thoby said, "because he always spoke the truth."

There was, of course, also Desmond MacCarthy, slightly older than the rest, a disciple of G. E. Moore, and, like Woolf and Strachey, a member of the secret Cambridge intellectual elite who called themselves the Apostles. MacCarthy was intelligent, handsome, and gifted. He was the promise of tomorrow; he would be the supreme English novelist of the century. Hearing him talk, for he was indeed loquacious, one could only conclude that he had "so charmed and domesticated that intractable creature the English language that it would do anything for him." But his promise came to nothing. After Cambridge he embarked on a career as literary journalist and drama critic, and never got very much beyond that. Despite his genial and expansive nature, he took life a little too casually, was unreliable in professional duties, and, socially or otherwise, was always just a little *too* late to produce his special effect.

Other young men attended the Thursday Evening gatherings who did not later become Virginia's intimate friends, but it was clear to her from the start that the young men Thoby knew were far different from those she had met in George Duckworth's circle—beautifully dressed young men who never got beyond banalities. The glittering evenings in Mayfair and Belgravia were social enterprises designed to facilitate the marriages of young women to eligible young men, whereas the evenings at Gordon Square were devoted to arguing ideas. "Love," "marriage," and other such abstractions had no place in Bloomsbury; here they spoke of "Truth," "Beauty," and "the Good." Those were the things that mattered. Thoby's friends did not dress for the occasion; they came prepared to use only their brains. And as time went on, Blooms-bury, with its shabby members, became increasingly unsettling to friends of the Stephen family. Kitty Maxse, who had introduced Vanessa to London society after George's failure to do so, moaned afterward, "I've no doubt they're very nice but, oh darling, how awful they do look!" Henry James, after seeing some of the young men in Rye, found them "deplorable!" How could the Stephen sisters have "picked up such friends?"

But this, in Virginia's eyes, was precisely the "proof of their superiority." She felt reassured by these gatherings. To her they meant casual dress for dinner, long hours arguing G. E. Moore, even longer, unembarrassed si-lences—everything, in short, that represented the exact opposite of 22 Hyde Park Gate. On Thursday evenings, said Virginia, when the front doorbell rang, she was in a "twitter of excitement" as Thoby's friends filed in, hesi-tantly, shyly, and folded themselves into chairs and sofa corners; it was late and the room was filled with pipe and cigarette smoke; there were coffee cups, plates of buns, and whiskey glasses scattered about. A long time might pass before anyone said anything. Clive was the exception; he was "always ready to sacrifice himself in the cause of talk." He would try various subjects, but almost invariably they were rejected with a quiet "No." Or "No, I haven't seen it"; or "No, I haven't been there"; or "I don't know." It was quite impossible for her to imagine such a thing happening at Hyde Park Gate, where a lapse in the conversation—however trivial, which it mostly was—would have been considered a serious breach of protocol.

But here at 46 Gordon Square, if someone was careless enough to use the word "beauty" casually, then a head would slowly lift and a voice would say: "It depends what you mean by beauty." And here, Virginia claimed, "it was as if the bull had at last been turned into the ring. The bull might be 'beauty', might be 'good', might be 'reality'." And so, once started, the argument might go on for hours—like a marathon, where runners gradually fell by the way-side as fewer and fewer pressed on to the finish line. It filled her with wonder to watch those who were finally left in the argument. Often they sat till two or three in the morning, when at last Sydney-Turner "would pronounce very shortly some absolutely final summing up." Then one would stagger off to bed "feeling that something very important had happened."

Such was the nature of these gatherings. They represented for Virginia much more than they did for Thoby, who did not come to Bloomsbury directly from Hyde Park Gate as she did, but by way of Cambridge, where distinctions were sharpest and least compromising. These Thursday Evenings, together with the "Friday Club" which Vanessa would organize in October, formed the nucleus of what would later be called the "Bloomsbury Group," though, of course, they never called or even thought of themselves as that. The short story "Phyllis and Rosamund," which Virginia wrote the following summer, would dramatize the opposing worlds of Bloomsbury and Kensington. The Kensington world of Kitty Maxse and George Duckworth would soon begin to fade into insignificance.

And even though "love" was rarely mentioned in Gordon Square, and Virginia felt that "marriage was a very low down affair," Clive Bell proposed to Vanessa during the summer of 1905, and was refused. But Clive, as they were soon to learn, was not a man to be put off. He would wait for another opportunity. He would even, Virginia said, "give up hunting if necessary in order to marry."

The Stephens' journey to Cornwall in August for the summer holiday was a journey in time, a step backward into childhood and memory. They had not been there since the summer of 1894, the year before Julia died. Here once again in St. Ives was Talland House, where Virginia had spent her first twelve summers, and here was the escallonia hedge, and there the Love Corner, and over there the stone urns. This cherished "little corner of England," on August 11, the evening of their arrival, had lost none of its enchantment. In substance and detail it had remained unchanged. Here Virginia was to find her "past preserved."

The sketches in her Cornwall journal—she was writing now every day from ten to one—were an attempt to infuse that past once more with the pulse and vitality of the present. The old woman in the church, recalling Julia Stephen's kindness, was a touching moment to be preserved. The visit to the Pascoes was another event worth recording. "Mrs. Pascoe was, I confess it here, chiefly memorable for some trouble in her 'pipes'; about which we used to inquire." Mrs. Pascoe, it appears, did most of the talking; but when she was told that George Duckworth would soon be visiting, "she gave up her attempt to wrestle with the English language, and covered her face with her hands." Having kept up with the fortunes of the Stephen and Duckworth families, the Pascoes naturally assumed that the Stephens' memory was equally sharp. Did Virginia remember Mrs. Pascoe's niece's husband? Did she remember the Whiteheads? Virginia, with only vague recollections of the natives, did not acquit herself very creditably: "Miss Whitehead," she said, with a touch of mockery, "I can at least remember, is now on the continent, recovering from a severe chill in her legs."

Other events caught her attention. The lively regatta, for instance, and the excitement of the fishing boats in action. But as Virginia observed, "these are rough notes to serve as land marks." Rough as they were, however, these evocations revealed the height to which she had grown as a writer. One essay, "A Walk by Night," published the following December, would come out of this journey. Not for another twenty years, however, would this visit to St. Ives fuse with earlier memories in an image of the Ramsay family in *To the Lighthouse*.

During their two months in Cornwall, although there were many visitors, the Stephens kept to a work schedule: Vanessa painted in the early part of the day; Adrian and Thoby worked at their law books; and Virginia wrote in the morning, took long walks in the afternoon, read before tea and dinner, and wrote to Violet in whatever hours remained. Violet was about to embark on a trip around the world with Nelly Cecil, and Virginia would miss them both, especially Violet. "I want to charge you to take the greatest care of every bone of your long and attenuated body," she wrote in August, ". . . try to come back an unspoilt virgin." She had written quite a lot, she said, but the others didn't take much interest. If only Violet were there to encourage. "Do you think I shall ever write a really good book? . . . I feel more than usually incompetent without you." But the *Times* kept her busy. They sent her a novel every week, which had to be read on Sunday, reviewed on Monday, and printed on Friday—the way, Virginia thought, they made sausages in America.

In the autumn Thoby's Thursday Evenings resumed, attracting new guests each week. In October, Vanessa launched the Friday Club, a group formed to discuss the fine arts. There was much overlapping in the membership. "The Club flourishes," Virginia wrote to Violet. "Old Nessa goes ahead . . . and manages all the business, and rejects all her friends' pictures, and don't mind a bit." Vanessa had a talent for organization; such an enterprise would have bored Virginia to death. With both groups in full swing and new friend-

ships under way, both sisters felt increasingly liberated from the stiff proprieties of Kensington.

As a journalist, Virginia now apparently felt sure enough of herself (or
reckless enough) to say to Violet with some audacity: "If I could get enough
work elsewhere I don't think I should bother about the Guardian." Violet
had found her this work, when work was desperately needed; but now in
December of 1905, Virginia was finding Mrs. Lyttelton a little short on literary taste—"she sticks her broad thumb into the middle of my delicate
sentences and improves the moral tone." Violet could not have felt gratified
by her egotistical young charge, whose career she had taken time and trouble
to launch.

During her Easter break from Morley, Virginia returned to Giggleswick in
Yorkshire to see Madge and Will Vaughan again. This time, too, she went
alone, with Gurth on his leash, and took lodgings at a place run by one Mrs.
Turner. The Vaughans lived ten minutes away if Virginia needed compan-
ionship; but it was solitude she wanted. Vanessa, now painting Lord Robert
Cecil's portrait, would join her for a few days when she finished.

"I promise not to bother you," Virginia wrote to Madge. "You shan't see
me at all . . . I am bringing a great box of books, and I shall shut myself in
my rooms and read." To Violet she wrote after settling in: "I lead the life of
a Solitary: read and write and eat my meal, and walk out upon the moor,
and have tea with Madge, and talk to her, and then dine alone and read my
book." There was a "Greek austerity" about her life in Yorkshire.

At about this time, Virginia gave a sample of her writing to Madge for
comment; and Madge found it cold and heartless. "My only defence," said
Virginia, "is that I write of things as I see them." She was perfectly aware
of her narrow and "bloodless" point of view. But this vague, ambiguous
world, Virginia added, "without love, or heart, or passion, or sex, is the world
I really care about . . . these things are perfectly real to me." It was better, she
went on, "to write about the things I do feel, than to dabble in things I
frankly don't understand in the least." But would Madge try to remember
that if she seemed "heartless" when she wrote, really she was very sentimental—"only I don't know how to express it . . . and I only want to be treated
like a nice child."

Virginia's two weeks up north were simple, quiet, and "mostly alone"; the
sketches written here reflect the mood of her unhurried wanderings through
the barren wilds of Yorkshire, at peace in the bleak grandeur of the moors.

When she rose, when she dined, where she walked, what she read—these were for her alone to decide. She was free. "I settle precisely according to my own taste and then the door is shut on me." In tone and texture, this little passage written in Giggleswick by the "solitary traveller" is only one short revision from the "Solitary Traveller" reverie of Peter Walsh in *Mrs. Dalloway*. The solitary Virginia, however, had traveled a long distance to be alone in this little northern town, "swept clean and simplified, out of all pettiness and vulgarity by the nobility of the country in which it lies."

In June Virginia wrote a two-column piece for *The Times Literary Supplement* called "Wordsworth and the Lakes," for which she received £9.7. "This is the largest sum I have ever made at one blow," she announced proudly to Violet. The *Times* "appreciates me!" Virginia also ventured into fiction now with her piece called "The Mysterious Case of Miss V." followed by "Phyllis and Rosamund." Apart from these, she wrote only book reviews.

The sisters rented Blo' Norton Hall in August. For four weeks they stayed in this lovely decaying moated Elizabethan manor house on the Norfolk-Suffolk border. They were like "rolling drunken sailors" with the money they were earning. "That blessed Lyttelton," said Virginia, "takes every word I write and corrects the spelling." Vanessa painted in the afternoons, and Virginia explored the countryside for miles around, leaping ditches, scaling walls, and "desecrating" churches, while inventing "beautiful brilliant stories every step of the way." There was one story in progress, she wrote to Violet, referring to the "Journal of Mistress Joan Martyn," of which she had written "40 pages of manuscript since I came here; that is about 3 a day." Thoby and Adrian went to see their sisters settle in before leaving on August 10 on horseback for Trieste by way of Montenegro and Albania.

At Blo' Norton, with her short dips into fiction, Virginia began for the first time to ponder the way her mind worked as a writer. In the past, she had made an occasional comment about her creativity, but had never developed her reflections. Here in Norfolk she did. "It is one of the wilful habits of the brain," she wrote in her journal, ". . . that it will work only at its own terms. You bring it directly opposite an object, and bid it discourse; it merely shuts its eye, and turns away. But in one month, or three or seven, suddenly without any bidding, it pours out the whole picture, gratuitously. Some such surprise may be in store for me still; on the heights of the Acropolis, the Norfolk fens may swim before me; and I know I shall have to wait many months before I can see Athens. Like the light that reaches you from the stars, it will only shine when some time after it has been shed."

Here in 1906 was the first bare statement of an important discovery. Thirty-four years later, in 1940, she would enlarge upon it: "Unconsciousness, which means presumably that the under-mind drowses, is a state we all know. We all have experience of the work done by unconsciousness in our daily lives." Let us suppose, she goes on, that we have been sight-seeing. Could we recall, upon returning home, all we have seen and done? Probably not. Our impressions are blurred, confused. But after we've turned aside and looked at something else, thought of something different, the sights and sounds we thought important and were previously a blur, now swim to the surface of their own accord; and what was not important remains sunk in oblivion. "So it is with the writer. After a hard day's work ... seeing all he can see ... taking in the book of his mind innumerable notes, the writer becomes—if he can—unconscious. In fact, his under-mind works at top speed while his upper-mind drowses. Then, after a pause, the veil lifts; and there is the thing—the thing he wants to write about—simplified, composed." Virginia Woolf, the essayist, had played out many variations on this theme.

On September 8, Thoby's twenty-sixth birthday, Virginia, Vanessa, and Violet Dickinson left London, traveled by train through France and Italy, and sailed to Patras. Thoby and Adrian, who had left England a month earlier on horseback, joined them in Olympia on September 13. It was a happy reunion. Virginia flourished in the classical world. She was soothed by its order and symmetry, and she began now to pause longer over what she saw.

There was the Apollo from the Temple of Zeus at Olympia, looking over his shoulder, "across and above the centuries. He is straight and serene ... has a human mouth and chin, ready to quiver or to smile." In Athens there was the Acropolis and the Parthenon and the sublime image one got by standing where once the Athena Parthenos had stood. They drove fourteen miles to Eleusis along the Sacred Way, and here Virginia imagined the Athenians two thousand years earlier, marching in procession to those yearly secret rites associated with the goddess Demeter. Then there was the five-hour climb up Pentelicus, and later the journey to Epidauros and its Temples of Asclepios and its great theater.

Virginia had her Homer with her and was reading the *Odyssey*; so that even if she was immersed in antiquity, when they reached Mycenae, historically the richest of Greek sites, she was at a loss. Where did the place begin? Where did it end? There was the Lion Gate, the Royal Circle Graves, the Treasury of Atreus, the Palace of Agamemnon. She imagined the King in purple robes and limbs shining in beaten gold and the air sweet with thyme;

and "in the evening they were all gathered in order in their courts, and perhaps a great beacon burnt; in case man or God beheld it." Mycenae was overwhelming.

Together with Adrian and Thoby, Virginia set off for the Noels, old family friends, in Achmetaga, Euboea, on October 1 for five days. Vanessa had fallen ill, and returned to Athens with Violet. She had begun feeling unwell when they landed in Patras. When Virginia got back to Athens she spent a good deal of time in the hotel tending her sister—and engrossed in Mérimée's *Lettres à une inconnue*. In two weeks, Vanessa was well enough to join the party now bound for Constantinople. Thoby left them and returned alone to England.

Turkey, too, was full of wonders. Here Virginia paid less attention to the scenery and more to the Turks and their habits. Their worship seemed barely distinguishable from ordinary life in the street. The voices of the recumbent figures in prayer in the mosque mixed easily with the clamor outside. Friends dropped in, "saluted each other, and turned as naturally to their devotions as, a few hours before perhaps, they had turned to their ledgers." The mingling of prayer and ordinary speech did not seem to falsify the sincerity of the worship, nor did it seem in any way strange that men should say "their prayer to rare carpets and painted tiles, without the figure of a saint or the symbol of a cross to inspire them."

Then there were the women of Turkey. It was well known, so Virginia wrote, that the female sex was so fiercely guarded in Constantinople that English women without a veil to cover their face might be severely chastised. The veil, she found, was a "frail symbol" and now had little meaning. Many Turkish women walked bare-faced, and the veil, when worn at all, was worn casually. Yet the veil had such virtue attached to it as to suggest that it "hides something rare and spotless, so that you gaze all the more at a forbidden face. And then the passionate creature raises her shield for a moment—and you see—a benevolent spinster, with gold rims to spectacles, trotting out to buy a fowl for dinner. What danger has she got to hide from?"

These Greek journals reveal a writer striving to capture the minutest details of people, places, manners, and morals. Something new and different was finding its way into her style, into the way she conveyed her impressions. Whether she was describing a site rich in ancient history or creating a portrait of some guest at the hotel, her imagery was becoming more impressionistic, ambiguous, and therefore more resonant, in sound and meaning.

In Greece, as in Turkey, she was beginning to model her perceptions in a way not evident in her earlier writing. She was now engaged in transforming simple visual impressions into verbal frames which had the power of evoking something residual and dormant in the reader, amplifying and heightening odd angles and relations which went *beyond* the object of contemplation and verged increasingly on the metaphoric. Something of this new mode of evocation she tried to express when at Mycenae she wrote: "There was never a sight, I think, less manageable; it travels through all the chambers of the brain, wakes odd memories and imaginations; forecasts a remote future; retells a remote past. And all the while it is—let me write it down—but a great congeries of ruined houses, on a hill side."

The visit in Turkey was cut short by Vanessa's illness. The doctor pronounced her well enough, however, to travel by train; and so on October 29, with Violet Dickinson in charge, the remaining Stephens returned by the Orient Express, arriving in England November 1. No one saw very much of Constantinople, and aside from a short piece published under the title "A Dialogue upon Mount Pentelicus," Virginia's only writing of substance was that of her 1906 journal. But the expedition to Greece would linger in her memory and surface once more in *Jacob's Room*. For just as Jacob Flanders would die after his tour of Greece, so too would Thoby Stephen, upon whom Jacob was fractionally modeled.

By the time the train reached Dover, Violet herself was ill. George met them with a nurse—and the news that Thoby was in bed at 46 Gordon Square with a high fever. By the end of that day, Violet went to bed in Manchester Street, where she remained desperately ill for several weeks with typhoid fever. Vanessa too was put to bed at Gordon Square with symptoms resembling those of appendicitis. It was Thoby who remained the mystery. The doctors, like so many in the past, were proving to be incompetent and, in their incompetence, overconfident. No one had any idea what Thoby suffered from—"it had been a sharp attack of 'something or other'." There was nothing to worry about, they were assured, no reason to think he had anything seriously wrong with him. He'd be up and about in no time. Still, it was better if he and Vanessa remained in bed. As Virginia wrote later: doctors were "a profoundly untrustworthy race; either they lie or they mistake." Even Dr. Savage was called in on the chance that Thoby's trouble had some neurological origin. But like the medics in charge, Savage dismissed any nervous disorder with a wave of the hand. Meanwhile, Thoby was not responding to treatment. This was hardly surprising since he was being treated for malaria, and it was only discovered after ten days, "through the discreet but desperate intervention of the nurse, to be typhoid fever."

"Thoby has a temp. of 103 and is a great deal bothered with his inside but [Dr.] Thompson is satisfied." This bulletin was sent to Violet on about November 7. A week later: "Visitors come and use their handkerchiefs a great deal; I begin by saying my brother has typhoid, my sister has appendicitis." But when the jokes were over, Virginia did not hesitate to let Violet know how much she needed her. "If you could put your hand in that nest of fur where my heart beats you would find the thump of the steadiest organ in London—all beating for my Violet."

Before long visitors began to stream to Gordon Square. Among them was Clive Bell, who came as often as he could. And so the days passed. Vanessa recovered. Thoby did not. He died on the morning of November 20, 1906. Two days later, Vanessa agreed to marry Clive Bell. There seemed no limit to the shocks Virginia suffered. She had just lost her brother. Now she was losing her sister. And there was still the chance of her losing her beloved Violet, who had not been told of Thoby's death. The news, they feared, might worsen her already weakened condition.

So from November 20, Virginia committed one of her grimmest acts of fiction and would keep it up for almost a month. She needed to keep Thoby "alive" for Violet's sake. "I must get out my pen again, and make that do its business." With her pen she would erase the tragedy. With words she would take away the pain. And so, without flinching, she began the unsavory invention. Two days after his death, November 22: "Thoby is well as possible," she wrote to Violet. "We aren't anxious." November 25: "Thoby is going on splendidly. He is very cross with his nurses, because they won't give him mutton chops and beer." On the twenty-ninth: "Dear old Thoby is still on his back—but manages to be about as full of life in that position as most people are on their hind legs." On December 10: "Thoby is going on well; he has chicken broth . . . and will be up for Christmas." On the thirteenth: "I check your stage by Thoby's; he is very cheerful today." On the fourteenth: Thoby "will have some minced chicken tomorrow." On the eighteenth, the deception came to an end. In the December issue of the *National Review*, Violet quite by chance saw a notice of Maitland's *Life* of Leslie Stephen. "This book," said the reviewer, "appeared almost on the very day of the untimely death of Sir Leslie Stephen's eldest son, Mr Thoby Stephen, at the age of 25 [26]."

"Beloved Violet," wrote Virginia. "Do you hate me for telling so many lies? . . . I never knew till this happened how I should turn to you and want you with me when no one else could help ... You are part of all that is best, and happiest in our lives. Thoby was always asking me about you. I know you loved him, and he loved you ... I can feel happy about him; he was so brave and strong, and his life was perfect."

Virginia was telling the truth; but something deeper and stronger seemed to be taking shape, something she herself could not yet put into words. For in his death, Thoby came into her full possession. She and Vanessa had fought over him in the nursery. Now that was over. Vanessa had Clive Bell, and Virginia had Thoby entirely to herself. One day, *with words*, she would resurrect this private and often melancholy brother who mattered so much to her. His early death had left him a mystery. There was much about him she had never known and now could never know. But in some corner of her mind, there was a frozen reservoir of feeling to which she would eventually return. She had her pen. She had words. With these alone she was fortified, and any disaster could be borne. Words had the power to alter reality. In a few years' time, she would once more get out her pen and "make that do its business." She would recover Thoby in all his beauty and splendor as Percival in *The Waves*.

At the moment, however, there was only grief and bewilderment. Thoby was dead. And Vanessa was engaged to marry Clive Bell and was "happier every day—though it's difficult to think that I can ever be much happier than I have often been at moments during these last few weeks." This was on December 18. A little earlier Virginia had received a letter from Maitland: two "distinguished people" had called her Note on Sir Leslie "beautifully done." On December 19, news came that Fred Maitland had died of pneumonia in Las Palmas. The future Mrs. Bell spent Christmas with Clive's family in Wiltshire. Virginia and Adrian went to Aunt Minna's house in the New Forest for the holiday. They took along with them a copy of Maitland's *Life and Letters of Leslie Stephen*.

For the rest of her life Virginia would carry with her the memory of Thoby. Her only recollections were of their youth. He had gone to university and she had not. He'd thought of her as an unprotected younger sister, "a very simple, eager recipient of his school stories; without any experience of my own." Though they argued, there was a great reserve between them. They never talked about themselves; there were no confidences or compliments or emotional scenes; and as for sex, "he passed from childhood to boyhood ...

to manhood under our eyes" without giving the faintest hint of what he was feeling. Surely a great many boys must have fallen in love with him, but "not he with them, I suspect." His sensibility and pride and love would have made him a good husband and father; and "publicly a Judge for sure: Mr Justice Stephen he would have been . . . with several books to his credit." He would have been a loved and respected figure, not a typical Englishman, for he was too "melancholy," too "original" for that. But all his promise was ended, and Vanessa was going to marry his best friend. Just as with Jack Hills, and then with their father's death, she was deserting Virginia again, betraying her now for the third time.

13 On New Year's Eve Virginia and Adrian joined their sister at the Bells' in Wiltshire, the refurbished Cleeve House, a rather hideous conglomeration of pseudo-Gothic and Jacobean styles. "The thickness of this nib and the luxury of this paper," Virginia wrote to Violet, would prove that she was in a "rich and illiterate house." Everything seemed barbaric. Even the inkwell was set "into the hoof of an old hunter." Mr. Bell was a jovial, uneducated country gentleman. The sisters wore satin bows in their hair at dinner and laughed at Adrian's jokes. It was an entirely new world for Virginia and she hated it. Exactly what the Bells thought of Virginia is hard to say; but she had a temper tantrum on New Year's Day and had to go outside "to trample it into the mud."

Vanessa's happiness was monstrous. When Virginia thought of her father and Thoby and then saw that "funny little creature twitching his pink skin . . . I wonder what odd freak there is in Nessa's eyesight." Clive had some good qualities. She knew he was sensitive and generous and understood how to make Vanessa happy. If Clive was artistic and clever, however, he was certainly no genius, "but then old Nessa is no genius" either.

Virginia was in turmoil. She would never see Vanessa *alone* again. Clive had stolen her away—picked her pocket. Virginia no longer had the sister she loved and the mother she needed. How could Vanessa be so cold-blooded? And this perverse happiness so soon after Thoby's death was treachery. These emotions churned in Virginia as the wedding day approached and she fell deeper and deeper into a pit of confusion. Her drugs were "a book" and "an ink pot." Only these could soothe for short periods.

When Clive and Vanessa were married on February 7—Julia's birthday—at the St. Pancras Registry Office, Virginia was floored. "I feel numb and dumb," she said. "I feel elderly and prosaic." And probably dispensable. Two years earlier, in February 1905, when Vanessa gave a dinner party at Gordon Square, Virginia had been excluded because the table would seat only eight. Now in March 1907 Virginia would be excluded again—she would have to give up her home because the Bells wanted 46 Gordon Square for themselves. Once again Vanessa was in and Virginia was out. The one important concession was Sophie Farrell, the family cook. She went along with Virginia. "I ought to be able to cut myself up among the lot of you," said Sophie, "but it must be Miss [Virginia]; she's such a harum scarum thing she wouldn't know if they sold her. She don't know what she has on her plate."

After the Bells set off for Manorbier for their honeymoon, Virginia began hunting for a place to live. She would be sharing the house with Adrian, even though they were "the most incompatible of people." But there was no choice. Besides, said Virginia, it was terrible that Adrian "should have no brother"; he should at least have a home.

Virginia had once described Adrian as a babbler who was "15 years younger than the rest of us." Born on October 27, 1883, Adrian was in fact twenty-one months Virginia's junior. As the youngest of the Stephen children, he had from the start to compete with three very precocious siblings; and at this he was not very successful: from the beginning he felt himself an outcast, different from and inferior to his brother and sisters. Julia took this frail, unhappy little boy under her wing and gave him special protection and an extra measure of motherly love. To Julia he was "My Joy"—a thin, often silent, almost stunted child—James Ramsay in *To the Lighthouse*.

Of the two boys, Sir Leslie favored Thoby and was often short-tempered and impatient with Adrian, whom he unfairly (and unfortunately) compared with his brother. At sixteen, the boy began to lengthen, and by the age of twenty, had grown to six feet five inches. But the growth was only physical, and at Cambridge "he appeared no more than an evening shade of his brother, less brilliant, less charming," altogether undistinguished intellectually and socially.

If Adrian occasionally suffered from depression, he was more regularly a depressing person to be with. Writing to Lytton Strachey from Cornwall on one holiday, Vanessa complained that Adrian visited her and was sunk in gloom almost the whole time. He has been "literally sitting in an arm-chair with his eyes shut all Saturday, Sunday and today . . . He occasionally grumbles at the weather or the food and last night roused himself for 10 minutes to explain to us how we had all combined to sit upon him in his youth and how much misery he has had in life."

It was one thing for brother and sister to take a house in a questionable neighborhood, but quite another for Virginia to claim that she needed to look after Adrian. It was Virginia who needed a guardian, the friends all said. What she really needed was a husband. Virginia must find a man to marry, the friends all agreed. It seemed to occur to no one that her father, the man she would always love best in the world, would never be replaced by a husband, no matter how intellectual or spirited or generous or good-looking he might be. And she was naturally irritated by the collective pressure to marry. In the meantime, she scoured the area for someplace to live and found, at last, 29 Fitzroy Square, which appealed to her (aside from its structural merits) because it was just close enough to Vanessa to lessen the sense of desertion she now increasingly felt.

It was not easy for Virginia to accept Clive Bell as a brother-in-law. She thought of him as an interloper and harbored grave reservations about his worthiness as Vanessa's husband; and Vanessa did nothing to ease the matter. In fact her behavior toward Clive particularly nettled Virginia. "Mrs Bell is struggling with the English language," Virginia wrote to Nelly Cecil; "there aren't enough words for happiness." "They sound so happy that they make noises like children," she said to Madge. "I can't believe that Nessa wasn't born married, because it seems so natural." Nevertheless she and Adrian joined the newlyweds in Paris.

Upon their return on April 12, Virginia and Adrian took up residence in their new home, where Virginia gradually settled down once more to writing, reviewing, and teaching. "Write me a nice letter," she said to Violet. "I want Affection. I don't get None." "I wish I could play with the children," she said to Madge, "and have you treat me as a child—a very nice child." She was longing for the embraces of a woman; Vanessa would no longer be there to supply them.

Before leaving for her summer holiday, Virginia sent Violet Dickinson the comic "Life" of her she had just "very hastily polished off this morning." It was indeed a hasty job and only Violet and Nelly were allowed to read it.

(The piece was eventually published as "Friendship's Gallery.") On the following day, August 8, Virginia and Adrian moved into the Steps, a cottage in Playden, about a mile north of the village of Rye. Vanessa and Clive joined them on August 26, staying at Curfew Cottage on Watchbell Street, in the middle of Rye itself.

Henry James, who had been living in Rye since 1898, wrote his friend Sara Darwin on September 7, 1907: "Leslie Stephen's children, three of them—the three surviving poor dear mild able gigantic Thoby... have taken two houses near me (temporarily) and as I write the handsome (and most lovable) Vanessa Clive-Bell sits on my lawn (unheeded by me) along with her little incongruous and disconcerting but apparently very devoted newly acquired sposo. And Virginia, on a near hilltop, writes reviews for the *Times*—and the gentle Adrian interminably long and dumb and 'admitted to the bar' marches beside her like a giraffe beside an ostrich—save that Virginia is facially most fair." James had gone to see Vanessa on the eve of her marriage and met her "sposo"—"the quite dreadful-looking little stoop-shouldered, long-haired, third-rate Clive Bell—described as an 'intimate friend' of poor, dear, clear, tall, shy, superior Thoby."

Here in Sussex, feeling marooned, Virginia began once more to write her journal—descriptions of the land, the sea, the salt marshes. It was presumably during this holiday that she also started to write the life of Vanessa, who was going to have a baby. The future Julian Heward Bell would one day have these reminiscences to help him understand his Stephen grandparents, life at 22 Hyde Park Gate, the story of Stella and Jack Hills, and a few anecdotes about George and Gerald Duckworth. Four chapters were completed that summer, but there is no evidence that Virginia ever returned to it.

They had a stream of visitors to Rye and of course there was work. Bruce Richmond had asked Virginia to review a novel by Marten Maartens "at once, at some length, for Friday's Times." Then Leo Maxse was racking his brain trying to think of subjects that might interest her. There was writing every morning and plenty of reading to do. She was now deep in Henry James's *American Scene*, a pleasant, tranquil book, but certainly "not the stuff of genius."

Virginia had tea with James on Sunday afternoon, August 25. Just before that she had met him in the street and described the encounter to Violet Dickinson: Henry James had fixed her with his penetrating eye and said: "'My dear Virginia, they tell me—they tell me—they tell me—that you—as indeed being your father's daughter, nay your grandfather's grandchild—the descendant I may say of a century—of a century—of quill pens and ink—ink—ink pots, yes, yes, yes, they tell me—ahm m m—that you, that you, that you *write* in short.' This went on in the public street, while we all waited, as farmers wait for the hen to lay an egg . . . I felt like a condemned person . . . But when I am old and famous I shall discourse like Henry James. We had to stop periodically to let him shake himself free of the thing."

Julian Heward Bell was born at Gordon Square on February 4, 1908. Almost immediately Vanessa seemed transformed from a mocking, overly confident, dry-humored sister and wife into a passionate, fiercely protective, almost primitive mother. Cradle-rocking, breast-feeding, diaper-changing suddenly became the focus of her universe. And just as suddenly, Virginia and Clive, feeling cut off from Vanessa's warm embraces, turned to each other for companionship. Their relationship had all the characteristics of a flirtation and it lasted a long time, resulting in Clive's becoming Virginia's most valued literary confidant.

Virginia may have thought of marriage, but no one of her acquaintances seems to have aroused any interest. Her passions, "her jealousies and tenderness," were reserved for her own sex, and above all for Violet. Since their move to Gordon Square and the Thursday Evening gatherings, a number of bright young Cantabrigians had come within close range, but none of them seemed interested in Virginia as a woman. Now why was that? she wondered. "Why were the most gifted of all people also the most barren? Why were the most stimulating of friendships also the most deadening?" What she didn't realize at the time was that the deadening effect came from an absence of physical attraction. The young men were for the most part homosexual— "buggers" was the word Virginia and her circle used—and with gay young men "one cannot . . . show off. Something is always suppressed, held down. Yet this showing off . . . is one of the great delights, one of the chief necessities of life."

Her first little intrigue had been with an old family friend, Walter Headlam, a Greek scholar old enough to be her father. Virginia liked him and respected his scholarship. He was eccentric enough to be interesting and flirtatious enough to attract her attention. But Walter Headlam had a special interest in little girls and in September of 1893 at St. Ives appears to have been sent away by Julia Stephen because of some perceived misconduct. It may have been precisely the childlike quality in Virginia that excited the aging Hellenist. For all her dazzling intelligence, Virginia was incredibly uninformed and inexperienced. But that was soon to change, and it was Lytton Strachey who helped pull down the bastions of Victorian prudery and suppression.

Virginia described in her memoir an incident which took place in 1908. "It was a spring evening," her recollection begins. She and Vanessa were sitting in the drawing room at 46 Gordon Square expecting Clive to appear at any moment. Vanessa was quietly doing something with a needle and thread as Virginia rambled on about her own affairs. Suddenly the door opened and at the threshold stood the long, uncompromising figure of Lytton Strachey. He pointed a finger at a stain on Vanessa's dress. "Semen?" he asked. Could one actually say that? Virginia wondered, as all three burst into laughter. With that single word the dams burst, flooding Bloomsbury with that "sacred fluid." "Sex permeated our conversation ... We discussed copulation with the same excitement and openness that we discussed the nature of good."

This was indeed an important moment "in the *mores* of Bloomsbury and perhaps in that of the British middle classes," wrote Quentin Bell. The alterations in Virginia's social climate and the new liberties taken in speech, however, had really very little "effect upon her conduct ... or her imagination." For Virginia, the important event of the years 1907–08 was "not the beginning of Bloomsbury bawdy talk, but the birth of *Melymbrosia*"—published in 1915 as *The Voyage Out*. And it is worth noting that the early stages of the novel's formation coincided with Virginia and Clive's flirtation. Had it been otherwise, the next few years might have taken a rather different, less arduous course.

From this distance in time, it appears that Virginia was thinking only of herself in this flirtation. There can be no doubt that with Vanessa's marriage Virginia felt shut out. And this sense of exclusion seems to have been in part the immediate incentive. For now with Julian's birth, Virginia seemed totally banished from Vanessa's life.

But the motive was not in the least so clearly defined. As Virginia groped her way through labyrinths of feeling, it may have occurred to her that through Clive she might once again reach her sister. She might even compete with Clive for Vanessa. Whatever the case, she could be more certain of Vanessa's attention if Clive was somehow implicated; and somewhere in this confusing maze, Virginia discovered that Clive was sufficiently sensitive to her as a writer to want to participate in her first large work of fiction. For this is what really mattered, and Clive would be flattered to see himself in so critical a role. If his sister-in-law needed him as literary adviser and confidant, he would come to her. She was a beautiful woman, after all. Now that Vanessa had a screaming baby in her arms, she seemed no longer to need her virile husband.

Whatever Virginia felt about her own breach of loyalty, if that was indeed how she saw it, she seems to have confided in no one. The emotional design of this curious love-triangle would fully emerge in a few years' time in one of the focal scenes between Rachel Vinrace, Helen Ambrose, and Terence Hewet in *The Voyage Out*. In that scene, Virginia would once more get her pen to "do its business."

On April 17, 1908, about a week before Virginia went to St. Ives, to be later joined there by the Bells and Adrian, she wrote to Clive: "I dreamt last night that I was showing father the manuscript of my novel; and he snorted and dropped it on the table, and I was very melancholy, and read it this morning and thought it bad." This was clearly an invitation. Poor Virginia needed his encouragement. She was being visited by the exacting ghost of Sir Leslie and was asking Clive for help. Well, Clive would read her pages. He wouldn't snort; he would see her gift, offer his sympathy, even affection. As though anticipating his response, Virginia went on: "I have been writing Nessa's life; and I am going to send you 2 chapters in a day or two. It might have been so good! As it is, I am too near, and too far . . . I never shall capture what you have, by your side this minute." The letter ended ambiguously: "Kiss her passionately, in all my private places . . . and tell her—what new thing is there to tell her? How fond I am of her husband?" Surely Clive was aroused. Was his sister-in-law a coquette? Or merely out to make mischief? Perhaps a little of both. He would soon find out.

Virginia did not lack suitors after Walter Headlam. There were several around with varying grades of qualification. The silent Saxon Sydney-Turner was one of them. Held in awe by his contemporaries, he was to Virginia a remarkable encyclopedia of useless facts. The hesitant, apprehensive Walter Lamb, who read Classics at Trinity and was to become Secretary of the Royal Academy, was another. (Lytton Strachey pursued, in vain, his younger brother Henry Lamb, the painter and determined heterosexual.) There was also Hilton Young, whose father had been a friend of Sir Leslie. He had become a regular visitor at both Gordon and Fitzroy Squares. And then there was Lytton Strachey himself. Thoby's death had brought him closer to the family, and Vanessa especially favored him as a potential brother-in-law. When Virginia stepped back to take a better look at him, she saw a self-flagellating creature, "slipping from one agony to another, a wretched, sighing, hand-wringing misfit, a quite impossible person." He was, further, Bloomsbury's most blatant homosexual and would therefore make no physical claims. That must have counted a good deal in his favor. But no one was forcing her to make a decision.

Clive, Vanessa, and baby Julian joined Virginia at St. Ives for Easter. Almost from the start, Virginia found herself surrounded by the noises and odors of infancy. The baby was constantly crying or screaming. To Vanessa this was as it should be; her maternal instincts were well developed. She had been initiated to small children in the nursery of Hyde Park Gate and was no stranger to the small, noisy world of infancy. Everything Julian did delighted her. But two people did not share her pleasure. Clive felt ignored and Virginia rejected. It was impossible now even to carry on a conversation with Vanessa in this ceaseless racket. Clive found the baby exasperating and Virginia was jealous of him.

"A child is the very devil," she wrote to Lytton; it seemed to blot out the rest of the world. When what little conversation they had got interesting, Vanessa's hand went up. Was that Julian crying? Or was it the cry of a baby who has "an abscess, and therefore uses a different scale"? Clive, for all his generosity, was driven beyond endurance with this boisterous bundle of babyhood. "Naturally anxious and easily alarmed for everyone's health," his second son, Quentin, later wrote, "he was disturbed by the fragility of babies. If a baby howled he would certainly conclude that it was desperately ill and if it continued to howl he would himself be made ill by the noise." He couldn't stop the noise, he couldn't adjust to it, but he *could* get away from it. And this he did, with his lovely sister-in-law as companion. If Virginia suffered feelings of guilt, she kept them to herself.

Away from the motherly wife and sister and the incredible mess of infancy, they comforted each other; and during the process, Virginia began for the first time to see some of Clive's good points—his sense of humor, his gallantry, his deference and sensitivity. Virginia was charmed. Always receptive to the attention of men and women alike, she seems to have encouraged Clive's advances. Certainly he was enchanted and, Don Juan that he was, would probably have taken advantage of the situation had not Virginia held back out of sexual cowardice. Clive, however, was the sort of man who was stimulated by resistance; and so began an intense and confusing emotional affair that would go on for many months and cause much unhappiness to both sisters and plenty of frustration for Clive himself.

Throughout the entire unpleasant drama, their friends assumed that Vanessa saw the whole business as being inspired by Virginia's "delight in mischief." It was more complicated than that, however. Part of what Virginia seems to have been doing with Clive was a more sophisticated version of the schemes she'd learned in the nursery. If Vanessa appealed to Clive's physical nature, then Virginia enticed his intellectual side. Aware of how much he wished to keep the wealthy Bell philistinism under cover, Virginia, with her first novel in progress, appealed to Clive's aesthetic ardor.

In childhood, outside the nursery Virginia had clung emotionally to her father in the distressing and frequent absences of her mother; now in adulthood she turned to Clive because of the maternal Vanessa's growing inaccessibility. It is not clear just how profoundly Virginia experienced her situation; but what is certain is that she needed Clive's help in keeping— with words, with writing—her increasingly fragmented world from flying apart. The price she would pay for thus enlisting Clive would be eloquently dramatized in the death of Rachel Vinrace in the terminal scenes of *The Voyage Out*.

Just as Virginia had begun a biographical account of Vanessa and left it unfinished, so she began a sketch of Clive in late 1908 which never progressed beyond a preliminary draft. A passage or two give some idea of how she saw him during this unsettled period. "He quoted Shakespeare in a shrill triumphant voice," she wrote, "when there was no occasion for it, and scorned the young lady who asked him for the name of the author." When he was sixteen, he suddenly discovered that he belonged to that special class of people called "clever." This discovery, Virginia observed, had a serious consequence: he saw at last his goal—he was certain now that his destiny lay in living the life of a scholar; only there was no one at home he could talk to. "Some of his efforts to find sympathy had grotesque results. The first young lady he danced with, at his first ball, had to hear a strange rhapsody—about art, and learning, and the only life worth living."

Despite the mockery in Virginia's sketch, Clive was self-assured and passionate, an odd contrast to the reticent, introspective males of the Stephen family. In the early days of Bloomsbury, to Thoby's Thursday Evenings, made up largely of tight-lipped, self-consciously intellectual Cantabrigians, Clive brought with him a blast of cold, fresh country air and an unflagging, convivial loquacity. He was energetic and robust and made no effort to conceal a vigorous heterosexuality which must at times have further silenced a room swarming with young homosexuals.

Despite Vanessa's initial marital raptures, Virginia had been convinced that no male was worthy enough to be her sister's husband. Suspicion and bitterness had distorted her perception. And though the marriage would inevitably diminish the time Vanessa spent before her canvas, Clive's attention made up for that loss by liberating her naturally sensual nature. She would soon become a kind of goddess of fertility and motherhood, and within this domain she would no longer suffer comparison with her younger, brilliant sister. He also kept Vanessa alert and vibrant with the fresh ideas that made up her painter's world and provided her, for a time, with artistic communion and intimacy, both of which would add to her later relationships with Roger Fry and Duncan Grant.

With all this, Vanessa was still becoming increasingly unsure where to turn or to whom. Virginia's love was unconditional. Clive's was not. When the realities of being a mother and wife finally crystallized, Vanessa began to see that Clive would not be made to wait for his gratifications; he would find them as easily now as in the days of his bachelorhood. Although Vanessa might be made unhappy by his roaming passions, Clive saw to his needs first. So until her affair with Roger Fry, three years later, Vanessa's emotional demands were satisfied only by the unlimited love that poured from Virginia's pen. In fact, Virginia's need for Vanessa now often seemed obsessive and her dependency morbid; and her letters to her sister were sounding more and more like Leslie's to Julia during the height of their courtship. Until the appearance of Vita Sackville-West, still many years away, Vanessa would remain Virginia's primary love object; and unable to upstage his wife, Clive enthusiastically assumed the office of nurturing the other great passion in Virginia's life, her writing. In retrospect he saw his encouragement as one of the important achievements of his career. Almost a half century later, he asked Leonard Woolf to quote a line from one of Virginia's letters to him: "You were the first person who ever thought I'd write well." That sentence, he said, "seems to me the finest feather I shall ever be able to stick in my cap."

The emotional haze of the moment, however, was too dense for Clive to see how adroitly Virginia was leading him on. For however romantically her letters began, they invariably ended on the subject of her writing—"I have been reading Lamb and Landor—and set beside them a page of my own prose. Lord! what vapid stuff! . . . I see all you say of my looseness . . . and verbosity . . . I think you will laugh at the natural trend of this letter." Clive would have been either blind or too proud not to notice it, not to see that Virginia flirted with her brain, not her body.

Throughout the spring and early summer of 1908, she wrote and rewrote and "cursed and burned." Adrian had gone with Saxon Sydney-Turner to Bayreuth for the Wagner operas. Left alone, Virginia went off with her dogs,

Hans and Gurth, to Wells, Somerset, on August 1, spending two weeks there and a further two weeks in Manorbier, Wales. She made some headway with her novel during this interval. And with Clive's continuing letters of advice and encouragement, the figure of Violet Dickinson drifted into the shadows.

Clive was sympathetic, spontaneous, and careful in his remarks, so that Virginia did not feel threatened or demoralized by the amount of material he did *not* like in the novel's early drafts. He inspired her with confidence in herself, something neither Madge Vaughan nor Violet Dickinson could do. But this was the only novel she would ever consult Clive about. All of her later work was done in complete privacy; no one saw a manuscript until it was finished. With Clive, however, she felt safe. She could be candid with him, and it was through the candor that her feelings for him blossomed, coloring her relationship in deeper tones than in reality it had. Virginia had no desire to arouse Clive sexually, but in the absolute solitude of writing her book, he became increasingly the only person she could turn to; and it was the emotional and cerebral closeness that looked so like—and on Clive's part indeed was—an affair of the heart.

As soon as she had settled into the Vicars' Close in Wells, a lodging she had arranged with the help of Violet, Virginia began writing separately to Clive and Vanessa. The Close, managed by a garrulous housekeeper called Mrs. Wall, was congested with theological students and altogether distracting. It was necessary, or so Virginia thought, in so ecclesiastical an atmosphere, to keep her cigarettes hidden. After a few days she moved to 5 Cathedral Green, into quieter rooms in a lodging run by a Mrs. Dorothy Oram, the wife of a verger.

"I walked to the top of a hill today, imagining that I was Christ ascending Calvary," she wrote to Vanessa on August 12. On the nineteenth, Clive received his letter with a Welsh postmark. She was now in Manorbier. "I think a great deal of my future," she said, "and settle what book I am to write— how I shall re-form the novel . . . Poor Clive! What a sister-in-law . . . There was a day when I never talked of my writing to you." And now she did almost nothing else. She was also, she informed him, reading ten pages of G. E. Moore's *Principia Ethica* every night, "feeling ideas travelling to the remotest part of my brain, and setting up a feeble disturbance, hardly to be called a thought." Moore's philosophy was hard work, but such holiday reading was an old habit.

On the twenty-eighth, again to Clive: "I am in a mood today to care very little what anybody says about Melymbrosia . . . But as you know, I count immensely on your encouragement." She announced to Violet Dickinson a day or so later that she had completed the first hundred pages of her novel. "I shall work hard at it this winter, and see ... whether I can finish it."

It seems odd that Virginia should go off to the wild and isolated Manorbier to write her book, but this was where Vanessa and Clive had spent part of their honeymoon. Perhaps she hoped to find for her novel some trace of connubial passion the newlyweds had left there. Perhaps she thought she might conjure up more easily the strange excitement Rachel Vinrace was beginning to feel for Terence Hewet. Perhaps she was beginning to see the resemblance Rachel, Terence, and Helen Ambrose bore to Virginia, Clive, and Vanessa. Whatever the reason, the elemental setting of Manorbier seems to have provided her with an atmosphere in which she felt both fertile and productive. For it is clear from the few sketches she wrote in the Wells-Manorbier journal that most of her energy was being siphoned off into fiction.

Virginia returned from Wales at the end of August and set off for Italy with the Bells on September 3. It was a strenuous expedition. When she was not seeing the sights, and there were a great many to be seen, she read and wrote in her journal. In some of its pages she recorded her impressions, but her mind was really on fiction. She had with her Hardy's *Two on a Tower* and Meredith's *Adventures of Harry Richmond*. Her comments on these two novels were no longer simple notes to remind her in future years of what she had read in Italy. Her remarks now were those of a novelist grappling with aesthetic problems; they were the observations of a writer struggling with the difficulties of transforming the ephemeral impressions of life into the more permanent stuff of fiction. Her criticisms were close, deep, and remarkably acute.

No less remarkable were the character sketches made of some guests at the hotel. "One old lady ... has spent her life, so far as she will reveal it, in travelling and testing the merits of different pensions. She pronounces the table here the best in Italy ... Poor, a spinster, who begins to grow old, to travel is really her most agreeable life ... and sets off on these long rambling peregrinations, from one cheap pension to another ... She sits all day in a corner of the dining room, knitting or writing in a fretful hand long letters to old friends; she waits for meals and watches the dish on its way round the table. Certain old gentilities forbid her to gobble openly, and in the pauses between the plates discharges a vast amount of faded learning ... her skin is like folds of old leather; creases are in the very flesh. But though the task seems so unnecessary, she will fill this torpid case with food and wine; what purpose they serve, let philanthropists declare ... Food consoles her." This "old lady" was to find her way into *The Voyage Out* as old Mrs. Paley, who, like her prototype, was consoled by food and fretfully watched the dish go round the dinner table.

Virginia generally said little about architecture or the paintings she saw, but in Perugia her attention was caught by the frescoes and she felt motivated to write about them. The impulse to record her impression seems to have been triggered by her comments about Meredith's faults as a novelist. He was not satisfying; he was flimsy; he was too concerned with verbal felicities to look squarely at the world and describe truthfully what he saw. Then she inspected the frescoes of Perugino and noted how everything in his vision of the world gave way to the expression of beauty. But was his way the only way? Wasn't there another kind of beauty? Another way of achieving it? This was the question that needed some thought. How did she as a writer achieve symmetry and wholeness, this finished state she called beauty? And was it of the same order as the artist's? This too she must ponder, for she would come back to it. On this warm September afternoon, however, she could say with some certainty only that her own scriptural beauty would be achieved "by means of infinite discords" and "shivering fragments." Only thus would she attain wholeness and harmony.

Just a few days earlier, she had said in her journal that she distrusted description in writing, surface matter, external appearance. In the end it was deceptive. Her aim was to "discover real things beneath the show." Discovering "real things beneath the show" and achieving wholeness through "infinite discords." Here was articulated for the *first time* the aesthetic principle which would guide her in the years ahead. Here in Italy in 1908 Virginia Stephen, a still untried novelist, had finally set down the foundation stone upon which all the rest would depend.

It is not surprising that this notion should occur to her while she was with the two people who would constitute the principal personae of her first novel. For Vanessa's abandoning Virginia after Thoby's death and rushing into the arms of Clive Bell had been an act of selfishness and cruelty; and the past year had been dissonant and fragmentary. This was what *Melymbrosia—The Voyage Out*—was meant to insinuate. Vanessa's dereliction and betrayal was almost a repetition of Julia's death. Rachel Vinrace, like Virginia, must somehow make sense of her motherless life, must find in Helen Ambrose all that was missing. And Virginia, the novelist, must now struggle out of the waters that threatened to close over her and assemble this unhappy story into a tale of beauty. Small wonder that the novel took so great a toll, and cost her so many years of labor. She had now to learn just how that transformation from life to art was achieved.

. . .

By 1909 Virginia was a hard-working journalist, and as her finances grew, so did her independence. Aunt Caroline Emelia died that spring, leaving Virginia in her will the sum of £2,500.*

Throughout the early months of the year, she wrote her novel and sent Clive chapters. Her intention, she said in February, was to finish the book; and then, "if that day ever comes, to catch if possible the first imagination ... Ah, how you encourage me! It makes all the difference."

Clive was the first to see in Virginia's writing a special prismatic quality that was difficult to achieve and even more difficult to explain. "How on earth," he asked, "by telling us what it is like at noon, do you show us what it was like at five, at sunset, and at night?" He was "seeing" what she wanted her readers to "feel." On the subject of gender, however, Clive had a word or two to say. "Our views about men and women are doubtless quite different ... But to draw such sharp and marked contrasts between the subtle, sensitive, tactful, gracious, delicately perceptive and perspicacious women, and the obtuse, vulgar, blind, florid, rude, tactless, emphatic, indelicate, vain, tyrannical, stupid men, is not only rather absurd, but rather bad art, I think."

Virginia trusted Clive enough to swallow such criticism. He saw a great deal more in Virginia's novel. He saw the life model upon whom Helen Ambrose was being molded—Vanessa herself. "Of Helen," he wrote, "I cannot trust myself to speak, but I suppose you will make Vanessa believe in herself." If he saw Vanessa in Helen Ambrose, could Clive *Heward* Bell not see a fragment of himself in Terence *Hewet*? And a lot of Virginia in Rachel?

 In an uncharacteristically expansive mood, Lytton Strachey, on February 17, 1909, made Virginia a proposal of marriage. No sooner had he uttered the words when he realized the appalling mistake he'd made. He was terrified she'd kiss him. He would die if she accepted him then and there. Virginia did accept him on the spot and the proposal

---

* Roughly equivalent today (1998) to £115,000; at the current exchange rate, the sum would amount to approximately $185,000.

was withdrawn—on the spot. By mutual consent. As it happened Lytton, having kept up a regular correspondence with Leonard Woolf in Ceylon, had written him about Virginia's holiday with Clive and Vanessa in Italy. Wasn't Clive lucky—being with the "two most beautiful and wittiest women in England!" Sometime earlier, Lytton had written that he might surprise everyone by marrying Virginia himself. No letters survive to tell how Leonard received this astonishing piece of news. He did, however, write to Lytton that marrying Virginia would mean perfect happiness. Did Lytton think Virginia would have him, Leonard, as a husband? Would Lytton put the question to her? "Wire me if she accepts. I'll take the next boat home."

"Your letter has this minute come—with your proposal to Virginia..." Lytton replied. "I think there's no doubt whatever that you ought to marry her. You *would* be great enough, and you'll have the immense advantage of physical desire... If you came and proposed she'd accept. She really would." On the following day, Lytton ended his letter with this final paragraph: "I've had an éclaircissement with Virginia. She declared she was not in love with me, and I observed finally that I would not marry her. So things have simply reverted."

Virginia had written to Clive on Christmas of the previous year: "We had Lytton last night; you will be glad to hear that I am not in love with him, nor is there any sign that he is in love with me." Yet when he proposed some two months later, she accepted without hesitation. We may guess that her motive for doing so originated, in part, in the unsavory memory of her half brothers' "malefactions." So abusive an experience of fondling no doubt tainted the physical side of marriage for her. With Lytton's frankly homoerotic life, she would not have to cope with the problem. "I was always sexually cowardly," she said many years later. "My terror of real life has always kept me in a nunnery." Sexual coward though she was and always would be, she still wanted to be married—but to someone whose mind she could respect—someone, perhaps, like her father.

Sensing how unhappy her sister was, Vanessa suggested that Virginia join her and Clive on their trip to Florence in April 1909. Virginia demurred. She was too busy, she said. There was Caroline Emelia's obituary to write for *The Guardian*; she was dining with a new friend called Lady Ottoline Morrell; there were books to review; she must work at her novel. Then (though she couldn't offer this as an excuse) tension built up whenever Vanessa, Clive, and Virginia came together. As April 23, their departure date, approached, Virginia changed her mind and wrote Clive a mildly coquettish letter: "Why should I excite you? Why should you be glad that I and my bundle of tempers come with you to Italy? ... When I have melted down the whole of my illusions, one or two things remain ... One is—well, that you care for me." And so in a few days, all three were off to Florence.

The brief sketches Virginia made in her journal during this trip reveal an apprentice learning to evoke character through "suggestion," leaving the reader to supply the rest. The apprentice was also attempting to get to the "essence" of one's character; and her dip into Florentine society provided her with fresh models. She said of Contessa Rasponi, for example: "Look at the conflict of lines on the brow—She is much like a peasant woman; and is a woman of cultivation ... Her talk is bold and free, also tentative." Janet Ross was the "friend of writers, and the character of the countryside. She sells things off her walls." Then there was a certain Mrs. Campbell, "who wrote devout books,—had done the life of Father Damien into rhyme." This particular guest would one day find a reference to herself in *The Voyage Out*: "I have an aunt called Rachel, who put the life of Father Damien into verse. She is a religious fanatic."*

The shy, nervous Virginia Stephen of Hyde Park Gate, now in Florence beside these formidable old ladies, was drawing them out to the limits of good manners. But in fact, she was becoming an observant novelist, surveying her cast of characters, probing their depths and ferreting out their secrets. The next day, when she returned to the pale blue page of her journal, all her observations would be cast in the integument of words and made permanent. Her natural shyness was concealed, went undetected, when the novelist, in quest of "copy," moved into territories which the twenty-seven-year-old Virginia would have been reluctant to tread.

But if Virginia was growing as a writer, she was shrinking in self-esteem. Watching Vanessa and Clive together, as husband and wife, was painful. The smallest, most natural show of affection made her feel "unloved, unwanted and excluded." On May 9, she cut her holiday short and returned to London, leaving the Bells to themselves. There was something pathetic about her position. "I think she would like very much to marry," Vanessa wrote to a friend. "I hope some new person may appear in the course of the next year or two for I have come to think that in spite of all drawbacks she had better marry."

A person did appear, though not a "new" one. It was Hilton Young. During Virginia's holiday in Wells the previous August, he had written to her several times. Vanessa evidently had some reservations: "I gather you

---

* In *Jacob's Room* too, there would be "Sally Duggan's *Life of Father Damien* in verse."

don't think much of Hilton Young...If I had had the chance, and determined against it, I could settle to virginity with greater composure than I can, when my womanhood is at question."

In May 1909, Virginia went to Cambridge, and while punting on the Cam, Hilton Young did finally propose to her. By this time, however, she had lost interest and said she would marry no one but Lytton in order to discourage Young from pursuing her further. But whatever hope she had of becoming Mrs. Lytton Strachey must have faded by now. So she continued to petition Clive and succeeded only in increasing his frustration, Vanessa's pain, and her own vague anxieties. If Clive's manhood suffered from this alliance, certainly his intellectual image prospered. How many people in future years would be able to claim being, for a time, Virginia's exclusive literary confidant?

It was at this juncture that Virginia's social life increased suddenly and substantially with the appearance of the inimitable Lady Ottoline Morrell, who had the "head of a Medusa" but was "very simple and innocent in spite of it" and worshiped the arts. Although Virginia had met her the previous December, it was not until January 16, 1909, that she wrote to "Dearest" Ottoline: "If you will have me for a friend it will be a great joy for me. Shyness, I suppose, makes it difficult to say that it is delightful to know you and like you as I do." Ottoline was becoming fond of her, Virginia wrote to Violet Dickinson. It was like sitting beneath a lily "with a thick golden bar in the middle dropping pollen, or whatever that is which seduces the male bee."

Lady Ottoline, born Cavendish-Bentinck, was a literary hostess, aged about thirty-six at this time. Her husband, Philip Morrell, was in the House of Commons. They made their home at 44 Bedford Square in Bloomsbury. Peppard Cottage was their weekend retreat. She came to one of the Thursday Evenings, which Virginia and Adrian were now holding, with the painter Augustus John and his wife, and found herself in an atmosphere as rebellious and unconventional as her own eccentric and flamboyant tastes, and not only enjoyed the company at 29 Fitzroy Square but also had money enough to offer her patronage.

Gertrude Stein described her as a "marvellous female version of Disraeli." But Ottoline was a generous-hearted woman whom Virginia and Lytton found fascinating. She had had a love affair with Augustus John and would later become involved in a more protracted intimacy with Bertrand Russell. She did not hesitate to ask Virginia for the names and addresses of all her "wonderful" friends, and soon all of Bloomsbury was swept into the "whirl-pool" of her extravagant Bedford Square parties. Lady Ottoline brought "petticoats, frivolity and champagne to the buns, the buggery and high thinking of Fitzroy Square." And much as she liked her, Virginia couldn't resist occasionally turning Ottoline into a figure of fun: ". . . her mind vapours off about friendship and love and literature—'I could never love anyone who does not care for literature—that is my cross—my refuge, Virginia—when people are cruel . . . And I suffer so terribly—my back gives me agonies—my feet are swollen with chilblains . . . What would I not give to be able to work as you do—to create—to be an artist—' imagine crossing Holborn with this dribbling out, as painfully as two old witches on crutches."

In August Virginia accompanied Adrian and Saxon Sydney-Turner to Bayreuth for the opera. She had never had any musical training, nor was she in any strict sense a musical person, but the pleasure she got from music was probably connected to her extraordinary sensitivity to sound and rhythm, which would become apparent in her later writing. At this point, however, her interest in opera was, like Adrian's, probably aroused by Saxon Sydney-Turner. For Virginia did not particularly care for the Germans she met at the sanctuary of Wagnerism. Nor, for that matter, did she care for the food or the lodgings. Even her two companions she found mildly uncongenial and comforted herself by writing her sister long, affectionate letters.

To Vanessa she described a typical day at the festival: first they read through the opera; then they listened to it; and afterward they discussed it. They made her read the libretto in German, she complained, "which troubles me a good deal." Adding to the petty irritations was the sphinxlike Saxon to contend with: he was dormant all day and irritable if one interrupted him. "He reminds me a little of father. He clenches his fists, and scowls in the same way." Even his conversation, laden with detail as it was, Virginia still found uninteresting. Talking to Saxon was like "reading a dictionary." His memory often threw up bits of very odd stuff: What did Virginia mean when she said three years ago that her view of life was like that of a Henry James novel, and his of a George Meredith? "I had to invent a meaning, and he actually told me that he thought me a very clever young woman—which is the highest praise I have ever had from him." Saxon's "purity of mind" Virginia found very attractive.

It may indeed have been his "purity of mind" and certain oddities of manner that brought Sir Leslie to mind, for at this time Virginia found herself thinking a great deal about her father. He had been very modest, she thought, and not at all self-conscious about his work—"He had very few sympathies though; and practically no imagination." His years of climbing the Alps may have contributed to her recollections, surrounded as she now was by Germans. Still, she found Germans uncongenial. Even the operatic performances, the finest in the world, she spoke of with mockery: "I can never quite get over the florid Teuton spirit, with its gross symbolism . . . Imagine a heroine in a nightgown, with a pig tail on each shoulder, and watery eyes ogling heaven." Neither Bayreuth nor Wagner appealed to Virginia's fastidious taste.

In September Virginia rented a cottage in Studland, Dorset, for two weeks to be near the Bells. Vanessa invited Lytton Strachey to join them in the hope that he might reconsider making Virginia his wife; but he was away at a Swedish sanatorium undergoing a cure of some sort, and so Walter Lamb was invited in his place. Lamb had been one of Clive's friends at Trinity and was now an assistant master at Clifton College. He had been a guest of the Bells at Gordon Square several times and Vanessa thought Virginia might find him interesting. But the plan failed. Lamb was dull, rather stale, and certainly no "substitute for Lytton."

The Christmas holiday this year was unusual. On the morning of Christmas Eve, while walking in Regent's Park, Virginia suddenly took it into her head to spend Christmas in Cornwall. The idea struck her at twelve-thirty and her train left at one—or so her story goes. She had only thirty minutes to prepare for the journey. Sophie was hysterical, Virginia wrote to Vanessa on Christmas day, "and I have no pocket handkerchief, watch key, notepaper, spectacles, cheque book, looking glass, or coat." The maid, according to Virginia, had packed "old amethyst necklaces" but not the bare necessities; so that the landlady's husband had to lend her his watch key, "and I borrow pencils and stamps." But it was worth the trouble, for no one else was staying at the Lelant Hotel, and all the festivals passed over her head "without a trace."

Just before the holiday, the *Times* had sent a copy of *Lady Hester Stanhope*, by Mrs. Charles Roundell, to review and Virginia had brought it along. The memoir made her "rock with delight," she wrote to Clive. Lady Hester had gotten into the habit of talking "so that she could never read . . . and took herself for the Messiah. Suppose I stayed here, and thought myself an early virgin, and danced on May nights in the British camp!" Wouldn't that provide little Julian with an eccentric relation, so that when he grew older he might nonchalantly bring her up on a Thursday Evening as a scandalous "aunt who copulates in a tree, and thinks herself with child by a grasshopper . . . She dresses in green, and my mother sends her nuts from the Stores."

. . .

Several years earlier, on March 4, 1905, the *Daily Mail* reported what at the time came to be known as the "Zanzibar Hoax." The Mayor of Cambridge had been wired that the Sultan of Zanzibar would arrive at Cambridge at 4:27 that afternoon for a brief visit and wanted to be shown all the buildings of interest. Would the Mayor send a carriage to meet the Sultan and his party? This was the opening scene of "one of the most audacious and carefully-planned practical jokes ever perpetrated by undergraduates." The leader of the hoax was none other than Adrian Stephen. The event caused a considerable stir and a good many municipal officials public embarrassment.

Now, on the morning of February 10, 1910, Adrian organized a second hoodwinking of the authorities called the "Dreadnought Hoax"—only this time Virginia Stephen would also be in active attendance at this equally well-publicized "practical joke." On the morning in question, Virginia, Adrian, and four companions, impersonating Abyssinian princes and their staff, took a train to Weymouth from Paddington Station. Virginia was rigged up with beard and moustache glued to her blackened face, wearing a turban, gold chains, and an embroidered caftan. Adrian wore a beard and bowler hat. The other four, all appropriately costumed, were Duncan Grant (Adrian's lover at the time), Anthony Buxton, Guy Ridley, and Horace Cole.

The hoax was essentially a repeat performance of the Zanzibar affair, only now the joke would be on the British Navy: the imposters wanted to penetrate naval security and be conducted on a tour of the HMS *Dreadnought*, the most impressive vessel then afloat. As in 1905, a telegram preceded them. The most audacious part of the scheme was the possibility of Adrian's meeting his cousin William Fisher, who was then flag commander of the *Dreadnought*. This itself, however, was an added incentive to Adrian's participation.

The scheme proceeded as planned. Adrian, in the role of interpreter, had several times to mumble something that sounded like Swahili interlarded with scraps of Virgil and Homer. They were given their tour; they politely refused a twenty-one gun salute; and with considerable ceremony they were escorted back to Weymouth. Throughout the entire elaborate imposture, with all its stiff machinery and gold-encrusted protocol, the officers of the British Navy must have seemed incredibly obtuse to Virginia, who spoke of the incident many years later with pride. Male figures of power and authority had been made to appear ridiculous. The tricksters' looks, their language, and their manners would have told the slowest-witted undergraduate that they had no more to do with Abyssinia than Adrian, five years earlier, had had to do with Zanzibar.

The joke should have ended with the return trip to Weymouth, but Horace Cole, itching for a bit of notoriety, leaked the story to the London press, which responded with full-page photographs and gigantic headlines. Virginia and Adrian were assaulted with letters of indignation from the Fisher and Stephen families. Letters of distress poured onto editors' desks, but Virginia's friends found it all very amusing. Cousin Dorothea Stephen, however, took time from her meditations to point out that it was God Virginia needed, to restore her to the path of righteousness and cure her recalcitrant waywardness. For Virginia, the incident left a lasting impression of "masculine honour, of masculine violence and stupidity, of gold-laced masculine pomposity." Some of the memory would find its way into a story called "A Society," but, more significantly, it would fuel the anger that pervaded an essay called *Three Guineas* she would write many years later.

The same year as the Dreadnought Hoax Virginia wrote to Janet Case— she was still "Miss Case"—to say how impressed she was by the campaign for women's votes. She was finally coming to see how intolerable the situation was. Would it be of any use if she spent an afternoon or two each week addressing envelopes for the Adult Suffragists? She felt ill-equipped to do more important work like bookkeeping or public speaking, "but I could do the humbler work if that is any good." This was to be her first active involvement in politics. Emmeline Pankhurst's campaign for the vote had been gradually gaining public support, but Prime Minister Herbert Asquith strongly opposed the feminist cause, and between 1910 and the outbreak of World War I, his opposition generated increasing protest and violence.

Something more personal was beginning to manifest itself at this time, however, which could not be ignored. Virginia was clearly entering a state of severe nervous temper. The symptoms may have been connected with any number of things: her troubled entanglement with Clive; Vanessa's defection to motherhood; herself now older and still mateless; the endless novel with its endless revisions. *The Voyage Out* was beginning to take final shape, but by early March she was on the verge of a massive breakdown. The nearer she approached completion, the less she would have (and presumably need) Clive's reassurances; and the more would she, alone, be held accountable for the life and death of her fictional but highly autobiographical character, Rachel Vinrace.

Dr. Savage was consulted. Predictably he ordered his usual regimen of avoiding excitement and getting plenty of rest, food, and sleep. If she observed his orders to the letter, the tension would decrease and the headaches disappear. Clive and Vanessa accordingly took her to Studland on March 26 for a three-week course of vegetable existence. On April 16 she returned to Fitzroy Square, thinking herself better. But she was wrong. Whatever improvement there was from the three weeks in Dorset quickly disintegrated with the pace and distractions of London. The symptoms returned, now with even greater force. Once again, Savage was called in. Convinced that his prescription was the only right one, he again ordered complete rest, anywhere *outside* London. Virginia by now had grown severely depressed.

This time, Clive and Vanessa rented a house near Canterbury—the Moat House, Blean—and here they settled in on June 7 and hoped for the best. Clive was particularly solicitous toward Virginia. He was sympathetic and perhaps a little relieved that she was away from Lytton Strachey, Walter Lamb, and Hilton Young—her suitors, his rivals. No matter how hopeful he was, though, it was obvious after two weeks that Virginia was getting no better. Vanessa, still in the role of guardian, returned to London to consult with Dr. Savage. The journey could not have come at a worse time, for she was expecting another baby; and with her own confinement imminent, she could no longer fully attend to Virginia. All of this she reported to Savage.

He now insisted that Virginia be admitted to a mental nursing home in Burley Park, Twickenham—"a kind of polite mad-house for female lunatics"—owned and operated by a Miss Jean Thomas. From London, Vanessa wrote on June 23 to inform Virginia of the decision. Virginia had obviously little choice in the matter. If this was what she must do, then she would do it, but it brought her to the depths of despair when she realized how little control she had over her own life in times of illness. Why hadn't Savage insisted on this in the first place? She would probably have been better by now instead of prolonging the matter. But it was too late to argue. She surrendered, swallowing her bitterness and disappointment. It would be "damnable" and the memory of nurses and food and boredom was "disgusting." But she also imagined the "delights of being sane again." Dr. Savage did not insist on "complete isolation, so I suppose I shan't be as badly off as I was before."

And so on June 30, she penetrated the sturdy walls of "Burley," and remained there until August 10, fluctuating between days of euphoria and days of melancholy, manifesting all the symptoms of classical manic-depressive psychosis. She suspected everything and everyone during her incarceration. Vanessa especially came under assault. The mistrust that was blocked from consciousness in times of good health rushed to the surface with terrifying violence in illness. "I gather," she wrote to Vanessa, "that some great conspiracy is going on behind my back . . . (Miss T.) won't read me or quote your letters. But I gather that you want me to stay on here." "[Y]ou can't conceive how I want intelligent conversation—even yours," she said to Vanessa, who was now the "Dark Devil." Because Virginia had a way of charming her medical advisers, she could be a difficult patient, and did her best to break all the rules and take liberties that a more aggressive supervisor than Miss Thomas would not have tolerated.

There were long talks with Jean Thomas, who had a "charming nature," was "rather whimsical, and even sensual." Apparently she did not need money and took patients as a kind of "spiritual work." Miss Thomas, Virginia assured her sister, led an immaculate life. "She has harboured innumerable young women in love difficulties . . . The utmost tact is shown with regard to our complaints; and I make Miss T. blush by asking if they're mad."

Miss T. was being seduced by Virginia and quite obviously was under her spell. For when Virginia was sufficiently recovered to leave Burley in mid-August, she went on a walking tour in Cornwall with the "spiritual" Miss Thomas in attendance. From Gurnards Head Virginia wrote to Clive thanking him for his letters. "One is a very nice animal, apart from books and culture, but almost dumb." She had been thinking of Thoby all the while there in Cornwall. "I suppose it's the birds," she wrote on September 4. "I lay awake till 5 this morning, for some unknown reason," she wrote again on the eighth. But the reason was not hard to find: September 8 was Thoby's birthday. He would have been thirty.

She returned to London for a few days and then, with Clive and little Julian, went to Studland to complete her convalescence. Vanessa joined them several days later with the new baby—who would eventually be called Quentin. Virginia seemed improved. She had warned Clive earlier that it took only one sleepless night to make her again "incapable." She resolved to be "cautious" with the Bells, and asked Clive "not to irritate the beast, for amusement."

 By late November Virginia resumed writing *The Voyage Out*, which had lain dormant since March. Her health was still precarious and she was encouraged by Vanessa to find some place nearby to have as a retreat. There must be a country house Virginia could rent if she looked hard enough. Virginia did look. She began her search almost

immediately in the vicinity of Sussex. She and Adrian (and later Duncan Grant) in fact spent their Christmas in Lewes at the Pelham Arms. It was a very bleak Christmas. No letters came, no parcels, nothing. Worse than that, Virginia was beginning again to suffer her usual symptoms.

Clive wrote several days later and the acerbity of her reply suggests her state of mind. She didn't deserve another letter from him, she said, "because that old Bitch left off suckling her whelps and wrote." But would Clive please write again. Communicating with Vanessa was like talking to a "stone wall." She felt even more deserted because Adrian was so happy. His lover, Duncan, was going to spend the holiday with him. It was easy and natural for Virginia to feel unloved and unrelated to anything.

She was spending Christmas in Lewes, she wrote to Violet on New Year's Day, with a very considerate landlady "who is so much struck by my incompetence to face life, that she always offers to lace my boots." Then the good Miss Thomas came to Virginia's side for the night, "in an interval between discharging a woman who wished to commit murder, and taking one, who wants to kill herself." And so Virginia succeeded in garnering all the affection she could get. Those who refused her were left to wallow in guilt. She was once more following in the footsteps of her father.

She also succeeded during this holiday in finding a semi-detached villa in the village of Firle, near Lewes. The downs behind the house were its principal attraction. She named it Little Talland House in memory of her childhood at St. Ives. Lewes and the surrounding area would remain her country base for the remainder of her life. In January of 1911, with Vanessa's help, she furnished and decorated the house and was in full possession by March when she moved in with Maud and Sophie Farrell, her two servants. She wrote all morning, walked all afternoon, and would "read and write and look out of the window the rest of the time." By April 17 she had rewritten the first third of her novel. She was working hard and having weekend guests regularly despite recurrent headaches and some sleeplessness. Though no one seems to have noticed, she was still very far from well.

In November 1910, Roger Fry, aged forty-four at the time, mounted the first Post-Impressionist exhibition (*Manet and the Post-Impressionists*) at the Grafton Gallery. Fry wanted to distinguish the painters he was showing as more "expressionist" in their treatment of color and form than their contemporaries. The painters here, as Fry's biographer writes, "were no longer content to record the shifting pattern of appearance but instead wanted to make the image more durable, either by emphasizing an underlying structure, as in the work of Cézanne, or by emphasizing an expressive response to the scene and therefore ... rearranging visual facts to create the desired effect." The show opened to an explosion of indignation. To the Edwardians who came to look, the paintings were vulgar, childish, and aggressive.

Roger Fry had been educated in the natural sciences and elected an Apostle at King's College, Cambridge. Before finishing his studies, he discovered that painting was to be his vocation, against the wishes of his Quaker father. When he was just twenty, however, he went to Italy to paint and in the following year managed to study for two months at the Académie Julian in Paris. While painting, he began to write art criticism and soon built himself a reputation in both England and America. In 1897 he married Helen Coombe, a fellow artist, who suffered from a recurring mental illness which required his seeking employment that would provide a regular income. In 1906 he became a curator of the Metropolitan Museum in New York and remained the Museum's British adviser until 1910. By this time, however, Helen had become incurably insane and was to spend the rest of her life institutionalized.

Vanessa and Clive had met Roger on a train from Cambridge in January 1910. Although he was a recognized authority on the Italian old masters, it was the modern French painters, particularly Cézanne, who attracted his attention. Vanessa, finding they had much in common, persuaded him to lecture to her Friday Club; so that by the autumn of 1910, when the Grafton Gallery asked him to mount the Post-Impressionist show, he already knew most of the Bloomsbury figures and had half of them on his committee. Desmond MacCarthy, as secretary to the exhibit, accompanied him to France to collect the paintings of Cézanne, Van Gogh, Gauguin, Matisse, and several others.

Although the British public was outraged—the painters were "bunglers" and "lunatics" and the paintings "pornographic"—Vanessa and Duncan Grant were among the first to adopt the French Impressionist style and Roger became a kind of father figure to the group. In fact the atmosphere he created made Vanessa's circle of painters "a little more conscious of being revolutionary and notorious." Bloomsbury was becoming "an object of public disapproval, a centre of disaffection ... and of incomprehensible aesthetics." The shifting planes and odd luminosities of modern French painters were gradually overpowering the recondite principles of G. E. Moore's philosophy.

Under Roger Fry's aegis a group was formed to visit the birthplace of Byzantine art; and in April of 1911, Clive, Vanessa, Roger, and the Cambridge mathematician Harry Norton all found themselves in Constantinople. Soon the trouble started, however. Vanessa, now pregnant for the third time, had not been feeling well even at the outset. By the time they reached Broussa, she collapsed. It was a miscarriage. When Virginia got the news, the horrors of Greece in 1906 flashed before her; without a moment's hesitation she made her way to Turkey.

She arrived to find Clive in a state of complete helplessness and Norton drawing "diagrams of Ovaries on the table cloth." Vanessa was convalescent and Roger was in charge. Virginia was correct in thinking he had saved Vanessa's life by his extraordinary reserves of energy and practical good sense. She wrote to Violet that she found Vanessa surrounded by men who "had to get a litter made, and carry her stretched on it, through Constantinople and home by the Orient Express."

Actually it was several days before Vanessa was well enough to be moved; and it was during this brief delay that Virginia began to look more closely at Roger. What she saw she liked. He was intelligent, attentive, witty, and extremely efficient. It was also apparent that he was in need of female companionship, and although Virginia knew of his brief sexual adventure with Ottoline Morrell (who had served on the exhibition committee), she could see as he nursed Vanessa back to health in the weeks ahead that they had fallen in love. That new realignment of feeling now cast everything in a different light. Clive's womanizing, and particularly their flirtation, no longer mattered. They could flirt as much as they liked—Vanessa now had Roger. So just as the bonds between Vanessa and Roger grew stronger, those between Virginia and Clive weakened.

The dissolution of the Bell marriage, the "transformation into a union of friendship" which took place in the following months, reduced the strain between the sisters. Whatever Virginia had earlier envied in Vanessa's domestic happiness now ceased to exist. Arrangements would now proceed on a new footing. In another and subtler way, Vanessa's falling in love with a man thirteen years her senior—almost the same difference in age as between Leslie Stephen and Julia Duckworth—put Roger in a different and altogether unexpected focus. With Clive now emotionally out of the way, Vanessa would resume her maternal function in Virginia's life, casting Roger, whether he was conscious of it or not, in the paternal role. It is unlikely that this occurred to Virginia with any definition or clarity, but it is possible that even at this early stage, she dimly felt a filial bonding with Roger. Vanessa knew that Roger thought highly of Virginia's gifts, and it may even have crossed her mind that Virginia would again set out to charm Roger away from her; for the younger sister had (almost) always wanted what the older sister had.

. . .

Despite the protective atmosphere Roger brought with him, however, with its accompanying aura of security, Virginia was descending into troubled waters. She was depressed, she said to Vanessa in early June; she was finding it hard to write—"all the devils came out—hairy black ones. To be 29 and unmarried—to be a failure—childless—insane too, no writer."

The world was changing too quickly and Virginia was having difficulty adjusting, establishing once more a sense of who she was. Only then could she escape that terrible feeling of dereliction. The atmosphere of freedom which clung to Roger may have had something to do with it. And the new lawless spirit of painters. And the extravagant world of Ottoline Morrell. It was all new and compelling. The reticence of old was quickly vanishing, perhaps too quickly. Only a few years earlier Virginia would have blushed when excusing herself to use the lavatory. Only a few years earlier Adrian wouldn't have dreamed of mentioning the love affairs of Cambridge undergraduates.

It no longer troubled anyone to hear Vanessa talking about one young man's "utter despair" because Rupert Brooke had been "twice to bed" with another young man. The old accepted views of marriage, too, were spinning out of bounds. Perhaps marital fidelity was not so keenly observed as one had been led to believe. "Of course Kitty Maxse has two or three lovers," said Clive. "Kitty Maxse, the chaste, the exquisite, the devoted!"

Old proprieties, old values, old beliefs and customs were fading. Indeed "the future of Bloomsbury was to prove that many variations can be played on the theme of sex." The Thursday Evenings with their long silences were now ancient history. Other very different parties took their place. The Post-Impressionists shed their multicolored rays on Bloomsbury—"we dressed ourselves up as Gauguin pictures" in bright printed cottons, and whirled around the dance floor, scandalizing members of an earlier generation. One old woman accused Vanessa and Virginia of appearing "practically naked." Reports began to circulate that at Bloomsbury parties everyone undressed. One particularly vicious story had it that Maynard Keynes had "copulated with Vanessa on the sofa in the middle of the drawing room." Here was sexual anarchy. The women were fast and loose. The men were dissolute. The world of Bloomsbury was immoral, arrogant, cold-blooded. So the rumors flew.

This was the public picture, and Virginia saw it only in hindsight. The private side of her still very chaste life at 29 Fitzroy Square was a world apart. There would be another proposal in November from Sydney Waterlow, Clive's Cambridge contemporary. He had somehow attached himself to the Thursday Evening visitors of Gordon and Fitzroy Squares and the previous September had been to Studland with the Bells and Virginia. Not yet divorced, he proposed to Virginia, and she refused him gently. She would never feel for him what she must feel for the man she married, her letter said. "It would be unpardonable of me if I did not do everything to save you from what must—as far as I can tell—be a great waste."

16 Leonard Woolf, on leave from Ceylon, where he had been since 1904, returned to England on June 11, 1911. He had dined with the four Stephens on November 17, the eve of his departure. Virginia was still recovering from the illness following her father's death. Leonard was twenty-four then and thirty-one now. He was the third of nine children in an Orthodox Jewish family, his father, Sidney Woolf, a barrister by profession. In October 1899, after St. Paul's School, he went to Trinity College, Cambridge as a classicist, where his closest friends, apart from Thoby, were Lytton Strachey, Saxon Sydney-Turner, Desmond MacCarthy, Maynard Keynes, and, more distantly, Clive Bell. Like his contemporaries, he was influenced by G. E. Moore, from whom he acquired a challenging intellectual skepticism and a firm belief in "personal affection and aesthetic enjoyments." He saw himself now as a reserved and sophisticated Cambridge intellectual. In 1902, like Lytton, he had been elected an Apostle. Unlike Lytton, Leonard was a staunch heterosexual and one of a handful of men Lytton did not see as a rival in matters of the heart.

When Leonard met the lovely Misses Stephen in 1904, they were about to become sideline observers of the Cambridge intellect and manner. But now in 1911, they had blossomed into the center of the Bloomsbury community with a certain intellectual and artistic arrogance of their own. After seven years of colonial administration, imposing order on chaos in "a wilderness of monkeys," Leonard found Vanessa and Virginia exhilarating and this newly altered Bloomsbury congenial. He quickly became a frequent visitor at 46 Gordon Square, and soon Virginia addressed "Dear Mr Wolf" to see if he would come for a weekend to her cottage in Firle. That was how the friendship between Leonard and Virginia began.

As it happened, the lease on 29 Fitzroy Square was up in July, and Virginia, perhaps to terminate her isolating domestic arrangement with Adrian, for they still irritated each other, suggested they find a house large enough to share with their male friends and thus help reduce the friction between them. The house they found meeting that general requirement was 38 Brunswick Square. The idea of renting out rooms, providing meals, and sharing the expenses of running a house was of course revolutionary, and one that raised a good many eyebrows. George Duckworth's rose highest and his protests were loudest. How could Virginia even consider sharing her living quarters with all those men? It was unthinkable! It violated everything they stood for. But Vanessa, who thought the plan a good one, wickedly reminded George that it was quite all right: Brunswick Square was near the Foundling Hospital. Even the broad-minded Violet Dickinson tried to dissuade Virginia. What would Julia Stephen have said if she knew her daughter was living in such a situation? Certainly she would disapprove. But Virginia went ahead with her plan over all objections.

By November 20, 38 Brunswick Square was ready for occupancy. The ground floor would be taken by the young economist, Maynard Keynes, whom Virginia had known since 1907. Although Maynard's Fellowship at King's College required his living in Cambridge much of the time, he would share his part of the house with Duncan Grant, who could use the space as a studio. Adrian would take the first floor, Virginia the second, and on December 4 Leonard Woolf would assume occupancy of the top floor.

Virginia set about organizing the daily schedule and distributed to each of the "inmates" a notice that breakfast would be served at 9 a.m. (tea, egg, bacon, toast or roll), lunch at 1 p.m. (meat, vegetables, and sweet), tea at 4:30 p.m. (tea and buns), and dinner at 8 p.m. (fish, meat, and sweet). The "Scheme of the house" said that trays would be placed in the hall punctually. The entire enterprise sounded as though it were being managed by someone highly organized, certainly not by someone who was not competent "to face life" and needed help lacing her shoes.

Leonard Woolf had been unable to accept Virginia's first weekend invitation to Firle in July. He had already engaged himself in seeing old friends. When his visits were over, however, he reminded Virginia of her earlier invitation and it was renewed. "It would be so much easier to use Christian names," she wrote him on the last day of August. "This is not a cottage," she added, "but a hideous suburban villa"; she had to prepare people for the shock. Leonard went to Little Talland House for the weekend of September 16. Desmond MacCarthy and Marjorie Strachey (Lytton's sister) were the other guests. It was on one of their walks that Virginia discovered Asheham (sometimes spelled "Asham"), "a strange and beautiful house in a lonely and romantic situation" a few miles to the west of Firle. She was enchanted by the house and set out to inquire if it could be rented from January 1912. Vanessa, equally attracted to the house, agreed at once to share the lease.

Shortly after that weekend, Virginia wrote to Leonard about her "spirited controversy about W.C.s and E.C.s [earth closets]" with Mr. Hoper, the owner. It only remained now to decide whether Mrs. Hoper should clean the earth closet or have a separate drain installed. "It seems to me that both must require cesspools: and W.C.s are certainly pleasanter in wet weather." At any rate she'd had a "splendid" day down there discussing all this—an occasion she would recall and inscribe many years later in the opening pages of *Between the Acts*.

The Asheham housewarming in early February 1912 was a disaster. It was one of the coldest days of the year; the pipes were frozen; perched on the windowsills were starving birds; the fireplace grates fell apart; and then suddenly Marjorie Strachey, while reciting Racine, decided (or discovered) she had chicken pox. A week later Vanessa gave a second party, with Adrian, Duncan Grant, Leonard, and Roger Fry in attendance. Despite the atmosphere of festivity, however, Virginia was in great distress. All of her symptoms had returned sometime in December. She had been foolish, working too hard, playing too hard; there had been too much excitement; her headaches returned and she couldn't sleep.

Since his move to Brunswick Square Leonard and Virginia saw a great deal of each other. He had come to know her as well as anyone not a member of the Stephen family and found himself falling deeply in love. Exactly how she felt about him, apart from her obvious fondness, he did not yet know and therefore kept silent. In early January, however, while visiting the Rector of Frome in Somerset, away from the distractions of London, Leonard saw that he must hesitate no longer. He must know, one way or the other, if Virginia would marry him.

On January 10 he sent a telegram to Brunswick Square: "I MUST SEE YOU FOR AN HOUR TOMORROW THURSDAY I SHALL ARRIVE TOWN 12.50 AND LEAVE AGAIN 5 IF I CAN COME TO BRUNSWICK SQUARE 1.15 CAN I SEE YOU THEN LEONARD." He left his host in the early morning, rushed to London, proposed to Virginia, got no definite answer, dashed back to Frome, and was at the Great Elm Rectory in time for dinner. Whether he ate anything or how violently his hands trembled we do not know. But Virginia's hesitation had fired him up sufficiently to put all his hopes and feelings on paper—in a two-part letter:

the first part dated January 11, 1912, the evening of the proposal: "My dear Virginia," it began, "I must write to you before I go to bed . . . I never realised how much I loved you until we talked about my going back to Ceylon . . . I got into a state of hopeless uncertainty, whether you loved me or could ever love me or even like me . . . It isn't, really it isn't, merely because you are so beautiful . . . that I love you: it is your mind and your character—I have never known anyone like you in that . . . And now I will do absolutely whatever you want."

On the following day, January 12, he continued: "I'm sure now that apart from being in love . . . it would be worth the risk of everything to marry you. That of course—from your side—was the question you were continually putting yesterday . . . God, I see the risk in marrying anyone and certainly me. I am selfish, jealous, cruel, lustful, a liar and probably worse still . . . I would never marry anyone because of this, mostly because . . . I felt I could never control these things with a woman who was inferior and would gradually enfuriate [*sic*] me by her inferiority and submission . . . It is because you aren't that that I risk so infinitely less. You may be vain, an egoist, untruthful, as you say, but they are nothing compared to your other qualities."

On Saturday, the following day, before rushing to her train, Virginia hurriedly replied: "There isn't anything really for me to say, except that I should like to go on as before; and that you should leave me free, and that I should be honest . . . I am very sorry to be the cause of so much rush and worry. I am just off to Firle." As she was posting her letter from Brunswick Square, Vanessa, from Gordon Square, was writing her own letter to Leonard, interceding for Virginia much the same way Julia Stephen would have done had she been witness to all this: "You're the only person I know whom I can imagine as her husband," Vanessa wrote, "which may seem to you a rash remark considering how little I know you. However I have faith in my instincts."

Virginia's resistance to Leonard's proposal may have been due in part to the passion he expressed and her fear of the physical aspect of marriage that passion implied. But whatever the cause, one thing was certain: her health was rapidly deteriorating. After the Asheham housewarming fiasco, her symptoms became so severe that on Dr. Savage's recommendation, she returned to the isolation of Jean Thomas's nursing home in Twickenham. This was on February 16. Leonard was told by Vanessa that he was not to write or attempt to see her while she was under Thomas's care. When Virginia was finally released two weeks later, Vanessa encouraged him to return to the rectory in Somerset. Whether she did this to prevent his seeing Virginia in one of her illnesses or whether she thought Leonard's imposing presence might aggravate her condition is not clear. From Vanessa's point of view, there was a distinct advantage in Leonard's marrying Virginia: he would assume her job of mental health custodian, and it was probably for this reason that Vanessa did not interfere with any of Dr. Savage's recommendations. The sooner Virginia recovered, the sooner she would be free to marry.

Virginia wrote Leonard a "crazy" letter from Brunswick Square shortly after returning from Twickenham which must have come as rather a shock. It begins with her promise to tell him "wonderful stories of the lunatics" and ends with her announcement of going out to buy "chocolates and a sleeping draught, if the shops are open, and I escape molestation. I shan't want the sleeping draught—in any case." This, from the brilliant Virginia he wanted to make his wife. "A tepid lover might have wondered what kind of woman he was wooing and might well have withdrawn from the undertaking," wrote Quentin Bell, "but there was nothing tepid in Leonard's love."

From late February through April Virginia was at Asheham, where she lived quietly and worked at her novel in peace and seclusion. Her companion was Katherine Cox (called Ka and sometimes Bruin), whom Virginia had met in early 1911. Ka was one of the younger generation of women from Newnham College and was at this time involved in a complicated love affair with Rupert Brooke. A "bright, intelligent, nice creature; who has, she says, very few emotions." She was soon to assume an important role in Virginia's life.

Leonard in the meantime was beginning to realize that he was in a difficult situation. He was officially on leave from his post in Ceylon but was expected to return there on May 20. He was also aware that Virginia's decision to marry might take a good deal longer than he had anticipated and was determined not to rush her. If she accepted his proposal, he would of course resign. Accordingly, he wrote to the Colonial Office on February 14 requesting a four-month extension. The reason was personal, he said. The Under-Secretary asked him what specifically that personal reason was. When Leonard refused to supply him with this information, the matter was referred to the Governor of Ceylon. If Mr. Woolf could not give details, the Governor would be in a position to deny the extension. To this Leonard replied on April 25 from Brunswick Square: "With reference to your letter number 12288/1912 of 23 April I have the honour to report that, as I am unable to assume duties on May 20, I regret that I must resign my post under the Ceylon Government from that date." He signed the letter: "I am Sir, Your obedient servant, L. S. Woolf."

After posting it, he went to Asheham for the weekend feeling that matters were not going at all well. Upon returning to London, he wrote Virginia another long letter, this one repetitious and rambling: "... I've read two of your MSS from one of which at any rate one can see that you might write something astonishingly good ... I know clearly enough what I feel for you. It is not only physical love though it is that of course ... It's true that I'm cold and reserved to other people ... We often laugh about your lovableness but you don't know how lovable you are ... I wouldn't have asked you to marry me if I thought it would bring you any unhappiness ... I have faults, vices, beastliness but even with them, I do believe you ought to marry me ... I shall never be content now with the second best ... You must finish your novel first and while you are doing it you must not try to decide ... After all, I've had more happiness in the last two months than in all the rest of my life put together."

It was a touching letter, in its openness and ardor very much like some her father had written to Julia; and Virginia must have seen at once that she would never find anyone to equal Leonard. He assured her that physical intimacy was secondary, that her work as a novelist came first. Most of all, he would always love her as a man loved a woman, and would never press her to do anything she objected to. All of which meant that in Leonard's eyes, she was first and she was best.

After sending off this letter, he received one from the Colonial Office. If he still wanted the four-month extension, they were willing to reconsider. Would he let them have his final decision? And so on April 30, he wrote to Virginia again at Asheham. He must talk to her, he said, before giving the Colonial Office a definite answer.

The urgency of having to make a final decision must have struck Virginia now as an ultimatum, one that in the course of events would wreak havoc with her nervous stability. She replied nevertheless on May 1: "I ought to be as plain with you as I can, because half the time I suspect, you're in a fog which I don't see at all ... I say to myself, Anyhow, you'll be quite happy with him; and he will give you companionship, children, and a busy life ... Then, of course, I feel angry sometimes at the strength of your desire. Possibly, your being a Jew comes in also at this point. You seem so foreign. And then I am fearfully unstable. I pass from hot to cold in an instant ... when I am with you, there is some feeling which is permanent, and growing ... But I don't know what the future will bring ... Again, I want everything—love, children, adventure, intimacy, work ... So I go from being half in love with you, and wanting you to be with me always ... to the extreme of wildness and aloofness ... and then—is it the sexual side of it that comes between us? As I told you brutally the other day, I feel no physical attraction in you. There are moments—when you kissed me the other day was one—when I feel no more than a rock . . . But it's just because you care so much that I feel I've got to care before I marry you. I feel I must give you everything."

When Leonard received this, he knew he must leave the Colonial Service. His resignation was accepted on May 7, and on the twenty-ninth—with *The Voyage Out* finished except for one chapter—Virginia told Leonard she would marry him. She announced the engagement to her friends with a mixture of apology and mockery, as if expecting to be ridiculed. To Violet Dickinson she wrote: "I've got a confession to make. I'm marrying Leonard Wolf [*sic*]. He's a penniless Jew." To Nelly Cecil and Janet Case, too, Leonard was a "penniless Jew." To Lytton Strachey her message was simply "Ha! Ha!" Only to Madge Vaughan did she change the tune: "At first I felt stunned, but now every day the happiness becomes more complete—even though it does seem a fearful chance—my having any man who gives me what Leonard does."

If Leonard saw this early Virginia's self-absorption, her need to be loved, and the difficulty she had returning it, he said nothing. If he had any notion how much his rigid, persistent, morally unyielding behavior resembled that of the high-principled and self-righteous Leslie Stephen, he gave no sign of it. If he imagined at this point the role he would serve as Virginia's mentor and nurse and doctor and companion and confessor and comforter, he kept his silence. In the end Virginia would make claims on Leonard equal to those Leslie had made on Julia.

As might be expected, the excitement began to tell on Virginia. In early summer she became once more "headachey" and sleepless. Despite these warning signs, she spent most of June and July introducing Leonard to her friends and relatives; and he brought her to meet his mother, Marie Woolf, living in Colinette Road, Putney, with her children. "Work and love and Jews in Putney take it out of one," Virginia wrote to Violet Dickinson. By mid-summer *The Voyage Out* was finished, or so she thought, and on August 10, 1912, Miss Adeline Virginia Stephen, aged thirty, and Mr. Leonard Sidney Woolf, aged thirty-two, became husband and wife at the St. Pancras Registry Office.

The wedding ceremony, like so much else in Virginia's life, contained a bit of spectacle. Duncan Grant was in borrowed clothes that threatened to slip off; Aunt Mary Fisher had come hobbling on a crutch; the painter Frederick Etchells "came bearded, bespectacled and uncouth, to lend a final touch of oddity to the scene." Getting married at the Registry Office was quick and efficient. One had only to repeat a few words and then sign a paper. "Nothing went wrong," said the bride. The only disturbance was about the names

Vanessa and Virginia, which the registrar "who was half blind ... mixed hopelessly and Nessa upset him worse by suddenly deciding to change her son's name from Quentin to Christopher." The entire ceremony was accompanied by thunder and lightning, but the assembly seemed to enjoy it. Afterward there was a "very odd" lunch party. George and Gerald Duckworth were in frock coats looking "suspiciously" at Duncan, and the "odd little painter" who talked of nothing but pawned clothes. Saxon Sydney-Turner and Roger Fry were also present. Leonard's mother did not attend.

INFINITE DISCORDS AND SHIVERING FRAGMENTS

1912–1919

17 Everything about the months leading up to that fateful morning of August 10, 1912, with Leonard by Virginia's side is inconsecutive, uncertain, and conflicted. "I began life with a tremendous, absurd, ideal of marriage; then my bird's eye view of many marriages disgusted me," wrote Virginia in March, just five months before her own wedding day. This "disgust" it appears was now causing the bride-to-be headaches and sleeplessness, and it seemed powerful enough to trigger a depression that would lead, a year later, to a second attempt to end her life. There are long stretches of *The Voyage Out* that read as though Virginia were trying to free herself from a predicament in fiction she found herself struggling with in reality. So overwhelmed and confused had Virginia become that dying appeared to be Rachel Vinrace's only alternative to marriage. Perhaps it was something deeper than that. Whatever it was, Stella Duckworth had shown her that marital happiness was fleeting and death its price. Love, it seemed, was incompatible with freedom. Intimacy and independence could not coexist. Love required submission, and submission destroyed autonomy and selfhood. What was the future of Virginia Stephen when she became Virginia Woolf? That was the unsettling question. The event of marriage now stood before her like a wall of granite.

Virginia began writing *The Voyage Out* at about the time of Vanessa's marriage. A year later she said that as a writer, she would *discover real things beneath the show*, achieve symmetry through *infinite discords*, make harmony and wholeness out of *shivering fragments*. Exactly thirty years later she would bring these incongruities to their finest arrangement in *Between the Acts*. For it was in this posthumous novel that she finally dramatized the fusion of opposites she saw at the heart of life.

But where did the fragmentation and opposition originate? What inconsistencies held the foreground of her mind? Why should her perception of the world be polarized? Was it from the knowledge that what seemed impossible could indeed happen? Was it from seeing Thoby and Stella, both still in their twenties, follow their mother to her burial ground? Was it connected to those years of heartbreak and loss from 1895 through 1906? We have only to turn back to her writing of this period to infer the reasons for her gathering despair.

It was perhaps, more than anything, Vanessa's sudden marriage to Clive Bell and the sense of dereliction this produced that prompted Virginia to "preserve" Vanessa for herself by writing her "life" (published as "Reminiscences" in *Moments of Being*) in Playden in 1907. To write Vanessa's life, however, Virginia had first to recall and record the marriage of Leslie and Julia Stephen; and it was here in 1907 that the stark reality of their lives came home to her like a roll of thunder: it was, in part, the realization that whatever harmony there was between her father and mother was achieved *only* "by rich, rapid scales of discord, and incongruity." For both were difficult people. How often had Virginia heard her father complain of Julia's "contempt" for all his practical opinions. How often had she seen her mother, when pressed or angered, withdraw into withering silences. And what did this mean to one in the total helplessness of infancy?

But that was only part of it. The other disturbance—this one much harder to describe—was the difficulty she had seeing her mother as her father's wife. Virginia was deeply troubled by her mother's attachment to the man she herself loved so completely and so desperately wanted to satisfy. At her mother's death, she had offered her outstretched arms: her father would be hers now.* But he had ignored her in his grief, excluded her, and turned to Stella for comfort. That was part of what Virginia would all her life have trouble coming to terms with. Not until she wrote *To the Lighthouse* would she see the depth of the dissonance and the effort required to overcome it. It was also only after her mother's death that she saw her father as the tyrant

---

* There is a vague reference (to which emphasis has been added) in the trip to the lighthouse with James, Cam, and Mr. Ramsay sitting in the boat. Ramsay says to Cam: "Tell me—which is East, which is West?" Cam, of course, doesn't know and looks perplexed. Ramsay "seeing her gazing, with her vague, now rather frightened, eyes fixed where no house was Mr. Ramsay forgot his dream; how he walked up and down between the urns on the terrace, *how the arms were stretched out to him*" (London, 258). Woolf then shifts us back to Cam's perspective: "For no one attracted her more; his hands were beautiful to her and his feet, and his voice, and his words, and his haste, and his temper, and his oddity, and his passion . . ." (262). Those outstretched arms and the realization of Virginia's extraordinary attraction to her father can be dated to May 5, 1895, the night of Julia's death.

he would become in her 1907 reminiscences. For it was only then that she began to see the differences between surface features and the reality they concealed. Still, how could she love so profoundly a man who represented so much of what she hated? This was the unanswerable question she would carry with her through life. How did one explain loving one's oppressor?

Her father, for example, the distinguished Victorian man of letters, was respected by the intellectual world and loved by his peers. This was the "show." The "real thing beneath the show" was Leslie Stephen behind the closed doors of Hyde Park Gate; here he was "the tyrant of inconceivable selfishness," who openly, heedlessly trampled on the feelings of others, whose endless incantations of grief transformed his second wife into an "unlovable phantom." Here was the same sickly little boy who had once hurled a flowerpot at his doting mother.

In the memoir written near the end of her life, Virginia Woolf drew upon these early journals, and saw again the two separate, incongruous fathers under whose tyranny she so often raged and suffered. Surrounded at home by his nest of women, he was ferocious, egotistical, devouring; yet to the outside world he was all intellect and lovable eccentricity. To his younger daughter, however, he was the "tyrant father . . . the alternately loved and hated father" who did not cease dominating her life at his death in 1904; who continued to govern from the grave—the most unpardonable of all tyrannies. Living with him was like "being shut in the same cage with a wild beast." But Virginia was still his favorite, and he took special pains with her, made her feel that "we were in league together." It was precisely because she loved him so much that she found these appalling inconsistencies so bewildering.

Beside him in the family archive was the remote, enigmatic Julia Stephen, commemorated in *To the Lighthouse* by her daughter and eulogized in the *Mausoleum Book* by her husband. As in her life, so too after her death some inevitable mystery eddied around her memory. Like Leslie, she was full of contradictions, a complex personality—"a mixture of simplicity and scepticism . . . sociable yet severe." She was, above all to her younger daughter, unpredictable and "dispersed," a "general presence"—"impetuous," "imperious," "ruthless"—rather than a specific, benevolent mother to a child of seven or eight. "Can I remember ever being alone with her for more than a few minutes?" Once or twice perhaps, and it is worth noting that the first of those "few minutes" was associated with pain—". . . the scratch of some beads on her dress . . . as I pressed my cheek against it." To the child Virginia, Julia was a woman obsessed with charity, visiting workhouses, carrying on her increasingly frail shoulders a mantle of sickness and death; a woman so extended in every direction that she had neither time nor strength "to concentrate . . . upon me or upon anyone."*

Julia's inconsistencies were baffling; for how could a woman love her children and yet disregard them so wantonly by nursing the sick, wasting herself so carelessly in the back streets of St. Ives or in the slums of London. Wasn't her philanthropy futile? And how could a woman of such deep sympathy be so severe with her own children? How did one reconcile the charity with the futility of this profoundly depressed woman who believed so completely in life's sorrow, who saw living as an endless procession "towards death"? How had she maintained so crowded and vital a world and kept it spinning throughout Virginia's childhood? Just as bewildering were her two husbands, both much older than she, and entirely different from each other; the first married for love, the second out of compassion.

Leslie's relationship to Stella had only made matters worse. That Virginia had lost her father to another woman was bad enough. But to find her father and Stella, in Virginia's eyes, betraying the woman they had both worshiped was beyond belief. More than that, if Virginia had had her first vision of love in Stella and Jack, Stella's death had robbed that love of its authority, had made marriage morbid and menacing; just as Jem Stephen's love for her would always be linked to madness and violence. This was Stella's legacy to the fifteen-year-old Virginia in 1897; and one needed no magnifying glass to see that fear written large in the pages of *The Voyage Out*.

· · ·

* In an apparently biographical little story by Julia Stephen called "The Monkey on the Moor," set in St. Ives, "little Ginia" is characterized as a "wicked little girl" who has been very "mischievous" by burying her shoes and socks in the sand and has "to be carried all the way home with her bare legs like a little beggar girl." But "poor little [Ginia]" is abandoned after the first page of the story and is not mentioned again until the closing paragraphs, where she is "ill in bed"; they "had all quite forgotten [her]." Evidently even in illness this "wicked little girl" could be deserted by her mother (*Julia Duckworth Stephen: Stories for Children and Essays for Adults*, 47, 63. Karin Stephen, as a practicing psychoanalyst, would have much to say on the subject of childhood rejection, disappointment, illness, and attention-getting in *The Wish to Fall Ill: A Study of Psychoanalysis and Medicine*).

Julia appears to have been fully aware of the effect her absences had on her children. In a story called "Cat's Meat," the young children of Sir Robert and Lady Margaret Middleton run away from home to live among the indigent, because only then would they see their charity-minded mother: ". . . if we were really poor children," they tell her, "we *should* see you because you are always with the poor." Lady Middleton often came home "chilled and tired," for there was "so much to be done for the poor women and little children"; but even at home she often behaved "as if she had left part of herself somewhere else" (*Stories for Children*, 187, 167).

The world was no easy place to live in. Always, just over the horizon, lay the promise of illness or annihilation. There was something else, however, deeper, more private, never very far from Virginia's mind, a subject she could only brood over or talk about in whispers; and that was the truth about her mental stability. She had collapsed now three times—in 1895, 1904, and in 1910—and it looked as though she might now in 1912 go over the edge once more.

All her life Virginia suffered unpredictable mood swings, passed from "hot to cold in an instant." Always there was more than one Virginia. In the nursery there was the vivacious little girl who kept her sister and brothers rocking with laughter; and there was the shy and frightened Virginia, often trembling with fear of one kind or another. 'Ginia shouldn't be so nervous, her father would say when he caught her peeking out the window, waiting for her mother to return home at night from her "good works."

There were other childhood incidents that might have warned her parents that little 'Ginia was no ordinary child. One terrifying event she remembered vividly. She had come to a puddle of water in her path which, for no reason she could discover, then or later, had made everything unreal: "I was suspended; I could not step across the puddle; I tried to touch something . . . the whole world became unreal." This episode was powerful enough to find its way many years later into *The Waves*: "I came to a puddle. I could not cross it. Identity failed me," reflects the suicidal Rhoda. There was another, equally vivid memory of an idiot boy who "sprang up with his hand outstretched mewing, slit-eyed, red-rimmed." Without saying a word, with a "sense of the horror in me," Virginia handed him her bag of toffee. That night in her bath the "dumb horror" came over her again, and again she felt a "hopeless sadness," a sense of utter helplessness and passivity. These were her predominant feelings. In much of her childhood world, regardless of the many happy memories, always there was the vague, pervasive sense of being small and weak and unprotected.

There was madness on Julia's side of the family. Leslie had written in his memoir of "poor Mary Fisher's troubles"—two sons had suffered episodes of insanity. And on Leslie's side there was the brilliant, pathetic Jem Stephen, who in Virginia's version of the story, "ran naked through Cambridge" and was committed to a mental institution where he later died.

Even the calm, even-tempered Thoby had succumbed to irrational violence in March 1894, attempting to jump from a window at his preparatory school. He had been in bed with influenza when the incident occurred. The Master, Mr. G. T. Worsley, wrote to Julia that Thoby was suddenly "attacked with delirium and before the nurse could get to him he was half way through the window which he had smashed to shivers! Luckily I was within call and I soon quieted him and got him into bed again and barricaded the window." There was a second episode in April, when Thoby was at Hyde Park Gate being looked after by Julia.

There were other signs of instability in the family. Julia herself, most prominently after Herbert's death, exhibited chronic depressive symptoms. Both Adrian and Vanessa, at some time or other, suffered debilitating depressions. Adrian especially was given to moods of despair and burying himself in the family's past. The most dramatic reminder, however, was Virginia's half sister, Laura Stephen, the "vacant-eyed girl whose idiocy was becoming daily more obvious, who could scarcely read . . . who was tongue-tied and stammered and yet had to appear at table with the rest of us." Although Virginia saw Laura as an oddity, perhaps at Vanessa's prompting even as a joke, there can be little doubt that Virginia felt moments of silent terror about her own state of mind after her first nervous collapse in 1895.

The possibility of a "hereditary taint" in the family preoccupied Sir Leslie. Laura's maternal grandmother, Isabella Thackeray, fell into a profound depression after Minny's birth from which she never recovered. She had once tried to commit suicide by throwing herself over the side of a ship. Thackeray had finally no alternative but to conclude that Isabella's melancholy had "augmented to absolute insanity," leaving her "quite demented." With this family history Leslie did not attempt to conceal his blasted hopes for his "poor little Meemee." He recalled the time they had sent Laura to a kindergarten and the teacher informed him that Laura would never learn to read. This had happened about 1879, when Laura was perhaps nine or ten. Then, in April 1897, he turned to his convalescing daughter to find 'Ginia "devouring books, almost faster than I like." It was almost as if Virginia were showing her father she would never be compared to Laura. She knew how pleased he was seeing her read books no child her age could possibly understand. "I was a snob no doubt, and read partly to make him think me a very clever brat."

The letters between Julia and Leslie which Virginia read in 1904 for Fred Maitland while she was convalescing in Cambridge revealed to her the full impact of Laura's deficiency. Perhaps one of her greatest fears was what happened to mad people. As she was recovering from her most protracted collapse in 1915, she recorded in her diary what she had seen while out for a walk with Leonard: "On the tow path we met and had to pass a long line of imbeciles. The first was a very tall young man, just queer enough to look twice at, but no more; the second shuffled, and looked aside; and then one realised that every one in that long line was a miserable ineffective shuffling idiotic creature with no forehead, or chin, and an imbecile grin, or a wild suspicious stare. It was perfectly horrible. They should certainly be killed."

She might have been echoing Julia Stephen's writing in 1883: "Whether it be a benefit to themselves or to others that pauper lunatics should be allowed to have their miserable existences prolonged though they cannot be improved, we would not venture to say. No one who has witnessed physical or mental suffering in its hopeless stages can ... repress the longing that it may soon be ended ... who has not heard the devout mother express her hope that the Lord will soon remove her idiot child? Who has not heard the pious ejaculation that 'It was a happy release'?"

Nor could Virginia have failed to note in her father's letters to Julia his matter-of-fact endorsement of suicide. On board ship to America on June 6, 1890, Leslie wrote of a passenger who had taken his life by jumping overboard—"It seemed the poor wretch was off his head or had been drinking." Not having known the man, he could not properly feel much sympathy; but going overboard, he thought, was "a cleaner way of committing suicide than most." In another letter, dated July 11 on his return voyage, he wrote of a fellow passenger—a Mrs. Gray—with whom he evidently engaged regularly in conversation. Mrs. Gray "to my disgust did not come on deck till this afternoon. She explained that she had been in the blues, I don't know why, but we had a long and agreeable talk in the evening, when I tried to convince her of the expediency of suicide on certain occasions. She is a clever little woman, as well as pretty." In still another, this one from the Alps, he wrote: "I feel a respect for the Duke of Bedford. To shoot oneself and be cremated is doing things handsomely." Such were his sentiments about the taking of one's life. It was all a matter of course.

There is a scene in *Mrs. Dalloway* in which Septimus Warren Smith recalls having observed "a maimed file of lunatics being exercised or displayed for the diversion of the populace (who laughed aloud), ambled and nodded and grinned past him, in the Tottenham Court Road." When Virginia threw herself from a window in 1904, she must have felt much the same as Septimus when he plunged to his death, convinced that "human beings have neither kindness, nor faith, nor charity ... They desert the fallen." With the threat of madness hanging over her from the age of thirteen, it is understandable that she thought those who suffered from a mental illness "should certainly be killed." Being mad, being powerless and unprotected—this was what she feared most. This was perhaps the most dissonant sound in her crowded, often confusing range of experience, especially as the child of a mother and father who had little sympathy with mental disorder, who condoned suicide and euthanasia. How incongruous it must have seemed to see the Madonna-like Julia die of exhaustion at forty-nine, and the beautiful Stella at twenty-eight, and yet watch the mentally deficient Laura go on year after year in an institution.

18   The deaths of Julia and Stella transformed Virginia's sense of impotence into a stark and irreversible fact. Her early years, full of excitement as they seem to have been, were also a time of tension and turbulence. Despite all that was good and beautiful in the distinguished Julia and Leslie Stephen, it was impossible for Virginia not to register a certain disturbing irregularity and inconsistency in the dispensation of their love and attention. The link was very weak between her parents' protection and her own infantile sense of vulnerability. She grew up never quite certain her mother and father would be there when she needed them. As a child, the sense of powerlessness was further exacerbated by the deep divisions and contradictions she perceived in Julia's and Leslie's behavior. In order to keep herself "in league together" with her father, she had to be athletic enough to join him in his long, strenuous walks. But to get her mother's fleeting attention, she must be "ill or in some child's crisis." For people in good health made Julia feel irrelevant. "I at once put people away on a mental shelf when they are bright again," she had said to Leslie. When they recovered from illness, "I cease to think about them." So that as a child Virginia was forced to act separate and contradictory roles for each parent—robust in the morning, sick in the afternoon—if she was to attract any attention at all. How could a child make so divided a world cohere?

During her opening years as a writer she discovered that with words she could bridge the gap between reality and expectation, and through imagination bring them under her control. Sydney-Turner had once said that Virginia made "brilliant and imaginative pictures of things as they ought to be." Vanessa claimed that "Virginia since early youth has made it her business to create a character for me according to her own wishes and has now succeeded in imposing it upon the world." Virginia would learn that she could transform the Granite of "is" to the Rainbow of "ought to be." This was what she meant in 1908—making wholeness out of shivering fragments, making harmony out of dissonance. This was the way to conquer powerlessness.

In the memoir she wrote toward the end of her life, she lingered over the significance writing had for her. It was the need to discover "some real thing behind appearances"—almost the same words she had used in 1908 about needing "to discover real things beneath the show." And it was her tolerance for shock that helped to make her a writer. "I feel that I have had a blow," she said, "but it is not, as I thought as a child, simply a blow from an enemy . . . it is or will become a revelation . . . it is a token of some real thing behind appearances; and I make it real by putting it into words." She rearranged what "was" into what "should be" and in the process changed reality into something of her own making—a reality that "lost its power to hurt me." Through writing, through words, "I take away the pain." With words, she could transform life's "orts, scraps, and fragments," as she wrote in *Between the Acts*, into wholeness and harmony. This was how she gained ascendancy over the "shocks" that had earlier made her a helpless pawn. It was with words that she brought coherence to a life that was otherwise contradictory and hopelessly fragmented. And she discovered that any sorrow could be borne so long as she had pen and ink within easy reach.

As she read through her early journals many years later, she was reminded again of "the years 1897–1904, the seven unhappy years." But why was 1906 not included—the year of Thoby's death? Surely his loss was as pointless and brutal as the earlier deaths in this palimpsest of memory. We need only remember that Virginia—the writer—emerged at the end of 1904; that from 1905, as a journalist, she had achieved an acknowledged self—an "I" that was verifiable. From 1905 she was no longer a helpless child in a capricious and intractable world.

Her three published pieces at the end of 1904 were symbolic of an autonomy she had never known before. Thoby's death did not devastate her in 1906, did not plunge her into a terrifying state of psychic paralysis. She was grief-stricken, yes, but no longer defenseless. When the time came, she would resurrect his memory and give him a more permanent reality in *The Waves*. She would make his life "real by putting it into words."

"I cannot remember a time," said Vanessa Bell years later, "when Virginia did not mean to be a writer . . . She was sensitive to criticism and the opinion of the grown-ups." She remembered putting the family newspaper called *Hyde Park Gate News* on the table by her mother's sofa while Julia and Leslie were at dinner. As they waited, Virginia trembled "with excitement." Eventually Julia picked it up, looked at it, and pronounced it " 'Rather clever,' . . . But it was enough to thrill her daughter; she had had approval and had been called clever." This extraordinary excitement reveals the degree to which, even as a child, Virginia gauged her own worth by the value set on her inventions. If what she had written was "clever," then she herself must be clever as well. The need for approval found its way into the nursery at bedtime. At Vanessa's bidding, Virginia told stories until "one by one we dropped off to sleep." Entertaining her sister and brothers nightly made them her friends: she could entrance them, absorb their affection, feel safe and wanted—and all this from storytelling. Her stories were valuable. She would invent more. And like all storytellers, she needed listeners. Bernard in *The Waves* would confess, "Soliloquies in back streets soon pall. I need an audience . . . I need the illumination of other people's eyes."

Captivating an audience meant approbation—and power. Nowhere is this made more explicit than in an early typescript of *Pointz Hall*. Miss LaTrobe, after a performance of her play, "was happy; triumphant. She had given the world her gift—with a village pageant. Take it from me, she said, addressing the world humbly, yet confidently. The world had taken it." Her audience had seen and believed what she meant them to see. She had imposed her will.

As with Miss LaTrobe, so too with Virginia Woolf: no triumph was possible without an audience. When it accepted the work of art, it accepted the artist as well. Overtly, this or something like it was what the gift of fiction meant. So that her success in the nursery was no small victory. Her need for acceptance made her, in ordinary life, overly sensitive to what others felt, quick to sense what might amuse, what might offend. Many of her "shocks" can be traced to her uncommon responsiveness to others.

It was in childhood that Virginia felt the dissonance that made daily life so disruptive—Leslie's irrational behavior and Julia's endless disappearances. How untrustworthy and erratic they must have seemed to a precocious child of six or seven. Julia's impromptu flights especially represented to Virginia an irreparable fracture between *fact* and *feeling*. In the child's mind, feeling— "I want my mother"—was in constant collision with fact—"Your mother has vanished." One of the consequences of this split generated an almost endless sense of frustration: Fact and Feeling were forever out of synchrony, at odds, in discord.

With such frequent disappointment, it was easy for the child to think that "the good" was fleeting and "the bad" more or less permanent. It was natural, therefore, that a certain amount of fear should eventually infiltrate the business of daily life. It follows too that the more persistent the fear, the greater would be the tendency to escape to the realm of imagination, where *fantasy* and *feeling* could be brought together in perfect alignment.

There were other ways of avoiding frustration, the young Virginia was soon to discover. Storytelling was a solitary occupation. It meant living, temporarily at least, in an atmosphere free of dependency, expectation, and, most of all, disappointment—free of that terrible feeling of hopeless passivity. For, after all, the realm of fantasy was entirely of her own making. In the fictional universe, Virginia was Boss Omnipotent. Whatever she bid her imaginary people to say or do, they said and did. Omniscience and power were hers for the taking. Here no one could meddle, hinder, or hurt.

But there was an even subtler value in writing which Virginia discovered going into London society with George Duckworth. The evenings out, the dances, the social rounds George insisted upon were ordeals forced upon her: "I remember of these parties humiliation—I could not dance; frustration—I could not get young men to talk." In *The Voyage Out*, Rachel Vinrace "felt herself surrounded, like a child at a party, by the faces of strangers all hostile to her, with hooked noses and sneering indifferent eyes." In *The Waves*, Virginia dramatized more powerfully those social ordeals through the powerless Rhoda—the "door opens and people come . . . Throwing faint smiles to mask their cruelty, their indifference . . . I am thrust back to stand burning in this clumsy, this ill-fitting body . . . A million arrows pierce me. Scorn and ridicule pierce me . . . Hide me, I cry, protect me."

Yet through all this, Virginia had one "good friend" and "that good friend has never deserted me—the scene as a spectacle to be described later." Sometimes, she was later to confess, "I could even find the words for the scene as I stood there." Writing was thus her shield, a necessary protection. So long as she could anticipate pen and ink, she would survive the squirming, the terror, and the humiliation. For she remained always observant, taking mental notes which next day would be recast into the more permanent stuff of fiction. Words were her defense against pain.

These aesthetic transformations, reaching back to adolescence, appear to have become her deepest and most persistent motive for writing. As we move forward through her fifty-nine years, it becomes evident that those years of greatest stress were also periods of greatest productivity. The greater the tension, the higher she soared into the airy spaces of imagination. What she said in *To the Lighthouse* of Lily Briscoe's art, she might have said of her own: that the pen was "the one dependable thing in a world of strife, ruin, chaos." And the godlike power she felt as a writer is perfectly embodied in a passage from that novel. On the beach one of the Ramsay children is crouched over a little puddle of water: "Brooding, she changed the pool into the sea, and made the minnows into sharks and whales, and cast vast clouds over this tiny world by holding her hand against the sun, and so brought darkness and desolation, like God himself."

Virginia's feeling of exclusion at Vanessa's marriage caused her much unhappiness. "You dwell in the Temple," she said to Clive, "and I am the worshipper without." Her need to make a place for herself once more in Vanessa's life involved Clive to the degree that Virginia hardly wished for and found its way into her novel.

In its barest outline, *The Voyage Out* is the story of Rachel Vinrace, aged twenty-four, motherless, sailing on her father's ship with her aunt and uncle, Helen and Ridley Ambrose. Helen Ambrose, whom Clive correctly identified as Vanessa, is determined to educate her niece to the world of adult experience. Under her tuition Rachel meets and becomes attached to Terence Hewet (representing Clive Bell, in part). After an expedition inland with some of the tourists, Rachel develops a headache and fever (origin withheld), becomes delirious then intermittently comatose, and finally dies. Life goes on. The story ends.

As the tale unfolds, we learn that Rachel has emerged from a sheltered life and feels a need for privacy—a peculiar need for solitude mixed with a defiant need for independence. Her room at the Ambrose villa is a "sanctuary" as well as "fortress," and she tends to avoid attachments which jeopardize her freedom. Hewet's determination to know her she perceives as an intrusion: "Why did he sit so near and keep his eye on her? Why did they not have done with this searching and agony?" It is soon apparent that though Rachel doesn't know how to give love, she desperately wants to be loved. But whatever form it appears in, her freedom must not be violated. This must always come first.

One scene in the novel—the most peculiar and ambiguous in any of Virginia Woolf's fiction—focuses on the group's expedition up the Amazon. It brings into close range Rachel's mixed feelings for Hewet as well as her strange attachment to Helen. By this time in the story Hewet has declared his love and made a proposal of marriage. Together they have separated from the group and are walking alone. The published version—the *only* one Vanessa would have seen—reads as follows:

> Voices crying behind them never reached through the waters in which they were now sunk. The repetition of Hewet's name in short, dissevered syllables was to them the crack of a dry branch

... they never noticed that the swishing of the grasses grew louder and louder ... A hand dropped abrupt as iron on Rachel's shoulder ... She fell beneath it, and the grass whipped across her eyes and filled her mouth and ears. Through the waving stems she saw a figure, large and shapeless ... Helen was upon her. Rolled this way and that, now seeing only forests of green, and now the high blue heaven, she was speechless and almost without sense ... Over her loomed two great heads, the head of a man and a woman, of Terence and Helen.

Both were flushed, both laughing, and the lips were moving ... She thought she heard them speak of love and then of marriage. Raising herself and sitting up, she too realised Helen's soft body, the strong and hospitable arms, and happiness swelling and breaking in one vast wave.

An earlier draft of this scene, one that Vanessa (still in the role of Helen) *would not have seen*, begins with Helen pursuing Rachel:

Suddenly Rachel stopped and opened her arms so that Helen rushed into them and tumbled her over on to the ground. "Oh Helen, Helen!" she could hear Rachel gasping as she rolled her, "Don't! For God sake! Stop! I'll tell you a secret! I'm going—to—be—married!" Helen paused with one hand upon Rachel's throat holding her head down ... "You think I didn't know that!" she cried. For some seconds she did nothing but roll Rachel over and over, knocking her down when she tried to get up; stuffing grass into her mouth; finally laying her flat upon the ground, her arms out on either side, her hat off, her hair down.

"Own yourself beaten," she panted. "Beg my pardon, and say that you worship me!"

Rachel saw Helen's head pendent over her, very large against the sky. "I love Terence better!" she exclaimed.

The scene is violent and brutally explicit. And most unflattering to Vanessa. But this draft too was revised on December 21, 1912, about five months after her marriage to Leonard—another draft Vanessa *would not* have seen. It runs as follows:

Before Mr. Flushing could do more than protest, Helen was off, sweeping over the ground ... shouting Rachel's name in the midst of great panting. Rachel heard at last . . . and at once took to her heels. Terence stopped and waited for her. But she swept past him . . . pulling handfuls of grass and casting them at Rachel's back, abusing her roundly . . . Rachel turned incautiously to look, caught her foot in a twist of grass and fell headlong. Helen was upon her. Too breathless to scold, she spent her rage in rolling the helpless body hither and thither, holding both wrists in one firm grasp, and stuffing eyes, ears, nose, and mouth with the feathery seeds of the grass . . . "Own yourself beaten!" she gasped. "Beg my pardon!" Lying thus flat, Rachel saw Helen's head pendent over her, very large against the sky . . . "Help! Terence!" she cried. "No!" he exclaimed, when Helen was for driving him away. "I've a right to protect her. We're going to be married."

In this revision too, Helen's behavior is monstrous. There is no question of her relationship to Rachel; nothing is left for the reader to surmise. And Vanessa, of course, remains grotesque. We have only to compare these two revisions with the published version to see the extent to which Virginia Woolf transformed the scene into something misty and ambiguous. She must protect Vanessa's image—and thus protect herself perhaps—from so disturbing an imputation. And the ambiguity encourages a metaphoric reading. All of Helen's abusive handling of Rachel is now called into question and relegated to the shadows of fantasy. There is still some erotic turbulence, still a mix of sensuality and violence—only now it appears discontinuous, dreamlike; part of Rachel's distorting consciousness. In effect it appears hallucinatory. Now Helen is the *real* woman; Rachel the mere observer—passive, remote—in this bizarre love triangle.

By the end of the novel, we know that no sacrifice is too great to safeguard Rachel's tragically useless independence; an independence so assiduously achieved that intimacy is no longer possible, sexual passion no longer within her reach. It is enough to say that Rachel's dying at the end of the story is the price she has paid for deserting Helen and turning to Hewet. The novel thus biographically dramatizes the price Virginia thought she must pay for betraying Vanessa by turning flirtatiously to Clive.

But there is a complication in the story of Rachel's fatal illness. The onset of her headache coincides with Terence's reading *Comus* aloud. The virgin Sabrina in Milton's masque is Locrine's daughter and the stepdaughter of Gwendolyn, who in a fit of jealous rage orders Sabrina "to be taken and drowned in the river." And it is at this point in *Comus* that Rachel's head begins to ache, before she slides into her fevered delirium. The lines insinuate a connection between Rachel and the virgin and her death at the hands of her jealous and overpowering stepmother, Gwendolyn—not unlike Helen's role as the jealous and overpowering aunt. So that in a series of small clues scattered throughout the text Virginia Woolf hints that Gwendolyn was to Sabrina what Helen was to Rachel, and what Vanessa was biographically to Virginia. Gwendolyn's rage at Sabrina was like Helen's rage at Rachel. It represented Vanessa's rage at Virginia for stealing Clive from her. It was almost as if Virginia were recovering memories of many years earlier when both sisters struggled in the nursery over Thoby; or more recently, of Virginia's struggle with the surrogate-mother Stella for her father's love.

Virginia, however, insisted upon keeping Rachel's death ambiguous. We are never told explicitly the cause of her illness. No proliferating organisms are named, no jungle fever, no unwashed vegetables—though a good many readers and critics have read them into the text, as indeed they were intended to do. And just as the allusion to *Comus* insinuates a larger, more oblique meaning of the novel, so too does the ambiguity of Rachel's death move the story onto a plane where rationality has no meaning, where contradictory forces haunt the twilit, often lyrical regions of dream and delirium and fantasy.

Rachel's pledging herself to Hewet in marriage, coupled with Helen's withdrawal after the proposal, leaves Rachel overwhelmed and destined to a life filled with uncertainty. Her only recourse then, on a level below consciousness, is to protect herself; and protection in Rachel's sequestered world is synonymous with withdrawal—extreme withdrawal. It is a death consciously unresisted, unconsciously sought—a self-willed death. Just as one escapes a life too threatening to tolerate through periods of unconsciousness or madness, so too can one escape it in death. Rachel has paid with her life for the mistake of betraying Helen Ambrose, just as Virginia dies in fantasy for betraying Vanessa. It was a very high price to pay. But symbolically the ledgers were now balanced.

19 The Woolfs' honeymoon began a few days after the wedding at the Plough Inn in Holford, Somerset, where William and Dorothy Wordsworth stayed in 1797–98, while Coleridge was living close by at Nether Stowey. From England they meandered to the South of France and from there to Spain—to Barcelona, Madrid, Toledo, and finally

Valencia, from where they took a boat to Marseilles. They then wandered into northern Italy. Virginia wrote to Ka Cox in early September that she couldn't understand why people made so much of sexual intercourse. "Possibly my great age [she was thirty] makes it less of a catastrophe; but certainly I find the climax immensely exaggerated." From the pension Biondetti in Venice, Leonard wrote to Molly MacCarthy: "Virginia is very lazy, she's lying on the sofa eating chocolates and reading and looking at pictures ... She ought to be writing to you, but as I'm sure she won't before tea, I'm doing it for her."

They returned to Brunswick Square on October 3. By this time both Virginia and Leonard knew that physical intimacy would not be easy. She was not "frigid," as her passion for Vita Sackville-West would show a decade later, but she was physically cold and unresponsive to men. She would always have trouble returning someone's love, but would never cease craving the love others gave her. So that with a husband as sexually intense as Leonard, it must have crossed her mind that he might now cease loving her. Leonard had several times assured her that sex would never be primary. But she could not have been certain of that in the autumn and early winter of 1912; it is reasonable to assume therefore that her unresponsiveness to Leonard caused her a good deal of anxiety.

Vanessa informed Clive that the Woolfs were "a little exercised in their minds about the Goat's coldness. I think I perhaps annoyed her but may have consoled him by saying that I thought she never had understood or sympathised with sexual passion in men. Apparently she gets no pleasure at all from the act." Virginia had told Leonard she felt like a "rock" when he kissed her; so Vanessa's comment could not have come as a surprise; nor could he accuse Virginia of deceiving him about anything so fundamental to their marriage. And until 1913 Virginia, despite her sexual difficulties, still wanted (or thought she wanted) to have children.

She and Leonard also hoped to earn their living from writing, but realized that running 38 Brunswick Square was too time-consuming to make that possible. Accordingly, soon after their honeymoon Leonard, having just written a novel called *The Village in the Jungle*, needed immediate cash and accepted a temporary post as part-time secretary to the Second Post-Impressionist Exhibition, again organized by Roger Fry at the Grafton Gallery, where he remained until January 2, 1913. The Woolfs then left Brunswick Square and moved into rooms at 13 Clifford's Inn, intending to divide their time between their new lodgings and Asheham House in Sussex.

Virginia wrote to Violet Dickinson on the twenty-ninth of October, the eve of their move to Clifford's Inn. There would be a week of "intense misery," two weeks of "profound discomfort," and, about Christmas, "absolute happiness." There was a "little patch of green for my brats to play in . . . I'm writing hard." The "patch of green" makes her intentions of maternity clear. Whatever other adjustments were made, the possibility of having children had not yet been ruled out.

Both Virginia and Leonard found Clifford's Inn on Fleet Street an exhilarating place to live. The rooms were "incredibly ancient" and from the continual rain of "smuts" they were also incredibly dirty; but though Fleet Street was noisy, all they heard was the muted hum of traffic. On the weekends the entire area was deserted. For forty-eight hours almost all traffic stopped. Only an occasional policeman or solitary pedestrian might be seen. Each night they had their dinner across the street at an old city eating place called the Cock Tavern, where Tennyson was still remembered. The restaurant was secluded during the evening hours, with only a handful of reporters from the dailies and lawyers dropping in from the Temple.

Virginia was "writing hard," revising *The Voyage Out* for the fifth or sixth or seventh time. Leonard finished *The Village in the Jungle* and Edward Arnold accepted it for publication. "It's triumphant to have made a complete outsider believe in one's figments," Virginia wrote to another writer. But she was irritated by Leonard's work at the Post-Impressionist Exhibition. He had to deal with art lovers who either exploded with laughter or roared with fury before the works of Picasso and Matisse. The people who came to the gallery were "incorrigibly philistine" and their taste "impeccably bad." It could not have been a pleasant job, but Virginia, more than Leonard, did the complaining. She found artists an "abominable race" and painting an inferior art. The commotion they made over their bits of canvas was "odious." In July 1913 a whole crew of jobless artists would be employed by the Omega Workshops, an enterprise launched by Roger Fry to give them work designing, building, and decorating chairs, tables, pottery, and other such items. The workshop was located in Fitzroy Square, and, after Roger, Vanessa and Duncan Grant would soon become its most influential artists.

Throughout the late autumn of 1912 and early winter of 1913, Virginia's novel was presenting what seemed to her insurmountable difficulties. She was writing the last chapters of *The Voyage Out* "for the tenth or, it may have been, the twentieth time." She was agonizing over the expedition scene and Rachel's death. In December the headaches returned. They went to Asheham for Christmas. Virginia needed a rest. The intensity with which she had driven herself was tortured and exhausting. In January Vanessa joined her there. And Leonard, still suffering bouts of malaria, was writing his second novel, *The Wise Virgins*, inevitably about Virginia and Vanessa. He had also begun to study the history of co-operation. His interest in the Women's Co-operative Movement was triggered by his growing friendship with Margaret Llewelyn Davies, its secretary.

In early 1913, the troubled question of Virginia's having a child came up again. With her headaches and now insomnia as well, he began on January 13 to keep a diary in which he recorded, minutely, all the details of her daily health. He noted symptoms of headache, sleeplessness, nervous irritability, refusal to eat—all the danger signals that augured an approaching breakdown. Shortly after that, he began making his entries in cipher, a code consisting mainly of Tamil and Sinhalese letters. As Virginia struggled on with her final revisions, Leonard himself began to investigate the possibility of her bearing a child. He spoke to Dr. Savage first, who dismissed the idea of danger entirely: "Do her a world of good, my dear fellow; do her a world of good!" But Leonard by this time no longer trusted Savage's judgment and went on to consult Maurice Craig, T. B. Hyslop, and Jean Thomas. Unable to get some consensus, he finally persuaded Virginia of the danger. "We aren't going to have a baby, but we want to have one and 6 months in the country or so is said to be necessary first," she said to Violet, cloaking in jest the seriousness of the matter.

On March 9, after reading through the manuscript of *The Voyage Out*, Leonard delivered it to Gerald Duckworth's publishing office in Henrietta Street and soon after that he and Virginia went on a tour of the industrial north; it was work for the Women's Co-operative Movement. As they visited one factory after another in York, Liverpool, and Manchester, witnessing every kind of "horror and miracle," Virginia began worrying once more about the book. They had heard nothing about it from Gerald. She was sure he had rejected it—"which may not be in all ways a bad thing."

On April 12, she went herself to Henrietta Steet and was told by Gerald how pleased he would be to publish it. His reader, Edward Garnett, had written a favorable report. But it's fair to assume, wrote Quentin Bell, "that she immediately had misgivings ... A book is so much a part of oneself that in delivering it to the public one feels as if one were pushing one's own child out into the traffic." Her anxiety became fierce. It was a worry no amount of reasoning could spirit away. Sleepless nights were followed by lingering headaches and deepening melancholy. Suddenly her novel, the whole "meaning and purpose of her life," might be jeered at, laughed at, ridiculed. There was nowhere to turn. A ravaging depression was imminent. To forestall catastrophe, Leonard decided it was better to spend as much time at Asheham House as possible. She was still writing reviews and articles for *The Times*

Literary Supplement but she could do those in the country. Leonard now saw to it that she would lead as healthy a life as he could manage.

In late April, she wrote to Vanessa that at nine o'clock "I begin to undress, Leonard then fetches me a great tumbler of milk which I wallop down. Then sleep 8 hours—then lie down in the afternoon—then bask in the garden." Like her father, Virginia needed the care and protection of someone whose devotion was unquestioned, and Leonard filled the bill to perfection. Being needed so much must have seemed to him almost as good as having his love returned.

There was no confinement this time, only precaution. When they returned to London, they saw friends and went to the theater and the opera. Her ears were dulled and her brain "a mere pudding of pulp," she said in the middle of May, after sitting through Wagner's *Ring* with all its "bawling sentimentality"; and she seemed well enough to accompany Leonard when he lectured on economics and politics to Co-operative Societies in the provinces. On June 9 they went to Newcastle-upon-Tyne to attend a Women's Co-operative Congress. When they returned to London on the twelfth, Virginia was just well enough to join Leonard at a luncheon to meet the Fabian Socialists, Beatrice and Sidney Webb.

Although they spent increasingly more time in Sussex, Virginia's health was rapidly deteriorating. By the middle of July Leonard consulted Dr. Savage, who advised a two-week rest at Jean Thomas's nursing home in Twickenham. Virginia entered on July 25 and was rational enough to write Leonard letters, pining for home and his company. "I do love you, little beast," she wrote on August 3, "if only I weren't so appallingly stupid a mandril. Can you really love me—yes, I believe it, and we will make a happy life." She added on the following day: "Nothing you have ever done since I knew you has been in any way beastly—how could it? You've been absolutely perfect to me. It's all my fault."

On August 11, she was moved to Asheham, where they would remain until the twenty-third. They planned then to go on holiday to the little village of Holford in the Quantocks, and to stay at the Plough Inn, where they had begun their honeymoon—perhaps not an altogether wise choice of accommodation. No sooner had they settled in at Asheham, however, than the serious trouble began, and continued for twelve days. Leonard could see that Twickenham had failed. If anything she was worse—depressed, sleepless, delusory, anorexic. By this time Leonard had observed her closely enough to know that in this state she might try to kill herself. What would he do if she made an attempt at the Plough Inn in the tiny village in Somerset, where there was no one to summon for help? To go there as planned was surely tempting Providence.

On the morning of August 22, the day before departure, they went up to London, intending to stay with Vanessa in Gordon Square. In the afternoon Leonard went alone to Savage to explain the situation. But once again the urbane, ever-confident Savage brushed aside Leonard's fears. If Virginia was in fact as bad as he said, to tell her suddenly she was not well enough for a holiday would certainly throw her into suicidal despair. Leonard left Savage's office filled with dread.

At Gordon Square he repeated his worries to Vanessa and Roger Fry. They agreed that a holiday at the moment was too risky. Roger suggested that Virginia be taken to Dr. Henry Head, not only a brilliant physician but an intelligent man—in fact, an intellectual. If anyone understood Virginia, he certainly would, far more at any rate than Savage evidently did. Arrangements were made and within an hour Leonard was explaining his predicament for the third time. Dr. Head saw the difficulty but maintained that if Savage had said she could go, then go she must, risky as it was. With rest and food and peace and quiet, her symptoms might gradually subside. Above all, however, Leonard must arrange to have some "second line of defence against an attempt at suicide." If he saw her depression deepen or her condition veering out of control, he must remove her at once to London and bring her to Head's office. In the meantime Leonard must keep him informed on how the holiday was progressing.

And so on August 23, having just observed their first wedding anniversary, off they went to the village of Holford, where Coleridge had composed "The Rime of the Ancient Mariner" a century earlier. The Plough Inn was the same in 1913 as it was in days gone by—the Somerset breakfasts as hearty, the joints as succulent, the cider as brisk. But Virginia was also just the same. She gave no sign of improvement. People were laughing at her, she said. Her body was grotesque. Food was repulsive. Like Septimus, she felt herself the cause of everyone's troubles. Leonard kept some veronal for sleep, and gave her some. By the seventh day he could see she was only getting worse.

Before leaving London, Leonard had arranged that Ka Cox should join them in Holford if the need arose. By the end of their first week, Leonard was exhausted. He wired Ka on September 1. She arrived on the second. Matters disintegrated further. Virginia's despondency deepened. She scarcely ate. Her nights were sleepless. He must induce her to return to London to see a doctor. That would be the hardest part. For as with every other episode of illness, Virginia insisted that nothing was wrong. She was not ill. Why couldn't Leonard see that? Eating and resting just made her fat and uncomfortable. Why did Leonard refuse to understand that?

Patiently, slowly, deliberately, he explained the need to return to London—to return to London to see a doctor—any doctor she chose. If the doctor said she was not ill, Leonard would rest his case and trouble her no longer. Was that fair enough? If, however, the doctor pronounced her ill, she must accept his verdict and undergo whatever treatment was prescribed. Was all this understood?

After some argument, Virginia agreed. She would submit. She would go to Dr. Head. Leonard thought it a miracle that she should even name the man Roger Fry had recommended. What Leonard may not have sensed at the time was the odd father-daughter bond that had been growing between Virginia and Roger since 1911. And there was something else—Roger *still* looked after his wife, Helen Coombe, now incurably insane, who had been in an asylum since 1910. If Roger recommended Head, then Virginia would go to Head.

An appointment was fixed for September 9. They left Holford on September 8—it would have been Thoby's thirty-third birthday. Leonard could see as they returned to London that Virginia was in the "blackest despair." During their consultation, Dr. Head convinced her that she was ill, but if she followed his advice, she would soon be able to read and write again. She must agree, however, to go to a nursing home. Virginia remained silent. They returned to Brunswick Square to spend the night in Adrian's rooms.

Leonard had committed a violation of doctor-patient protocol in seeking Head's advice without first telling Savage. And so, leaving Virginia in the care of Ka Cox, he went off with Vanessa to see Dr. Savage. They were still in his office when at 6:30 the telephone rang. It was Ka. She had just discovered Virginia in a deep sleep. Leonard raced back to Brunswick Square to find her unconscious, her breathing labored and heavy. He guessed immediately what had happened. He had forgotten to lock the medicine chest in which he kept the veronal tablets. She had discovered them and swallowed a lethal dose. He called Head.

As it happened, Maynard's brother, Dr. Geoffrey Keynes, a house surgeon at St. Bartholomew's Hospital, had taken over Leonard's rooms at 38 Brunswick Square. With Leonard in the passenger seat, Keynes tore through the streets of London to the hospital to get a stomach pump. "The drive," wrote Leonard many years later, "like everything else during those days, had the nightmare feeling about it. It was a beautiful sunny day; we drove full speed through the traffic, Geoffrey shouting to policemen that he was a surgeon 'urgent, urgent!' and they passed us through as if we were a fire engine."

The small medical team at No. 38 were soon in a frenzy of work pumping Virginia's stomach until one in the morning. At 1:30 she was still close to death, but Leonard, by now exhausted, dropped off to sleep and was awakened by Vanessa at six o'clock. Dr. Head returned at nine—it was now Wednesday, September 10—and found Virginia practically out of danger. She remained comatose until Thursday. On Sunday Leonard wrote to Lytton Strachey that Virginia had regained consciousness, and that there was "every reason to believe that by tomorrow or Tuesday no effect of having taken the veronal will remain." Her state of mind was the same as it had been at Holford, but she was now "inclined to see that it is illness and nothing moral. She remembers everything . . . and talks quite calmly about it." In fact, she was bearing up courageously.

Another letter was written that Sunday, September 14, this one from Jean Thomas to Violet Dickinson: "It is the novel which has broken her up. She finished it and got the proof back for correction . . . [she] couldn't sleep and thought everyone would jeer at her. Then they did the wrong thing and teased her about it and she got desperate—and came here [to Twickenham] a wreck. It was all heart rending . . . They will blame Sir George [Savage] probably, but they have never really done what he advised, except get married."

No doctor in 1913 would run the risk of leaving a suicidal patient in a private facility, and this was the problem Leonard Woolf immediately faced. It was customary at that time to certify anyone in Virginia's condition. The procedure, wrote Leonard, took place before a magistrate who, on a doctor's certificate, "made an order for the reception and detention of the person either in an asylum or in a nursing home authorized to take certified patients." Leonard's heart sank when he inspected the huge dark mental homes which had been recommended. The doctors agreed not to certify her if he could arrange to take her to the country accompanied by two or three trained nurses. Asheham House was out of the question; it could not accommodate that many people living in. It was also too inaccessible should another emergency arise.

George Duckworth stepped in at this moment and offered Leonard the use of Dalingridge Place, a large, luxuriously appointed, fully staffed house near East Grinstead. It seems odd that Vanessa and Leonard should agree to accept Duckworth's hospitality if he was in fact, as they seemed to think, Virginia's childhood sex abuser. One would have thought that in Virginia's state, Dalingridge was the last place on earth to bring her. But that is exactly what they did. On Saturday, September 20, Ka and one nurse went ahead, followed by Leonard, Virginia, and a second nurse. By this time Virginia's condition had grown worse than ever. She had completely lost touch with everything around her; she was outside the world and beyond time, starving, sleepless, alternating between violent excitement and profound melancholia. The worst problem during the first week was food. She was convinced that she was fat and ugly, that there was something disgusting about food and eating. When the nurses came near her with meals she grew violent. They must leave her alone! Had Leonard not taken endless hours coaxing one spoonful of food at a time, at all three meals each day, she would probably have died of starvation just as her cousin James Kenneth Stephen had twenty-one years earlier at St. Andrew's Hospital. And just as he had sat in his enclosure, wildly suspicious of some conspiracy against him, or silent and sunk in the blackest melancholy, so Virginia sat at Dalingridge for hours at a time, overwhelmed in misery, hopeless, responseless, in some wilderness of her own.

By this time Leonard had given up on Dr. Savage and saw him only occasionally in later years as a gesture of courtesy. He now began consulting Dr. Maurice Craig, a leading Harley Street specialist in neurological disorders. The medical profession was still in its infancy where nervous diseases were concerned. No one had the slightest idea of the nature or cause of Virginia's trouble. Everyone agreed that she suffered from "neurasthenia"; but as far back as 1894, Sir George Savage had amused members of the British Medical Association by saying, "I am inclined to think that if I gave, in brief only, the many symptoms which are attributed to neurasthenia . . . there are very few of my audience who would not be inclined to believe that they have got it themselves." His colleague, T. C. Allbutt, former Commissioner in Lunacy, said in 1910, "To make neurasthenia everything is indeed to make it nothing." With so many symptoms ascribed to neurasthenia, it became almost impossible to maintain its existence as a discrete, recognizable disorder.

At the time of Virginia's collapse, however, there was a type of mental illness known as manic-depressive psychosis. "People suffering from it," wrote Leonard Woolf, "had alternating attacks of violent excitement (manic phase) and acute depression (depressive). When I cross-examined Virginia's doctors, they said she was suffering from neurasthenia, not manic-depressive insanity." Yet in all the months he observed her, he noted the bipolar nature of the illness, always alternating between extreme opposites. In one stage there was depression, starvation, suicidal urges; at another stage were violent excitement, wild euphoria, ceaseless volubility—the "raving mad" stage. There were times during these weeks at Dalingridge when she was so hostile toward Leonard

she refused to see him. She was as violent with her nurses. Regardless of
what the doctors said, Leonard concluded, Virginia was indeed suffering from
manic-depressive disorder.

The weeks passed and Virginia began slowly, intermittently, to feel a little
better. The "manic" days gradually became fewer and she could be made to
eat a little. The days also got quieter and the nights more restful. So that at
last, after two grueling months—on November 18, to be exact—Leonard was
allowed, after much consultation, to move her to Asheham. He was required
to take two nurses with him. They settled down in Sussex and remained
there in nearly full residence until August 1914. He gave up the rooms in
Clifford's Inn and Virginia improved sufficiently to have only one nurse in
January. By February 1914 the second nurse was also discharged. Leonard
had occasionally to go up to London on business and it was during these rare
separations that Virginia wrote the few letters to him that remain. In one of
them, dated December 4, 1913, still believing that her illness had some moral
provenance, she wrote: "I wish you would believe how much I am grateful
and repentant." In another, she implored her "Dearest Mongoose"—Leonard
himself—to "be a devoted animal, and never leave the great variegated creature [Virginia herself]. She wishes me to inform you delicately that her flanks
and rump are now in finest plumage, and invites you to an exhibition."

With Virginia's suicide attempt, Duckworth & Co. put off the date of
publication of *The Voyage Out*; and although there seemed to be some improvement in the new year, the horizon was still gray and uncertain. More,
and worse, was still to come. When Virginia's breakdown exploded into a
major catastrophe, Vanessa wrote to Leonard, "I'm afraid you're having a
very bad time of it just now . . . I am sure she will get quite right again but
you'll need patience for months I expect . . . you looked to me frightfully tired.
But it's no use saying this for you haven't much choice as to what you will
do." She was right. He had no choice, and he had no choice because neither
Vanessa nor Adrian had warned him about what he was getting into in
marrying Virginia. Her insanity "was clothed, like some other painful things
in that family, in jest." It had been swept up in lighthearted phrases like "the
Goat's mad" or the Goat's "off her head." It is unlikely that being told about
Virginia's illness would have influenced his decision to marry her, but allow-
ing him to proceed in ignorance was inexcusable on Vanessa's part and selfish.
A married Virginia would no longer hang round her neck like an albatross.
Vanessa was now largely free from future responsibility. And Leonard found
himself in the worst crisis to date, learning day by day how to keep Virginia

alive and himself from going "off his head"; for in the early part of 1914, after months of close and uninterrupted surveillance, he too began having "violent and disabling" headaches.*

Adding to Leonard's troubles was Sir George Savage's annoyance at the way he had solicited additional medical assistance. Sir George understood his anxiety and why he sought further and younger advice. "I am not professionally jealous," he wrote, "but that, while I was supposed to be looking after her, several others were also being consulted without reference to me caused me pain. This was made greater when another specialist was called down and I heard nothing from anyone."

Leonard was also having troubles with his family over his second novel, *The Wise Virgins*. The new book was about a young man (Leonard) and a young woman (Virginia) and a conflict in values between the world of Bloomsbury and the world of Putney; that is, the Stephens and the Woolfs were poised against each other in a fictitious setting. He sent the manuscript to his sister Bella, who responded with a nine-page critique, harshly condemning much of it as an unpardonable attack on the Woolf family and their Putney neighbors. His brother Philip liked the book but was depressed by the accuracy of Leonard's portrait of their mother.

Marie Woolf herself finally read the manuscript and returned it with a very explicit letter: "My dear Leonard," she wrote, "I am returning you the manuscript ... which has given me more pain than evidently you intended ... You thought fit to hold us all up ... to ridicule, contempt and pity ... You have not convinced me one jot that the people at Rickstead [Putney] are one bit less valuable to the common working of the Universe, than the people at Bloomsbury. I don't know what the Lawrences [Stephens] are developing into in your next chapters but as far as I have made their acquaintance I have discovered nothing especially attractive, useful, or great. That God had made the Ladies [Vanessa and Virginia] tall and beautiful, was not their fault ... No, Leonard, this style of writing is unworthy of you, you can do better, if only you would give first preference to the finer part of your nature and intellect. If you publish the book as it stands, I feel there will be a serious break between us."

.   .   .

* In 1967 the Hogarth Press published Leonard Woolf's *A Calendar of Consolation: For Each Day of the Year a Profound, Original, and Often Surprising Quotation*. The Quotation he chose for Virginia's birthday, January 25, was Charles Dickens's "Anythin' for a quiet life," from *Pickwick Papers*.

The early months of 1914 were often clouded by setbacks and false hopes. Virginia was far from recovered. She could read a little, but serious writing was forbidden. Whenever Leonard had to be in London for a day or two on business, either Ka Cox or Janet Case or Vanessa came to Asheham; but the strain on him was beginning to tell. His headaches became so incapacitating that by March it was necessary to go on a ten-day break to Marlborough, Wiltshire, where he stayed with Lytton Strachey.

Lytton amused him during this respite by indulging in gossip and reading him sections of "Cardinal Manning," which would eventually become the first of his *Eminent Victorians*, published in 1918. (Lytton had already engaged Virginia briefly to typewrite the manuscript of his "naughty novella" called *Ermyntrude and Esmeralda*, an erotic exchange of letters satirizing the sexual hypocrisy of the English Establishment.) Leonard slept well, ate "hugely," and took long walks. During this absence, he wrote to Virginia daily. "Sometimes in the last few days," he wrote on March 11, "I've thought it may be a bad thing to love anyone as much as I love you . . . Listening to Lytton and Norton, I sometimes almost hugged myself to think what you are to me and I to you."

Clive Bell's *Art* was published in March, marking him now as a serious art critic; and Leonard's *The Wise Virgins* was accepted, again by Edward Arnold. By April both Virginia and Leonard were well enough to go to Cornwall for three weeks. Virginia was not fully recovered: she still suffered from delusions and was nervous around strangers. Food and sleep continued to be a problem, but the nostalgia associated with Cornwall calmed her "jangled mind and nerves."

They returned to Asheham House on May 1, and for the next three months Virginia resumed her routine existence of "milk, green fields, early bed, and contemplation." Leonard was with her all of this time except for two Co-operative Guild Conferences, when Janet Case came to stay with her. "It's quite clear from what [Dr.] Craig said," Leonard wrote to Janet Case, "that Virginia cannot be left completely alone yet, and . . . it naturally depresses her to feel that I get people to come here when I want to go off." Craig had warned him that Virginia would deteriorate very rapidly if she were left on her own.

The declaration of war on August 4, 1914, might not have happened at all so far as Virginia was concerned. Certainly it had little or no effect on her slow recuperation. On August 6 they went to the Cheviot country in Northumberland for a month's holiday, staying at the Cottage Hotel in Wooler until September 4. From there they crossed the border to Coldstream for a further ten days, renting rooms from a woman "appropriately called Miss Scott."

20

In the middle of September Leonard began looking for a place for him and Virginia to live. Virginia wanted to stay in London, but Leonard firmly refused. The excitement of the city would be bad for her. He concentrated his efforts on the outskirts, and eventually found temporary rooms at 17 The Green, Richmond, run by a Belgian woman, Mrs. le Grys, "an extremely nice, plump, excitable flibbertigibbet, about 35 to 40 years old." They moved in on October 16 and sent for the furniture and books they had in storage. It was a comfortable house and far enough out— ten miles from Bloomsbury—not to entice Virginia. After more house-hunting in the vicinity of Richmond, they found, toward the end of the year, in Paradise Road a large handsome eighteenth-century house with paneled rooms and a large garden. It had been divided into two separate dwellings: Suffield Place (named after Lord Suffield, who built it in 1720) and Hogarth House, the part they wanted. Matters were left to stand; no firm plans were made.

During the remaining months of 1914, Virginia continued to improve, reading and helping Leonard with his new book on international government the Fabian Society had commissioned. Her medical expenses had been enormous, and although she and Vanessa regularly received a little money from Stella's marriage settlement, she considered herself "the wife of a poor man." Thinking she ought to have some domestic skill, Virginia enrolled in a cooking school. The institution was in Victoria Street, she said to Janet Case, and run by an "adorable" young woman who had canine eyes and was "really stupider than I am." There were a few gray-haired ladies of "great culture and refinement, dabbling in the insides of chickens . . . I distinguished myself by cooking my wedding ring into a suet pudding!"

By December she was well enough to see a few friends for short periods, take walks, go to the library, and occasionally attend a concert. Leonard was especially anxious to avoid Bedford Square and Lady Ottoline's parties. With

Virginia's recovery he was able to give more time to his own writing and to the political activities which interested him. He was now being asked increasingly to speak on co-operation and international relations. And so the days passed. They spent a weekend in Wiltshire in a cottage Lytton had lent them and celebrated a quiet Christmas near him at Marlborough. On January 1, 1915, Virginia began keeping a diary which she would inscribe with few interruptions for the remainder of her life.

The first interruption, however, came on February 15 with the longest and most harrowing of Virginia's psychotic episodes. There had been no signs of danger except for the nervous anticipation of the March 26 publication of *The Voyage Out*. Otherwise the year had begun well. Leonard was writing a pamphlet on arbitration* for the Fabian Society, as well as lecturing to the women of the Co-operative Movement and working closely with Margaret Llewelyn Davies.

Virginia often went out on her own to the London Library, and when Leonard was occupied she went alone to the Sunday afternoon concerts at the Queen's Hall. On the afternoon of January 17, for instance, she recorded going to Queen's Hall and staying for "three beautiful tunes"—the "tunes" being a Bach Brandenburg Concerto, the César Franck symphony, and Edouard Lalo's *Symphonie Espagnole*. She also liked to explore the streets and squares of London, which she did by the hour, and later record her observations. In her diary she kept herself in practice writing exercises and little gossipy scenes, such as Marjorie (Gumbo) Strachey's unfortunate love affair with Josiah Wedgwood of the famous Staffordshire family, a married man and the father of seven children; or Molly MacCarthy's equally unfortunate eighteen-month affair with Clive Bell; or the difficulties of a servant girl unable to resist the charm of the British army.

At about this time Virginia was finally allowed to read *The Wise Virgins* and found it a remarkable book, "very bad in parts; first rate in others." It was a writer's book; only a writer could see why the good parts were so good and the bad not "so very bad." The novel pleased her. It revealed Leonard's "poetic side," the side that got "smothered" in politics and pamphlets.

January 25 was Virginia's thirty-third birthday. Leonard "crept" into her bed with a little parcel which contained a green purse. He later brought up breakfast and a three-volume edition of Sir Walter Scott's *The Abbot* inscribed:

---

* This would become his influential book *International Government* (1916), used by the British Government in its proposals for a League of Nations.

"V.W. from L.W. 25th Jan. 1915." It was indeed a "very merry" morning; in the afternoon she was "taken up to town, free of charge, and given a treat, first at the Picture Palace, and then at Buszard's [tearoom] . . . I was also given a packet of sweets to bring home." They decided that day that if Hogarth House could be had, they would take it. They also agreed to invest a little money in a small printing press.

Two days later she told Janet Case that her friends would praise her novel to her face and condemn it behind her back, as indeed it deserved to be condemned. Had Leonard been aware of this remark, he would have become immediately watchful. It was an early sign. If he had read her diary he would have seen a number of other strange, uncharacteristic comments. A house they were looking over, for instance, had rooms "rank with the smell of meat and human beings." This was followed by others: "I begin to loathe my kind, principally from looking at their faces in the tube. Really, raw red and silver herrings give me more pleasure to look upon." Something was brewing, an odd pressure was building up and being stored in her diary. "I do not like the Jewish voice; I do not like the Jewish laugh." "I can imagine . . . how she [Mrs. Sydney Waterlow] cursed that dreadful slut Virginia Woolf." This was not the voice of the sane Virginia Woolf. These remarks were like escaping gas from a balloon about to explode. Her last words were written on February 15. She would not open her diary again until August 1917, two and a half years later.

On February 17 Leonard accompanied Virginia to London for a dentist's appointment. Later they went to see about the printing press they'd thought of buying. Everything seemed fine. The next day, however, February 18, she suddenly developed a severe headache. At once, Leonard began the treatment of rest and food, with veronal at night for sleep. Shortly afterward—it might have been February 22 or 23—he came to her room as she was having break-fast in bed, and suddenly, without any warning, she became very excited, distressed, as if something frightening were happening, as if the clock had suddenly begun to spin backward. Her mother was in the room. She became more agitated and remote by the minute. This, Leonard wrote, was "the beginning of the terrifying second stage of her mental breakdown . . . com-pletely different from, almost the exact opposite of, the first stage"—the de-pressive, suicidal stage of the autumn of 1913.

In a day or two the symptoms subsided, and Virginia, thinking she had avoided the crash this time, and all it had previously cost emotionally and materially, wrote Margaret Llewelyn Davies on February 25. It was a letter of thanksgiving. "I am now all right though rather tired . . . And I wanted to say that all through that terrible time [in 1913] I thought of you, and wanted to look at a picture of you, but was afraid to ask! . . . It seems odd, for I know you so little, but I felt you had a grasp on me, and I could not utterly sink. I write this because I do not want to say it, and yet I think you will like to know it." This was followed by two more letters to Margaret, now dictated to Leonard, with a postscript by him saying he thought Virginia "a little better."

But Virginia was not a little better and she was not getting better. Nature was just taking its time, gathering terrible hurricane force. On March 4, with renewed violence, she plunged once more into chaos; and almost immediately, Virginia passed beyond Leonard's care. Trained nurses had to be called in. This was the most terrifying period of illness yet. Daily, hourly, it seemed, she grew worse. She was violent with the nurses, violent with Leonard, and soon entered a phase of garrulous mania, as Leonard described it, talking incessantly, without pause for two or three days, ignoring or not hearing anything said to her. On the first day her speech was still intelligible, the words still meant something, the sentences still coherent. Then gradually her speech disintegrated to a jumble of disjointed sounds. This went on for another twenty-four hours, until the meaningless chatter diminished and she descended finally into the shadowless regions of coma.

Generous as she was, Mrs. le Grys, the landlady, was not about to convert her house into a lunatic asylum. Measures had to be taken. More help was needed. Accustomed to emergencies, Leonard acted quickly and correctly. As soon as Virginia was in a nursing home on March 25, Leonard took possession of Hogarth House, their new residence. He was badly in need of money and applied to Jack Hills for help. Would Jack immediately send the hundred pounds Virginia received quarterly from Stella's marriage settlement rather than wait until the end of March? "The expenses with nurses &c. are so heavy and much of it one has to pay at once." The year past had left them with very little money, "but if the £100 can be paid earlier I can get along for a month or two."

Leonard then had their furniture and books transported to Hogarth House, persuaded the servants from Asheham (Annie the cook and Lily the parlor maid) to come live in Richmond, and engaged four professional nurses, two by day and two by night, who were in attendance and ready when Virginia was brought home on April 1.

The move to Hogarth House took place on March 25, and *The Voyage Out* was published on March 26. It would be many weeks before Virginia reentered the real world to register these two important facts. The next two months were desperate. Unlike the soundless suicidal melancholy of 1913, April and May of 1915 were filled with deafening screams and terrifying rage. Leonard was again the chief object of Virginia's abuse. For two months he dared not face her lest he arouse the irrational fury that threatened to rip open at any moment. "She is worse than I have ever seen her," he wrote to Violet on April 28. "She hasn't had a minute's sleep in the last 60 hours."

Dr. Craig was pessimistic. There were times when Leonard was certain Virginia would never regain her sanity. His only hope was not to have her certified and placed in an asylum; and as long as the nurses tolerated her behavior there was no immediate danger of that. Though he did all he could to maintain his own sanity, Leonard "seemed to have reached a state when he didn't much care what happened," Vanessa wrote to Roger Fry on May 27. Jean Thomas, who knew Virginia's case intimately, was not very sanguine. She was certain Virginia would never be the same again. This opinion was evidently shared by Vanessa too; in another letter to Roger on June 25, she said that her sister seemed "to have changed into a most unpleasant character." Virginia refused to see Leonard, but worst of all, she had "simply worn out her brains." It showed in her letters, which had always been so brilliant. Those of the past year or two had become dull, commonplace, by comparison. What would become of Virginia if she could no longer write? It was inconceivable.

By late June, under the best medical supervision Leonard could find, Virginia began slowly to show signs of recovery. Dr. Maurice Craig had several times come to Richmond from London and seemed reassuring. By August, when Leonard was able to take Virginia out in a wheelchair, they had reduced the number of nurses from four to two; and from September 11 to November 4 they lived at Asheham House with only one nurse and the two servants. The one remaining nurse was allowed to go on November 11, when Virginia was at last declared out of danger. She emerged from her illness fatter, dazed, and looking pathetically vulnerable.

Jean Thomas had told Violet Dickinson in September 1913 that Virginia was terrified "everyone would jeer at her" when the book came out. The little

'Ginia who stood trembling with excitement over her mother's verdict of a piece of childhood writing was the same Virginia who now stood trembling with the horror of rejection. For she was one of those people who equated work with Self—the writer with the written. So that if her novel was attacked or misunderstood or minimized, it was in her mind Virginia Woolf herself who was attacked, misunderstood, minimized. It was as though she herself would be led by a jeering crowd on March 26 to some public square to be humiliated, so fused in her mind had Virginia Woolf and *The Voyage Out* become.

Though she would not know this for many months to come, the novel was well received. *The Times Literary Supplement*, the most influential of the major journals, said her people were "brilliantly drawn—particularly that aunt [Helen Ambrose], who is so real and baffling." The *New Statesman* singled out the characters' sophistication and introspection; the *Spectator* predicted that some readers would "hail the author as a genius and the story a classic." A good many reviewers commented on Rachel's illness in the concluding chapters. "No reader," said one, "will ever forget her description of a girl's bewildered falling into the depths of love or of the unbelievable approach of death."

There were some unfavorable reviews. That was to be expected; but when she was well enough to see them all, it must have been clear to Virginia that not only had she survived the ordeal, she had triumphed as well. She had imposed her will; her readers had seen what she wanted them to see. She had offered her gift (like the future Miss LaTrobe) and it had been accepted. Most important of all, her book had not been seen as the raving of a lunatic. Her small departures from narrative convention were not the inventions of a disordered mind. Her novel was sane. It was the work of a *sane* woman. Her worst fear was at last dissipated.

She had also survived the ordeal of marriage, and Leonard, apart from being her husband, had become and would remain the principal mainstay in her life. Even though there would be no physical intimacy, it was clear that he loved her profoundly. When all this settled in her mind in the ensuing months of recovery, the figures of Clive and Vanessa and even Violet Dickinson would all assume different positions in the intricate constellation of Virginia's emotional life. She could never tolerate losing people; so with each new inroad Leonard made into her life, those upon whom she had relied in the past would undergo some readjustments to accommodate for Leonard's insistent priorities.

Despite the zeppelin raids over London on moonlit nights, 1916 was a quiet and sheltered year for Virginia. She was allowed to read and occasionally write a review for *The Times Literary Supplement*, but many of her friends were scattered. Ka Cox was in Corsica caring for Serbian refugees. Clive Bell had settled as a farm laborer at Garsington, now Ottoline Morrell's country retreat; he had also fallen in love (and would remain so for many years) with Mary Hutchinson, wife of the barrister St. John Hutchinson. Duncan Grant and David (Bunny) Garnett, both also pacifists (and now lovers too), took jobs as fruit farmers in Suffolk, where Vanessa kept house for them. Maynard Keynes and Saxon Sydney-Turner were both at the Treasury dealing with the intricacies of wartime spending. And with what time she could spare, Virginia looked for a farmhouse where Vanessa, Duncan (her lover also since 1913), and the two children could live.

In early May, Duncan and Bunny Garnett both appeared before the local tribunal in Suffolk. Part of Bunny's case for military exemption was that his mother had been a lifelong pacifist who had visited Tolstoy in Russia.* The chairman, thinking Tolstoy was a town, refused their claim. They were, however, finally exempted from service on the condition that they work as farm laborers for the duration of the war. They were not permitted to remain in Suffolk, where they were self-employed. This led them to Charleston, where they were hired by an established farmer four miles from Asheham House.

When Leonard with his permanent hand tremor saw that he might be called to service, he consulted the doctor who had tried and failed earlier to treat his condition. But more important, it would have been disastrous to Virginia if Leonard was drafted. He was therefore provided with a letter he produced at his medical examination. "Mr. L. S. Woolf," it said, "has been known to me for some years and has previously been under my care. Mr. L. S. Woolf is in my opinion entirely unfit for Military Service and would inevitably break down under the conditions of active service. Mr. L. S. Woolf has definite nervous disabilities, and in addition an Inherited Nervous Tremor which is quite uncontrollable." Virginia characteristically added a little zip to the story in her letter to Ka Cox. Leonard, she said, "went before the military doctors trembling like an aspen leaf, with certificates to say that he would tremble and has trembled and will never cease from trembling."

Leonard's brothers Cecil and Philip were in the military. In the following year Cecil would be killed and Philip wounded—both from the same shell. But here at Asheham and now in the summer of 1916, the war had no appreciable impact on his or Virginia's life, save for fuel and food shortages.

* Constance Garnett was Tolstoy's English translator.

Occasionally, from the downs above Asheham, they could hear the pounding of guns in France.

At about the time Virginia and Leonard were moving to Richmond in October 1914, Adrian married Karin Costelloe. He had stayed on at Brunswick Square for a while and although he'd studied law, he was still without a career, and would remain so until 1919, when he and his wife entered the medical profession and became practicing psychoanalysts. Karin Costelloe was a graduate of Newnham College, Cambridge, where she now held a research fellowship. Her sister Rachel (Ray), a women's rights activist, was married to Lytton's brother Oliver Strachey. As a conscientious objector, Adrian was required to engage in farm work, but there was a hitch. He was six feet five inches tall and not very sturdy. Any form of strenuous manual labor, his doctor said, would put a dangerous strain on his heart. He was thus freed from farm work as well as military service.

Virginia had never been at ease with Adrian, nor he with her. He was too shy even to tell her he'd liked *The Voyage Out*. At any rate, his marriage seems to have changed him a little in Virginia's eyes. She was tolerant of Karin and perhaps even a little fond, the way one is fond of a bushy-haired schoolboy with a barnyard appetite. Leonard, however, was intolerant of both, but of Karin in particular. During her pregnancy, she and Adrian came to stay for a few days at Asheham. Shortly after their departure, Leonard ventilated himself in a letter to Lytton Strachey. He didn't like "these pregnant women," he said. "Karin has the appetite of ten horse-leeches. For seven days I tried to fill her up and make her refuse something. I increased the helpings until I thought no human being could possibly stand it. She blew and puffed and heaved and swelled but it all went down; so I told Virginia to order a very heavy suet pudding for lunch and when it appeared, I heaped Karin's plate." Halfway through the meal, she put her fork down, sighed, and a "curious twitching appeared to take place about the stomach and abdomen. We sat expecting either an explosion or a premature birth, but after another deep sigh, she finished her plate of suet."

Leonard couldn't see why Adrian married her, but Virginia could. Adrian had always felt himself an amateur among professionals, and Karin did her best to block that "outsider's" feeling. She provided him with a home, children, and all the flutter of daily life, so that to all appearances he was "just like other people." Virginia shared some of his feelings. This was perhaps what made them so shy with each other when they were alone. With others present they got along better. Adrian had told Virginia a little about Karin—

how deaf she was; how depressed her deafness made her; how she often felt that people lowered their voices on purpose. All of it was painful, but Karin had vitality; and it was precisely this vitality that gave Adrian "a good deal of the stuff of life, which he does not provide for himself."

In the middle of September, Virginia and Leonard went to Cornwall. Margaret Llewelyn Davies and her companion Lilian Harris went with them on this two-week holiday. They made rather an odd party, the four of them, Virginia said to Vanessa. Miss Harris was "an old creature of 50, extremely sensible and unselfish . . . who smokes a pipe, and lives alone in lodgings." When Margaret got worked up she called her "John" and Miss Harris called Margaret "Jim." Miss Harris, Virginia reported to Sydney-Turner, apart from smoking eight pipes a day was also very fond of "good wine and cigars" and wanted to meet him. Would Saxon oblige and come to tea?

They returned to London in October, and Virginia resumed once more her quiet life. Occasionally she went with Leonard into London to borrow books from the public library. Often they went to tea with Bloomsbury friends at the Omega Workshops in Fitzroy Square. And it was about this time that Virginia began holding monthly meetings at Hogarth House of the Women's Co-operative Guild's Richmond branch. It was her job to engage speakers, and by tapping the talents of a good many friends, she managed to keep the talks lively and interesting. Leonard, for his part, was becoming influential among the Fabians, especially in international relations. Before the year was out he was invited to serve as Secretary to the Labour Party's advisory committees on international and imperial questions, a post he eventually accepted.

During the autumn Vanessa, Duncan, and Bunny Garnett moved from Suffolk to Charleston in Sussex, which would eventually become Vanessa and Duncan's permanent home. In October two Slade students appeared on the scene who would become Leonard and Virginia's friends. One of them, Dora Carrington, was called simply Carrington by her friends; and she adored Lytton Strachey. The other was Barbara Hiles, with whom Saxon Sydney-Turner was in love. As it happened, Carrington, Barbara, and Bunny Garnett, one day in early October, were on their way to look over Charleston, where Bunny and Duncan were to live with Vanessa while they worked on a neighboring farm. When the three found themselves without a place to sleep for the night, they made their way to Asheham and broke in. Leonard and Virginia were furious when their caretaker reported the incident to them. Virginia immediately wrote to Carrington and asked her to Hogarth House to explain herself—and to dine. Explanations were eventually offered by all three in their turn, and a year or two hence, when the Hogarth Press was established, each would make a contribution that more than compensated for the damages incurred in their escapade: Carrington with woodcuts, Barbara with typesetting, and Bunny with a number of small services.

It was Virginia who found Charleston, a farmhouse about a mile from Firle. It was a large dwelling with a vegetable garden and fruit trees—and four miles from Asheham "so you won't be badgered by us." When Vanessa finally took occupancy in October, Leonard began to have grave doubts about the move. His first fear was that Virginia would be forever going to Charleston to be with Vanessa, and an eight-mile roundtrip walk was far more exercise than her doctor thought good for her. She was already losing weight too quickly. Then there was the fear that Vanessa would surround herself with a group of young, irresponsible art student—"cropheads" Virginia called them—who were noisy, untidy, and with too flexible a moral sense. Breaking into Asheham House confirmed that fear, certainly, and Leonard was not anxious for a repeat performance, nor indeed of having such people as his neighbors.

He made no effort to conceal his disapproval of Vanessa's way of life, which was "a trifle ramshackle, a little desperate." The roof of Charleston would not only cover the heads of Vanessa's lover Duncan, and Duncan's lover Bunny, but also of the two children living there. And the prospect of having Julian and Quentin and their nurse constantly making their way to Asheham for one thing or another Leonard did resent and said as much to Virginia. Asheham was after all their "retreat," the place they went to for rest and quiet. Too much talk could still land Virginia in bed with excruciating headaches, and that Leonard would not tolerate. He was thus put in the disagreeable position of dictator, tyrant, and "family dragon." It was his job to discourage visitors, shorten visits, subdue excitement. His law enforcement created a good deal of friction and certainly more than one argument. But Virginia, however much she protested, knew he was right.

21 By 1917 Virginia was reviewing more frequently for *The Times Literary Supplement* and Leonard, apart from his increasing involvement in politics, was now writing *Empire and Commerce in Africa*. They both worked hard during the week and over the weekend left time for what they called a "treat": a long bus ride through London, a leisurely walk along the river, tea in Hampton Court, a stroll through Kew Gardens. They had inherited Roger Fry's two servants: Nelly the cook and Lottie the housemaid, who stayed with them for many years despite endless squabbles. But having help meant seeing people again. Guests came to Richmond for lunch or dinner and spent the night.

During this interval, Virginia's health became more stable, and she had either begun or was about to begin a new novel called *Night and Day*. When she was writing fiction, her concentration was intense, and Leonard, always watching for signs of exhaustion, witnessed her absorption. Although she worked only in the morning from ten to one and generally typed out in the afternoon what she had written by hand in the morning, she never stopped working. All day long, whether she was walking through London or on the Sussex downs, "the book would be subconsciously in her mind or she herself would be moving in a dream-like way through the book." It was the intensity of her concentration that made writing so exhausting. Throughout her life she kept two kinds of writing going on simultaneously, fiction and criticism. After a stretch of work on a novel she would turn to criticism for relief, "because, though she devoted great care and concentration to even a comparatively unimportant review, the part of her mind which she used for criticism or even biography was different from what she used for her novels."

It had occurred to Leonard some months earlier that if he could find some occupation that would engage Virginia enough to take her mind off writing, they would both profit immeasurably. And so one day he suggested they learn the art of printing. Virginia had already as a youngster learned some of the rudiments of bookbinding, but the idea of creating a book filled her with excitement. Her medical expenses had been so high, though, that even the cheapest printing press available was beyond their means. Even if they could afford a press, moreover, printing was strictly regulated and only a limited number of trade union apprentices could be trained. Neither obstacle stood in their way for long, however.

On one of their walks up Farringdon Street—the day was March 23, 1917—they passed the Excelsior Printing Supply Company, and in its window were some printing implements. Both stared "like two hungry children gazing at buns and cakes in a baker shop window." They found that not only could they buy a printing machine and type and all the rigging but also that a sixteen-page instruction manual accompanied the apparatus. There was no need to go to a printer's school or to become an apprentice, so long as they could read and follow directions. By the time they left the shop, Leonard and Virginia found themselves owners of a small handpress, some Old Face type, and all the necessary gear for the sum total of £19 5s. 5d.

When the equipment was delivered on April 24, they set up the press on the dining-room table and after a month acquired sufficient skill to set up and print an entire page of a book. This was the beginning of the Hogarth Press. Within the next twenty years the Press would become one of the most prestigious in England and claim a roster of authors the best publishers in Europe and America would have been proud to have on their lists.

The Woolfs devoted what little spare time they had to becoming not only printers and publishers but their own authors as well. Leonard wrote a story called *Three Jews* and Virginia's was called *The Mark on the Wall*. These first two works became Publication No. 1 of the Hogarth Press. Carrington was asked to do four woodcuts. On May 3 they began printing an edition of 150 copies of this thirty-two-page pamphlet which they bound themselves. They made a small additional investment in Caslon Old Face Titling for printing the covers, and drew up a circular offering their first number for 1s. 6d. net, explaining that the Press proposed to print other such items that "would have little or no chance of being published by ordinary publishers."

This was no small victory, and Leonard, clearly, was hooked. So was Virginia. Becoming her own publisher would significantly influence her as a novelist. It would make all the difference in the world to write whatever she liked and to experiment however much she chose—and not worry about "editors, or publishers."

The success of their first venture encouraged them to go on to something more ambitious. First they planned to buy a larger press with their income tax refund, but that plan would not materialize for another few years. In the meantime Virginia's attention was drawn to a young short story writer, Katherine Mansfield. Mansfield had been publishing stories for seven years and since 1911 had been associated with the critic John Middleton Murry. Lytton Strachey had been Lady Ottoline's weekend guest at Garsington when he met her for the first time. She had spoken highly of *The Voyage Out* and wanted to meet its author.

This had all happened somewhat earlier. Virginia now lost no time getting her to write a story for the Press. It would be an enormous undertaking, however, because what Mansfield offered them was a sixty-eight-page story called *Prelude*. A small edition was planned nevertheless, and Virginia herself set all the type. But it was too long for Leonard to machine. That part of the operation would have to be done at a nearby jobbing printer called McDermott. Once again, the Woolfs did all the advertising, hand-binding, packing, and dispatching with no outside help.

This was more work than two people with other primary occupations could do. Leonard was still editing, lecturing, and writing on international relations. Virginia was again reviewing regularly, writing *Night and Day,* and trying generally not to exhaust herself. For however hard they worked side by side, Leonard kept one watchful eye on her, and the slightest danger signal brought his immediate intervention.

Air raids over London driving them to the cellars night after night did not lessen the pressure of their daily lives. But more than once Leonard was "in rather a state again" because Virginia was not leading as quiet a social life as she should have. When he began lecturing to Co-operative Societies in the north, Virginia wanted him to know just how much she depended on his care and equally how much she could be trusted. Her letters reveal an obedient child writing to a harsh, uncompromising guardian: "I promise faithfully to do everything as if you were there [at Asheham]." "I have rested and done everything as if you were here. It's no good repeating that I adore you, is it?" "I am drinking my glass of milk and ovaltine as I write . . . and slept perfectly . . . and then had a hot bath; and then walked for 5 minutes on the terrace . . . I eat exactly as if you were here, and I think it's done me good."

What is so remarkable about these few letters, something which would have been more apparent had they separated oftener and more letters passed between them, is their familiar ring. They might indeed have been written by Leslie to Julia, sending her one of his daily health bulletins. For in matters of health, as in so much else about her, Virginia bore the unmistakable imprint of her father; and just as Leslie depended upon Julia, so Virginia depended on Leonard. He was now in exactly the same custodial position that Vanessa had once occupied, and just as Virginia could not bear to be separated from Vanessa, so could she not tolerate Leonard's few and brief separations.

Katherine Mansfield had gone to Asheham in the middle of August 1917, and stayed from Saturday to Wednesday. There is scarcely any record of how she and Virginia got on except that they walked and talked a great deal. Seven weeks later, on October 9, Leonard took a proof of the first page of *Prelude,* and on the following evening Katherine dined with them. This time she did not, apparently, make a very favorable impression. Virginia thought she stank like a "civet cat," seemed "hard and cheap"—a regular street-walker—yet "intelligent" and "inscrutable." At the end of the evening a munition worker called Lesley Moore (the pseudonym of Ida Constance Baker) came to fetch Katherine—"another of these females on the border land of propriety, and naturally inhabiting the underworld."

S. S. Koteliansky, a Ukrainian Jew, had come to England in 1910 and knew Katherine Mansfield and her circle. When he met the Woolfs in January 1918 he had a lot to say about her—"not all to her credit," noted Virginia. According to Koteliansky, Mansfield lied and posed a lot; and her writing, he thought, was second-rate. "I don't know that this last pleases me however, though it sounds as if I wrote it down for that reason."

Mansfield was suffering from tuberculosis and periodically left England for a warmer climate. In March 1918 she had a hemorrhage in France and had to be brought home by her companion Middleton Murry, who up until this time was not bound to her legally. She had married George Bowden on May 1, 1909, and left him on the morning of May 2, but remained nevertheless technically his wife. It was not until April 1918 that her divorce from Bowden was made absolute. On May 3 she and Murry were married (though they had been living together since 1912) and on the ninth they lunched with the Woolfs. Katherine was her usual "marmoreal" self, pretending her marriage to Murry was "a matter of convenience." She looked terribly ill and, Virginia found, was not an easy person to know.

Prelude was published in July in an edition of 300 copies. According to Leonard's business accounts, 247 copies were sold. Virginia had set almost every one of the story's sixty-eight pages and when it was dispatched took a moment to assess the achievement. *Prelude* was a little "vapourish . . . and fully watered with some of her cheap realities"; but still it bore the trademark of a serious writer. When the now-famous story "Bliss" came out in August in the *British Review*, Virginia was less sympathetic. It was a failure—thin, superficial, and impoverished in conception. It was not the work of an "interesting mind." She wrote badly too, and the effect was "to give me an impression of her callousness and hardness as a human being."

The real truth was, Virginia saw for the first time a rival of consequence in the art of fiction. The one thing Katherine was guilty of as far as Virginia was concerned was her excessive sentimentality. Apart from that, though their fictional worlds were very different, they created them in much the same way—obliquely, through insinuation and allusion, always skirting the central idea; building up scene and character cumulatively through sound repetition, visual image, and resonating metaphor. When she had a clearer sense of her own method, Virginia would acknowledge this; and when Katherine died she would recognize her for the kindred spirit she was.

But in 1918 there was the new press to launch, writers to discover, weekly reviews to write, and *Night and Day* grown now to over 100,000 words. By late November Virginia reached a state she'd never known before. When there was no book to review, she was free to turn to her novel. Writing for her own press became a cushion against futility. It was the surest means she had of coping with life. But it was also a writer's "curse" to need acceptance so desperately; to be floored by "blame or indifference." The one thing she must remember was that "writing is after all what one does best; that any other work seemed to me a waste of life; that on the whole I get infinite pleasure from it; that I make one hundred pounds a year; and that some people like what I write."

Virginia Woolf's diary was important to her, and entries like this were usually made after it had been neglected and she suddenly needed a place to siphon off excess nervous energy. "Since I am back ... and waiting for Leonard I had better assuage my fretfulness with pen and ink." "Another lapse in this book, I must confess it," she had written earlier; but if she wrote against her will, she would begin to loathe it; "so the one chance of life it has is to submit to lapses."

Virginia liked the diary better than letter writing. There was usually an "awkward moment" between coming home and dinner which was its "salvation." Often she couldn't settle down to reading; and writing seemed the best channel for the unsettled "irritable condition one is generally in." She liked doing character sketches fresh after an interview; but that too presented problems. When people came to tea, she couldn't very well say to them: "Now wait a minute while I write an account of you." They left and it was too late to begin. And often when she was brimming with ideas and descriptions "meant for this page I have the heartbreaking sensation that the page isn't there."

But when there *was* time, when the page *was* there, and her pen *was* poised in readiness, she could make quick character sketches of extraordinary penetration. Here is a miniature of Clive, for example, done in three brief installments. "Clive starts his topics—" she begins, "lavishing admiration and notice upon Nessa, which doesn't make me jealous as once it did, when the swing of that pendulum carried so much of my fortune with it." "On Sunday," she continues later, "Clive came to tea ... and we spent an hour or so in gossip. When one sees Clive fairly often, his devices for keeping up to the mark in the way of social success and brilliance become rather obvious. We were all talking of the 17 Club:* upon which he rapped out 'I was among the haughty who wouldn't join when they were asked, now of course I find it's the thing to do, and I've had to climb down' the truth being that he wished to join and was blackballed by Leonard and others. Such would be the truth of many of his stories I daresay . . . His habits are like those of some faded beauty; a touch of rouge, a lock of yellow hair, lips crimsoned." In her third installment, Clive was in his "best man-of-the-world vein . . . and inclined to think himself one of our foremost. He sent me his book [*Potboilers*], where I find myself with Hardy and Conrad . . . He babbled and prattled and hinted at all his friends and parties and interests . . . He gives, or wishes to give the impression that he sits drinking in the Café Royal with Mary [Hutchinson], and the young poets and painters drift up, and he knows them all, and between them they settle the business. His book is stout morality and not very good criticism. He seems to have little natural insight into literature. Roger declares that he doesn't know about pictures." Such was the devastating sketch of her brother-in-law who, ten years earlier, had been her literary mainstay, her most valued critic.

Harriet Weaver, who financed a periodical called *The Egoist*, had published James Joyce's *A Portrait of the Artist as a Young Man* in installments and later in book form. In 1918, with T. S. Eliot as her assistant editor, she wished to arrange the publication of Joyce's *Ulysses*, the first episode of which her printers had set in type but (open to prosecution under the law of obscene libel) refused to print. Eliot had suggested to her that the Woolfs might accept the book at the Hogarth Press.

Miss Weaver acted on his suggestion and on a fine April day in 1918 made her way to Hogarth House with the explosive manuscript under her arm. Virginia, apart from her interest in Joyce's novel, used the occasion to add a new sketch in her portrait gallery. "I did my best to make her reveal herself, in spite of her appearance," wrote the insatiably curious Virginia, "all that the Editress of the Egoist ought to be," but without effect. Miss Weaver remained "inalterably modest, judicious and decorous. Her neat mauve suit fitted both soul and body; her grey gloves laid straight by her plate symbolised domestic rectitude." Conversation was difficult, the pauses awkward. "Possibly the poor woman was impeded by her sense that what she had in the brownpaper parcel was quite out of keeping with her own contents." How on earth had she met Joyce? What did she hope to gain promoting his work? She was certainly not competent from the business point of view. "We both

* The 1917 Club, located in Soho, was newly founded; its membership consisted mainly of left-wing politicians and Bloomsbury intellectuals.

looked at the MS. which seems to be an attempt to push the bounds of expression further on, but still all in the same direction. And so she went."

Although she found the language shocking, Virginia saw vaguely what Joyce was trying to achieve. His "method," she said to Lytton Strachey, consisted chiefly of "cutting out explanations and putting in the thoughts between dashes." Yet they were willing to publish *Ulysses*. Leonard searched for a printer but no one would touch it. Two large printing firms said publication of the novel would certainly lead to prosecution. So in the end, they had to turn the novel down.

Virginia would in time revise her initial impression of the book. Only later would she appreciate Joyce's essential inwardness, his repeated violations of mechanical time, and his effort to render the content and flow of human consciousness. In the early 1920s, when the Hogarth Press began publishing the translations of Sigmund Freud, she would better understand the methods by which Joyce achieved his peculiar concentrations of introspection and subjectivity.

The year thus far had been productive. They had published Katherine Mansfield's *Prelude* and, stimulated by Lytton Strachey's enormously successful *Eminent Victorians* (published in May), Virginia finished a draft of *Night and Day* on November 21, in addition to writing an experimental piece called *Kew Gardens*. Leonard was now editing the *International Review* and deep in the writing of *Empire and Commerce in Africa*. The final months of the year ended auspiciously with the Armistice on November 11 and the birth of Vanessa's baby, Angelica, on Christmas Day. Duncan Grant was her father.

On November 15, a few days before the completion of Virginia's second novel, T. S. Eliot came to dine at Hogarth House in Richmond. Virginia had never met him before. Mr. Eliot "well expressed his name," she wrote in her journal. He was a "polished, cultivated, elaborate young American" who talked very slowly and was clearly an intellectual—serious, intolerant, with strong opinions—who thought highly of James Joyce. He brought several of his own poems for the Woolfs to look at—"the fruit of two years, since he works all day in a bank, and . . . thinks regular work good for people of nervous constitutions." As the evening wore on, Virginia became increasingly conscious of "a very intricate . . . framework of poetic belief; owing to his caution, and his excessive care in the use of language, we did not discover much about it." What she did discover was that he believed "in observing all syntax and grammar; and so making this new poetry flower on the stem of the oldest."

After dinner, Eliot read aloud the poems he had brought with him, and these they agreed to publish in the spring. It would be the third of two other slim volumes already planned: Murry's *The Critic in Judgment* and Virginia's *Kew Gardens*. So that on May 12, 1919, the Hogarth Press would publish simultaneously three separate titles of two already important writers; Virginia's and Eliot's volumes were printed and bound by hand; Murry's piece, owing to its length, had to be sent out for printing. The next few months would be busy, and it was during this interval that Virginia began visiting Katherine Mansfield regularly. "What a queer fate it is—" she wrote in her journal, "always to be the spectator of the public, never part of it. This is part of the reason why I go weekly to see K. M. up at Hampstead, for there at any rate we make a public of two."

22 Shortly after finishing *Night and Day*, Virginia slipped into a mild depression, pronounced enough not to pass unnoticed. They discussed the cause of her melancholy, and she was reassured by Leonard, "so that here I sit comfortable and secure; once more established in that degree of belief which makes life possible." Regardless of how "reassured" she was, however, she was still incapable of sitting idle. The manuscript of *Night and Day* was not submitted to Gerald Duckworth until April 1; she had consequently to rely on book reviews and articles to keep herself busy writing and "afloat."

Even her work at the Press was not enough. She was now reviewing two or three books a week for *The Times*. "It fills up the time while Night and Day lies dormant." For some reason, however, she was always racing against the clock, no matter how much time she allotted herself. "I write and write; I am told to stop writing; review must be had on Friday; I typewrite till the messenger from the Times appears; I correct the pages in my bedroom with him sitting over the fire here."

This little confession sounds as if she purposely engineered an atmosphere of rush and inconvenience; as if intentionally creating a situation that made her appear busier than she was, in demand, holding up the press of a major journal. So that if her piece was not up to her standard, well, she'd had too much pressure exerted; she'd been sent too much work. Regardless of the circumstances, somehow she must find herself in the middle of chaos, at the center of some confusion. Perhaps it was her way of testing others' feelings for her, or measuring her own worth; perhaps it was some variation of the excitement she felt as a child awaiting her mother's approval. Whatever the cause, it was to become her modus operandi, and the key to this maneuver is in her admission that "this sort of writing is always done against time; however much time I may have." As she grew older, this tendency penetrated many of her personal relationships and created difficulties that might have been avoided, that sometimes forced people who deeply cared for her into a state verging on alienation. It was as though she needed to test their loyalty or love at regular intervals. It was the insecure child in her clamoring for assurance—just as her nervous, thin-skinned father kept plucking for reassurance at Julia's sleeve.

After making final corrections Virginia handed *Night and Day* over to Leonard. This was on March 20. Leonard spent two mornings and two evenings reading the manuscript and then gave her his frank appraisal, a system they would follow for the rest of her life. A few days later she wrote in her diary: "I own that his verdict, finally pronounced this morning gives me immense pleasure: how far one should discount it, I don't know." It was, she knew, a more "finished" book than *The Voyage Out*; still she didn't "anticipate even two editions." It is not clear from these contradictory statements exactly how Virginia herself felt about this novel. Quentin Bell explained that *Night and Day* was, and "was intended to be, a fairly pedestrian affair." Virginia was in a sense testing her skills to see if she could write a "perfectly orthodox and conventional novel." If that was her aim, she succeeded in full measure. Her motives were probably mixed, however, and we can assume that *Night and Day* was regarded as a piece of apprenticeship she must endure before graduating to larger, more intricate designs. Once she'd taken that fence she would be free to experiment. She would proceed along the lines of *Kew Gardens*, and Leonard would be there to judge. First, however, she must get through the exercises of conventional form and style.

She delivered the manuscript to Gerald Duckworth on April 1. They had a little "half domestic, half professional" meeting in his office. She didn't like his "Club man's view of literature." But Gerald was reassuring. He would almost certainly want to publish the novel; and with the book off her hands she began to feel unanchored once more. She had just finished a long novel. Was she content? Had something worthwhile been achieved? Was she happy? But—"what, I wonder constitutes happiness? I daresay the most important element is work." Gerald had just sent his acceptance letter. He had read the novel "with the greatest interest." She was perhaps more relieved than pleased, for the "first impression of an outsider, especially one who proposes to back his opinion with money, means something."

The Hogarth Press was now in the thick of the publishing season. "Murry, Eliot, and myself are in the hands of the public this morning," she wrote on May 12, feeling depressed. She reread *Kew Gardens* and found it "slight and short." Why had it impressed Leonard so much, she wondered? His judgment prompted her to reread *The Mark on the Wall* and in that too she found "a good deal of fault." The worst part of writing was that "one depends so much upon praise." She was sure there'd be none for this story, and "unpraised, I find it hard to start writing in the morning." Orders came in for Murry and Eliot—"and not me." But whatever the story's fate, it was the writing that mattered. Work alone, words, made the business of living tolerable.

She was in for a surprise, however. While they were away at Asheham, *Kew Gardens* had been enthusiastically reviewed by *The Times Literary Supplement* (on May 29). So that when they returned to Richmond in early June they found the hall table piled high with orders for *Kew Gardens*. There were over 150 which they opened all through dinner. "And then ten days ago I was stoically facing complete failure." There was also a letter from Macmillan in New York, so impressed by *The Voyage Out* they wanted to read *Night and Day*.

The first edition of *Kew Gardens* sold out immediately and a second edition was ordered. The flurry of publicity had also resuscitated interest in *The Mark on the Wall*, and that too was reissued in an edition of 1,000 copies. That two stories, the first about a snail on a wall and the second about a snail in a flower bed, should have excited such enthusiasm must have seemed to Virginia something close to miraculous. The public was taking her literary experiments seriously. They didn't think she was mad; in fact, with these two "stories" she'd passed the acid test.

In the rush of success and relief, there was only one dark cloud—Vanessa. She was not satisfied with the way her woodcuts for *Kew Gardens* had come out and was disproportionately upset by the entire operation. She and Virginia quarreled, and Vanessa refused to illustrate any more stories of Virginia's under present conditions. Vanessa didn't stop there: she went on to "doubt the value of the Hogarth Press altogether." In her opinion, an ordinary printer would have made a better job of it. "This both stung and chilled me . . . I left in rather a crumpled condition."

Changes were about to take place in living arrangements. On the last day of February 1919, the Woolfs were given notice to vacate Asheham by the end of September. Virginia was naturally upset, but her sense of adventure was sparked. At once, she began looking for another house. Throughout April and May the search was on. Then, on Thursday, June 26, they saw a placard tacked up on the wall of the auctioneer's office which read: "Lot 1. Monks House, Rodmell. An old fashioned house standing in three-quarters of an acre of land to be sold with possessions." Virginia decided to inspect the place alone on the following day. The house, she realized, had many drawbacks, but the possibilities of the garden were limitless. There was an amazing variety of fruit-bearing trees, bushes freighted with berries, random flowers sprouting among cabbages. How Leonard would love this. How she loved it already. She calmly told him of her discovery, and they went there together the following day. It was agreed between them that they would buy the place if they could and settled on £800 as their limit. The auction took place on Tuesday, July 1, at the White Hart Hotel, and throughout the bidding, Virginia held her breath. When the gavel came down for the last time, the house was theirs for £700—Virginia "purple in the cheeks, and Leonard trembling like a reed." On September 1, with two farm wagons, they moved from Asheham to Monks House, Rodmell, which was to be their country house for the rest of their lives.

Night and Day was published on October 20, 1919, and was dedicated to Vanessa Bell. Clive called it a "work of the highest genius"; but in fact didn't like the novel as much as he claimed. His comment pleased Virginia all the same. The opinion of only three or four people mattered to her; the rest, "save for a senseless clapping of hands or hissing, are nowhere." No intelligent reader, she was certain, apart from her friends would pick up so long a novel.

E. M. Forster's opinion meant a great deal to her and she paid attention to his criticism. What he said in substance was that *Night and Day*, being "strictly formal and classical," required more "loveability" in the characters than a book like *The Voyage Out*, which was "vague and universal." Then Katherine Mansfield wrote what to Virginia was a spiteful review. "A decorous elderly dullard she describes me; Jane Austen up to date." What mattered, however, was that now Virginia could "write with the sense of many people willing to read." The anticipation of willing readers was important, and so ultimately *Night and Day* was more than an academic exercise. For while she observed the conventions of the traditional novel, she paid closer attention to motivation—"to discover what aims drive people on, and whether these are illusory or not." It was always in the foreground of her mind, this business of illusion and reality. Indeed, "life without illusion" could be "a ghastly affair."

By the end of 1919, Virginia had offers from two American publishers, Macmillan and George H. Doran, to bring out editions of *Night and Day* and *The Voyage Out*. For the moment, she was riding a crest. "It was certainly your doing that I ever survived to write at all," she wrote to Violet Dickinson; "and I suppose nothing I could say would give you an idea of what your praise was one night . . . O how excited I was and what a difference you made to me! But I don't suppose you realise how often I think of it, or how grateful I am."

AN ORDINARY MIND ON AN ORDINARY DAY

1919–1924

23 The reception of *Night and Day* stimulated Virginia to begin a series of short experimental stories to be published in 1921 under the title of *Monday or Tuesday*. She had mastered traditional narrative form. The new stories would now provide her with an opportunity to create a method flexible enough to convey a new kind of fictional reality—the experience of an "ordinary mind on an ordinary day." Two of the stories she had written already—*The Mark on the Wall* and *Kew Gardens*—encouraged her to "grope and experiment" further.

The turning point came unexpectedly on January 26, 1920, while she was writing *An Unwritten Novel*. It was the day after her thirty-eighth birthday. "Well, I've no doubt I'm a great deal happier than I was at 28; and happier today than I was yesterday." Only a few minutes earlier that afternoon, she had arrived at an idea of a new kind of novel: "Suppose one thing should open out of another—as in An Unwritten Novel—only not for 10 pages but 200 or so . . . conceive Mark on the Wall, Kew Gardens and Unwritten Novel taking hands and dancing in unity. What that unity shall be I have yet to discover."

What was there in *The Mark on the Wall* and *Kew Gardens* to facilitate their joining hands? *The Mark on the Wall*, published three years earlier, signaled the beginning of a mode of perception that would yield a new kind of fiction. The narrator of the piece sees a spot on the wall and begins to speculate what it might be. Each guess triggers what appears to be a random series of personal associations—not unlike Freud's concept of "free association." That the mark on the wall is finally identified as a snail is, by itself, entirely irrelevant. What matters is the way in which Virginia Woolf has stopped the ticking of the mechanical clock in order to fill the piece with a rich spectrum of thought and feeling, all of it stimulated by the indefiniteness of the mark under observation. The story was one of the earliest to attach importance to the way each human being perceives the world and gives it its singularly personal coloration and emotional weight. It is also a persuasive rendering of mental time—mind time that simulates the way human beings experience the linear flow of sequence and consequence.

Virginia gently pried her snail off the wall and set him down in a flower bed to function as her principal narrative point of view in *Kew Gardens*. Here an unspecified narrator is used sparingly to contextualize the piece. Most of the physical details of the flower bed, however, and the people walking by—a pair of feet walking "about six inches in front of the woman"—are filtered to us primarily from a consistent but highly restricted snail's-eye view. The same restriction is placed on the seemingly offhand speeches of the four groups of people who pass the flower bed of the resident mollusk. We hear only those snatches of conversation the snail "hears" as they pass; we see only what the snail "sees." *Kew Gardens* was an entirely new way of storytelling. It was a piece of snail impressionism. Time and space appear fragmented and scrambled, speech and thought fractured and random. This was mere simulation, however. Time and space and speech and thought were under the strictest narrative control, with the aim of creating a natural, "unedited" impression of a hot July afternoon in a public garden.

An Unwritten Novel, unlike its two predecessors, was an attempt at simulating the complicated process by which one human being gets to know another. Omniscience is as false and out of place here as it is in real life. And so the unnamed narrator of the story, sitting across from an elderly woman in a commuter train, begins to fantasize who this woman is, what her circumstances are, what triumphs and tragedies she has known. "Life's what you see in people's eyes." Such is the story's opening line. This proposition reduces finally to the idea that *the nature of the object is always colored by the nature of the subject*. Scene after scene is conjured up; feeling runs high; varied and fertile possibilities are set in motion—all of this the *imagination* of the observing passenger. When the train reaches its destination the elderly woman alights and joins her waiting son. The narrator's guesswork is all wrong; the entire invention collapses like a house of cards. And the old warning, soon to be articulated in Virginia Woolf's first experimental novel, *Jacob's Room*— "It's no use trying to sum people up"—holds true. If life itself is as "bare as bone," what gives it its vitality and color is the creative imagination, a purely human phenomenon.

If Virginia Woolf could join the separate technical methods utilized in each of her three pieces, she would achieve the freedom of mental association and interior monologue, the freedom of shifting narrative points of view, and finally the freedom to create fictional worlds built on pure narrative invention which did not promise the "Truths" of omniscient storytelling. The making of truth, the making of meaning, the making of sense—something was only true, after all, if you believed it—would now be relegated to readers themselves. Truth would now be both relative and contingent upon the reader's subjective perception of the world. Equally important was the notion that all the fragmentation and discordance and splintering of an ordinary day could be made to come together under the controlling hand of the writer into fictional segments closely resembling moments of real human experience.

This was perilous ground for the novelist to tread. The whole weight of convention was against her. All the same, the hall table had been littered with orders. Readers wanted *Kew Gardens*; they clamored for *The Mark on the Wall*. It was a dangerous risk, but one she must take. These three experiments would soon join hands in *Jacob's Room*; and the freedom that union yielded would provide Virginia Woolf with certain technical possibilities she would bring to perfection in *Mrs. Dalloway* and *To the Lighthouse*.

Ten years later she would write about this extraordinary breakthrough in a letter to a friend: "I shall never forget the day I wrote Mark on the Wall—all in a flash, as if flying, after . . . stone-breaking for months. The Unwritten Novel was the great discovery however. That—again in one second—showed me how I could embody all my deposit of experience in a shape that fitted it . . . Jacob's Room . . . Mrs Dalloway etc—How I trembled with excitement; and then Leonard came in, and I drank my milk, and concealed my excitement, and wrote I suppose another page of that interminable Night and Day."

The year 1920 was crowded and adventurous, for Leonard especially. He became editor of the international supplement of the *Contemporary Review* and leader-writer on foreign affairs for the *Nation*. *Empire and Commerce in Africa* was published by Allen and Unwin in January; he was writing *Socialism and Co-operation* for the Independent Labour Party's Social Studies Series; he was also preparing *Stories from the East* for the Hogarth Press while translating with S. S. Koteliansky Maxim Gorky's *The Note-Books of Anton Tchekhov* . . . ; and in May, he was adopted as Labour candidate for the Combined English Universities.

The Hogarth Press had started out as a hobby to keep Virginia occupied in the afternoons, but now it was expanding too rapidly and consuming more time than they wished to give. Short books by Hope Mirrlees, E. M. Forster, and Logan Pearsall Smith were scheduled for publication. There was type to be set, machining, cutting, binding, making up parcels—the work was endless. Certainly it was more than Leonard and Virginia could do alone. They needed help, and that help took the shape of a part-time assistant named

Ralph Partridge, the joint lover of Carrington and Lytton Strachey. From the time Partridge arrived in October 1920 to the time he left in March 1923, there was friction in the air. There always seemed to be some large discrepancy between Ralph's performance and Leonard's expectation. He was crude and stubborn and drove Leonard wild. They were forever at odds. His two love alliances complicated matters further by putting a strain on the Woolfs' long friendship with Lytton. Somehow they got through their two-and-a-half-year ordeal.

Having labored through the intricacies of *An Unwritten Novel*, Virginia launched into *Jacob's Room*. This would be a full-scale experiment requiring all the courage and skill she possessed. It would also require long stretches without interruption. Her plan was to write in prescribed blocks of time, not beginning a chapter unless she was certain of enough days to complete it. This was her plan in April 1920. By early May the novel was under way, and to her diary she confided an important fact for "future reference"—that "the creative power which bubbles so pleasantly on beginning a new book quiets down after a time, and one goes on more steadily." There were days of doubt and days of resignation, but she kept at it all the same.

With some long breaks for reviewing and working at the Press, Virginia stuck resolutely to *Jacob's Room*. Each day's work was like an obstacle race, with a number of hurdles to clear—with "my heart in my mouth." Some days she succeeded and some days she didn't. Through it all, however, she watched herself closely. Her own creativity, like a lifeline, was of the greatest importance. "Yesterday broody and drowsy all day long, writing easily, and yet without strict consciousness, as though fluent under drugs: today apparently clear headed, yet unable to put one sentence after another—sat for an hour, scratching out, putting in, scratching out." This was in August. Toward the end of September the novel came to a halt. A headache threatened. "It was this [headache], not Eliot [his comment on Joyce] I suppose, that broke off Jacob." She was bothered by the notion that her experiment in fiction was "probably being better done by Mr Joyce." Hadn't she been assured by Mr. T. S. Eliot that James Joyce was an artist to the fingertips and *Ulysses* brilliant?

But who, after all, was this Mr. T. S. Eliot to pass so sweeping a judgment? And what was there about Mr. T. S. Eliot that made Virginia ill at ease? She had been wondering this for some time now and decided to get a better look at him. She'd ask him to Monks House for a weekend. It would be like making a "scientific observation." Eliot came and Virginia observed. She found it odd that his eyes should be so youthful and vivacious, and the rest of him so precise and ponderous. "We talked—America, Ottoline, aristocracy ... 'And I behaved like a priggish pompous little ass,' " he'd said of his visit to Garsington. Virginia liked that. He got better as the day wore on. (Leonard found him intellectually disappointing.) Eliot, she noticed, completely ignored her claims as a novelist; and "had I been meek, I suppose I should have gone under—found him and his views dominant and subversive." He was more interested in people than in anything else, he confessed. "A personal upheaval of some kind came after Prufrock, and turned him aside from his inclination—to develop in the manner of Henry James. Now he wants to describe externals."

Virginia's "inspection" of Eliot was finished. He was a writer. He was her contemporary. He had to be watched. She had done the same with Katherine Mansfield, another promising literary figure who aroused certain feelings, some of them most uncharitable. She was the only writer Virginia had ever been jealous of, and Mansfield too had been put under a magnifying glass. "It is at this moment extremely doubtful whether I have the right to class her among my friends," Virginia had written earlier.

Months had passed without a word from Katherine. They had been open, intimate, intense. Virginia had taken the trouble to see her regularly. It was hardly convenient traveling up to Hampstead every week. "And then what happened? I go away for Christmas, and we send small bright presents, carefully timed to arrive on Christmas day. I add to mine one if not two long and affectionate letters ... I get no thanks, no answers, no enquiries."

Sometime later, Virginia resumed her meditation: "... I find with Katherine what I don't find with other clever women ... her caring so genuinely ... about our precious art." But Katherine had reviewed *Night and Day* and disliked it. In the *Athenaeum* (November 26, 1919) she had been ambiguous: "We had thought that this world vanished for ever, that it was impossible to find on the great ocean of literature a ship that was unaware of what has been happening; yet there is *Night and Day*, new, exquisite—a novel in the tradition of the English novel. In the midst of our admiration it makes us feel old and chill. We had not thought to look upon its like again."

Virginia had felt the sting, but she was fascinated. She couldn't keep away from Katherine. In May of 1920, she went to see her again. Mansfield had spent four months at Ospedaletti on the Italian Riviera literally on the verge of death. There was a "steady discomposing formality and coldness at first ... No pleasure or excitement at seeing me." She was like a cat: remote, aloof, poised, watchful. "Then we talked about solitude and I found her expressing my feelings . . . Whereupon we fell into step, and as usual, talked as easily as though 8 months were minutes." Unable to resist mentioning her novel, Virginia at some point steered the conversation to *Night and Day*. "An amazing achievement," said Katherine. "But I thought you didn't like it?" Virginia pressed her. Well, they would meet again in a week for lunch and talk about it. This was what Virginia needed to hear—some sign that she cared. So that once more she felt "a common certain understanding between us—a queer sense of being 'like'—not only about literature . . . I can talk straight out to her."

Katherine was going away in August for two years. Virginia met her in London to say goodbye—"Do I feel this as much as I ought? Am I heartless? Will she mind my going either?" Then suddenly she felt the "blankness" of not having Katherine to talk to. "A woman caring as I care for writing is rare enough I suppose to give me the queerest sense of echo coming back to me from her mind the second after I've spoken . . . But we propose to write to each other—She will send her diary. Shall we? Will she? If I were left to myself I should; being the simpler, the more direct of the two . . . Strange how little we know our friends."

Bliss and Other Stories was published in December. The *TLS* reviewed it favorably and Virginia wrote to congratulate her on its success. A week earlier she had said in her diary: "I was happy to hear Katherine abused last night. Now why? Partly some obscure feeling that she advertizes herself . . . yet in my heart I must think her good, since I'm glad to hear her abused." She returned to her private page a week later to say that she had "plucked out" her jealousy of Katherine. *Bliss* had been praised at length. This was the prelude of "paeans" to come. The book would sell; then she would be awarded the Hawthornden prize next summer. "So I've had my little nettle growing in me, and plucked it . . . I've revived my affection for her somehow, and don't mind . . . But I've not read her book."

Vanessa, years later, in a letter to Julian wrote about Virginia's attitude toward her contemporaries. David Garnett's theory, she wrote, "is that Virginia lives so precariously (in nerves and brain) that she can't face any other writer of any real merit . . . That is why she always gives absurd praise to obscure females and one never hears her really enthusiastic about any of her own generation, such as Lytton or Morgan [E. M. Forster] or Joyce or Eliot, who may conceivably be of real importance. Bunny thinks it's not exactly jealousy, but some need to keep her own poise."

One could feel in Virginia's letters for some time now an undercurrent of melancholy as if the world were somehow passing her by. Life was "like a little strip of pavement over an abyss." She was feeling impotent and small and "cutting no ice." "Melancholy diminishes as I write [the diary]. Why then don't I write it down oftener? Well, one's vanity forbids. I want to appear a success even to myself. Yet I don't get to the bottom of it. It's having no children, living away from friends, failing to write well, spending too much on food, growing old."

24 June, July, and much of August of 1921 were consumed in illness. *Jacob's Room* was still not finished. Virginia had been getting a collection of short stories together called *Monday or Tuesday*. Because of some blunder about the publication date, *The Times* did not adequately review it; and Doran, the American publisher, recently so anxious to publish *The Voyage Out*, now refused the stories.

Meanwhile Lytton Strachey's *Queen Victoria* made its debut in a blaze of glory and was selling in large numbers. Lytton had asked Virginia for permission to dedicate the book to her. He would use only her initials, he promised. Nothing would make her happier, she replied, but she objected to the initials. She wanted her name spelled out. With "V. W." some "Victoria Worms or Vincent Woodlouse" might claim the book as theirs and she wanted all the glory. And there was much to be had. The book was an unconditional success; there were rumors that 5,000 copies had been sold in one week. She enjoyed the book enormously. It was "quite magnificent." But Lytton's success made her collection of stories seem "a damp firework." She was a failure, old, out of fashion. And there was Lytton with column after column of solid praise—"how my temper sank and sank till for half an hour I was as depressed as I ever am." To make matters worse, at a large publication party, Lytton himself failed to mention her book. Not a word was said. So "for the first time I have not his praise to count on." If only the *TLS* had said she was a "mystery or a riddle," she'd have been satisfied. But she was not a mystery and not a riddle. She was "plain as day, and negligible."

In a calmer moment Virginia would realize that her feeling had less to do with vanity than with the old nursery fear of being deserted, forgotten in some corner because she had told her sister and brothers a dull story; and there was nothing worse than being irrelevant or not "interesting," as she euphemistically phrased it. This sense of dereliction she invariably connected with feelings of jealousy. Even with Leonard she felt it. His *Stories from the East* had come out on the same day as *Monday or Tuesday*. "And suppose every one (that is to say the 6 people who matter) praise Leonard, shall I be jealous—" A little later: "the Daily Mail says that Leonard's story 'Pearls and Swine' will rank with the great stories of the world. Am I jealous? Only momentarily." But more important, a novel had just been published which would certainly win the Hawthornden prize, "thus robbing Katherine [Mansfield] of it: so I have some cause for pleasure. I write this purposely to shame it out of me."

Despite intermittent illness, Virginia finished the first draft of *Jacob's Room* on November 4, 1921 (having begun it on April 16 the previous year). Now she would put the manuscript aside and let the dust settle before revising it for an October 1922 publication. *Jacob's Room* would bear the Hogarth Press imprint, its first full-length book. The Woolfs were now confident enough of their future as publishers to invest in a much larger printing machine, a secondhand Minerva platen machine worked by a treadle, which they set up in the basement of Hogarth House.* So successful were they by December 1921, they could boast of Roger Fry's volume of woodcuts going quickly and efficiently into three editions.

The early months of 1922 were again lost to illness. Virginia was suffering from a lingering case of influenza, an elevated temperature, and an irregular pulse. All three, singly or in varying combinations, kept her in bed much of the time. For weeks she was unable to stray from the immediate vicinity of home. S. S. Koteliansky was translating Tolstoy and Dostoyevsky. Both Leonard and Virginia had learned enough Russian to rewrite Koteliansky's literal but awkward transcriptions into grammatical, idiomatic English. During these months Virginia was allowed to help Koteliansky for short periods with his translation of *Stavrogin's Confession*, the two "newly found chapters" from Dostoyevsky's *The Possessed*. She also dipped occasionally into a story called "Mrs Dalloway in Bond Street," which would eventually grow into *Mrs.*

---

* This press was given by Virginia to Vita Sackville-West in 1930 and still stands at Sissinghurst Castle in Kent.

Dalloway. But for the most part she was never very far from her bed, where one or two late unfavorable reviews of *Monday or Tuesday* reached her. "I have made up my mind that I'm not going to be popular, and . . . look upon disregard or abuse as part of my bargain," she wrote on February 18.

The illness and discomfort dragged on. "God knows what is happening to my influenza germs," she wrote to Violet Dickinson in May. "I can't get rid of this miserable little temperature, and last week it flared up into another attack and laid my heart flat again." Sometime during this interval, after she had seen three physicians, the idea struck one of them that her influenza germs may have collected at the roots of three teeth. "So I'm having them out, and preparing for the escape of microbes by having 65 million dead ones injected into my arm daily." Needless to say, this radical procedure did nothing to improve her condition, and she was missing three teeth into the bargain. The medical speculation went on until, in the natural course of events, the fever subsided. But the whole process was exhausting, expensive, and ultimately useless. Once more, Virginia's faith in the medical profession was severely taxed, whether they were general practitioners from Richmond or Harley Street specialists. Some of her disillusionment would be siphoned into *Mrs. Dalloway* with Septimus Warren Smith's so-called medical experts. By late spring she was able to return to the revisions of *Jacob's Room*.

By early summer a plan was brewing that would lead to endless hours of wasted effort. On a Sunday in late June, T. S. Eliot spent an evening with the Woolfs in Richmond. After dinner he read them a poem he had just finished. Virginia found it deeply moving. "He sang it," she said in her diary, "and chanted it, rhythmed [*sic*] it. It has great beauty and force of phrase: symmetry; and tensity. What connects it together, I'm not sure. But he read it till he had to rush." She was left, however, "with some strong emotion. The Waste Land, it is called," and it was said to be his "biography—a melancholy one."

Eliot, at the time, was employed by Lloyd's Bank of England, a job his friends saw as a deplorable waste of talent. Ottoline Morrell thought it was time someone did something about it. So she and Virginia and Richard Aldington (and Ezra Pound abroad) attempted to raise enough money to free Eliot from his work in the Colonial and Foreign Department of Lloyd's and enable him to devote himself to poetry. Not far in the background was also his chronically ill wife, Vivien, who was running up huge medical expenses.

Ottoline and Virginia's plan took up entire mornings in writing letters, distributing circulars, and soliciting friends (and strangers). Almost from the start, the Eliot Fellowship, as it came to be called, was doomed. After several months, the total sum collected was seventy-seven pounds, with many uncertain promises for more later. Virginia, if not the extravagantly generous Ottoline, saw almost immediately that the people she approached were not able, or indeed willing, to subsidize a fellow writer. Both women persisted with the appeal, against increasing odds; but in the end it failed, and it would be five years before all the money was returned to subscribers.

25 In the spring of 1922, Virginia discovered Marcel Proust— his novel *A la recherche du temps perdu* was published in an English translation by C. K. Scott-Moncrieff—and she was swept off her feet. "Oh if I could write like that!" she said to Roger Fry. "And at the moment such is the astonishing vibration . . . that I feel I *can* write like that, and seize my pen and then I *can't* write like that." Scarcely anyone had ever before so stimulated her poetic sense.*

Virginia had also parted with four pounds for a copy of *Ulysses*, she told Eliot, who still maintained James Joyce's artistic supremacy. But it was to Lytton Strachey that she made her criticism explicit. "Never did I read such tosh . . . merely the scratching of pimples on the body of the bootboy at Claridges. Of course genius may blaze out on page 652 but I have my doubts. And this is what Eliot worships." Joyce, however, remained very much on her mind throughout the summer of 1922, as she revised her novel.

Jacob's Room was a highly innovative experiment and she was growing anxious about its reception in England. Her deepest fear, the old familiar one, was that it would be thought the effusions of a crazy woman. The novel was being typed and would cross the Atlantic on July 14. Then would begin

---

* Part of her fascination with Proust was his handling of mental time, which linked him to Henri Bergson and the concept of *durée*, loosely interpreted as ceaseless durational flux or fluid time. Virginia would develop and concretize the concept in *Mrs. Dalloway* with the method she called her "tunnelling process," by which she stopped the mechanical clock to capture selected moments of the past—implying in the Bergsonian sense the "presence of all the past states of consciousness in the present moment of experience." See Kumar, 157. It might also be noted that her sister-in-law Karin Stephen had published a book this year (1922) entitled *The Misuse of Mind—A Study of Bergson's Attack on Intellectualism*. This is not to say that Virginia read Karin's book, for Bergson was fairly common knowledge in Virginia's circle. Certainly T. S. Eliot was under Bergson's influence during the years 1910–11, when he attended Bergson's lectures and studied whatever published material was then available. The Hogarth Press would publish Clive Bell's book *Proust* in 1928.

her "season of doubts and ups and downs." If readers said it was a clever experiment, she would publish "Mrs. Dalloway in Bond Street." If they said, "You can't make us care a damn for any of your figures—I shall say, read my criticism then. Now what *will* they say about Jacob? Mad, I suppose: a disconnected rhapsody."

Some of the pressure let up at the end of July when Leonard read the typescript and pronounced it her best work to date. It was also "amazingly well written," he thought. "There's no doubt in my mind that I have found out how to begin (at 40) to say something in my own voice." She could proceed now "without praise." No sooner had she written those words, however, than Joyce once more intruded upon her serenity. She had read 200 pages of *Ulysses*—"not a third; and have been amused, stimulated, charmed, interested by the first 2 or 3 chapters . . . and then puzzled, bored, irritated, and disillusioned . . . And Tom, great Tom, thinks this on a par with War and Peace! An illiterate, underbred book it seems to me . . . and ultimately nauseating." Why eat raw meat if one could have it cooked? But Eliot, she thought, was anemic and therefore attracted to blood. She was prepared to go on with her own novel, however, even if it was "rejected in America" and "ignored in England."

In this state of mind it wouldn't be long before she once more skirted the verges of depression. When the galley proofs of *Jacob's Room* arrived, her mood dipped further. The book now seemed "thin and pointless"; and again she returned to *Ulysses*. It was "pretentious." A good writer didn't startle or play tricks or insist on so many stunts. And then, one afternoon, Leonard brought her an "intelligent review" of Joyce's novel which, for the first time, "analyses the meaning; and certainly makes it very much more impressive than I judged."

And so the days drew on. Her book was scheduled for publication on October 27, and she would very likely have worked herself up into a frenzy by that time had it not been for a letter she received from her American publisher, Donald Brace: "We think *Jacob's Room* an extraordinarily distinguished and beautiful work. You have, of course, your own method, and it is not easy to foretell how many readers it will have; surely it will have enthusiastic ones, and we delight in publishing it."

This was the first testimony of its value from an outside source and she was greatly relieved. The novel had made *some* impression; it could not be "wholly frigid fireworks." She began to grow calmer as the public day approached. It was better to go on working during this interval of waiting. The one great remaining anxiety was how the book would be received by *The Times Literary Supplement*—for that review would be the most widely read and "I can't bear people to see me downed in public"; she became very resolute, however. *Jacob's Room* was a full-scale departure from tradition. Her readers would be baffled, bewildered, impatient, even hostile. To sit quietly in a London suburb, prepared to take the consequences, whatever they might be, required plenty of courage.

October 27 came and went. Her friends, with their usual candor, let her know what they thought, for better or worse. Mostly, however, they were full of praise. Desmond MacCarthy, although puzzled by the book, marveled at her virtuosity. E. M. Forster found her treatment of Jacob himself a remarkable achievement. Lytton Strachey was lavish in his praise. "I breathe more freely now that I have your letter," Virginia wrote him back.

On November 1, she told Ottoline that the Press had just ordered a second edition of a thousand, "and now I look forward to sneers and jeers in all quarters and a loss of so many pounds." But more soberly to her diary on November 27: "Jacob has now sold 850 copies... People—my friends I mean—seem agreed that it *is* my masterpiece, and the starting point for fresh adventures." At dinner the night before, Roger Fry had praised her "wholeheartedly... for the first time." She knew *Jacob's Room* was no masterpiece; she had said repeatedly it was an experiment. But it *was* the necessary step to the "fresh adventures" that would soon make her one of England's most revolutionary and accomplished novelists.

Not all reviewers welcomed the innovations. Many were lost. How could one review a novel that had no plot, no structure, no solid characters? There were "vivid glimpses" and "snapshots"—yes, but certainly that did not constitute a novel. Perhaps this was a new form, something that might be called literary impressionism. But how did one evaluate impressionism? *Jacob's Room* was a "rambling, redundant affair, in which the commonplace details and motives of ordinary people are divided and subdivided until they form a series of atoms." A good many other reviewers—and readers—were simply baffled and angry.

The Times Literary Supplement, however, offered an intelligent explanation of the book. "Jacob Flanders," the reviewer asserted, "absorbed with the half-savage, half-winning absorption of youth... is in the brief career which we follow by glimpses the mutest of all heroes. He is the 'silent young man'; Mrs Woolf's method increases his silence. But there is his room, his behaviour, his impressions; there are the scenes, the numerous people who float into the story for a moment or eddy round its centre."

It was a poet, however, who came closest to defining Virginia's perceptions of the world she had created in *Jacob's Room*. The poet was Siegfried Sassoon. "Your novel gave me an immense apprehension of your subtlety of intellect," he wrote in a letter. "But I was able to follow your meaning—instantly— every time, because you visualise everything you write." And it was to a young man named Gerald Brenan, in the wilds of Spain, who had abandoned civilization to live and write in a remote cottage in the Sierra Nevada that Virginia explained her position as a novelist and her method in *Jacob's Room*. Her letter is dated Christmas Day 1922. "I have been thinking a great deal about what you say of writing novels ... I don't see how to write a book without people in it. Perhaps you mean that one ought not to attempt a 'view of life'?—one ought to limit oneself to one's own sensations ... one ought to be lyrical, descriptive: but not set people in motion, and attempt to enter them, and give them impact and volume? Ah, but I'm doomed! ... The best of us catch a glimpse of a nose, a shoulder, something turning away, always in movement. Still, it seems better to me to catch this glimpse, than to sit down with Hugh Walpole, Wells, etc. etc. and make large oil portraits of fabulous fleshy monsters complete from top to toe."

She could not have given a more succinct or more precise justification for what she had done in *Jacob's Room*. She wanted Brenan to see that her aesthetic problem was poised on the conviction that the novelist conveys "character without realism"—a problem of immense complexity. One of those novelists who create "fleshy monsters"—Arnold Bennett, specifically—challenged that conviction. As far as he could determine, Virginia Woolf's characters, despite the exquisite writing, did "not vitally survive in the mind," because she was obsessed "by details of originality and cleverness."

Virginia met his challenge, theoretically and practically, first by writing her now-famous essay *Mr. Bennett and Mrs. Brown* repudiating his claims, and second by systematically dismantling his argument with her next novel *Mrs. Dalloway*, in which she created two of the most memorable characters in contemporary British fiction—Clarissa Dalloway and Septimus Warren Smith. But all that was still to come.

Virginia met Vita Sackville-West (Mrs. Harold Nicolson) for the first time at a dinner party given by Clive Bell on the evening of December 14, 1922. On the following day, she recorded her impression: she was a little "muzzy headed" from meeting the "lovely gifted aristocratic Sackville West last night ... Not much to my severer taste—florid, moustached, parakeet coloured, with all the supple ease of the aristocracy, but not the wit of the artist. She writes 15 pages a day ... publishes with Heinemann's—knows everyone."

There was no "false shyness or modesty" in Vita; she had her "hand on all the ropes—makes me feel virgin, shy, and schoolgirlish . . . She is a grenadier; hard, handsome, manly."

Vita had apparently shot like a comet through Virginia's evening sky. For the moment, however, there would be only an exchange of each other's novels and a few chaste dinners. After March of 1923 they would not meet again for a very long time.

Virginia had spent endless hours in correspondence over the failed Eliot Fellowship Fund. Now in the early months of the new year she would again devote herself to his welfare. Would she help him find some sort of permanent work more suited to his talents than what he was at present doing at Lloyd's? He had finally decided that if circumstances were right, he'd leave the bank.

Virginia wasted no time in applying to Maynard Keynes, now a major shareholder and Chairman of the Board of the *Nation*. Leonard had been a regular contributor to that journal and had served it well, but Keynes wanted to change its policy and its staff. Eliot was anxious to get work "connected with literature," Virginia said, that would "bring him in £3 or £400 a year." Was there any chance of the *Nation*'s giving him employment as a literary editor with an assured income? Eliot was well qualified. If he could depend on a regular income he would risk leaving Lloyd's. He'd have left long ago if it weren't for Vivien's chronic illness.

In her next letter, Virginia patiently explained that should Eliot be given the job, he would have to give the Bank three months' notice. Also he would like a holiday first. This of course would postpone his assuming the editorship at the time compatible with Keynes's plans, but Eliot thought Keynes ought to know this before making an offer. "He had tried to write you," she labored on, "but being consumed with gratitude and diffidence had failed, and so asked me."

By spring matters were getting, if not desperate, at least incredibly intricate. Insecurity kept Eliot vacillating, indecisive, riddled with doubts. His new fear was that if the *Nation* dismissed him within a year, he would not have sufficient experience to qualify for another literary post and would end up without any work whatever. "Do you think it would be impossible to assure him a guarantee for the first two years at any rate?" she asked Keynes, pressing as far as she dared. Personally she wished the great poet "had more spunk in him." His behavior was disillusioning. All the egotism and complication made "one feel that he dreads life as a cat dreads water . . . It's American,

Leonard says; that and neurotic." Keynes did make an offer in March, and when Eliot, after all his conditions, turned it down, it was offered to Leonard, who accepted the post and remained literary editor until 1930.

During this period Adrian and Karin Stephen were in the middle of their medical studies, and Adrian was having a particularly bad time of it. He was devastated by his psychoanalysis, Virginia wrote in her diary. The doctor said "his tragedy consists in the fact that he can't enjoy life with zest. I am probably responsible. I should have paired with him, instead of hanging on to the elders. So he wilted, pale, under a stone ... Had mother lived, or father been screened off—well, it puts it too high to call it a tragedy."

Virginia started 1923 off "in one of my moods." She was feeling elderly, alone, "suffering inwardly, stoically." And then the shocking news came. Katherine Mansfield had died in France of a massive pulmonary hemorrhage on January 9. Murry had been visiting her at the Gurdjieff Institute for the Harmonious Development of Man at Fontainebleau, where she had been living since autumn. Everyone knew how ill she was. Still the announcement was stunning, and all Virginia's submerged, ambivalent feelings came swimming to the surface. She faced them, analyzed them, and, when she was ready, wrote them out in the privacy of her journal.

"Katherine has been dead for a week," Virginia wrote on January 16, "and how far am I obeying her 'do not quite forget Katherine' which I read in one of her old letters. Am I already forgetting her? It is strange to trace the progress of one's feelings ... A shock of relief?—a rival the less? Then confusion at feeling so little ... And I was jealous of her writing—the only writing I have ever been jealous of. This made it harder to write to her; and I saw in it, perhaps from jealousy, all the qualities I disliked in her ... Probably we had something in common which I shall never find in anyone else."

Virginia had developed another friendship, this one in letters only, with the French painter Jacques Raverat, who in 1911 had married Virginia's friend Gwen Darwin. Although he'd been educated in England, the Raverats now lived in Vence, near Nice. Jacques was slowly dying of multiple sclerosis and would become the only person Virginia chose to write to about her work—and about personal matters she would have found awkward with someone else. But to Jacques she could say anything. And to him she recommended Mansfield's stories. She wanted his opinion.

"Please read Katherine's works," she wrote him at the end of July. "My theory is that while she possessed the most amazing *senses* of her generation so that she could actually reproduce this room ... to the life, she was weak as water . . . when she had to use her mind." Whenever she needed to create a serious character, the result was "hard"; when sympathy was required, the result was "sentimental. Her first story which we printed, Prelude, was pure observation and therefore exquisite."

Whether Virginia was correct in her assessment is hard to say; but why should she ask a painter about a writer whose work was as submerged as her own? It was almost as if she were urging Raverat to take the place Katherine had just left empty; as if she wanted him to see her perform the heroic feat of literary impressionism she was about to undertake with *Mrs. Dalloway*. If he understood Mansfield's impressionism, he would also understand hers. Clarissa and Septimus, however, were still gestating.

In early spring the Woolfs went abroad for a month's holiday, traveling through France and Spain. It was their first trip since their honeymoon eleven years earlier. During their travels they paid a ten-day visit to Gerald Brenan in his Spanish village. "Virginia seemed," he said later, "though quiet, as excited as a schoolgirl on holiday." When they returned, Leonard took up his new duties as literary editor of the *Nation* and Virginia turned to her writing. For both it would be a period of intensive work. "Here we are with our noses to the grindstone," she wrote Brenan in the middle of May.

Apart from work on the novel, Virginia was correcting Koteliansky's translation of *Tolstoi's Love Letters* and of (A. B. Goldenveizer's) *Talks with Tolstoi*, both volumes soon to be published by the Hogarth Press. There was also her work every afternoon—reading manuscripts, setting type, tying parcels, in addition to writing reviews regularly for the *Nation*. The Press itself, though, was worse than breast-feeding six children "simultaneously." More than that, it affected domestic life at Hogarth House. They lived almost apart—Leonard in the basement and Virginia in the printing room. They met only at meals, "often so cross that we can't speak . . . His triumphs always coincide with my disasters."

What most consumed her energy, however, was writing two books simultaneously: a book of critical essays called *The Common Reader* and *Mrs. Dalloway* (then called *The Hours*), both begun shortly before the publication of *Jacob's Room*. There was a reason for two kinds of writing at the same time. As she explained: ". . . now I'm writing fiction again I feel my force flow straight from me at its fullest. After a dose of criticism I feel that I'm writing sideways, using only an angle of my mind." A shift from creative to critical thinking, and vice versa, was enough to keep her going, therefore, for long

periods of time with undiminished concentration. It was almost p[...]
that exhausting though her writing was, it was only when she was [...]
in a book that she felt free, safe, and secure. The virgin page vali[...]
identity by providing her with a place to express feelings that might otherwise
find no outlet. She said in June, for example, that she wanted "to bring in
the despicableness of people like Ottoline: I want to give the slipperiness of
the soul ... The truth is people scarcely care for each other"—words very
close to those uttered by Septimus in *Mrs. Dalloway*: "For the truth is ...
human beings have neither kindness, nor faith, nor charity beyond what
serves to increase the pleasure of the moment ... they desert the fallen."

Septimus's mad scenes—built from Virginia's memories of her summer
illness in 1904 at Violet Dickinson's house in Burnham Wood—were the
most difficult to write. They were vivid and harsh and based in fact. By June
they made her "mind squint" so badly she could scarcely face those memories.
The writing became slow and arduous. By November she had reached "the
100th page." "I am now in the thick of the mad scene in Regent's Park. I
find I write it by clinging as tight to fact as I can." There were days when
fifty words were all she could manage. The character of Mrs. Dalloway was
also troublesome: she was becoming "too stiff, too glittering and tinsely."

Virginia's principal discovery in the writing, however, was in learning how
to turn the clock and the calendar backward through narrative retrospec-
tion—"what I call my tunnelling process, by which I tell the past by instalments, as I have need of it." The process involved learning the technique of
stretching time—stopping the clock's horizontal movement in the service of
vertical (historical, experiential, psychological) exploration. It was essentially
discovering how to render the backwardness of *mind time* while simultaneously moving the narrative forward; that is, as content moved forward, memory meandered backward. It was the Bergsonian way of presenting an eternal
present of all past states of consciousness in a "moment of being."

In early September, Virginia resigned from the Richmond Women's Co-
operative Guild and, with Leonard, joined Maynard Keynes in the spacious
seaside house he had rented in Studland, Dorset. The Russian ballerina, Lydia
Lopokova, whom Keynes would shortly marry, was one of the party. She
would soon be Virginia's model of Rezia, Septimus's unlucky wife. The other
two guests were George (Dadie) Rylands, who would (for a brief time) be
Leonard's assistant at the Hogarth Press, and the bright young literary critic
Raymond Mortimer (Dadie's lover), who had just moved from Chelsea to

Gordon Square and would soon become Virginia's friend. It was a short three-day holiday, but enough to revive Leonard for his work at the *Nation* and Virginia for her two unfinished manuscripts.

Though she seldom mentioned it, Virginia was unhappy living in Richmond. Hogarth House had seen her through a terrible illness, and much had happened there she could look back on with satisfaction. But it was time to leave. It worried her to think of spending her life there "mute and mitigated." She wanted to live in London, not "on the verge" of things. Leonard, however, far from being sympathetic, insisted that her health came first. "And I can't sacrifice his peace of mind." It was dreary having to dwindle in Richmond away from the center of life—"always to catch trains, always to waste time, to sit here and wait for Leonard to come in" when she might be at a concert, or a gallery, or simply among people. None of that was now possible. She was "tied, imprisoned, inhibited." Leonard didn't mind life in the suburbs, and "Lord! ... what I owe him! What he gives me! Still, I say, surely we could get more from life than we do—isn't he too much of a Puritan, of a disciplinarian."

Slowly, with determination and patience, Virginia made Leonard see the need for a house in central London. About her sense of social privation, she was especially eloquent. Gradually he began to see her point of view. For he too was beginning to feel the strain of (almost) daily travel between Richmond and London. Yes, it was perhaps time to leave the large comfortable house which had sheltered them for nine years. And so in the autumn Virginia set out once again, searching through Chelsea and Maida Vale and Battersea, without success. Then, as though drawn by a magnet, she found a house in Bloomsbury.

On January 9, she recorded in her diary that "fifteen minutes ago, to be precise, I bought the ten year lease of 52 Tavistock Square, London W.C.1." This was, of course, subject to the lease. But if all went well, the house was theirs "and the basement, and the billiard room ... and the view of the square in front ... and Southampton Row, and ... music, talk, friendship, city views ... all this is now within my reach, as it hasn't been since August 1913, when we left Clifford's Inn, for a series of catastrophes which very nearly ended my life."

It was too large a house for just the two of them; so the sitting tenants, Messrs. Dollman and Pritchard, Solicitors, continued their occupancy of the ground and first floors. Leonard and Virginia took the upper two floors and installed the printing press in the basement. Saxon Sydney-Turner took over the lease of Hogarth House, where he lived with his widowed mother. The Woolfs completed the move back to Bloomsbury on March 15, 1924. The mission was at last accomplished. And for Virginia it was a victory of some magnitude, for in this new dwelling the love of her life would also be played out.

 After their meeting in December 1922 and the few dinners that followed, the budding friendship between Virginia and the magnificent Vita had come to a halt. Whether their first steps had been taken too quickly or Vita grew impatient is not clear. But for many months an almost complete silence separated them.

Early in March, three days after moving into Tavistock Square, Virginia asked Vita to lunch—but warned that she must be prepared for a picnic among books and "dirt and dust and only fragments of food." This was their first time alone together and there is no record of what transpired, but the luncheon took place as scheduled and Vita went away with her "head swimming with Virginia."

Something of importance was in the offing, however: an opportunity that would serve Vita's ambitions as a novelist. The Hogarth Press was anxious to know if Vita would write a book for them. "If so, what and when? Could it be this autumn?" Virginia's request came in late May. This was rather a challenge, being asked to produce a book out of thin air on three months' notice. But Vita flourished on challenges. Of course she would give them a book. In fact she would write it during her holiday on the peaks of the Dolomites!

Three or four days before her departure, Vita took Virginia to lunch at Knole, the great 365-room ancestral house which Queen Elizabeth had granted to Thomas Sackville in 1566. It was a visit that impressed Virginia very much. "Knole crushed me," she wrote to Vita on June 6, the day following the visit. Her journal got a fuller account. One walked through miles of galleries, past endless treasures, "chairs that Shakespeare might have sat on—tapestries, pictures, floors made of the halves of oaks." Knole was a cluster of buildings half the size of Cambridge. Many of the rooms were roped off; the chairs and pictures "look preserved"; and there was Mary Stuart's altar, where she knelt in prayer before execution. Thomas Sackville had been elected to present the death warrant. "All these ancestors and centuries, and silver and gold, have bred a perfect body. She is stag like ... save for a face, which pouts ... All very free and easy ... no inhibitions, no false reserves; anything can be said." But it was Vita's breeding that cut the sharpest impression; she was an aristocrat and "supple jointed."

There was something strong and protective in Vita, and whether Virginia was conscious of this at the time, we don't know; but clearly she was responding to the nurturing, custodial atmosphere that surrounded Vita; and it was the maternal aura that attracted the thirteen-year-old child in Virginia. For it may have been more than sheer coincidence that this year, on May 5, just a few weeks *after* their picnic and *prior* to the Knole visit, Virginia recorded for the first time in twenty-nine years the anniversary of her mother's death. It had happened early on a Sunday morning and Virginia had looked out the nursery window and seen Dr. Seton walking up the street with his hands behind his back. "I was 13, and could fill a whole page and more with my impressions of that day ... how I laughed, for instance, behind the hand which was meant to hide my tears."

It is hard to tell whether Vita triggered this memory. Would she understand the terrible story of Virginia's desperate, unnatural love for her father or the gnawing ambivalence she harbored for her absent mother? Could she give Virginia all the things that Julia never gave, could never give? This was to become the bond joining Virginia to Vita. The tall, arrogant Vita would lavish her privilege and protection on the lost and wandering child living inside Virginia.

All this was still half hidden from them both. On July 8 Vita left for the Italian Alps and produced in those breathless altitudes the better part of a long story called *Seducers in Ecuador*. It turned out to be her most "interesting" book to date, and she dedicated it to Virginia, who was proud and indeed touched "with my childlike dazzled affection for you, that you should dedicate it to me." With that dedication, the first step was taken toward a deeper friendship.

"I enjoyed your intimate letter from the Dolomites," Virginia had written a week or two earlier. "It gave me a great deal of pain—which is I've no doubt the first stage of intimacy ... Never mind: I enjoyed your abuse very much." Vita had written about a place in the Basque provinces she wanted to visit with Virginia. Look upon the expedition "as copy," she had said, "as I believe you look upon everything, human relationships included. Oh yes, you like people through the brain better than through the heart."

When Vita delivered her story in September, Virginia again turned to the privacy of her journal: "Vita was here for Sunday, gliding down the village in her large new Austin car, which she manages consummately." She wore a large hat, and carried a case "full of silver and night gowns wrapped in tissue." Virginia was interested in her story but marveled more at its author: "for is she not mother, wife, great lady, hostess, as well as scribbling? How little I do of all that: my brain would never let me milk it to the tune of 20,000 words in a fortnight."

But, she went on after some reflection, Vita "is like an over ripe grape in features . . . she strides on fine legs, in a well cut skirt . . . has manly good sense . . . Oh yes, I like her; could tack her on to my equipage for all time; and suppose if life allowed, this might be a friendship of a sort." And so, little by little, letter by letter, and visit by visit, Aphrodite began exerting her influence.

At the rear of the new house was a large billiard room which Leonard had intended to rent out for seventy-five pounds a year. This became Virginia's workroom as well as a storeroom for the Press. Here Leonard was able to observe her closely during sustained periods of writing and to intervene at the first signs of exhaustion.

The doctors of Harley Street had, like Sir William Bradshaw advocating Proportion to Septimus, urged Virginia to "practice equanimity"—something she had never learned to do. When she was in good health she went every day to her workroom to write with the same "regularity of a stockbroker" going to the office; but the room she wrote in bore little resemblance to a stockbroker's office. She was extremely untidy and her work space was cluttered. She had a tendency to accumulate what Lytton Strachey called "filth packets"—an assortment of debris consisting of burned matches, rusty paper clips, pieces of string, and bits of paper strewn everywhere. She was comfortable in this mess; in some ways it resembled the clutter of her father's study; even as a child she was happiest in a small mountain of litter.

In this workroom was a large plain wooden table "covered with filth packets, papers, letters, manuscripts, and large bottles of ink." She never used this table, however. In fact she rarely sat at it to write. In composing her novel, she sat in a low, dilapidated armchair with the stuffing and springs hanging out. Balanced on her lap (also like Sir Leslie) was a writing board with an inkstand glued to it. She wrote the first draft of all her novels in large notebooks of plain unlined paper with pen and ink, every day from ten to one. In the afternoon (or sometimes beginning the next morning's work) she typed out what she had written in the notebook, revising it along the way; and it was her habit to make all subsequent revisions at the typewriter.

In his memoir Leonard explained the different phases of the writing and Virginia's frame of mind accompanying each. In the regularity of this schedule, she did practice a certain "measure of equanimity." In many ways her attitude "was extraordinarily controlled, dispassionate, coldly critical." When she was writing fiction, there were "long periods of, first, quiet and intense dreamlike rumination when she drifted through London streets or walked across the Sussex water-meadows or merely sat silent by the fire." The second phase was entirely different: here she was intensely critical of what she had written. Both the dream state and the revision phase required a certain tranquillity and detachment.

There was also a period of passion and excitement, Leonard goes on to explain. When she was working, Virginia was "almost the whole time writing with concentrated passion." When composing the first draft of a novel, she was in a state he described as "emotionally volcanic." It was this terrific, persistent tension that exhausted her, that made her writing "a perpetual menace to her mental stability." Whenever her symptoms began—headache, insomnia, racing pulse—he forced her to stop. The creative stage was always emotionally violent. He could tell "by the depth of the flush on her face" whether she had been writing fiction or criticism or was in the process of revision.

When the novel was finished, other worries descended. There would be galley proofs to face, a publication date that threatened, then finally delivering herself "artistically naked to the public." Virginia was morbidly "sensitive to criticism of any kind and from anyone. Her writing was to her the most serious thing in her life." She felt about her books the same way a mother feels about a child. And just as a mother feels acutely any criticism of her child, "so any criticism of her book, even by the most negligible nitwit, gave Virginia acute pain. It is therefore hardly an exaggeration to say that the publication of her books meant something very like torture to her." Rejecting her book was the same as rejecting Virginia herself—Virginia Woolf and the writing of Virginia Woolf were the *same* thing.

As soon as she finished a book, the torture began and "continued off and on until the last reviewer, critic, friend, or acquaintance had his say." Yet despite the punishment, she was both tough and resilient, and this combination manifested itself in the "dogged persistence with which she worked at every word, sentence, paragraph of everything she wrote, from a major novel to a trumpery." And though she was forever saying she didn't care,

Virginia did care very much and by the time she died had faced the ordeal seventeen times, with seventeen books, not counting hundreds of essays.

With *Jacob's Room* Virginia began her full-scale offensive against the forms and methods of her contemporaries, most notably Arnold Bennett. She would create her own realism with *Mrs. Dalloway* and bring it to perfection in *To the Lighthouse*. This was to begin the most fertile period of her life as a writer. But before she could forge ahead she had to defend herself against the charge that she was incapable of creating character. That defense took shape in public in a lecture to undergraduates at Cambridge University in May of 1924.

The first version of *Mr. Bennett and Mrs. Brown* was written in December 1923 as a reply to an article by Arnold Bennett claiming that the "foundation of good fiction is character-creating and nothing else." He went on to say that Virginia Woolf's characters—he was referring specifically to those in *Jacob's Room*—"do not vitally survive in the mind because the author has been obsessed by details of originality and cleverness." Virginia's original essay, enlarged and revised, was read to the Society of Heretics in Cambridge under the title "Character in Fiction." It was finally revised and published as *Mr. Bennett and Mrs. Brown* by the Hogarth Press in October 1924.

Now considered a kind of literary manifesto, the essay repudiated the novels of the earlier generation on the ground that they invented all kinds of trivia with which to fill their pages and, in doing so, denied their readers even the scantiest insight into human nature. The earlier novelists, Virginia Woolf asserted, never bothered to look at Mrs. Brown in her corner—never bothered to look "at life, human nature"—and in consequence foisted upon the reader the job of imagining for them, making us believe that because they have described a house, there must be a human being living in it for us to invent.

The significance of *Mr. Bennett and Mrs. Brown* becomes clearer if we move back a little to the letters in which Virginia and Jacques Raverat tried to work their way through the problems which differentiated painting from writing. "The method of writing smooth narrative," she said, "can't be right; things don't happen in one's mind like that." The difficulty came down essentially to this: painting was *spatial*—ideas and images could be expressed simultaneously. Writing on the other hand was *linear*—that is, a series of ideas and images followed one another in *time*, in *sequence*. Writing, therefore, did not naturally possess the aesthetic force of *simultaneity*. A word like "Neo-Pagan," for instance, triggered clusters of ideas and images. But the closest a novelist could come to achieving the spatial dimension of the painter was similar to casting a pebble into a pond. "There are splashes in the outer air in every direction," Raverat said, "and under the surface waves that follow one another into dark and forgotten corners." Graphically, it would be the same as writing "a word in the middle of the page and surrounding it with associated ideas." This was the only (unusable) way the writer might approximate the simultaneity of the painter.

But trying to catch and consolidate those "splashes" was precisely what the novelist had to do, insisted Virginia, because "the falsity of the past (by which I mean Bennett, Galsworthy and so on) is precisely I think that they adhere to the formal railway line of sentence," those time-bound, linear, sequential verbal utterances—"never reflecting that people don't and never did feel or think or dream . . . in that way; but all over the place, in your way"—in those simultaneous "splashes" of experience, those jumbles of irrelevant and incongruous ideas which crowd into one's head in unending radiations of ordinary human experience. It was this crowding, these "splashes," these incongruous and irrelevant juxtapositions of idea and image that more closely approximated reality; and here was an elaboration of the aesthetic credo Virginia Stephen had formulated sixteen years earlier in Italy in 1908—to attain beauty and symmetry through "shivering fragments." Her artistic aim had remained steadfast during those sixteen years. From the very start she knew, if not the means, certainly the direction her writing would take.

This was the kernel out of which *Mr. Bennett and Mrs. Brown* grew. Virginia used Arnold Bennett's novel *Hilda Lessways* as the text of her argument. She began by saying that Bennett, in describing Hilda Lessways, described not Hilda herself but the view from her window, and that was the wrong way. But how should the novelist describe his character—his Mrs. Brown—she asked. Mr. Bennett answered: "Begin by saying that her father kept a shop in Harrogate. Ascertain the rent. Ascertain the wages of the shop assistants in the year 1878. Discover what her mother dies of. Describe cancer. Describe calico. But I cried: Stop! Stop! . . . I threw that ugly, that clumsy . . . tool out of the window, for I knew that if I began describing the cancer and the calico, my Mrs. Brown, that vision to which I cling though I know no way of imparting it to you, would have been dulled and tarnished and vanished for ever." Mr. Bennett's tool was inadequate. For novels were first and foremost about people, and only incidentally about the houses people live in. And in those houses, rooms were furnished not with chairs and tables and chests but with human emotion, eddies of feeling, the press of sensation—all of this expressed in the language of thought and feeling; in verbal "splashes," that simultaneous spatial expressiveness and shimmer of Impressionist painting.

The more expressive—that is, the more fragmentary and splintered the verbal utterance—the further removed it was from the domain of public discourse, and consequently the more demanding it was on the reader. The more demanding the text, the more personal the aesthetic experience; the more personal the aesthetic experience, the more individual and unique the interpretation. The argument Virginia Woolf was advancing depended largely upon our accepting the premise that "on or about December 1910, human character changed." This change meant that all public utterance implying shared values and common assumptions about reality was no longer valid. Who or what was behind this? Psychoanalysis? The failure of traditional values? Scientists insisting on the distortions of human perception?

There was no single answer. What seemed clear, though, was that this phenomenon called Reality had been misconstrued. The world was no longer perceived by everyone in the same way. There were no longer fixed points of reference, no common grounds of agreement, no shared beliefs or communal experience as of old. Every perceiving subject was now an individual; and every individual was unique. Every human perception was therefore different; so that every perceived object was inevitably processed and interpreted differently by each unique perceiving subject. The world was fragmented, unstable, asymmetrical. For the advance-guard writer, it must therefore now be represented verbally by grammatical and syntactical violations and unexpected ruptures in logic and coherence. Life must no longer be seen as "a series of gig lamps symmetrically arranged."

We, as readers, had to synthesize the broken pieces for ourselves. We had to make our own harmony, our own wholeness. The success or failure of the literary experience was now largely dependent upon the reader's perception of fictional texts which no longer offered stable photographic reproductions of the world. The reader could no longer rely upon commonly accepted descriptions of cancer and commonly agreed upon measures of calico. For these were public conventions, and reality was no longer public: it was, from December 1910, so Virginia Woolf claimed, private, personal, idiosyncratic, subjectively construed. This meant that the reality constructed by one reader would inevitably differ from that of another, even while both were reading the same words, on the same page, in the same book, at the same time. Conventions were gone, as were previously agreed upon notions of Truth.

Virginia Woolf's argument continues: "We must reflect that where so much strength is spent on finding a way of telling the truth, the truth itself is bound to reach us in rather an exhausted and chaotic condition." Ulysses, Queen Victoria, and Prufrock—"to give Mrs. Brown some of the names she has made famous lately—is a little pale and dishevelled by the time her rescuers reach her."

The haystacks and lily ponds of Giverny were as visible to French citizens as they were to Monet. In the same way, Mrs. Brown was as visible to readers who remained silent as she was to novelists who told stories about her. It was now the reader's responsibility to note the countless aesthetic experiences this visibility made possible. Readers could no longer remain passive recipients of a novelist's story: they now had to participate actively in the story's evocation. Nothing was more mistaken than the notion that the writer knew more about Mrs. Brown than the reader. "It is this division between reader and writer, this humility on your part, these professional airs and graces on ours, that corrupt and emasculate the books which should be the healthy offspring of a close and equal alliance between us."

The essay closes on a brilliant summing up, which sweeps in the major premises she set forth in her three experimental pieces: "You have overheard scraps of talk that have filled you with amazement" [*Kew Gardens*]. "In one day thousands of ideas have coursed through your brains; thousands of emotions have met, collided, and disappeared in astonishing disorder" [*The Mark on the Wall*]. "You should insist that she [Mrs. Brown] is an old woman of unlimited capacity and infinite variety; capable of appearing in any place; wearing any dress; saying anything and doing heaven knows what" [*An Unwritten Novel*]. It was these three experiments, joining hands, that prepared her to write the novels which would mark her technical virtuosity and ensure her fame.

It's a curious coincidence that Jacques Raverat spoke of the writer's not being conscious "on page 259" of what had been written "on page 31." For Virginia Woolf in *Mrs. Dalloway* was to provide English literature with an example of precisely that consciousness. Clarissa, during her morning hour on Bond Street, has what appears to be a random memory. It is on page 11 of the Hogarth Press Uniform Edition: "She remembered once throwing a shilling into the Serpentine." This is the memory in its entirety. What precedes and what follows it have no apparent connection with the memory itself. It only becomes significant (if the reader is lucky enough to recall it) some 191 pages and many fictional hours later, when Clarissa is told of Septimus's suicide. Alone in an upstairs room, she relives his death in her imagination, and remembers that "she had once thrown a shilling into the Serpentine, never anything more. But he had flung it away," connecting Septimus's fatal plunge and her *own suicidal impulse*. What motivated that impulse and how it relates to Septimus's death is left to be worked out in another series of closely related images. So when Virginia Woolf spoke of the reader's participation in the reading event, she meant precisely that. If readers were not prepared for this kind of *reflexive* reading and missed the connections, then there would be a good deal of frustration and confusion. Many readers would dismiss her highly fragmented, overly elliptical scenes as Arnold Bennett had and, like Bennett, altogether miss her point. For Virginia Woolf was now creating a text that reverberated with deliberate, calculated ambiguities which could be interpreted or resolved (or tolerated) only in accordance with the individual reader and all the past experience that reader brought to the reading act.

Few indeed have sensed in *Jacob's Room* the strange sequences Virginia Woolf created to insinuate the story of Jacob as a young man who has lost his footing in life, a young man emotionally crippled by a possessive, over-protective, and adoring mother. To experience *that* particular story—for there are certainly other readings—readers would have had to hold conventional assumptions about mother-son relationships in abeyance and surrender themselves to the peculiar series of images that suggest Jacob throughout his young life—a little boy with weak legs, the captive crab circling on "weakly legs" the water bucket; and later Jacob's difficulty dancing, managing his feet socially; still later, his disillusionment with a woman old enough to be his mother; and the elliptical final gesture of Betty Flanders dangling Jacob's shoes before the homosexual youth who adored her now-dead son.* It was not by accident, surely, that Virginia Woolf introduced recurring images throughout the novel referring to Jacob's *feet*, Jacob's *shoes*, Jacob's *footing*, Jacob's *stand* in life. For like the little crab of his childhood, Jacob's ascent to adulthood and emotional maturity has failed.

To have experienced this unusual reading would not have been easy for readers in 1922 who were still turning the pages of Trollope and Dickens and Thackeray, who still had faith in Omniscient Narration, who still believed it was the author who made them laugh or cry, and not something deeply buried in themselves—readers still largely unaware that it was principally their own perceptions that determined and colored their evocation of ambiguous texts.

---

* In fact, Betty Flanders and Jacob had much in common with Julia Stephen and Adrian; but one might as easily read Vanessa and Julian into this hermetically sealed mother-son relationship.

The method was brought to perfection in *Mrs. Dalloway*. Here Virginia Woolf created a complex, deeply troubled, suicidal woman behind a glittering exterior, who in loving Sally Seton had violated one of her society's moral codes; who freely admitted that kissing Sally Seton "on the lips" was the "most exquisite moment of her whole life"; who in the end would have only her memory of that love to cling to. We have only to imagine how Arnold Bennett would have gone about creating Clarissa, to gauge Virginia Woolf's success in insinuating throughout the entire novel the woman residing inside Clarissa Dalloway who is never made explicit.

The same is true of Septimus Warren Smith, Clarissa's "double." Like Clarissa, Septimus is bound by a morally and socially unlawful love for his officer Evans. Like Clarissa he is an "outsider" who married his wife in a panic rather than out of love; who could not acknowledge, so great was the pressure of society, his forbidden love for another man; who took his own life to escape the tormentors pursuing him. Here Virginia Woolf would once more create, through a series of images—birds singing in Greek, men cutting down trees, dogs "busy" at railings, dogs "busy with each other," dogs turning into men—and through ever-increasing radiations of fear and self-hatred and self-glorification, one of the most memorable characters in contemporary fiction.

One of the non-linear ideas Virginia Woolf would "splash" on her page was the name "Septimus"—the name "Septimus" coupled with an allusion to Dante's *Inferno*. This seemingly negligible detail appears in parentheses: "('Septimus, do put down your book,' said Rezia, gently shutting the *Inferno*)." Virginia Woolf's first readers would not likely have realized the significance of the allusion, so quietly is it introduced. But the juxtaposition of Septimus and the *Inferno* is rich and resonant. For the Seventh Circle of the Inferno—the Septimus Circle—is the place where punishment is meted out to those guilty of violence and brutality. In the First Round of Circle Seven, those engaged in *war* are tormented (Septimus and Evans in the trenches); in the Second Round, those guilty of *violence against themselves* (Septimus's suicide); and in the Third Round, those guilty of crimes against God, *nature*, and art (Septimus's homosexual love for Evans)—in Canto XIV, sodomites are specifically singled out.

Certainly, as with all her novels, other readings are possible, and even encouraged. But one fact remains: Virginia Woolf did not introduce these details as decoration. Every detail was there *not* by chance but by *choice*. The novel is full of such deliberate details; for her aim was to create small "shocks" of feeling, sudden "moments" of being, small "splashes" of emotion that would have been recognizable (because expected) to readers of poetry. T. S. Eliot had earlier written in an essay on *Hamlet* (1919) that "the only way of expressing emotion in the form of art [was] by finding an 'objective correlative'; in other words, a set of objects; a situation, a chain of events which [would] be the formula of that *particular* emotion; such that when the external facts, which must terminate in sensory experience, [were] given, the emotion [was] immediately evoked." In much the same way Virginia Woolf's "tunnelling process" and handling of mind time made it possible for her to express her characters' values and feeling states; and by creating multiple sequences of idea- and image-clusters, she might dramatize those feeling states and the values they implied. *But only with the help of the reader*.

By the time she had written most of *Mrs. Dalloway* Virginia realized how difficult it would be to continue with her method. She turned repeatedly to her journal, sometimes in satisfaction, more often in despair. In September she was writing sloppily, "using nothing but present participles." She had reached the party scene, however, and decided how the novel would end: with the words "For there she was." On those four words would rest the burden of bringing all the "tunnels" together so that each would illuminate the other, a task of monumental difficulty. But there were those dreaded mad scenes of Septimus to be revised. The novel presented what now appeared to be an insurmountable problem of form: the success of the design depended entirely on getting each character's emotional inflections in the correct relation to those of all the other characters. At bottom it was a problem in time sequence that Roger Fry would have understood in terms of spatial relations.

"But how entirely I live in my imagination," she said in her journal; "how completely [I] depend upon spurts of thought, coming as I walk, as I sit; churning up in my mind and so making a perpetual pageant which is to me my happiness." On October 8 she wrote the last four words of the novel.

By mid-December, she was "galloping" over *Mrs. Dalloway*, typing it over entirely from the beginning. Reviewers would say the book was "disjointed because of the mad scenes not connecting with the Dalloway scenes"; others would see only its "superficial glittery writing." But no matter what they said, the book was real; it was more than verbal acrobatics. It had been dug up from the "richest strata of my mind." And with that vein tapped she could "write and write and write now: the happiest feeling in the world." Four days before Christmas, she was "putting on a spurt to have Mrs. Dalloway copied for Leonard to read at Rodmell; and then in I dart to deliver the final blows to the Common Reader,* and then—then I shall be free."

But she would not be very free, or free for very long. Since the early months of 1924, the distinguished psychoanalyst Dr. James Glover (who was also Adrian Stephen's training analyst), acting on behalf of the British Psycho-Analytical Society, had been negotiating with Leonard the terms on which the Hogarth Press would undertake all future publication and distribution of the papers of the International Psycho-Analytic Library. It was the Agreement which led to Leonard and Virginia's becoming the publishers of Freud's complete works in English translation. In November of 1924 the Hogarth Press had published the first two volumes of Freud's *Collected Papers*. Thus the Press, which had begun as a therapeutic hobby in 1917, had suddenly become "monstrous, kicking and sprawling." But it was perhaps the most extraordinary coincidence of the decade that the Press took over the work of Sigmund Freud—who was exploring free association, dream analysis, unconscious motivation, and the like—at the very time when Virginia was herself developing a literary method in many ways similar to Freud's; certainly it was as difficult to comprehend, and almost as hostile to a skeptical public. Both Sigmund Freud and Virginia Woolf were being prepared for a public debut under the same roof, literally and metaphorically, during the second half of 1924.

The year 1925 marked the beginning of a five-year period that would be the richest, most productive, and most satisfying time in Virginia's life. There would be illnesses and setbacks and frustrations—"some intensities of pleasure, some profound plunges of gloom"—but on the whole they would be years of contentment, and even happiness. As a writer, she would reach her peak of artistic maturity.

---

* The book of essays called *The Common Reader* and *Mrs. Dalloway* would be published within a few weeks of each other.

VITA

� 1924 - 1928 ✗

27 Sometime before the publication of *Mrs. Dalloway* and *The Common Reader* Virginia felt the first stirrings of another novel inside her. This was to be *To the Lighthouse*. The moment of conception, though it was unknown to Virginia herself, can probably be dated to October 17 of the previous year, 1924. Too many ideas for stories were impinging, she complained, when she should be finishing the two books at hand; but she had difficulty keeping the lid shut. "I see already The Old Man." Who this mystery figure was, she didn't say, but he did not appear again until January 6, 1925: "Here I conceive my story—but I'm always conceiving stories now. Short ones—scenes—for instance The Old Man (a character of Leslie Stephen). The Professor of Milton . . ." This fragmentary evocation of her father led, some ten or eleven weeks later, after a bout of influenza, to a seemingly irrelevant comment: "I can only note that the past is beautiful because one never realises an emotion at the time. It expands later, and thus we don't have complete emotions about the present, only about the past." She was happiest and lived most fully when the moment was backed and filled with the past; only then did the experience of living seem rich and deep, as when she was thinking of childhood and her father. "This is why we dwell on the past, I think." She was to say a few months later: "I can't write about people I am in the habit of seeing, anymore than I can describe places until I have practically forgotten them. It's not humour; it's simply the way my mind works."

It is important to remember that while Virginia was composing *Mrs. Dalloway*, Tolstoy was fresh on her mind. Only a little earlier she and Kotelian-sky had translated Goldenveizer's *Talks with Tolstoi*. In one of those talks the great Russian had said: "All that a man has felt remains with him in memory. We all live by memories." Wasn't this also true of Proust, who, for Virginia, was "far the greatest modern novelist"?

• • •

Sometime in February, Virginia sent Jacques Raverat advance proofs of *Mrs. Dalloway*. He was dying of multiple sclerosis and had to dictate his reply. The novel, he said, made him want to live a little longer, if he knew he'd continue to receive such books. In early April, Virginia turned to her diary. "Since I wrote . . . Jacques Raverat has died." But he had written her a letter that had given her one of the "happiest days" of her life. "I wonder if this time I have achieved something? Well, nothing anyhow compared with Proust, in whom I am embedded now."

Upstairs in his study, Leonard had been correcting proofs of Freud's *Collected Papers*, and downstairs in her workroom Virginia was digging into the past of her characters, to strata very near the baseline of consciousness. At this moment in her career, one thing was beyond dispute: "I have at last, bored down into my oil well, and can't scribble fast enough to bring it all to the surface . . . I have never felt this rush and urgency before . . . Oddly, for all my vanity, I have not until now had much faith in my novels, or thought them my own expression."

What the new "tunnelling" method showed her was that the past blossomed naturally into the present. The bloom of all her yesterdays tinged everything she saw, everything she wrote. While walking by herself in Cambridge in early May, she remarked that the old city was a "lovely place full, like all places, now, of this wave of the past. Walking past the Darwins I noticed the willows; I thought with that growing maternal affection which now comes to me, of myself there." Ten days later, on May 14, after meandering through the past since October 17 of the previous year, the creative explosion happened. "I'm now all on the strain with desire to . . . get on to *To the Lighthouse*. This is going to be fairly short: to have father's character done complete in it; and mother's; and St Ives; and childhood . . . But the centre is father's character, sitting in a boat, reciting We perished, each alone, while he crushes a dying mackerel." But she must hold back and let the novel simmer, "adding to it between tea and dinner till it is complete for writing out."

This was what Virginia Woolf's preoccupation with the past had been leading to, and how odd that she herself seemed unaware of where it was headed. For the novel even had a title. Some months later, as she was thinking through *To the Lighthouse*, she said, in complete parenthetical innocence: "(how I begin to love the past—I think something to do with my book)." *To the Lighthouse* was to be about her childhood, so that whatever she experienced of the adult world, she now saw in relation to her mother and father, and to her earliest years. Riding on a bus one afternoon, she heard a little girl asking her mother how many inches there were in a mile, and the child, excited and eager "to grasp the whole universe reminded me of myself, asking questions of my mother." Leonard settled a minor dispute in the Press one morning and Virginia noted his firmness: "Here I salute Leonard with unstinted, indeed childlike, adoration . . . But then I have a child's trust in Leonard." He made her feel secure. He had behaved like a father—*her* father, while her mother was still alive. "I snuggled in to the core of my life . . . feeling entirely immune." Leonard had become a version of an idealized Leslie Stephen; and much of the child's world she was resurrecting would soon carry over into her imminent relationship with the radiant and protective Vita Sackville-West, an idealized mother.

Meanwhile Virginia prepared herself for the publication of *The Common Reader* on April 23. Eight days passed before the silence was broken. Then came a mocking review in *Star* poking fun at Vanessa's cover design. *The Times Literary Supplement*, however, gave her two columns of "sober and sensible praise—neither one thing nor the other." "From Mrs Woolf," the critic said, "we get that valuable thing, a true perspective. It implies the sanity of criticism which is common sense enlightened." The *Manchester Guardian* reviewer found in the essays that "combination of brilliance and integrity which is so rare . . . until we read this volume we credited Virginia Woolf with more charm and vivacity than vision."

On May 4, two weeks later, *Mrs. Dalloway* was published, and its reception was sharply divided. Readers contrasted the accessibility of the criticism with the impenetrability of the novel. Letters from baffled readers piled up on the hall table. All the "old gentlemen," she wrote to a friend, said she was a born critic and not a novelist; and all the "young gentlemen" assured her that she was a born novelist and not a critic. It was all quite bewildering. Readers who liked one book hated the other.

Leonard had said that *Mrs. Dalloway* was her *best* work to date, "but then has he not *got* to think so?" she said, almost dismissively. Gwen Raverat asked her about the madness and suicide parts, and Virginia replied that she could scarcely touch those scenes "without bursting into flame." Those memories of the summer of 1904 were still "a raging furnace . . . madness and doctors and being forced." It was better not to talk about it.

Mrs. Dalloway was not at first well received. It was a "bewildering jumble" to one reviewer; although the book did not much interest him personally, he thought that "readers of preternaturally nimble intellect [might] discover a consecutive story." To another: "None but the mentally fit should aspire to read this novel . . . It may be said such is life, but is it art?" A reviewer for *The Independent* claimed that while most readers are not "proficient in the difficult gymnastic of jumping in and out of other people's skins," the novel would be "highly praised by the sensitive minority."

Part of the division stemmed from the novelty of the book's narrative method. Any text that required the reader's full participation (as Virginia Woolf had explicitly warned in *Mr. Bennett and Mrs. Brown*) would necessarily be interpreted according to each reader's preoccupations. Such participation was the natural consequence of a method in which the writer "suggested" and the reader "supplied." But this critical blindness was something Virginia either did not foresee or found difficult to accept, as her letter to Gerald Brenan implies: "I shan't answer your criticisms . . . because at the moment I can only pit them against other people's criticisms, and cannot make them refer to Mrs Dalloway itself"—by which, presumably, she meant *her own interpretation*.

She had just had a long criticism from Roger Fry "and he gave me an entirely different view of Mrs D from yours," she said to Brenan. In fact, they contradicted each other on almost every important point—"the two I now remember being Septimus: to him [Fry] the most essential part of Mrs D:"—the natural reading for a man whose wife was in an insane asylum—and Brenan's reading, with his entirely different orientation, seeing Septimus as having "no function in the book." Such was the dilemma she had created for herself. In this letter to Brenan, she was speaking as a novelist who wanted to *communicate* what she thought she had *expressed*.

On the whole, however, Virginia was in high spirits and had good reason to be. Her American publisher had accepted both books "without seeing" them and increased her royalty to fifteen percent; the German publisher, Tauchnitz of Leipzig, was interested in bringing out a translation of *Mrs. Dalloway*; and soon Ann Watkins, the New York literary agent, would be coming to see Virginia about some stories for America. Never had she felt "so much admired." But more important than that, as half owner of the Hogarth Press, "I'm the only woman in England free to write what I like."

Apart from the excitement of having two books published within weeks of each other, there were now social demands resulting from the sudden leap in reputation. There were dinners and teas, weekends away, people to see, letters to answer, parties to grace. Altogether from May through early August she led a far more social life than Leonard might have been expected to allow. "I never ask a soul here," she said in mid-July, "but they accumulate.

Tonight Ottoline; Tuesday Jack Hutchinson [the barrister]; Wednesday Edith Sitwell, Friday dine with Raymond [Mortimer]." These were her fixed invitations: there'd be plenty more before long. "I run out after tea as if pursued." Too much was happening and she wasn't thinking of the future—"I feast on the moment."

In early August the Woolfs went to Rodmell for their annual eight-week holiday. They were both exhausted, but Virginia had some "superstitious wish" to begin writing *To the Lighthouse* on the first day at Monks House. She planned to write the entire first draft in those two months. But nature, at last, intervened. On Wednesday, August 19, when she and Leonard were at Charleston to celebrate Quentin Bell's fifteenth birthday, Virginia collapsed. She fainted at the dinner table. The newly married Keyneses were there, and Maynard drove her back to Monks House. Leonard put her to bed and there she remained for two weeks in "that odd amphibious state of headache." Not until September 5 was she allowed to write in her journal: she'd used up all her reserves; she'd been "riding on a flat tire." The illness had "rammed a big hole" into her eight weeks. But she'd made a "very quick and flourishing attack on To the Lighthouse . . . 22 pages straight off in less than a fortnight"—that is, between August 6 and the 19th.

September crept by slowly and on October 2, a Friday, they returned to Tavistock Square. By Monday Virginia was so ill her new doctor, Elinor Rendel, Lytton Strachey's niece, was sent for. She was immediately "tumbled into bed" and did not move very far from it for the remainder of October and most of November. "I have not been unhappy; but not very happy; too much discomfort . . . rat-gnawing at the back of my head."

There was something else gnawing at Virginia—and that was Vita Sackville-West. Vita's husband, Harold Nicolson, had been in the Foreign Office in London from 1920. He was now posted as Counsellor to the British Legation in Teheran. Vita had just told Virginia about joining him in Persia for two months in the spring of 1926, and this upset her greatly: "I minded the thought so much (thinking to lose sight of her for 5 years) that I conclude I am genuinely fond of her." Virginia was not being entirely straightforward about her feelings, however; for she didn't need this piece of news to tell her she was "genuinely fond" of Vita. Only a few days later she was quoting some lines of Shelley:

> *I could lie down like a tired child,*
> *And weep away the life of care*

Which I have borne and yet must bear,
Till death like sleep might steal on me.

"Most children do not know what they cry for; nor do I altogether." What she did know was that her tears were due partly to that "devil Vita. No Vita. No letter. No visit. No invitation to Long Barn." Vita had been to London without calling her. "So many good reasons for this neglect occur to me that I'm ashamed to call this a cause for weeping. Only if I do not see her now, I shall not—ever: for the moment for intimacy will be gone." What Virginia meant by "intimacy" was really the maternal coddling she wanted from Vita. *To the Lighthouse* had pushed her back into the past, with all her childhood needs; and they would remain acute while the novel was in progress. Leonard would give her the love and intellectual camaraderie of Leslie Stephen, and Vita would provide the protective embraces Julia Stephen could never find the time to give.

Before Virginia's tears were dry, Vita called and arranged to carry her off to Long Barn on December 17, where she stayed three nights. It was during this weekend that the goddess Astarte descended upon them and marshaled their friendship to the higher stratum of love. In her diary Vita made a note for December 17, 1925: "A peaceful evening." But for the eighteenth: "Talked to her till 3 A.M.—Not a peaceful evening."

Virginia too made a record of the "unpeaceful evening"—it was a very defensive and not altogether candid note: "These Sapphists *love* women; friendship is never untinged with amorosity." But, she went on, "I like her and being with her, and the splendour—she shines in the grocer's shop in Sevenoaks with a candle lit radiance . . . pink glowing, grape clustered, pearl hung. That is the secret of her glamour, I suppose." The inventory didn't stop there. "There is her maturity and full breastedness: her being so much in full sail on the high tides, where I am coasting down backwaters; her capacity I mean to take the floor in any company . . . to control silver, servants, chow dogs; her motherhood . . . her being in short (what I have never been) a real woman." There were deficits, too, that Virginia had no trouble identifying. "In brain and insight she is not as highly organised as I am. But then she is aware of this, and so lavishes on me the maternal protection which, for some reason, is what I have always most wished from everyone."

Virginia's early "crushes" on Madge Vaughan and Violet Dickinson had in them a large component of longing for this cosseting and maternal solicitude. But they could never give, nor could the younger Virginia ever accept, what Vita had to offer. It was almost inevitable that the relationship with Vita would become the longest and most passionate in Virginia's adult years. Apart from Leonard and Vanessa, Vita would mean more to her than anyone else in the world for the remainder of her life. And for the next three years Vita would occupy that emotional center out of which everything else radiated. Not many weeks would pass before their perceptions of each other became more focused.

From Long Barn, Vita wrote about her side of the adventure to Harold. Having only a few years earlier survived Vita's devastating affair with Violet Trefusis,* Harold Nicolson was understandably worried. He had no reason to be, Vita assured him, for she would not "fall in love with Virginia," nor would Virginia fall in love with her. On December 18, Vita assured Harold again: "She says she depends on me. She is so vulnerable under all her brilliance. I do love her, but not b.s.ly [back-stairs-ly; i.e. homosexually]." And still again on the nineteenth: "We have made friends by leaps and bounds in these two days. I love her, but couldn't fall 'in love' with her, so don't be nervous."

Vita left London to join Harold in Teheran on January 20, 1926, bidding goodbye to a disconsolate Virginia on the doorstep at 52 Tavistock Square. Her first "Persian" letter to Virginia was written in the train to Dover. Virginia replied, purely and simply: "I have missed you. I do miss you. I shall miss you." The letters during Vita's Persian expedition chronicle the early chapters of this extraordinary love affair in which Vita quested for glory, with Virginia stumbling after her in childlike devotion.

In the next four months, letters would be exchanged that on the surface effervesced with excitement and verbal caress, and below stammered with uncertainty and apprehension. Both were women of formidable resilience and determination; and during these early months of alternating confidence and doubt, Virginia reviewed all the adverbs of motive and manner, while Vita conjugated every known verb for love and passion.

In Virginia's earliest impressions, Vita was "virginal, savage, patrician" and wrote constantly and competently—"with a pen of brass." To Vita, Virginia was simply the "gentle genius"—lovely, idolized, and remote. But even in

---

* See Nigel Nicolson, *Portrait of a Marriage*, and *Violet to Vita: The Letters of Violet Trefusis to Vita Sackville-West*, ed. M. A. Leaska and J. Phillips (New York: Viking, 1990).

January 1926 it would have been apparent to anyone who looked closely that Virginia was completely in Vita's thrall. What was perhaps not so apparent was just how large, complicated, and obsessive this enterprise of the heart would become.

Even through the calculated medium of letters exchanged at this time, where verbal risks were minimal, it was evident that Vita's attention settled on Virginia with obstinate concentration, and Virginia responded with a mix of nervous mockery and guarded acquiescence. Each clearly needed something from the other. Vita was the superior woman in Virginia's eyes, and Virginia was the superior writer in Vita's. It was obvious to both that just as one was questing for literary fame and glory, the other craved the maternal embrace; and in those dual pursuits large loyalties and high proprietorial claims would emerge—and with them four distinct personalities as well. Some of the time Vita would appear to Virginia the voluptuous aristocrat, and at other times she was the protecting mother figure, crooning affection and reassurance. Virginia, to Vita, would at one moment represent the mistress of English letters, and in the next the helpless, grasping child, soliciting Vita's strong custodial arms. The rapport between them was by no means simple, and both would soon realize that in the chiaroscuro of human needs, neither loved the other for herself alone. So that just as passion and promise flourished in the beginning, so in the end there would be compassion and compromise.

In no relationship, before or after, would Virginia emerge so clearly and consistently defined. Vita saw Virginia as someone whose perceptions were swift, incisive, on the mark—an intellectual who probed and analyzed human act and utterance. There were times when Virginia seemed unattainable, unpredictable, even unapproachable. With so much of her emotional side kept under cover, she could indeed appear reserved and mysterious. Strangely though, Virginia's insatiable curiosity could often be misconstrued as friendliness. Sometimes she gave the impression, especially in social gatherings, of being a part of everyone yet accessible to no one. Her deepest and most persistent difficulty was an overwhelming need for intimacy often in conflict with an equally overwhelming need for independence. To the restless Dionysian figure lurking in Vita, this Apollonian frieze of intellect and intuition was an irresistible challenge.

The part of Virginia which Vita more readily responded to was the childlike, affectionate side: the self-absorbed, insecure, demonstrative little girl who forever needed her confidence bolstered; the vulnerable child so prone to emotional bruising, who hated criticism, demanded directness, and craved affection, the little 'Ginia of 22 Hyde Park Gate who got knocked down over and over again by Thoby and Vanessa but refused ever to admit defeat. This was the Virginia Vita loved and protected and mothered.

Vita, on her side, was a mass of contradictions. She was rebellious and she was reticent; she was fearless and yet frightened; sociable yet reclusive; bold one moment, shy the next. She was a woman who concealed a naturally timid disposition under a lustrous husk of managerial competence and extravagant courage. And, as with all contradictory personalities, there was something deceptive about her. Not far from the surface one could touch the stargazer, the solitary Vita who sought privacy and shunned emotional embroilments. It was this same woman who seemed forever fanning the embers of passion, yet forever stepping back from its blaze. Much of this Virginia sensed as the weeks went by.

But some traits stood out too much to be ignored. Vita's indomitability, for instance. She had a tendency to take charge of people's lives. Her arrogance flattened obstacles, and her vanity renounced shabbiness. This was the exalted Vita who spoke her own mind with devastating simplicity, who worked like a slave and played like a prince. And directly beside this imposing figure was the gentle, compassionate Vita who held the moth and nursed the swallow. All of these Vitas, wrapped into one, held Virginia magnetized in a bright circle of romance and adventure.

In this network of emotional cross-currents, something like an enormous paradox began to shape itself. As soon as Virginia realized she had fallen in love with Vita, two simultaneous and contradictory searches were set in motion: the first was the attempt to make Vita show her all the maternal affection and care she had expected in her earlier years; the second was the expectation that Vita would "correct" all the errors of the past and somehow fulfill the promise Virginia's childhood figures, Julia Stephen principally, had failed at. The feeling for Vita which crystallized in December 1925, then, was doomed from the start, for it contained simultaneously both an attempt to return to her past as well as an attempt to undo and rectify that past. This was essentially what Virginia was trying to do in writing *To the Lighthouse*— to disinter personal history and transform its cold granite into mists of rainbow. That she should be engaged in that large effort while simultaneously clinging to Vita was bound to create tidal waves.

· · ·

Virginia had thought through the design of her novel more thoroughly than ever before. As early as July 1925, she had set it down in her journal: the outline of *To the Lighthouse* would be "father and mother and child in the garden: the death; the sail to the lighthouse. I think, though, that I shall enrich it in all sorts of ways... (I conceive the book in 3 parts: 1. at the drawing room window; 2. seven years passed; 3. the voyage)." For many weeks Virginia remained submerged in this haunted world. She rekindled and remembered and reimagined that stretch of phantom history: "... things are crowding into my head: millions of things I might put in—all sorts of incongruities."

And the "incongruities" were legion. There was the hot-tempered, "tantrumical" father and the imperious, often-absent mother; a father who slammed doors and sent dinner plates whizzing through windowpanes; a mother who often withdrew into accusing, deathlike silences, who could be contemptuous of everything and everyone around her; who denied little Virginia, the most precocious of the four, the maternal affection and caressing security any sensitive child needed in so conflicted a household, whether at St. Ives or in London. It was natural that a youngster of her temperament should gradually feel unlovable and unworthy and even "bad" in so tense and unpredictable an atmosphere, and form a deep attachment to the more responsive, but highly moralistic, father. It was equally natural that the young Virginia should turn to storytelling, to fantasy, in search of satisfactions the real world refused to provide, and in the making of fantasy begin to notice that appearances, if one looked closely, were sharply different from the darker realities which lay beneath them.

Much of the fantasy life she created in childhood would naturally be siphoned into this autobiographical novel. And one of the premises upon which the satisfactions of this fantasy world of childhood depended was keeping alive her mother's first love, Herbert Duckworth, thus freeing her father to love her, Virginia, in a deeper, more vital way as a grown man, as well as a father. But the guilt such a pairing might be expected to generate could be minimized, though never fully eradicated, if Virginia kept herself a child throughout the novel, and told that story from a child's perspective. But such a tale, Virginia Woolf realized, could never be stated explicitly: it could only be rendered through innuendo, metaphor, suggestions of the faintest kind. Yet how lyrical and tender that story would be.

· · ·

When she surfaced long enough to rejoin the real world, Virginia wrote letters, long letters to Vita, letters calculated to entice, to divert, to amuse. There was a dinner party, for instance, given by Rose Macaulay, the novelist. She and Leonard had been invited, but arrived late, covered with ink. While seated around the noisy table, Virginia mistook something that had been said by Macaulay's lover, an ex-Catholic priest by the name of O'Donovan. He had evidently said something that sounded to Virginia like the "Holy Ghost," whereas what he was in fact talking about was the "whole coast." Where was the Holy Ghost? Virginia shouted above the babble of voices. That was all she wanted to know. "Where ever the sea is," came the reply. "Am I mad," thought Virginia, "or is this wit?" "The Holy Ghost?" she repeated. "The whole coast," he shouted back. And so the exchange went on, "in an atmosphere so repellent that it became like the smell of bad cheese . . . Leonard shook all over, picked up what he took to be Mrs Gould's napkin, discovered it to be her sanitary towel," by which time this "tenth rate literary respectability . . . shook to its foundations. I kept saying 'Vita would love this.' " (According to Leonard, it was the hem of Mrs. Gould's petticoat that he mistakenly picked up; but of course Virginia's "towel" adds a little spice to the anecdote.)

In another letter, this one meant to give Vita something to ponder, Virginia took up the subject of writing. "As for the *mot juste*, you are quite wrong. Style is a very simple matter; it is all rhythm. Once you get that, you can't use the wrong words. But on the other hand here am I sitting after half the morning, crammed with ideas and visions . . . and can't dislodge them, for lack of the right rhythm."

And there was business too. Vita had promised to write a travel book while she was in Persia. Virginia now wanted to know if she would let the Hogarth Press have it, when actually Heinemann was Vita's publisher. "I don't want to press you, if you feel . . . that Heinemann's has a right," said Virginia. "At the same time I don't want these refinements of feeling to lose us a chance which would give a great fillip to our autumn season. So consider." Vita did consider and in the end broke her contract with Heinemann to publish *Passenger to Teheran* with Hogarth. It was a magnanimous gesture, but Virginia was big-hearted too. She would soon insist that she had used the royalties of *Mrs. Dalloway* to install, in Vita's honor, two water closets and a bathroom with hot running water at Monks House.

28 For much of 1926 Virginia was submerged in the ancient world of St. Ives. By mid-April she had finished the first part of the novel and was just beginning the "Time Passes" section. "I cannot make it out," she said in her diary— "here is the most difficult piece of abstract writing—I have to give an empty house . . . the passage of time, all eyeless and featureless . . . at once I scatter out two pages. Is it nonsense, is it brilliance?" In five weeks' time, she had sketched a draft of the novel's second part.

But Vita was now back. She had returned in May, and Harold, who remained in Teheran, once more needed Vita's reassurances. "Oh my dear," he wrote, "I do hope that Virginia is not going to be a muddle! It is like smoking over a petrol tank!" But there was no muddle, Vita insisted. "I love Virginia—as who wouldn't? But really, my sweet, one's love for Virginia is a very different thing: a mental thing; a spiritual thing." She inspired tenderness. She was an odd "mixture of hardness and softness—the hardness of her mind, and her terror of going mad again. She makes me feel protective." Her love naturally flattered Vita, but Virginia was "not the sort of person one thinks of in that way. There is something incongruous and almost indecent in the idea. I *have* gone to bed with her (twice), but that's all. Now you know all about it, and I hope I haven't shocked you."

Just before leaving London for the summer, the Woolfs paid a visit to Thomas Hardy in Dorset on July 25. Virginia made a lengthy record of the occasion in her journal; it was, after all, her father, Leslie Stephen, who, as editor of the *Cornhill*, had encouraged Hardy in his first years as a novelist.

After the parlor maid had brought in the silver cake stands, the second Mrs. Hardy appeared and began talking to the Woolfs about her dog. "How long ought we to stay? Can Mr Hardy walk much &c I asked, making conversation, as I knew one would have to." They couldn't go very far, Mrs. Hardy said, because the dog wasn't able to walk much, but they did go out every day. He bites, she told them, becoming more animated about the dog, who was "evidently the real centre of her thoughts." The door opened again and in "trotted a little puffy cheeked" old man, addressing them cheerfully like an old doctor or lawyer might, "saying 'Well now—' or words like that as he shook hands."

Hardy was dressed in gray tweed with a striped tie. He had a hooked nose and a round white face, with faded watery eyes—a vigorous little man. It was a substantial tea and old Hardy enjoyed his one cup, sitting on his three-cornered chair. He was extremely easygoing and talked of Sir Leslie. "Your father took my novel—Far From the Madding Crowd. We stood shoulder to shoulder against the British public about certain matters dealt with in that novel . . . I think he broke all the Cornhill laws—not to see the whole book; so I sent it in chapter by chapter, and was never late. Wonderful what youth is! I had it in my head doubtless, but I never thought twice about it—It came out every month."

Hardy was "not interested much in his novels, or in anybody's novels; took it all easily and naturally. 'I never took long with them' he said. The longest was the *Din*nasts (so pronounced). 'But that was really 3 books' said Mrs Hardy. Yes: and that took me 6 years; but not working all the time . . . Did you write poems at the same time as your novels? I asked. No, he said. I wrote a great many poems. I used to send them about, but they were always returned, he chuckled . . . 'You must give Mrs Woolf one of your books,' said Mrs Hardy, inevitably. Yes, I will. But I'm afraid only in the little thin paper edition, he said. I protested that it would be enough if he wrote his name." It was time to go, however. So Leonard and Virginia got up and signed Mrs. Hardy's visitors' book; and Hardy took "my Love's Little Ironies off, and trotted back with it signed, and Woolf spelt Wolff . . . There was not a trace anywhere of deference to editors, or respect for rank . . . He seemed very 'Great Victorian' doing the whole thing with a sweep of the hand . . . Mrs Hardy thrust his old gray hat into his hand and he trotted us out on to the road."

Virginia reached Monks House on July 27 this year, exhausted and mildly depressed. After a week's rest she plunged back into the novel and by September 3 was "easily within sight of the end." She was by this time writing "with heat and ease till 12.30" each day, completing her daily quota of two pages and had just finished the scene with Lily Briscoe painting on the lawn and was now about to begin the concluding chapter of Mr. Ramsay and the two children in the boat on their way to the lighthouse.

One more problem had to be faced, however. "I had meant to end with Ramsay climbing on to the rock." But then what would happen to Lily and her picture? Could she somehow present Lily and Carmichael summing up Mr. Ramsay's character at the end while simultaneously showing the Ramsays at the lighthouse—"so that one had the sense of reading the two things at the same time?" It was again the problem of time. (As she puzzled this out, she suddenly felt the impulse for a new story—"Slater's Pins Have No Points"—in which the first and last sentences would be direct statements, the remaining text, essentially the whole story, given over to recollection, 2,000 words of a remembered past: interior monologue or what Virginia referred to as "oratio obliqua.")

She finished the novel, provisionally, at the end of September. The thought of saying goodbye to the enchantments of childhood, even temporarily, was disheartening. And something else was in the air; something that involved Leonard was intruding upon her domestic life. She noticed that whenever Vita appeared, Leonard "shut up" and tended to be "caustic." He reminded Virginia that their "relationship had not been so good lately." The power Vita exerted over Virginia obviously and naturally bothered him. Was all the excitement she stirred up good for Virginia? And where did he stand in this peculiar liaison? All of this remained unspoken, and because those questions lay silent and smoldering, they made themselves felt all the more forcefully. That was all it took to dip Virginia into a trough of despondency. Once again she felt herself "an elderly, dowdy, fussy, ugly, incompetent woman."

Back in London, as she revised the novel, it occurred to her that life in middle age was "quicker, keener at 44 than at 24." Opportunities were multiplying, her fame was growing; she had even developed a new vision of death—"active, positive . . . exciting." The one experience "I shall never describe," she had said to Vita. For there was Vita now to consider—who'd begun coming to see Virginia in Tavistock Square. In November she'd spent the afternoon "sitting on the floor in her velvet jacket and red striped silk shirt, I knotting her pearls into heaps of lustrous eggs. She had come to see me—so we go on—a spirited, creditable affair . . . rather a bore for Leonard, but not enough to worry him"—so she hoped. But even Vita would soon be causing anxiety, for beneath the shimmer and flourish Virginia knew that Vita was an adventurer, always seeking new spoils. She knew that the adoring, mothering Vita was the appearance; behind that appearance was another Vita, sexually aimless, on the lookout for new conquests, fresh pleasures.

For the moment, however, she must concentrate on her novel. It was moving quickly, but there were still too many scenes; it was too sketchy, too disjointed. By late November, she had resolved most of the difficulty. It was now "easily the best of my books . . . not complicated with all that desperate accompaniment of madness." But time was running out. There was only December left. Then in the new year Vita was going away again. Virginia thus found herself once more in one of those states which kept her under the threat of headache. In fact on November 19 she reported one to Vita. It was the result of seeing too many people, she claimed, and not a bad one; "but I tell you, to get your sympathy: to make you protective," she said to her beloved Vita, just as Leslie Stephen had so often said to his beloved Julia. There might have been another, deeper reason for the headache—a worry that Virginia saw as inevitable and could do nothing about—the ten-year difference between them and what that gap implied: "you'll be tired of me one of these days (I'm so much older) and so I have to take my little precautions."

Then from out of the blue: "And isn't there something obscure in you?" Virginia said; "...something that doesn't vibrate in you: It may be purposely—you don't let it: but I see it with other people, as well as with me: something reserved, muted—God knows what...It's in your writing too... The thing I call central transparency—sometimes fails you there too." It was a serious matter, this flaw in Vita, tantamount to some congenital character defect. How Virginia came to sense what Vita had tried so hard to conceal was baffling. It was a block nevertheless which Virginia thought muffled her feeling for people and impaired her writing.

Vita couldn't find her pen fast enough to write Harold: "Damn the woman, she has put her finger on it. There is something muted...Something that doesn't vibrate...doesn't come alive...It makes everything I do (i.e. write) a little unreal; gives the effect of having been done from the outside. It is the thing which spoils me as a writer...But how did Virginia discover it? I have never owned it to anybody, scarcely even to myself. It is what spoils my human relations too."

Virginia discovered the flaw, Vita should have realized, because she suffered from the same affliction. What it amounted to was the need for intimacy in combat with the need for distance. There was one big difference between them, however. Virginia, like many another writer, shielded herself from the "shocks" of living with pen and ink; but her intellectual superiority, coupled as it was with her emotional submissiveness, permitted her as a novelist to surrender completely to the mental atmosphere of her characters, as she was now doing in *To the Lighthouse*. With astonishing ease she could crawl in and out of her characters' minds, however different from one another they might be, to record their deepest feelings. A few years hence, she would write a biography of Elizabeth Barrett Browning from the point of view of her cocker spaniel, Flush; and this would require a complete abdication of human attributes in the service of a canine perspective, representing an enormous stretch of imagination. What this meant was that Virginia Woolf was sure enough of herself as an artist, and submissive enough emotionally, to surrender her Self during the creative act, to imagine, freely, without inhibition, the thoughts and feelings of her characters. This was something Vita simply could not do.

Vita's orientation to the world was too competitive, too domineering; hers was the aggressive stance. She was very much like Julia Stephen in this respect. The very idea of submission was foreign to her nature. It threatened her most vulnerable sensibilities. In consequence, she could write lavish descriptions *about* her characters' feelings; she could describe them in elaborate detail, *but always and only from the outside*. She could never genuinely experience those feelings because she was incapable of getting to the deeper strata of her characters' inner lives. A fundamental lack of confidence concealed under the carapace of aggression did not permit access to the minds of her fictional people in order to experience *their* feelings. This was what Virginia meant by something that did not "vibrate." Vita could only write "from the outside"; and the external quality of the writing was *un*lifelike and *un*real.

That Virginia had ferreted out Vita's "secret" made a difference in their relations in the months ahead. Vita would have given anything to be able to write "from the inside"—this, after all, was at the very heart of Virginia's "tunnelling" method—and so she began to study Virginia's writing with greater concentration. Virginia found Vita's attention flattering, but not very satisfying. For now the affection-craving child would have to make room for Virginia, the "gentle genius" of fiction. She would now assume the role of literary mentor, and Vita would follow her like a "puppy on a string." In this vaguely defined office, Virginia now became "essential": that is, on Vita's side the bond had now become as professional as it had earlier been personal.

Harold Nicolson wrote to Virginia from Teheran: "I am glad that Vita has come under an influence so stimulating and so sane . . . You need never worry about my having any feelings except a longing that Vita's life should be as rich and as sincere as possible. I loathe jealousy as I loathe all forms of disease."

In the middle of January Virginia spent two nights with Vita at Knole, and on the twenty-eighth, after a morning with her alone, Vita left for her second visit to Persia. She was accompanied this time by two friends. One of them was the wealthy Lady Dorothy Wellesley, the wife of Lord Gerald Wellesley, who was on more intimate terms with Vita than Virginia liked. Leigh Ashton was the other—to Virginia "that putty faced low voiced rather beaten cur"— who would later become Director of the Victoria and Albert Museum.

"I don't know how I shall get on without you," Vita wrote on the day of her departure. "Put 'honey' when you write—Darling, please go on loving me—I am so miserable—Don't forget me." On the next day: "I shall work so hard, partly to please you, partly to please myself . . . It is quite true that you have had infinitely more influence on me intellectually than anyone, and for that alone I love you . . . You do like me to write well, don't you? And I do hate writing badly—and having written so badly in the past."

What seems not to have crossed Vita's mind was not that her writing was bad, for she was a competent novelist, but that her writing was so different from Virginia's; and that difference had its origin in the structure of her personality, not in verbal performance. Eventually she would find a subject for which her "exterior" writing would be not only appropriate but necessary. That novel would be *The Edwardians* and it would make a small fortune for Vita and the Woolfs.

Virginia's principal concern at this time, however, was *To the Lighthouse*, scheduled for publication in May. When she wasn't working she wrote long, amusing letters to Vita and to Vanessa, who was in the South of France painting with Duncan Grant. Her chief bit of news was her haircut. She'd been shingled, she told Vanessa. "We got slightly merry the other night on Spanish wine," and out came the scissors. "I can't describe the delight when the long coil of hair fell off . . . I think however hideous it makes me look it is worth it . . . It was none of Vita's doing," she assured Vanessa. "For you, of course, beautiful as you are . . . But then I was always a second rate work . . . so it don't matter." To Vita: "It's off; it's in the kitchen bucket: my hair-pins have been offered up like crutches in St Andrews, at the high altar . . . You shall ruffle my hair in May, Honey: it's as short as a partridge's rump . . . I have bought a coil of hair, which I attach by a hook. It falls into the soup, and is fished out with a fork."

29 All her life, Virginia had a tendency to make herself the butt of jokes; she was the family jester. She made others laugh, but mostly at her own expense. If she kept herself amusing and silly, she aroused interest; one liked circus clowns. This propensity to keep others entertained was a familiar variant of her childhood storytelling instinct. The

more she valued one's affection the more inclined she was to pay for their attention. She had always done this with Vanessa, and now she was beginning to play the same role with Vita—neither of whom, too dictatorial to tolerate self-mockery, would have dreamed of joking about themselves.

She wrote to Vita, for instance, about a party she had been to at Ethel Sands and Nan Hudson's, both wealthy American painters whom Virginia would soon visit in France. Lytton Strachey's young lover, Philip Ritchie, was one of the guests and at some point during the evening told Virginia that she was "the chief coquette in London. 'Allumeuse' Clive corrected him. Then my suspenders came down, dragging with them an old rag of che-mise—why didn't you tell me one must fasten one's suspenders properly?" Always "some misery like suspenders clips my wings of glory."

But Virginia's "clipped wings" had another, quite different function. They provided her with an alibi for her helplessness in carrying on the business of daily life. When she needed to buy clothes, for instance, a chore she dreaded, she invented scenes calculated to arouse pity and recruit assistance. "I've got to buy skirts, hats, shoes, boxes, mackintoshes. I find myself in the wrong department. I dream. I saunter. People trample on me—they inflict the most dreadful insults . . . It's humiliating to be in the Babies Sock Dept. when one wants Ladies hand bags." At one point she felt so incompetent in a clothing store, she paid Vanessa a fee to buy a dress for her.*

This ineptitude and self-belittling were pieces of a larger scheme created to give the impression that Virginia was always desperate. After all, if she lived in such a state, surely she must deserve something in return. (She was very much like her father in this respect.) The claims she made had once been only wishes. But with time those wishes developed into something she now felt entitled to. Her persistent sense of unworthiness also encouraged a too-ready willingness to forgive—Vita a great deal of the time, and Vanessa all of the time. Running parallel to this was a tendency to glorify the person she clung to—Vita some of the time, Vanessa all of the time. The greater their glory, the freer she was to feel helpless, subordinate, dependent, and therefore, again like Sir Leslie Stephen, more entitled to be cradled, protected, and loved.

One conspicuous correlate to such self-minimizing was the difficulty Vir-

* The most authentic basis for Virginia's clothes "complex" may perhaps be explained in a passage from her short story called "The New Dress." Mabel, the story's principal narrator, had always had the sense "ever since she was a child, of being inferior to other people." She was conscious of "her own appalling inadequacy"; often she "dared not look in the glass." People laughed at her; she felt despised, condemned. How familiar she was with "humiliation and agony and self-loathing." *The Complete Shorter Fiction*, 164–65, 168–69.

ginia had coping with success. She never, for very long, felt worthy of praise. The reason for this was simple enough: if she succeeded too consistently she would be denied the privilege of making extravagant claims on others. But if she was a failure, then she suffered, and suffering justified an ever-increasing tendency to make demands. If she lived in such torment, shouldn't Leonard and Vanessa and Vita come to her side? rescue her? love her forever? It was easy to be selfish and egotistical if she experienced the goodwill of others as something unconditionally her due. And if those benefactors on occasion appeared hurt or became uncooperative, even that had a function: she was now free to feel exploited. She was the victim, the outcast, an outsider. She had Nothing. They had Everything. Virginia was like Septimus Warren Smith, "the Lord who had come to renew society . . . suffering for ever, the scapegoat, the eternal sufferer." And much of Virginia's suffering allowed her to impose always further and larger claims. She paid so dearly, she was convinced, for the little she got in return. Wasn't she entitled to a little happiness? She was indeed her father's daughter.

In this childish spirit of egocentricity, Virginia insisted upon an unbroken stream of letters from Vita and became testy and querulous when her mailbox was empty. Even the office manager, she claimed, "noticed my melancholy and offered me a plain bun. At last, just as hope seemed extinct and the waters of despair were shut about my head two arrived . . . satisfying every desire of my soul." But the letters contained no words of love! No endearments! "To punish you, I shan't call you Honey once this letter. So there." Virginia's demands on Vita were not those of a grown-up lover: they were the demands of a lost child looking for a mother she never had and would never find. They were the demands of a child who was frightened.

One day a figure from the past turned up—George Duckworth, to wit. He was "swollen, affable, overdressed, beyond belief," Virginia wrote to Vanessa now in Cassis. He could only mumble, it seems, for he'd just fallen flat on his back in Berkeley Square. He'd gone to see Vanessa, but without success, and now lingered with Virginia, telling her endless stories "of his own glory: how he's on some committee, and has cheques made out to him for £122,000 'to me, mark you, in my name: all the taxpayers' money!' So I said, 'Well George they'll be making you a K.C.B. next.' 'Making me? I should rather think so. Why my name's been on the list these 12 years.' I never saw anyone so completely self-satisfied."

But for all that, George was better than those other relations who showed their contempt by calling to see if Vanessa "ever sells a picture" and if Virginia has "been in a lunatic asylum lately." These odious cousins evidently couldn't forgive Vanessa for "living in sin" with Duncan Grant—or Virginia for writing *Mrs. Dalloway*, which amounted to the same thing.

The Woolfs left London on March 30 for a month's vacation in France and Italy. They traveled by train through Paris to Cassis, where they stayed (in hotel rooms) for a week with Vanessa, Duncan, and Clive. (Clive, now in a hopeless muddle with his mistress Mary Hutchinson, was trying, also hopelessly, to write a book called *Civilization*). From the South of France they went on to Italy, where Virginia enjoyed herself immensely. She wrote to Vanessa from Palermo about seeing D. H. Lawrence sitting on a bench beside Norman Douglas: "Lawrence pierced and penetrated; Douglas hoglike and brindled—They were swept off by train one way and we went on to Rome."

They had crossed over to Palermo during the night and Virginia had had to share her cabin with a Swedish woman whose virtue was in distress because of no lock on the door. At length Virginia poked her head through the curtain and said in her best French: "Madame, we have neither of us any cause for fear." It was odd, Virginia thought, how much the Scandinavians scraped, scented, gargled, and cleaned at night, considering the results next morning— "as hard as a board, and as gray as a scullery pail." And much though she cared for her sex, Virginia's patience ran thin with traveling females: they had two with them from Toulon to Mentone, "arch and elderly, with handbags packed with face powder and complexions that not all the thyme and mint of England could sweeten—elderly virgins from Cheltenham, playing golf in France."

The subject of motherhood was a sensitive one with the sisters, and Vanessa wrote to Virginia in Sicily: "I wonder how you'd really like the problems of children added to your existence. I don't feel at all equal to dealing with it myself." "I should make a vile mother," Virginia replied, adding a remark which suggests the underlying emotion that had earlier motivated *Jacob's Room*. "For one thing (though I try to hide it from you) I slightly distrust . . . the maternal passion . . . You would fry us all to cinders to give Angelica a day's pleasure . . . In fact what you feel about marriage I feel about motherhood, except that of the two relations motherhood seems the more destructive and limiting." Virginia almost certainly had Julia's attachment to Adrian in mind when she created Betty Flanders and Jacob; but Vanessa's extraordinary relationship to Julian could now have served equally well as her model of destructive bonding. For in both cases—Julia and Vanessa—Virginia was portraying the deadly, crippling reality lurking behind the excessively maternal façade.

Certainly Vanessa was in the forefront of Virginia's mind when she created Susan in *The Waves*. It was Vanessa, in fact, who inspired this novel yet to come, which Virginia first called *The Moths*. It originated in an episode Vanessa had reported from Cassis on May 3. One evening while sitting with Duncan, she heard a loud tapping on the windowpane. When she went to look she discovered a moth with a half-foot wingspan. "We had a terrible time with it. My maternal instinct which you deplore so much wouldn't let me leave it. We let it in, kept it, gave it a whole bottle of ether . . . all in vain." Next day they took it to a chemist who dosed it with chloroform, again in vain. Finally it did die. Vanessa then remembered the French entomologist Jean Fabre's experiment. He had shut up in a room just such a moth—a female—which had attracted all the neighboring males. "I wish," said Vanessa, "you would write a book about the maternal instinct." Virginia was fascinated. Yes, she would write a story about it. "I could think of nothing else but you and the moths for hours after reading your letter. Isn't it odd?"

But there was more than maternal instinct bothering Virginia at the moment—and that was the violation of her privacy. It evidently took Vanessa's fancy on occasion to read aloud Virginia's letters, some of them very personal, for Duncan's and Clive's amusement. The fun stopped with Duncan. It did not stop with Clive. He retailed the contents of Virginia's letters to friends in London, making her appear sentimental and ridiculous. In fact Clive had kept his friends amused for hours with Virginia's letters from Italy. When she got wind of this, she wrote to Vanessa in a way that made Clive appear the culprit—and Vanessa herself blameless: "Of course nothing was said about your reading my letters aloud or showing them, so I suppose I've no right to complain." But the likelihood that her letters were being shown around, she said, reduced her to silence.

The matter went beyond that. When the Woolfs returned to London, stories were circulating and Clive was still at it. He continued to entertain his friends at Virginia's expense. "I should be much interested to know why he does this," Virginia wrote to Vanessa. "There must be some obscure jealousy at work I think. He grudges not your affection for me which doesn't exist, but mine for you." Vanessa had tactlessly written that "Clive simply raved about your brilliance and we discussed your gifts as a letter writer." This must have come as a slap in the face, for Virginia responded coldly: "You are kind but foolish to hand me on his praises, by way of solace." If Vanessa wanted to be amused, she could read Virginia's new novel about the lighthouse and "laugh at [Lily Briscoe's] painting bits."

30 *To the Lighthouse* was published on May 5, the anniversary of Julia's death. It had a considerable advance sale and was clearly a success. But Virginia wanted most of all Vanessa's opinion. And this she got on May 11 in a letter from Cassis: "You have given a portrait of mother which is more like her to me than anything I could ever have conceived of as possible. It is almost painful to have her so raised from the dead...It was like meeting her again with oneself grown up and on equal terms and it seems to me the most astonishing feat of creation...So you see as far as portrait painting goes you seem to me to be a supreme artist and it is so shattering to find oneself face to face with those two again that I can hardly consider anything else." And no, neither she nor Duncan laughed at the "bits about painting."

Virginia had been relieved when Leonard called it her "best book," but Vanessa's verdict was more than she had hoped for—"I can never believe that you approve of me in any way." So incredulous was she of Vanessa's letter, she consulted Leonard—Yes, Vanessa meant it, he was certain. "I'm in a terrible state of pleasure that you should think Mrs Ramsay so like mother." But wasn't it a mystery, bringing her to life like that?—"How could a child know about her: except that she has always haunted me... *Probably there is a great deal of you in Mrs Ramsay.*"*

Many years earlier, for Virginia, Vanessa had—in fact *and* in fiction—taken the place of the beautiful, haunting Mrs. Ramsay and had become the living substitute for Julia Stephen. And if Vanessa was the model for both Helen Ambrose and Mrs. Ramsay, then it would appear that Virginia saw both women having many traits in common. If this is true, then the parallel goes a long way in explaining Virginia's conflation of the maternal Vanessa *and* the elusive mother Julia Stephen herself represented; and just as the child Virginia rivaled Julia, so would the adult Virginia rival Vanessa.

When she returned from Persia, Vita found waiting for her at Long Barn a copy of the novel which Virginia had inscribed: "In my opinion the best novel I have ever written." The copy she sent Vita was a dummy with all the pages blank. This was of course half joke, half modesty. For as she was finishing the novel Virginia herself saw "how lovely some parts of The Light-

---

* Emphasis added. This admission explains the absence of a Vanessa-figure in the novel; although Lily Briscoe is a painter, she is Virginia's deputy, not Vanessa's; she is also not Mrs. Ramsay's daughter.

house are! Soft and pliable . . . and never a wrong word for a page at a time."
When Vita read it she was "dazzled and bewitched. How did you do it?
how did you walk along that razor-edge without falling?" Virginia was naturally flattered but confessed to being doubtful of her portrait of Mr. Ramsay—Leslie Stephen. "Do you think it sentimental? . . . I should like to know.
I was more like him than her, I think; and therefore more critical: but he
was an adorable man, and somehow, tremendous."

Virginia had thought of dedicating the novel to Roger Fry, who seemed
most to understand the thing she was striving for: "You're no longer bothered
by the simultaneity of things," he said, "and go backwards and forwards in
time with an extraordinary enrichment of each moment of consciousness."
This was a remarkable insight. He had hit the mark precisely. The simultaneity of the moment was exactly what Virginia had been struggling toward—and that achievement was finally being acknowledged by someone
who knew more about the problems of time and space relations than anyone
else among her contemporaries.

She was moved by Roger's letter and wrote back. "I am immensely glad
you like the Lighthouse. Now I wish I had dedicated it to you. But when I
read it over it seemed to me so bad that I couldn't face asking you. And
then, as it happened, I met you somewhere—was so overcome (did you guess
it?) by your magnificence, splendour and purity . . . that I went home and was
positive it was out of the question—dedicating such a book to such a man."
Of all his private virtues, Roger had kept Virginia "on the right path, so far
as writing goes, more than anyone." And now here was *To the Lighthouse*, a
novel to celebrate that fateful day in December 1910 when "human character
changed."

In this same letter Roger had said: "I'm sure that there's lots I haven't understood and that when I talk it over with Morgan [E. M. Forster] he'll have
discovered a lot of hidden meanings. I suspect for instance that arriving at
the Lighthouse has a symbolic meaning which escapes me." Virginia's reply
to this remark constitutes the clearest, most succinct statement of aesthetic
purpose she had tried at greater length to express in *Mr. Bennett and Mrs.
Brown*—that the reader supplied what the novelist suggested; that interpretation was a highly personal matter; that a lighthouse to one reader was not
the same lighthouse to another reader; that each of us brought to the reading
act our entire personal history; that at its deepest level, all one could say was
that reaching the lighthouse was vaguely the generalized expression of all
human quests—experienced in one way or another by all human beings.

Whether one called reaching the lighthouse "symbolic" or not was irrelevant to the idea of quests and questing, which in some vague yet absolute way represented the striving of all human beings in pursuit of self-realization.

What Virginia did actually say in her letter was this: "I meant *nothing* by The Lighthouse ... I saw that all sorts of feelings would accrue to this, but I refused to think them out, and trusted that people would make it the deposit for their own emotions—which they have done, one thinking it means one thing another, another. I can't manage Symbolism except in this vague, generalised way. Whether it's right or wrong I don't know, but directly I'm told what a thing means, it becomes hateful to me."

The multiple interpretations Virginia Woolf's method made possible, indeed stimulated, would always create problems of meaning for critics and readers alike. She intended no fixed or single interpretation of the book: that was too narrow a way to experience her view of the world. She meant different readers to make different meanings along some broad, generally accepted semantic axis. As the author she of course had her own specific plan, but it was not of the kind to restrict interpretive freedom. It was a plan full of suggestion, full of insinuation, meant to encourage various inferences, meant to spark differences among readers professing common beliefs and shared values.

That plan, in its most general outline, might be seen as consisting of three parts. In part one, "The Window," where the trip to the lighthouse was suggested, the quest itself is suggested but not realized: there is too much discord among the principal characters: they are too close to one another. The middle section, "Time Passes," is the dramatization of nature's indifference to human effort. In this stretch of time, linking the first section to the third, death and decay and destruction are rampant. In the final section, "The Lighthouse," the promised expedition to the lighthouse is made. With time and distance now separating the once-dissonant elements, harmony is possible and resolution assured. James, now sixteen years old, "finds" his father on the trip. Lily Briscoe on shore now adjusts to a new perspective. It was Mrs. Ramsay who suggested the trip ten years earlier, but Mr. Ramsay who makes it a reality. It was Mrs. Ramsay whom Lily worshiped. It is Mr. Ramsay who now commands her vision. Implicit in the changed perspective is the idea that real harmony was not possible while Mrs. Ramsay (and her phantom lover) lived. So that on both the literal and metaphoric levels, the novel's most general symmetries organize around the conviction that human experience means involvement with the living, while artistic achievement requires detachment. Only then, when the dissonance and incongruity have been confronted, can one surrender to the chaos of reality and compose wholeness and harmony. For art, in Virginia's mind, was essentially an act of submission—an act in which one's private vision is transformed into the more permanent structures of public design. And only with distance in time and space could Virginia Woolf, at the most personal level, exercise the solipsistic power of *re-creating on her own terms* a world in which, as a child, she had once felt so powerless. Only by giving voice and pattern to that past could she bridge the gap between *feeling* and *fact*, and experience the triumph of having exhumed from those ancient vaults of private history the tableaux vivants which the outside world might be persuaded to accept as a work of art.

Virginia had always been obsessed with her mother. In writing *To the Lighthouse*, she said later, she had done for herself what psychoanalysts did for their patients. They expressed "some very long felt and deeply felt emotion," and in expressing it "explained it and laid it to rest." But that simply did not happen here. She did not lay Julia to rest. In resurrecting Herbert Duckworth, she fueled once more her mother's passion for her phantom lover and, in so doing, freed her father to express his love for the child Virginia. She could say, with a mixture of joy and relief, that for Mr. Ramsay "life did not consist, after all, in going to bed with a woman!" With her child's perspective, she muffled her rivalry with Julia, obscured her ambivalence, and poeticized the conflicted story of the Stephen family and, along with it, her own forbidden—and bewildering—incestuous fantasies. Only later would it become clear to her that the divisions which split and polarized her world were beyond reconciliation. Her lyricism in *To the Lighthouse* merely smothered the feeling and weakened the volume of the prevailing dissonance. What still burned in her memory was the terrible shock of exclusion—when her father had stumbled out of Julia's death room and brushed past her, ignoring the outstretched arms. Even that scene she purified and rearranged parenthetically in the novel—"[Mr. Ramsay, stumbling along a passage one dark morning, stretched his arms out, but Mrs. Ramsay having died rather suddenly the night before, his arms, though stretched out, remained empty.]" She would eventually come to realize that she had not really told the whole story and would try again in *The Years*; and after that still again in "A Sketch of the Past." Much as she tried to lay her mother and father to rest, she could not. Their sour music would continue to assail her from the grave, haunt her to the very end. As long as she could write, however, she would protect herself by resurrecting them in benign worlds of her own making.

To the Lighthouse was on the whole favorably received. The press was sympathetic. Even Arnold Bennett found the novel "the best book of hers that I know." He had reservations of course, but still there was "stuff in it strong enough to withstand quite a lot of adverse criticism." Once again, however, it was the poet who saw the play of Virginia's mind on the reel of time. The poet was Conrad Aiken. The moment comes in one's reading of *To the Lighthouse*, he said, "when at last one ceases to be aware of something persistently artificial in this highly feminine style, and finds oneself simply immersed in the vividness and actuality of this world of Mrs. Woolf's—believing in it, in fact, with the utmost intensity, and feeling it with that completeness of surrender with which one feels the most moving of poetry . . . She makes her Mrs. Ramsay—by giving us her stream of consciousness—amazingly alive; and she supplements this . . . by giving us also, intermittently, the streams of consciousness of her husband, of her friend Lily Briscoe, of her children . . . We live in that delicious house with them—we feel the minute textures of their lives with their own vivid senses—we imagine with their extraordinary imaginations, are self-conscious with their self-consciousness— and ultimately we know them as well, as terribly, as we know ourselves . . . Nothing happens, in this houseful of odd nice people, and yet all of life happens. The tragic futility, the absurdity, the pathetic beauty, of life—we experience all of this in our sharing of seven hours of Mrs. Ramsay's wasted or not wasted existence. We have seen, through her, the world."

There were headaches in June, but the reception of the book gave Virginia no cause for anxiety. By July over 3,000 copies had been sold. She had "taken her fences." Now the Woolfs could indulge in a little luxury. Just as *Mrs. Dalloway* had paid for the installation of modern-day plumbing at Monks House, so *To the Lighthouse* would now buy them an automobile. On July 15, they became owners of a secondhand Singer for £275. The husband of Angelica's nurse was a chauffeur who taught Vanessa to drive her secondhand Renault. He now taught Leonard. It took only six lessons. By July 31 he was able to manage the car on his own. Virginia had lessons, too, but with decidedly less success.

"On the backs of paper I write down instructions for starting cars," Virginia wrote in her diary on July 23. With this nice little car they were free to go anywhere. "The world gave me this for writing The Lighthouse . . . All images are now tinged with driving a motor. Here I think of letting my engine work, with my clutch out."

To her friends she was more effusive, promising Ethel Sands "24 hours" of talk "mostly about motor cars." She could think of nothing else. "I've driven from the Embankment to the Marble Arch and only knocked one boy very gently off his bicycle." "I have been wobbling round and round Wind-mill Hill, every day, trying to avoid dogs and children," she wrote to Janet Case. Her whole life was "spent motoring with Harris," she said to Vanessa. She was "competent to drive alone in the country, he says." Harris also said that "I'm well above the average. We both have the same fault—you and I—we keep too much to the left. But my changing gear is very good." Harris was going to drive her to Charleston next day. "Then you will see me take the wheel . . . It is an awesome sight."

How Vita would have laughed to see them at it. They were off for their first drive in the Singer and "the bloody thing wouldn't start. The accelerator died . . . All the village came to watch—Leonard almost sobbed with rage." At last they had to bicycle into Lewes to hire a repairman who told them the magnetos were off. Would Vita have known that? "Leonard will shoot himself if it don't start again."

"Back from Long Barn," wrote Virginia a little earlier that summer. "Such opulence and freedom, flowers all out, butler, silver . . . wine, hot water, log fires, Italian cabinets, Persian rugs, books—this was the impression it made." And then there was Harold, whom Virginia liked. He was a "spontaneous childlike man" with a lively mind; he opened his eyes wide when he spoke to you. He wore a little boyish mustache, had curly hair, and was generous and gentle and kind.

She looked at Vita too, now perhaps a little more critically. Vita was as usual free and easy and a pleasure to be with. Her poetry, though, was another matter. There she was not an adventurer and never broke the rules—or "fresh ground." She picked up and used whatever she could find, instinc-tively, from inherited tradition. Her adherence to custom was evident even in the way she lived. Her house was "gracious, glowing, stately, but without novelty or adventure. So with her poetry."

"Darling, it makes me afraid of you," wrote Vita to Virginia shortly after reading *To the Lighthouse*. "Afraid of your penetration and loveliness and genius." In tunneling back into the lives of those who made up her past, Virginia had performed one of her most brilliant analyses of human mind and motive. "Only if I had read it without knowing you, I should be fright-ened of you," Vita added. Virginia's "penetration" was indeed frightening, for in Vita's mind it translated into domination. It meant power, something Vita as a surface writer lacked. Hadn't Virginia's penetration already uncovered her own weaknesses? Wasn't it possible that she would ferret out more? There was something terrifying about finding oneself under Virginia's moral and intellectual scrutiny.

But there was another, more immediate worry. Vita was frustrated. She needed an adventure, not Virginia's minute dissections. Her months away from England had lowered what little immunity she had to Cupid's darts, Virginia or no Virginia, and the adventure she hankered for at this particular moment appeared in the person of Mary Campbell, the wife of the South African poet Roy Campbell. Vita had a history of wrecking marriages. Danger was part of the attraction to married women. She had been partly responsible only a few years earlier for the marital warfare between Violet and Denys Trefusis; she had certainly been the cause of Geoffrey Scott's divorce; and there would soon be some suspicion that she was implicated in separating Dorothy Wellesley from her husband.

At any rate Vita met Roy and Mary Campbell on May 22. On the twenty-third they dined with her, and on October 1 moved into the gardener's cottage at Long Barn, by which time Vita had become Mary's lover, and a kind of mother to her as well. In the coming years there would be a small train of new love affairs and passionate encounters, with Margaret Voigt, Hilda Matheson, and Evelyn Irons leading the procession. Yet Vita's relations with Virginia would continue as though no one else in the world existed.

Vita was an impresario of passion and there were times when her life rang with a chorus of lovers. She respected Virginia too much, however, to encourage these dangerous love games. Virginia had artistic genius, which Vita valued. It is true that the dozen or so sexual encounters between them flattered Virginia's vanity—for she was ten years older—but their real emotional center lay elsewhere. Vita idolized the mistress of letters and felt protective toward the child who lurked within; and with Vita's extraordinary competence so much on display, it was easy for Virginia to forget that beneath the surface there was a woman who also needed attention. The old conflict, therefore, once more reared its stubborn head. So long as intimacy and independence both claimed equal ascendancy, Vita would never be on open and equal terms with anyone, Virginia included.

Nor, it seems, in the days and months ahead, did Virginia, immersed in her own conflicts, realize how often she threatened Vita's loyalty with her inquisitorial cross-examinations and exasperating demands. Little wonder that below the patrician grandeur Vita felt love-starved and solitary; and even less wonder that she was promiscuous, and ruthless with her lovers. They didn't understand her and there was nothing she could do about it. To have confessed her own needs would have been a confession of weakness. It was easier to act the warrior in a world of strife and struggle. Maintaining her magisterial pose at least satisfied her craving for autonomy. And so she continued to force the people in her universe to conform to her own limitations. The more Virginia badgered, the deeper the real Vita went into hiding, the higher the sovereign Vita climbed, hardening further the already brittle structure of her inner conflict.

The nicknames they used with one another indicate the alternating roles they assumed. When Virginia addressed "Dearest Vita," she was appealing to the maternal figure; when "Donkey West" was summoned, she sought the haughty novelist and poet. On Vita's side, when a letter began "My dearest Virginia," she was addressing the lovely and remote mistress of letters; when "Potto" (a nickname Virginia gave herself, meaning a lemur) was called upon, it was the child in Virginia being invited out for a romp.

Thus at least two Virginias were in constant negotiation with at least two Vitas. Their age difference really mattered very little, although Virginia, perhaps oftener than was necessary, resorted to her seniority when she was jockeying for sympathy. There was plenty of room for surprise in the intense, and often untidy, game of love they so beautifully dramatized. How often Virginia, in one breath, shouted at "Donkey West" for muddling personal relations and, in the next, implored her "dearest Vita" to assure her of which "rung on the ladder" Potto stood in her affections. Phrased differently, at any given moment, the elegant novelist called upon the aristocrat and wheedled her into repeating how much the domineering mother loved her anxious, often submissive child. This could be very confusing. Harold Nicolson was accustomed to Vita's gambolings and usually stood behind whatever made her happy. Leonard however was new to all this, and just how he responded, apart from an occasional growl, we can only surmise.

Vita had several years earlier written a novel called (fittingly) *Challenge*. It was based on her spectacular love affair with Violet Trefusis—Eve the heroine of the novel and Julian (Vita) its hero. From Dorothy Wellesley's country house in Hampshire, Vita wrote to Virginia on June 11: "Do you know what I should do if you were not a person to be rather strict with? I should steal my own motor out of the garage at 10 pm. tomorrow night, be at Rodmell by 11.5, throw gravel at your window, then you'd come down and let me in; I'd stay with you till 5, and be home by half-past six. But, you being you, I can't; more's the pity. Have you read my book? *Challenge*, I mean. Perhaps

I sowed all my wild oats then. Yet I don't feel that the impulse has left me; no, by God; and for a different Virginia I'd fly to Sussex in the night. Only with age, soberness, and the increase of consideration, I refrain."

"You see I was reading Challenge," Virginia coolly replied, "and thought your letter was a challenge; 'if only you weren't so elderly and valetudinarian' was what you said in effect 'we could be spending the day together' whereupon I wired 'come then' to which naturally there was no answer and a good thing too . . . as I am elderly and valetudinarian,—it's no good disguising the fact. Not even reading Challenge will alter that." And so came the first wrench of pain. Vita still had a great many "wild oats" to sow—but not with Virginia.

Fear sharpens one's perceptions and by July of 1927 Virginia sensed that something was amiss. That something was Mary Campbell, with whom Vita was now hopelessly infatuated. Virginia had warned her to be careful in her "gambolling" or she would find Virginia's "soft crevices lined with hooks." Little did Vita know that when Virginia felt menaced by her lapses in fidelity, she would seize whatever means she could find to protect herself from losing the woman she loved; and the most natural means of protection for Virginia came in the form of pen and ink. The result was to become what Vita's son Nigel Nicolson called "the longest and most charming love letter in literature"—a fictional biography of Vita Sackville-West.

The Campbells had moved into Long Barn cottage on October 1. On the fifth Virginia noted in her diary the idea for a biography that would begin in the year 1500, continue to the present day, and be "called Orlando: Vita; only with a change about from one sex to another." She had earlier planned to start work on a serious, mystical novel—The Waves—and the Press had been expecting her to produce a critical book called Phases of Fiction. Both these projects, however, were pushed aside.

On October 9 Virginia wrote to inform Vita that she was quite aware of the beautiful Mary Campbell's existence—and also about Orlando. "But listen," she said, "suppose Orlando turns out to be Vita; and all about you and the lusts of your flesh and the lure of your mind (heart you have none, who go gallivanting down the lanes with Campbell) . . . Shall you mind? Say Yes, or No. Also, I admit I should like to untwine and twist again some very odd, incongruous strands in you." Vita was "thrilled and terrified" at the prospect, gave her "full permission," and thought the least Virginia could do was dedicate the book to the woman she intended to untwine and retwist. What Virginia was essentially asking Vita was, Would she mind having the nasty story of her rampant lust and reckless promiscuity show through the glittering surface pageant of personal glory? For such was the tale her biographer intended.

Five days later Virginia wrote, now in a more tranquil mood: "Never do I leave you without thinking, it's for the last time . . . Since I am always certain you'll be off and on with another . . . All our intercourse is tinged with this melancholy on my part and desire to . . . keep you half an instant longer." Vita had, just a day or two earlier, said that she was good and industrious and loving, but how long would it be before she was out prowling again on some adventure of lust? "I would never break out if I had you here, but you leave me unguarded." That was the way things stood between them, at least from Vita's point of view. Virginia was adamant, however: "If you've given yourself to Campbell, I'll have nothing more to do with you, and so it shall be written, plainly, for all the world to read in Orlando."

There was more truth in that statement than Virginia herself could have known at the time. She knew of Vita's past love affairs; and she knew too that temperamentally and psychologically unsuited as she was, she had never and could never satisfy Vita's ravenous appetite; and about that little could be done. But there was nothing in the world of fiction or fantasy to prevent her from inscribing for posterity Vita's lusty delinquencies, fierce ambitions, and yearning for fame and glory. And so, with all the elegance at her command, Virginia Woolf would show the world a Vita Sackville-West in full plumage and in all her magnificent contradiction. Just as she had redeemed from the ravages of time a lyrical version of her mother and father in *To the Lighthouse*, so now would she memorialize for generations to come the one great love of her life.

Thus, in much the same proprietorial spirit as Browning's jealous Duke, preserving for himself his "Last Duchess" in a portrait, so Virginia preserved the Vita she loved in the fantastic world of *Orlando*. No matter how many excursions into lust or how much gamboling there might be in the months and even years ahead, Orlando—the seductive aristocrat of Virginia's imagination—would remain inviolate, safely out of reach of rapacious women, and forever beyond the threat of loss. The Orlando of Virginia's book had stepped outside the irrelevancies of life and into the purer chamber of art, where she would remain for all time. Others might seduce Vita in the flesh, but no one could sully the Vita that Virginia had created.

.   .   .

While *Orlando* was in the making, Virginia grew distant. So much of what Vita had done was *not* an affirmation of love—whatever "love" meant—and that realization now came as a crushing disappointment. But pen and ink, words and phrases—these would "take away the pain," soften the "shock"; for art, not life, now consumed Virginia's attention. "I'm not afraid of your not wanting me," she wrote to Vita in late October, "only of what one calls circumstances . . . My questions about your past can wait till London."

By November Roy Campbell had found out about the affair. First he threatened Mary's life, then demanded a divorce. Once more Vita had made a hash of it and went to her biographer with the whole dreadful story. Virginia bowed her head and listened. She weighed the pros, considered the cons, and then scolded Vita roundly for disrupting so many lives, her own included. Vita left in tears. "You made me feel such a brute," Virginia wrote next day, "and I didn't mean to be . . . And I'm half, or tenth part, jealous, when I see you with the Valeries and Marys: so you can discount that . . . I'm happy to think you *do* care: for often I seem old, fretful, querulous, difficult."

Yet, however generous the grown-up Virginia wanted to be, the jealous child inside inevitably erupted in little bursts of misery. "Promiscuous you are," she would soon write, "and that's all there is to be said of you. Look in the Index of Orlando—after Pippin [Vita's spaniel] and see what comes next—Promiscuity *passim*." In the meantime, as the months passed, the liaison with Mary Campbell gained in momentum. By early December Vita had written fourteen sonnets to her, while Virginia retreated into fantasy to spin out the spectacular centuries of *Orlando*.

On January 11, 1928, Thomas Hardy died at home. As far back as February 14, 1919, Bruce Richmond had asked Virginia to prepare an article on Hardy's novels that might be used at his death. He hoped it would be "many years before it comes to anything," but all the same he wanted the piece ready "whenever the evil day comes." Virginia had prepared an essay called "Thomas Hardy's Novels" and this was published anonymously on January 19 as the leader in *The Times Literary Supplement*. Leonard and Virginia attended Hardy's funeral at Westminster Abbey. His heart was buried in his own parish churchyard at Stinsford and his ashes were placed in the Poet's Corner, both funeral ceremonies taking place at precisely the same hour.

Another death was about to occur in January. While Virginia was pressing on with *Orlando*, Vita's father, Lionel, the 3rd Baron Sackville, aged sixty, lay slowly and painfully dying at Knole. The end came a few minutes after midnight on January 28, and with Harold away in Berlin, Virginia tried to

Julia Duckworth

(*Julia Cameron*)

Sir Leslie Stephen, K.C.B.,

1902

Virginia Stephen (*Berg Collection, New York Public Library*)

The Stephen family, circa 1894. *Back row*: Gerald Duckworth, Virginia, Thoby, Vanessa, George Duckworth. *Front row*: Adrian, Julia, Leslie (*Berg Collection, New York Public Library*)

Vanessa, Stella, Virginia, circa 1896
(*Berg Collection, New York Public Library*)

Virginia, 1903

George Duckworth

Violet Dickinson

Thoby Stephen, 1906

Adrian Stephen at Fitzroy
Square

Roger Fry

T. S. Eliot

Asheham House
(*Barbara Bagenal*)

Clive, Virginia, and
Julian at Blean, 1910
(*Tate Gallery Archive*)

Virginia and
Leonard Woolf
(*Tate Gallery
Archive*)

Lytton Strachey and Virginia

Vita Sackville-West in the garden at Sissinghurst Castle
(*Nigel Nicolson*)

Vita Sackville-West, 1924
(*Nigel Nicolson*)

Julian Bell, 1932

Leonard and Virginia at Cassis, 1928

Monks House, Rodmell
(*Leonard Woolf*)

Virginia with Ethel Smyth
at Monks House

console Vita. Lord Sackville was buried, as all the Sackvilles had been since the fourteenth century, in the family chapel at Withyham Church. Since he had no son, his title and estates passed to Vita's uncle Charles and would in turn eventually fall to her cousin Edward Sackville, and not to Vita, who worshiped Knole and everything it stood for. "I find it difficult to say anything about it all—" wrote Vita two days after the death. "I will tell you some day," she said to Virginia. "In the meantime nothing but the most grotesque ideas come into my mind, such as what good copy it would all be for Virginia's book. The whole thing is a mixture of the tragic, the grotesque and the magnificent."

In the early months of 1928 Virginia's work was interrupted first by headaches and then by a bout of influenza. Somehow between the illness and the work, she managed to see people. T. S. Eliot came to talk with her about his religious conversion. She was not a sympathetic ear, however, and wrote to Vanessa about "poor Tom Eliot," who should be considered "dead to all of us from this day forward." He had become an Anglo-Catholic, believed in God and immortality, and now went to church. Virginia was "shocked." (Later in the year he would read the Woolfs a new poem called "Ash Wednesday," written under the spell of his newfound faith.)

Then there was Clive Bell, still talking about his ubiquitous and sometimes embarrassing love affairs. And a little later came Rebecca West, who had "knocked about with all the mongrels of Europe" but was very "intelligent and engaging." So was Noël Coward, just twenty-eight at the time, who could sing, dance, act, write plays, and compose music. "He is in search of culture," she wrote Vanessa, and was thinking of Bloomsbury as a "place of pilgrimage." She also saw Desmond MacCarthy and Dorothy Todd, both of them now launching new magazines.

After five months of work Virginia was getting "headachey" and tired of *Orlando*. "The futility of it all," she wrote in her journal. Spinning out a sentence was almost beyond her. It was time to stop work and retire to bed for a day or two. The blankness would not last. A rest was all she needed. A few days later she tried to get on with her book, but once more "not a drop came . . . It is the oddest feeling: as if a finger stopped the flow of ideas in the brain." The finger was soon removed, however, and the last flood of ideas came rushing out, so that by one o'clock on Saturday, March 17, 1928, the first draft of *Orlando* was finished—"begun 8th October, as a joke."

But she was troubled. *Orlando* was too long for a joke and too "frivolous" to be taken as a serious book. Which was it? And how much time should she invest in making it a book that wouldn't harm her reputation? "At 46 one must be a miser; only have time for essentials." Before doing anything, however, she must rest. Then she would begin revising—rewriting, actually— "10 pages daily" if the book was to be published in the autumn.

"Did you feel a sort of tug, as if your neck was being broken on Saturday last at 5 minutes to one?" she asked Vita. "That was when he died—or rather stopped talking, with three little dots..." At the moment the book was messy, sprawling, incoherent—and she was sick of it. "The question now is, will my feelings for you be changed? I've lived in you all these months— coming out, what are you really like? Do you exist? Have I made you up?" Had the granite become rainbow? Or merely random splashes of meaningless color?

Vanessa and Duncan had acquired for themselves a secure base in Provence from this year on. It was a small house, "La Bergère," reconstructed from a ruin on the property of Colonel A. S. H. Teed at Fontcreuse, near Cassis. In late March Virginia and Leonard, in their Singer, made the Newhaven-Dieppe crossing. Their drive took them to Beauvais, Troyes, Beaune, Vienne, Orange, and Aix, reaching Cassis on Sunday, April 1. They stayed in rooms at the Château de Fontcreuse and ate their meals with Vanessa's family at the new villa.

It was altogether a satisfactory holiday marred only by another argument between Virginia and Clive—caused, Virginia suspected, by his having read her letters to Vanessa, many of them containing remarks not entirely flatter-ing to his immense but tender vanity. Mountain roads and bad weather made the return journey a little alarming at times, but they arrived in London on April 16 unharmed, and Virginia plunged at once into her revisions of *Or-lando*.

On the day after her return she wrote in her diary that Clive "smacked me in public—curse him for an uneasy little upstart." He had presumably insulted her in front of others, and Virginia wasted no time getting the incident out of her system and into a letter to Clive himself. "I sometimes wonder what itch this smacking gratifies—" she said, "why I'm so often the victim. Psychologically, I'd like to understand it. And if I ought to remember that you've been unhappy, so you ought to remember that I've been mad. These slaps and snubs...annoy me more than they should. But enough."

Vita too got a chastening rap on the nose. "I always said you were a promiscuous brute—Is it Mary again; or Jenny this time or a Polly?" Virginia wasn't going to wear her heart out for a woman who "goes with any girl from an Inn!" Actually Vita's new flame was Margaret Voigt, an American writer married to a British journalist. But Virginia needn't have been so upset, for as usual the intimacies with both Margaret Voigt and Mary Campbell came to an end in the early summer of 1928, much to the distress of both women, when Vita returned to Long Barn. The "promiscuous brute" had taken up still another new lover—Hilda Matheson, Talks Director of the BBC, for whom Vita had frequently broadcast.

When Vita returned from Germany, however, she had her hands full with another problem. Her mother was now behaving monstrously. Lady Sackville, illegitimate daughter of the 2nd Baron Sackville and Pepita, a Spanish dancer, had married her cousin Lionel in 1890. She had been a woman of beauty and charm. With age and the accumulation of wealth, however, she became increasingly nasty, demanding, and capricious. When Vita's father installed his mistress, the singer Olive Rubens (and her husband), in the house in 1919, Lady Sackville left her husband and Knole, moved into an enormous house in Brighton, and refused to set Lionel Sackville free to marry Mrs. Rubens. His death in January set off a series of explosions.

In February Virginia wrote to Vanessa that Lady Sackville had done her best to upset everything, had "insulted Vita, made off with Marie Antoinette's diamond necklace, won't answer lawyers' letters, and holds up the whole will." In April Vita had a terrible row with her mother. Lady Sackville had ordered her to remove a pearl necklace, cut it in two with a pocket knife, surrender the twelve central pearls, and then deposit the remainder into an envelope her solicitor had given her. "Thief, liar, I hope you'll be killed by an omnibus"—so Lady Sackville had addressed her daughter in the presence of a horrified secretary, solicitor, and chauffeur. Lady Sackville would henceforth consider Vita dead and stop every penny of her allowance. By May she was filing a suit against the new heir, Eddy Sackville's father, which meant "all their characters will be blackened in the Law Courts." Already she was broadcasting Harold's homosexuality and Vita's too. Such was the life of wealthy aristocrats, but Virginia had troubles of her own.

"So sick of Orlando," Virginia wrote on June 20. She had corrected the proofs in a week and found it impossible to "spin out another phrase . . . This is the worst time of all. It makes me suicidal. Nothing seems left to do. All seems insipid and worthless." Virginia had warned Vita that her feelings might change when *Orlando* was finished, and it appears that some realignment was in fact taking place. In surrendering *Orlando* to the public Virginia was losing the figure of her fantasy and now felt again childlike and deserted. "I go back to words of one syllable."

Vanessa had mercifully returned from France—"She is a necessity to me— as I am not to her. I run to her as the wallaby runs to the old kangaroo," she wrote in her diary. "You must take me in your arms and cover me with kisses," she said to Vanessa herself. With Orlando's model temporarily in the shade, Vanessa once more took up Vita's place. How masterfully Vanessa managed "her dozen lives; never in a muddle, or desperate, or worried." This was Virginia's idealization of her sister and it was nonsense. She was trans- ferring to Vanessa all the qualities she had imagined in Julia; whereas Vanessa was often desperate and worried and muddled; only, like Julia, she was too proud to let anyone see it. Nor, it appears, did she do much to correct Vir- ginia's exaggerated perception of her goodness.

 Each year two Femina Vie Heureuse Prizes were awarded, one to an English book and one to a French. In 1927 the English prize had gone to Radclyffe Hall for *Adam's Breed*. This year it went to Virginia for *To the Lighthouse*. The prize, a check for forty pounds, was presented to Virginia by her contemporary the popular novelist Hugh Walpole at the Institut Français in South Kensington on Wednesday, May 2. She had met Walpole once in November of 1923 at a luncheon given by the indefat- igable London hostess Sibyl Colefax, the deadly name-dropping Sibyl whose gatherings Virginia mostly enjoyed. But the Femina award to Virginia was "my show dog prize." Vita attended the ceremony. "Mrs Nicolson and Mrs Woolf gave some offence on Wednesday by coming to the prize as if dressed for a funeral," wrote Virginia in a subsequent letter. "Still it *was* my funeral."

The one lasting impression of the event for Virginia, however, was meeting Elizabeth Robins, the American actress. "I remember your mother—" Miss Robins said to her, "the most beautiful Madonna and at the same time the most complete woman of the world. Used to come and see me in my flat . . . Never confided. She would suddenly say something so unexpected, from that Madonna face, one thought it *vicious*." It is almost as if Robins were corrob- orating Virginia's insinuations about the beautiful, maternal, loving Mrs.

Ramsay—that behind the saintlike appearance, the real woman, Julia, was vicious, flawed—a malicious Madonna.

Two other literary events that spring claimed Virginia's attention. One was the publication of Clive Bell's *Civilization*. The previous November, Virginia had "galloped through" parts of the essay and told Clive it was the best thing he'd done. He bristled at this and accused her of insincerity. His reaction offended Virginia. "I am enough of a prig and conceited enough to attach some importance to my judgment of books and don't like it to be assumed that though I may lie about everything else, I lie about them." Leonard, on the other hand, thought the book "very superficial" and said so in his weekly page, "The World of Books." Both Bell's "method and assumptions are wrong and are bound to lead to wrong conclusions," wrote Leonard with his usual detachment in the June 9 issue of *Nation & Athenaeum*.

The other event was the publication of Radclyffe Hall's *The Well of Loneliness*, a novel about lesbian love. The popular press voiced the public's outrage, and, under pressure from the Home Secretary, the publisher, Jonathan Cape, withdrew the book. E. M. Forster and Leonard Woolf were in principle opposed to such suppression as being a violation of the freedom of the press, and on September 8 published in the *Nation & Athenaeum* a letter of protest, written jointly by Virginia and Forster. Then the question arose whether evidence of the novel's literary merits was admissible. Vita, Bernard Shaw, MacCarthy, Forster, Walpole, and Virginia were all prepared to testify in its favor. As a possible witness Virginia was faced with questions of definition: How did one define obscenity? What constituted a literary work? How did one distinguish between subject and treatment, between the What and the How? To the author of *Orlando* these questions were indeed troublesome.

Jonathan Cape and a London bookseller were finally required to show why *The Well of Loneliness* should not be destroyed for being obscene. When the case came before him, the Chief Magistrate ruled that he alone would decide on the question of obscenity and, further, that no evidence of literary merit would be admissible. This had all been determined by November 9. One week later, he ordered the book to be seized and destroyed. On December 14, an appeal was entered, and dismissed. The court concluded that the book was obscene, offensive, and morally prejudicial. From the start Virginia had thought the novel a "Well of all that's stagnant and lukewarm."

.   .   .

Virginia had earlier written a lesbian story for America called "Slater's Pins Have No Points." It had been published in *Forum* in January 1928. Now in September, with all the publicity stirred up by *The Well of Loneliness*, there was danger of her being thought "the mouthpiece of Sapphism"; throughout the summer she and Vita had been planning a tour of Burgundy together, which meant further publicity. But with *Orlando* scheduled for publication on October 11, she decided to run the risk. This might be her last romp with Vita. When the book came out, Vita might vanish forever.

Still, Virginia had reservations, and they concerned Leonard. How did he feel about this expedition? Would he mind being left alone? Would he feel rejected, ignored? This bothered her in a way that Vita, with her history of multiple elopements, found difficult to sympathize with. "You see," Virginia said to her, "I would not have married Leonard had I not preferred living with him to saying good bye to him." Then there was also the worry that Vita might be bored with her company, become disillusioned. In her journal she said: "This is written on the verge of my alarming holiday in Burgundy. I am alarmed of 7 days alone with Vita: interested; excited, but afraid—she may find me out, I her out."

The two of them set off, nevertheless, on September 24. It was the first and only expedition they would make together, and the first sample of what living together might have been like. On the morning of departure, Virginia and Leonard "had a small and sudden row" about the trip—and Vita. But Virginia's fears and the row notwithstanding, the holiday was a success. The French countryside was spectacular, the food exquisite, and the days full of adventure. From Vézelay Virginia wrote to Leonard: "Vita is a perfect hen, always running about with a hot water bottle, and an amazingly competent traveller, as she talks apparently perfect French."

To Harold, Vita wrote: "Virginia is very sweet, and I feel extraordinarily protective towards her. The combination of that brilliant brain and fragile body is very lovable. She has a sweet childlike nature, from which her intellect is completely separate." In her diary, for September 27, she wrote: "In the middle of the night I was woken up by a thunderstorm. Went along to Virginia's room thinking she might be frightened. We talked about science and religion for an hour ... and then as the storm had gone over I left her to go to sleep again."

Virginia was right on the mark in describing the dominant-compliant character of their relations when she said to Vita just following their holiday: "I have seen a little ball kept bubbling up and down on the spray of a fountain: the fountain is you; the ball me. It is a sensation I get only from you."

A ROOM OF HER OWN

1928-1932

32 The women returned to London and to terrible embarrassment: Lady Sackville had been soliciting her friends to give her "a small cheque or postal order" to help defray the expenses of a new house. By early October she had collected some 400 pounds and had no intention of building a house or anything resembling one.

Virginia returned also to the publication of *Orlando*. Vita had, up to this time, been kept in the dark about the book and not been allowed to read a word of it. But now, on October 11, 1928, it was here, finished, for all the world to see. It was an immediate sensation. Booksellers, however, weren't sure how to display it. Was it biography? Or was it fiction? This confusion was a high price, Virginia confessed, for the "fun" of calling it a biography. There was no need to worry, however, for the book was in reality as much a biography as Sterne's *Tristram Shandy* or Defoe's *Moll Flanders*, and prospective readers did not mind the uncertainty.

Orlando had all the features of a biography—a preface, acknowledgments, even an index; but in tone and spirit, it was of course a fantasy based on Vita personally. It begins in the reign of Queen Elizabeth, with its titular hero a full-blooded youth, and ends on the chiming of midnight, October 11, 1928, with Orlando now a woman—the hero turned heroine. Above all, the book is filled with audacity and irreverence. Time and place become mere abstractions in a profusion of detail, and the concept of androgyny is dramatized with playful pedantry. Critics and poets are satirized. Conventions are ridiculed. Biographers are instructed in biography. Nothing was sacred in these pages; no one immune. And *Orlando* was soon the talk of the town. One of the London papers said the book in Bloomsbury "was a joke, in Mayfair a necessity, and in America a classic."

On her first reading of *Orlando*, Vita wrote from Long Barn: "My darling, I am in no fit state to write to you ... I can't say anything except that I am completely dazzled, bewitched, enchanted, under a spell. It seems to me the loveliest, wisest, *richest* book that I have ever read ... It is like being alone in a dark room with a treasure chest full of rubies and nuggets and brocades ... how you could have hung so splendid a garment on so poor a peg ... Virginia, my dearest, I can only thank you for pouring out such riches."

Harold wired Virginia from Berlin on October 13: "Orlando has filled me with amazed excitement. I feel deeply grateful to you Virginia for having written something so lovely and so strong." This was followed two days later by a letter: "It really *is* Vita—her puzzled concentration, her absent-minded tenderness ... She strides magnificent and clumsy through 350 years." Most of the reviews were full of praise. Rebecca West in the *New York Herald Tribune* (October 21) called the book "a poetic masterpiece of the first rank." Hugh Walpole reviewed it in the *Morning Post* (October 25) under the title "On a Certain New Book" and mentioned neither its title nor its author, so sure was he that readers wouldn't need to be told. Only Arnold Bennett was baffled: "Orlando at the end of the book has achieved an age of some four centuries. Which reminds one of the Wandering Jew and the Flying Dutchman ... Orlando is intended to be the incarnation of something or other."

One storm cloud dampened the event—again it was Lady Sackville. "You have written some beautiful phrases in Orlando," she wrote to Virginia, "but probably you do not realise how *cruel* you have been. And the person who inspired the book, has been crueller still." Beside a photograph of Virginia that she had pasted into her copy of *Orlando*, Lady Sackville wrote: "The awful face of a madwoman whose successful mad desire is to separate people who care for each other. I loathe this woman for having changed my Vita and taken her away from me."

Apart from her extraordinary pleasure in the book, Vita was affected by *Orlando* in a very private way. It had come to birth at the time her father lay dying, so that in a way it became a kind of memorial she alone had been allowed to observe. Further, Lord Sackville's death made a reality of the one thing Vita most dreaded: her permanent loss of Knole. That loss and all it represented to Vita was beyond utterance. With the birth of *Orlando*—and Orlando—however, its edge had been dulled, for in a symbolic sense the ancestral home had been restored to her, their pasts reunited. "You made me cry with your passages about Knole, you wretch."

There was something else, however, that Virginia had done in *Orlando* which was harder to talk about, and that was laying bare a hidden side of her subject. Virginia had said earlier that she would "exhibit the most profound and secret side" of Vita's character. And indeed she did just that. There for all the world to see was Orlando's violence; his lust for glory and swings of temper; his rages, his dreams, his wish for solitude. And there was that large and terrible flaw in his nature—his tendency to substitute the phantom for the actual, to mix illusion with reality. Virginia came nearest the very soul of her subject when she said that Orlando would surrender everything he owned in the world "to write one little book and become famous." "Desire for fame"—that was the vital force in Orlando's life. And in Vita's too.

So much of Vita's life, her past as well as her future, could be understood if one realized just how much fame meant to her. With it she had recognition and power and acceptance, the very things Lady Sackville had denied her. It was the achievement of glory that excited her most extravagant passions. If she could not be remembered in the histories of England as the successor to Knole, surely she could take her place as one of England's poets. Fame was the key. Virginia had unearthed it. And Vita saw this at once. If Virginia's penetration into the human heart in *To the Lighthouse* had made Vita "afraid" of her, how naked and vulnerable she must now have felt, with *Orlando* staring out at the world from the windows of every bookshop. Virginia had been relentless in her search and brilliant in her exposition. Indeed the entire creation had about it a ruthless virtuosity. And though *Orlando* was not a serious book, Virginia had nevertheless succeeded once more in transforming the hardness of fact into the magnificence of fantasy.

Now, Vita realized, there was nothing either too personal or too private she could withhold from the "gentle genius," and with this realization her feelings for Virginia once more began to shift. Toward the artist Vita's adoration increased, but so did the distance now separating them. "Darling, you are my anchor," said Vita, following the book's debut. "An anchor entangled in gold nuggets at the bottom of the sea." And with that new orientation, she began to drift more openly from Virginia. The anchor would remain forever steadfast; of that she was certain, and with that certainty the restless Vita would again bob and dip and plunge in the sea of passion. Virginia would continue to love her, perhaps with more ease, now that Vita had been captured in an edifice of words. So that while the child remained cradled in Vita's affection, the author of *Orlando* stood poised, watchful, just a little apprehensive.

In the often bewildering interplay of their multiple roles, there was always a danger: the more openly Virginia tried to monopolize Vita or tried to curb her sexual frolics, the greater the strain she put on their relations. Vita was generous with everything except her personal freedom—the emotional franchise her biographer repeatedly put to the test. Virginia, however, was reasonably assured of Vita's yielding to her whenever—like Julia Stephen—her maternal susceptibilities were touched, and frequently she took advantage of that weakness. How often she waved goodbye to Vita feeling like an infant having drunk sweet milk. Even in her chronic illnesses, Virginia knew she could arouse Vita's protective instincts more effectively by pretending she was well when she wasn't—and Vita *knew* she wasn't—than by acting the simpering, propitiatory invalid. Vita never failed to come to her side. Vita the lover posed all kinds of difficulties, but Vita the mother was as stable as the Rock of Gibraltar. Sir Leslie Stephen had behaved in exactly the same way when he wanted Julia's attention all for himself. Father and daughter were indeed mirror images.

Virginia had sent Roger Fry a copy of *Orlando*, and after the flurry of success died down, Roger wrote her a letter from Paris, not so much about the book as about Virginia herself, Virginia the artist. "There seems no doubt about your genius," he said. "How odd that must be . . . I've never doubted its existence. No doubt genius doesn't insure one against doing a bad work of art, but, all the same, there must be a curious security about it. Whatever you do must come out with a certain gushing impetus like an instinctive act."

There was something very comforting in this, for Roger had said it, as he had said so much else to her, in his deep, rich fatherly voice—the voice she would hear over and over again when the time came for her to reconstruct *his* life. "I venerate and admire you to the point of worship," she wrote him on December 4. "Lord! you don't know what an awful lot I owe you!" It would be difficult to express "a thousandth part of the devotion I have for you." Virginia respected the opinions of Forster and Strachey and Leonard, but it was Roger Fry alone who knew what she was after in all her literary experiments and departures from tradition. He had explained for painting what she was trying to achieve in writing—a method of expressing an essentially new way of seeing the world. "Roger is the only civilised man I have ever met, and I continue to think him the plume in our cap . . . If Bloomsbury had produced only Roger, it would be on a par with Athens at its prime."

Shortly after the publication of *Orlando*, Virginia gave two lectures at Cambridge University. The first was read for the Arts Society at Newnham and a week later the second was read for the ODTAA (One Damn Thing After Another) Society at Girton. "Thank God, my long toil at the women's lecture is this moment ended," she wrote in her diary on Saturday, October 27. "I am back from speaking at Girton . . . Starved but valiant young women—

that's my impression. Intelligent, eager, poor; and destined to become school mistresses ... I blandly told them to drink wine and have a room of their own." These two papers on "Women and Fiction" were expanded and published a year later as *A Room of One's Own* and destined to become the classic essay on feminism.

By the end of 1928 Virginia Woolf was among the best-known writers of the day. She was now what one called a "successful novelist." In its first six months *Orlando* sold over 8,000 copies in England and over 13,000 in America. There could be no question now of fame. During that autumn, the Hogarth Press also brought out Vita's second travel book called *Twelve Days: An Account of a Journey Across the Bakhtiari Mountains.*

Virginia was now earning a great deal of money in royalties. For the first time since her marriage, sixteen years earlier, she was able to afford certain luxuries. The spending habit did not come any more naturally to her than it had to her father (or to Leonard). There was always some reservation involved, some tendency to put off, to wait. But now at least there was the "agreeable luxurious sense of coins in my pocket beyond my weekly 13/– which was always running out." For many years now, with so many medical expenses, she had denied herself even the smallest comforts. "All this money making originated in a spasm of black despair at Rodmell 2 years ago [September 15, 1926] ... part of my misery was the perpetual limitation of everything; no chairs, or beds, no comfort, no beauty." She appealed to Leonard, who controlled household accounts, and they eventually agreed to share whatever money they made after reaching a sum necessary for basic living expenses. Virginia would now have her own bank account as a result and two hundred pounds of her own by January 1. The important thing was "to spend freely, without fuss or anxiety; and to trust to one's power of making more."

The promise of future earning power, however, was highly conditional, and the subject of yearly income and expenditure would always be a sensitive subject to both Virginia and Leonard. Medical doctors and nursing care were costly, and Virginia, since her marriage, had suffered three major bouts of illness. There could never be a guarantee of future income. It was her own mental health that made her so dependent, and the older she got the more serious this worry would become. For old age would increase dependency, and the more dependent she became the more she would need to lean on Leonard. It was not a pleasant prospect.

There must have been times, numerous times, when, despite all her claims of freedom and independence, she realized that the *only* real freedom she had was the freedom of her imagination. If illusion failed her, if the power of invention faltered, the only meaningful life she knew would be effectively over. And of this stark and ugly fact she needed no reminding.

Virginia waited for her cisterns to fill before beginning *The Waves* (still called *The Moths*), and during that interval finished her short book called *Phases of Fiction* which, although originally intended for the Hogarth Press, would be published in New York in three installments of *The Bookman* in the spring of 1929. During the Christmas holidays Vita and her sons, Benedict and Nigel, went to Germany to be with Harold, now Counsellor at the British Embassy in Berlin. Unfortunately, she spent most of the holiday in bed with influenza. When Virginia got word of this, she wrote her immediately to "let me have one line on receipt of this to say how you are . . . If I don't hear, I shan't sleep; then I shall get a headache; then I shan't be able to come to Berlin." Virginia was once more blackmailing her beloved Vita, oddly echoing her parents' relationship.

" 'Joy's life's in the doing'—I murder, as usual, a quotation: I mean it's the writing, not being read that excites me." Virginia was trying to quote a line from Shakespeare's *Troilus and Cressida*—"Things won are done; joy's soul lies in the doing." She was referring, of course, to *Orlando*. "How odd to think that I have given the world something that the world enjoys." With these words she opened her 1929 diary. *Orlando* had been called a masterpiece by the *Manchester Guardian*, but Vanessa's paintings, now showing at the New Burlington Galleries, had not even been mentioned. "So I have something, instead of children," Virginia reflected, comparing once more her life with Vanessa's. She had said once to her: "You have the children, the fame by rights belongs to me." There had always been a certain rivalry between them, and Virginia had always diminished herself in her need to idealize Vanessa. But that was now beginning to change. If Virginia was sure about her gift to the world, she was no longer so sure about her shifting relations with Vanessa.

 On January 16 the Woolfs went for a week to see the Nicolsons in Berlin, where they were joined by Vanessa, Duncan, and Quentin. From every point of view the holiday was a failure. It was, first of all, too large a party to blend harmoniously. Second, Leonard disliked the Germans (and here Virginia sided with him) and he disliked Berlin. Third, and most important of all, he hated the social obligations—the dinners and luncheons Harold had arranged—and refused to go.

Leonard had sworn he would go to no parties and insisted that Virginia make this clear to the Nicolsons, Vanessa wrote to Roger Fry. Virginia evidently did not make this clear and the result was a series of exploding tempers. "We spent one of the most edgy and badly arranged evenings I can remember with them," she went on. It was indeed a party of "unrelated passions."

At some point during the visit, Virginia and Vita dined alone at the Funkturm, the radio-tower which overlooked the city. In a letter to Virginia after she'd returned to England, Vita reminded her of "feelings to which you gave such startling and disturbing expression in the Funkturm." There is no record of what exactly transpired during this dinner, but it appears that Virginia renewed her declaration of love for Vita and Vita had tried to say she no longer loved Virginia in the passionate way she had in the beginning. The rapture was over. This strange paradox seems to have resulted from the brilliant *Orlando*. Vita felt defeated by Virginia's intellectual indomitability. The childish figure of "Potto" was difficult to respond to with so much brainpower behind it; in a sense, the genius of *Orlando* effectively killed the childlike Virginia in Vita's mind.

There was another equally baffling paradox in their relations. Much of the maternal benevolence Vita carried into all her intimacies made her curiously inaccessible to the women she attracted. For in secretly guarding her privacy Vita never permitted her lovers to know her well enough (as Virginia had) to meet her on an open and emotionally equal footing. Her generosity, her protective affection tended to deny her partners the privilege of behaving maturely and responsibly toward her. They all became, to some extent and each in her own way, like dependent and loving children. For this reason, in none of her love affairs could Vita feel fulfilled, for in none was she allowed to experience herself as a valued human being in her own right. In other words, she was unable to feel herself loved and valued by an adult woman, because any lover, in submitting to Vita's protective caresses, simultaneously forfeited her status of equality.

As if still under the feudal system of old, the lord dispensed her bounty and guardianship, and her vassals pledged their fealty in return. Vita offered. They took. Vita demanded. They supplied. The intimacies were skewed, unbalanced, and decidedly unsymmetrical. And so *Orlando* put Vita in an awkward corner. When Virginia once more reached out for love, Vita was made to realize once more that love itself was simply not hers to give. It was sad. But it was also true. Somewhere she had written that her mother, Lady Sackville, for all her passion and extravagance "was a dictator: not a colleague." In a much subtler way, this applied to Vita as well. The woman who created *Orlando* understood all this. Virginia the child did not.

Vanessa described the week in Berlin as "rackety," and Virginia, in her heightened state of excitement, felt it most; so that by the time they reached London on January 25, she was in a state of collapse. On board the ship from Holland to Harwich, after taking some seasickness medicine Vanessa had given her called Somnifène, she drifted into what appeared to be a coma.

Leonard wrote to Vanessa from Tavistock Square on the twenty-eighth that when he woke Virginia in Harwich she was "giddy" and scarcely able to walk. He managed with difficulty to get her into the train, for she seemed still drugged. "The giddiness lasted off and on for another 24 hours and she has now one of the old fashioned headaches and a rather bad one." He was certain her condition was the result of too many late nights.

For the next two weeks she lived the life of an invalid, bedridden most of the time. She saw few people, and her letters for the most part were to Vita, who was not due back from Germany until the end of February. Dr. Ellie Rendel treated her during this collapse. "It's odd how I want you when I'm ill," Virginia wrote toward the end of January, just as Leslie had so often said to Julia. Everything would be "warm and happy" if Vita came in. On the following day: "I'm afraid I shall be very strictly kept under for a time. No parties—no romances. But that suits you very well . . . You want Potto and Virginia kept in their kennel," she wrote, trying pathetically to believe that Vita still felt a lover's jealousy.

When Vita failed to respond to that ploy, Virginia—in a now familiar pattern—began pointing the finger of blame at Vita: "I've had this sort of thing before . . . But of course the Dr and Leonard say it's all the Berlin racketing (I daresay it was)." In early February she could write a long enough letter to elaborate. The doctor maintained that Virginia was in "a state of nervous exhaustion" with all the usual symptoms of "pain, and heart jumpy, and my back achy, and so on. What I call a first rate headache." But of course Leonard was there to nurse her, she said, with large wholesome meals. "He sits on the edge of the bed and considers my symptoms like a judge ... I should have shot myself long ago in one of these illnesses" if Leonard had not been there. But—"How I love you."

Vita became impatient at this point, and defensive. "I can't believe it's the 'racketing' of Berlin; really, you might have spent every night for a week till 5 in the morning indulging in orgies—to hear you talk—or Leonard talk, rather, and the doctor. No, no ... Do you know what I believe it was, apart from 'flu? it was SUPPRESSED RANDINESS. So there—you remember your admissions as the searchlight went round and round [on the Funkturm]?" Virginia tried to stand her ground. But it was no use. The passionate Vita was gone.

By mid-February she began to recover, and was anxious to be writing *The Waves*. She had been out for a walk and was now composing this letter to Vita "sitting up like a woman of the world, over a little gas fire." She would be in "rude health" when rude health was needed. On February 23: "I've been down to the Studio and done a mild morning's work." So the illness was over, and next week she'd be risen "like the morning star."

And as always happened when Virginia's sense of well-being seemed threatened, she turned to her pen. Words would restore balance and harmony. Writing would soften the facts. But what were the facts? Would she discover them in *The Waves*? It was too soon to tell. There were adjustments to be made: Vita now stood at a different angle to her. So did Leonard. So did Vanessa. She needed time and introspection. "I am going to enter a nunnery these next months," she wrote on March 28, "and let myself down into my mind ... I am going to face certain things." It was going to be a time of adventure, but "rather lonely and painful I think." Solitude would be good for the new book. Outwardly she would seem unchanged; but for the entire duration she was going to "attack this angular shape in my mind" which was now so restless, "in some ways so desperate." She was on the verge of breaking into some large "strenuous adventure" that would need all her courage.

Virginia was just finishing her revision of the two lectures on "Women and Fiction" she had given the previous October. Soon it would be published in England and America as *A Room of One's Own*. It would make money; it would increase her freedom. Hadn't she just finished insisting that freedom depended on so much money a year and a room one could call one's own? Well, now she had five hundred pounds—indeed she had four times that;

and she would build with that money, not one but two rooms: a bedroom for herself on the ground floor and a writing room directly above it at Monks House.

Freedom aside, however, there was still old age to face. But did age matter when she felt still bubbling inside her that creative, "impetuous torrent"? If she saw "ugliness" in the looking glass, she was inwardly "more full of shape and colour" and bolder as a writer. If she needed courage she had only to remind herself that she earned money—a lot of money. People now looked forward to her books. They sought her out. She was in demand. The "Uniform Edition of the Works of Virginia Woolf" was in preparation. The Hogarth Press would soon issue four volumes. And what about the Press? For the first time, it made over £400 profit. "And 7 people now depend on us; and I think with pride that 7 people depend, largely, upon my hand writing on a sheet of paper. That is of course a great solace and pride to me. It's not scribbling; it's keeping 7 people fed and housed." Next year when *A Room of One's Own* was published—for which she predicted a large sale—they would continue to depend on Virginia for their livelihood. All of this meant independence. It meant power. Still, *Orlando* had lost her Vita. Had that loss been inevitable? How she would miss being in love with Vita. If only she could soar into the airy spaces of imagination and "get some pull on this horrid world of real life!" But she remained calm, for when she counted up her blessings, they far outweighed her sorrow.

"Now about this book, The Moths. How am I to begin it? And what is it to be?" she asked herself in late May. The earlier urgency to begin writing had passed. There was now only a "great pressure of difficulty." And so beginning *The Waves* was again postponed. A longer incubation period was needed; and while she waited, she read Proust, did some journalism, wrote letters, considered her friends, made character sketches.

There was Clive, for instance. She would write to Quentin about his father. Since Clive's long love affair with Mary Hutchinson had ended a short time earlier, he had become a fierce womanizer. Love and women were all he talked about, and Virginia wished he would progress beyond love "where he has been stationed these many years to the next point in the human pilgrimage." Everyone was beginning to think Clive's endless tales of debauchery were becoming rather tiresome.

Her annual conversation with George Duckworth was also preserved. He was now Sir George Duckworth. It was lunchtime, but he kept Virginia for almost half an hour—"asking me to lunch to meet some literary bores . . .

and then going on and on and on. 'Where's dear old Nessa? In France? But who's she living with? Clive, d'you say? And her boy? Which boy? The painter? Is he a good painter? . . . How I should like to run over and stay with her! I've just had my last tooth out; and they've put in what they call a transformation—temporary of course—to last three months. Meanwhile my teeth fall out when I talk; when I eat; when I telephone. Margaret and I want to come and see you. We're hoping to settle in Connaught Square—' At last, at last I dropped the telephone; he puffs and blows like a sea-horse; I daresay all his teeth were on the floor at the end."

The Woolfs left England by train for Cassis on June 4 for a ten-day holiday. During this visit, they found a three-room dwelling in the woods near Vanessa's small villa that they wanted to buy. It would be a place they could come to for part of each year. The negotiation was never completed, however. Leonard saw the practical disadvantages of having three houses and did his best to convince Virginia of them as well. She was financially fortified at the time, however, and eager to complete the sale.

Life was very pleasant in an old French farmhouse in a vineyard. Vanessa's villa was five minutes off; Virginia and Leonard went to her for meals—"a delicious life, with a great deal of wine, cheap cigars, conversation, and the society of curious derelict English people, who have no money and live like lizards in crannies." Whether she realized it or not, Virginia was putting a great deal of emphasis on money during this period of her career. It was a touchy subject with Vanessa, who was now and would always be a little pinched financially, and it put a further strain on their relationship. Virginia's success as a popular writer, her fame, made comparisons with Vanessa's reputation as a painter inevitable and unpleasant. Virginia dealt with this material difference by constantly pointing out that Vanessa had children and she did not. But the score remained far from even, for Virginia still felt herself stiffen when her sister lavished too much attention on her children. This habit Virginia referred to as Vanessa's "almost overpowering supremacy"; and the object of that supremacy was of course Vanessa's favorite, Julian: "My elder son is coming tomorrow; yes, and he is the most promising young man in King's; and has been speaking at the Apostle's dinner." Maternal boasting never failed to raise Virginia's dander. "All I can oppose that with is, And I made £2,000 out of Orlando and can bring Leonard here and buy a house if I want." To which Vanessa never failed to reply: "I am a failure as a painter compared with you, and can't do more than pay for my models." And so they went on.

Much as she cared for Julian, Virginia saw the limitations his mother could not. "I daresay he'll give you a lot of trouble before he's done—" Virginia said to Vanessa; "he is too charming and violent and gifted altogether: and in love with you." She was naturally sensitive to Julian's power over Vanessa and jealous of Vanessa's extravagant love for him. Virginia watched them closely. Julian must often have seemed dimly like Thoby, usurping Vanessa's attention, depleting the fountain of love. Vanessa and Julian were always hinting at very "intimate things." Virginia resented this. He was really a "simple crude boy—whom I shall now never know, I daresay." One of these days she would say to Vanessa: "You are a jealous woman, and don't want me to know your sons, don't want to take, but always to give; are afraid of givers." If Virginia was her father's daughter, Vanessa was most assuredly her mother's.

Vanessa had her children, however, and as a painter had been forced to sacrifice a great deal to motherhood; and it was to the mother in her that Virginia always appealed. "Now if you sometimes kissed me *voluntarily* perhaps I would not be afraid." Virginia was perhaps justified in feeling afraid, for her success seemed to be working against her. *Orlando* had driven a wedge between her and Vita; and now the money *Orlando* was earning was upsetting her relations with Vanessa. Public success meant private failure. The higher one went, the lonelier it got. The grown-up genius and the love-starved child were at war with each other; and much of the battle in the months ahead would be played out in the pages of *The Waves*.

"I would rather fail gloriously than dingily succeed." How easy it is to imagine those sensational words coming from Orlando. In fact, they were written by Vita Sackville-West herself when the idea for *The Edwardians* (six weeks before the publication of *Orlando*) flashed into her mind. In the early months of her research on the book, Virginia had recruited Vita's help in collecting facts about Knole—tracing its history, taking photographs, wandering through its great halls. In the process of Virginia's writing, Vita's own imagination caught fire. What was there to prevent her from making up her own story of Knole? In early February 1929, Vita wrote from Germany, with a Tauchnitz edition of *Orlando* before her, that she couldn't read without shedding a tear. "Whether it is the mere beauty of the book, or whether it is because of you, or because of Knole," she didn't know. By late June, however, she began writing at top speed about her magnificent Knole, and *The Edwardians* would signal a major change in her life as a writer.

· · ·

Meanwhile, back from Cassis, Virginia was pitched in melancholy. "Lord, how deep it is!" she wrote on June 23 in her diary. "What a born melancholic I am! The only way to keep afloat is by working. A note for the summer; I must take more work than I can possibly get done . . . Directly I stop working I feel that I am sinking down, down . . . I feel that if I sink further I shall reach the truth . . . that there is nothing—nothing for any of us. Work, reading, writing are all disguises; and relations with people. Yes, even having children would be useless."

This was Virginia Woolf, the novelist, despairing. Had she listened to the child within, she would have heard her longing for Vita; felt an emptiness about the heart. Vanessa had her family; Vita had her new lover. Virginia had nothing. She had better plunge very soon into fiction; into the past. "I must grind on with Proust," she said. He knew how to re-member the scattered limbs of history. Proust alone knew how to transform the granite of "this horrid world of real life" into pale rainbows of feeling.

34 On Sunday, June 23, 1929, Virginia saw the opening of her next novel. "I think it will begin like this: dawn; the shells on a beach . . . then all the children at a long table—lessons . . . this shall be childhood . . . the sense of children; unreality . . . there must be great freedom from 'reality'." Now she would need peace and quiet to let the mind expand. Like the changing positions of the sun on Monet's haystacks, the monochrome of melancholy would soon shimmer as some submerged part of her urged *The Waves* on. The work now would be in making a private feeling public. Just as Cézanne made one feel the solid rocks and rhythms beneath his carpet of landscape—the invisible structures behind appearances—so Virginia would pattern her novel; so she would attempt to express the emotion of human experience *without* communicating its meaning. For many months she had put off the novel. During the last week of June, she thought it through. Finally the notebook was open; the pen poised. On July 2, she set down the first words. The writing was slow, difficult, very private.

· · ·

By the end of July, however, Virginia was sent to bed with a headache. Part of it was the strain of *The Waves*; part of it was discovering that Vita was in France on a walking tour with Hilda Matheson. In Savoy she planned to write some of *The Edwardians*. Virginia had once complained that her letters were not very intimate. Vita now responded to that charge. "This is perhaps not what you call an intimate letter? But I disagree. The book one is writing at the moment is really the most intimate part of one, and a part about which one preserves the strictest intimacy. What is love or sex, compared with the intensity of the life one leads *in* one's book? A trifle ... Therefore if I write to you about my book, I am writing intimately ... But you would rather I told you I missed Potto and Virginia, those silky creatures with a barb under their fur—and so I do."

It was an endearing letter, but Vita made the mistake of saying Hilda Matheson was with her. This brought on a spasm of jealousy Virginia could scarcely conceal. She got it into her head that the tour had been secretly planned months earlier and was upset to be so ruthlessly deceived. On her return Vita, now equally upset by the accusation, attempted to reassure Virginia that the holiday had been an impromptu affair. And with some effort, she succeeded. Virginia later confessed to being relieved "that her story to me is precisely true." Vita had even brought documents to prove it. "Indeed I was more worried and angry and hurt and caustic about this affair than I let on." But now she could rest.

Not for long, however. The suspicion returned, and with it, a severe headache. On August 12, two days after Vita's visit, despite the documents and telephone calls and letters, Virginia's badgering started up again. "I've had to retire to bed with the usual old pain ... the price of the value I set on your honesty. Lord! ... Meanwhile will you send me at least a line to say what happened about Hilda—I particularly want to know the situation."

Vita was, in fact, having a love affair with Hilda Matheson, but Virginia, her self-esteem bruised and battered, was prepared to accept any excuse Vita might offer. The fact that Vita even took the trouble to explain was, to Virginia's mind, proof of her affection—or something. Little wonder that she fled to her manuscript. Only in a world of her own making could she find peace and satisfaction.

A Room of One's Own was published, to almost universal acclaim, on October 24. It was to become, and remain, the classic essay on feminism. Virginia Woolf had made a full-scale attack on male economic dominance in England, on the pressure to keep women out of universities and uneducated, and on the effort to keep women chained to their kitchen stoves or in confinement with endless pregnancies. The essay actually went much deeper than that.

Writers of fiction, so Virginia Woolf asserted, must free themselves of the hatred and bitterness that originate in sexual politics. They must be able to express a larger, more comprehensive sympathy which embraces the feelings of both men and women, a sympathy that fosters gender harmony. The militant feminist was as incapable of producing worthwhile fiction as the male chauvinist, precisely because her artistic powers were forever inflamed with ill feeling. Great artists were androgynous; their minds were unimpeded and their imaginations incandescent. But androgyny could flourish only when one had intellectual freedom, and that freedom depended upon certain material comforts, the most fundamental of which were money in one's pocket and a room of one's own.

On October 31, in her BBC broadcast on new books, Vita, reviewing *A Room of One's Own*, said that Virginia Woolf enjoyed "the feminine qualities of . . . fantasy and irresponsibility, allied to all the masculine qualities that go with a strong, authoritative brain." Vita's voice over the air waves "was a trumpet call, moving me to tears . . . It's an odd feeling, hearing oneself praised to 50 million old ladies in Surbiton by one with whom one has watched the dawn and heard the nightingale." It was rather a surprise— "your praise at once sells 100 of my book . . . So you will have me at your skirts for ever." Virginia was now richer and more celebrated than ever.

But nothing of this busy exterior world touched the silent interior of her new novel. With each passing day it was becoming a long, solitary journey into her self. Earlier, when *The Waves* was just underway, she commented on the oddness of it all: "I'm not writing with gusto or pleasure," she said, "because of the concentration. I'm not reeling it off; but sticking it down. Also, never, in my life, did I attack such a vague yet elaborate design; whenever I make a mark I have to think of its relation to a dozen others." This was a problem of literary impressionism, the effect of collective relations on the mind, getting the design to contain the vision. It was a lonely struggle, and these October days were "strained and surrounded with silence." The silence wasn't physical. It was nothing she could point to. It was rather a strange, remote sense of aloneness—like a fin far out in a waste of water. As she walked up Bedford Place, one afternoon, she suddenly felt—"How I suffer, and no one knows how I suffer, walking up this street, engaged with my anguish, as I was after Thoby died—alone; fighting something alone." Vanessa had fled into the arms of Clive Bell. She had left Virginia to grieve alone. But Thoby was now being re-collected, image by image. He was being re-membered, and part of *The Waves* was to become a monument to his memory.

Early in 1930 someone new came into Virginia's life. The person was Ethel Smyth, aged seventy-two, a composer and a feminist. She blew into 52 Tavistock Square with the same hurricane force as she had lived most of her life. Dame Ethel had been to Germany to study music with the Brahms circle. She had composed several operas, been imprisoned for militant feminist activism; and already written several volumes of her autobiography. Virginia had read her two-volume *Impressions That Remained* in 1919, and had reviewed her *Streaks of Life* in 1921.

Ethel had written to Virginia, praising *A Room of One's Own*. Virginia had replied, suggesting they meet: ". . . you might like me. Who knows?" she said flirtatiously. The meeting was postponed several times because of illness; but it finally took place on February 20, and a friendship developed with lightning speed. Dame Ethel was an impatient woman. "She has descended upon me like a wolf on the fold," said Virginia in a note to Saxon Sydney-Turner. "I like her—she is as shabby as a washerwoman and shouts and sings." But what Virginia really wanted to know about was Ethel's music. Was it any good? she asked Saxon.

Ethel Smyth had an insatiable curiosity and was in this respect almost worse than Virginia herself, who made a record of their first meeting. Not entirely recovered from her recent illness, Virginia had been lying on the sofa when she heard the bell ring and then a "brisk tramp" up the stairs, and then—"behold a bluff, military old woman . . . bounced into the room . . . in a three cornered hat and tailor made suit. 'Let me look at you'. That over, Now I have brought a book and pencil . . . First I want to make out the genealogy of your mother's family. Old Pattle—have you a picture? No. Well now—the names of his daughters." The interrogation lasted throughout tea. In fact they talked without pause until seven, when Leonard appeared. Almost from the start they were using Christian names. Ethel turned to her music. " 'I am said to be an egoist. I am a fighter. I feel for the underdog' . . . Her cheeks redden. Her faded eyes flash. 'I've thought of nothing but seeing you for 10 days. And this friendship has come to me now'." There was a lot to Ethel beyond the flourish and the egotism. She had a passion for sports: she played golf, rode a bicycle, had been thrown from a horse two years earlier. A very strong woman she was—"which she proved by talking till 7.30; then eating a biscuit and drinking a glass of vermouth and going off to eat a supper of maccaroni when she got to Woking at 9."

E. F. Benson had written the once-celebrated novel *Dodo* in 1893, using Dame Ethel as the model for Edith Staines. Ethel was still playing the vigorous games of life at seventy-two. She *was* life, Virginia said, "and I am only a spectator." Ethel next asked about Virginia's marriage, and got the laconic reply: "What about marriage? I married Leonard Woolf in 1912, I think, and almost immediately was ill for 3 years." But Ethel persisted and in several months got a fuller account. Virginia told her about meeting Leonard in November 1904, on the eve of his departure for Ceylon. She was recovering, she said, from her second major breakdown and was in London between visits to Cambridge and Giggleswick. "And I heard stories of him; how he trembled." Lytton said he was like Jonathan Swift and would murder his wife. Someone else said Leonard had married a black woman. "That was my romance—Woolf in a jungle. And I set up house alone with a brother and Nessa married, and I was rather adventurous for those days; that is we were sexually very free." Despite that freedom, however, Virginia admitted to being a sexual coward. "My terror of real life has always kept me in a nunnery." All of her talk on Thursday Evenings with the young Cantabrigians had been "narrow, circumscribed; and leading to endless ramifications of intrigue."

But all that stopped when she married Leonard. Then "my brains went up in a shower of fireworks." As an experience, madness was "terrific I can assure you . . . and in its lava I still find most of the things I write about. It shoots out of one everything shaped, final, not in mere driblets, as sanity does." During the six months she lay in bed, she learned a great deal about "what is called oneself. Indeed I was almost crippled when I came back to the world . . . Think—not one moment's freedom from doctor discipline . . . 'You shan't read this' and 'you shan't write a word' and 'you shall lie still and drink milk'—for six months."

Ethel's insatiable appetite for Virginia's history may have fertilized the novel's breeding ground; for Virginia continued assiduously writing *The Waves*, and although she was making slow progress, she managed to finish the first draft on April 29, typing in the afternoon what she had written in the morning. It was a hard book to write and it would be an equally hard book to read. She began even at this early stage to predict that no one would possibly understand what she'd written even if they took the time. "Oh you can't think what gibberish my next book will be," she'd written to Quentin earlier in the year. "I fancy you tactfully apologising and tapping your forehead when you hear people say, Is that your Aunt?"

Virginia persevered, however. She was buoyed up by the record-breaking success of *A Room of One's Own*. On January 26—she was now forty-eight—she marveled at having earned "about £3,020 last year—the salary of a civil servant: a surprise to me, who was content with £200 for so many years." On February 16 the book's sales had reached 10,000 copies. There was every reason to feel confident. There was also every reason to mull over Ethel Smyth's declaration of love: "Odd as it may seem to you I did love you before I saw you, wholly solely because of 'a room of one's own,'" she wrote to Virginia in May.

Vita had finished *The Edwardians* in early March, submitted it to the Hogarth Press, and immediately went out real estate hunting. As it happened, the view from the terrace of Long Barn was being threatened by poultry farmers who were negotiating the purchase of a neighboring farm. The prospect of having to look out on chicken coops was appalling, and so Vita began looking for another house. On a rainy April 4 she discovered Sissinghurst Castle, a monumental ruin set gloriously in acres of mud and debris. "Fell flat in love with it," she wrote in her diary. She made an offer of £12,375 and Sissinghurst was hers.

The Edwardians was published on May 29 and became an immediate best-seller both in England and in America. Hugh Walpole, a member of the selection committee of the Book Society, had read the novel in typescript and recommended it. Clemence Dane, another popular novelist, did the same; so *The Edwardians* appeared as the Book Society's Choice for June. It was selling so fast, they were "hauling in money like pilchards from a net," Virginia wrote Quentin in early June. The Press was filling orders of about 800 copies a day. On June 16 Virginia recorded the sales as verging on 20,000 copies— "And it is not a very good book." On July 4, she said to Vita: "We have passed the 20,000." A few days later: "Lord! What a go! £5,000 at least I imagine." The novel had been chosen by the American Literary Guild as Book of the Month for September.

Virginia had her reservations, however. The trouble with Vita was that she wrote with such "incredible ease" that she could fill up a few spare weeks "by dashing off a book." *The Edwardians* was done to "wile away a few months' leisure" and she succeeded in making six thousand pounds. In early August Virginia again reported the book's sales to Vita. It was breaking all Press records. "I don't see any reason why we shouldn't sell 25,000; and what the sales will be in America—heaven help us—the imagination boggles, as they say."

But Vita had private plans she confided to no one. The royalties now pouring in would go toward realizing her most cherished and persistent dream—to transform the ruined Sissinghurst Castle into her own private version of Knole. Sissinghurst's traceable history went back as far as Orlando's. Was it not an act of fate that Sissinghurst should eventually come into her hands? Orlando had sought fame and glory through writing a book. Now Vita's book had earned her that fame, and Sissinghurst would transform her glory into something tangible. Thus the dream and the quest of a lifetime converged in *The Edwardians*, materially and metaphorically. There was one further premium, a very personal one: Sissinghurst had a rose-brick tower that shot up above all the other buildings. This would soon become Vita's most guarded sanctuary and citadel. If she wanted solitude, she would have it, but now with a certain lofty splendor.

In the summer of 1930, Virginia turned to her diary to enter some remarks about her curiously "unnatural" friendship with Ethel. "I say unnatural because she is so old, and everything is incongruous." Ethel had been badly treated in the music world and clung to a few faded compliments "often repeated to herself at dead of night." There was a conspiracy against her, she claimed. The press was determined to do her in. Over and over she repeated these stories to Virginia. "Lying in my chair in the firelight she looked 18; she looked a young vigorous handsome woman. Suddenly this vanishes; then there is the old . . . humane battered face that makes one respect human nature: or feel that it is indomitable and persistent."

Ethel confessed that she didn't like other women being fond of Virginia. "Then you must be in love with me, Ethel." "I have never loved anyone so much." Was there something senile in this, Virginia wondered. She may not have returned her love, but with Ethel's two letters daily, she was certain that the "old fires of Sapphism" were "blazing for the last time." What Virginia wanted—as she always had and always would—was to be possessed by an "indomitable and persistent" mother figure. She made no secret of this, and Ethel somehow knew how to get Virginia into a state of childish, egotistical loquacity. She knew somehow which nerve to press to get Virginia started. Then in profusion came "the usual chaos of pictures of myself—some true, others imaginary." There was something in Ethel that penetrated Virginia's "stumbling and fitful ways: my childish chatter." And for that reason she saw in Ethel "that maternal quality which of all others I need and adore."

"If I were ill," Virginia said to Ethel, "I should be quite as ready to come to you as to Vita, though for entirely different reasons." When Virginia was ill several years earlier and had to spend three months in bed, Vita took her to Long Barn where she lay "in Swansdown and recovered." If Vita was "soothing," Ethel was "supporting." It was important that Ethel understand that Virginia was "diverse enough to want Vita and Ethel and Leonard and Vanessa and oh some other people too." Over a month later, Virginia added: "I can't conceive that you would ever tire me; no; or agitate me." Perhaps she spoke a little prematurely, for before long Ethel would prove not only tiring but downright exhausting.

Now Ethel wanted Virginia to tell her about her headaches and her health in general. This whole area she must have clear in her mind. Virginia was just recovering from a mild headache in June, so she could gratify Ethel's curiosity with a fresh example. First, she explained, there was pain; then numbness; and last, the onset of visions. This most recent headache had stopped at the pain stage, "and only a little pain at that. And it's gone; and I've been working, for me very hard." She went on with her "sordid" medical history: "it is 10 years since I was seeing faces, and 5 since I was lying like a statue."* She was now much stronger than ever: "I had a perpetual temperature, after influenza, for some years: this has now gone; and a heart that was always leaping 5-barred gates; this is now as steady as a cab-horse."

Virginia had driven herself ruthlessly in re-writing *The Waves*. And exhausted from both the effort and the sweltering heat, she collapsed again as she had in August five years earlier at Charleston. This time it was at Monks House on Friday, August 29. Maynard and Lydia Keynes were there at the time. She was walking in the garden with Lydia, she wrote in her diary four days later. "If this don't stop, I said, referring to the bitter taste in my mouth and the pressure like a wire cage of sound over my head, then I am ill." Maynard carried her into the sitting room. Leonard hovered over her, very frightened. She attempted to climb the stairs, but her heart was drumming so painfully she fainted again. It was not until eleven o'clock that she recovered enough to crawl up to bed. It had been a "brush with death."

Virginia wrote Ethel about the incident. It was her old problem of irregular heart rhythms, she said. It stopped and jumped "like a mulish pony." It had nothing to do with the heart; it was all nerves; and Ethel, "valiant" old woman that she was, rushed to Virginia's side.

With the illness came once more the special claims, the small demands. Nothing unreasonable, but demands all the same. Virginia wanted letters—

* From the middle of August to November 1925, Virginia had been intermittently in bed after collapsing at Charleston during Quentin's birthday party.

letters every day—they were essential. Letters about everything. If Ethel saw a sunset or the butcher's boy or a shop full of cabbages, she must write it all down in a letter. Virginia was not well enough to resume work, and so must be kept amused. "Tell me all you do—in spite of my inaccuracy, every fact is valuable"—the time she got up, bathed, had breakfast; what she talked about, what she wore, read, ate; where she walked, and when—"have you a sitting room; how furnished; wine for dinner? . . . In short please Ethel, think, I shan't be working or walking for another week seriously; and gape like a baby cuckoo for Ethel's words."

Virginia was fascinated by Ethel's vigor; by her generosity and the vehemence with which she scattered the floor with hairpins and fumbled for eyeglasses and embraced foreign dignitaries and swept up everyone in her path. Ethel yielded to the demands and accepted the flatteries, but she was not blind to Virginia's faults. Her passion for Virginia did not cloud her vision or dull her judgment. She saw the shortcomings and recorded them in her diary. Virginia, she said, was absolutely "self-absorbed . . . jealous of literary excellence . . . Ungenerous, indeed incapable of knowing what generosity means, I had almost said, but she recognizes it in others. In Vita, for instance, who I think is the only person except Vanessa . . . and Leonard . . . whom she really loves . . . She is arrogant, intellectually, beyond words yet absolutely humble about her own great gifts. Her integrity fascinates me. To save your life, or her own, she would not doctor what she thinks to be the truth." This very "integrity," authentic as it was, would be devastating when she came to chronicle the Stephen family history in *The Years*. Her lyrical *To the Lighthouse* had been a masterpiece, but in it she had not told the *whole* truth: the story of Cam's intense, unnatural love for her father, her ambivalence for her mother.

 It was a full three weeks before Virginia recovered sufficiently to resume work on *The Waves*. For some reason she scarcely mentioned the book to anyone except perhaps Ethel. Her struggles with it, however, she confided to her journal almost from the start. It was the "most complex, and difficult" of all her books, she had said in the spring. "I have not yet mastered the speaking voice . . . I propose to go on pegging it down . . . then re-write, reading much of it aloud, like poetry." Then two

weeks later: "What I now think (about the Waves) is that I can give in a very few strokes the essentials of a person's character. It should be done boldly, almost as caricature."

When she finished the first holograph draft on April 29, 1930, she recorded for her own information that the novel was the "greatest stretch of mind" she'd ever known, especially in the last pages—"this is a reach after that vision I had, the unhappy summer—or three weeks—at Rodmell, after finishing The Lighthouse." It was in July 1927, with success still ringing in her ears, that she realized Vita had fallen in love with another woman, in fact with Mary Campbell. She was once more excluded, pushed out into the cold. It must have been painfully reminiscent of Leslie's rejection after Julia's death. What good was success then if one was deserted. There had also been some hurt feelings with Vanessa about reading her letters aloud for fun. And there'd been some harsh words with Leonard. Then on September 4, 1927, she had written in her diary the song of Shelley she'd been thinking of a year earlier ("Rarely rarely comest thou, spirit of delight"), which in fact she had been singing in September 1926. And she had sung that Shelley song so poignantly she'd never forgotten it or her "vision of a fin rising" out of the sea. "No biographer could possibly guess this important fact about my life in the late summer of 1926." He or she would have to go back to September 30, 1926, to discover what Virginia had written about the mystical side of solitude—that it was "not oneself but something in the universe that one's left with . . . One sees a fin passing far out." Never before had she felt or thought this. "Life is . . . the oddest affair; has in it the essence of reality. I used to feel this as a child—couldn't step across a puddle once I remember, for thinking, how strange—what am I?"

This life event was transferred whole and unaltered into The Waves. There is a scene in which the suicidal Rhoda too cannot step across "the puddle"— "There is the puddle," said Rhoda, the one mad voice in the novel paralyzed by helplessness, "and I cannot cross it." So that when Virginia wrote now in 1930 that The Waves was a "reach after that vision," she was referring to the accumulation of feeling states stretching back to 1926, and perhaps even earlier. It was the repeated experience of dependency, vulnerability, and exclusion. Having one's outstretched arms left empty. And the terror of madness. People with mental illness were deserted, locked away in asylums, isolated, and—again—excluded.

This cluster of feelings appears to have struck Virginia most powerfully after Thoby's death, and it was terrifying. If she went mad, she might be abandoned. Did anyone now in 1930 in the Stephen family—Vanessa, Adrian, the aunts and uncles and cousins—did they know where Laura Stephen was? How she was? Who was looking after her in this year of 1930?

It was in June that Virginia began the second draft of *The Waves*. The re-writing required as much concentration as the original draft, but by August 20, she saw the book resolving itself into a series of "dramatic soliloquies." The question of design was still troublesome. Was the book coherent? Could the soliloquies be read consecutively? She would have to wait and see. "Yet I respect myself for writing this book." And with that respect came a few months of happiness. Indeed it was a free and "occasionally sublime" summer. Even with her "brush with death," she felt secure and in command. She could continue to work on her novel "with a new picture in my mind; my defiance of death in the garden."

On October 4 they returned to Tavistock Square. Soon the days would shorten, curtains would be drawn, fires lit, and steady work to attend to. It was in this mood that Virginia drove her pen through the second draft of *The Waves*. She meditated on it in the evenings while the gramophone was playing. "It occurred to me last night while listening to a Beethoven quartet that I could merge all the interjected passages into Bernard's final speech, and end with the words O solitude." She could thus emphasize the theme of effort, for that was what she wanted most to stress. *The Waves* must show that "effort, effort, dominates: not the waves: and personality: and defiance." The Beethoven quartets, in particular, would weave rhythmically into the last part of the novel. More than that, music—a string quartet—would become part of one of its most abstract and ambiguous images. It would constitute the image that linked the vulnerable, long-suffering Rhoda to the mystical experience of living that Virginia was attempting to express concretely.

The autumn of 1930 was on the whole agreeable. There were more social engagements than Leonard would have wished, but these events—"seeing" and "being seen"—were, when Virginia was in good health, always salubri-ous. There was one in particular that found its way into one of Virginia's gossipy letters. It was a very smart party in Belgrave Square "old Ethel" had taken her to. Immediately upon arriving, Ethel began to unpeel herself "of sweater, jersey and mothy moleskin before all the flunkeys, knocking her pasteboard hat to right and left and finally producing from a cardboard box fastened at the edge by paper fasteners a pair of black leather shoes." "The truth is I'm a snob, and like to be smart," said Ethel, bending over to put on her shoes. Then when the music began, she turned to Virginia and said in a voice that carried farther than it should, " 'Isn't this slow movement sublime—natural and heavy and irresistible like the movement of one's bowels.' All the dapper little diplomats blushed."

With Julian now aged twenty-two and a published poet—Chatto and Windus had just brought out his first collection—Virginia could not resist telling Vanessa about her tea with the great poet himself, T. S. Eliot and his wife, Vivien, whose mental illness was becoming unmanageable. An engagement to see Eliot alone had been arranged weeks earlier; but at the last moment he telephoned to say Vivien wanted to come too, so would Virginia pretend she had invited her as well. "This sounded ominous, but was nothing to the reality. She is insane. She suspects every word one says. 'Do you keep bees?' I asked, handing her the honey. 'Hornets' she replied. 'Where?' I asked. 'Under the bed.' That's the style, and one has to go on talking, and Tom tries, I suppose, to cover it up with longwinded and facetious stories." Vivien, it seems, also opened Eliot's mail and suspected Virginia of being his mistress.

It was not an easy or pleasant tea. But it is odd that Virginia was not more sympathetic to the bizarre behavior for which Vivien Eliot could hardly be held accountable. It is almost as though someone else's madness had a peculiar fascination for her, for on that same day Virginia continued her account in the privacy of her diary. "Was there ever such a torture since life began!— to bear her on one's shoulders, biting, wriggling, raving, scratching, unwholesome, powdered . . . reading his letters, thrusting herself on us . . . trembling—Does your dog do that to frighten me?" Perhaps Virginia was remembering her own departures from reality in 1904 and 1913—or even as far back as 1895—now making Vivien Eliot an object of ridicule and disgust, someone to be kept out of sight.

This was more than a reaction to madness, however. There seemed to be, as Ethel Smyth had said, a chilling arrogance about Virginia. Perhaps it was her way of "protecting" herself; for it appeared again in her account of Somerset Maugham's unpardonable treatment of Hugh Walpole, who had been maligned in Maugham's new novel, *Cakes and Ale*. All London was ringing with it, Virginia said to Vanessa. He had been maliciously and "unmistakably and amusingly caricatured [as Alroy Kear]." Hugh had been sitting on his bed, with only one sock on when he opened the book; and there he remained until eleven o'clock the next morning, reading and weeping.

Clive, Vita, and several others were present when Walpole told his story, on the verge of tears and unable to stop. "Whenever we changed the conversation he went back. 'There are things in it that nobody knows but Willie

[W. S. Maugham] and myself... There are little things that make me shudder. And that man has been my dearest friend for 20 years. And now I'm the laughing stock of London... You don't know the kind of life Willie has led. I do. I could put him in a book. But then I call it a dastardly thing to do.' And so on, round and round... like a dog with a tin on its tail." It was indeed a vicious thing to do. Even Maugham's allusion to Walpole's lover, the Danish tenor Lauritz Melchior, failed to gain her sympathy.

There were numerous interruptions both at Tavistock Square and at Monks House, but work on *The Waves* continued. Virginia was precisely at that stage in the writing where the world seemed full of promise and fatigue, the result of good hard work. All of this was effort. Effort dominated. That was her point in *The Waves*. Throughout January 1931 Virginia forged ahead with her revisions. She was now working with such intensity she could write for only an hour each morning.

Then suddenly something entirely unexpected happened. A new book burst into view—"a sequel to a Room of One's Own—about the sexual life of women: to be called Professions for Women perhaps—Lord how exciting! This sprang out of my paper to be read on Wednesday [the following day] to Pippa's society." The new work would begin as *The Pargiters*; and eventually it would become *The Years*.

Philippa (Pippa) Strachey, one of Lytton's five sisters, was secretary to the National Society for Women's Service and had invited Virginia and Ethel Smyth to speak at the London branch on January 21. The event was reported a week later in the *New Statesman and Nation* by Vera Brittain, whose column was called "A Woman's Notebook": "I was interested... to hear both Dame Ethel and Mrs. Woolf attribute their success largely to the possession of a private income, which enabled the one to take up a non-lucrative career, and the other to flout the displeasure of authors and editors by writing honest reviews. Women, Mrs. Woolf maintained, had succeeded better in literature than in the other arts because paper was cheap and pens made no noise." The audience immensely enjoyed both "hilariously serious" speakers.

On Saturday, February 7, Julia's birthday, Virginia finished *The Waves*. "I wrote the words O Death fifteen minutes ago, having reeled across the last ten pages with some moments of such intensity and intoxication that I seemed only to stumble after my own voice... (as when I was mad). I was almost afraid, remembering the voices that used to fly ahead. Anyhow it is done;

and I have been sitting these 15 minutes in a state of glory, and calm, and some tears, thinking of Thoby . . . Whether good or bad, it's done."

There had been "freedom and boldness" in the last stages of writing. She had discarded "all the images and symbols" she had prepared. That was the right way—simply suggesting images, "never making them work out." The reader would supply, fill in, complete what the writer had merely hinted. That was the poetic method—complete reliance on ambiguity; making multiple meanings possible; freeing different readers to see different things. And *that* was her method. Just as the Impressionists painted only what they *saw*, not what they *knew* was there, so Virginia Woolf wrote what she felt, not what tradition said she *should* feel.

With this novel she had pushed literary impressionism to its limit. *The Waves* expressed a *shared feeling*, without communicating a *shared meaning*. She had at last "netted that fin in the waste of waters" which had appeared before her on September 30, 1926, when she was nearing the end of *To the Lighthouse*. She had created a Reality more real than that manufactured by the methods of the self-proclaimed "realists"—Arnold Bennett, H. G. Wells, John Galsworthy. No two readers would ever read *The Waves* in the same way. That was the significance of impressionism. Each reader would bring his or her unique experience to the novel. Each subject would color the object differently.

And behind it all was her beloved Thoby, who had not lived long enough to fulfill his own private quest. But that no longer mattered. For Virginia, with *The Waves*, had floated him across that vast expanse of water and given him a completion in art that he had been denied in life. Her effort had defied death. She had resurrected him with mind and heart as she had (almost) done with her father. No one could hurt him now. He belonged to Virginia in his death as he had never belonged to her in life. It had been a mighty effort, but his commemoration and his monument were now permanent.

If the form of *The Waves* for Virginia Woolf was structurally simple, the formal relations were not. The novel consists of nine chapters, each describing a stage in the lives of six people—six voices—three female, three male, from childhood to old age. On the female side were Rhoda, the mentally unbalanced; Jinny, the sensualist; and Susan, the rapacious maternal figure. On the male side were Louis, the builder of empires; Neville, the love-starved homosexual; and Bernard, the novelist manqué, maker of phrases. Each stage in their life is preceded by a poetic interlude in which the position of the sun and the ebb and flow of the tides are described. Although all of them share the same world, each perceives it in a different way. Their differing perceptions are implied in their values and life choices. The language of their soliloquies is compressed and ambiguous and resists fixed interpretation. Like a sequence of Impressionist cathedral façades, each section of the novel is fluid and changing and shifting in the different lights of day; and each reader comes to it from a different personal angle and epistemological orientation. One feels throughout the book an invisible substructure, an almost palpable manifestation of that "real thing behind appearances." A veil of impersonality is cast over the novel's universe, endowing it with a large and haunting vitality. No novel like it had ever before been written, and it is hard to think who other than Virginia Woolf could have conceived and brought to life a work of such resonance and finality. Quentin Bell said that on this morning of February 7, 1931, the moment of finishing *The Waves*, Virginia Woolf reached the "culminating point in her career as an artist." Never again would she scale such heights.

But for the time being, the novel was put away. It was far from ready. A great many corrections and alterations still had to be made. Virginia, however, needed a change of pace and took advantage of this break to write six articles on the London scene for *Good Housekeeping* in America. She also, against her better judgment and Leonard's warnings, indulged herself far too much in London's "chatter and clatter." She threw herself into the social whirlpool with reckless vigor, almost as if she were making up for lost time. The novel had left her physically fatigued but in a state of high excitement, a combination both unpredictable and dangerous.

Ethel Smyth's *The Prison*, a work for voice and orchestra, was to have its first London performance this spring. With her customary zeal, Ethel insisted that Virginia not only attend the rehearsal but come three weeks later to its Queen's Hall debut and to the party afterward given in Ethel's honor by Lady Rosebery. The party was evidently the fuse that caused Virginia to explode with a volley of abuse and protest, almost pathological in its intensity. "It was the party," wrote Virginia in molten fury. It was the party that did it. Never had she suffered more, dragged as she was "to that awful exhibition of insincerity and inanity against my will . . . And I felt betrayed." Ethel, so Virginia thought, had deliberately and for no discernible reason "inflicted this hideous indignity." She felt herself wantonly mauled. "I who was reeling and shocked . . . by my struggle with The Waves . . . and you forced me to it and you didn't mind. I went home therefore more jangled and dazed and out of touch with reality than I have been for years." After a sleepless night she spent a day "of horror and disillusionment." How could Ethel have been so unfeeling? It was being hauled about like this and being made to exhibit herself that brought on this frenzy of madness.

The rage wore itself out. Virginia was now skirting that dangerous, vulnerable state that usually accompanied finishing a book. Her moods swung from one extreme to the other without warning. Life was bright one minute and black the next. "I look at you," she said, "and . . . think if Ethel can be so downright and plainspoken and on the spot, I need not fear instant dismemberment by wild horses. It's the child crying for the nurse's hand in the dark." It was also what some people paid "£20 a sitting to get from Psychoanalysts—liberation from their own egotism."

"Arnold Bennett died last night; which leaves me sadder than I should have supposed," wrote Virginia in her diary. Bennett had died at his Baker Street home on March 27 of typhoid fever contracted through drinking tap water in Paris earlier in the year. Virginia had met him last at a dinner party given by Ethel Sands on December 1—"a lovable genuine man; impeded, somehow a little awkward in life; well meaning; ponderous; kindly; coarse; knowing he was coarse . . . Glutted with success." Never again, she thought, would he sit down to write his daily 1,000 words. He would never again compose his "regulation number of pages in his workmanlike beautiful but dull hand."

Leonard and Virginia attended the memorial service on March 31 at St. Clement Danes in the Strand, and on April 6 left England for a French motor tour, crossing at night from Newhaven to Dieppe, and returning on April 30. They drove slowly to the Dordogne. The weather was bad. It rained; it hailed; it was cold; they had flat tires along the way; their hotels and inns were without heat or hot water. They could keep warm only by going to bed early and staying under covers. But Virginia enjoyed it all immensely.

"Lord, how you'd laugh at my voluble sanguine French—" she wrote Ethel from Brantôme, "half Madame de Sévigné; half schoolgirl English: but I can't resist branching out." And to Vita from Chinon: "Almost enough castles here for you." Despite the unsuitable accommodations, the holiday held two special attractions for Virginia: the first was visiting the tower of Michel de Montaigne, whom Leonard considered the first civilized modern man. It was on Thursday, April 23, that they reached the château, located to the west of Castillon. "Rang at Castle door," Virginia wrote in her journal. "No one came. Woman tending cows in ancient stables. A tower at one end. A garden of flowering trees." Another woman finally came and took them up narrow stone steps at the top of which was a thick nail-studded door. This was

Montaigne's bedroom, where he died in 1592. They then went down to see the chapel and climbed upstairs again to look over his library, his table and chair, and his inscriptions on the beams. They wandered onto the terrace and saw the vineyards below and a farm or two—"much his view—the curious musing man must have halted to look at what we saw."

The second highlight of the trip was the high unroofed room where Joan of Arc had stood before the King. This was the Great Hall of the Château du Milieu at Chinon where Joan, on March 9, 1429, recognized Charles VII hiding among his courtiers. They sat on the steps and heard the clock which had been striking the hour since the thirteenth century. The clock Joan heard. "Rusty toned. What did she think? Was she mad? A visionary coinciding with the right moment?" Virginia was entranced. The rain, the cold, the bad roads—they were all worth it.

The manuscript of *The Waves* awaited her in London. A firm timetable had to be devised. The socializing must stop. A great deal of work still lay ahead. On May 13, she began typing out, from start to finish, her 332-page novel. If she typed (and revised) seven or eight pages each day, the book would be finished by late June. "This requires some resolution; but I can see no other way to make all the corrections, and keep the lilt, and join up, and expand and do all the other final processes. It is like sweeping over an entire canvas with a wet brush." Resolute Virginia was, and though she worked steadily, the schedule was wrecked by Ethel Smyth on one of her rampages.

Sir Adrian Boult, Director of Music at the BBC, had earlier conducted *The Prison*. Ethel now picked an especially inopportune time to ask him to repeat the performance. He refused. She exploded. And Virginia caught most of the flying debris. On May 20 Ethel appeared for tea "stamping like a dragoon" and her purse filled with documents. "For 3 hours she nailed me to my chair" repeating Boult's "iniquitous" treatment. He had been conducting a Bach Mass for six hours at the time of Ethel's assault, and, in no mood for her demands, he apparently insulted her in the presence of "the finest artists in Europe." Finally, after a "screaming and scratching which rang through Queen's Hall," Sir Adrian ordered her out of the place.

Ethel now insisted that Virginia hear her entire history of persecution, and brought out old letters and papers and read them aloud, beating on a chair with her fists. Finally Virginia had to shout that she had a headache. But this didn't stop Ethel. " 'You've got to listen to me—You've got to listen' she kept saying and indeed the whole of 52 rang with her vociferations." This happened on May 20. On the twenty-eighth Virginia was in the grip of a headache: "flashes of light raying round my eyes and sharp pain; the pain cut into me by Ethel's voice . . . And then to Rodmell, where the same thing happened—the light around my eyes . . . If it were not for the divine goodness of Leonard how many times I should be thinking of death."

36 Virginia recovered quickly however and was well enough to tell Vita that her latest novel, *All Passion Spent* (published on May 27), was going to be another best-seller. The money Vita was making for the Press was paying for more new conveniences at Monks House—a new refrigerator, electricity, two new rooms, a garage, and soon a new car. Orders were again coming in "like pilchards in a net." Before the rush of sales was over, *All Passion Spent* surpassed the success of *The Edwardians* a year earlier.

But however much rejoicing, the rift between Virginia and Vita was still widening, on Vita's side mainly. Having resigned from diplomatic life, Harold was now living permanently in London and about to turn his talents to literature and politics, and would therefore consume more of Vita's time. Vita herself now had Sissinghurst Castle to renovate, a garden to create, and a great deal more money to earn. Virginia felt the growing separation but could do nothing to check it. Her love simply folded itself up and waited in silence. Or almost in silence.

In July Virginia sent Vita a brief pitiful letter. "Potto is dead," she said. "For about a month . . . I have watched him failing . . . The other day coming unexpectedly into the room, I found him wiping away a tear . . . 'Tell Mrs Nick that I love her . . . She has forgotten me. But I forgive her and . . . (here he could hardly speak) die . . . of . . . a . . . broken . . . heart!' Then he expired." Here was the child, Virginia, pleading for a maternal embrace, so much like the letters she had written in 1907 begging for Vanessa's love. The real "Mrs Nick"—the promiscuous Vita lurking behind the idealized aristocrat—had deserted them. She was engaged with a new lover. Her name was Evelyn Irons, a journalist for the *Daily Mail*. They had been intimate since February of this year and Vita was now planning a holiday with her in Provence in the early autumn.

• • •

Virginia was meanwhile trying to stay clear of Ethel Smyth's "remorseless fangs." In June Dame Ethel began revising a number of her articles for a collection to be published in 1933 as *Female Pipings in Eden*. She sent Virginia the most recent piece she'd written and asked for criticism. Virginia read the article and returned it on June 27 with a letter "written in a hurry." It was a long, thoughtful letter. Virginia reminded Ethel again that it was not a good idea to place so much emphasis on praise and recognition when in fact she had both in ample measure. Artists who dwell on their injuries, she added, seem "infinitely sterile" and sometimes worse. Also, blowing one's own trumpet made a "harsh, raw, noise." The letter ended with her usual banter, but on the whole Virginia's criticism was sound and certainly not meant to offend.

Ethel, unfortunately, did not read it in quite that way. She misinterpreted the tone entirely and responded with a hysterical letter, which Virginia found "sordid and ridiculous." Virginia then wrote another long, careful letter, plainly and powerfully stating her case. With all its grievances Ethel's letter, she said, had made a large demand on her sympathy. "I had the sense afterwards to reflect that such demands ... are inevitable." That was to be expected, and certainly Ethel's complaints were real enough. Such scenes and rages were a bore, but they would pass. "What does not pass, and is not forgotten is the feeling that one is prevented from intimacy. Your extreme susceptibility to criticism and your vast ... need of sympathy inevitably make one feel that one cannot be ... free and careless with you." She had had years of such experience, she said, with a father she adored. His deafness, his widowerhood, his sense of failure were never far below the surface. He thus demanded perpetual sympathy and was apt to fly into violent rages if one said a "careless" word about his work. One had to be so careful of what was said to him. "And I think this queered the pitch and made us much more formal and cautious with him than was right ... I don't care for unreal friendships; and if one thing emerges from this it is the extreme unreality of a relationship which leads to all these words."

Two or three days after receiving this letter, a penitent Ethel paid Virginia a visit and explained herself in a speech "which lasted 20 minutes by my watch." One had to stand up to her or be overwhelmed—so "I shout obloquies at her like gun shots" and Ethel had little choice but to take them. Virginia had driven her point home and could once more resume her playfulness. "Lord! how I like the thud of my abuse upon your hide ... Ethel, d'you know you're a damned Harlot." And so the friendship wobbled on.

.   .   .

On the morning of Friday, July 17, *The Waves*, which had been moving slowly but inexorably forward, was at last finished. That is to say, Virginia had for the eighteenth time copied out the opening sentences. "Leonard will read it tomorrow; and I shall open this book to record his verdict." They drove to Rodmell in the afternoon for the weekend. On Sunday morning, Leonard walked out to Virginia's garden hut and pronounced the book "a master-piece." The first hundred pages were difficult and readers would have trouble following, but all that at the moment didn't matter. The verdict had been pronounced. A masterpiece. "Lord! what a relief! I stumped off in the rain to make a little round to Rat Farm in jubilation."

The Woolfs returned to Rodmell on Thursday, July 30, for their two months in the country. By August 7 Virginia had begun writing another book for relaxation. It was to be called *Flush*, a biography of Elizabeth Barrett Browning's cocker spaniel. But she was soon interrupted. For on Monday, August 10, the galley proofs of *The Waves* arrived. "I have now 10.45, read the first chapter of The Waves, and made no changes, save 2 words and 3 commas... And see that for once my proofs will be dispatched with a few pencil strokes... I will now write a little at Flush."

The proofs were sent off on August 18—"never, never to be looked at again by me, I imagine." The book was scheduled for an October 8 publication. The days between proofs and publication were always filled with anxiety, and although she tried to divert herself with a new rubber dinghy to paddle down the river, the inevitable headache descended, forcing her to bed for a week in early September. During this period of waiting, she had plenty of time to imagine every possible horror she would have to live through until the first reviews came in.

By 1931, Virginia Woolf's reputation stood as high as any living writer's. Yet she had chosen to write an impressionist novel so compressed and ambiguous as to be almost inaccessible. No two readers, certainly, would experience or interpret the book in even remotely the same way. For on every page there was "—a whole flower to which every eye brings its own contribution." It is almost as if Virginia Woolf were "testing" her readers and her reputation. If They really cared for her, They would take the Trouble with her book—or something like that.

John Lehmann, the young poet, who had joined the Hogarth Press in January of 1931 to serve an eight-month apprenticeship preparatory to enter-ing a partnership, was among the first to receive an advance copy. "Lord!" Virginia wrote him. "To think you are reading The Waves! Now I shall be immensely interested to have your opinion—brutally and frankly—so please write it down for me. At present it seems to me a complete failure." To Vita, too, Virginia called the book "a complete failure." Vanessa was sent a copy of the "unfortunate book" and told she "needn't read it."

Virginia was evidently preparing herself for the worst, and by advertising its failure beforehand, she could not later be accused of laboring under grand delusions. Just as she had trembled as a child awaiting her mother's verdict, so she trembled now with tortured anticipation. "I mean John Lehmann is about to write to say he thinks it bad—I mean Leonard accuses me of sensibility verging on insanity—I mean I am acutely depressed . . . The Waves, I predict, marks my decline in reputation."

The next morning, however, found a very different Virginia—"I'm like a bee in the ivy bloom—can't write for pleasure." Lehmann had written to say he "loved" the book; it was an amazing achievement. Only the thinnest wall separated her novel from poetry. She had somehow maintained "the speed of prose and the intensity of poetry." His letter came like rain in a desert; she felt "flushed and flooded" and inspired now to write *A Letter to a Young Poet.*

"What I want," she said a few days later, "is to be told that this is solid and means something. What it means I myself shan't know till I write another book." She was here affirming once more her hope that *The Waves* expressed a shared feeling without encouraging a fixed meaning; she wanted an emotional response closer to music than to poetry.

Vanessa was among the first to confirm Virginia's effort. The novel was "as real an experience as having a baby . . . Of course there's the personal side—the feelings you describe on what I must take to be Thoby's [Percival's] death . . . if you wouldn't think me foolish I should say you *have* found the 'lullaby capable of singing him to rest.'" Goldsworthy Lowes Dickinson, the Cambridge don and friend of Bloomsbury, wrote her a flattering letter: the novel dealt with a theme that was "perpetual and universal." To which Virginia replied: "What you say you felt . . . is exactly what I wanted to convey. Many people say that it is hopelessly sad—but I didn't mean that. I did want somehow to make out . . . a reason for things . . . I did mean that in some vague way we are the same person, and not separate people . . . I wanted to give the sense of continuity."

A good many readers completely failed to see this. Some saw only poetic, unintelligible grandeur; others saw only futility and nothingness. To Ethel, for instance, *The Waves* was the saddest book she'd ever read. At the other end was E. M. Forster: "It's difficult to express oneself about a work which one feels to be so very important, but I've the sort of excitement over it which comes from believing one's encountered a classic." Dorothy Wellesley and Vita found "the first 100 pages boring in the extreme." To Hugh Walpole the whole novel was "unreal." Even Lytton Strachey, who should have seen what Virginia was doing, found *The Waves* "perfectly fearful. I shudder and shiver—and cannot take the plunge. *Any* book lying about I seize up as an excuse for putting it off." And *The Times Literary Supplement* in its long review had also missed the point. "Odd, that they (The Times) should praise my characters when I meant to have none." This unintelligible book was being better " 'received' than any of them... And it sells—how unexpected, how odd that people can read that difficult grinding stuff!"

But they did. Even in the provinces reviewers were saying with almost "one accord, here is Mrs Woolf doing her best work; it can't be popular; but we respect her for so doing; and find The Waves positively exciting." That was something to think about. "I'm in danger of becoming our leading novelist, and not with the highbrows only." Before the flurry was over, nearly 10,000 copies were sold. "Everybody's taken to writing to me about The Waves. After 3 months they've just been able to get to the end, and write in triumph to say so."

There is a little footnote to the *The Waves* supporting Virginia Woolf's claim about resonance in imagery. It was E. M. Forster who, some years later in the course of his Rede Lectures, said that Virginia Woolf "belonged to an age which distinguished sharply between the impermanency of man and the durability of his monuments... She respected and acquired knowledge, she believed in wisdom. Intellectually, no one can do more; and since she was a poet, not a philosopher or a historian or a prophetess, she had not to consider whether wisdom will prevail and whether the square upon the oblong which Rhoda built out of the music of Mozart, will ever stand firm upon this distracted earth. She cared for these abstractions, and tried to express them through symbols, as an artist must, though she realised the inadequacy of symbols."

Forster was referring to the scene in Part V of *The Waves* where Percival's death is announced. Rhoda's soliloquy about the square and oblong image begins here: "There is the puddle... and I cannot cross it... I shall be blown down the eternal corridors for ever... I am alone in a hostile world. The human face is hideous... I ride rough waters and shall sink with no one to save me. Percival, by his death, has made me this present, has revealed this terror . . . Here is a hall where one pays money and goes in, where one hears music . . . Then the beetle-shaped men come with their violins; wait; count; nod; down come their bows . . . but what is the thing that lies beneath the semblance of the thing . . . Percival by his death, has made me this gift, let me see the thing. There is a square; there is an oblong . . . The structure is now visible . . . we have made oblongs and stood them upon squares . . . I will set aside this afternoon. I will make a pilgrimage to Greenwich." In the earlier, less ambiguous draft of the novel, this passage reads: ". . . Percival is dead, and this is my funeral service. I will set aside this evening and make it a pilgrimage, and go to Greenwich."

In the March 6, 1954, *New Yorker* review of *A Writer's Diary*, entitled "A Consciousness of Reality," W. H. Auden wrote: "If I had to choose an epitaph for [Virginia Woolf], I would take a passage from *The Waves*, which is the best description of the creative process I know: 'There is a square; there is an oblong. The players take the square and place it upon the oblong.' " That the poet should have chosen from the entire novel—indeed, from the entire body of her work—this particular passage as an *epitaph* at once moves the square-oblong image out of Forster's abstraction of order and justice and locates it more literally in the province of death—for it was Percival's death which initially generated the image. Further, Auden's choice of word—*epitaph*—for the square and oblong suggests the simple death image of "square" crematorium door (or tombstone) upon "oblong" casket.

But there is also the link between music and death in this passage. For it is the musicians who were maneuvering the square and the oblong. How music and death coalesce can be explained by one detail Virginia made in her diary on June 18, 1927: "Now the Moths [*The Waves*] will, I think, fill out the skeleton which I dashed in here . . . I do a little work on it in the evening when the gramophone is playing late Beethoven sonatas [and quartets]." In another entry made on November 28, 1928: "The Moths still haunts me, coming, as they always do, unbidden, between tea and dinner, while Leonard plays the gramophone. I shape a page or two; and make myself stop." Quentin Bell noted that "another important addition to Virginia's life was the gramophone . . . Virginia, who had a fairly catholic taste, developed a particular interest in Beethoven's late quartets, and they assisted her in those meditations which finally resulted in *The Waves*."

Finally, in the fifth volume of his autobiography, *The Journey Not the Arrival Matters*, Leonard Woolf, in a passage about Virginia's death, wrote: "I had once said to her that, if there was to be music at one's cremation, it ought to be the cavatina from the B flat quartet, op. 130, of Beethoven. There is a moment at cremations when the doors of the crematorium open and the coffin slides slowly in, and there is a moment in the middle of the cavatina when for a few bars the music . . . seems to hesitate with a gentle forward pulsing motion—if played at that moment it might seem to be gently propelling the dead into the eternity of oblivion. Virginia agreed with me."

And it was probably for this reason that Virginia connected the square-oblong image with Rhoda in the music hall, who, apart from Bernard, is the one voice that most closely approximates that of Virginia's throughout the novel. With this constellation of interlocking images, Virginia seemed to have been writing out in fantasy, through Rhoda's madness and suicide, a fictional version of her own death just a little over a decade later.

Toward the end of November a headache forced Virginia to bed. After her month's confinement, she set *Flush* aside, resumed work on the collection of essays that would make up a second *Common Reader*, and began her *Letter to a Young Poet*. John Lehmann, now managing the Hogarth Press, was beginning to attract from among his friends such young writers as W. H. Auden, Stephen Spender, and C. Day Lewis.

In October, at about the time *The Waves* came out, the first of Leonard's three-volume study of communal psychology, *After the Deluge*, was published. It had taken him ten years to write. Goldie Dickinson had written a qualified letter of praise: the ideas were new and important, but the style was "repetitive and tedious." Harold Laski, professor of political science at the London School of Economics, had called it "a masterpiece," but *The Times Literary Supplement* gave it only a half-column review which was not in the least complimentary. Leonard knew this was the book's death. Ten years of work wasted. He had written it for that larger audience who read what public libraries ordered. Librarians took "their orders from the Lit Sup; . . . they judge[d] by the length of the review." No librarian would invest 15/– after that.

If Leonard was crushed or humiliated, Virginia saw no evidence of it. For he had a "pessimistic temper" that went deeper than reason; it was somehow connected "with centuries of oppression. The world against us . . . And when I say this morning incautiously, 'I'm reviewed in the Manchester Guardian,' Leonard says 'Is it a long review?' And I say, feeling like a mother to a hurt and miserable little boy, Yes."

Over the Christmas holidays this year hung the news of Lytton Strachey's illness. It was Carrington who wrote Virginia about him in mid-December.

Typhoid fever had been the first diagnosis. Then a second doctor said the trouble was an ulceration of the colon, with the danger of perforation. By December 22 his condition was very grave. Then another specialist examined him: it was toxic fluid from the ulceration affecting his heart, he said.

The entire family had gathered at a nearby inn and Virginia called daily from Monks House for news of his condition. "I seem to have lived about 20 years in the past week—" she wrote to Ethel Smyth two days before Christmas, "so much we have shared—so many states of mind; such intimacy. I find myself now talking to him whatever I read or think." On Christmas Eve, the family thought he was dying; but he regained consciousness on the following day and was able to drink some milk. It was clear to everyone that Lytton was fighting for his life; he was doing his utmost not to sink into unconsciousness. Another specialist came on the twenty-eighth, and there was more speculation.

At this point Virginia was becoming very tense. She needed something to calm her. She needed to write. Something, anything. If she didn't write soon she would "whizz into extinction." The headache that had been bothering her had subsided, so that she might be able to "glide into words" in a day or two. But how badly she wanted Lytton not to die; how she wanted to think of the future with him in it—"to laugh at, to abuse: I shall read his book on Shakespeare . . . I shall tell him how Leonard and I sobbed on Christmas Eve."

A few days after Christmas Ethel Smyth made the mistake of accusing Virginia of caring for "so few" people. It was an insensitive thing to say, especially at this time, and struck an exposed nerve. "No," Virginia replied, "I think you grossly underrate the strength of my feelings—so strong they are—such caverns of gloom and horror open round me I daren't look in . . . Do you know how I cared for Katherine Mansfield, for Charlie Sanger [barrister]—to mention friends only? No, you don't." She had learned silence, she said, from the people she most honored: Vanessa, Leonard, Lytton—and also from "the terror I have of my own unlimited capacity for feeling . . . I never cease to feel that I must step very lightly on top of that volcano. No, Ethel, there's a mint of things about me . . . you've no idea of." Before the ink was dry, Virginia turned to her diary. She couldn't get Lytton off her mind. She had gone through "every grade of feeling—how strong, how deep . . . Soon the whole being can suffer no more"—and then like Septimus Warren Smith, "I can't feel anything," she said on that bitter windy morning of December 29, 1931.

.   .   .

At 2:30 p.m. of January 21, four days before Virginia would turn fifty, Lytton Strachey died in his sleep at Ham Spray, his house in Wiltshire. The anxious family who had congregated at the nearby Bear Inn soon dispersed. There were no services of any kind for him. Virginia felt his loss deeply. To Carrington she wrote on the afternoon of his death: "We are all thanking you for what you gave Lytton . . . This is our great comfort now—the happiness you gave him—and he told me so." They would miss him. She would miss him. She couldn't write now without suddenly thinking, "Oh but Lytton won't read this," and suddenly it all seemed pointless. But what it must be for Carrington. "I wish I could see you," Virginia wrote on the last day of January.

On March 10 the Woolfs drove to Hungerford to see her. That evening after they returned to London, Virginia wrote her again: "You can't think how close Lytton comes when you're there: you keep him for me more than anyone. So go on dearest . . . because you do what no one else can do. I'm so lonely sometimes without him, so old and futile and merely dried up, and then with you I feel . . . what I was when Lytton was there."

On March 11, the following morning, Carrington shot herself and died, after six hours of great pain. Virginia's letter was the last thing she read before taking her life. The news reached Tavistock Square sometime in the afternoon. On the next day Virginia turned to her private page to describe their final meeting. It had been a lovely bright day when they arrived, just after one in the afternoon. Carrington had hot soup ready and gave them a succulent lunch. Then Leonard suggested a walk. Carrington accompanied them for a short way and excused herself. When they returned to the house, Virginia asked to see Lytton's sitting room, and there Carrington "burst into tears, and I took her in my arms . . . 'There's nothing left for me to do. I did everything for Lytton. But I've failed in everything else. People say he was very selfish to me. But he gave me everything. I was devoted to my father. I hated my mother. Lytton was like a father to me. He taught me everything I know. He read poetry and French to me.' " She seemed so helpless and small and abandoned. Lytton had been silly about his flock of young men, but he really "loved his old friends best," she said. They had tea and when Virginia said they must go, Carrington showed no inclination to detain them. As they were leaving, she picked up a little French box with a picture of the Arch of Triumph on it and said " 'I gave this to Lytton. Take it. James [Strachey] says I mustn't give away Lytton's things. But this is all right. I gave it him.' " Virginia took the box and saw how "frightened she seemed of doing wrong—like a child who has been scolded." She followed them to

the front of the house and kissed Virginia. "I said 'Then you will come and
see us next week—or not—just as you like?' 'Yes, I will come, or not' she
said. And kissed me again, and said Goodbye." At 8:30 the next morning the
gardener heard a report from her bedroom. He hurried in and found she
had shot herself "through the thigh. She died in 3 [6] hours."*

* Carrington's death is said to have been more violent than what Virginia described: she is
alleged to have inserted the nozzle of the gun between her thighs, and then fired.

PARGETING

❖ 1932 - 1937 ❖

37 Virginia had put aside *Flush* the previous August, and had resisted beginning *The Pargiters*, which was still "incubating." Now she focused her attention on the essays for her second *Common Reader*, taking time out to read and comment on each of the essays Ethel Smyth was revising for her *Female Pipings in Eden* collection. On the last day of February 1932, Virginia received a letter from Sir Joseph Thomson, Master of Trinity College, Cambridge, inviting her to be Clark Lecturer in 1933. The prestigious Clark Lectures on English Literature were founded in 1883, when her father gave the first series in honor of William George Clark, the Shakespearean scholar and Vice-Master of Trinity. Virginia was the first woman to be honored by the invitation. "Think of me," she wrote in her journal, "the uneducated child reading books in my room at 22 Hyde Park Gate—now advanced to this glory." But she would refuse. To accept the honor would mean preparing six lectures and forfeiting a year's time away from her own publishing schedule. No, that was impossible; but she was pleased to have been asked and even more pleased to refuse—"and like to think that father would have blushed with pleasure" had she told him thirty years earlier that his poor little 'Ginia would be invited to succeed him.

Three days later, however, she had second thoughts. Actually, she had already written six lectures in her "Phases of Fiction"—the introduction and six sections which had been published in the New York *Bookman* in 1929. Those could be refurbished and delivered as the Clark Lectures and "win the esteem of my sex, with a few weeks' work." Now her refusal seemed "lazy and cowardly." But in the end the refusal stood and the lectures were never delivered. She was going to spend the next few years writing about the position of women in a man's world, in *The Pargiters* (*The Years*) and *Three Guineas*.

. . . .

"Listen, long ears," Virginia wrote Vita in early April. An American collector was interested in buying the manuscript of *Orlando*. Vita might get one or two hundred pounds for it, which was better than "to keep it mouldering at Long Barn." Virginia had given Vita the bound manuscript of *Orlando* soon after its publication in 1928. It remained in her writing room, first at Long Barn and then at Sissinghurst Castle, until her death in 1962, when it was given by her sons to the National Trust, to be kept in perpetuity at Knole.*

Vita was shouldering the expenses of the Nicolson family almost single-handedly. This was a particularly difficult time financially, with two sons at Eton, the upkeep of Long Barn, and the expenses of rebuilding Sissinghurst. More than that, Vita was generous to a fault and could never resist helping those who appealed to her—another trait she shared with Julia Stephen. She worked hard writing her novels, reviewing books, and broadcasting. This was what prompted Virginia's suggestion of selling the manuscript. Vita of course refused.

Earlier in the year Hugh Walpole asked Virginia if he could dedicate a new book to her. Yes, of course, she replied. It would be an honor. As it happened, 1932 was the centenary of Sir Walter Scott and Hugh had written a long introduction to his anthology of Scott's novels called *The Waverley Pageant*, to be published later in the year. His dedication read: "For Virginia Woolf who does not scorn Sir Walter."

Of course, she didn't "scorn" Sir Walter. Quite the opposite. Leslie Stephen had read the family the Waverley novels in their entirety at least once, and for Virginia there were many "warm, scattered" memories. A few months later, she found *The Waverley Pageant* lying on the hall table. "I shall read the Monastery again and then I shall go back to [*The Heart of*] Midlothian," she said in her thank-you letter. "I can't read the Bride [*of Lammermoor*], because I know it almost by heart: also the Antiquary (I think those two, as a whole, are my favourites)." Hugh had done a splendid job: to inspire "a harassed hack to this wish to kick up her heels"—what better proof was there?

On the morning of Friday, April 15, Virginia and Leonard went on holiday to Greece with Roger Fry and his sister Margery (Ha). Leaving from Victoria

* Virginia also bequeathed to Vita in her will any other manuscript she wanted; Vita chose *Mrs. Dalloway*, which is now preserved in the British Library.

Station, they traveled by way of Dover-Calais, had dinner in Paris, journeyed overnight, and reached Venice on Saturday in the afternoon. At noon on Sunday, they boarded the SS *Tevere* and sailed down the Adriatic and round the southern coast of Greece to Athens, where they took rooms at the Hotel Majestic. They visited Daphne and Sounion and Marathon, and then drove to Corinth, Mycenae, Nauplia, and back again to Athens. Then came the expedition to Delphi. It was by far the best holiday she'd had in years.

On the first or second day in Athens Virginia began recording in her journal: "Yes, but what can I say about the Parthenon—that my own ghost met me, a girl of 23 [24], with all her life to come." She was thinking back to the autumn of 1906, to the autumn of Thoby's death, when the four Stephens and Violet Dickinson had gone to Greece and Turkey. "Perhaps I've washed off something of the sentimentality of youth, which tends to make things melancholy ... now I'm grey-haired and, well through with life I suppose."

There was no time for brooding, however. Her companions were too busy exploring, painting, botanizing. The Frys were indefatigable, knowledgeable, and extremely talkative. Roger in particular was a "shower bath of erudition." They kept the expedition a little breathless and in high spirits. Virginia suspected that Margery Fry, for five years the Principal of Somerville College, Oxford, thought her an "intellectual and moral and social snob; so I do my best to climb off my perch and roll on the floor; and sometimes she likes me."

"Now we are at Delphi," she wrote to Quentin on May 1. It was Easter Sunday. The Greeks were roasting sheep over wood fires and "marching about with candles and corpses on biers." Roger had settled the question of Greek art for all time. The Byzantines were the "real swells." There was so much to see and Roger was painting everything in sight. In fact he never went out without his paint boxes. Margery painted too. But even so, brother and sister never stopped talking. They spoke Greek "on a system, so that tonight we were almost landed with two black kids and a pail of sour milk" because of a misunderstanding between the Frys and a shepherd.

The trip was a great success, she wrote to Vanessa on the following day. The inns were clean: no bedbugs, no fleas. The food, though, was not especially to Virginia's liking—"too many olives and sardines for me; but Leonard and Roger love them and plunge into octopuses and lizards—I mean they eat them, fried—oily lengths like old rubber tires cut into squares." Yes, Greece was perfect. People didn't sneer; the natives were sympathetic; there were almost no beggars; friendly peasants crossed their fields to chat. Only there was a language problem. Leonard's and Roger's Greek dictionaries did not coincide, and often it was impossible to get a drop to drink because they couldn't agree what the word for wine was.

And of course Vita got her letter too, even more imaginative than the others. Virginia had to tell her "how we've been off in a car jolting and jumping to Nauplia, Mycenae, Corinth . . . Sea was around us at Nauplia— waves lapped my balcony door"; how they crossed an appalling pass, winding round and round, "every sweep higher, and one wheel . . . balancing over a precipice 3,000 feet of sheer rock beneath. How I trembled!" This was Virginia's blood-curdling version.

In the few moments she could escape from the inexhaustible Frys, Virginia turned to her journal. The Greece she now saw was ancient. It was like wandering on the surface of the moon. The Greeks were no longer, as they had been in antiquity, masters of their native land. It was too barren, too stony, too precipitous. One saw them now on high mountain passes with their donkeys "in search of some herb, some root . . . Such solitude as they must know, under the sun, under the snow . . . is unthinkable in England." The centuries had left no trace. There was "no 18th, 16th, 15th century all in layers as in England—nothing between them and 300 B.C." It was a country "lit by a dead sun." Even the bays were deserted, and the hills and the valleys; "not a villa . . . no wires, no churches, almost no graveyards."

Such were her parting impressions—"And I could love Greece, as an old woman . . . as I once loved Cornwall, as a child." In August 1906, a quarter of a century earlier, Virginia had noted in her journal how her mind worked: "You bring it directly opposite an object, and bid it discourse; it merely shuts its eye, and turns away. But in a month, or three or seven, suddenly without any bidding, it pours out the whole picture, gratuitously."* And now on May 15, twenty-six years later, she repeated almost the same words: "Already my mind is hard at work (in my absence) arranging, editing, bringing forward, eliminating, until it will present me, unasked, with visions . . . of Aegina, of Athens—the Acropolis . . ." As Leonard had said in his memoir: Virginia never stopped working or thinking about her work.

The Woolfs returned from Greece by the Orient Express via Belgrade and reached Monks House on May 12, where they stayed for two days before motoring to London. At Tavistock Square Virginia found the May issue of *Scrutiny*, edited by F. R. Leavis (and his wife Queenie), with an essay by

---

* She would return to this idea in her essay "The Leaning Tower," in *The Moment and Other Essays*, 109–10.

Muriel Bradbrook, a young Cambridge graduate, criticizing her for certain stylistic tricks. Bradbrook had discovered the means by which Virginia Woolf protected herself from making overt value judgments. Giving as one of her examples a line from *A Room of One's Own*—"But for women, I thought, looking at the empty shelves, these difficulties are infinitely more formidable"—Bradbrook said that Woolf softened the directness of her statement by inserting the "aside" ("I thought, looking at the empty shelves") and by so doing lessened or often evaded the responsibility of an otherwise questionable assertion. This was camouflage, she protested, and it saved Woolf "from committing the indelicacy of putting a case or the possibility of her being accused of waving a banner." The arguments were both serious and personal, and yet "dramatised and surrounded with all sorts of disguises to avoid an appearance of argument."

This was a perceptive observation and had Bradbrook known Virginia personally she would have noted exactly the same "disguises" in her relations with those closest to her. Words spoken in moments of anger or retaliatory responses of consequence were invariably interlarded with verbal "asides" that diminished their starkness and muffled their brutality. It was a kind of verbal defense. The horrors which kept Virginia awake at night before publication, the fear of being "found out"—this, Bradbrook, it seems, had "found out" and made public with all the impersonality of professional criticism; and Virginia felt the full force of the blow. "It is perhaps true," she wrote in her diary, "that my reputation will now decline. I shall be laughed at and pointed at." Had not Miss McAfee of the *Yale Review* just recently rejected her essay about the Reverend Skinner?* Had she not recently felt the need to go on with the *Common Reader* "by way of proving my credentials"?

There were other worries too. John Lehmann, who had written so sympathetically about *The Waves*, was now becoming difficult at the Press, and the worst of it was that Vanessa (that "wonderful woe-receiver," like their mother, Julia) had sided with John, who worshiped her, against "the irascible Leonard . . . And today we have to discuss with him his 'feelings'—and I'm not specially sympathetic." This was the John Lehmann to whom she had addressed *A Letter to a Young Poet*, to be published in a month or so. Lehmann had come to the Hogarth Press in January 1931 as assistant to Leonard and would eventually become a partner. At this time in May 1932 the partnership did not look as promising as it had a year earlier. Apart from his needing more money, it was becoming increasingly apparent that he could not work satisfactorily with Leonard.

* "The Rev. John Skinner," published later in *The Common Reader (Second Series)*.

From Lehmann's perspective, the difficulty was Leonard's emotional attitude toward the Press—"as if it were the child" his marriage had failed to produce. In one of his diary entries at about this time, he wrote: "Leonard very difficult today, haggard, abrupt, twirling bits of string, a touch of hysteria in his voice, in fact suffering from a severe nervous crisis . . . This manifests itself in repeated invasions of the office, anxious examinations of work being done, nagging tirades and unnecessary alarms and impatience about what is progressing steadily and in advance of the time-table."*

In the back of John Lehmann's mind was the idea of making the Hogarth Press—apart from Dorothy Wellesley's Hogarth Living Poet series—the center for the emerging talent of young poets of his generation—W. H. Auden, Christopher Isherwood, Stephen Spender, Louis MacNeice—all or most of whom would, under the right circumstances, give their work to Lehmann, and hence to the Press. But Leonard was resistant to many of Lehmann's suggestions and most of his efforts in the end came to nothing.

Toward the end of June (*A Letter to a Young Poet* was scheduled for a July 1 publication), Leonard wrote out the new arrangement that would go into effect on September 1, 1932. It stipulated that Lehmann would be required to do two hours of work daily, his average daily attendance during the year not to exceed two hours. From September 1, 1932, to September 30, 1933, he would receive as remuneration ten percent of the profits, and would monthly receive £16 13s. 4d. as an advance on this ten percent. Leonard ended the agreement letter: "The question of any guarantee or advance after September 30, 1933, is left completely open and it is understood that I do not pledge myself to any guarantee or advance after that date. The present agreement shall be terminable at three months' notice, by either side."

Virginia could not have looked serenely at these proceedings, for so much of her freedom to write what she pleased depended upon the successful continuation of the Press. At the time of this "agreement" she wrote in her journal: "My advice is that he [Lehmann] shall be more malleable, and less persnickety. He craves influence and authority, to publish the books of his friends . . . He says Leonard is 'so deep: he plans things; and never comes out at once with what he means; so I don't know how to behave.'" A great many hours were given over to the problem of John Lehmann and the Press, and

---

* A youth by the name of Richard Kennedy, who worked at the Hogarth Press in the late 1920s, recalls an example of Leonard's temper. Kennedy had been invited to Monks House one weekend, and after dinner a discussion had somehow got on to quadratic equations. Leonard found the boy mistaken on some point and "shouted 'Liar!' 'Absurd!' 'Why!' until Mrs Woolf had to pour oil on troubled waters by reminding him that 'Richard is a guest'." *A Boy at the Hogarth Press*, 52.

in whatever disputes came up, Virginia, rightly or wrongly, never failed to take Leonard's side.

Three books about Virginia Woolf were published this year. One was *Le roman psychologique de Virginia Woolf*, by Floris Delattre. (Virginia asked one of the young Hogarth novelists, William Plomer, to investigate Delattre's "credentials" and was pleased to find him "highly respectable.") Another, a doctoral dissertation devoted almost entirely to grammatical features of the writing, was *Die Sprache Virginia Woolf*, by Ingeborg Badenhausen. The third was Winifred Holtby's study. Holtby was a novelist herself and an intimate friend of the journalist Vera Brittain. She had reviewed *The Waves* the year before and had once met with Virginia in the course of writing her book. When Hugh Walpole asked if she had read Holtby's study, Virginia replied: "No, I've not read Miss Holtby: Prof Delattre (in French) almost did for me; I suppose Winifred has merely added another kind of tombstone." She was the daughter of a Yorkshire farmer "and learnt to read, I'm told, minding the pigs—hence her passion for me." Later, she added a little harshly, "vain though I am, I cannot read about myself, and my parents and my education—all lies too." Harcourt Brace had proposed commissioning a more biographical book about her and had approached E. M. Forster. When nothing came of that, Harold Nicolson was suggested, but that plan too failed to materialize. If anything was to be written about Virginia Woolf and the Stephen family, it would be written by Virginia Woolf herself—as fiction.

Earlier in the year, Virginia had received a letter from an undergraduate in an American university who had written an essay for a competition and wanted to clarify some questions on method and influence. Virginia clearly wanted to set the record straight. "I have not studied Dr Freud or any psychoanalyst," she replied. Indeed she had read no books on the subject. Her knowledge came from "superficial talk." Therefore any use of their methods was purely "instinctive"; further, she had never written a line of verse. "But the decision to write prose and not verse was made without any deliberation." So far as she knew, her methods were her own and "not consciously at any rate derived from any other writer."

A Letter to a Young Poet was published in England in July, one month after its appearance in the *Yale Review*. Sustaining the illusion of playful informality throughout the essay, Virginia charged young poets with excessive self-indulgence, and with relying too heavily on the actual and the colloquial. The result was far too much stress on the differences that separate the poet from his world and not enough on the similarities common to all human beings. "How can you learn to write if you write only about one single person?"

The *Letter* elicited little response from the popular press. Harold Nicolson, who had always been lavish in his praise of Virginia, said vaguely in the *New Statesman* (July 9) only that the piece would "be read by posterity with curiosity and pleasure." The young poets themselves, however, might have said a great deal more but chose to remain silent. They were indignant. As far as they were concerned, Virginia Woolf had shown an astonishing lack of understanding and justice. Her suggestion that they should wait until they were thirty before publishing seemed especially ludicrous. Where would Keats and Shelley have been had they followed this preposterous advice? What particularly irritated them was the fact that in picking out the numerous faults she had listed in the *Letter*, Virginia had quoted from the poems of Auden, Spender, and Lewis without giving their names—probably feeling thus freer to criticize their limitations.

John Lehmann wrote to her about the *Letter* toward the end of July, and Virginia did not attempt to defend herself: "I admit . . . that my quotations aren't good illustrations: but as usual, I couldn't find the ones I wanted when I was writing; and was too lazy to look." In March, a few months earlier, when Julian Bell's dissertation on Pope had been rejected by the Electors of King's College and failed to win him a Fellowship, Virginia recorded in her diary: ". . . they say Julian's dissertation is no good, quite uneducated—" And to Julian himself she blandly wrote: "I don't think it much matters, not getting the fellowship—I expect I am foolish—but still I don't like Fellows, as fellows. Much better write on your own." When Julian submitted his dissertation to the Hogarth Press for publication, Leonard also rejected it. For some members of the younger generation for whom Virginia professed so much interest, there seemed to grow an ever-widening gap between her advice and her credibility. In the youthful world of letters she was beginning to appear both unsympathetic and misleading.

Ten days after returning from Greece, Virginia began feeling "screwed up into a ball." There was no single cause one could pinpoint—residual exhaustion from *The Waves*, the deaths of Lytton and Carrington, the growing tension between Leonard and John Lehmann—perhaps an accumulation of these. "Lord how I suffer!" she wrote in her diary in late May. "What a terrific capacity I possess for feeling with intensity . . . myself only an organ that takes blows, one after another . . . hatred of my own brainlessness and indecision . . . contempt for my lack of intellectual power . . . buying clothes . . . how I hate Bond Street and spending money on clothes; worst of all is this dejected barrenness."

That evening she analyzed her depression with Leonard: "How my brain is jaded with the conflict of two types of thought, the critical, the creative; how I am harassed by the strife and jar and uncertainty without." In that little analysis Virginia had put her finger on the problem that would trouble her for the next five years, once she began—a few months later—to write *The Pargiters*.

In early summer she began to suffer from fainting spells. On the evening of July 6, she collapsed at the table in the Ivy Restaurant at a dinner party given by Clive Bell. She was full of explanations: it was seeing too many people; it was being asked out too often; it was never having enough time for herself. These were her excuses. In her diary she described the faint two days later as a "curious sensation. Feeling it come on; sitting still and fading out: then Clive by my side and a woman with salts. And the odd liberation of emotion in the cab with Clive."

She was well enough to finish the *Common Reader* essays in mid-July, but with "no sense of glory; only of drudgery done" before going to Rodmell. On August 11, at Monks House, it happened again: "Here I am in bed," she wrote, "after falling in a faint among the roses on Thursday evening precisely as I fell 2 years ago"—on August 29, 1930. "I was looking at Caburn . . . when suddenly my heart leapt; stopped; ran away, like a four in hand. I can't stop it, I said. Lord, now it's in my head. This pounding must must must break something." And with that she slid to the ground. Leonard rushed to the house for an ice tray to put under her neck, but it was thirty minutes before the pounding diminished.

In London, as she was writing *Flush*, she suffered two other similar episodes: one in October and the other in November. According to her physicians, the fainting spells, the racing pulse, the low-grade temperatures—all were due to "nerve exhaustion" and had nothing to do with her heart. But what was "nerve exhaustion"? she wanted to know. "Ah, that we cannot say," replied the medical experts. She was told to take digitalis, avoid excitement and overwork, and get plenty of rest. Apart from taking the medicine, however, such advice was not easy to follow. Work and worry were part of her life.

The Press was a constant worry, for instance, and so was John Lehmann. On the day his old agreement expired, August 31, he decided it would be useless to continue the "long-drawn-out acrimonious arguments." He therefore left the job and informed the Woolfs in a letter addressed to Monks

House. Leonard was outraged and refused to reply; Virginia, who in business matters always followed Leonard's example, called his decision a "blessing!" By the end of the year he'd be in tears calling on his lawyers, she predicted.

Another source of concern was the impending publication of the second *Common Reader* on October 13. The work had brought her no deep sense of satisfaction. From the start it had been menial and unrewarding. Virginia prepared herself by starting a new book two days before its debut. When the reviews appeared, they were on the whole polite but little else. No one seemed overly enthusiastic about the *Reader* except Vita, who devoted her book review broadcast, cutting out three other titles to leave more time for Virginia. "Pinka [the spaniel] and I sat erect, blushing, as our praises poured forth from the trumpet," Virginia wrote her on the following day. "Anyhow you said what I most wanted—not that I'm an enchanting gossip, but that my standard is high."

Vita's novel *Family History*, published also on October 13, turned out to be another best-seller for the Hogarth Press—the third consecutive commercial success. "I've just bought the 6,000th copy of Family History," Virginia wrote to Vita, "6000 sold before publication—my God!" Her fingers were sore from doing up parcels for three days, orders were pouring in, the clerks were exhausted, the telephones were ringing off the hook. "Oh Lord, what it is to publish a best seller."

On the next day, suddenly, without any warning, Virginia's mood exploded into destructive rage. Hilda Matheson and her walking tour with Vita in Savoy in July 1929, in some mysterious way, twisted to the surface like a volcanic eruption: "Oh I was in such a rage of jealousy the other night, thinking you had been in love with Hilda that summer you went to the Alps together! because you said you weren't. Now were you? Did you do the act under the Dolomites?" Did Vita remember coming to confession in Virginia's lodge? Was she guilty or not? Vita had sworn she wasn't, that she was innocent. Virginia then added, a little pitifully, "Anyhow my Elizabeth [Bowen]* comes to see me, alone, today."

At the time of this mood swing, Virginia was feeling exposed and vulnerable and "revealed." Wishart, Holtby's publisher, had used for its frontispiece not the professional photograph by Lenare which Virginia had sent them but a snapshot taken by Leonard. The switch greatly upset her. The image she had cultivated and adjusted to, the photo of herself she was willing to let the

---

* The Irish-born novelist whom Virginia had met at Lady Ottoline Morrell's in 1931.

public see, had been ignored: "I feel that my privacy is invaded; my legs show; and I am revealed to the world...as a plain dowdy old woman... Now I'm all of a quiver—can't read or write...The complex is: privacy invaded, ugliness revealed."

This single outburst to Vita probably represented a whole array of irritations that had been accumulating, and Virginia was feeling inadequate. Feelings of inadequacy almost without exception generated a sense of dependency, often accompanied by some degree of depression; and depression was invariably experienced as worthlessness and self-contempt. The inherent contradiction of the whole scheme was what made it so perplexing. For here was Virginia Woolf, feeling deserted and unloved and unlovable, when in fact she was a novelist at the top of her form, a woman of considerable consequence in the world of letters. She had only recently sold 10,000 copies of an incomprehensible novel. And yet none of this seemed to matter.

Never before had she been able to be so generous with Vanessa, for instance. In May she bought her a refrigerator for her birthday. In July she sent her a check for a hundred pounds. She'd earned so much money that she was sending "a very small crumb," she said. But Vanessa needed money and in November Virginia gave her another hundred pounds to cover the expenses of a Private View party. "Poor little 'Ginia" had once gained her siblings' affection with stories. Now she was trying to maintain a place in Vanessa's heart with donations. No matter how great her success, however, in her own mind she was still the Scapegoat in the Stephen tragedy—the story she would soon begin to write under the title of *The Pargiters*. If she had poeticized the Stephen family in *To the Lighthouse*, she was now determined to tell the true story, reveal the harsh underlying reality behind the deceitful domestic façade.

38 Twenty months earlier, on the morning of January 20, 1931, the day before Virginia was to deliver her speech on professions for women, she noted in her diary that she had just "this moment, while having my bath, conceived an entire new book." It would focus on the sexual life of women. The idea for the book grew out of the paper she had prepared for the National Society for Women's Service. So now on the morning of October 11, 1932, after almost two years of waiting, Virginia

opened a fresh manuscript volume and wrote on the pale blue unlined sheet: "THE PARGITERS: An Essay based upon a paper read to the London National Society for Women's Service." Sometime between October 11 and November 2, 1932, she returned to the title page, deleted the "An" and revised the subtitle to read "A Novel-Essay."

The insertion of "A Novel-" tells us a good deal about her original plan. *The Pargiters* would be an extension of *A Room of One's Own*, but the design of the book would be another experiment in form. Each essay of fact would alternate with a chapter of "vision"—that is, a fictitious chapter from a non-existent novel—each chapter being a set of ideas ranging from sex and feminism to politics and education; and this fictional illustration would be followed by another essay explaining how the woman novelist deals with certain controlling ideas from real life and transforms them into fiction.

Virginia Woolf was ready to express her views on the social arrangement of the sexes, which, to her mind, had smothered the aspirations of women, corrupted humane values, and contaminated human relations. She would describe a world in which the male represented power, status, and authority; in fact, the very world in which she grew up. She would write about herself as a novelist, a profession which did not intrude upon domestic peace and needed only the cheapest of materials—all of this so different from the profession practiced by men who made up great armies and navies, requiring large and expensive instruments of warfare.

She would go on to explore the manifestations of sexual polarization. Why were healthy young middle-class women in 1880 confined to the tea table and sighing in boredom? Because the privilege of a university education was denied them; and without that education, the professions were closed to them; and without a profession, there was no opportunity whereby a healthy young woman might earn a living and have the money and the independence to make choices, express opinions, and contribute in significant ways to the society in which she found herself trapped.

The only path open to a young woman of the Pargiter social class, where a well-to-do father looked after her material needs, was to become a model of virtue, and repress any attraction to members of the opposite sex until the day came when a man slipped a wedding ring on her finger. From that day on, all her passion would be channeled to her husband for the remainder of her married life. And repression to that degree, Virginia Woolf insisted, ran counter to the patterns of nature, caused rivalry among sisters over an available male, forced them into concealment and duplicity; and in the end, riddled with guilt, these young women suffered from distortions in development which made their behavior unnatural and their lives a prison. Virtue became synonymous with chastity. Caring got confused with caressing. Love and lust became hopelessly muddled. In a sense, Virginia was telling, in part, her own story. She began these alternating sections of fact and fiction on October 11 and by December 19 had written 60,320 words. On that day she finished what she considered to be the first draft of "Chapter One," consisting of six essays and five fictional extracts—that is, the complete first draft of what was eventually to become the "1880" section of *The Years*.

But *The Pargiters* was not completed as originally conceived, and no one can say at precisely what point she realized the futility of going on with her original plan. There are two details in a diary entry of July 13, 1932, however, that hint at the cause of her difficulty. In that entry she spoke of "sleeping over a promising novel," which we can assume refers to *The Pargiters*; and almost directly beside it is a passage about Dr. and Mrs. Joseph Wright: "Old Joseph Wright and old Lizzie Wright are people I respect . . . He was a maker of dialect dictionaries: he was a workhouse boy—his mother went charing. And he married Miss Lea a clergyman's daughter. And I've just read their love letters with respect . . . Odd how rare it is to meet people who say things that we ourselves might have said."

Conscious of Virginia's tendency to play with names, one opens Joseph Wright's *English Dialect Dictionary* in search of the word "pargiter." "Pargiter" is not there, but "pargeter" is; and its infinitive form, "to parget," means "to plaster with cement or mortar, esp. to plaster the inside of a chimney with cement made of cow-dung and lime." In the *Oxford English Dictionary*, the nominative form of the word—"pargeter"—refers to "a plasterer; a whitewasher," and, by figurative extension, to one who "glosses and smooths over."

Just how the word "pargeter" connects to *The Pargiters* becomes clearer from the diary entry Virginia made on November 2, 1932: the Essay-Novel called *The Pargiters* would "take in everything, sex, education, life &c; and come, with the most powerful and agile leaps, like a chamois across precipices from 1880 to here and now." In effect, she had at this point determined with some finality the novel's design. The book would progress from one "precipice" to another: that is, from 1880 to 1891 to 1907 to 1908 to 1910 to 1911 to 1913 to 1914 to 1917 to Present Day (1930s). The years *between* those precipices would remain buried in the valleys and she would have to "gloss" them over, "parget" those troughs.

Without explaining her reasons for selecting these particular years, she began writing the book in a state of exhilaration. But her record of the book's progress suggests that she soon came to see that its factual and imaginative components collided with each other and made the writing strained and angular. The truth of fact and the truth of fiction refused to come together in wholeness and harmony. "For though both truths are genuine, they are antagonistic; let them meet and they destroy each other ... Let it be fact ... or let it be fiction; the imagination will not serve under two masters simultaneously." So that in a sense the novel was destined to become a remarkable specimen in fiction where fact and feeling would begin and end in deadly combat. And throughout its course, she would face the problem of leaping from one precipice to another, while simultaneously "glossing" over those deep valleys which separate impersonal fact from personal feeling. To achieve this, Virginia Woolf herself would have to do some pargeting.

There were as usual many interruptions, but Virginia worked steadily at *The Pargiters*. During the Christmas holiday at Rodmell, she resumed work on *Flush*, revising ten pages a day, and finished that "silly" book on January 26. She was anxious to get back to her novel. There was a "torrent of [biographical] fact" to flood its pages. The book had become so important, she said, that "I mustn't take risks crossing the road" till it was finished. She was in what appeared to be an elevated state of excitement, leaping from one dizzying "precipice" to another—"scarcely seeing anything but the Pargiters."

The book was liberating and she was euphoric. Perhaps this mood was in some way linked to the "tremendous revelation" she recorded in her journal on the last day of 1932, when "all impediments suddenly dropped off ... Everything appeared very distinct, amazingly exciting." She felt no restrictions whatever and forged ahead with a vigor and certainty she had scarcely known before. It may have dawned on her that if she could get the dying Mrs. Pargiter dead and buried, she would be free at last to reveal Eleanor Pargiter's feeling for her father, reveal at last the real thing behind appearances.

With *Flush* out of the way, she returned to her manuscript on January 31, 1933, with a fresh page, beginning: "The Pargiters (additions to Chapter One)." Two days later, February 2: "Today I finished—rather more completely than usual—revising the first chapter. I am leaving out the interchapters [the Essays]—compacting them in the text: and project an appendix of dates." We know from the published text that the "appendix of dates" did not appear; and as far as "compacting" the interchapters was concerned, she had eventually to confront the problem of transforming their weighty emotional substance into poetic dramatizations of the characters' lives through a dense maze of overlapping images and interrupted metaphors.

Virginia seemed by this time convinced that the truth of fact and the truth of fiction would not come together in that queer "marriage of granite and rainbow." So that the whole idea of the "Novel-Essay," this "novel of fact," was essentially abandoned by February 2, 1933, and from that date on the novel form would govern the book's design.

But there was another reason for giving up the original plan. In her speech of January 21, 1931, Virginia made a point of singling out her difficulty as a woman writing about the minds and sexual passions of women. Because men were prudish where women were concerned, a woman was not expected to speak out with the same candor a man was permitted. Therefore, if she was going to describe the restrictive taboos and inhibitions to which her own generation of women were conditioned, the very act of daring to write them out would, on the contrary, disprove the existence not only of the taboos but of the inhibitions in describing them as well. And if she did not describe those repressions with the directness they required, she would be unable to analyze and explain their debilitating effect upon the minds and bodies of women. So as a novelist, Virginia Woolf found herself trapped in both directions, and the only avenue of escape was to relieve that pressure of fact against "vision" by recasting her material in such a way as to create an aesthetic tension from documented (and reduced) vision in union with poeticized (and diminished) fact—that is to say, by documenting fancy and beautifying reality—an artistic task carrying enormous risk and difficulty, and ultimately transforming her into what she wanted least to become—a Pargeter. During the early part of 1933, however, still unaware of the problem that lay ahead, she was enjoying the adventure. Headache and heartache would come later.

 While Vita and Harold were in the United States on a lecture tour, Virginia wrote her long, bantering letters loaded with her twisted views of America—"an unattractive land, largely sprinkled with old tin kettles." She imagined Vita in a train racing across "vast slabs of plate glass" to a town called Balmoralville where "after a brief snack off clams" with a Mayor named Cyrus K. Hinks, she'd pop into a Baptist hall and give her lecture. Then Vita would have to "clear a space among the spittoons" to write Virginia a long letter about "all those virgins you've ravished—teas you've eaten, shrines you've visited, fat old women you've intoxicated." All London was buzzing with Vita's "raging success" in the United States despite the grave economic crisis. But "Please Vita darling come back soon."

If Vita was too often absent, Ethel was too often present. Virginia continued to read and comment on her essays, but Ethel sometimes went too far. She could be imperious and demanding. Being with her, Virginia felt, was sometimes like "being a snail and having your brain cracked by a thrush." She was "a general's daughter," to be sure, and too much of the time her story came across like a smack in the face by "an aggressive charwoman." The most serious problem in Ethel's writing, however, was her egotism. Her world revolved around "I" and "Me." And "I hate it," Virginia wrote, "I don't think it adds anything . . . I hate any writer to talk about himself . . . And this may be an obsession . . . I blush, I fidget, I turn hot and cold. I want to pull the curtain over this indecency." She said a great deal more; and Ethel, always grateful, took some of the advice. Much of it she ignored.

The Pargiters commanded Virginia's attention in the early months of 1933, and she discovered that scene-making caused her heart rate to increase "with uncomfortable rapidity." Now why should that be? "Why should the Pargiters make my heart jump . . . What connection has the brain with the body?" No Harley Street specialist could explain that. Yet the symptoms were purely physical and as distinct as "one book is from another." As she pondered this question, a letter arrived from Vice-Chancellor Walter Moberly of Manchester University offering her an honorary degree of Doctor of Letters. Nothing, she said in her diary, would induce her to "connive at all that humbug." Three days later her "polite" refusal was sent off. The novel need not be interrupted now just to have "a tuft of fur put on my head." She observed on the same day that Julian Bell failed to become a Fellow at King's College. It must have occurred to her, entering this note, that Julian of the

Bell clan had failed to win what Virginia of the Stephen family refused to accept.

By April Virginia was worn out—"I've written myself out over The Pargiters this last lap . . . and so shall bury it for a month"—and turned to the essay on Oliver Goldsmith she'd begun during the Easter break. She had intended to finish the first draft of *The Pargiters*—an estimated 100,000 words—by the end of September. The book would be "a terrific affair . . . the whole of the present society—nothing less: facts, as well as vision." Never had she worked so quickly. Nor apparently did she see, even after seven months, that by combining fact and vision she was setting a deadly trap for herself. Unaware of what lay ahead, she went off with Leonard in early May for a three-week holiday on the Continent.

They returned to England, actually to Monks House, on the twenty-seventh; and by Wednesday, May 31, Virginia had established a strenuous work schedule; she had reached the stage where she could "write for 4 months straight ahead at the Pargiters. Oh what a relief—the physical relief!" *Flush*, Oliver Goldsmith, motoring through Italy—they were like "butting against a blank wall." She ended her diary entry with a statement she had made before and would make again—there was something profound about "the synthesis of my being: how only writing composes it: how nothing makes a whole unless I am writing." Throughout most of June she was brimming over with her novel.

Squeezed into this frenzy of writing was a social life perhaps more active than it should have been. "By God's grace we may get 10 or 12 days without visitors," she wrote in Rodmell. "The truth is, I like it when people come; but I love it when they go." This was as true in London as it was in the country. Yet constantly she got herself into these whirlwinds of people, as if she were deliberately creating an atmosphere in which Virginia Woolf was in demand, for certainly she could have managed a less exhausting social calendar had she wished to.

Soon after returning from their holiday, Leonard and Virginia drove to Sissinghurst to collect Pinka, whom Vita was looking after in their absence. In the course of their visit, Benedict, Vita's older son, took Virginia aside and told her about the interview he'd had with his grandmother. Lady Sackville had filled his head with stories about Vita's love affairs with women—Violet Trefusis, Virginia, and others—and assured him that Harold was not much better; only he went after men. Very attentively Virginia listened, and when he had finished she looked up—"That old woman ought to be shot," she said.

Lady Sackville was a determined troublemaker, and frequently in the newspapers for some kind of mischief. Sometime during the summer, Virginia had read that she was again in a court of law. This latest instance was an action brought against her by a certain Thomas Seller, whom she'd hired to act as a security guard over her property. She then refused to pay his wages of £3 10s. because he had neither a loaded pistol nor a straining bloodhound. He was therefore incompetent in her opinion. But Lady Sackville was sued so often for "libel, wrongful dismissal, unpaid bills, etc., that she named her house at Brighton the Writs Hotel."

"Yes, Vivienne [Eliot] seems to have gone crazy, poor woman," Virginia wrote Elizabeth Bowen in July. "Tom however is back and safe." Eliot had been appointed the Charles Eliot Norton Professor of Poetry at Harvard University (1932–33). During those six months in America he decided to separate from Vivien. Upon reaching England, he went off to Surrey to stay for several months with a fellow director of Faber and Faber. During this interval Vivien had been sent a Deed of Separation along with a letter from Eliot's lawyer. The whole affair was most interesting "to one who loves the smell of the rubbish heap as I do," Virginia wrote to a friend. Vivien sat in her flat "under a crowned effigy—that is, Tom's photo . . . and a wreath of daisies—saying that he was drowned: whereas he was editing the Criterion round the corner." The question was, would he "drop Christianity with his wife, as one might empty the fishbones after the herring." Eliot did not drop Christianity, however. Indeed, he embraced his God ever more fervidly. Eventually he found lodgings in South Kensington, and later became a "paying guest" of the Vicar of St. Stephen's on Gloucester Road, where in 1934 he became Vicar's Warden. On the last day of the year, Virginia received for the first time a "remarkable letter" from Vivien herself, saying that Tom refused to come back to her; and that was "a great tragedy." She made Leonard her executor.

In July of 1933, Dorothy Brett sent Virginia a copy of her recently published *Lawrence and Brett: A Friendship*. "I looked into your book and shut it," Virginia wrote her a few days after receiving it. She had not read D. H. Lawrence, she said, but one day soon she would read him through seriously— "We saw his grave in Vence—what a fate for a man who loved beauty—a kind of plum pudding...raised by the local mason." Dorothy Brett, the painter, had been an intimate friend of Katherine Mansfield and a frequent guest of Lady Ottoline Morrell at Garsington Manor. When Mansfield died in 1923, Brett became a "disciple" of Lawrence and followed him to Taos, New Mexico, in 1924, where he hoped to found an ideal community, and there Brett remained for the rest of her life.

Virginia's acquaintance with Lawrence was long-standing but very slight and a little curious. She had read his book *The Trespassers* in Spain while on her honeymoon in 1912, and once at Asheham House in December 1915 Leonard had read her one of Lawrence's newly published poems, which "made Max [their dog] sick." Several years later, in London, Koteliansky tried to introduce Virginia to the novelist, but she hesitated—"tempted, but alarmed." Then Leonard and Virginia had at one time considered renting one of the two cottages at Tregerthen in Cornwall, where Lawrence and his wife Frieda had lived in 1916–17 and most of *Women in Love* was written. Katherine Mansfield and Murry had occupied one of them briefly. In January 1919, Lawrence wrote to Koteliansky, suggesting that if the Woolfs wanted to take the Cornwall cottage he would be willing to exchange it for the Woolfs' house in Richmond. Through all this, Virginia and Lawrence never met face-to-face.

In December of 1920 she had reviewed his *The Lost Girl* in *The Times Literary Supplement*. But it was only when *Women in Love* was published in 1921 that Virginia got a stronger sense of the man. Lawrence had drawn an ugly portrait of Ottoline Morrell in the character of Hermione Roddice; and it was apparently his nastiness that "lured" Virginia on to read the novel. Ottoline/Hermione "has just smashed Lawrence's head open with a ball of lapis lazuli—" wrote Virginia in a letter, but then "balls are smashed on every other page...There is no suspense or mystery: water is all semen." It was all a little boring; the writing was superficial, the imagery too transparent. There must be something wrong with the man to account for his preoccupation with sex. Still he was "honest" and therefore "100 times better than most of us."

A typescript volume of Lawrence's poems called *Pansies* had been seized in the post in February 1929. The poems, posted from abroad, had been opened at Customs and then forwarded to the Home Secretary, who described them in Parliament as "grossly obscene." Leonard Woolf and the barrister St. John Hutchinson immediately drew up a protest. Yet, when

Lawrence died on March 2, 1930, aged forty-five, Virginia confessed she had never spoken to him and had only twice laid eyes on him: "once, swinging a spirit lamp in a shop in St Ives, and once ... when our train stopped outside Rome in the early morning."

It was only after Lawrence's death and the publication of some personal papers that Virginia began to assess the work of this intense and often-misunderstood writer. Aldous Huxley, a close friend, was among the first to step in to advise Frieda, or, as Virginia put it, "persuade her not to make love to every waiter ... and not to sell all Lawrence's MSS. twice over to every publisher in London."

In April 1931 Middleton Murry, toward whom Virginia had an intense dislike after Katherine Mansfield's death, had written a book about D. H. Lawrence, *Son of Woman*, "making out that he is Judas and Lawrence, Christ." At about the same time, she read *Sons and Lovers* and realized with some regret that "a man of genius wrote in my time and I never read him. Yes, genius obscured and distorted I think." Still, *Sons and Lovers* was in her estimation a worthy book.

When Huxley's edition of Lawrence's letters was published in 1932, Virginia again shifted her ground: sympathetic she might be, but still—"a thin exaggerated affair it is to be sure! and all on the same string." When Vita broadcast an adulatory review of Lawrence for the BBC in November, Virginia accused her of overdoing it: "I admit the genius, in Sons and Lovers ... the rest is all a dilution, a flood, a mix of inspiration and prophecy." He was a genius all right, "but not first rate." And this was her estimate of Lawrence when Dorothy Brett sent Virginia her book in the summer of 1933.

In August, without the slightest warning, Virginia succumbed to a state of complete exhaustion, a fatigue so debilitating she could hardly lift her pen to write. At the time, she was reading a book called *Oxford Apostles: A Character Study of the Oxford Movement*, in which its author, Geoffrey Faber, described the 1820 and 1827 nervous breakdowns of John Henry Newman. There were a number of details about his collapses that caught her attention: she pondered Newman's condition and compared it to her own. In Newman's case it was "the refusal of some part of the mechanism." Is that what happened to her? "Not quite. Because I'm not evading anything. I long to write the Pargiters." This was a curious observation, for she had written four years earlier: "Clearly the mind is always altering its focus, and bringing the world into different perspectives. But some of these states of mind seem ... to be less comfortable than others." There is discomfort when the writer "is unconsciously holding something back, and gradually the repression becomes an effort. But there may be some state of mind in which one could continue without effort because nothing is required to be held back."

It appears that at the time of this entry in August 1933, Virginia had convinced herself that whatever needed to be stated of a factual nature in this novel of fact she would state—assuming she did not connect unconscious censorship with imagination. So when she wrote a few days later, "I have just killed Mrs Pargiter," she was convinced she was writing what she remembered of her own mother's death in 1895. And that past was true. What Virginia appears not to have realized was the consequence of that death and what it meant to the relationship of one of Mrs. Pargiter's ambivalent daughters to the surviving spouse and father, Colonel Abel Pargiter. For in the published novel, one of the daughters is impatiently awaiting her mother's death, and when it comes she is relieved, but scornful of the nurse's sobbing, the nurse who had come only that afternoon. At Mrs. Pargiter's funeral, the scornful young woman "stared down into the grave. There lay her mother; in that coffin—the woman she had loved and hated so. Her eyes dazzled. She was afraid she might faint; but she must look; she must feel; it was the last chance that was left her . . . As for her father he was so rigid that she had a convulsive desire to laugh aloud."

Nine years earlier, on the anniversary of her mother's death, Virginia had written in her diary "how I laughed . . . behind the hand which was meant to hide my tears; and through the fingers saw the nurses sobbing." Again she would recall "turning aside at mother's bed, when she died . . . to laugh, secretly, at the nurse crying. She's pretending, I said: aged 13 and was afraid I was not feeling enough." And she would describe still again her laughing behind her hands at her mother's death, when, in 1939, she began writing her memoir. With these "confessions" Virginia Woolf had every reason to believe that now, in writing *The Pargiters*, she was "holding nothing back," "evading nothing." And this is where her difficulties would begin. For while she was open and candid about *some* things, she had deluded herself into believing in her own candor, and was therefore not aware that there was so much *other* material she was still holding back, much of it having to do with her father. And when she came to make this discovery in a year's time, she would see, finally, the impossibility of combining fact and vision. They would simply not come together, and the novel that resulted, called *The Years*, would be a fatal compromise which would call into question not only her honesty but her technical virtuosity as well.

Some remarks Virginia made at this point in the novel's composition suggest that there was some confusion in her own mind about what exactly she was doing. In late October, fatigue forced her once again to stop work. A rest, she hoped, would again float her into a state that was "full and calm and unconscious." It was impossible to stress "how tremendously important unconsciousness is when one writes." Certainly the function of the unconscious in writing *fiction* was understandable. "Vision," as she called it, depended to a very large extent upon her mind's unconscious processes. But if she was writing a novel which mixed "vision" with (conscious) *fact*, then problems were bound to arise. For unconsciousness in writing fact would seem the very last thing she wanted. Unless she was referring to *facts* that had been *transformed into reality* by her own private creative machinery. And if that was the case, then her novel would certainly give her trouble because transformed facts were not facts at all: they were poeticized versions of the truth which Virginia Woolf had made tolerable, had purified.

In other words it would be difficult to talk about the *reality of fact* if that *reality* was of her own *invention*. And this is what seems to have been taking place. For although she had succeeded in creating Mr. and Mrs. Ramsay in *To the Lighthouse* by writing almost entirely in the realm of "vision," to attempt to repeat that performance in *The Pargiters* would inevitably falsify the Stephen family history. Had she not said: "I prefer where truth is important, to write fiction." Had she not said: "Fiction . . . is likely to contain more truth than fact." And if writing became an effort when a writer was "unconsciously holding something back," then would it not follow that the effort she was just beginning to feel resulted from, and would increase in proportion to, what she herself was actually—and unconsciously—repressing? Stated differently: the facts she presented, or thought she was presenting, were material that she had unconsciously censored or edited or poeticized and therefore not really facts at all. And since *un*consciousness can only be inferred or deduced, and never rendered directly, Virginia Woolf was getting herself into a position where the line between "fact" and "vision" was becoming increasingly blurred.

 In late August, about five weeks before publication, *Flush* was chosen by the American Book Society as its premium selection for October. This would bring in a great deal of money that Virginia had not anticipated. Now Leonard could build his new pond at Monks House, have the old one regrouted, and even pave the front garden. "Flush, I think with some pleasure, has made these extravagances possible." The book would net about two thousand pounds from that "six months dogged and dreary grind." What would readers think of the book, she wondered without much anxiety.

Indeed, she was still relatively untroubled by *The Pargiters*. The only incident to bother her was the sudden fit of exhaustion and the insatiable need for sleep which accompanied it. But this she attributed to the interferences of the real world while she was creating her fictional one. That was the cause, or so she believed. "I only want walking and perfectly spontaneous childish life with Leonard and the accustomed when I'm writing at full tilt: to have to behave with circumspection and decision to strangers wrenches me into another region; hence the collapse." But the perfectly "childish life with Leonard" could not of course go on without intrusions of one kind or another; and in the autumn months it was Vita Sackville-West who would wrench her out of her reverie, and destroy the calm and monotony necessary to the novel in progress.

As it happened Vita's novel *All Passion Spent* had been dramatized and was being performed under the title *Indian Summer* at Croydon. Virginia wrote to her about it. She also wanted to see Vita. She missed her. Would she come to Monks House? Virginia then casually brought up Clive's old lover Mary Hutchinson, with whom she had recently dined—and again, suddenly and without warning, came a burst of violence—"Mary makes love to me—" Virginia wrote with mounting fury, "yes: other people don't. I daresay at this very minute you're couched with some herring griller in the straw, God damn you." It was identical to the burst of rage in October when Virginia flew against Vita for doing "the act under the Dolomites" with Hilda Matheson. This sudden mood swing would have alerted Leonard had he seen the letter. But he missed the signal, and the mounting trouble went unchecked.

On Wednesday, October 3, two days before the publication of *Flush*, Virginia, more for Leonard's sake than her own, accompanied him to the Labour Party Conference at Hastings. It was for her "a queer experience," this other world of politics. "I sat rather half witted and heard things that I didn't understand.

But I always enjoy it." There were ships passing by outside, while the "tub thumping" went on inside with Beatrice and Sidney Webb sitting "like idols" on the platform. The next day she spent in bed with a headache, "infinite weariness" in her back, and "clouds forming" in her neck. *Flush* would be out the next day and she anticipated becoming depressed by the kind of praise it would get. The reviewers would say it was "charming, delicate, ladylike." There was no question of its being a success; but she disliked that sort of success, the work of a "ladylike prattler." Above all she must concentrate on *The Pargiters*.* That would sail her through the next few days.

If Virginia did not take *Flush* seriously, the important reviewers didn't either. It was, as she predicted, like *Orlando*, a commercial success. "It amused Mrs Woolf to write and it has brought out her delightful humor as nothing else has done," wrote Bunny Garnett in the *New Statesman and Nation* (October 7). Another reviewer thought *Flush* "entirely beautiful" but saw it as a "necessary pause" in Woolf's career and not a "*tour de force* as its predecessor [*Orlando*] was." But it was Rebecca West who punched a hole in Virginia's "jubilant" indifference. *Flush* would not be met with enthusiasm by Woolf's admirers, she said. "It sometimes produces the effect . . . of a family joke that has been too hardy in leaving the four walls of its origin, and facing the rude airs of the great world." Then Geoffrey Grigson bit Virginia with his "coarse yellow feeble teeth" in the *Morning Post* (October 6): "Its continual mock-heroic tone, its bantering pedantry, its agile verbosity make it the most tiresome book which Mrs Woolf has yet written." There was one review, however, that might have given Virginia serious pause, for it hinted at the trouble she herself would be facing in the next few years—facile writing for indiscriminate readers: ". . . the deadly facility of [*Flush*] combined with its popular success mean . . . the end of Mrs Woolf as a live force. We must mourn the passing of a potentially great writer who perished for lack of an intelligent audience."

No matter how critical or adulatory her public at the moment was, however, she felt a kind of half-hearted security of having "plenty of money anyhow." The "perpetual little spatter of comment" might keep her awake, but only for a little while. For on December 19, 1932, she had written in her diary: "I will be free . . . mistress of my life by Oct. 1st 1933." This was the "freedom" she was referring to now on October 29. But did she really think herself free? Certainly the question of having "plenty of money" entered into it. Like so much else in her life, however, her sense of security and autonomy

---

* She had changed its title to *Here and Now*; there would be eight or nine changes of title altogether.

held good only when her writing was progressing favorably. When her "vision" faltered, then all freedom and independence instantly vanished. A new wrinkle in her relations with Vita would soon show her just how *unfree* she was; how morbidly dependent she remained. Very far indeed was she from being the "mistress" of her life. She had every reason to read "rather vainly" the Book of Job.

When Virginia went to Sissinghurst in early October, she met Gwendolen St. Aubyn, Harold's sister, for the first time—the Honourable Mrs. Francis St. Aubyn, aged thirty-seven at the time. Virginia could not have failed to notice Vita's regard for her sister-in-law, the new woman in her life. An affair of the heart had sprung up between them, and Gwen was to remain by Vita's side for the next several years. What Virginia sensed was perhaps mere suspicion, but it was enough to trouble her sleep. For once more she was faced with the terror of losing Vita altogether.

At a dinner party on October 31, St. John Hutchinson had casually said in Virginia's presence that he had seen Vita lunching at the Café Royal that day. All Virginia's coveted freedom and independence went flying out the window at this announcement, and the frightened child once more suddenly materialized. "Oh such a pang of rage shot through me!" she wrote Vita on the following day. "All through dinner . . . it burnt a hole in my mind, that you should have been lunching at the Café Royal and not come to see me . . . But who were you with? You knew I should get wind of it—yes and it was a woman you were lunching with, and there was I, sitting alone . . . Dearest Creature, do write and tell me who you were lunching with at the Café Royal . . . oh the Café Royal! When Jack said that—not to me, but to the company, you could have seen my hand tremble . . . and the candles were lit and I chose mine, a green one, and it was the first to die, which means . . . I shall be the first to wear the winding sheet." But even then, even if Virginia died, Vita would still "be lunching at the Café Royal!"

Her reaction may have appeared excessive, even to Vita, and in ordinary circumstances it would have been. But this, Virginia could now see, was no fleeting love affair. She'd grown accustomed to those. No, this was a serious matter. It was no Mary Campbell or Hilda Matheson or Evelyn Irons Vita was pursuing. This was Gwendolen St. Aubyn, Harold's sister, a member of the family; with Gwen there would be close and constant contact.

In the middle of December, Virginia wrote to Vita about meeting her in London: "What fun to see you at the bottom of the stairs, like at the fishmonger's shop again. Wasn't it about this time of year we saw the porpoise?

You wore a pink shirt and pearls. Lord how I remember it!" She was re-membering December 18, 1925, the scene of Vita, pearl hung and seductive, in a Sevenoaks shop, ordering fish—it was the day their friendship turned into love; but that love was for Vita, though by no means so for Virginia, becoming more and more a thing of the past.

On the last day of the year, Virginia wrote a long letter to Ottoline Morrell. She had just seen Vita with her sons, Nigel and Benedict, one at Eton and the other at Oxford, which explained the financial pinch and her need to spin out "those sleepwalking servant girl novels." But, Virginia went on, "I remain always very fond of her—this I say because on the surface, she's rather red and black and gaudy, I know: and very slow . . . but she is incapable of in-sincerity or pose, and digs and digs, and waters, and walks her dogs, and reads her poets, and falls in love with every pretty woman, just like a man . . . But do let her come down from her rose-red tower where she sits with thousands of pigeons cooing over her head."

By the middle of February, after ten days of headache, Virginia plunged once more into the Pargiter world to live "strongly and quietly there for 6 weeks." This was cut short, however, for the year opened with an Ethel Smyth festival of sorts. There were concerts, luncheons, dinners, and tea parties, some of which Virginia felt obliged to attend. On March 3 the celebration culminated in a performance at Albert Hall of Ethel's Mass in D, conducted by Sir Thomas Beecham in the presence of Queen Mary. Virginia thought it rather a joke seeing Ethel in her three-cornered hat seated by the Queen in the Royal box among all the court. Afterward Ethel gave a tea party at Lyon's— and "a more sordid 6d. affair you can't imagine; marble slabbed tables . . . and the populace munching their cream buns." Among the guests were the American-born hostess, Lady Cunard, Lady Diana Cooper, and Laura, Lady Lovat, "all eating thick bread and butter . . . and Ethel bellowing, as red as the sun, entirely triumphant and self satisfied."

Ethel Smyth was indeed triumphant, and much as Virginia wanted her affection, Ethel's egotism and pertinacity got in the way. She had almost a talent for saying the wrong thing at the wrong time. At any rate she provided Virginia with an outlet for her accumulating tensions; for one could fire as many cannonballs as one liked without moving a hair on Ethel's impenetrable hide.

41

That spring, Nelly Boxall, the Woolfs' cook for eighteen years, once more caused Virginia the "most disagreeable six weeks" of her life. Nelly had a history of "tempers and glooms" and Virginia had for a long time considered dismissing her. Then one day during the winter, matters reached flash point. There was an argument over an electric oven and Nelly made herself more disagreeable than usual. Suddenly for Virginia this was the last straw; if she permitted her to remain, she would "grow on us and wither and decay." But Virginia couldn't endure Nelly for a whole month under notice; so she devised a scheme to which she stuck for six weeks—"and almost died of it—that is, I kept serenely but severely at a distance; and again and again she tried to break me down; cajoled and apologised, and half suspected what was up, but not quite." Some weeks passed before Virginia finally told her straight out that the strain of having her in the house was too much and she would have to go. This brought on a "storm of abuse and apology, and hysterics and appeals and maniacal threats." Nelly refused to go, and refused the handsome severance check Virginia offered her, pleading and clutching and "following me about the house, till I was driven in the cold wind to spend yesterday morning parading Oxford Street."

Why, Virginia wondered, did this long, drawn-out struggle with a servant "demoralize one more than any love or anger scene with one's own kind?" A good question, for it sheds a little light on Virginia's self-esteem, on how she saw herself in terms of power and control in other human relationships. It is hard to imagine either Julia Stephen or Vanessa Bell being driven out of her own house by the hysterics of an obstinate domestic. With both Julia and Vanessa the situation would have been reversed: Nelly herself would have been shot out into the cold. But this was unfortunately not the case with Virginia. Despite her bravado on paper, the sharpness of her mind and tongue; despite the razor-keen logic and rhetorical brilliance of her arguments, Virginia was in many ways submissive, compliant, yielding. At the deepest levels of her being, she experienced herself as small, weak, and dependent. The image she saw in the mirror was not strong or confident enough to manage even ordinary day-to-day mistress-servant confrontations. How could she be expected to engage in the daily combats of life when she herself was so defenseless and vulnerable?

"I cannot describe how the Nelly situation weighs on my spirits," she wrote in her diary. She could not get back into the writing mood, because "Nelly spoils it all." She dined with Vanessa, and in the presence of all her sister's force and determination, she felt "so old, so cold, so dumpish, nothing flowery or fiery in me, owing to Nelly." On March 26, the day before Nelly's departure, she wrote again in her journal: " 'The worst is yet to come'—that is with Nelly. Well it is coming very near—by this time—3.30—tomorrow it will be over . . . I feel executioner and the executed in one."

The underlying feeling of punishment and degradation and passivity would explain, a few months later, her response to Wyndham Lewis's brutal attack on her. "Already I am feeling the calm that always comes to me with abuse," she would confess to her diary; ". . . there is the queer disreputable pleasure in being abused . . . in being a martyr." This secret "pleasure" manifested itself most dramatically in her relationship with Vita. Almost from the start, little phrases scattered throughout her letters point to the dominant-compliant lines along which their love relations developed. A few words here and there, often cushioned in deceptive contexts, reveal how devalued and weak Virginia felt herself. "Is it true you love giving pain?" she asked Vita in mock seriousness. "I enjoyed your intimate letter," she had written. "It gave me a great deal of pain . . . Never mind; I enjoyed your abuse very much." Later she would beg Vita not to "snuff the stinking tallow out of your heart—poor Virginia to wit." Still later: "Chuck me as often as you like, and don't give it a moment's thought." And running parallel to this was the "childlike dazzled affection." She appears to have enjoyed being Vita's helpless "victim."

As was said earlier, that role served a protective function in Virginia's interior world. Her helplessness allowed her to shift the responsibilities of life onto someone else's shoulders. If this was, as Julia Stephen believed, a cold, hostile, begrudging world, then Virginia learned almost from the cradle to put herself at someone else's mercy. Others would take care of her; and with their care, she might also expect a certain measure of affection and charity reserved for the martyr, the messiah, the "scapegoat, the eternal sufferer." The domestic squabble with Nelly was merely a symptom of a much larger, more pervasive problem which would become unmanageable in the next few years when Virginia became convinced that her writing—her *only* means of survival—was beginning to fail her. For if her pen stopped doing "its business," she would become entirely defenseless and in perpetual danger of being destroyed by her own internal rage.

The money Virginia might have been enjoying during this period of her life continued to unsettle her relations with Vanessa. From the start Vanessa had been the person she idealized and depended upon, as she now depended upon Leonard. But with money now in Virginia's coffers—a financial state Vanessa would never achieve as a painter—the sisters' positions were materially reversed. The greater Vanessa's need of money, however, the more aloof and standoffish she appears to have become. To be otherwise would have been humiliating, and Vanessa, like Julia Stephen, was not a woman to countenance humiliation. Virginia on her side knew that Vanessa was "very hard up," and though "afraid to impose" she did what she could to help, while maintaining her pose as the needy, helpless younger sister, which indeed she was still in many ways. A year or so earlier, she had begun giving her niece Angelica a regular dress allowance. It was not an extravagant sum, but enough to remind Vanessa—unintentionally on Virginia's part—that it was something she herself could not afford.

During the spring of 1934, Virginia used the occasion of Vanessa's fifty-fifth birthday to give her a hundred pounds to buy a new car. Duncan and Vanessa were to accept the money as a joint birthday present. "I am much better off than I expected owing to Flush, and it would be a great pleasure," said Virginia, trying to cover up the smell of charity, "to think of you attending family funerals in style." Virginia knew, of course, that if Vanessa accepted (and she eventually did), she would become even more distant from Virginia out of vanity. While Virginia understood this sore spot in their relations, what she did not anticipate was the necessity of soon becoming more openly judgmental of Vanessa's precious Julian and his poetic gifts.

"Julian is rather bothered about his fellowship which will be out next week," she wrote casually to Quentin. As it turned out, Julian would soon discover he'd failed in his second attempt to become a Fellow of King's College. It must have been a terrible disappointment to have his hopes dashed twice. Now he would live in London, without any paid employment, writing poems before going off to China to settle his future. It was pretty clear to Virginia and to Leonard, however, that neither Julian's poetry nor Julian's scholarship was up to the Hogarth Press standard. Virginia's relationship with him, critical as it was, would thus increasingly interfere in her relations with Vanessa in the coming years.

On Wednesday, April 25, Virginia, Leonard, and Pinka left for southern Ireland for a two-week holiday. Virginia had never been there and looked forward to the journey. They set out from Rodmell and drove to Fishguard in Pembrokeshire, where they crossed overnight in the stormy channel for the Irish Free State. They spent one night at Bowen's Court in Kildorrery, the eighteenth-century mansion inherited by the novelist Elizabeth Bowen, where she and her husband Alan Cameron lived part of the year. On Sunday they continued to the southwest of Ireland, then turned north to Galway, saw the Aran Islands, and headed east to Dublin, where they spent two nights.

Irish life to Virginia was "ramshackle ... empty and poverty-stricken" and the Irish themselves the most talkative people she had ever met. With the ear of a novelist, she listened and recorded the garrulous Mrs. Ida Fitzgerald, proprietor of the Glenbeigh Hotel, where they stayed. She was one such talker who found her way into Virginia's journal. "But why isn't Mrs F. a great novelist? ... She said one could never understand the Irish: one had to live as they did. They sit in cottages talking about politics; they don't dance; they have no amusements ... 'Oh, as my grandmother said, one becomes able to read people's characters before they step over the door, and one's never wrong' ... Her quickness was amazing. This morning the talk began and Leonard very slightly put out his hand. 'Oh I know that means you're wanting to be off'— and so we parted from the last representative of the French salon of the 18th Century, this strange mixture of country lady, peasant, and landlady."

On the homeward journey they stopped in Stratford-on-Avon. The distant past held a peculiar fascination for Virginia; and here the spirit of Shakespeare hung over everything she saw. This was New Place, one of the largest houses in Stratford, which Shakespeare had purchased in 1597; and here he came to retire until his death in 1616. " 'That was where his study windows looked out when he wrote the Tempest' said the man. And perhaps it was true ... and when the clock struck, that was the sound Shakespeare heard ... Yes, everything seemed to say, this was Shakespeare's ... but you won't find me, not exactly in the flesh. He is serenely absent-present; both at once; radiating round one ... in the flowers, in the old hall, in the garden; but never to be pinned down."

They wandered from the house to the church, Holy Trinity Church, where a colored bust was erected on the chancel wall. On the floor stone over his grave was inscribed:

> *Good friend for Iesus sake forbeare,*
> *To digg the dvst encloased heare!*
> *Blest be ye man yt spares thes stones,*
> *And curst be he yt moves my bones.*

In the church too Virginia felt his presence—"he seemed to be all air and sun smiling serenely; and yet down there one foot from me lay the little bones that had spread over the world this vast illumination ... to think of writing The Tempest looking out on that garden; what a rage and storm of thought to have gone over any mind."

While they were in Ireland, Leonard saw quite by chance in an outdated copy of the London *Times* an announcement that George Duckworth, aged sixty-six, had died on April 27 at Freshwater on the Isle of Wight. Later in the day Virginia turned to her journal to record her reaction. Curiously, she felt at first the "usual incongruous shades of feeling ... how great a part he used to play and now hardly any." But as she wrote and meandered back through the years, she began to remember the good and happy things of her earliest years and "how childhood goes with him—the batting, the laughter, the treats, the presents, taking us for bus rides to see famous churches, giving us tea at City Inns."

These affectionate memories of George Duckworth are so different from the monster she would make of him later when she was writing her memoir. In that "Sketch of the Past" George Duckworth was painted as the offensive child-molester who deserved every punishment imaginable for the wrongs he (and Gerald) had inflicted on Virginia during the tenderest years of her childhood. If she was recalling the facts accurately, one would have expected his death to come as a relief, that she was at last free of that nasty pedophilic sex offender now finally in his grave and out of harm's way. But this was not what she remembered. Here we have only the benign recollections, memories of generosity and kindness.

Many years earlier, when she was fifteen, Virginia recorded impressions of him that were bright and intimate, impressions that did not support the claims she would make of him in 1939. Her journal for 1897 is filled with references to George that are like those recorded in 1934. Page after page describe her jaunts with him, meetings for lunch, cricket matches he took her to, days he would be away, presents he was sure to return with, and so on. Her entries then, like her memories now, did not sound like those of a sexually abused victim writing about her abuser. Nor would there have been any need for concealment now after nearly forty years. Virginia's perception of her Duckworth half brother in 1939, when she was writing under great stress, clearly does not coincide with her perception of him in 1934.

The most eloquent scene of childhood sexuality Virginia Woolf ever wrote can be found in the "1880" section of *The Pargiters* that she had finished writing just a year earlier. It centers on the ten-year-old Rose Pargiter, who has been nearly molested on her way to a neighborhood shop, and on the way home confronts the sex offender again, only now with his pants unbuttoned, exhibiting himself. Rose was traumatized by the incident and Virginia Woolf, in the first draft of the novel, insinuated the real trouble. Rose's instinct, when her older sister Eleanor came to her room that night, "was to turn away and hide herself. She felt that what had happened was not merely 'naughty' but somehow wrong." The image of the man unbuttoning his clothes "somehow suggested to her a range of emotion in herself of which she was instinctively afraid; as if, without being told a word about it, she knew that she was able to feel what it was wrong to feel. *For also by instinct, she knew that her father would be angry — yet not angry in the way that disobedience angered him — if he knew what she had seen.*" (Virginia was later to recall that her own father's "waistcoat was often unbuttoned; sometimes the fly buttons.") "So that she did not mind . . . being found out about her disobedience—what she could not say to her sister, even, was that she had seen a sight that puzzled her."

The passage goes on: "At ten years old, tomboy though she was, she was beginning to feel the desire, which was much more highly developed in her sisters, for the approval of the opposite sex. When her father had said 'grubby little monster' and pointed to the stain on her pinafore, she at once covered it with her hand; although when Milly noticed it, she did not care in the least, and she said what was a lie."

The text makes clear that Rose's adoration for her father, her fascination with the "shiny knobs" of his mutilated hand, her standing "erect" in imitation of him, her trying to conceal from him the stain on her pinafore—all these details point to a strong sexual component in her attachment to her father, whose approval as a grown man she, a budding female, hopes to gain. The sexual aspect of Rose's attachment is so powerful, and thus frightening, that even to the trusted older sister she must remain silent. Rose's thought that "Papa . . . would be angry if he knew what she had seen" is the clearest evidence we have to the erotic nature of that thought. For she imputes feelings to her father which she alone imagines; and those feelings, were she able to articulate them, would run something like this: "Papa would be angry if he knew that I'd seen *another* man's private parts—I haven't been loyal to the man who calls me 'grubby little monster,' who loves me in the same way I love him."

In the end the sexual scene at the pillar-box is traumatic for Rose, *not* because of what she has seen but because that exposure suddenly becomes a shocking *actualization* of her profoundly forbidden and dimly perceived sexual fantasy; and the shame resulting from that fantasy is so great that the episode in which Rose is really the innocent victim becomes transformed and magnified in her ten-year-old mind as *her* crime, a crime so horrible it is choked off from speech.

In writing *The Pargiters*, then, Virginia Woolf had got herself into a corner: How could she write about this crucial scene with all the candor it required without suggesting her own intimate knowledge of Rose's feelings? Didn't she love her father equally? Identically? As enduringly? A few months later, Virginia wrote a scene in which one of the young Pargiter women sees her father across a crowded room and muses: "... love of father and daughter. Spontaneous. Rather suspect all the same. Of mixed origin. Do I love my father sexually?"* Nowhere in the Woolf canon is the suggestion of father-daughter incest made more explicit. For in the world of imagination, there is no right or wrong.

Thus it was not only possible but highly probable that the transformation which took place in Rose Pargiter's mind also took place in Virginia's *adult* imagination at about this time in 1934, *after* George Duckworth's death. The Duckworth brothers, guilty as they probably were, became the loathsome creatures to whom Virginia could attach the deeply disturbing fantasies which she herself harbored for her father. It was easier to lay the weight of those unmentionable crimes on the shoulders of her half brothers than to acknowledge in her "Sketch of the Past" the private shame generated by her equally unmentionable incestuous fantasies. The body of *fact* that was to go into *The Pargiters* bore down on her like a ton of granite, and the futility of attempting to transform it to rainbow would almost cost Virginia Woolf her sanity in the coming months. Such was the nature of her conflict and the depth of her trouble in writing this so-called "novel of fact."

In the middle of May, after several days of flu, Virginia gently worked her way back into the novel. "Now, self-confidence, conceit, the blessed illusion by which we live begin to return." By September 2 she was in a state of high excitement: "my cheeks burn; my hands tremble." Though she was making progress, the old problem of shifting between the real world and the world of the Pargiters was becoming daily more like "a smash in a car."

---

* In the published text this is changed to: "And what's this? she asked, for the sight of her father in his rather worn shoes had given her a direct spontaneous feeling. This sudden warm spurt? she asked, examining it. She watched him cross the room. His shoes always affected her strangely. Part sex; part pity" (p. 378).

Her "smash" with reality was certainly real enough. Vita had submitted a new novel to the Press written, presumably, under the influence of Gwen St. Aubyn, so Virginia believed, which contained scenes of physical sadism—a naked woman being whipped in a cave. It was an ugly scene in a disturbing novel. Virginia expressed her disappointment to Vita, but offered her criticism with "diffidence"; her knowledge of the real people, she suspected, had "queered the pitch" for her and undoubtedly she was "jealous." For Gwen in the flesh, not the novel's sadism, was the thorn in Virginia's pillow. A second thorn was Julian Bell. He had applied for the Chair of English at National University of Wuhan in China, and if he succeeded he would be away for several years. The prospect of losing Vanessa to sadness and worry lay like a stone on Virginia's mind.

A terrible blow descended on September 9. Roger Fry suddenly and unexpectedly died. He had fallen and broken his pelvis at his home in Bernard Street and died of heart failure at the Royal Free Hospital two days later. "I feel dazed: very wooden. Women cry, Leonard says: but I don't know why I cry ... I think the poverty of life now is what comes to me; a thin blackish veil over everything." Since 1911 Roger had assumed a significant place in Virginia's life. He had a deep and abiding interest in her gifts and, apart from Leonard, understood better than anyone what she was after as a novelist. When *Orlando* was published, he had said to her: "... you happen to have genius, my dear Virginia. It might have happened to any of us but it didn't. But it doesn't matter where it happens so long as it does happen somewhere quite near to one in time and space, which makes me desperately glad that you have it."

In the shock of Roger's death, Virginia recalled her mother's final hours: "I remember turning aside at mother's bed, when she died ... to laugh, secretly ... and was afraid I was not feeling enough. So now." If Virginia had once before cut off feeling in a moment of crisis, as she was now doing with Roger, it was only for the moment. But there was one fact that could not be suppressed. On September 9, 1913, with an overdose of veronal, Virginia had brushed the sleeve of death for the second time in her life. It must have come to her as a sign of dark significance that exactly twenty-one years later to the day—September 9, 1934—Roger Fry's death should occur, fixing forever in death the father-daughter bond which held them together in life.

The funeral was at Golders Green Crematorium on the afternoon of September 13. Leonard and Virginia came up from Rodmell that morning and drove Desmond and Molly MacCarthy home when it was over. The ceremony was "all very simple and dignified. Music. Not a word spoken." Roger lay under an old red brocade and two branches of flowers. Bach was played and, after "the coffin moved slowly through the doors," Frescobaldi. Then Desmond suggested they walk in the garden, and for "the first time I laid my hand on his shoulder, and said don't die yet. Nor you either, he said."

The death of Roger Fry, like the death of Leslie Stephen, ended a life but not a relationship. Virginia would eventually be asked to write his life, and the task of resurrecting him for posterity would demand a formidable price. For in making her way into the past once more, she would have to shoulder her way through the crowded obliquities of a private history that quickened to life the memory of Leslie Stephen as well. Roger Fry and her father seemed to coalesce in her mind almost from the day of his death. Her letters now about Roger carried almost the same tone of grief as the letters about her father had in 1904. "The dreadful thing," she had written thirty years earlier, "is that I never did enough for him all those years . . . I never helped him as I might have done." And again: "I can't believe that all our life with Father is over . . . If one could only tell him how one cared." And here in 1934 were her words for Roger: "I still find myself thinking I shall tell him something." ". . . I have felt since his death how little one gave him—how much I wished I had told him what he meant to me."

In some dim but absolute way Virginia held in reserve for Roger Fry the very phrasing of sorrow she had uttered for Leslie Stephen. How much must have passed through her mind as she stood at Golders Green in this autumnal month of 1934 that recalled the leafless trees of February 1904, when she had stood at Golders Green for her father. And just as she had sifted through the spectral love letters of Julia and Leslie in 1904 for Maitland's *Life*, so now, thirty years later, would she break the silence of the past in going through the love letters of Roger and Vanessa in readiness for her commemoration of him.

However dark her sky in the following weeks, Virginia pressed on with *The Pargiters* and for a short interval, at least, achieved once more "the exalted sense of being above time and death which comes from being again in a writing mood." On the morning of September 30, at Monks House, she wrote the last words of her book, calmly, peacefully, with "no tears and exaltation at the end" as with *The Waves* and no "beautiful writing."

On the following day, October 1, "the old rays of light set in; and then the sharp, the very sharp pain over my eyes." The headache did not last but it was warning enough to make her realize how monumental a strain the book had been. Before long she would be dreading the day the rewriting would begin. One month later, November 2, she wrote to her American publisher, Donald Brace: "With regard to the novel"—it was now nameless— "I am in rather a perplexity. I have finished it—that is to say I have written what appears to be about 200,000 words; but my feeling is that it will have to be considerably shortened and re-written." She had put it away and would not look at it for another month. As to how much revision and how long it would take, she didn't know. But she did not expect to have it ready before next autumn. "And it is always on the cards that I shall tear it up."

The October 11 issue of *The Times Literary Supplement* advertised Wyndham Lewis's new book, *Men Without Art*, which contained a chapter on Virginia Woolf. She knew instinctively that it was an attack on her—"I am publicly demolished; nothing is left of me in Oxford and Cambridge and places where the young read Wyndham Lewis." Also instinctively, she reached for the *Letters of John Keats* and copied out the following passage in her journal:

> Praise or blame has but a momentary effect on the man whose love of beauty in the abstract makes him a severe critic of his own works. My own domestic criticism has given me pain beyond what Blackwood or Quarterly could possibly inflict . . . This is a mere matter of the moment—I think I shall be among the English poets after my death. Even as a matter of present interest the attempt to crush me in the Quarterly has only brought me more into notice.

Would she, Virginia Woolf, be among the English novelists after her death? Was it even worth thinking about? And why should she shrink from Lewis? Why was she so sensitive? Was it vanity? Was it the idea of being laughed at? "Perhaps I feel uncertain of my own gifts: but then I know more about them than W. L. . . . What I shall do is craftily to gather the nature of the indictment from talk and reviews: and, in a year perhaps, when my book is out, I shall read it [*Men Without Art*]." But again that twisted pleasure from pain came to the surface—that queer "disreputable pleasure in being abused

... in being a martyr." Lewis had made a mockery of *Mr. Bennett and Mrs. Brown*. He had attacked her logic, her example, her femininity, and her eloquence. But his malice went deeper. He had prefaced his argument with the claim that to "certain critics" Virginia Woolf was "extremely insignificant ... a purely feminist phenomenon ... taken seriously by no one any longer." Lewis's venom could not have been more potent. For in calling her insignificant he had blotted out her identity as a writer, and if she was not a writer, she was nothing, nobody, a mere object of contempt—self-contempt.

By the middle of October she was sunk in depression and dug out old diaries to see if the "blackness," the "blankness" came from finishing *The Pargiters*. Yes, that was it, she tried to persuade herself. She had gone through the same thing after finishing *The Waves*. It was right there in her diary. And after *To the Lighthouse*: "I was I remember nearer suicide, seriously, than since 1913." Finishing a book meant there was nothing left of the imaginary people, of the ideas, "of the whole life in short that has been racing round my brain." Again she was grateful for Leonard. It was "an immense relief to talk to him! What a simplification. What an egress to open air and cold daylight ... and I have him every day, as I so often think." But with the idealized Virginia Woolf image torn to shreds, the inevitable self-denigration crept in once more to assert itself: "I'm so ugly. So old. No one writes to me." Wyndham Lewis did indeed have the power to sting.

Several days passed before Virginia discovered that Stephen Spender had come to her defense in a review of *Men Without Art*: "This is a book in which *The Waste Land* is referred to with some contempt, as are also the novels of Mr. E. M. Forster, and in which Mrs. Woolf is attacked with a great deal of malice and without any show of evidence that Mr. Lewis has read either of her best works, *The Waves* or *To the Lighthouse*." Lewis, of course, answered Spender with another attack in the *Spectator*: Spender's charge of malice was absurd, wrote Lewis, and went on to rub salt in the wound. But Lewis could say what he pleased, said Virginia. She could brave his ill temper. Leonard had said it would be contemptible to mind. But she did mind and tried to console herself with all her blessings: "I have Leonard: and there are his books; and our life together and freedom, now, from money paring." She must try to forget herself and her fame and her "sink in the scale—which is bound to come now." She must remember the unfinished novel overboiling in the wings.

So she braced herself: "And am now, 10.30 on Thursday morning, Nov. 15th [1934], about to tackle re-reading and re-writing The Pargiters. An awful moment." There would be many such moments, some much worse than this, in the coming months. But only writing would restore some degree of equi-

librium in her life even though the work was sure to be "damnably disagreeable." That didn't matter. "I'm using my faculties again. And all the flies
and fleas are forgotten."

Other troubles were brewing, however. Roger's death had come as a terrible blow to Vanessa, and Virginia tried to console her: seeing her more
often, talking about Roger, asking about Julian. Reminiscing made her less
lonely. But whenever Julian's name came up Vanessa ruffled "like a formidable hen." This was irritating. Julian was a special topic with Vanessa and
she guarded him jealously. To Virginia that kind of partiality exemplified
"the religion and superstition of motherhood." When Leonard spoke of him
"emphatically but reasonably," she was also reasonable "but cold." Vanessa
was by now aware that both Virginia and Leonard were critical of her son—
and his poetry. He had recently sent Virginia some poems in manuscript;
and she had read them, with no hint whatever that they might be good
enough for the Hogarth Press to publish. And so naturally Vanessa felt injured, perhaps more than Julian himself did. She was blind to his faults. In
her eyes, anyone with sense could see that he was talented, charming, gifted,
and so on—thus increasing Virginia's annoyance. If he was so charming and
gifted, Virginia asked herself, then why does he "beg us to get him a job?"

On a rainy Sunday morning in early December, Virginia went to see her
friend Francis Birrell, now slowly dying of brain cancer in his hotel room in
Russell Square. She sat with him for an hour and noted the large lump on
his forehead. He was conscious of his danger, aware that he might not survive
a second operation, that he might stiffen slowly into complete paralysis; aware
that his brain might go and his body live on. "All this he knows; and there
it was between us, as we joked. He came to the verge of it once or twice.
But I can't feel any more at the moment—not after Roger . . . I kissed him.
'This is the first time—this chaste kiss' he said. So I kissed him again. But
I must not cry, I thought, and so went." He died one month later.

"I am pained . . . about Vita and Gwen," Virginia wrote to Ethel Smyth in
early January 1935. Harold thought Vita had "grown very slack. So I said
'she sits in her red tower—and dreams.'" And he agreed. Vita refused "to
see anyone but _____." And that was true. With Gwen St. Aubyn
now living at Sissinghurst, Vita had achieved that conjugal serenity she had
tried, and failed, to gain with Violet Trefusis fourteen years earlier. With
Gwen now by her side, Vita increasingly cut herself off from others.

Virginia tried, in vain, to rekindle the embers. "I'm longing for an adventure, dearest Creature. But would like to stipulate for at least 48½ minutes alone with you. Not to say or do anything in particular. Mere affection." She was filled with romantic dreams. Did Vita remember once sitting in Kew Gardens in a storm? "So let me know, and love me better and better, and put another rung on the ladder and let me climb up."

In early February, the long-suffering T. S. Eliot came to Tavistock Square for tea. Virginia's heart went out to him. He seemed so flat and forlorn. Leonard questioned him on a piece he'd written about A. A. Milne's antiwar tract, *Peace with Honour*. Eliot responded with a surge of feeling, releasing a passion he seldom revealed to anyone. "A religious soul," Virginia thought, listening to him, "an unhappy man; a lonely very sensitive man, all wrapt up in fibres of self torture, doubt, conceit, desire for warmth and intimacy." She was so like him in her own "reserves and subterfuges."

Some six or seven weeks later, she went to see him at the home of Father Eric Cheetham, Vicar of St. Stephen's Church, where Eliot had been living for about a year as Vicar's Warden. Here in South Kensington Eliot had a small angular room which Virginia found shabby and dismal. There were bookcases with missing shelves, gloomy wallpaper, chairs too hard for comfort, nothing pretty to look at. "I forgot to ask you to drink sherry," said Eliot, pointing to the bottle and glasses. But it was time to go and Virginia felt they were both glad the visit was over. "A pallid very cold experience. He stood on the steps—it is the Kensington Rectory and he shares the bath with curates . . . our great poet."

It was more than the "decorous ugliness" of Eliot's room that disheartened Virginia. She was feeling a "vast sorrow" with all of life this winter. Roger was dead; Vanessa was away; Ethel Smyth was wearing thin; the novel had become a torment. And then there was Vita. Leonard and Virginia had driven in a blinding snowstorm to Sissinghurst on Sunday, March 10. On the following day Virginia turned to her diary: "My friendship with Vita is over. Not with a quarrel, not with a bang, but as ripe fruit falls. No, I shan't be coming to London before I go to Greece, she said . . . But her voice saying 'Virginia?' outside the tower room was as enchanting as ever. Only then nothing happened . . . Well, it's like cutting off a picture: there she hangs, in the fishmongers at Sevenoaks, all pink jersey and pearls," wrote Virginia, recalling again that December day almost ten years earlier—"and that's an end of it." There was no bitterness or disillusion, "only a certain emptiness."

The friendship was not over. It was Virginia's depression that spoke. She was in her fifty-fourth year and feeling old and redundant. All of her troubles had gathered and pressed her into a state of vulnerability not far from despair. Her rapport with Vita had now reached a more realistic footing that would endure the remaining years of her life; the voluptuous aristocrat she loved so much, the large maternal protecting figure, was drifting beyond her reach, and there was nothing she could do to stop it.

Sissinghurst Castle, with all its symbolic meaning, was becoming the center of Vita's world, a safe, reclusive world of continuity and pattern, with Gwen St. Aubyn securely settled within its walls. Vita strode her own grounds now, dressed in breeches and high boots. Her earliest fantasies of manhood were swelling to life, and her craving for self-governance was now taking the shape of solitude in the guarded privacy of her tower room. There she sat, alone, writing her books and scanning her poems "with thousands of pigeons cooing over her head." And from all this Virginia was now excluded. Long ago, Julia, preoccupied with her dead Herbert, had kept Virginia outside her emotional orbit; now Vita, with Gwen on her arm, was doing the same thing; it was almost as if Mrs. Ramsay and Orlando were in league together.

As Virginia contemplated her altered relations with Vita, the attack which Wyndham Lewis had inaugurated a few months earlier was now resumed by two new hostile combatants. They would make her feel not only excluded and unwanted but despised as well. Prince Dmitri Mirsky was the first of these. In a book called *The Intelligentsia of Great Britain*, published in English in 1935, he gave a Marxist analysis of Bloomsbury that was both contentious and abrasive. Members of Bloomsbury, being "theoreticians of the passive, dividend-drawing and consuming section of the bourgeoisie . . . are extremely intrigued by their own minutest inner experiences, and count them an inexhaustible treasure store of further more minutious inner experiences . . . Having 'one's own room' in which one can escape from the outer world and its racket is, so we are informed by a book written by Virginia Woolf on the emancipation of women, the first condition of civilised creative work." Woolf's lyrical method, Mirsky went on to say, "is devised in order to master the particular suffering and dissolve it away. The suffering is wrapped up in self-contained rhythms and sublimated from the world of reality to a world of esthetics"—from the world of granite to the world of rainbow, he might have said. "Her lulling rhythms are a fine example of the narcotic function which art takes on in the hands of liberal esthetes, who turn it into a new and more perfect form of dope, though of course one not intended for the people."

The second assault came from Frank Swinnerton in *The Georgian Literary Scene*. To him Virginia Woolf was "on the whole creatively unimportant."

She was essentially "an impressionist, a catcher at memory of her own mental vagaries, and not a creator. She is aware, too, of many of the latest scientific facts and theories about human beings, but she is unable to imagine, to create, a human being who is not exactly like herself." Psychologically, she "is as much at fault as the so-called realists, in thinking that if she chases every detail she will find truth." Perhaps Jane Austen "was wiser and less anxiously exploratory; but Jane Austen had more creative imagination than cultivated brains. How odd that Virginia Woolf cannot see this."

All these "blasts from the outer world" affected her as "a robin affects a rhinoceros—except in the depths of the night." She was resilient but she was also fatalistic. However much she tried to brush these sneers aside, the scorn of Mirsky and Lewis and Swinnerton made her feel "hated and despised and ridiculed . . . If I didn't feel so much, how easy it would be to go on." If she hadn't *The Pargiters* to occupy her with its endless problems, the "severe swingeings" of her three tormentors, coupled with her "loss" of Vita, might have had a far more devastating result.

On May 1, a Wednesday, Leonard, Virginia, and Mitz, the marmoset Leonard had acquired during the previous summer, set off by car for their annual holiday. They crossed from Harwich to Holland by the night boat and motored through much of Germany to Austria. In almost every German town, they met with anti-Semitic placards and in one city found themselves on the verge of a Nazi demonstration. From Innsbruck they crossed the Brenner Pass into Italy on May 13 and drove leisurely through Florence and Perugia, reaching Rome by the sixteenth, where they spent a week with Vanessa, Quentin, and Angelica, now living there in a rented studio. The Woolfs left Italy on the twenty-fourth and drove through the Italian and French Rivieras and through central France to Chartres and Dieppe, arriving at Monks House on the last day of May.

In preparing for the tour through Nazi Germany, Leonard had consulted a member of the Foreign Office, Ralph Wigram, who lived in nearby Southease. Virginia wrote in a letter just before departing that "Leonard's nose is so long and hooked, we rather suspect that we shall be flayed alive." In fact, the Woolfs were provided with a letter from Prince Otto von Bismarck, "since our Jewishness is said to be a danger." Bismarck was Counsellor at the Embassy in London. On April 22 Wigram and his wife, Ava, came to tea at Monks House. He'd just returned from Berlin, where he had met with Hitler. When they left, Virginia recorded their conversation in her journal: "I want room to move about, Hitler said . . . No ideals except equality, superiority, force, possessions . . . Talks of himself as the regenerator . . . Wigram and the rest frightened. Anything may happen at any moment . . . And if we have only nice public schoolboys to guide us, there is some reason I suppose to expect that Oxford Street will be flooded with poison gas one of these days."

Undaunted by Hitler or by "our Jewishness," the Woolfs set off as planned. A few days before their departure Virginia confessed that "all desire to practice the art of a writer has completely left me." A change was necessary, no matter how perilous it might prove to be. After all, Leonard had in his pocket an impressive letter from Prince Otto von Bismarck, telling all German officials to show the Englishman and "his distinguished wife, Virginia Woolf, every courtesy and render them any assistance which they might require." In addition to this precious letter, Leonard had the equally precious marmoset, Mitz, sitting on his shoulder or nuzzled in his waistcoat, accompanying him wherever he went. And Mitz, it appears, was a great hit—"wherever we went little groups of people would surround the car and go into ecstasies" over this nervous, chattering handful of fur.

When they reached Bonn, they found themselves facing an excited German policeman, shouting orders to retreat; the road was closed to traffic: Herr Präsident was coming—that is, Hermann Wilhelm Goering. The main thoroughfare was lined with uniformed Nazis and rows of schoolchildren waving flags. The Woolfs found themselves in precisely the kind of situation Ralph Wigram had advised them to avoid. Luckily, it was a warm day and Leonard had wound the roof back so that they were driving in an open car; and on his shoulder sat Mitz, engrossed with the noisy crowds. "When they saw Mitz, the crowd shrieked . . . Mile after mile I drove between the two lines of corybantic Germans, and the whole way they shouted 'Heil Hitler! Heil Hitler!' to Mitz and gave her (and secondarily Virginia and me) the Hitler salute with outstretched arm." They could forget about Bismarck's letter: Mitz carried them through triumphantly. "Pig-tailed schoolchildren, yellow-haired Aryan Fräuleins, blond blowy Fraus, grim stormtroopers went into ecstasies over *das liebe, kleine Ding* . . . It was obvious to the most anti-Semitic stormtrooper that no one who had on his shoulder such a 'dear little thing' could be a Jew."

When they reached Rome, Virginia found a letter awaiting her from the Prime Minister, Ramsay MacDonald, asking if he could submit her name to the King for inclusion in his Birthday Honours as a member of the Order of Companions of Honour. She refused the honor. It was all "d_____d nonsense."

Virginia had departed from England exhausted from *The Pargiters*. Now toward the end of the holiday, she was anxious to return to it. But as they made their homeward journey, she couldn't get her mind off Wyndham Lewis and Prince Mirsky and Frank Swinnerton—"how I'm disliked, how I'm laughed at." By May 29, she was feeling imprisoned and couldn't wait for the "cage doors" to open.

The last two days had become as intolerable as the first two had been rapturous. "How insipid life is without—writing is it?" It would be a long time before she went touring again, looking endlessly at scenery. It meant no talking, no writing, no reading. It was like having "a pane of glass" pressed over one's brain. Her mood was beginning to fluctuate; she was becoming irritable; she was about to begin a downward spiral. When they reached Monks House, they found Pinka dead. She had died just the day before. "So that's what's bound to happen," wrote Virginia in her journal; she had learned from her mother that misfortune struck when one least expected it.

By June 1, she was dipping into a depression and desperately needed to return to her book. Only that would help. Her hand was shaking. She must get back to regular working hours. "I can't get into the swim by saying it is Saturday morning and I will write . . . All sorts of habits, of being unconscious of the surface, attentive to other things, have to settle naturally."

This was nothing new. It happened every time. "Every time I say it will be the devil! but I never believe it. And then the usual depressions come. And I wish for death." There was so much to be depressed about—Roger gone; Vanessa away; Vita with Gwen; Mirsky, Lewis, Swinnerton all hating her. Collectively these reminders forced her into dark corners where everything looked distorted and ugly; and in these "incurable moods" she tended to become overly critical, especially of those she needed most.

Leonard, for instance, was too "hard on people," especially on the domestic help. He was harsh and rigid and unduly severe; he expected too much; he was dictatorial. Not with Virginia. No, she wouldn't stand for it. But where did this acerbity come from? "Not being a gentleman partly." He was uneasy around working-class people; he suspected them, was never cordial with them. His brothers were the same. Then too, there was his "desire, I suppose, to dominate. Love of power." Even if he preached against it, Leonard himself was power-hungry and that made domestic life sometimes rocky. He was also excessively "touchy" about his family: "an inferiority complex I call it."

Tension was building up in the Bell household and once again Julian was behind it. Despite the mutual adoration of mother and son, Vanessa could no longer keep Julian tied to her apron strings. He was now twenty-seven and had to think about a future. In the middle of July he was offered the teaching job he had applied for the previous year. It was the post of Professor of English at the National University of Wuhan, four hundred miles up the Yangtze River in China. He would be gone for three years and return a "full grown mature man, with a place in the world," wrote Virginia in her journal. She would miss him, of course, but Vanessa's pining away, her languishing for Julian, would bother Virginia most. She adored mothers and babies, she said, but detested a "child being covered with maternal spit" after the age of ten. "That's what queers the pitch, and makes Aunts detest their nephews. But up till 10—there I am with you." She quite understood that Vanessa's children were her most prized possessions and would forever infringe upon the love she craved for herself. Even so, at the age of fifty-three she was still imploring Vanessa to "please love me—I'm such a darling—and getting very wild without you."

During the summer months Virginia was once more in the thick of *The Pargiters*. She finished a "first wild retyping" and found the book came to 740 pages. Much of it would need to be rewritten, but that could wait. Meanwhile Leonard and Virginia had a "reconciliation" dinner with John Lehmann. He had always admired Virginia's work too much to let his difficulties with Leonard stand in the way; but more than that, he still wanted a career in publishing; and by this time the "indignation and injury on both sides had faded."

The most wearisome task of the summer, however, was Margery Fry's asking Virginia to open the Roger Fry Memorial Exhibition at the Bristol Museum and Art Gallery on July 12. This was a request she could not refuse, and it turned out to be an ordeal. It was a stifling day and Leonard somehow misread the map and got lost. They arrived, sticky and crumpled, just in time for the proceedings to begin. There was a large audience of the "most stodgy and respectable" kind, and because of the heat an electric fan was kept going, so that Virginia could scarcely make herself heard. More important, she felt that neither Margery nor Pamela, Roger's daughter, much liked what she had to say. It all seemed rather a waste of time and effort. Margery, it appears, never wrote to thank Virginia for all the trouble; and Virginia was left with the unsettling impression that the Frys' view of Roger was "completely different" from hers and Vanessa's. And this difference, whether real or imagined, would be a source of endless doubt and anxiety in the months ahead.

A few weeks later, Margery Fry sent Virginia three large boxes of Roger's letters and papers. Sometime in the early winter of 1935 it was evidently settled that Virginia would write his life—not "a whole big life" but something "lesser and slighter." Still, what difficulties she would have to face. Worse than that, "what a time it'll take."

Virginia was pushing herself to the limit. By mid-August she was typing *The Pargiters* out at a rate of one hundred pages a week. While the typewriter clicked away, ideas for *Three Guineas* (the sequel to *A Room of One's Own*) kept swimming to the surface and she had all she could do to keep the lid shut tight. By September 5, she was exhausted. "I've had to give up writing The Years—that's what it's to be called—this morning. Absolutely floored ... Can't pump up a word ... so I shall wait, a day or two, and let the well fill. It has to be damned deep this time—740 pages in it." By September 12, the writing had become a mixture of Ecstasy and Hell: "never have I had such a hot balloon in my head as re-writing The Years; because it's so long; and the pressure is so terrific." The trick was to steady herself, keep herself sane, avoid a headache, ration the work a little—"I will broach the three boxes of Roger; very staidly, merely beginning to drop a few facts into my brain."

And so a schedule was established. She rewrote *The Years* all morning and read Roger Fry's papers with a notebook in hand between tea and dinner. When the novel became too demanding, she turned to Roger, an "admirable sedative and refresher." Some mornings she spent typing out her Fry notes; but now *Three Guineas*—the book had no name yet—again began surfacing. It was becoming an obsession; it was "like being harnessed to a shark."

The truth was all of her work was becoming a little frenzied. She contemplated finishing *The Years* in January, then dashing off *Three Guineas* in six weeks, then writing the Fry biography during the summer. Some deep, driving force was propelling her remorselessly. It was as though her world were falling apart and the only way she could hold it together was with words, with writing—any writing; it didn't matter what. The world of the Pargiters, the world of Roger Fry, the world of Virginia Woolf—all of these were beginning to tilt, to collide, to slip out of control. Only by fitting words together could she regain coherence and wholeness.

By November 1, again she was floored—"can't concentrate on The Years." It seems not to have occurred to her, during her rewriting of the novel, that she was still attempting to transform fact into fiction, trying still to conceal the smell of the past with incense, whitewashing the truth—in fact *pargeting* this Pargiter chronicle. It was a problem she would again have to face in Roger's life in dealing with his wife's madness. And how was she to talk about his love affair with Vanessa? to tell that story without hurting her sister? How could she betray the trust of a man who had believed in her so implicitly?

More and worse was yet to come. If there was anyone now, apart from Leonard, she could talk to it was Vita. But Vita was sealed up in her tower, with Gwen still in the shadows. Their letters had dwindled. And sadly, Vita in her cherished solitude had gone to seed, had grown heavy. The beautiful expressive eyes were now hidden in flesh, the sensuous mouth slack, all her loveliness gone.

But there were difficulties of another kind now pressing for attention. The Hogarth Press was going through a lean period, Leonard said, and they had to begin thinking about money. Perhaps Virginia would consider journalism again. After all, she hadn't written a "serious" novel since *The Waves*—over four years ago. But with all the abuse she had suffered recently, what ought she to expect from her readers? And what would the literary public think of her writing articles again? And there was Hitler to think about, and Mussolini, both disturbing the balance of European power; an international crisis was brewing; as a writer, how would she be affected? That was still another worry.

Toward the end of December Virginia was "almost extinct." She had just finished another revision—now a 797-page version of *The Years*. But was it any good? She didn't know. Did it hang together? Was it whole? Who could tell? Only one thing was certain: a great deal of work still remained to be done, and how long it would take she didn't know. This was critical work and it was drudgery. She must prepare "another creative mood, or . . . sink into acute despair." But it was too late. By December 30: "I can't write a word . . . Can only look back at The Years as an inaccessible Rocky Island which I can't explore, can't even think of." Was she remembering the out-stretched arms her father had ignored? The concealed laughter at her mother's death? Was it the rivalry, the jealousy, the feeling of exclusion she'd felt on May 5, 1895? Was it the guilt and the shame these thoughts engen-dered? No one could say. The dissonance was intolerable, however, and the headache returned, this time in earnest.

With excruciating pain she met the new year. It was now 1936 and *The Years* was laboring into its fourth year, still unfinished. More eagerly now, she returned to the mountain of documents Margery Fry had entrusted to her. Reading through the letters had become part of her working day. She wouldn't begin writing *Roger Fry* until April 1, 1938.

Then money suddenly became an urgency. Leonard opened the account books and pointed out that for the first time in many years Virginia had not earned enough to pay her share of their joint expenses. She had to withdraw seventy pounds from her "hoard," which had now dwindled to £700. "Amusing, in a way, to think of economy again," she wrote in her journal. "But it would be a strain to think seriously; and worse—a brutal interruption—had I to make money by journalism." What she now wanted most was to have the novel out of the way—it would be like having a "bony excrescence" cut out of her brain.

In mid-January, she read over the last part and sank into a trough of despair. It was feeble, diffuse, long-winded. "I could only plump it down on the table and rush up stairs with burning cheeks to Leonard." This always happened, he calmly reminded her. "But I felt, no it has never been so bad as this." Bad as it was, however, she fought fatigue and headache and forced herself to press on, writing each morning from ten to one and again in the afternoon from five to seven. The most extraordinary thing about writing was that "when you've struck the right vein, tiredness goes. It must be an effort, thinking wrong." Whether the thinking was right or wrong, she per-sisted in telling her ugly story of the Pargiters, working every day with com-plete concentration. By the end of February, she had written at *The Years* with such absorption the outside world began to seem "a kind of amplifica-tion, variation in another key."

On March 10, the first 132 pages of the novel were sent to the printers, R. & R. Clark of Edinburgh. This was an unusual step for Virginia. Normally Leonard read her novel in typescript first before sending it off; the printer then supplied them with page proofs for final correction. This time, Leonard would read the book in galleys before sending it to Harcourt Brace in New York. Perhaps seeing the book at the galley-proof stage made its publication seem a little more inevitable. Or perhaps it was easier to throw galleys into the fire than page proofs. Whatever the reason, work on *The Years* went on at a relentless pace.

 King George V died at Sandringham on January 20 after a short illness. His body was taken through London to lie in state at Westminster Hall. Leonard and Virginia waited outside in the Square to watch the hearse go by. All London was suddenly in an orgy of emotion. "Old greybearded ladies" were taking flying leaps over the railings, "and though some stalwarts held the gates, the mob was on us." Leonard got crushed between "5 fat grocers." Still it was a magnificent sight—"the crown glittering blue and white, and the long yellow leopards stretched over the coffin." There was something strangely primitive, even barbaric, about public grief. All England was "deluged in tears and muffled in crape." So much raw emotion, such extravagant ritual for the King, that "very commonplace man who was like ourselves."

The new King, Edward VIII, Virginia had been told, was a "cheap little bounder" who kept two mistresses and shunned marriage. He enjoyed "dropping in to tea" with the wives of miners. And he had been so abused by his father, it was said, that when King George died, all Edward could do to express his emotion was have the clocks put back by thirty minutes. One of the King's little eccentricities was to keep the clocks at Sandringham a half hour fast. Edward's first royal decision therefore was to restore them all to Greenwich time.

Vita's mother, aged seventy-three, died in Brighton on January 30. Lady Sackville's ashes were strewn on the nearby waters, Virginia wrote to Hugh Walpole, now in Hollywood working on a movie. Vita and Harold had hired a steam launch and "are at this moment tossing up and down" with the remains of this eccentric and quarrelsome woman. But this was all local gossip. Of great national consequence to Great Britain was now the power-mad figure of Adolf Hitler. All England was under his shadow.

On March 7, he marched his troops into the demilitarized zone of the Rhineland in defiance of the Treaty of Versailles and the Locarno Pact. Neither Britain nor France had taken steps to force his withdrawal. It was a time of foreboding; each day passed under the threat of disaster. Small groups of French and British intellectuals were convening to discuss the ever-worsening international crisis. Virginia was a member of a group called For Intellectual Liberty, roughly comparable to the French organization of anti-Fascist intellectuals known as the Comité de Vigilance; and Leonard found himself submerged in politics and committee meetings—"all day, every day ... I might be the charwoman of a Prime Minister," said Virginia.

However inconvenient and unsettling all this was, it did not compare to the torture Virginia was forcing herself to endure with *The Years*. "I have never suffered, since The Voyage Out, such acute despair on re-reading, as this time," she noted in her diary on March 16. She was facing "complete failure," she was certain, and thought more than once of destroying the manuscript. "Then I set to: in despair ... but went on typing. After an hour, the line began to taughten. Yesterday I read it again; and think it may be my best book." Rarely had there ever been such wild fluctuations. Now there were also headaches and insomnia. Still she persisted. On April 8, she posted the final section to the printer, who by this time had begun returning the earlier parts. She could still make large changes in the galleys, but that was small consolation. "The horror is that tomorrow, after this one windy day of respite ... I must begin at the beginning and go through 600 pages of cold proof." The book was a "complete flop." The earlier revision had been a terrific strain. By April 14 she was flattened with pain, lying on two chairs, "befogged, utterly vacant and vapid."

Leonard had been observing her closely and now, fearing she might be headed for a nervous breakdown, took her to Monks House to recover. As soon as they heard that the American edition would not come out before October, Leonard persuaded Virginia to postpone publication until 1937. This was a temporary relief. So as the galleys arrived from the printer, Virginia stuffed them away without looking at them, and took a four-week break from the book. For the remainder of April she was confined either to her bed or to the sofa, tortured by headaches, unable even to look at a newspaper. Whenever the pain subsided, sleep took its place. This was the "cursed irritable head piece" she had inherited from her father, who had in turn inherited his from his father.

Virginia's doctor, Ellie Rendel, agreed with Leonard that a change of atmosphere might do Virginia some good. So from May 8 to the 20th they made a tour of the west country. When they got back to London, they decided to move to Rodmell and remain there for the entire summer. The past two months, and the months to come, were to be darkened by depression. Not for many years had Virginia been so close to suicide.

On Thursday, June 11, Virginia took out her diary, unopened since April, and made the following entry: "I can only, after 2 months, make this brief note, to say at last after 2 months dismal and worse, almost catastrophic illness—never been so near the precipice to my own feeling since 1913." Much of the novel, she knew, would have to be cut and revised further—"Oh but the divine joy of being mistress of my mind again!" Her relief lasted only a week, however. Then came the "intense suffering—indeed mornings of torture."

But what was behind this tortured writing? The answer is embedded in this June 11 diary entry—"never been so near the precipice of my own feeling since 1913." As it happens, the 1913 section of *The Years* is one of the shortest in the novel. More significant, it deals with the servant Crosby and the dog Rover. In two years' time, when she was composing *Three Guineas* and assaulting the adult male's "infantile fixation," her examples would point to domineering fathers and submissive daughters: ". . . we [the daughters of educated men] . . . become aware at once of some 'strong emotion' on your side . . . by a ringing of an alarm bell within us . . . The physical symptoms are unmistakable . . . there is a strong desire . . . to change the conversation, *to drag in . . . some old family servant, called Crosby, whose dog Rover died . . . and so evade the issue*" (emphasis added).

The year 1913 in Virginia's life was a critical one. After delivering her manuscript of *The Voyage Out* to Gerald Duckworth, we recall, she suffered a prolonged nervous breakdown which culminated in her suicide attempt in September of that year. Yet, in *The Years*, this novel of fact, there was no hint of any corresponding horror. Virginia instead dragged in Crosby, the old family servant, and her dog Rover, and in doing so *evaded* some "strong emotion." That is to say, she had pargeted some deep well of feeling. How many other deep wells she plastered over and locked away from recognition only Virginia herself could say—and evidently wouldn't. For those feelings probably had more to do with her longing for her father than with her mixed feelings for Leonard.

During these revisions she made numerous changes in narrative perspective and characterization; but the most conspicuous alteration was in the character of Abel Pargiter—the generalized Abel Pargiter of the original draft reshaped into the more particularized Abel Pargiter of the published novel. That is, in *The Pargiters*, it appears that *all* fathers with *all* their faults had been siphoned into the person of Abel Pargiter, the Victorian prototype which called forth from Virginia a flood of abuse and accusation; whereas the Abel Pargiter of *The Years* was more the particular father she knew and loved, and was attempting desperately to recover.

Subtleties of characterization, needless to say, get lost in so heavily populated a novel; but if Virginia Woolf had been conscious of the changes she was making in the person of Colonel Pargiter, then it is highly probable that as the book advanced from one revision to the next, she became increasingly conscious that she was writing into her novel more about the ugly truths of the Stephen family at 22 Hyde Park Gate than about "one of those typical English families" she described in the First Essay of *The Pargiters*. The more aware she became of exhuming damaging confessional material, the more she had to be on her guard against turning her father into a loathsome ghost upon whom too much blame was being heaped for the wrongs she herself had suffered in childhood and now saw with the terrible clarity of an adult.

For in writing this "novel of fact" she was compelled to deal with long-"forgotten" memories which forced her to plumb the subterranean world of emotion; to grope and stumble through darkened nurseries; to revisit sweet-scented death rooms; to relive ancient facts of childhood and adolescence; to reawaken states of feeling, sometimes benign, more often morbid—feelings of exclusion and jealousy and rivalry—and somehow capture them all in the intricate tissue of words. It was the shaping and molding of all these antiquated and mildewed relics that most ravaged her. For if the facts in the finished novel were to be stated—all of them verifiable—then the *truth* of those facts had to be phrased poetically, adorned, softened, made eloquent through ellipsis and metaphor. She would have to rely more heavily on the "disguises" Muriel Bradbrook had earlier described, deliberate "asides" calculated to diminish their starkness and brutality. However one chooses to phrase it, those recognizable "facts" that would finally appear in cold print had to be *pargeted*; had in some way to be veiled and varnished if they were to be made public and palatable.

Revising *The Years* thus became not so much a labor of literary skill, though it was certainly that too, as a monumental mission which called into action her moral character both as a woman and daughter and as an artist. She must tell the truth; but how was she to do so without blackening the Stephen family history and a social system from which she herself had sprung and of which she herself was altogether a product? If *The Years* failed, its author would be morally exiled.

And so, day by day, during this long, tortured summer, when it was possible, Virginia concentrated for just one hour at a time correcting proofs. The rest of the day she lay out in the garden, took short walks, wrote a few notes, rested at intervals, and did her best to avoid people and talk and excitement. By late August, having stuck faithfully to this convalescent regimen, she began slowly to get better.

By November she was able to tell Julian she had cut the novel from 700 to 420 pages. But it was pretty bad, and probably not worth publishing. When the Woolfs returned to London in early October, Virginia had still not finished correcting. By November 2, however, she was again in such misery Leonard decided he had better begin reading the novel. To his enormous relief, it was not so bad as she had led him to expect. On the following day she wrote in her long-neglected diary: "Miracles will never cease—Leonard actually likes The Years! He thinks it so far . . . as good as any of my books."

Two days earlier, Virginia had begun reading proofs and was soon in such despair she carried them "like a dead cat" to Leonard and told him to burn them unread. A great deal of money had already been invested in the book. The proofs alone would cost about three hundred pounds, which she would have to pay out of her own funds. She would call Bruce Richmond and ask for books to review. There were seven hundred pounds in her savings account; this would leave her with a balance of four hundred. It was on that same evening that Leonard began reading. He "read and read and said nothing"; and she began to feel one of her "horrid heats and deep slumbers, as if the blood in my head had been cut off." Then Leonard put the proofs down and said he thought it "extraordinarily good—as good as any of them" and went on reading. By Wednesday he reached the end of the "1914" section and still thought it "extraordinarily good."

It was an interesting but very sad book, he thought. Virginia couldn't bring herself to believe him. "It may be simply that I exaggerated its badness, and therefore he now, not finding it so bad, exaggerates its goodness." By Thursday, however, the miracle was accomplished. "Leonard put down the last sheet about 12 last night; and could not speak. He was in tears." He said it was "a remarkable book" and hadn't the slightest doubt that it must be published. His judgment was all she could cling to, but her relief was overwhelming.

Many years later in his memoir, Leonard Woolf confessed that his verdict of *The Years* was "not absolutely and completely what I thought about it. As I read it I was greatly relieved . . . most publishers would have been glad to publish it as it stood. I thought it a good deal too long . . . To Virginia I praised the book more than I should have done if she had been well." But Leonard's verdict was like waking "from death." It was indeed an incredible night. "Whatever happens I don't think I can be destroyed. Only work, work is essential." She made this diary entry on November 24.

For the rest of the month she revised *The Years* mercilessly. She cut out "bodily two enormous chunks." Scarcely a page escaped some drastic alteration. On November 30 part of the proofs was sent off to the printers, and at the end of December the final pages were dispatched. "There is no need whatever in my opinion to be unhappy about The Years," she wrote soon after. But she was whistling in the dark, for no one knew its dodges and omissions better than its author. In reality she was preparing herself for the horrors that would descend as she waited through the long, anxious months for publication.

With her gradual disburdening of *The Years*, the world outside, held so long in abeyance, was allowed once more to enter daily life. The Spanish Civil War, which had broken out in July, now became a source of worry, for Julian, still in China, was brimming with youthful patriotism. The Fascist uprising in Spain was expected to continue into France, and Julian was anxious to participate in the effort to resist Fascism. In England, now preoccupied with the growing power of Hitler and Mussolini, Winston Churchill was calling for rearmament to bolster the ineffectiveness of the League of Nations.

Troubles were also multiplying in the Royal Family. On December 2, some northern provincial newspapers reported the Bishop of Bradford's regrets that King Edward was not a more ardent member of the Church. The London press, having until now kept respectfully quiet on the subject, broke out with a flood of commentary about the King and his determination to marry the twice-divorced American, Mrs. Wallis Simpson. Fascinated by the imminent abdication, Virginia recorded Prince Edward's broadcast from the Augusta Tower of Windsor Castle on the evening of December 11: " 'Prince Edward speaking from Windsor Castle'—as the emotional butler announced. Upon which, with a slight stammer at first, in a steely strained voice . . . the King . . . began: 'At long last . . . I can speak to you . . . The woman I love . . . I who have none of those blessings . . . ' Well, one came in touch with human flesh, I suppose . . . a very ordinary young man; but the thing had never been done on that scale. One man set up in the Augusta Tower at Windsor Castle addressing the world on behalf of himself and Mrs Simpson."

The Instrument of Abdication had in fact been signed by the King the day before, on the morning of December 10. His message to Parliament was read to the House of Commons in the afternoon. King Edward VIII's reign was technically terminated with the passage of the Abdication Bill through both Houses of Parliament on the next day, December 11, when Edward's brother, Albert, Duke of York, succeeded him as King George VI.

By the strangest of coincidences, just as Virginia thought she had finished with private history in packing off *The Years*, Violet Dickinson from the distant past momentarily entered her life again. From 1902 to about 1907 Violet had been one of Virginia's most intimate friends. Virginia had found in her a mother and protector and, after 1904, even a father-substitute. For almost three years Violet was the center of Virginia's world. She advised her on everything from bedroom slippers to the tone of her writing exercises, and it was through Violet that Virginia met Mrs. Arthur Lyttelton, who published her first essays at the end of 1904 in the *Manchester Guardian*.

In early December Virginia received typescript copies of some 350 letters, bound in two volumes, she had written to Violet in those early years. Enclosed in the parcel was also a little silver peacock she had given Violet as a gift. Virginia thanked her friend, now in her seventies: ". . . all those scattered fragments of my disjected [*sic*] and egotistic youth. Do you like that girl?" she asked. "I'm not sure that I do, though I think she had some spirit in her, and certainly was rather ground down harshly by fate . . . At points I became filled with such a gust from her tragic past, I couldn't read on . . . But one thing emerges whole and lucid—how very good you were to me, and how very trying I was . . . so full of storms and rhapsodies . . . Well, thank you for everything—if I were to write out what I mean by that, I should need many many pages."

A second echo from the past came in a Christmas letter from Janet Case, who had many years before taught Virginia Greek and now lived with her sister Emphie in the New Forest, where she earned a meager income writing Nature Notes for the *Manchester Guardian*. In 1914 when Virginia was recovering from her breakdown and staying at Asheham House, Janet Case had come to look after her in Leonard's absence. She was now slowly dying from Graves' disease. On Christmas Eve Virginia wrote her to "please do get well." She and Leonard wanted to visit. "I've been thinking so much of you this past month, that if thought were visible you'd have seen something luminous in the middle of the laurel bush." She told Janet about the "2 huge volumes" Violet had just sent her. Janet Case's name came up so often in the letters: "I could see you coming up to my room at the top of the house and saying, You've not done any work! ... And what a bore I must have been ... I think the young have easier lives than we had, but then I don't believe they have such affection as I had, and have, for Janet Case." (Miss Lucy Craddock, Kitty Malone's tutor in *The Years*, appears to have been modeled on Janet Case.)

And evoking more recent history was the fish Vita sent for Christmas, as though to refresh Virginia's memory of the image of December 1925 so frequently recalled: "... d'you think it's the very same that got caught and hung in the fishmonger's shop at Sevenoaks?" It looked like the same fish that "winked at you in your pink jersey and white pearls." It was an image Virginia would never let go of.

The opening of 1937 was filled with anticipation anxiety, and the only remedy Virginia could think of was "work, work, work." She was writing *Three Guineas*, begun the previous November, and intended to go on with it at full tilt, or so she said. But in fact she was steeling herself against March 15, the official publication date of *The Years*. *Three Guineas* was her protection from the "dull cold torture" during the days of waiting.

In the middle of February a new worry materialized. Leonard became suddenly ill and no one, it appears, could diagnose his trouble. He might be suffering from diabetes; or it might be a prostate disorder; or it might be nothing at all. On the day of his appointment with a Harley Street specialist to hear some test results, Virginia was frantic: "I must face facts: how to keep cool, how to control myself if it is a bad report. Work is my only help." On that cold Friday afternoon, outside the doctor's office, she paced the street for an hour; "people looked at me; I bought a paper; dropped my handkerchief; always returned to the swing door ... People kept going in and out. And I hardly could make myself turn my back." As it turned out, Leonard was given a clean bill of health. But her extraordinary response to his health is an eloquent testament of their relations at this time. Virginia never had trouble manufacturing disasters of the worst kind; and in the midst of all this Miss Margaret West, the efficient manager of the Hogarth Press, suddenly died of pneumonia, thereby increasing the work hours for both Leonard and Virginia until some new replacement could be found.

Despite her reading and note-taking of Roger's papers, her journalism, and her work on *Three Guineas*, Virginia still could not divert an anxiety that

threatened to descend at any time with devastating effect. One new acquaintance, Christopher Isherwood, briefly attracted her attention during this interval. She liked Isherwood. He was "very small, red cheeked, nimble and
vivacious." The Hogarth Press had already published two of his books and
would bring out an additional two. He had been living abroad with his
German lover and was now in London for rehearsals at the Mercury Theatre
of *The Ascent of F6*, the play he had written with W. H. Auden. Isherwood
has "put some colour into my cheeks," Virginia wrote in her journal. "He
said Morgan [E. M. Forster] and I were the only living novelists the young
... take seriously." This pleased her enormously, but Isherwood and his
friends brought Julian Bell once more into the foreground.

At the end of January, Julian had given up his professorship at Wuhan
University and sailed for Marseilles, intending to go to Spain to enlist in the
International Brigade. It was a rash, emotional decision and came as a terrible
shock to Vanessa who begged him to return to London to talk with her
before going any further. This he agreed to do and made arrangements to
return on March 14.

Relieved as she was that Julian was coming home, however, Virginia's
preoccupation with the approaching "fatal day" was causing her to become
daily more apprehensive. "I must dig myself deep in 3 Guineas ... It will be
immensely depressing." The *Saturday Review* (February 6) had just published
an article called "Virginia Woolf and Feminine Fiction," and in it Herbert
Muller had described her as "a maker of films and laces; a sitter in shaded
dark rooms." The next lap of her life would be accompanied by "whistlings
and catcalls." Reviewers would say she had "written a long book all about
nothing." They would say it was a "tired book ... a last effort." Well, if she
had to exist in the shade, she would do so. But it was necessary to keep hard
at work. Writing would protect her. That was the secret. She had written in
the original holograph of *The Pargiters*: "Probably people who have been
bullied when they are young, find ways of protecting themselves. Is that the
origin of art? ... making yourself immune by making an image!"

By March 1, the worry was beginning to produce physical symptoms. "I
wish I could write out my sensations at this moment. They are so peculiar
and so unpleasant. Partly Time of Life [menopause]? I wonder. A physical
feeling as if I were drumming slightly in the veins: very cold: impotent: and
terrified ... Very lonely ... Very useless. No atmosphere round me. No
words. Very apprehensive. As if something cold and horrible—a roar of
laughter at my expense were about to happen. And I am powerless to ward
it off. I have no protection ... And I want to burst into tears, but have nothing

to cry for . . . And my own little scraps [of writing] look dried up and derelict. And I know that I must go on doing this dance on hot bricks till I die."

On the following day the "doomed, discarded, ridiculed novelist" continued in the same vein: "I'm going to be beaten, I'm going to be laughed at, I'm going to be held up to scorn." A few days later, even with 5,300 copies of the novel sold before publication, the woeful monotone went on—with this curious variation. The book may be "damned with faint praise; but the point is that I myself know why it's a failure, and that its failure is deliberate. I also know that I have reached my point of view, as writer, as being."

If the "deliberate" failure was due to deliberate pargeting, if she had consciously tampered with the truth, then this was the closest she ever came to saying so. We have only to look at the sequence of chapters in *The Years*— "1880"—"1891"—"1907"—and so on—to realize how much *during* and *in between* those years she had glossed over. *The Years* was unlike *To the Lighthouse*. In the earlier novel she had cast into a poetic mold those prosaic angers and fears of earlier years, and in so doing had bridged the gap between fact and feeling; she had also repressed the ambivalence she felt for her mother and the special relationship she longed to have with her father. So that in writing the *Lighthouse* she came to discover the solipsistic power of the artist, re-creating *on her own terms* that childhood world of helpless passivity. Nothing like this had happened in *The Years*.

In *The Years* she had abandoned the child's vision. The characters were now seen from an adult perspective, and seen from that perspective, all the contaminations of personal history were swept into the narrative. For in shifting away from the child's point of view in *To the Lighthouse* to the presumably more "objective" stance, she discovered that she was giving biographical rather than "aesthetic facts," that she was documenting granite instead of creating rainbow. Virginia in *The Years* had divided herself up into several of the Pargiter daughters: there was Delia, hurrying up her mother's death and laughing secretly at the graveside; there was Rose, filled with both shame and guilt from her public street scene, and the sexual feelings for her father that scene provoked; and there was Eleanor, with a slip of the tongue— buying a gift "For my niece—I mean cousin"*—becoming emotionally and incestuously Abel Pargiter's wife rather than his daughter. In the documentation of all these sordid details, lyrical fluency gave way to factual truculence. "Reality had become too strong," Miss LaTrobe of *Between the Acts* would later say. The truth behind appearance, from the adult point of view, loomed

* See Leaska, 1977, p. 206.

up before her as unalterable and foul and squalid. As one of her detractors had said, Virginia Woolf's lyrical method was devised to "dissolve" human pain—suffering was "wrapped up in self-contained rhythms and sublimated from the world of reality." The beauty of her writing was like a narcotic dulling the pain of truth. But all this, although perhaps true for *To the Lighthouse*, was not true for *The Years*.

45 *The Years* was a battle between poetic expression and factual documentation. The latter won, and in the process Virginia Woolf was forced to plunder the Stephen family cemetery. If by writing she got at the truth, she did so by her own method and on her own private terms. The wholeness she achieved was consequently hers alone; and that "truth" and "wholeness" were not Truth and Wholeness in the abstract Bloomsbury sense. Here, finally, was the crux of the difficulty which probably crystallized at her mother's death, almost certainly at Stella's, and would persist, varying only in intensity, for the remainder of her life. When the first reviews of *The Years* began to appear, we must try to imagine their effect on Virginia Woolf: first, there was relief, then, later, a disappointment so overwhelming that nothing could assuage the disillusionment which followed. It was a bitter achievement and a hollow triumph.

"Oh the relief!" she cried when Leonard brought home the first reviews* in *The Times Literary Supplement* and *Time and Tide*, on Friday, March 12, three days before the scheduled publication. Readers were "in contact not only with a first-rate novelist, who can summon human personalities to her page in the flick of a sentence, but also with a great lyrical poet," wrote Theodora Bosanquet, once Henry James's amanuensis; the *TLS* reviewer called the novel's finale "a brilliant fantasia of all Time's problems, age and youth, change and permanence, truth and illusion." Virginia was ecstatic; to think that her book was "*not* nonsense"; that it *did* have an effect. Now, after all the agony, "I'm free, whole; round. Can go full ahead." This was Friday, March 12. On Sunday: "I am in such a twitter owing to 2 columns in the Observer praising

* The publication date appears to have been changed to March 11.

The Years that I can't . . . go on with 3 Guineas." Just a year earlier she had suffered "the worst summer" of her life. That was now all history.

Virginia Woolf did not differ from other creative artists in the degree to which she depended upon public approval. Part of what seemed to differentiate her from other artists, however, was the extent to which she identified herself with her writing. She had given the Stephen family chronicle in *To the Lighthouse* in lyrical strokes, and the sour strains of parental conflict had been muffled in poetry. The praise had shown her readers to be discriminating. Her identity as a writer, the self who maintained its integrity with words, had been reaffirmed. That was all well and good. But now with *The Years*, a presumably factual account of the same family, that earlier affirmation had become invalidated. For in this later novel, a cacophonous chronicle of discord had been served up to the public. Virginia Woolf had blurred fact with fantasy, had failed artistically in vision and design, had offered the world a pargeted, ill-conceived, overwritten book; and her readers had not only accepted it but had applauded as well. She was caught on the horns of a dilemma: praise for *The Years* invalidated her public. Her readers were indiscriminate, unreliable. If she could make them swallow this book, then the public "echo" she needed so desperately was suddenly worthless. With these readers, there was really no writer, no verifiable self. Their enthusiasm had virtually destroyed their significance. In that collapse, the writing "I" who had spent so many years creating wholeness out of shivering fragments collapsed as well. Her weakest book had catapulted her into the dizzy altitudes of a best-selling novelist.

There was still another complication. Writing was the *only* reality in Virginia Woolf's world, as necessary to her as air and water. Only with words, with writing, could she hold together a world forever threatening to fly apart. And the deepest satisfaction behind her invention was the feeling of self-sufficiency and independence it gave her. But just as love and ambition are incompatible for some people, so for Virginia was success incompatible with her need to be cradled. That is to say, while she needed public recognition, the success her writing brought conflicted with the private image she had of herself as someone needing to be taken care of in a begrudging world. So too did the freedom and independence her writing brought conflict with her incessant demands for love. How could she claim independence when she leaned so heavily on Leonard and Vanessa and Vita? Her need for independence and her tendency toward submission and self-effacement would create insurmountable barriers in the months ahead. A successful woman chained to a helpless child, living side by side, was a combination bound to cause trouble.

"Now at any rate money is assured: Leonard shall have his new car," she wrote after the first flurry over *The Years* had settled. "And my last lap—if I've only 10 years of life more—should be fruitful. Work—work." Her uncertainty in the burst of excitement notwithstanding, Virginia enjoyed the praise—" 'they' say almost universally that The Years is a masterpiece." Her brief moment of glory had come. "And I'm so steeled now I don't think the flutter will much worry me." But she was wrong. In some hidden corner of her mind, she still knew the book was no good.

When the "flutter" did come, all the bright lights went out. Writing for *The Spectator* (March 17), John Sparrow said that Virginia Woolf had "neither retreated nor advanced along the path of her own development"; she had simply written an ordinary book. R.A.S. James in the April issue of *The London Mercury* said she had "not removed from the picture the sense of dreariness and fatuity, however brightly coloured the strands with which the pattern [was] woven." Edwin Muir, in *The Listener* (March 31), found *The Years* "a disappointing book." "Dead and disappointing—" she repeated in her diary, "so I'm found out and that odious rice pudding of a book is what I thought—a dank failure . . . Now this pain woke me at 4 a.m. and I suffered acutely."

This was followed almost immediately by that curious pleasure she got from suffering: "One feels braced for some reason; amused; roused; combative; more than by praise." It provided her once again with a certain license to feel just a little exalted and *immune*. "That is the achievement . . . of my 55 years," she said on April 9. "I lay awake so calm, so content, as if I'd stepped off the whirling world into a deep blue quiet space . . . armed against all that can happen." By early May over 10,000 copies of *The Years* had been sold; and while Virginia was reluctant to buy a coat for herself, she thought nothing of buying Leonard a new car.

Julian Bell had returned from China on March 12, a grown man, Virginia thought. But he seemed to her a little saddened, with lines of tension on his face. They all had dinner together at Charleston and Leonard felt his usual spasm of irritation at Julian's egotism—in fact, the egotism of the whole family. Vanessa thought only of her children; Julian thought only of himself. They were not a very considerate crowd. There was some uneasiness at the dinner table due in part to Leonard's "family complex," or so Virginia claimed.

Behind the uneasiness, however, something else was brewing and that something was Julian's immediate future. Not himself a member of the Communist Party, Julian nevertheless felt compelled to join forces in the fighting in Spain. It was his duty to do so, he was convinced, regardless of the distress such a move would cause his mother. It was a serious decision and Vanessa implored him to abandon the idea, but he was determined. He wouldn't argue. Virginia found him "peppery and pithy—making his strange faces . . . keeping something up his sleeve." In the end there was a compromise. Julian would go not as a soldier in the International Brigade but as an ambulance driver for the Spanish Medical Aid Organization. He must do *something*. He was bitter and disillusioned. Cambridge had given him "only a vague literary smattering"; and now, aged twenty-nine, he found himself with no special training and entirely unprepared for any sort of professional life. He left for Spain on June 7.

By June 1 the American edition of *The Years* had sold 25,000 copies, and remained for many weeks at the top of the best-seller list. For the next several months Virginia kept a running account of the book's sales in her diary: "Monday 14th Jun. The Years still top of the list. Monday 12th July The Years still top of the list. And has been weekly. Aug. 23rd: Years now 2nd or 3rd. 9 editions. Yesterday, October 22nd, it was last on the list." Even William Faulkner, future Nobel laureate, "most intelligently (and highly) praised" *The Years*.* In this same entry Virginia noted that the *New Republic* had rejected her article on Gibbon, "so I shall send no more to America."

With Julian now in Spain and soon in the war, Virginia gave her attention to *Three Guineas*. On June 8, the day after his departure, Rosamond Lehmann's husband, Wogan Philipps, also a member of the Spanish Medical Aid Organization, had suffered a concussion and a fractured arm during an air raid just outside Madrid; the man next to him was killed. "So, a strain: which I cannot now go into: and it must last—how long? A year? Who knows?" She was already very near the point of doing anything "to keep talking, inventing, distracting."

In late June on her way home, Virginia saw a long line of men, women, and children tramping through Tavistock Square like a caravan—"Spaniards flying from Bilbao, which has fallen . . . Somehow brought tears to my eyes." There were children shuffling along, and women in cheap jackets and kerchiefs on their heads, and young men—all laden with cardboard suitcases

---

* Faulkner's notice has not been traced.

and pots and pans. It was a melancholy sight, this "shuffling trudging procession ... clasping their enamel kettles." Bilbao fell on June 18 to the rebel Spanish forces. Earlier, however, as the Fascist attacks grew in force, thousands of mothers and children had fled to England, disembarking at Southampton in late May. In the weeks following, these refugees would be transported to various country shelters. The people Virginia saw were probably Basques staggering from one London railway station to another.

On Thursday, July 15, Janet Case died. Virginia wrote her obituary for *The Times* (July 22). It was titled: "Miss Janet Case: Classical Scholar and Teacher. By an Old Pupil." "Today they are cremating her," she noted on the nineteenth, "and she had printed a little funeral service—with the death day left blank. No words; an adagio from Beethoven, and a text about gentleness and faith, which I would have included had I known." Janet Case, for Virginia, had always been a steadfast, contemplative woman, "anchored in some private faith which didn't correspond with the world's." She was also an inhibited woman. Only in her last letter did she begin with "My beloved Virginia." But "how I loved her, at Hyde Park Gate; how I went hot and cold going to Windmill Hill: and how great a visionary part she has played in my life, till the visionary became part of the fictitious, not of the real life." No one, not even Leonard, knew how much she had to thank Janet for.

LIFE, LIFE, LIFE

1938–1941

46

Julian Bell was killed on July 18, 1937. As an ambulance driver he was attached to a medical unit, based at the Palace of the Escorial, that was set up to obstruct the supply route of the Nationalist forces surrounding Madrid. He was struck by a shell outside the village of Villanueva de la Canada and died in the dressing station at the Escorial. News of his death reached his family two days later, on Tuesday, July 20. On Friday, the twenty-third, an account in *The Times* said further that Julian Bell had "died during the offensive at Brunete. He was in one of the British ambulances when it was hit by an insurgent bomb. The ambulance was badly damaged and a fragment of the bomb entered Mr Bell's lung. He died in hospital 8 hours later."

In the days immediately following, Virginia remained by Vanessa's side, doing what she could to console her inconsolable sister. "It has been an incredible nightmare," she wrote to Vita. "We had both been certain he would be killed, and the strain on her is now, perhaps mercifully, making her so exhausted she can only stay in bed ... I'm not clear enough in the head to feel anything but varieties of dull anger and despair." It had been useless arguing with Julian about going to Spain. His own feelings were mixed. "I mean, interest in war, and conviction, and a longing to be in the thick of things." Then there was "dear old Clive," so pathetic, cracking jokes, trying to make them all laugh.

The Woolfs drove Vanessa to Charleston on July 29 and installed themselves in Monks House so that Virginia might go to her every day. Vanessa's suffering was terrible—to see it was like watching "an accident, and someone bleeding." At the first shock of Julian's death Virginia had felt the outsider's isolation, the unwanted spectator looking on, but that diminished with her coming daily to the family. She also realized, once more, that her one chance of surviving this blow was work. Work was all that remained. "Directly I'm not working ... then nothingness begins."

Julian had "every sort of gift," Virginia had said to Vita. But what did she, Virginia, think of that gift? What was her private estimate of Julian as a writer, a poet, a future man of letters? In a diary entry of August 6 she wrote of her "relief when Tom [Eliot] rejected his essays, for I felt I had not been merely spiteful, merely jealous." But why was she "relieved" when Eliot, acting as literary adviser for Faber and Faber, had to reject Julian's work? Was it relief from her fear of being "spiteful" and "jealous" as she suggested? Or was it something deeper?

Before Julian left for China in late August 1935, Virginia had encouraged him to write down his memories of Roger Fry, something she might include in the biography she would soon be writing. Julian enthusiastically agreed to do so and wrote out his recollections in the form of "A Letter to A.," sending it to Virginia in March 1936. He hoped Leonard might publish it in its entirety in the Hogarth Letters series. Virginia, who was ill at the time, had the piece professionally typed but didn't get around to reading it until early summer. In a letter to Julian, dated June 28* Virginia praised Julian's letter briefly and generally, but had longer, specific criticisms: first, "that you've not mastered the colloquial style, which is the hardest, so that it seemed to me . . . to be discursive, loose knit, and uneasy in its familiarities and conventions." The letter was also much too long. "Leonard has read it and agrees with me on the whole . . . What L. suggests is that you should send it to . . . the Mercury, who might do it in two parts. Even so, I expect he [R. A. S. James, editor] would ask you to shorten it." In fact, both Virginia and Leonard thought Julian's piece contained too much of him and too little of Roger.

Julian was stung by Virginia's response and didn't write to her again until the end of the year, on December 5, 1936, from Wuhan: "I was hurt at your not liking my Roger letter better—which was most unreasonable of me, but I think your letter caught me at the moment when one feels most sensitive about one's work, when it's finished past altering and at the same time is still a part of oneself."

Just before leaving for Spain, Julian assembled his longer essays, including the rejected "A Letter to A.," and asked his mother to send them to T. S. Eliot, whose firm might publish the collection. After Julian's death Eliot

---

* The letter was not published in the original six-volume Nicolson-Trautmann edition of Virginia Woolf's letters, but was included in *Congenial Spirits*, No. 3146a, 375. It is preserved at King's College, Cambridge.

wrote to Virginia to tell her—and Vanessa, indirectly—that though he personally found the essays interesting, Faber and Faber unfortunately had to reject them for publication.* It was this letter from Eliot that Virginia was now referring to in her diary. She was perhaps feeling guilty for not having been more generous to Julian. It is also likely that she was now feeling utterly alone. For Leonard had been excluded from the family sorrow and was now stony and silent; and Vanessa had said with morbid finality, "I shall be cheerful, but I shall never be happy again."

Thus Virginia was left with no one to confide in but her diary. The "extraordinary extinction" of Julian's life, and all it represented beyond Julian himself, had momentarily drained life of its substance. "I do not let myself think. That is the fact. I cannot face much of the meaning. Shut my mind to anything but work." To the end of the year, work was once again her "only refuge." There were days in the country when Virginia walked herself into a state of calm. She played bowls with Leonard. She read. But there wasn't much to say that had not already been said a thousand times before. The only life this summer was "in the brain." Writing alone quickened her: "3 hours pass like 10 minutes." Yet she could write nothing about Vanessa— she must keep herself even from thinking about her.

But that was impossible. She couldn't avoid thinking about Vanessa, or about Julian either. And the more she thought, the more critical she became; the less natural their relations seemed to her. These were deep, troubling thoughts. "Julian had some queer power over her—the lover as well as the son. He had told her he could never love another woman as he loved her." Even as a child he needed more sympathy than the others; he "had a kind of clumsiness...I think I mean lack of judgment...We should have respected him more if he had stayed in England and faced the drudgery. I often argue with him on my walks, abuse his selfishness in going."

There was something of the dabbler in Julian. He could "never force himself to think to the bottom of an idea." But if Julian's dilettantism annoyed Virginia, what she found upsetting was his and Vanessa's feeling for each other, for it represented to her the all too familiar pattern of exclusion. When he was in China Vanessa wrote him letters that might have been written by Julia Duckworth to Leslie Stephen at the height of their courtship. "Darling," she wrote on November 1, 1935, "I think it's *much* better to tell me everything ...I can't help suspecting too that it's easier and better for you to tell me

---

* The Hogarth Press did eventually bring out the essays in 1938, along with a number of other items, in *Julian Bell: Essays, Poems and Letters*, edited by Quentin Bell.

and not keep things to yourself. Of course it does make me want terribly to be with you . . . Oh Julian, I can never express what happiness you've given me in my life. I often wonder how such luck has fallen my way." Being a mother was by itself an "incredible delight," but having children who should "care for me as you make me feel you do, is something beyond all dreaming of."

"I've found out," Julian had earlier written to his dearest Nessa, "more than ever how much our relationship matters to me. And we both know it. I feel about it rather like Donne going religious after his profane mistresses, except that I can love you without having to believe nonsense."

On board the *Fushimi Maru*, before reaching China, Julian wrote two letters to Vanessa and sent them for safekeeping to a friend who was instructed to send them to Vanessa on two conditions: one, if he should be killed in an accident or die of some fatal disease; or two, if the friend should hear that Julian was involved in some revolutionary activities. Both letters were dated September 26, 1935, and intended as "confessions of faith." What Julian wanted to convey to his mother was essentially that: "I've had an extremely happy life"; that "I love you more than anyone else, and always have done so"; that "whatever happens I shall try to put up a fight. I'd much rather a violent finish in hot blood . . . indeed, I wouldn't mind losing a few years for one." In his second letter, he wanted Vanessa to know that "I do feel as if action and excitement were in some way necessary to me, as if I should never be perfectly at peace and happy unless I had experienced them."

At the time of Julian's death, Virginia was condemning this very "masculine" revolutionary spirit in *Three Guineas*. What did she think when she later read Julian's letters from Spain, saying that war was "rather fun . . . boyscoutish in the highest" (June 10, 1937); that "one of the reasons one enjoys war and travel is getting back into male society" (June 13); that "I find [war] perpetually entertaining and very satisfactory . . . It's a better life than most I've lived" (June 22).

Maynard Keynes wrote a brief obituary of Julian for the Annual Report of King's College (November 13, 1937). Julian, he said, had "the utmost openness of character and purity of motive, simple and gentle, with truth and sincerity stamped upon him, and was gradually learning to form his character and to express it. He developed to maturity slowly and was still but a grown and clumsy child whose final accomplishment, now cut off, might have greatly exceeded his apparent early promise."

Ten days after the announcement of Julian's death, Virginia went out to her garden hut at Monks House and wrote a memoir of him.* "I am going to set down very quickly what I remember about Julian," she said, "partly because I am too dazed to write what I was writing: and then I am so composed that *nothing is real unless I write it* . . . I know by this time what an odd effect Time has: it does not destroy people—for instance, I still think perhaps more truly than I did, of Roger, of Thoby: but it brushes away the actual personal presence." She had said only recently that she would leave Julian Roger's papers in her will; and Julian had replied in his abrupt way: "Better leave them to the British Museum." Virginia realized at once that he had said this because he thought he might be killed in Spain. But she was determined to erase this from her mind, because "subconsciously I was sure he would be killed; that is I had a couchant unexpressed certainty, from Thoby's death I think; a legacy of pessimism." At their last meeting she had asked Julian if he would write something in Spain and send it to her—"(This referred of course to my feeling, a very painful one, that I had treated his essay on Roger too lightly.)" He said he would, abruptly, and drove off with Vanessa by his side. This was the last time Virginia saw him alive.

They went back into the house, she remembered, and the talk naturally got round to Julian again. Clive said that as a father he was glad his son should be a "character"—being cool, dressing haphazardly, wearing large floppy hats—it was even good that Julian should have no profession: there would always be enough money to live on. Julian, Clive said, "was a character, like Thoby." Virginia heard this and was offended. "I did not like any Bell to be like Thoby"—apart from his obvious youth and very good looks. "I said that Thoby had a natural style, and Julian did not."

What bothered Virginia most, however, was her being so critical of Julian's writing. Could she justify the hard line she had taken with him? Certainly she was jealous of his youth, and both she and Leonard envied Vanessa's having two healthy, vigorous boys. Then there was Leonard's family "complex," which made him always eager to find some deficiency, some weakness in Vanessa's children; he didn't like the idea that Virginia thought her family better than his, or something like that. But where writing was concerned, Virginia thought Julian "very careless, not 'an artist', too personal in what he wrote, and all over the place." He had faults as a writer, and she regretted not having encouraged him more; still it was hard to sympathize with his egocentricity, his wishing to be published, to be in the public eye. "But how could he know why I was so cool about publishing his things."

What Virginia only hinted at was her reluctance to brighten Vanessa's life

* It is printed in QB II, Appendix C. Emphasis added.

by helping Julian. She knew how much Vanessa wanted this, and yet she refused. Her encouragement, when it came, had been lukewarm. She had treated his work casually. Did it really make any difference in the end whether he had the makings of an artist? Did she have the right to act as his judge? She seemed to have forgotten how much she herself had once wanted Violet's encouragement. Nor does she appear to have remembered relying so heavily on Clive's criticism when she was Julian's age and struggling with her first novel. Perhaps it was inevitable that she should feel a little remorse now that Julian would come to her no longer. Perhaps, too, some distant voice from the past told her that Vanessa had at last paid the price for having abandoned her at Thoby's death, at their father's death—and, yes, at Stella's too.

On a mild clear morning in late August Virginia and Leonard drove to London from Rodmell to see Archie Cochrane, a Cambridge contemporary of Julian's, and Dr. Philip Hart. Both men had joined the British Medical Unit in Spain and were attached to the Escorial Hospital where Julian had died. Cochrane had been in the receiving room when Julian was brought in and Hart had removed the shell splinter from his chest. Julian had been conscious when they got him to the hospital and "anxious to explain that the road was dangerous: then anxious to get on with the operation." He lost consciousness, rambled deliriously in French about military matters, and died four hours later. But why was Virginia recording all this? It belonged to an unreal world now. What reality there was had become "very shallow."

When she wasn't sitting by Vanessa's side, Virginia was writing her long, loving letters—love letters, in fact—"Yes, I'll come tomorrow . . . my own darling creature. You shan't be rid of me for long. In fact I can't bear not seeing you." "My love has always been fuller than your thimble." ". . . I'm more nearly attached to you than sisters should be. Why is it I never stop thinking of you . . ." "My darling honey how I adore you, and . . . what it means to me to come into the room and find you sitting there." "I wish my dolphin were by my side . . . But then I've always been in love with her . . . and so shall remain . . . dearest love, how I adore you." In some perverse way, Vanessa's loss had become Virginia's gain. Little wonder Leonard should feel left out.

Vanessa had once said that when Virginia "is demonstrative, I always shrink away." Indeed, some of Virginia's epistolary *longueurs* were so saturated that Vanessa might well recoil at their childlike artlessness. Virginia nevertheless persisted. "I want to see you without someone to distract you from me: jealousy pure and simple." Her dependency was morbid—"when you're not there the colour goes out of life, as water from a sponge; and I merely exist, dry, and dusty."

Her wanting to see Vanessa without someone distracting her is perhaps the most revealing sentiment of all. It is almost as if Virginia were reclaiming the right to *all* of Vanessa now that Julian was out of the way. That baby, that extravagantly cherished son, was gone. Now the jealous, love-starved sister could be taken once more into Vanessa's arms. How Vanessa, in the privacy of her grief, responded to this, we will never know. But early in September she wrote to Virginia: "Please don't exhaust yourself by coming here if it's too difficult—I really need not be visited like an invalid now." She later wrote to Vita that Virginia had helped more than she could say. Would Vita please make Virginia believe this. When the message was conveyed, Virginia replied: "Isn't it odd? Nessa's saying that to you ... meant something I can't speak of. And I can't tell anyone ... But that message gives me something to hold to."

Despite all this, something came between the sisters with Julian's death. A barrier had been erected, a metaphoric hedge separating them just as certainly as the "hedge" in the *Lighthouse* was insinuating the emotional barrier cutting off Mrs. Ramsay from her husband, and barricading Julia from Leslie Stephen. In 1904 Vanessa had left Virginia to grieve alone after their father's death, and had done so again after Thoby's. Julian's death reawakened those memories in Virginia. "When Thoby died I used to walk about London saying to myself Stevenson's verses: 'You alone have crossed the melancholy stream, Yours the undiminished gladness, undecaying dream [*sic*].' " All this summer of 1937, however, she found herself speaking the verse of Lowell's *Biglow Papers* (second series) "about those coming steps we listen for: the verse about the nephew killed in the war ... With Thoby though I felt we were the same age. With Julian it is the old woman, saying that she won't see the young again. It is an unnatural death, his. I can't make it fit in anywhere."

Julian's death had revived Thoby's. It also resurrected the ancient nursery struggles between the sisters. Virginia might have brains, but Vanessa had beauty. "Thank God," Virginia said to her lovely niece, "you haven't an elder sister to take the winds of March with beauty, as I had, and so force you to be a modest violet on a shady bank." But for several years now that "modest violet" status had been replaced by a major literary reputation, with a lot of money to go with it. Virginia was a best-selling novelist. And Vanessa was "querulous sometimes about my 'success'. When I told her the actual figures—40,000 [copies of *The Years* sold in the U.S.]—she was, I think relieved

... to find them less than reported." The old competitive struggle was coming to life again.

At the end of November, when Virginia added up the money she was earning from the magazines "for a handful of old sketches," she felt a little ashamed. Vanessa, in comparison, earned so little from her paintings—"but then I reflect, I put my life blood into writing, and she had children." Even Vanessa's domestic life was in tatters. Her soi-disant "companion," Duncan Grant, was still pursuing young men, some of them from an assortment of criminals; so Vanessa never had the security of a shared life with him. With each new infatuation, he might go off and never return. She thus stiffened with dread each time a handsome face or a lithe body crossed Duncan's line of vision: she might easily end up an abandoned old woman. The solidity of Virginia's life with Leonard—a "child's life" though it seemed—together with Virginia's extraordinary success at this time, made her acutely uncomfortable when she sat with Vanessa. "No, no, I will not describe that: don't I dread it? But I make myself all the same stay on when she's alone."

And so doors were beginning to shut in Virginia's life. She still had the first draft of *Three Guineas* to finish and a great deal more reading to do before beginning Roger Fry's life. There were requests for articles from various English and American magazines and periodicals. And there were global concerns that would soon impinge first upon her private and eventually upon her public life. Hitler was exerting pressure for the return of those German colonies lost to the Allies during World War I; and at the same time, he and Mussolini continued active intervention in the Spanish war.

By December Leonard's suspected prostate ailment flared up again and once again Virginia was frantic. In fact on December 28 he was forced to retire to his bed with a fever. The one bright spot in Virginia's Christmas holiday was the present from Vita—a large Strasbourg *pâté de foie gras*. "Heaven above us," wrote Virginia, "what immortal geese must have gone to make it! ... It was so divine, I could forgive any treachery." Tom Eliot was dining with them the night it arrived, and complete silence reigned. "The poet ate; the novelist ate. Even Leonard, who had a chill inside, ate ... But Orlando, pink porpoise, isn't it against our Covenant to do this sort of thing?" Didn't Vita remember the night of December 18, 1925, at Long Barn—just twelve years ago—when she gave Virginia a silver paper knife that had belonged to the Duke of Dorset, and Virginia had said, "... with this knife you will gash our hearts"? But that was all history, and however much Virginia complained, Vita's thoughtfulness brought her a moment of happiness in this season of sorrow. She ended her letter with a little fillip—"12,000 copies of *Pepita** sold. I'm thinking of buying a fur coat."

The very cold New Year began with a chill of anxiety. For several days after Christmas, Leonard's temperature remained above normal. It was clear by this time he needed to be seen by a physician. They drove to London where he was examined, X-rayed, and left with the same "professional" vagueness: it might be prostate trouble; it could be a kidney infection; or it might be nothing at all. It would be at least five days before the doctor knew anything. And again Virginia was rigid with worry. What would her future be without Leonard? To whom could she turn if she needed help? By mid-January, however, Leonard was once more given a clean bill of health. "I'm so beside myself with relief," she wrote from Tavistock Square, "it was a damnable nightmare." And she coped with this emergency in her usual way: with intense, uninterrupted work: "incessant writing, thinking, about 3 Guineas— as I did the summer after Julian's death . . . And the result of writing this [diary] page is to make me see how essential it is to steep myself in work."

In the middle of January, Virginia took the final pages of *Three Guineas* to Chancery Lane to be typed, and on the evening of February 1 Leonard was given the completed typescript to read. He went through it carefully and "gravely" approved. It was "an extremely clear analysis." And so on the whole she was satisfied with his opinion. It was "a good piece of donkeywork" and didn't affect her as the novels did. At this point in her career, she had evidently convinced herself that with her critical writing she was immune to the torture she suffered with her fiction. But this was not entirely true, as she was soon to discover.

With the book now finished, she had once more to "ward off the old depression"; and within weeks the familiar doubts began: "I suspect I shall find the page proofs (due tomorrow) a chill bath of disillusionment." Yet, she added later, she'd never written a book with such gusto. All the same, Leonard didn't seem enthusiastic. She was correcting absolutely the worst book she'd ever written, she said to Vanessa, "let alone that I shan't, when published, have a friend left."

.   .   .

* Vita's most recent best-seller: a biography of her grandmother.

In the summer of 1937, when Leonard and Virginia thought again of giving up the Press, John Lehmann was once more searching for a publisher for his biannual miscellany called *New Writing*. One plan was that Lehmann, Stephen Spender, W. H. Auden, and Christopher Isherwood would buy the entire Press for six thousand pounds, of which Lehmann would put up three thousand. The other three investors, however, could not raise their half share. Leonard then conceived a plan whereby Lehmann would become his partner in the Press by buying Virginia's share for £3,000. This was the decision they finally arrived at, and on February 23, 1938, the agreement was signed, even though the partnership would not become effective until April. Whatever grumbles Virginia had over the time the Press took from their private industries, she was proud of the enterprise they had launched on the dining-room table in 1917. They had suffered a good many trials and had helped along, with painstaking care, authors that many commercial publishers would now have been proud to have on their list. More than that, the Press had earned them a great deal more money than they might otherwise have earned pursuing more conventional careers.

After completing the negotiations, Lehmann wrote to Virginia that "Leonard was very rugged the other day when I signed the Partnership Agreement, and to my proposal that the event be marked by a mutual health-drinking, replied that he only had cold water. Nevertheless I refuse to be dashed, and think that at any rate I owe you a letter, in which joy at reaching such an honourable position in such a distinguished and old established firm is mixed with tears for the departure from the same position of its co-founder and chief literary glory...I hope the new arrangement is going to release you and Leonard for a steady stream of masterpieces. I stand with both hands extended, waiting for them."

"I'm full of sanguinity about the future," Virginia replied. "Nor can I see myself any reason why we should quarrel; or why we should drink the Toast in cold water. What about a good dinner . . . at Boulestin or some such place? You are hereby invited to be the guest of Virginia Woolf's ghost—the Hogarth ghost." This was followed by a note from Leonard himself: "I am sorry that I was 'gruff' over the signature of the agreement, and I certainly did not grudge you a glass of wine. It was emotion!"

In Europe, just across the Channel, a frightening growl was beginning to make itself heard. It was Nazi Germany. "Hitler has invaded Austria," Virginia noted in her diary on March 12: "that is, at 10 last night his army crossed the frontier, unresisted." The Austrian national anthem would never be heard on the radio again. Before the Chancellor could determine the sentiments of his people about a Nazi presence in the Austrian government, Hitler's determination to annex Austria to the German Reich was put into action on March 11. Within hours of the invasion, an all-Nazi cabinet was announced in Vienna.

47 Virginia began writing *Roger Fry* on April 1 and *Pointz Hall* (eventually called *Between the Acts*) on April 2, both under the ominous shadow the Fuehrer was casting on the fate of the civilized world. Behind that shadow was still the terrible reminder of Julian's death. Indeed life itself was beginning to seem pointless and provisional. Ottoline Morrell, having suffered a stroke the previous year, died on April 21, aged sixty-four, in a clinic in Tunbridge Wells. Philip Morrell asked Virginia whether as one of Ottoline's oldest friends she would like to send "some short account of her to the Times." Soon after the funeral service, Virginia reached for her diary: "Odd how the sense of loss takes this private form: someone who won't read what I write. No illumination in Gower Street, an intimacy abolished."

Then Ka Cox (now Arnold-Forster) died unexpectedly at the age of fifty-one. She had helped Leonard through Virginia's suicide attempt in September 1913 and ministered to her in the full horror of madness. "I was self-conscious; remembering how she had seen me mad," Virginia wrote in her journal. Her role in life had always been "to help; to lift lame dogs...to arrange; manage; receive confidences." Virginia had thought of her often, and of her love affair with Rupert Brooke, but that memory too had faded into the shadows of history.

Will Vaughan, Virginia's cousin, was also dead. He had been sent to India as a delegate to the Indian Science Congress. While visiting the Taj Mahal he fell and broke his leg. It was amputated, and he died of pneumonia soon after. Virginia harbored many potent memories of the visits she had made to Giggleswick in 1904, almost a quarter of a century earlier, when she was recovering from her nervous breakdown, and later in 1906 when she had become a budding journalist. And now that chapter too was ended.

But June 2, the publication date of *Three Guineas*, was fast approaching, and Virginia kept herself safely immersed in "the solid world of Roger" and "the airy world of Poyntz [Pointz] Hall." Once more she found herself wavering between "fact" and "vision"—between biography and fiction—"like a spider's web with nothing to attach the string to." The solid world of Roger was beginning to create problems: "How can one cut loose from facts, when there they are, contradicting my theories?" It would not be many weeks before the biography grew into an appalling and monumental grind.

The days passed slowly. Leonard warned Virginia that *Three Guineas* would provoke some "very angry reviews from men." She braced herself. But on May 30, before official publication day, she received a letter from Philippa Strachey, Secretary to the National Society for Women's Service. She had read the book "with rapture—It is what we have panted for for years and years." The letter brought a short wave of relief, but there was still the press with its huge deadly jaws open. So she took a deep breath, and prepared herself to "face the music."

Three Guineas was a passionate denunciation of wars and the men who fought them. Julian had been killed less than a year after Virginia began writing it. His had been a senseless death, and for Virginia the shock was a compound of fact and memory. It was a fact that somewhere in Spain Vanessa's beloved Julian now lay buried. In memory, Virginia lived through once more the death of her own beloved Thoby, who, like Julian, had died a young man with all his hope and promise blighted. The double sorrow moved backward and forward on the shuttle of time and sought release across the pages of *Three Guineas*. And the result was grim. Grief and logic were mortal contestants: they refused to mingle except in a surge of unmitigated rage. The book was intended to arouse anger, stir up complacency, raise hackles, make readers think.

Objections were indeed roused. Although most of her friends were silent when the book appeared, newspapers and periodicals tended to print empty ceremonial reviews. Virginia's subtle ironies, cushioned in lyrical phrasing, made the argument sometimes difficult to pinpoint. *The Times Literary Supplement* called Woolf "the most brilliant pamphleteer in England," but said little beyond that to justify such a claim. Theodora Bosanquet said in *Time and Tide* (June 4) that it was "not as Amazons but as Antigones that Mrs Woolf sees the daughters of educated men." But a good many reviewers, as Leonard predicted, were not so generous.

Public sneers may have given Virginia some anxiety, but it was a letter from Vita that caused the genuine wince of pain. "You are a tantalising writer," Vita said, "because at one moment you enchant one with your lovely prose and the next exasperate one with your misleading arguments ... And far be it from me to cross swords with you publicly ... though if it came to fisticuffs I might knock you down ... In the meantime, let me say that I read you with delight, even though I wanted to exclaim, 'Oh BUT, Virginia . . .' on 50% of your pages."

Virginia replied: "You say you don't agree with 50% of it—no, of course you don't. But when you say that you are exasperated by my 'misleading arguments'—then I ask, what do you mean?" Did Vita mean that Virginia had been dishonest in order to produce an effect which she knew to be untrue? "If *that's* what you mean by 'misleading' then we shall have to have the matter out." Because *Three Guineas* might be "a silly book" and it might not be a well-written book, but it was certainly an "honest" book: and "I took more pains to get up the facts and state them plainly than I ever took with anything in my life."

Despite her vigorous self-defense, however, Virginia began to have doubts. Perhaps she'd gone too far, said too much. Then letters began to pour in: some hostile, some incredulous, some baffled. Many, far too many, demanding an explanation—"Letters . . . from that hysterical and illiterate ass the public." To Margaret Llewelyn Davies she confessed it was impertinent to air her views on such a subject; but to remain silent and agree to all the silly letter signing and "vocal pacifism" with Hitler and Mussolini in their midst led to Virginia's "usual ink-spray." Too much accumulated material had led to verbosity. One had to "secrete a jelly in which to slip quotations down people's throats." She was writing for the "very common, very reluctant, very easily bored reader"—not for people like Margaret Llewelyn Davies.

This was not quite the case, however, for in writing *Three Guineas* Virginia had in mind a privileged class of women, the daughters of educated men; and it was Queenie Leavis's attack in *Scrutiny* that most challenged Virginia's argument. "This book is not really reviewable . . . because Mrs. Woolf implies throughout that it is a conversation between her and her friends, addressed as she constantly says to 'women of our class' . . . *A Room of One's Own* was annoying enough, causing outpourings of disgust in the very quarters in which Mrs. Woolf . . . expected to earn gratitude; but this book is not merely silly and ill-informed, though it is that too, it contains some dangerous assumptions, some preposterous claims and some nasty attitudes . . . It seems to me the art of living as conceived by a social parasite."

The principal weakness of *Three Guineas*, wrote Quentin Bell, was its "attempt to involve a discussion of women's rights with the far more agonising and immediate question of what we were to do in order to meet the ever-growing menace of Fascism and war. The connection between the two questions seemed tenuous and the positive suggestions wholly inadequate."

· · ·

Storm clouds were gathering, tension was building, and "—how I bless Roger, and wish I could tell him so, for giving me himself to think of . . . in this welter of unreality," she wrote in her diary on September 10. The welter of unreality was real enough. A crisis was brewing in Czechoslovakia. On September 7 the pro-Nazi Germans in the Sudetenland broke off their fake negotiations with the Czechoslovak Government for self-determination; France, pledged to assist Czechoslovakia, now threatened by German invasion, enlisted her military reserves. On September 9 France's ally Great Britain announced that part of the Royal Navy would be put into service. On September 15, the Prime Minister, Neville Chamberlain, had flown to Germany, and agreed in principle to the secession of these areas to Hitler. On September 22 Hitler stepped up the pressure, and five days later the French army and British fleet were mobilized. At the very last moment, while the Prime Minister was describing these events to the House of Commons on the twenty-eighth, he received from Mussolini a proposal to settle the crisis.

The conference met the next day in Munich. Chamberlain, French Prime Minister Edouard Daladier, Hitler, and Mussolini were the principal participants. Neither Russia nor Czechoslovakia was invited to attend. An agreement was signed at 1 a.m. on the thirtieth, and Hitler regained power over almost all the territory he demanded. A triumphant Chamberlain returned to London, waving a piece of paper signed by himself and Hitler, by which Britain and Germany pledged themselves "never to go to war with one another again." From Downing Street he assured the cheering crowds that he had brought back "peace with honour." As the following weeks would show, the Munich Agreement turned out to be an act of betrayal—the dishonorable sacrifice of Czechoslovakia.

A few days prior to the Munich Agreement, Leonard, still Secretary of the Labour Party's Advisors Committee, was in great demand. Kingsley Martin, editor of the *New Statesman*, called on him endlessly for meetings, for advice, for decisions on political issues and party policy. He implored Leonard to return to London. In a torrential rain, Leonard and Virginia drove up from the country. The streets were jammed with people; everyone talked of war; small mountains of sandbags congested the streets; trenches everywhere were being dug; loudspeakers moved slowly through the squares exhorting Londoners to get fitted for gas masks; long weary lines waited outside dispensing centers. In the event of an air invasion, all poisonous snakes at the Zoo were to be destroyed and dangerous animals shot. Kingsley Martin himself, by the time they reached him, was on the verge of hysteria and melodramatically hinting at suicide.

The following day Virginia went to the London Library to collect material for *Roger Fry*. She needed to consult the *Times* of November 1910 for the first Post-Impressionist Exhibition. As she sat in the basement reading, an old janitor approached her: "They're telling us to put on our gas masks." "Have you got yours?" Virginia asked. "No, not yet." "And shall we have war?" she wanted to know. "I fear so, but I hope not. I live out in Putney. Oh they've laid in sand bags; the books will be moved; but if a bomb strikes the house . . . May I dust under your chair?"

From the Library, she made her way to the National Gallery. Walking down Pall Mall, she heard the megaphones once more urging Londoners to get fitted for gas masks. Over and over the warning was repeated. At the Gallery a lecture on Watteau and French painting was in progress. A large crowd was following a flushed, perspiring lecturer. "I suppose they were all having a last look."

Back at Tavistock Square in the Hogarth office, arrangements were being made with the staff about shelter, wages, filling out orders, and keeping the business going generally. The atmosphere was tense. Everyone seemed uncertain. And what would the Woolfs need if they were marooned in Rodmell without gasoline or bicycles? Leonard took his mackintosh and a heavy winter coat. Virginia took Roger's letters and a stack of stamped envelopes. When she said goodbye to the Press, she "felt rather a coward . . . But the Gov't. asked all who could to leave London . . . So off we went."

They left London, just as they had arrived, in a torrential rain. The streets were still congested; wooden shutters were being nailed up over shop windows; sandbags were stacked; the air was thick with fear and flight. It took them three hours to get to Rodmell. At 10:30 that night a member of the district council responsible for civil defense in Rodmell brought them gas masks. Then another council member stopped by to say that 9,000 children had been billeted in Sussex, fifty in Rodmell. How many of them could the Woolfs manage? "We arranged to take two. By that time, the nightmare feeling was becoming more nightmarish . . . for no one knew what was happening; and yet everyone was behaving as if the war had begun." Virginia couldn't be sure what Leonard was feeling, but she herself felt angry, ashamed, and cowardly.

Vanessa was in Cassis at this time and Virginia kept her informed of the day-to-day developments. Vita had written that it was almost certain that London would be attacked by German air fighters at twenty-minute intervals for twenty-four hours with gas and bombs. "We came back, half expecting to find our refugees waiting us at Monks House . . . Then the BBC kept on saying that nothing was safe; we were all to go on expecting war." Then Chamberlain returned from Munich with his fantastic news of the agreement. Maynard Keynes had told the Woolfs that the whole thing had been staged by Chamberlain; that there never was any fear of war; that it was a planned deception between him and Hitler. So in the end it was, as Leonard had said, "peace without honour." Whatever the truth was, the feeling of "despair and coming death was very genuine in London, however irrational." In Rodmell, they prepared themselves for the worst. Candles were purchased; an extra supply of coal was ordered; when the time came, they would live off cabbage, apples, and honey.

During this interval of "peace without honour," Virginia retreated once more into the solid world of Roger Fry. She didn't like having to stick to facts. Biography was a grind. It was her favorite reading, but difficult to write. There were details of Roger's life—his wife's insanity, for example—that she was reluctant to deal with, no matter how important the woman and their love were to his life. "All the morning I work my brain into a screw over Roger—what did he do in 1904—when did his wife go mad, and how on earth does one explain madness and love in sober prose, with dates attached?" Helen Fry's was a tragic story—her brilliance, her uniqueness, her disintegration—but "not much in detail can be said of her." If Virginia was prepared to gloss over Helen Fry's illness as she appears to have been, then the biography would require once more the delicate art of pargeting. More consequentially, if she chose to deal principally with the public, socially acceptable parts of Roger Fry's life, she must surely have known how pedestrian the result would be. But as she said in the biography, ". . . what Roger Fry could not say that evening . . . must be left unsaid by another."

And "What am I to say about you?" she asked Vanessa. "It's rather as if you had to paint a portrait using dozens of snapshots . . . Either one ought to dash it off freehand . . . or toil like a fly over a loaf of bread. As it is I'm compromising; and it's a muddle; and unreadable . . . But Roger himself is so magnificent, I'm so in love with him . . . reading his books one after another I realise that he's the only great critic that ever lived." But the problem remained: "how to deal with love so that we're not all blushing." In the published text, Virginia referred to Roger and Vanessa's love affair simply as "their friendship." She had once more succumbed to glossing over certain facts, just as Leslie Stephen had many years earlier glossed over the madness of his nephew James Kenneth Stephen in *The Life of Sir James Fitzjames*

Stephen. She had learned to *sublimate*, to make "socially acceptable" the un-compromising starkness of the truth.

After Julian's death, Leonard and Virginia agreed to publish a memorial volume of his work in 1938, *Julian Bell: Essays, Poems and Letters*, with Quentin as its editor. But here, too, social form reared its incorruptible head. John Lehmann was "crowing over your rather imperfect index," Virginia wrote to Quentin. He claimed further that there were misquotations and erroneous attributions. All that could be fixed; the real problem now was with the printer. Although he was a personal friend of John's, he objected at the last minute to "printing bugger, fuck, balls and piss." John offered to use initials, but the printer refused. The matter was still in dispute. "And it's all John's fault for engaging a . . . notorious prude."

But here was the equally prudish Virginia agonizing over Vanessa and Roger's love affair. She was "stuck at 1911." Would Quentin please "tell Nessa to write and tell me how I'm to deal with Roger . . . [I] plunge daily deeper into despair." There were now days when *Roger Fry* became that "cursed biography." How did one square the facts with Roger's family? How did one "euphemise 20 different mistresses?" How did one write "the truth about friends whose families are alive?"

These questions were still unresolved when Virginia learned on Christmas Eve that her brother-in-law Jack Hills was dead.* And during the night, Leonard's marmoset, little Mitz, died of the cold. "It was very touching— her eyes shut and her white face like a very old woman's." On Christmas Day, however, the atmosphere brightened when Virginia's beloved Vita, her "extravagant Prince," sent another Strasbourg pâté jeweled with black truf-fles—very much in the style of the voluptuous aristocrat who had once stood, pearl-hung, in a Sevenoaks fishmonger's shop.

As the calendar moved forward into 1939, Virginia became steadily encased in the labor of fitting together the pieces of Roger Fry. The task was both personal and complicated, and she began to doubt her skill as a biographer. Over and over the book seemed doomed. The raw materials were massive.

---

* After Stella Duckworth's death in 1897, Jack Hills gave Virginia and Vanessa the income from her marriage settlement. On his death, he left the capital sum to be divided equally among Virginia, Vanessa, and Adrian.

Would she choose the right letters? Quote the appropriate passages? Interpret his writing creditably? Could she darken here and lighten there the long years of his life in a way that would restore him whole and harmonious to those who knew him? The doubts were endless. It must have crossed her mind countless times that the father figure she wished to resuscitate was decidedly discrepant from the man she knew him to be. His ineluctable figure stared at her. Facts glared at her. To these she must suppress her imagination. For there was his family waiting in the shadows. Documents held her in their grip and pressed her into a state of vulnerability not far from despair.

The struggles over his reincarnation grew steadily deeper and more impairing. How could she, cluttered with letters and testimonies and confirmations, light up the dim passages of his most private affairs—his small successes, his major failings, his permanent failures? The relics obstructing her path were as monumental as those that might have blocked her way had she been asked to write the life of Sir Leslie Stephen. She might rewrite the words, but she could not revise the emotion.

At the end of January 1939, Virginia and Leonard, as his publishers since 1924, went to see Sigmund Freud in the last year of his life. Under the protection of some influential friends, he and his daughter Anna, the child psychologist, and his son Martin were able to leave Nazi-controlled Vienna in the summer of 1938. With the help of Princess Marie Bonaparte, wife of Prince George of Greece, Freud was installed in 20 Maresfield Gardens, a "great silent solid Hampstead mansion." At the time of their visit, Saturday, January 28, he had been suffering from cancer of the mouth, for which he had undergone more than thirty operations. He was a compulsive smoker of cigars and the irritation they caused provoked malignant recurrences of the condition. When the time came, Freud would die, as previously arranged with Dr. Ernest Jones, from an overdose of morphine. The suicide took place at his Hampstead home early in the morning of September 23. He was eighty-three.

"Dr Freud gave me a narcissus," Virginia recorded in her diary the day after the visit. "Was sitting in a great library with little statues at a large scrupulously tidy shiny table." She and Leonard sat "like patients" in chairs. He was a white-bearded, wizened, very old man with "a monkey's light eyes, paralysed spasmodic movements, inarticulate: but alert ... About his books. Fame? I was infamous rather than famous; didn't make £50 by his first book." It was difficult to talk, but Anna and Martin Freud helped the conversation along. Leonard found him extremely courteous in a formal, "old fashioned way . . . There was something about him as of a half-extinct volcano, something sombre, suppressed, reserved." But there was also a great gentleness behind which one felt enormous strength. Freud brightened when Leonard told him about a man who had recently been charged with stealing books from Foyle's, among them one of Freud's. The magistrate fined the thief and decreed that he should read all of Freud's books as punishment. This brought a smile to the old man's face. But it was a strange, slightly strained visit. Leonard left with the feeling that Freud was a "formidable man." Virginia, who had presumably not read much of his work, would soon begin reading seriously, and finding much in Freud that was both fascinating and disturbing.

During this interval, T. S. Eliot sent Virginia a copy of his new play, *The Family Reunion*, which was having a limited run at the Westminster Theatre. She read the play and then saw it performed. It was a failure. Eliot was a lyric, not a dramatic, poet. More specifically, he was a "monologist," not a dramatist. The speeches were cold, stiff, disembodied. One London critic called it a "barren, arid, gritty wasteland" devoid of dramatic impulse and continuity. Virginia was relieved that the play was a flop. Was that proof of an idea she was evolving about the drama in *Pointz Hall*? Or was it again simply a matter of jealousy? There was no doubt that Eliot himself knew his play had failed. He dined with the Woolfs several days later and Virginia found him pale and heavy-lidded. In the course of the evening, he confessed that his three Boutwood lectures at Corpus Christi, Cambridge, on church and state (later published as *The Idea of a Christian Society*) were "very bad." Perhaps that was proof that "all his work now seems so."

There were days now when Virginia could write neither *Roger Fry* nor *Pointz Hall*. When she was in this state she rushed to her diary. On one such occasion, she had had a long three-hour visit alone with Hugh Walpole. When he left, her blank page was open and ready to receive the rich outpouring of nuggets the conversation had produced. Hugh "gave me a full account of his sexual life, of which I retain these facts." For many years Hugh had been the lover of the Danish tenor Lauritz Melchior. Sometime in 1926, Melchior was replaced by a Cornishman, Harold Cheevers, who was at the time a constable in the Metropolitan Police force. Cheevers was nine years Walpole's junior and a married man with two little boys. He remained for the rest of Walpole's life his chauffeur, secretary, and companion.

All of this fascinated Virginia. It smacked of the "male urinals" she alluded to when gossiping about her gay friends. Hugh "only loves men who don't love men. Tried to drown himself once over Melchior . . . Told me too of the Baths at the Elephant & Castle. How the men go there." He had seen Lord C_____ naked, prowling the premises in search of a partner. He had seen Lord B_____ having sex with a boy. He had seen a number of distinguished figures stark naked at the baths at four in the afternoon and then showing up at their clubs two hours later, looking immaculate and unapproachable with all their medals and ribbons on display. Once Hugh himself had "had a father and son simultaneously." And he had now been living "a married life with Harold [Cheevers] for 15 years without intercourse. All this piles up a rich life of which I have no knowledge: and he can't use it in his novels." His novels were about lives he "hasn't lived which explains their badness." He lacked the courage to write about his real life. It would shock and hurt the people he cared for. But it was true, as Walpole had said: "Copulation removes barriers. Class barriers fade." He now lived at Hampstead with Harold's family and friends openly and naturally. It was odd to Virginia that he had never had any feelings for a woman. Yet his sister was "a suppressed Lesbian; and his brother entirely without sex—a schoolmaster."

Hugh had been to Rome for a month on a Hearst Press assignment to report on the funeral of Pope Pius XI and the installation of his successor, Pius XII. Following the assignment, he wrote an autobiographical account of his stay in Italy called *Roman Fountain* and sent Virginia a copy. (Both Desmond MacCarthy and Harold Nicolson had written condescending reviews of the book.) "I like some of Roman Fountain very much," Virginia wrote him after finishing the book. "I dislike some very much. Oh to disentangle these questions with you by word of mouth—how that would interest me!"

Virginia copied out part of his reply into her journal: "As to my book . . . of course I knew that you would dislike some of it very much, but hoped you would like some which apparently you do. MacCarthy speaks to me as to a child, so does Harold Nicolson talking of my babyish love of my toys . . . But do you care to hear the truth? Half of me is very mature, half has never grown up at all. I can't help my excitement which irritates you all. I never had anything when I was young . . . As to my writing, you and I are the opposite ends of the bloody *stick*? You are the supreme example of the aesthetic-conscience—there has never been such another in English fiction. But you *don't* write novels. What you write needs a new name. I am the *true* novelist—a minor one but a true one. I know a lot about the novel and a lot about life seen from my very twisted child-haunted angle. Had I been normal I might have been a major novelist. As it is I am a Siamese twin."

. . .

The first draft of *Roger Fry* was at last finished on March 10, 1939, with "innumerable doubts, of myself as biographer." Extensive revisions were still to come, and this was when the "terrible grind" would begin. A few days earlier Liverpool University had offered her an honorary doctorate, which she refused. This was hardly the time for such frivolities. In the middle of March Hitler, in violation of the Munich Agreement, invaded Czechoslovakia and annexed it to the Reich; and on April 7, Good Friday, Mussolini attacked Albania. England and France agreed that if Hitler attacked Poland (which he did), they would support the Poles.

Suddenly, however, a new wrinkle appeared in the uncertain spread of war, and it was personal. The Press and Virginia herself were beginning to lose their reading public. "At the moment we are finding it very difficult to continue our publishing for nobody will read anything except politics." It might be necessary to move the Press outside of London—or to shut it down altogether. "It is very difficult to go on working under such uncertainty." Then another problem arose: this one too on the home front. In February Virginia found her writing hours wrecked each morning by hammers and drills. Some nearby buildings in Tavistock Square were being torn down. This noise was deafening, and the dust and dirt intolerable. They considered moving to another square, but their lease on No. 52 would not expire until 1941. The adjacent demolition created so much disturbance, however, they had no choice but to flee. In May, after some searching, they found 37 Mecklenburgh Square, into which they would not move until August. Unable to persuade their landlords to free them of their current lease, and unable to find someone to take over 52 Tavistock Square, however, meant they would soon find themselves paying rent for two houses.

Virginia had been giving Vanessa's daughter, Angelica, one hundred pounds a year as a dress allowance, but she would have to decrease the amount. "I'm afraid it's possible that I may have to send you less," Virginia explained; "Leonard says we shall be a good deal poorer, owing to taxes, not having let 52, the Press not paying etc." A few months later, Angelica's allowance was cut to sixty pounds: "The thing is, I can't at the moment make money in America, and my life of Roger won't I'm afraid pay at all."

In early June Leonard and Virginia made a two-week motor tour of Normandy and Brittany. They stopped at Les Rochers, Madame de Sévigné's château near Vitré (Virginia was preparing to write about her), and went on slowly to Vannes and around the Brittany peninsula to Dinan and Bayeux. The holiday made for a change of scenery but not much else. In her bag

Virginia kept a small notebook in which to make notes about the places they visited; and on her return to England she decided it was important to keep her notebook with her when she walked the streets of London. It was almost as if she were afraid of drifting into a void if she had no writing implements on her person, ready for use—the way a cardiac patient would never be without nitroglycerine. She was descending slowly into a mild depression. Writing was becoming difficult and *Roger Fry* would in a month or two become "the worst of all my life's experiences." The world of meaning and substance was slowly disintegrating. "I took up my watch this morning and then put it down. Lost."

Leonard's mother fell and broke some ribs toward the end of June and was taken to a nursing home. She was now almost ninety, and Virginia reflected on her enormous will to live—her "terrible passive resistance to death"; she had the "immortality of the vampire." But Marie Woolf fooled her. She died a few days later on July 2. To the very end she tried to be cheerful—"Virginia must write a book called 'The Fallen Woman'." It was sad watching her die, however. She was such a spirited old lady who just stopped breathing. She wanted so much to live and had asked the matron if she'd known any old women to recover.

The day after the funeral, July 6, Virginia would make her mother-in-law "real" for the last time *with words*: she would capture her on paper with pen and ink. "What was she like then? Let me see—She was small, narrow shouldered—things slipped off—she wore a low blouse with pearl necklace— and rather heavy. Her head nodded. She had stiff curled grey black hair. She would say as we came in 'And Virginia?' My joke was, 'Conceal your disappointment'... Then she would laugh, kiss me, and give me a little pat ... A great joy in family; in society; she could make friends out of anyone: was very popular with elderly gentlemen. One at Worthing stood her dinners, took her to the theatre ... She could tell the whole plot of Gone with the Wind for example; talking as if they were real ... The truth was, age had taken everything away that was real, I think: only age left the pathetic animal, which was very real; the body that wanted to live."

The move to Mecklenburgh Square began on Thursday, August 17, with the removal of the Press from Tavistock Square to the new house. The following Thursday their furniture and books would come. Aside from the usual chaos, Virginia was in a strange state, owing partly to the disorientation of the move, and partly to the trouble the biography was giving her. The revisions were tedious enough; but to make matters worse, new material kept pouring in. "At least today I wrote ten sentences of Roger, but each word was like carrying a coal scuttle to the top of the house." Then there was her dispute with Leonard over the greenhouse he wanted built at Monks House to which Virginia objected: she thought it would be an ugly structure and spoil her view. It was either the greenhouse or the view. The view won. And the result was "headache; guilt; remorse." The argument weighed so heavily upon her, she couldn't read and couldn't write. It was that bad.

Walking through the new London house a little earlier, a grim thought crossed her mind: which of these rooms, she wondered, would she die in? "Which is going to be the scene of some—oh no. I won't write out the tragedy that has to be acted there."* Suddenly she recalled a line from Spinoza: "A free man thinks of death least of all things." That meant she wasn't free. She was dazed. She was depressed. With increasing frequency she thought of death and old age. Old age meant dependency. And that was worse than death. Madness meant dependency. Therefore madness was worse than death. Months earlier she had begun to sink, to give way to morbid feelings. "Why am I so old, so ugly, so—and can't write." She must stick to short books. That was the only way to "keep off the settling down and refrigeration of old age." But *Pointz Hall* was becoming perhaps the longest suicide note in English literary history.

Over everything hung the war. "The Poles vibrating in my room. Everything uncertain . . . Work, work, I tell myself." But she couldn't work. There was too much distraction, too much discomfort. Her hand was palsied from writing pages over and over again and not getting them right. "Roger seems hopeless. Yet if one can't write . . . one may as well kill oneself. Such despair comes over me." But it was not just *Roger Fry* that brought on these feelings. The declaration of war, which up to this time had been a terrible anxiety, was about to become a grim reality with all its companion horrors.

---

* But she had already or was soon to write that scene in the earlier typescript of *Pointz Hall*: "It was the first act of the new play. But who had written the play? What was the meaning of the play? And who made them act their parts? Then, the rage which they had suppressed all day burst out. It was their part—to tear each other asunder, to fight" (188).

48

Germany attacked Poland in the early hours of September 1 and declared the incorporation of Danzig into the Reich. On the second, the British announced to Mussolini that there could be no talks unless Hitler first withdrew from Poland; but the time for compromise was over. Hitler had not responded to the ultimatum. It was England's duty now to honor her guarantee of help. In a broadcast on Sunday, September 3, Prime Minister Chamberlain announced at 11:15 a.m. that Great Britain was now at war with Germany.

"Our first air raid warning at 8.30 this morning," Virginia noted in her diary on Wednesday, September 6. "Yes, it's an empty meaningless world now ... This war has begun in cold blood." The killing machine had been set in action. London, after sunset, looked like a city of darkness in the Middle Ages. Civilization was shrinking; amenities were disappearing. "There's no petrol ... so we are back again with our bicycles at Asheham 1915." Money too was increasingly a worry. They would have to turn to journalism again. "My old age of independence is thus in danger."

They would have to begin hoarding—sugar, butter, firewood. The fallen elm tree would be cut up to see them through two winters. But the war would last three years they were told. In the midst of all this, the second volume of Leonard's work on communal psychology, *After the Deluge*, was published, and scarcely noticed. The revisions on *Roger Fry* were erratic. There were good days. And many bad ones. Virginia kept at it, however, accepting short assignments from the journals to earn money. "I've been slipping into the frying pan of Journalism." It was degrading.

They were now living entirely at Monks House, with occasional trips to London on Press business. What a queer place London had become. Only a few buses were operating; the underground was closed; there were ambulances everywhere; everyone carrying a flashlight and "humped with a gas mask." Huge Caterpillars were digging trenches in Bloomsbury. Shops were shutting up early. Many windows remained darkened all day. When night descended, it was all "strain and grimness"—a retreat into the medieval age with the space and "silence of the country set in this forest of black houses"; and in the gloom one expected "a fox to prowl along the pavement."

Vita, at Sissinghurst, was becoming Virginia's "constant presence." If "I'm dumb and chill, it doesn't mean I don't always keep thinking of you ... how I go on seeing you, tormented." In the background, too, was Ethel and her stream of letters. Virginia saw her once in December and was saddened by the visit. Ethel had declined. She was now "shut up quite alone in her old age—talks to herself, about herself." It was pathetic. Her clothes were shabby and crumpled; she was untidy, talking still of her genius. How terrible it was to be reduced to that "feeblemindedness—at 84."

Hitler was still certain Britain and France were unwilling to fight and so no real warfare had yet begun. It was a fearful time of anticipation, however. Toward the end of the year, Virginia began reading Freud; she wanted to make her brain work harder. She was tired and depressed and cross. "Roger a failure—and what a grind . . . I'm brain fagged and must resist the desire to tear up and cross out." Freud would help her through this interval. His books would give her mind a "wider scope . . . Thus defeat the shrinkage of age." But Freud was disturbing; his notions of instinct and the unconscious were wholly incompatible with the idea of civilization and freedom.

In times of war, as in all times of social stress, private feelings gave way to herd instinct. Hadn't Freud said this? And to her artist's mind, the herd instinct was intolerable. Her stature as a writer, her financial independence, and, above all, the freedom she had won through years of struggle were now in danger. A regression to herd membership would be unthinkable. By her books alone had she become free. If they were now in peril, so then was her freedom.

This apprehension was not solely the result of war. Old age was becoming an obsession. It meant the decline of reputation, the dwindling of artistic power, the failure of illusion, and the shame of dependency. She must shut her ears to the sounds of slaughter and with pen and ink give reality that elegant coloration only she could achieve. Beyond that, nothing was certain. Julian's death was a daily reminder of that ugly fact, and her whole world stood poised in doubt.

However these shades of mourning assembled themselves, though, one thing was irrefutable: she must live more fully in the high spaces of imagination. She must ascend once more to "that exciting layer so rarely lived in: where my mind works so quick it seems asleep; like the aeroplane propellers."

Pointz Hall, as she called her novel at this time, was to become that extraordinarily inaccessible novel about the periods of England's literary history, enacted in the novel's village pageant, and reflected in the lives of three generations of the Oliver family living at Pointz Hall. Because so much of the book was devoted to the historical pageant, Virginia Woolf allowed herself, as she had in no other work, the freedom to explore the problems of art and the artist, and to illuminate the relationship between culture and creativity.

As she rummaged through the diaries and documents of biography, she began to siphon into her novel images and emotions which had no other outlet; and many of these fragments of daily life found their way into the novel before undergoing the alchemy of aesthetic transformation. Rumors of war were now coming to her so stretched and distorted that golfers were being mistaken for parachutists, and innocent tourists for the enemy. This showed what a "surplus of unused imagination" the English possess. "We—the educated—check it: as I checked my cavalry on the down at Telscombe and transformed them [in *Pointz Hall*] into cows drinking."

How many other such fantastic transformations were woven into the novel we have no way of knowing. But there is one in particular which can be traced. It is about an incident that took place in December 1939 and how that incident emerged, some six months later, in the pages of *Pointz Hall*. On page 218 of the earlier typescript of the novel, there is a short scene in which an unidentified character says: "The Brookes have gone to Sicily, in spite of everything [war, etc.] . . . If the worst should come—let's hope it won't—they'd hire an aeroplane . . . Yes, I was saying they've gone to Sicily . . . They've seen the volcano. Most impressive in eruption."

On Sunday December 17, 1939, Virginia noted in her diary: "Oh the Graf Spee is going to steam out of Monte Video today into the jaws of death. And journalists and rich people are hiring aeroplanes from which to see the sight." The *Graf Spee* was a badly damaged Nazi German battleship which took refuge in the harbor of Montevideo and, after releasing her crew and unloading her supplies, was blown up on December 17 to prevent its being captured by the English. Its commander, Hans Langsdorf, draped the ship's flag across his bed and committed suicide in a Buenos Aires hotel two days later. And so, just as the soldiers at Telscombe were transformed into cows drinking, so too was the *Graf Spee* turned into a volcano. Aerial photographs of the battleship's fiery end show how easy it was to imagine the scene as the smoky belchings of a volcanic eruption.

The Woolfs remained at Monks House throughout 1940, paying only occasional visits to London. Virginia was working too hard and worrying too much about the still unfinished *Roger Fry*. It was too thin, and unless she could add a little body to the text, "it'll have no interest, even for an old woman, turning the pages." By the end of January she was trying, with little success, to rewrite the last chapter. The exacting members of the Fry family were never very far from her mind. They would have to approve the book, and she expected "endless objections."

Virginia thought often of London, and the walks she might be taking to the Tower, to the Library, to the Strand. What would it be like when German bombers began to drop their deadly load—"I mean, if a bomb destroyed one of those little alleys with the brass bound curtains and the river smell and the old woman reading, I should feel—well, what the patriots feel."

By early February she was putting the finishing touches on *Roger Fry*. It could have been a better story, but she knew she'd caught a good deal of that "iridescent man" in her net of words. "I daresay I've written every page—certainly the last—10 or 15 times over." On February 23, she plunged into the icy waters of family approval, feeling like a schoolboy showing his exercise book to a teacher hard to satisfy. She also sent Vanessa a copy of the typescript—and sat upright holding her breath.

Vanessa wrote back immediately: "Since Julian died I haven't been able to think of Roger. Now you have brought him back to me. Although I cannot help crying, I can't thank you enough." Margery Fry approved too. The life was "very alive and interesting . . . It's *him* . . . unbounded admiration." A little later, she wrote a formal letter which appeared as the book's Foreword. In it she said: "Years ago, after one of those discussions upon the methods of the arts which illuminated his long and happy friendship with you, Roger suggested, half seriously, that you should put into practice your theories of the biographer's craft in a portrait of himself. When the time came for his life to be written some of us who were very close to him, thinking it would have been his wish as well as ours, asked you to undertake it. I have now begged to have this page to tell you of our gratitude to you for having accepted, and for having brought to completion a piece of work neither light nor easy."

Virginia almost gave a sigh of relief. "Almost" because something happened that had never happened before and would have considerable consequence. In March Leonard read the first half of the biography and refused to endorse it. Never before had he been so openly severe about Virginia's writing. The method was wrong. It was mere analysis. There was too much dead quotation. If one didn't already know Roger, the book would be dull and boring. One did not write biography that way! His criticism was rational, impersonal, and emphatic. This, at least, was how Virginia heard it. It was a very severe "lecture." It was like "being pecked by a very hard strong beak." The more he pecked the deeper went the hard, fatal beak. Virginia used the very image she had reserved twenty years earlier for Mr. Ramsay/Leslie Stephen: "the fatal sterility of the male plunged itself, like a beak of brass, barren and bare . . . the beak of brass, the arid scimitar of the male, which smote mercilessly, again and again." This was the tyrannical version of her father. But there was always another image of Leslie Stephen trailing behind this one—the image of the father she loved; the absentminded philosopher whose "fly buttons" were often undone, the adorable man who agreed that "the whole of life did not consist in going to bed with a woman"; the father who was so often away in the Swiss Alps with his guide Melchior Anderegg on her birthday. Whatever she thought, it is clear that re-creating Roger Fry's life had rekindled the ashes of Leslie Stephen.

And whether Leonard's criticism was justified or not matters little today. What mattered then was the effect it had. For despite the approval the biography won from Vanessa and Margery Fry, Virginia was privately more convinced than ever that her years of labor had been largely wasted. The book was a failure; and as a failure it did nothing to justify her either as a writer or even as a human being. Little wonder, then, that she turned to *Pointz Hall* in such desperation. If she failed at biography, surely she would succeed in fiction? But nothing now was certain. Leonard disliked the book. Perhaps he disliked Roger too, and the aura of paternity he radiated. Perhaps he resented Roger's influence over Virginia, resented the gratitude she felt as a writer. He may still have been fuming over losing his greenhouse. Whatever Leonard felt, his blast came like a spray of cold rusty water. It was brutal.

It is hard to imagine suffering such a blow from someone so close without feeling a certain degree of mortification. But whatever Virginia felt she expressed only in mild sneers in the privacy of her diary. As they labored through Good Friday and the Easter weekend, she occasionally looked up from her page and saw "poor Leonard . . . so bothered with fetching and carrying, and so serious, and with the old roadmaster's bucket of red coal smouldering in him." But sneers did nothing to soften his verdict. She had failed. Now she must work harder than ever. Only work would save her. Only effort.

A letter from Vita had come a few days earlier almost as a miracle. How was Virginia? Where was Virginia? What was she doing? Why had they drifted apart? Her beloved Vita still cared. Virginia reached for her pen— ". . . how I long to hear from your own lips what's been worrying you—for you'll never shake me off—no, not for a moment do I feel ever less attached." When Vita didn't reply, Virginia wrote again. Vita *must* write at once to reassure her: "One line on a card—that's all I ask."

During the remainder of March and April, when there was time and inclination, Virginia mulled over the "Sketch of the Past" she had begun writing in April of the previous year. And often she turned to her diary. It was becoming her sole companion in this vast and vacant country life. Neither guns nor bombs had yet begun to thunder; but each day was lived in grim expectation. In early May, Vanessa told Virginia a "very tiresome piece of family news": Angelica (Duncan's biological daughter) was in love with Bunny Garnett (Duncan's former lover). They had gone off together to live alone for two months in Yorkshire—the beautiful young Angelica passionately in love with a man old enough to be her father. "Pray God she may tire of that rusty surly slow old dog with his amorous ways and his primitive mind." What might Angelica be thinking this May evening as their train hurled its way to Yorkshire with all "the nightingales singing from that rusty canine jaw?"

On May 10, without warning, German land and air forces invaded Holland, Luxembourg, and Belgium. On the same day, Neville Chamberlain, having by this time lost his credibility, resigned as Prime Minister. Winston Churchill stepped in to lead the national coalition. "But though Leonard says he has petrol in the garage for suicide should Hitler win, we go on." Leonard offered his services as Local Defence Volunteer and assumed fire-watching and air-raid-precaution duties in the village. On the morning of May 15 he and Virginia discussed "suicide if Hitler lands. Jews beaten up. What point in waiting? Better shut the garage doors. This a sensible, rather matter of fact talk." But Virginia resisted the idea of dying in the garage: she wanted to live "for 10 years more, and to write my book." On May 29 she resumed *Pointz Hall*.

As the weeks drew nearer to July 25, publication day of *Roger Fry*, doubt grew to dread; and the familiar fears took hold. Virginia was veering into a state where concentration was becoming difficult. Her brain was wilting. She was feeling irritable and depressed. She had not done her best work. Like Isis, trying to bring the scattered pieces of Osiris together, she continued to struggle with the assemblage of Roger Fry. This was her present to Vanessa. It was her homage to Roger himself. It was also a proof of her ability as a biographer. But somehow the tension generated by these separate motives created further confusion and only increased the uncertainty.

On June 10, she sent off the page proofs of *Roger Fry* "and thus have read my Roger for the last time," she said—and began sinking into the doldrums. By this time she was convinced by Leonard's coolness that the book was "one of my failures." The phrase "one of my failures" suggests that she had begun to think of her two earlier books—*The Years* and *Three Guineas*—as failures too. *Pointz Hall* was now her only outlet and into it she poured all her remaining energy.

A decade and a half earlier Virginia had said in a piece called "Life and the Novelist"* that the "writer's task is to take one thing and let it stand for twenty: a task of danger and difficulty." She had performed this technical maneuver beautifully with the "hedge" in *To the Lighthouse* and repeated it with even greater virtuosity with the famous "crimson chair with gilt claws" image in *The Years*. She would now create one for *Pointz Hall*, but on a grand historical scale, and call her strategy "playing with words." With that wordplay she attempted to dramatize some Freudian concepts of ambivalence, herd instinct, primitive regression, and incest; and in so doing, she obliquely introduced into her novel one of the greatest love stories of all time—the Egyptian myth of Isis and Osiris, a tale of passion and betrayal and death and resurrection. With that story appeared a theme never before treated in any of her fiction: the brother-sister (emotional) incest of Lucy Swithin and Bartholomew Oliver, a coupling that replaced the implied father-daughter incest of *The Years*.

Pointz Hall (Between the Acts) is a historical, multilayered novel comprising many separate but interrelated strands of idea and image; and the Isis-Osiris myth is just one of those strands, but one connecting all the others in varying degrees of significance. Virginia Woolf introduced the myth in the earliest draft of the novel and retained it, unaltered, throughout all its revisions.

In a seemingly inconsequential transitional scene toward the end of the novel, Lucy Swithin, the old widowed sister of Bartholomew Oliver, seeks out Miss LaTrobe to thank her for her village pageant—and adds at the end of her short speech: "... you've made me feel I could have played ... Cleopatra!" This is perhaps one of the boldest strokes in the entire book, for Lucy's identification with Cleopatra also implies her identification with Isis, the most famous of Egyptian goddesses. There are numerous variations to the Isis legend, but in its most general outline, Isis is the sister-wife of Osiris, Pharaoh of Egypt, with Isis his Queen. A jealous brother traps Osiris in a chest and drops him into the Nile. Isis, transformed into a swallow, flies off and finds Osiris. The brother discovers him too, cuts the body into fourteen

* *New York Herald Tribune*, November 7, 1926.

pieces and scatters them across Egypt. Isis once more goes in search of her brother-husband and re-collects and re-members—remembering is healing—thirteen of the pieces. The fourteenth piece, the phallus, has (according to Plutarch) been swallowed by a fish. Isis not only re-members the body but also magically conceives a son called Horus.

Cleopatra, historical accounts tell us, was trained from childhood to dramatize herself in the role of Isis; and the swallow, one of the manifestations of Isis, thus became a major religious and ceremonial symbol. If Lucy Swithin identified with Cleopatra, she would also have had to assume a number of characteristics of Isis, the most conspicuous being the swallow. So that in the novel, Virginia Woolf was careful to insert one detail after another to give Lucy Swithin the cosmic quality she cumulatively assumes, and these details clarify her special relationship to her brother Bartholomew. Throughout the novel, therefore, the swallows in the temple-like barn Lucy repeatedly comments on, her fascination with fish, her perching like a bird, her "fly-away" clothes, her settling "like a bird . . . before starting out for Africa," her chirruping sounds, her brother's puzzlement at how she had ever borne children—all these details lose their randomness when Lucy is seen in the context of Cleopatra and Isis.

The Isis reference, one of many scattered throughout the novel, proliferates further and connects to the "huge symbolical figure" of Charles Budge. For it is Budge who waves "his truncheon" at Lucy Swithin. With the Cleopatra reference still echoing in the reader's mind, the character named Budge would have summoned the recently deceased E. A. Budge, Keeper of Egyptian Antiquities in the British Museum; and the "truncheon pointed markedly at Mrs. Swithin" also points to Isis's search for Osiris's phallus, the fourteenth missing part. So that Budge and Lucy and Cleopatra and Isis all gradually become inextricably and fundamentally bound up in the allusive deliberations of the novel.

With *Roger Fry* now in the hands of the printers, Virginia Woolf was again feeling unanchored and despondent. "I must put my head to the gallop, so as to cover these weeks"—the weeks to July 25, publication day. The first draft of *Pointz Hall* was still unfinished. She had her memoir to occupy her. But even these two manuscripts were not enough. It was almost as if something compulsory and self-governing had been set in motion. She had brought Roger Fry back to life and to utterance. But with *Roger Fry* begun on April 1 alternating with *Pointz Hall* begun on April 2—just as she had alternated chapters of fiction and essays in *The Pargiters*—Virginia was once more fluctuating between fact and fiction. This parallel by itself was a grim reminder of *The Years*, which cost her nearly five years of labor and almost her sanity. For somewhere there lurked still that corrosive sense of failure she had felt after *The Years* soared into publicity.

She had "killed" Mrs. Pargiter too soon in the novel; she had thus dodged her rivalry with Julia, her ambivalence; she had not been sufficiently candid about the father-daughter incest theme that just perceptibly runs through the novel; she had glossed over too much—much too much—of the sexual component so muffled in the relationship between Abel Pargiter and his sacrificial daughter Eleanor.

In early summer Adrian supplied Leonard and Virginia with a lethal dose of morphine should Hitler prevail. "This, I thought yesterday, may be my last walk," she wrote on Saturday, June 22. With a diminished readership she was feeling unvalued and especially vulnerable, with nothing to hang on to. Her readers, that "outer wall of security," were no longer there to validate her as a writer. "No echo comes back. I have no surroundings. I have so little sense of a public . . . those standards—which have for so many years given back an echo and so thickened my identity are all wide and wild as the desert now." Without that "wall of security" it was easy for Virginia to disparage herself, to become self-condemnatory. Still, those readers who had sent her soaring into success with *The Years*, those readers who had "thickened" her identity, had proved tasteless, indiscriminate, not entirely literate. If they served to ratify Virginia Woolf as a novelist, then Virginia Woolf's identity as a novelist was in serious danger.

On July 24, one day before *Roger Fry* was to appear, she returned in weary anticipation to the idea of being alone in a void, with nothing to shield her. "The veil will be lifted tomorrow, when my book comes out. That's what may be painful: may be cordial. And then I may feel once more round me the wall I've missed." Vacancy was all she felt. There was "No audience. No echo. That's part of one's death." In the "I and thou" of writer and reader, her "thou" was gone, and so the tension grew.

On the next day, to her relief, the biography's reception was cordial. So once more the protecting wall—for the moment—stood firm, the echo briefly heard, and immunity temporarily restored. With the scant assurance of only a few press notices, she felt vaguely shored up again and able to stand back for a moment to consider the book she had just written of this magnificent father figure. "What a curious relation is mine with Roger at this moment—I who have given him a kind of shape after his death—Was he like that? I feel very much in his presence at the moment: as if I were intimately connected with him; as if we together had given birth to this vision of him: a child born of us." She had given him back to the people he loved. Her offering, like Miss LaTrobe's, had been accepted. Surely that was a victory? And "poor Leonard" was wrong. The strong, hard, pecking beak had miscalculated. At the moment Leonard's judgment didn't seem very much to matter. She had "given birth" this time without his help. As the weeks wore on, Virginia appeared to feel increasingly cut off from the husband who had for so many years helped to make her work and success possible.

But how long would the immunity last, would she feel protected by the echo? How long before she felt once more the hireling of a random and recalcitrant world? Not very long, said the voice inside. She must soon leave this mild, this momentary celebration of Roger Fry and flee once more to *Pointz Hall*. Only in the open circuits of imagination would she again find stability and set those fluctuating interior scales in balance. But she had grown very tired, her hands shook; the new novel would require long stretches of sustained effort and all the assurance of her craft.

Where would that assurance come from? She had brooded too long in the twilight margins and worked too hard to propitiate Roger's shade. In pargeting Vanessa's love affair with him, she had, as with *The Years*, performed once more "an experiment in self-suppression." Then there was Leonard's chilling comment that the book was lifeless and dull. Virginia Woolf had always been her own severest critic; certainly she must have seen this for herself. So even with Vanessa and Margery Fry's approval, even with the generous letters of her friends, she soon began to feel a haze of defeat closing over her.

During the second half of 1940, faded recollections of 1913 began to gather; memories of childhood and madness and suicide began moving toward her like a procession of omens. The terrible conflicts of her mother and father were deafening—Leslie's infantile selfishness, Julia's pathological selflessness. Those were facts. That was reality. What stood behind it were two stern people, one of whom had made life intolerable. The Ramsays and their beautiful children—they were all made up, invented, counterfeit. That harmony suddenly turned sour, meretricious, a facade. Leonard too had failed her. And Vanessa. And what about Vita? Where did she stand in this museum of mannequins? Would Virginia ever recover the elusive mother, the lost father? Would she, now approaching sixty, remain the pathetic, needy orphan?

The ancient noise of war was everywhere. A quarter of a century earlier, almost half her lifetime, whatever else might be wanting, she had at least a greater physical durability to sustain her. But here, now, in 1940, a glance into the past showed her incontestably how tough a fiber she would need to survive the impending crisis. And here, now, there was something else to furrow her brow: What did the public care for the books of Virginia Woolf? for the elegance of her mind and pen? There were trenches to dig, shelters to build, the sick and the wounded to nurse. Did anyone care in this time of crisis for prose or poetry or the refinements of sentiment? It was in this state of mind—barely perceptible in her diary, and not at all in her letters—that she plunged headlong into *Pointz Hall*.

 In August, with the Battle of Britain, all the imagined horrors of war suddenly materialized. There were German air assaults over Kent and Sussex, and night bombing over London. On the sixteenth, and for many days to follow, German bombers flew directly over Rodmell. "We lay down under the tree . . . flat on our faces, hands behind head. Don't close your teeth said Leonard . . . Will it drop I asked? If so, we shall be broken together. I thought, I think, of nothingness . . . Hum and saw and buzz all around us."

And there was Vita at Sissinghurst with enemy planes overhead. She was in Kent as a volunteer ambulance driver. Virginia had been expecting her to come to Monks House for the night. "I'd just put flowers in your room. And there you sit with the bombs falling round you. What can I say—except that I love you and I've got to live through this strange quiet evening thinking of you sitting there alone . . . You have given me such happiness."

Virginia, finally, was beginning to see that Vita was really the only person in this strange lifelike drama whose appearance and whose reality were one and the same. Through all the years of love and disappointment and frustration, Vita remained the real thing behind the appearance. She was Mrs. Manresa in *Between the Acts*, who alone had the courage to stare into the looking glass without flinching. Mrs. Manresa alone "preserved unashamed her identity, and faced without blinking herself. Calmly she reddened her lips."

On September 10, Mecklenburgh Square was hit. The house adjacent to the Woolfs' was demolished and still smoldering. Under tons of brick were people who'd gone down to their shelter, now trapped. There were shreds of cloth clinging to bare walls, mirrors swinging in midair. "I sometimes think about violent death," she wrote in her diary. A few days later a time bomb exploded in the Square, badly damaging their house. Windows blew out, ceilings collapsed, china was smashed, and books lay in piles of broken glass and plaster. The place was now uninhabitable. Plans were made to transfer the Hogarth Press and its staff to Letchworth in Hertfordshire. The move took place on September 23. Through early November about 200 German bombers attacked London nightly.

In Rodmell, matters were no better. They saw a plane shot down before their eyes over the Lewes race course—"a scuffle; a swerve; then a plunge; and a burst of thick black smoke." Every night, about 8:30, they waited for the air raid and listened for the "sinister sawing noise" overhead; and in the midst of all this destruction, Virginia conceived an idea for a new book. It was to be a "Common History book—to read from one end of literature, including biography; and range at will, consecutively."*

London began to resemble a doomed city of craters. Vast holes were torn in the streets; squares were split asunder, office buildings demolished, shops destroyed. Some hotels, still standing, were mere shells of brick and mortar; windows were shattered; water pipes burst; broken gas lines fed open fires. It was a ghastly, sepulchral sight. In mid-October 52 Tavistock Square was destroyed by a bomb. It was in this house that Virginia had brought so many pages to life. Now there was only rubble. The rooms were now only hanging walls and shards of glass.

As the days passed, the fighting grew more intense. Lists of the dead lengthened. Rodmell, situated as it was on the south coast, came increasingly in the line of fire. Lewes felt the bombs, and planes overhead were now a daily sight. Virginia had already seen her first hospital train, gorged with the broken bodies of soldiers; each car "grieving and tender and heavy laden and

* See Brenda Silver, "'Anon' and 'The Reader': Virginia Woolf's Last Essays," *Twentieth Century Literature*, vol. 25, Fall/Winter 1979. Virginia Woolf began this book on social history and worked on it intermittently throughout the remaining months of her life; it was unfinished at her death.

private." This was the full pressure of war, the long slow train, carrying its terrible burden through green fields. Did the wounded look out and see what she saw? Were they afraid? Did they think of death? She did.

If Hitler conquered, she and Leonard had a great deal to fear. They were sure to face torture and humiliation. And so there was gasoline in the garage and morphine in the house. But that was little comfort. Death lay behind everything during these weeks of chaos and expectation. It was almost fitting that she should be sitting alone with her diary on a fading October day when a line from Gray's "Elegy" breasted its way, unbidden, onto the page—"And all the air a solemn stillness holds." In the twilight of her imagination, everything now seems to have grown still and solemn.

Her response to the war took on a special meaning which she alone understood. War and civilization were incompatible. She knew that. She also knew privation and loss. She had mourned the death of Julian. She had seen her London home destroyed and all the souvenirs of shelter and civilization destroyed with it. Certainly she feared the bombs dropping outside her window. Certainly the daily toll of human slaughter horrified her. But privately, war had for her its own sinister rhetoric. It meant that readers at the doors of the London Library would soon become barbarians at the gate—indifferent, even hostile, to art, to literature, to Virginia Woolf.

Without the endorsement of a civilized people, her identity—as an artist and as a woman—was denied ratification. With no "Thou" there could be no "I." That was war's special meaning. Hadn't Freud confirmed her sense that uniqueness was flattened to herd instinct in times of stress? Was she not also certain that for every group claim imposed by war, she would have to surrender some requisite part of herself? So as a novelist, Virginia found her sense of Self—her identity, both public and private—in greatest jeopardy. "It's odd to feel that one's writing in a vacuum—no one will read it . . . the audience has gone," she wrote in 1940. And just fifteen days before her death: "It's difficult, I find, to write. No audience. No private stimulus, only this outer roar."

She had always needed public approval. Yet no matter how spirited the ovation, it was never enough. Even in times when fame was secured, praise ran high, and editions piled up, she required continual reassurance. Within weeks, more often within days, she was off again, her brain "on the boil," making up a new book.

But there were times when the public—and her friends too—were reticent, even a little petulant; and these were dangerous times. The first wrench of fear always seemed to set in motion some obscure mechanism very close to self-contempt. Rarely, it seems, did it occur to her that she had deliberately written something to arouse antagonism—*Three Guineas*, for instance—and that the response was entirely natural and justified. On the contrary, too often she heaped upon herself more blame than was reasonable. She had been too reckless. When failure seemed inevitable, punishment quickly confiscated the place pain would more justifiably have occupied. In such circumstances, the *ideal* novelist set about flogging the *real* "hack." If failure exacted such punishment, she would be more severe with herself next time. This, or something like it, appears to be how her interior penal system operated. She had only to be careful to avoid exhaustion. For if her energy ran dry and a book failed, she would not have sufficient strength to prevent her *idealized* image from crushing the *real* Virginia Woolf under the weight of condemnation.

Running parallel with this process was a growing sense of guilt. When the idealized "I" was in danger, every movement of the pen, every phrase pinned down on paper, became a matter of large consequence. Had she not already delivered one failure after another? Had she not already provoked shouts of protest and derision with *Three Guineas*? And had her fill of worthless praise in *The Years*? Had she not discovered her "echo" tasteless and untrustworthy, applauding a book that should have been condemned? That appalling triumph had renewed her sense of dependency, usurping what little security there remained. And even then, in 1937, she was losing her way.

She must now, in 1940, somehow justify herself as a writer. Only through writing could she "put the severed parts together"; only with words could she "take away the pain" and reconcile those deep divisions, bring together in wholeness and harmony those ancient warring factions within. But every time the chilly propositions of reason failed, the force of emotion gained ascendancy and terrifying ideas took over—she was declining as a novelist; her powers were shrinking, her fame eroding; old age and dependency were gaining ground. She must shut her ears to the sounds of slaughter and once more force her pen to "do its business." She had only to review her yearly income to verify her decline: she had earned £3,426 from her books in 1937; in 1938 the figure dropped to £2,972; by 1939 the figure dipped to a mere £477.

In the eddies of imagination, her obsession with money spilled over into *Pointz Hall*. Isa, the wife of a stockbroker, hid her poetry in an account book; old Bartholomew worried about the exchange rate while the world crumbled around him. Much of this concern with money was a regressive slide to 1900, when Vanessa held out the weekly accounts and Sir Leslie groaned. There were other small signs throughout the novel, however, that as Virginia moved artistically forward, her story slid backward to tarnished memories and the primal enchantments of childhood. *Re*-membering was healing. Her memorial "A Sketch of the Past," written at the same time as *Pointz Hall* and tinging its pages with these hoary details, thus became a palimpsest of those opening years long gone and presumably forgotten.

But they were not forgotten. Some mysterious force kept her turning back. England's past—could she not find it disguised in the private ledgers of personal history? Were we not all Victorians, only dressed differently? In some curious way, this became her single line of reason, and the more she pursued that line, the more autobiographical *Pointz Hall* became. It was as though to her past she must return, in search of some sponsorship there and then, vital to her here and now.

In writing her memoir, Virginia was forced once again to re-visit 22 Hyde Park Gate. She had said once that writing *To the Lighthouse* had exorcized those memories, but it is clear from her aborted attempt in *The Years* that those ancient residues still troubled her. She could not put her mother and father to rest. She was trying now for the third time to come to terms with those two people. Whenever she tried to press fact and feeling together, she heard only discord. For as long as Virginia competed with Julia for Leslie's love, as long as she persisted in keeping alive Julia's love for Herbert Duckworth, and as long as she felt a love for her father that *for an adult* was unnatural in its intensity, there would be shame and guilt and despair. Whenever she returned to the past, she would somehow have to "correct" this strange twist in father-daughter coupling. For it was *only* in childhood that her love seemed natural and pure. And so she returned to that past with ever-increasing urgency. It was this child's vision she must cling to.

But the divisions in her past were too deep for reconciliation. They could never be brought together, never be joined in a truce of amity. *The Years* had emerged as a block of cold granite. It had shown her how ephemeral the *Lighthouse* rainbow had been. Now in her "Sketch of the Past" she was trying again. But perhaps it was too late. Only the child's vision held good. And she was no longer a child.

50 "Oh my Violet," the young Virginia had implored her friend thirty-six years earlier, just after her father's death, "if you could find me a great bit of solid work to do . . . I should be so grateful. I *must* work." And later, again to Violet Dickinson: "I know I can write, and one of these days I mean to produce a good book." At the age of twenty-two, her anodyne was work. Her longing to write was not simply to divert her mind from morbid thoughts. The inner executives of her being had inaugurated a much more complex process. For within a few short months of her father's death, the need to write usurped the place of loss. Her father's death had plunged her into a sea of helplessness and she tried to check that terrifying feeling in the only way she knew—by writing, by arranging words in sequences, by creating something outside herself that did not exist before. Writing thus became her restorative and would grow into the most deeply wrought and emancipating enterprise in her life.

"Haddock and sausage meat," she wrote twenty days before her suicide, "I think it is true that one gains a certain hold of sausage and haddock by writing them down." Was this a joke? Or was she, at the age of fifty-nine, admitting half-heartedly that even her dinner must be spelled out?

Writing imposed symmetry and coherence on a world of chaos and discord. This had come to her as a stunning discovery and in it lay the key to her continuance. Writing meant transforming a dissonant world of granite into lyrical arcs of rainbow. It was her one supreme act of sublimation—making reality poetic, benign, bearable. Anyone reading her diary will notice almost at once that the more menacing life became, the higher and oftener she soared into the airy spaces of imagination. It was in some such state of mind that she made her way into the world of *Pointz Hall*. After her disillusionment with *The Years*, the abuse of *Three Guineas*, her absolute aloneness in resurrecting Roger Fry, and her increasing sense of having lost Vita, only more work could fill the emptiness and assuage the crippling sense of impotence. No matter how random her days might become, she was a writer. She would bid her pen to "do its business," and reinstate order and purpose.

As the calendar moved relentlessly forward, Virginia persisted in driving herself almost to her limit. She would soon have to submit to fatigue and depression, its deadly companion. But still she went on at full speed. Day after day, as though flirting with disaster, she continued to write and write and write. Nothing could quiet her pen. Before the first draft of *Pointz Hall* was completed, she was making notes for her new book, adding new sections to her memoir.* In a frenzy of work, the pages mounted. And daily the demon force drove her further down the familiar slope to collapse.

From this distance in time, it appears as though a cycle had been set in motion. As the need to conquer powerlessness grew, the need to write grew; and the greater the need to write, the greater the fatigue; the greater the fatigue, the less satisfactory the production; the less satisfactory the production, the greater the sense of impotence, and the greater the need to conquer it by writing, and on and on it went.

Something happened at about this time that added to the turmoil. Virginia had impulsively lent £150 to Helen Anrep, Roger Fry's last mistress, who was in some kind of financial difficulty. As soon as she handed over the money to Helen, Virginia began to regret her rashness. She would never be repaid. She had worked so hard for that £150. It had been foolish to squander hard-earned money that way. (In fact Helen finally repaid her only £25 of the total sum.) Money at this time was an especially sensitive point. Still, Virginia's reaction was out of proportion, and having learned from the cradle the symbolism of the pound sterling, she worked herself into a highly excited state.

This same troublesome Helen Anrep was also the source of friction which now involved Vanessa. With Leonard's help, Vanessa had found a furnished cottage for rent in the village of Rodmell and told her about it. Helen took the cottage and with her two children, Igor and Anastasia, assumed occupancy on September 23. Virginia exploded. "I'm in a rage," she said to her diary. "Nessa has told those d_____d Anreps they can come to the cottage for a fortnight." And Vanessa had solicited Leonard's help. The thought of having that "spawn in the village" was offensive. Imagine having to look at Anastasia Anrep's "great gargoyle gutter dripping" for two weeks. Not for years had Virginia so violently lost her temper with Vanessa, and both were "cold and distant" after their wrangle. On the following day: "A rather strained talk on the phone with Nessa. She hasn't forgiven the Anrep conversation."

A circle of quiet began to surround Virginia, and within its circumference a barely perceptible congress of trouble. With Leonard's "pecking" condemnation of the Fry biography still smoldering, she realized just how much he

---

* She revised the description of her relationship to her father from "an odd fumbling fellowship" (*Moments of Being*, 1st ed., 117) to "a passionate fumbling fellowship" (*Moments*, 2nd ed., 137).

could hurt her when he chose to. And Vanessa too. She had acted carelessly, selfishly; she seemed heedless of Virginia's feelings. Vanessa and Leonard— like mother and father—the two people (apart from Vita) who mattered most in her life, had acted almost as if they wanted deliberately to hurt her; and she felt more alone than ever. Only work would numb the growing sense of isolation.

In the autumn of 1940, dying was becoming a preoccupation. "Last night a great heavy plunge of bomb under the window . . . I try to imagine how one's killed by a bomb. I've got it fairly vivid—the sensation . . . then scrunching and scrambling, the crushing of my bone shade in my very active eye and brain . . . painful? Yes. Terrifying. I suppose so—Then a swoon; a drum; two or three gulps attempting consciousness—and then, dot dot dot."

She was also drifting into strange terrain. But only in her diary was this discernible. "If it were not treasonable to say so," she wrote in the middle of October, "a day like this is almost too—I won't say happy: but amenable. The tune varies, from one nice melody to another." Several days later, when Tavistock Square was destroyed by bombs, Virginia looked at the ruins "with a sigh of relief." A change of mood was taking place. Their Mecklenburgh Square house too was all rubble and shattered glass, and again she felt "exhilaration at losing possessions." The devastation was liberating, exciting. She was no longer tied down to material things. She'd miss her books and chairs and carpets, but still it was "odd—the relief at losing possessions." Then in mid-November, she felt "infinite delight" when enemy planes bombed the nearby river. Flooding water roared over the marsh. "All the gulls came and rode the waves." It was "an island sea, of such indescribable beauty . . . that I can't take my eyes off it."

Virginia was feeling something close to euphoria. She seemed to be moving into the exalted stage of her illness, which would reverse itself a few months later. But in this autumn of 1940, her moods, though often elevated, were beginning to fluctuate. One day she was high; the next low. Some days were bursting with energy, others were exhausting and torpid. The fluctuations were unpredictable; but for the most part she was feeling elated and in that state she continued to write away at *Pointz Hall*. When she was not writing, the reality of war "seep[ed] in"; hence the "necessity of living in the upper air." On November 23, she finished a second typescript draft of *Pointz Hall* and, without pausing for breath, plunged into her manuscript on social history.

Then, at the end of November, she dipped abruptly into a mood of rage.

For some reason it suddenly occurred to her that the villagers of Rodmell were bloodsuckers draining her and Leonard of their vitality. The Woolfs were educated; they had money; they were well-known figures in the political and literary world. "Anyone with 500 a year and education, is at once sucked by the leeches. Put Leonard and me into a Rodmell pool and we are sucked—sucked—sucked. I see the reason for those who suck guineas. But life—ideas—that's a bit thick ... The simple envy us our life. Last night Leonard's lecture attracted suckers. Gwen Thompsett [a villager] is a sucker."

Had Leonard seen this entry, he would have acted immediately. He would have seen just below the surface some disturbance sending up signals that would lead to an eruption. Her exhaustion was becoming palpable. Her hands were now shaking visibly. "As you can see, my hand trembles," she wrote to Ethel Smyth, "... my mind is churned and frothed; and to write one must be a clear vessel." To Angelica: "I write in haste, with a trembling paw." To her diary, on Christmas Eve: "I note with some dismay that my hand is becoming palsied."

Christmas always brought Sir Leslie to mind. For it was during this season that he recited Milton to the family, and his image returned to Virginia with a long trail of memories. Death had ended his life, but not her love. Even now she could feel his presence. Did it matter how much he had failed her? How much she'd hated some of the things he'd stood for? Did it matter how much unhappiness he had caused? How excluded he'd once made her feel? All she knew was that the word "Father" would always touch something deep and precious. His memory would always matter.

"I detest the hardness of old age—I feel it. I rasp. I'm tart.

The foot less prompt to meet the morning dew,
The heart less bounding at emotion new,
And hope, once crushed, less quick to spring again."

These lines from Matthew Arnold's "Thyrsis" she copied out in her last entry for 1940. She was winding down. Exhaustion would soon step in to take its toll.

In writing *The Years* and *Roger Fry*, Virginia had lingered too long in the precincts of history, where memories of childhood weakness and passivity had been roused and were now crowding and menacing. She had intruded too much upon the ranks of the dead and left behind her too many cenotaphs. Ghosts of long ago were now stepping round her as in a danse macabre, pointing fingers of blame for disturbing what should have been left to slumber. In both *The Years* and *Roger Fry* she had pargeted her story in the name of family propriety, and had rushed headlong from one book to the next without pause or rest. Now she was worn out, depleted. To those near her she appeared serene, in possession. Leonard said she was "calmer and happier than usual." Perhaps she was a little too calm. For no one seems to have guessed that she had drifted into a kind of exhausted euphoria which would within weeks veer into the blackest of depressions.

In the meantime, concentration grew increasingly difficult. The shapely sentence resisted the pressure of her pen. The fountain of words began to subside. Little ruptures in logic tore into the coherence of daily life, and the battle against weariness grew every day more futile. She seemed to waver now on that thin line of indifference that separates hope from despair. It was too late now to attempt a balance of the forces without and the pressures within. The urge to rid herself of so much inner dissonance had become too powerful. No longer was it possible to catch in the rainbow of words those granitic chunks of feeling that so troubled her. The bottom had become untouchable. The past unreachable. Doors shut. Keys turned. Whatever remained locked within was left to do its predatory work.

It has been said that when every promise in one's world is lost, a person will search for something that will furnish him with some small reason to go on. One shred of hope, one dim ray of light—that is all one needs to persist in the struggle. That ray in Virginia's life, apart from Leonard and Vanessa, was Vita Sackville-West.

When the retrenchment of Vita's passion mellowed their love into friendship, a large and vital piece of Virginia's life had somehow got lost without hope of being recovered. Try as she might to push aside her vague sense of estrangement, she could not. Reason gradually made Virginia realize that she no longer had the luxury or the right to claim from Vita anything beyond the measured bounds of camaraderie; and there was a certain grimness about this realization. It was perhaps for this reason that Virginia not only "wrote" Vita into *Pointz Hall* in the loving and lusty character of Mrs. Manresa—that "cornucopia of bounty"—but also inserted into her script certain lines that only Vita would recognize, lines copied from *The Edwardians*, betokening love, loss, and death. Whatever it was that life refused to furnish, surely one could find in the larger globe of imagination.

Orlando, published in October 1928, had been Virginia's letter of love to Vita. And now woven into its multiple themes, *Pointz Hall* (*Between the Acts*) would contain her letter of farewell. Into the script of her novel, Virginia had inserted a line from *Orlando* ("Life, Life, Life! cries the bird as if he had heard") which was meant for Vita alone to identify—"birds syllabling discordantly life, life, life . . ." Virginia meant Vita to translate "life, life, life" into its Latin equivalent—"Vita, Vita, Vita." And Vita did indeed catch the message, but by the time she did, it was too late.*

On a glistening Thursday in January 1941, Virginia opened her diary and entered a line from Walter de la Mare's "Fare Well"—"Look your last on all things lovely." The entry was prophetic, for her own valediction was not far off. By this time she was worn out, unable to ward off the confederate fears of old age and servile dependency and palsied hands and the dread of madness. Her relations with Vanessa were still strained. In her mind, her fame and reputation had declined; before long she would be anonymous. The memory of all her yesterdays now showed her only a desolate girl "ground down harshly by fate."

As the days passed, her mood of serenity turned into "a battle against depression." The ostensible reason was *Harper's Bazaar*'s rejecting her story "The Legacy"; but the trouble had a deeper source, and she fought it with what remaining strength she had. "This trough of despair shall not, I swear, engulf me." It was becoming daily more evident that she lived now "without a future," and was trying to deny her despondency. Hadn't she told Ethel Smyth she was reading through the whole of English literature? "By the time I've reached Shakespeare the bombs will be falling. So I've arranged a very nice last scene." But her voice was thin and her joke hollow. Ethel also heard the truth—that Virginia could no longer concentrate: "I read and read like a donkey going round and round a well; pray to God some idea will flash . . . I can no longer control my brain." But with all that, did Ethel still love her? Did Vita and Vanessa and Leonard still love her? "Do love me," she implored Ethel. Someone must.

---

* Four years after Virginia's death Vita and Harold Nicolson compiled an anthology of poems called *Another World than This*. In it, Vita took this passage, as it was written in *Orlando*, and lineated it to resemble a poem; she had indeed interpreted the lines correctly.

Once fertile tracts of feeling and fancy were now pressed dry. She had trouble writing, and without writing Virginia's world suddenly became unreal, menacing, and she herself reduced once more to a state of helpless passivity. Without words there was nothing to "take away the pain." It was the failure of illusion—a fate worse than death. "Little donkey, kneel down. Fill your pannier," she had just written in *Pointz Hall*. "Then rise up, little donkey, and go your way . . . till the heels blister and the hoofs crack. There's no lying down, laying aside, or forgetting." For such was the "burden laid on me in the cradle." The lament was not only for Leonard and Vanessa and Vita. It spoke now for everything else that was missing or lost in the ledgers of her past.

On Wednesday, February 26, the third draft of the novel was finished— she now called it *Between the Acts*—but still something was wrong. She must erase from its pages certain harsh indictments, tone down her dangerous wordplay and name games; she had slipped in too many verbal tricks, swept in compromising allusions that might easily be traced. The novel was "silly and trivial." A fourth draft would repair these faults. "But shall I ever write again one of those sentences that gives me intense pleasure?"

Time was running out. And exhaustion had now begun to do its final work. Virginia saw it coming and in her diary remembered Henry James's injunction: "Observe perpetually. Observe the oncome of age. Observe greed. Observe my own despondency. By that means it becomes serviceable . . . I will go down with my colours flying . . . Occupation is essential." And so her soliloquy drew to an end. This was written at seven in the evening, Saturday, March 8. It was time for her to cook dinner—haddock and sausage meat. She would "conquer this mood." By this time, Leonard could not have failed to see how depressed she had become.

Virginia's final descent had begun in late December 1940; and as it happened, Dr. Octavia Wilberforce, distantly related to Virginia on the Stephen side of the family, had started visiting the Woolfs regularly at about this time. Octavia lived with the retired actress Elizabeth Robins in Brighton. Robins had a farm in Henley and Octavia brought milk and cream to the Woolfs during this period of wartime shortage. It was thus as a friend and doctor that Octavia Wilberforce became involved in the last months of Virginia's life.

It seems that either on the twenty-second or the twenty-third of December, Virginia read through her father and mother's love letters. For what exactly, she wasn't sure. What she clearly saw, however, was Leslie's love for Julia, the "general presence" Virginia had tried without success to capture all her life. Reading through those letters was disturbing, unsettling. "I shall lose my child's vision, and so must stop." If she didn't stop, she would be forced as a grown-up daughter to face her forbidden feelings. And like Septimus Warren Smith, she could not bring out into the open those "hidden thoughts which are the most diseased."

Elizabeth Robins, who had returned to America during the war years, was receiving letters daily from Octavia, and news of Virginia became one of the chief items of interest. Octavia wrote on December 23, for instance: "She [Virginia] had been sorting papers, love letters from her father to her mother. Had been swept away by them. 'Poor Leonard is tired out by my interest in my family and all it brings back.'"

Many years earlier, Virginia had heard of the British Society for the Study of Sex and Psychology, and had written in her diary that it was a group in which people of all ages discussed all manner of things "without shame"; for instance they talked about incest—"Incest between parent and child when they are both unconscious of it." "I think of becoming a member," she added quietly on that very private page. Whether she said this seriously or as a joke is irrelevant. It was her idea, and that's all that mattered. If this was still festering in her mind in December 1940, it is not surprising that she should look upon Julia and Leslie's bed as the "sexual centre"—and the "death centre"—of 22 Hyde Park Gate; that she should return so many times in her diary and fiction and memoir to the scene of her mother's death. It was like a malignancy that would not go away.

When Octavia saw her on December 31, Virginia said that *Pointz Hall* was a complete failure, a worthless book: "I've lost all power over words—can't do a thing with them." On another occasion Octavia brought up *Roger Fry*. "I can imagine no more really expert biographer," she said. "Have you been thinking of writing your father's life?" Octavia had become convinced that Virginia was "haunted by her father." And Leonard agreed with her. Virginia could not stop thinking of her father or her childhood.

On March 1, 1941, just twenty-seven days before her suicide, she was revising a story called "The Symbol." Several months earlier—in fact, on November 23, 1940, five days before Sir Leslie's birthday—she had in her diary expressed the hope of writing something whose starting point would be her "mountain top—that persistent vision." In "The Symbol"—the mountain peak being a symbol of something that "remained almost unspeakable even to herself"—the narrator, an elderly Englishwoman, staying at an inn in the Swiss Alps (its owner, Herr Melchior, named very likely after her father's

Alpine guide, Melchior Anderegg), is writing a letter to her sister confessing how once she had wished her mother to die—"I never told you...how I longed when the doctor came, that he should say, quite definitely, She cannot live another week." Here was Virginia trying, still, to work through the terrible intensities of her "unspeakable" feeling, trying still to lay the ghosts of Leslie and Julia to rest. But time was short.

Less than two weeks later, on March 12, Octavia came to Monks House to tea and had a long private talk with Virginia, who confessed to "feeling desperate—depressed to the lowest depths." After her mother's death, she said, her father "threw himself too much on us. Made too great emotional claims...and that I think has accounted for many of the wrong things in my life. I never remember any enjoyment of my body." Octavia could see how haunted Virginia was by her past—with her father its principal ghost.

On Tuesday, March 18, before going to the tidal river Ouse, Virginia wrote a note (undated) to Leonard on the upper right-hand corner of which "Tuesday" is clearly inscribed,* and left it for him to find. It reads as follows:

Tuesday

Dearest,†

> *I feel certain that I am going mad again: I feel we cant go through another of those terrible times. And I shant recover this time. I begin to hear voices and cant concentrate. So I am doing what seems the best thing to do. You have given me the greatest possible happiness. You have been in every way all that anyone could be. I dont think two people could have been happier till this terrible disease came. I cant fight it any longer, I know that I am spoiling your life, that without me you could work. And you will I know. You see I cant even write this properly. I cant read. What I want to say is that I owe all the happiness of my life to you. You have been entirely patient with me. If anybody could have saved me it would have been you. Everything has gone from me but the certainty of your goodness. I cant go on spoiling your life any longer.*
>
> *I dont think two people could have been happier than we have been.*

V.

---

* A facsimile of this letter is published in Spater and Parsons, 185.
† In the third volume of his autobiography (1st American edition), written some twenty-two years later, Leonard said that in 1941, Virginia "wrote the last words of *Between the Acts* on February 26 and 23 days later on March 21 she committed suicide" (*Beginning Again*, 81). In his memory, Virginia appears to have died (even after his characteristic calculation) one week earlier—on the date closer to March 18, the day presumably of her aborted attempt.

At about 11:30 a.m. she took her walking stick and made her way through the water-meadows to the river, where she tried—and failed—to drown herself. It appears that Leonard did not see the letter she'd left him and went out to meet her. In his own diary for that Tuesday, March 18, he noted that she was "not well and in the next week I became more and more alarmed. I am not sure whether early in that week [the phrasing is ambiguous, but he must be referring to that Tuesday, March 18] she did not unsuccessfully try to commit suicide. She went for a walk in the water-meadows in pouring rain and I went, as I often did, to meet her. She came back through the meadows soaking wet, looking ill and shaken. She said that she had slipped and fallen into one of the dykes. At the time I did not definitely suspect anything, though I had an automatic feeling of desperate uneasiness." (If the letter to Leonard was still where she'd left it, she must have assumed that he had not seen it and therefore removed it herself upon entering the house.)

Leonard presumably then communicated his "uneasiness" to Vanessa on that or the next day. For on Thursday, March 20, Vanessa came to see Virginia's condition for herself. Upon returning to Charleston she wrote the following (excerpted) letter, dated Thursday, March 20:

> You *must* be sensible. Which means you must accept the fact that Leonard and I can judge better than you can. It's true I haven't seen very much of you lately, but I have often thought you looked very tired and I'm sure that if you let yourself collapse and do nothing you would . . . be only too glad to rest a little. You're in a state when one never admits what's the matter—but you must not go and get ill just now. What shall we do when we're invaded if you are a helpless invalid . . . Both Leonard and I have always had reputations for sense and honesty so you must believe us . . . I shall ring up sometime and find out what is happening.

What indeed would Leonard and Vanessa do with her if she became "a helpless invalid"? That was the last thing in the world Virginia wanted to hear. What would they do with a mentally deranged woman of fifty-nine? That was her worst fear. She might be put away and forgotten, like her half sister, Laura.

On Friday, March 21, Octavia came to tea. Virginia told her she could no longer write. "I've lost the art." And if she couldn't write, she was completely defenseless. Only with words could she "take away the pain." "She said she had taken to scrubbing floors when she couldn't write," Octavia confided to

Elizabeth Robins. Leonard had told Octavia privately that afternoon that he
thought Virginia was in great danger. It was arranged that if the situation
got worse, they would come to her in Brighton for consultation. Then on
Sunday, March 23, Virginia replied to Vanessa's letter:

Sunday

Dearest,

    *You cant think how I loved your letter. But I feel that I have gone
too far this time to come back. I am certain now that I am going mad
again. It is just as it was the first time, I am always hearing voices and
I know I shant get over it now.*

    *All I want to say is that Leonard has been so astonishingly good, every
day, always; I cant imagine that anyone could have done more for me
than he has. We have been perfectly happy until the last few weeks, when
this horror began. Will you assure him of this? I feel he has so much to
do that he will go on, better without me, and you will help him.*

    *I can hardly think clearly any more. If I could I would tell you what
you and the children have meant to me. I think you know.*

    I have fought against it, but I cant any longer.

Virginia

Virginia wrote the letter but didn't send it. She must have been quite certain by this time that both Leonard and Vanessa had surmised the extrem-
ity of her condition and had between them decided upon the best course of
action. She would wait and see. On Monday, March 24, Leonard thought
Virginia "somewhat better." Two days later he changed his mind. On
Wednesday, March 26, he wrote: "I knew that the situation was very dangerous. Desperate depression had settled upon Virginia; her thoughts raced
beyond her control; she was terrified of madness. One knew that at any
moment she might kill herself." Virginia's condition was more serious than
it had been since August and September in 1913. His task was now to persuade her to admit that she was ill; and to do that he needed the help of
Octavia Wilberforce. So arrangements were made to see her in Brighton on
the following day. In the meantime, the words "rest cure" and "nursing
home" must not be uttered. They were the magic words that might set off
the worst possible reaction.

On Thursday, March 27, before setting out to see Dr. Wilberforce, Virginia wrote to John Lehmann, who had read the typescript of *Between the
Acts* and wanted to publish it that spring. (The letter may have been written earlier; but Leonard posted it on the twenty-seventh with his own cov-

ering letter telling Lehmann "that Virginia was on the verge of a complete nervous breakdown." Lehmann did not receive the letter until Saturday, March 29, when it no longer mattered.) Virginia's letter of the twenty-seventh read:

> Dear John,
> I'd decided, before your letter came, that I cant publish that novel as it stands—its too silly and trivial.
> What I will do is revise it, and see if I can pull it together and so publish it in the autumn. If published as it is, it would certainly mean a financial loss; which we dont want. I am sure I am right about this.
> I needn't say how sorry I am to have troubled you. The fact is it was written at intervals of doing Roger with my brain half asleep. And I didn't realise how bad it was till I read it over. Please forgive me, and believe I'm only doing what is best ... Again, I apologise profoundly.
> Yours,
>
> Virginia Woolf

On that Thursday afternoon, the interview with Octavia Wilberforce took place. It was a difficult and awkward meeting. Virginia began insisting almost at once that nothing was wrong with her, that the visit was entirely unnecessary, and she refused to answer any questions. Octavia convinced her that all she needed to do was give Leonard a little peace of mind. To do this, would she permit herself to be examined? "Will you promise if I do this not to order me a rest cure?" Virginia pleaded. She desperately needed this reassurance. Hadn't Vanessa threatened her already with the mandate to "not go and get ill"? "What I promise," said Octavia, "is that I won't order you to do anything that you won't think it reasonable to do. Is that fair?"

The interview, Leonard thought, had gone as well as could be expected. Octavia agreed to come to see her in a day or two. "We felt," Leonard wrote, "that it was not safe to do anything more at the moment. And it was the moment at which the risk had to be taken, for if one did not force the issue—which would have meant perpetual surveillance of trained nurses—one would only have made it impossible and intolerable to her if one attempted the same kind of perpetual surveillance by oneself." But it was the wrong decision.*

---

* In Virginia's September 9, 1913, suicide attempt, Leonard assumed the blame for having left unlocked the medicine case in which he kept the veronal, but—"I seem to be mentally and morally unable to cry over spilt milk."

And what was Virginia thinking during all these deliberations? That her mother had ignored her; that her father had excluded her; and now Leonard, and Vanessa too, the people she loved most, and Vita—had they all deserted her? Were these deserters the *real* people behind the show?

On the next day, Friday, March 28, at eleven in the morning, Leonard walked out to the lodge. Virginia said she would do some housecleaning and then go for a walk before lunch. She left the second suicide letter to him on her writing table and accompanied him back to the house. Leonard left her to work in his study. Virginia then placed the first "Tuesday" (March 18) letter to Leonard and her Sunday (March 23) letter to Vanessa in separate blue envelopes and left them for Leonard to find. She then put on her fur coat, took her walking stick, and left the house. It was now about 11:40 a.m. When she reached the river, she left her walking stick on the bank, put a large stone in her coat pocket, and walked into the Ouse.

Later in the day, Leonard found the second letter to him, this one on the writing pad in her lodge, written presumably on that morning of March 28:*

> *Dearest,*
>
> *I want to tell you that you have given me complete happiness. No one could have done more than you have done. Please believe that.*
>
> *But I know I shall never get over this: and I am wasting your life. It is this madness. Nothing anyone says can persuade me. You can work, and you will be much better without me. You see I can't even write this, which shows I am right. All I want to say is that until this disease came on we were perfectly happy. It was all due to you. No one could have been so good as you have been, from the very first day till now. Everyone knows that.*
>
> *V.*
>
> *You will find Roger's letters to the Maurons in the writing table drawer in the Lodge. Will you destroy all my papers.*

---

* On May 11, 1941, Leonard wrote on the reverse side: "This letter was not the one left for me by V. I found it later in the writing block on which she was writing when I went out to see her in the Lodge about 11 on the morning of March 28. She came into the house with me, leaving the writing block in the Lodge. She must, I think, have written the letters which she left for me and Vanessa in the house immediately afterwards." See Virginia Woolf, *Letters* VI, Appendix A.

The last line of the March 18 suicide letter—"I don't think two people could have been happier than we have been"—echoes that of the death-room scene in *The Voyage Out*—"No two people have ever been so happy as we have been"—written almost thirty years earlier.

POSTSCRIPT

Three weeks later, some children found her body by the river. The identification took place on April 18 in the Newhaven mortuary, and the inquest on the nineteenth. On Monday, the twenty-first, Virginia was cremated in Brighton. Leonard was alone at the cremation, and that night, alone, he played a recording of the cavatina from the Beethoven Quartet in B flat, op. 130, as they had many years earlier agreed upon. He buried her ashes beneath one of the two great elm trees they had christened "Leonard" and "Virginia" in the Monks House garden.

CHRONOLOGY

FAMILY TREE

NOTES

SELECTED BIBLIOGRAPHY

INDEX

CHRONOLOGY

1832	November 28	Birth of Leslie Stephen
1833	May 19	Birth of Herbert Duckworth
1846	February 7	Birth of Julia Duckworth (née Jackson) in India
1848		Julia returns with her mother to live in England
1855		Dr. John Jackson, Julia's father, joins his family; they live until 1866 at Brent Lodge in Hendon; Leslie Stephen is ordained a deacon
1856		Leslie Stephen becomes a tutor at Trinity Hall, Cambridge
1863		Leslie Stephen visits the United States and befriends James Russell Lowell
1866	December 14	Birth of Roger Fry
		Jacksons move to Saxonbury, a country house in Frant, near Tunbridge Wells
1867	May 4	Marriage of Julia and Herbert Duckworth
	June 19	Marriage of Leslie Stephen and Minny Thackeray
1868	March 5	Birth of George Herbert Duckworth
1869	May 30	Birth of Stella Duckworth
1870	September 19	Death of Herbert Duckworth
	October 29	Birth of Gerald Duckworth
	December 7	Birth of Laura Makepeace Stephen
1875	November 28	Death of Minny Thackeray Stephen on Leslie's forty-third birthday
1878	March 26	Marriage of Leslie Stephen and Julia Duckworth; they settle in Julia's house, 13 Hyde Park Gate South, which becomes 22 Hyde Park Gate in 1884
1879	May 30	Birth of Vanessa Stephen
1880	September 8	Birth of Thoby Stephen
		Between 1880 and 1884, Julia writes her children's stories
	November 25	Birth of Leonard Woolf
1881	November–December	Leslie Stephen purchases lease of Talland House, St. Ives
1882	January 25	Birth of Adeline Virginia Stephen (AVS)

	November	Leslie Stephen, editor of *Dictionary of National Biography*
1883	October 27	Birth of Adrian Leslie Stephen
		Julia publishes *Notes from Sick Rooms*
1887	March 31	Death of Julia's father, Dr. John Jackson
1889	June	Julia as "Mrs Leslie Stephen" signs "An Appeal Against Female Suffrage"
	Summer	Laura consigned to Earlswood Asylum for the Imbecile and Weak-minded
	Winter	Madge (Vaughan) Symonds stays at 22 Hyde Park Gate for several months
1890	Summer	Leslie Stephen in the United States, awarded honorary doctorate from Harvard
1891	January	Thoby begins Evelyn's Preparatory School
	February	*Hyde Park Gate News* begins publication
	April	Leslie Stephen retires from *Dictionary of National Biography*
1892	January	Adrian begins Evelyn's Preparatory School
	February 3	Death of James Kenneth Stephen, St Andrew's Hospital, Northampton
	April 2	Death of Julia's mother, Maria Jackson, at 22 Hyde Park Gate
1894	March 11	Death of James Fitzjames Stephen, Leslie's brother
	September	Thoby goes to Clifton College, Bristol
1895	May 5	Death of Julia Stephen
	Summer	AVS's first nervous breakdown
	November	Lease on Talland House sold
1896	August 22	Stella Duckworth engaged to Jack Hills
	September 24	Adrian enters Westminster School
1897	January 3	AVS begins writing a journal, still convalescent
	April 10	Stella marries Jack Hills
	April 28	Stella returns ill from honeymoon to her house at 24 Hyde Park Gate
	June 22	Queen Victoria's Diamond Jubilee
	July 19	Death of Stella
1898	January	AVS takes Greek classes at King's College, London
	July 28	Madge Symonds marries Will Vaughan
	October 17	AVS also takes Latin with Clara Pater
1899	Summer	Stephen family at Warboys, Huntingdonshire
	October 3	Thoby enters Trinity College, Cambridge; also entering: Lytton Strachey, Saxon Sydney-Turner, Leonard Woolf, and Clive Bell

1900	Summer	Stephen family to Fritham House, Lyndhurst
	Autumn	AVS returns to King's College
1901	Summer	Stephen family returns to Fritham House
	October	AVS learns bookbinding
	November	Leslie Stephen receives Hon. D. Litt., Oxford
1902	January	AVS begins private Greek lessons with Janet Case
	June 26	Leslie Stephen created Knight Commander of the Bath in Coronation Honours
	Summer	Family again to Fritham House; AVS meets Violet Dickinson; Clive Bell visits
	October	Adrian enters Trinity College, Cambridge
	December 12	Sir Leslie operated on by Sir Frederick Treves
1903	Summer	Family to Netherhampton House, Salisbury
	October	Sir Leslie dying of cancer; Thoby reading for the bar
	November 14	Sir Leslie dictates last entry in *Mausoleum Book* to AVS
1904	February 22	Death of Leslie Stephen
	February–March	Four Stephens and George Duckworth to Manorbier, Pembrokeshire
	April 1	Four Stephens to Venice with Gerald Duckworth
	May 1	Vanessa, AVS, and Violet Dickinson to Paris, where they are entertained by Clive Bell; Thoby is also there
	May 10	AVS's second nervous breakdown begins
	Summer	AVS goes to Violet Dickinson's house in Welwyn for about three months; first suicide attempt by throwing herself from window
	September 10	Marriage of George Duckworth to Lady Margaret Herbert
	October	AVS stays with Aunt Caroline Emelia Stephen in Cambridge; Stephens move from 22 Hyde Park Gate to 46 Gordon Square, Bloomsbury
	November 17	Leonard Woolf dines with Stephens on eve of departure for Ceylon for seven years
	November 18	AVS goes to Giggleswick to Madge and Will Vaughan
	December 3–10	AVS returns to Aunt Caroline Emelia in Cambridge
	December 14	AVS's first published book review in *The Guardian*
1905	January 14	AVS pronounced well by Dr. George Savage, can begin teaching at Morley College
	February 16	Thoby begins Thursday Evening "At Home"; Saxon Sydney-Turner is the only guest
	March 29	AVS and Adrian to Spain and Portugal; they return April 23

	June/July	Clive Bell proposes to Vanessa and is refused
	Summer	Four Stephens to Cornwall for two months
1906	August	AVS and Vanessa to Blo' Norton Hall, Norfolk
	September 8	Four Stephens and Violet Dickinson to Greece
	October 21	Thoby returns to England
	November 20	Thoby dies of typhoid fever
	November 22	Vanessa agrees to marry Clive Bell
1907	February 7	Marriage of Vanessa and Clive
	April 10	AVS and Adrian take up residence at 29 Fitzroy Square; the Bells remain at 46 Gordon Square
	October	AVS begins work on first novel, *Melymbrosia* (published in 1915 as *The Voyage Out*)
	December	AVS resigns from Morley College
1908	February 4	Birth of Julian Bell
	April 24	Cornwall: AVS's flirtation with Clive Bell begins
	June 20	Death of Walter Headlam
	August	Holiday: Wells and Manorbier; one hundred pages of *Melymbrosia* completed
	September	AVS to Italy with the Bells
1909	February 17	Lytton Strachey proposes marriage
	March 30	AVS dines for the first time with Ottoline Morrell
	April 7	Death of Caroline Emelia Stephen; AVS inherits £2,500
	April 23	AVS to Florence with Bells; AVS returns May 9
	August	AVS to Bayreuth Wagner festival with Adrian and Saxon Sydney-Turner; returns September 3
	December 24–28	AVS spends Christmas alone in Lelant, Cornwall
1910	June	AVS shows signs of depression
	July	AVS at Jean Thomas's private nursing home
	August	AVS on walking tour of Cornwall with Jean Thomas
	August 19	Birth of Quentin Bell
	November 8	First Post-Impressionist exhibition; closes January 15, 1911
	December 24	AVS finds house to rent in Firle, Sussex; Christmas at Pelham Arms, Lewes, with Adrian
1911	February 4–6	AVS completes furnishing Little Talland House in Firle
	April 22	AVS sets out for Broussa, Turkey, where Vanessa (with Clive and Roger Fry) has fallen ill
	October	AVS negotiates lease on Asheham House
	November 20	AVS moves into 38 Brunswick Square
	December 4	Leonard Woolf, returned from Ceylon, moves into Brunswick Square
1912	January 11	Leonard Woolf proposes marriage

	January 16–19	AVS's symptoms of mental illness begin
	February 3	Housewarming party at Asheham
	February 16	AVS enters Jean Thomas's nursing home for two weeks
	March 9	AVS consults Dr. Maurice Wright, a psychologist whom Leonard had seen about his trembling hands
	May 29	AVS agrees to marry Leonard Woolf
	August 10	Marriage of Virginia and Leonard (henceforth VW and LW)
	August 18	Leave for six-week honeymoon in Italy and Spain
	October	Move into rooms at 13 Clifford's Inn
	December	Headaches threaten VW
1913	January	Headaches and insomnia; LW consults doctors about having children
	March 9	*The Voyage Out* delivered to Duckworth & Co.
	April 12	Novel is accepted by Duckworth
	June–July	VW increasingly unwell
	July 24	Enters nursing home again
	August 22	LW consults Drs. George Savage and Henry Head
	August 23	To Holford, where VW gets worse
	September 8	Return to London
	September 9	Suicide attempt with veronal
	September 20	To George Duckworth's Dalingridge Place, where VW convalesces until mid-November; moves to Asheham House until August 1914
1914	March	LW suffering from severe headaches
	April 8–30	Woolfs to Cornwall for holiday
	May	Leonard reads Freud's *The Interpretation of Dreams*
	October	Move to 17 The Green, Richmond
	December	Discover Hogarth House, Richmond
1915	January 1	VW begins to keep diary
	January 31	Reads Leonard's *The Wise Virgins*
	February 16	Early signs of another breakdown
	February 23	VW incoherent for two days
	March 4	Becomes violent; nurses called in
	March 25	LW moves possessions to Hogarth House
	March 26	*The Voyage Out* is published
	April–May	VW is violent and raving mad
	August 31	Allowed to write postcards
	September 11	Moves to Asheham with LW and one nurse
	November 4	Returns to Hogarth House
1916	March 16	LW exempted from military service

	October	Vanessa recently moved to Charleston, four miles from Asheham
1917	January	VW again reviewing for the journals
	March 23	Purchase of printing press; delivered April 24 to Hogarth House
	July	First published texts by Hogarth Press: *Mark on the Wall* (by VW) and *Three Jews* (by LW)
	July 29	Woolfs dine with Katherine Mansfield at Hogarth House
	November	VW writing second novel, *Night and Day*
	November 15	Woolfs buy larger printing press; Mansfield's long story *Prelude* to be published by Hogarth Press
1918	March 2	VW has written over 100,000 words of *Night and Day*
	April 14	Harriet Weaver comes to tea with Joyce's *Ulysses*
	May	Publication of Strachey's *Eminent Victorians*
	September 8	LW becomes editor of *International Review*
	November 15	First meeting with T. S. Eliot
	December 25	Birth of Angelica Bell (father is Duncan Grant)
1919	February 28	Woolfs given notice to leave Asheham House
	April 1	VW submits *Night and Day* to Duckworth; it is accepted on May 7
	May 12	Publication of *Kew Gardens*
	July 1	Woolfs buy Monks House, Rodmell
	September 1	Move from Asheham to Monks House
	October 20	Publication of *Night and Day*
1920	January 26	VW conceives "new form" for the novel
	April 16	Begins writing *Jacob's Room*
	September 10	Writing chapter 6 of *Jacob's Room*
	December 19	Reading Roger Fry's *Vision and Design*
1921	January 9	Writing chapter 9 of *Jacob's Room*
	March	*Monday or Tuesday*, a collection of stories, published
	December 17	Roger Fry discusses Henri Bergson and Proust
1922	April	VW develops racing pulse and irregular heartbeat
	May	Persistent fever and arrhythmia; has three teeth extracted
	September	Reading Joyce's *Ulysses*
	October 4	Harcourt Brace accepts *Jacob's Room*
	October 27	*Jacob's Room* published by Hogarth Press
	December 14	VW meets Vita Sackville-West at Clive's dinner party
1923	January 9	Death of Katherine Mansfield
	February 8	Writing *Mrs. Dalloway*
	June 24	VW sets type for *The Waste Land*
	October 15	Writing mad scene in Regent's Park in *Mrs. Dalloway*

1924	January 9	Purchases ten-year lease on 52 Tavistock Square
	March 15	Woolfs move to 52 Tavistock Square
	Spring	LW negotiates contract for publishing the International Psycho-Analytical Library (and the complete works of Freud in English translation)
	August 2	VW Writing death scene of Septimus in *Mrs. Dalloway*
	October 9	First glimmer of *To the Lighthouse*
	October 20	Begins second draft of *Mrs. Dalloway*
	October 30	Publication of *Mr. Bennett and Mrs. Brown*
1925	April 23	Publication of *The Common Reader*
	May 14	Publication of *Mrs. Dalloway*
	July 20	Conceives *To the Lighthouse* in three parts
	August 19	VW faints at Quentin's birthday dinner
	September 5	Has written first twenty-two pages of *To the Lighthouse*
	October–November	Ill and bedridden most of the time
	December 17–20	Beginning of love affair with Vita Sackville-West
1926	January	Writing *To the Lighthouse*
	February 22	Writing scene of Mrs. Ramsay watching the lighthouse
	April 30	Begins Part II, "Time Passes"
	May 27	Begins Part III, "The Lighthouse"
	September 6	Writing scene in boat approaching the lighthouse
	November 23	Revising *To the Lighthouse* on typewriter at the rate of six pages per day
1927	January 14	Finishes *To the Lighthouse*
	May 5	Publication of *To the Lighthouse* (thirty-second anniversary of Julia's death)
	July 8	Finishes lesbian story "Slater's Pins Have No Points"
	September 18	Writes review ("A Terribly Sensitive Mind") of Katherine Mansfield's *Journal* (edited by J. M. Murry)
	October	Begins writing *Orlando*
1928	January 17	Vanessa and Duncan leave for Cassis (near Toulon), where henceforth they will spend winters
	March 17	VW finishes draft of *Orlando*
	April 24	Revising *Orlando* at ten pages per day
	May 2	Hugh Walpole presents VW with Femina Vie Heureuse Prize for *To the Lighthouse*
	August	VW reading Proust
	September 24	To Burgundy with Vita for a week
	October 11	Publication of *Orlando*
	October 17	Eliot visits and reads "Ash Wednesday"
	November	Clive Bell's *Proust* is published by Hogarth Press

1929	September	Hogarth Uniform Editions issued of *Voyage Out, Jacob's Room, The Common Reader*, and *Mrs. Dalloway*
	October	VW slowly writing *The Moths* (which becomes *The Waves* on October 23)
	October 24	*A Room of One's Own* published in England and the United States; its sales for the next few months are unprecedented
1930	February 16	Writing Hampton Court scene of *The Waves*
	February 20	Meets Ethel Smyth for the first time
	April 29	Finishes first draft of *The Waves*
	July 30	Rewriting Rhoda on summer holiday scene (chapter 2) of *The Waves*
	August 29	VW faints in garden at Monks House and is ill for 10 days
	November 24	Rewriting chapter 8 of *The Waves*, the reunion dinner
1931	January 21	Speech to National Society for Women's Service, which grows into *The Pargiters*
	February 7	Finishes second draft of *The Waves*
	April 16–30	Motor tour of western France
	May 13	Typing *The Waves* at a rate of seven to eight pages per day
	July 21	Begins *Flush*
	October 8	Publication of *The Waves*
	December (mid)	Woolfs learn Lytton Strachey is seriously ill
1932	January 21	Death of Lytton Strachey
	January 31	VW finishes *A Letter to a Young Poet* (begun October 1931, to be published in June)
	March 11	Carrington commits suicide
	April 15	Woolfs, Roger and Margery Fry holiday in Greece to May 12
	August 11	VW finishes *The Common Reader (Second Series)*
	October 11	Begins *The Pargiters*
	November 1	Racing pulse; Dr. Rendel advises restricting activities
1933	March 27	VW refuses honorary doctorate from Manchester University
	May 5–27	Woolfs motor to France and Italy in new car
	October 5	*Flush* published in England and the United States; VW meets Gwen St. Aubyn at Sissinghurst
	November	Writing hard at *The Pargiters* since early spring
1934	February 8	Has written 130,000 words of *The Pargiters* in ten months
	April 26	Two-week motor tour of Ireland; Woolfs visit Elizabeth Bowen; VW reading Proust's *Sodom and Gomorrah*

	September 9	Death of Roger Fry
	September 30	VW finishes first draft of *The Years* (*The Pargiters*)
	November 15	Begins rewriting *The Years*, now with days of alternating euphoria and despair
	December 30	Rewriting "1907" chapter of *The Years*
1935	March 25	Rewriting "1917" chapter of *The Years* in desperation
	April 25	Suffering from headaches
	May	A month's motor tour of Holland, Germany, Italy, and France; reads *The Letters of Katherine Mansfield*
	July 12	Delivers opening address for the Roger Fry Memorial Exhibition at Bristol Museum and Art Gallery
	August 16	Trying to rewrite one hundred pages of *The Years* per week
	August 28	Julian Bell's farewell dinner; he has a teaching post in English at National University of Wuhan in China
	December	VW reading through Roger Fry's letters in preparation for writing his biography
1936	January 6	Begins final revision of *The Years*
	March 10	Sends first batch of *Years* typescript to printers before Leonard has read it
	April 8	Sends off last batch of *Years* typescript
	May 8–22	Motor tour of Cornwall on Dr. Rendel's advice
	May 26	Allowed to correct *Years* proof for forty-five minutes per day
	June 11	Writes diary for first time since April 9; notes that last two months have been the worst since 1913 nervous breakdown and suicide attempt
	November 1	Leonard reads *The Years* and declares it "extraordinarily good" but has many private reservations; VW relieved
	November (mid)	VW cuts *The Years* from 700 to 420 pages
	November 23	Begins *Three Guineas*
	December 10	Edward VIII abdicates; George VI succeeds
1937	February 12	VW working steadily at *Three Guineas*
	March 11	*The Years* published; VW relieved next day by good reviews
	May 7–23	Tour of western France
	June 1	*The Years* has reached top of best-seller list in the United States
	June 6	Farewell dinner for Julian Bell, who leaves next day to drive ambulance in Spain
	July 18	Julian Bell killed by a shell fragment

	August–September	VW devotes herself to consoling Vanessa
	October 12	Finishes first draft of *Three Guineas* and spends most of November with revisions
1938	January 9	Finishes rewriting *Three Guineas*
	January 23	John Lehmann buys VW's half share of Hogarth Press for £3,000
	April 1	VW begins writing *Roger Fry*
	April 2	Begins writing new novel, *Pointz Hall* (eventually called *Between the Acts*)
	June 2	Publication of *Three Guineas*
	June 16	Motor tour through Scotland and the Western Isles; return on July 2
	August 17	Begins reading seventeen volumes of Madame de Sévigné's letters
	September 20	Sketches chapter 7 ("Post-Impressionists") of *Roger Fry*
	November 14	Works on *The Art of Biography*
	December 1	Resumes writing *Roger Fry*
	December 19	Has brought *Roger Fry* to 1919 and completed one hundred pages of *Pointz Hall*
1939	January 28	Visits Sigmund Freud (and his son and daughter)
	March 10	Finishes rough draft of *Roger Fry*
	April 18	Begins writing memoir "A Sketch of the Past"
	April 26	Has revised one hundred pages of *Roger Fry*
	May 15	Writes portrait of Julia Stephen in "Sketch . . ."
	June 5–19	Motor tour of Normandy and Brittany
	August 17	Woolfs move the Press to 37 Mecklenburgh Square, and their possessions on the twenty-fourth
	September 1	Hitler invades Poland
	September 3	Britain declares war
1940	April 27	VW delivers "Leaning Tower" lecture to Workers' Educational Association in Brighton
	June 9	Correcting *Roger Fry* proofs
	July 25	*Roger Fry* published
	August	Battle of Britain for next two months, with daily air raids
	September 10	Bomb drops on Mecklenburgh Square, badly damaging Woolfs' house when it explodes a day or two later
	September 13	Hogarth Press and staff move to Hertfordshire
	November 23	VW finishes later typescript of *Pointz Hall*
	December 4	Woolfs move furniture and books from Mecklenburgh Square to Monks House
1941	January 13	James Joyce (a week younger than VW) dies in Zurich

January 26	*Harper's Bazaar* rejects a story called "The Legacy"
February 26	LW reads (*Pointz Hall*) *Between the Acts*
March 18	First suicide note probably written on this day
March 28	VW ends her life in the River Ouse

1942–1969		LW continues to live at Monks House
1948	May	Death of Adrian Stephen
1953		LW edits VW's *A Writer's Diary*
1960–69		LW writes his five-volume *Autobiography*
1961	April 7	Death of Vanessa Bell
1962	June 2	Death of Vita Sackville-West
1964		Death of Clive Bell
1966–67		LW edits VW's *Collected Essays* in four volumes
1969	August 14	Death of LW

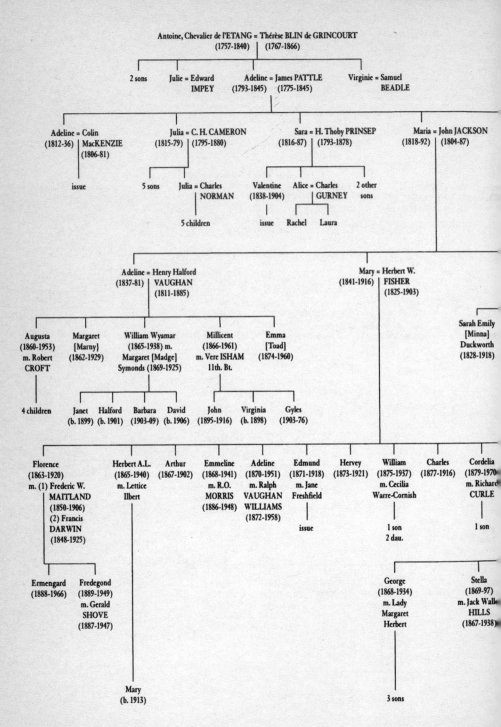

Antoine, Chevalier de l'ETANG = Thérèse BLIN de GRINCOURT
(1757-1840)　　(1767-1866)

2 sons　　Julie = Edward　　Adeline = James PATTLE　　Virginie = Samuel
　　　　　　IMPEY　　(1793-1845) (1775-1845)　　　　BEADLE

Adeline = Colin　　Julia = C. H. CAMERON　　Sara = H. Thoby PRINSEP　　Maria = John JACKSON
(1812-36) │ MacKENZIE　(1815-79) (1795-1880)　(1816-87) (1793-1878)　(1818-92) (1804-87)
　　(1806-81)

issue　　5 sons　Julia = Charles　　Valentine　Alice = Charles　2 other
　　　　　　　　NORMAN　　(1838-1904)　　GURNEY　sons

　　　　　5 children　　issue　Rachel　Laura

Adeline = Henry Halford　　　　　　　Mary = Herbert W.
(1837-81) │ VAUGHAN　　　　　　　(1841-1916) │ FISHER
　　(1811-1885)　　　　　　　　　　　(1825-1903)

　　　　　　　　　　　　　　　　　　　　　　　　　Sarah Emily
　　　　　　　　　　　　　　　　　　　　　　　　　[Minna]
Augusta　Margaret　William Wyamar　Millicent　Emma　　　Duckworth
(1860-1953)　[Marny]　(1865-1938) m.　(1866-1961)　[Toad]　(1828-1918)
m. Robert　(1862-1929)　Margaret [Madge]　m. Vere ISHAM　(1874-1960)
CROFT　　　　Symonds (1869-1925)　11th. Bt.

4 children　Janet　Halford　Barbara　David　John　Virginia　Gyles
　　　　(b. 1899)　(b. 1901)　(1903-09)　(b. 1906)　(1895-1916)　(b. 1898)　(1903-76)

Florence　Herbert A.L.　Arthur　Emmeline　Adeline　Edmund　Hervey　William　Charles　Cordelia
(1863-1920)　(1865-1940)　(1867-1902)　(1868-1941)　(1870-1951)　(1871-1918)　(1873-1921)　(1875-1937)　(1877-1916)　(1879-1970)
m. (1) Frederic W.　m. Lettice　　m. R.O.　m. Ralph　m. Jane　　m. Cecilia　　m. Richard
MAITLAND　Ilbert　　MORRIS　VAUGHAN　Freshfield　Warre-Cornish　CURLE
(1850-1906)　　　　(1886-1948)　WILLIAMS
(2) Francis　　　　　　　(1872-1958)
DARWIN　　　　　　　　　　　　issue　　　1 son　　　1 son
(1848-1925)　　　　　　　　　　　　　　　　2 dau.

Ermengard　Fredegond　　　　　　　　　　　　　George　　　Stella
(1888-1966)　(1889-1949)　　　　　　　　　　　(1868-1934)　(1869-97)
　　　　m. Gerald　　　　　　　　　　　　m. Lady　　m. Jack Wall
　　　　SHOVE　　　　　　　　　　　　Margaret　　HILLS
　　　　(1887-1947)　　　　　　　　　　Herbert　　(1867-1938)

　　　　Mary　　　　　　　　　　　　　　3 sons
　　　　(b. 1913)

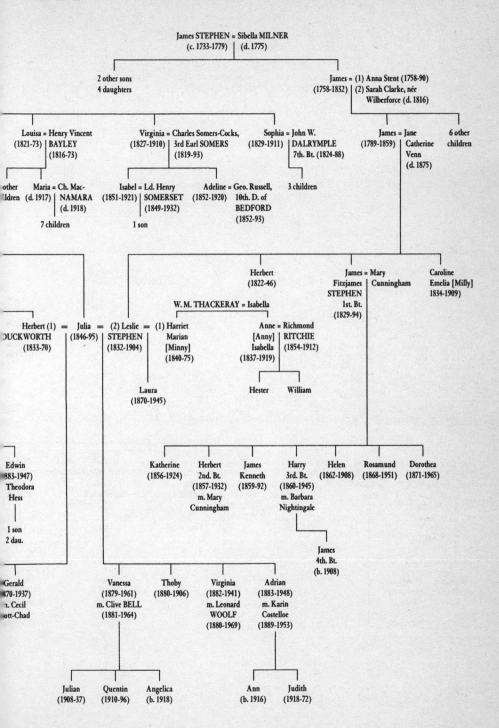

James STEPHEN = Sibella MILNER
(c. 1733-1779)   (d. 1775)

2 other sons
4 daughters

James = (1) Anna Stent (1758-90)
(1758-1832) | (2) Sarah Clarke, née
          Wilberforce (d. 1816)

Louisa = Henry Vincent
(1821-73) BAYLEY
          (1816-73)

Virginia = Charles Somers-Cocks,
(1827-1910) 3rd Earl SOMERS
          (1819-93)

Sophia = John W.
(1829-1911) DALRYMPLE
          7th. Bt. (1824-88)

James = Jane
(1789-1859) Catherine
          Venn
          (d. 1875)

6 other
children

other
ldren   (d. 1917)

Maria = Ch. Mac-
       NAMARA
       (d. 1918)

Isabel = Ld. Henry
(1851-1921) SOMERSET
          (1849-1932)

Adeline = Geo. Russell,
(1852-1920) 10th. D. of
          BEDFORD
          (1852-93)

3 children

7 children

1 son

Herbert
(1822-46)

James = Mary
Fitzjames Cunningham
STEPHEN
1st. Bt.
(1829-94)

Caroline
Emelia [Milly]
1834-1909)

W. M. THACKERAY = Isabella

Herbert (1) = Julia = (2) Leslie
DUCKWORTH (1846-95) STEPHEN
(1833-70)   (1832-1904)

(1) Harriet
Marian
[Minny]
(1840-75)

Anne = Richmond
[Anny] RITCHIE
Isabella (1854-1912)
(1837-1919)

Laura
(1870-1945)

Hester   William

Edwin
883-1947)
Theodora
Hess

Katherine
(1856-1924)

Herbert
2nd. Bt.
(1857-1932)
m. Mary
Cunningham

James
Kenneth
(1859-92)

Harry
3rd. Bt.
(1860-1945)
m. Barbara
Nightingale

Helen
(1862-1908)

Rosamund
(1868-1951)

Dorothea
(1871-1965)

1 son
2 dau.

James
4th. Bt.
(b. 1908)

Gerald
470-1937)
. Cecil
ott-Chad

Vanessa
(1879-1961)
m. Clive BELL
(1881-1964)

Thoby
(1880-1906)

Virginia
(1882-1941)
m. Leonard
WOOLF
(1880-1969)

Adrian
(1883-1948)
m. Karin
Costelloe
(1889-1953)

Julian
(1908-37)

Quentin
(1910-96)

Angelica
(b. 1918)

Ann
(b. 1916)

Judith
(1918-72)

NOTES

ABBREVIATIONS

LS/JD   Leslie Stephen's letters to Julia Duckworth are housed in the Berg collection of the New York Public Library

JD/LS   Julia Duckworth's letters and extracts are in the British Library

MB   *Sir Leslie Stephen's Mausoleum Book*. Ed. Alan Bell. Oxford: Clarendon Press, 1977.

MoB (1976) Virginia Woolf. *Moments of Being*. Ed. Jeanne Schulkind. New York: Harcourt Brace Jovanovich, 1976.

MoB (1985) Virginia Woolf. *Moments of Being*. Ed. Jeanne Schulkind. 2nd ed. New York: Harcourt Brace Jovanovich, 1985.

QB I   Quentin Bell. *Virginia Woolf: A Biography*. Vol. I (1882–1912). New York: Harcourt Brace Jovanovich, 1972.

QB II   Quentin Bell. *Virginia Woolf: A Biography*. Vol. II (1912–1941). New York: Harcourt Brace Jovanovich, 1972.

APA   Virginia Woolf. *A Passionate Apprentice: The Early Journals 1897–1909*. Ed. Mitchell A. Leaska. London: Hogarth Press; New York: Harcourt Brace Jovanovich, 1990.

VWD I   *The Diary of Virginia Woolf*. Vol. I, 1915–1919. Ed. Anne Olivier Bell, assisted by Andrew McNeillie. London: Hogarth Press; New York: Harcourt Brace Jovanovich, 1977.

VWD II   *The Diary of Virginia Woolf*. Vol. II, 1920–1924. Ed. Anne Olivier Bell, assisted by Andrew McNeillie. London: Hogarth Press; New York: Harcourt Brace Jovanovich, 1978.

VWD III   *The Diary of Virginia Woolf*. Vol. III, 1925–1930. Ed. Anne Olivier Bell, assisted by Andrew McNeillie. London: Hogarth Press; New York: Harcourt Brace Jovanovich, 1980.

VWD IV   *The Diary of Virginia Woolf*. Vol. IV, 1931–1935. Ed. Anne Olivier Bell, assisted by Andrew McNeillie. London: Hogarth Press; New York: Harcourt Brace Jovanovich, 1982.

VWD V   *The Diary of Virginia Woolf*. Vol. V, 1936–1941. Ed. Anne Olivier Bell, assisted by Andrew McNeillie. London: Hogarth Press; New York: Harcourt Brace Jovanovich, 1984.

VWL I	*The Letters of Virginia Woolf*. Vol. I, 1882–1912. Ed. Nigel Nicolson and Joanne Trautmann. London: Hogarth Press; New York: Harcourt Brace Jovanovich, 1975.
VWL II	*The Letters of Virginia Woolf*. Vol. II, 1912–1922. Ed. Nigel Nicolson and Joanne Trautmann. London: Hogarth Press; New York: Harcourt Brace Jovanovich, 1976.
VWL III	*The Letters of Virginia Woolf*. Vol. III, 1923–1928. Ed. Nigel Nicolson and Joanne Trautmann. London: Hogarth Press; New York: Harcourt Brace Jovanovich, 1977.
VWL IV	*The Letters of Virginia Woolf*. Vol. IV, 1929–1931. Ed. Nigel Nicolson and Joanne Trautmann. London: Hogarth Press; New York: Harcourt Brace Jovanovich, 1978.
VWL V	*The Letters of Virginia Woolf*. Vol. V, 1932–1935. Ed. Nigel Nicolson and Joanne Trautmann. London: Hogarth Press; New York: Harcourt Brace Jovanovich, 1979.
VWL VI	*The Letters of Virginia Woolf*. Vol. VI, 1936–1941. Ed. Nigel Nicolson and Joanne Trautmann. London: Hogarth Press; New York: Harcourt Brace Jovanovich, 1980.
LWL	*Letters of Leonard Woolf*. Ed. Frederic Spotts. New York: Harcourt Brace Jovanovich, 1989.
LW III	Leonard Woolf. *Beginning Again: An Autobiography of the Years 1911–1918*. New York: Harcourt Brace Jovanovich, 1964.
LW IV	Leonard Woolf. *Downhill All the Way: An Autobiography of the Years 1919–1939*. New York: Harcourt Brace Jovanovich, 1967.
LW V	Leonard Woolf. *The Journey Not the Arrival Matters: An Autobiography of the Years 1939–1969*. New York: Harcourt Brace Jovanovich, 1969.
VSW/VW	*Letters of Vita Sackville-West to Virginia Woolf*. Ed. Louise DeSalvo and Mitchell A. Leaska. London: Virago Press, 1992.
M&M	*Virginia Woolf: The Critical Heritage*. Ed. Robin Majumdar and Allen McLaurin. London: Routledge & Kegan Paul, 1975.

For reference purposes the Hogarth Press Uniform Edition pagination is used throughout, unless otherwise noted:

VO	*The Voyage Out*
JR	*Jacob's Room*
MD	*Mrs. Dalloway*
TW	*The Waves*
TTL	*To the Lighthouse*
TY	*The Years*
BA	*Between the Acts*
AROO	*A Room of One's Own*

3 "the looking-glass shame": *MoB* (1985), 68.

"Out and bought": *APA*, 242.

"fascinating": Clive Bell, *Old Friends: Personal Recollections* (New York: Harcourt Brace and Company, 1956), 97.

"a vast posterity": Ibid., 99.

4 "Who was I then?": *MoB* (1985), 65.

5 "she would discuss": *LW III*, 79.

"I ceased to be": *MoB* (1985), 81.

6 "Each part has": *APA*, 392.

6 "Those who indulge": Roger Fry, *Vision and Design* (New York: Brentano's, 1925), 49–50; published originally in the *Athenaeum*, 1919; see also John Hawley Roberts, " 'Vision and Design' in Virginia Woolf," *PMLA* 61 (September 1946): 835–47, and Jonathan R. Quick, "Virginia Woolf, Roger Fry and Post-Impressionism," *Massachusetts Review* 26 (Winter 1985): 547–70.

"some view of beauty": *APA*, 392–93.

7 "I should like": Ibid., 384.

"desperate search": Roger Fry, *Cézanne: A Study of His Development* (New York: Noonday Press, 1958 [1927]), 38.

"I make it real": *MoB* (1985), 72.

8 "I prefer, where truth": *Pargiters* (London: Hogarth Press, 1977), 9.

9 "Communication is truth": "Montaigne," *The Common Reader* (London: Hogarth Press, 1925), 93.

11 "an incessant shower": "Modern Fiction," *Common Reader*, 189.

12 "record the atoms": Ibid., 190.

"on or about December, 1910": "Mr. Bennett and Mrs. Brown," *The Captain's Death Bed and Other Essays* (New York: Harcourt Brace Jovanovich, 1950), 96.

13 "formal railway line": *VWL III*, October 3, 1924.

"Structure is still": Fry, *Cézanne*, 75.

"Beautiful and bright": *TTL*, 264.

"grassy bank is almost": Fry, *Cézanne*, 61.

"I must move": *TTL*, 135.

"You're no longer": in *QB II*, 128–29.

"I meant *nothing*": *VWL III*, May 27, 1927.

14 "to take one thing": "Life and the Novelist," *Granite and Rainbow* (New York: Harcourt Brace Jovanovich, 1975), 45.

"ignorant girl": *Pargiters*, xxxvii.

"invisible progress": Henri Bergson, *Matter and Memory*, trans. N. M. Paul and W. S. Palmer (New York: Macmillan, 1911), 194.

15 "the shadow of the past": Shiv K. Kumar, *Bergson and the Stream of Consciousness Novel* (New York: New York University Press, 1963), 52.

"these monsters up from the deep": Clive Bell, *Proust* (London: Hogarth Press, 1928), 50–53.

16 "more fascinating": *MD*, v–vi.

19   "No father, no mother": *APA*, 211–13.

20   "natural inclination": *QB I*, 6.

        "not at ease": Frederic Maitland, *The Life and Letters of Leslie Stephen* (London: Duckworth and Company, 1906), 40.

        "most independent-spirited": Ibid., 23.

        "is naughty": Ibid., 24.

21   "suspect because": Noel Annan, *Leslie Stephen: The Godless Victorian* (New York: Random House, 1984), 18.

        "One day this week": Maitland, *Life and Letters*, 30.

        "the difference between": Leslie Stephen, *The Life of Sir James Fitzjames Stephen* (London: Smith, Elder & Co., 1895), 78.

23   "tall, gaunt, and shy": Maitland, *Life and Letters*, 48.

        "never really believed": Ibid., 133

        "I now believe": Ibid., 144.

        "I mean to live": Ibid., 145.

24   When he felt the need: Annan, *Leslie Stephen*, 52.

        "up by the roots": Maitland, *Life and Letters*, 158–59.

        "This is my": Ibid., 185–87.

25   "heart and soul": Ibid., 188.

        "My dearest Minny": Ibid., 189.

        "hopeless mummy": Annan, *Leslie Stephen*, 61.

        "This day Leslie": Maitland, *Life and Letters*, 196.

        "playing with children": *The Letters and Private Papers of William Makepeace Thackeray*, Vol. IV (Anne Thackeray to Mrs. Baxter, April 25, 1861), ed. Gordon N. Ray (Cambridge, Mass.: Harvard University Press, 1945–46), 230.

        "tenuous, charming": *QB I*, 10–11.

26   "I have never": Maitland, *Life and Letters*, 223.

        "I found my darling": *MB*, 22.

27   "Both proposals": *MoB* (1985), 88.

        "as I might have": *MB*, 31.

        " 'superstition' that": Ibid., 29.

        "Her mother's judicious": Ibid., 33.

        "had had a life": Ibid., 25–27.

28   "devoted himself": Ibid., 39.

        "plenty of moral": *QB I*, 19.

        "who could match": Annan, *Leslie Stephen*, 113.

29   "not hard to find": *QB I*, 20.

        "most depressing": *MB*, 55–56.

30   "I came home": LS/JD, April 5, 1877.

        "I had another argument": LS/JD, April 7, 1877.

        "The chief sufferer": LS/JD, July 16, 1877.

        "but it is silly": LS/JD, July 17, 1877.

30–31   "I am in love": *MB*, 47.

31 "It was revealed": LS/JD, February 5, 1877.
    "on terms of the closest": *MB*, 49.
    "As for myself": LS/JD, March 31, 1877.
    "fresh life": LS/JD, April 4, 1877.
    "too well": *MB*, 55.
    "Things are quite": LS/JD, April 6, 1877.

32 "I am doing": JD/LS, April 7, 1877.
    "your ingenious notion": LS/JD, April 7, 1877.
    "I have felt": JD/LS, April 8, 1877.
    "Let me say one": LS/JD, April 9, 1877.

33 "I like to think": JD/LS, July 18, 1877.
    never again to tell: LS/JD, July 19, 1877.
    "I don't know": JD/LS, July 20, 1877.
    "My comfort depends": LS/JD, April 5, 1877.
    "I have learned": LS/JD, April 11, 1877.

34 "Love me, dear . . .": LS/JD, July 23, 1877.
    "I shall lay": LS/JD, February 7, 1877.
    "My own": LS/JD, December 29, 1877.
    "for which I hope": LS/JD, July 19, 1877.
    "I shall find": LS/JD, August 9, 1877.
    "Dearest, are you": LS/JD, July 11, 1877.

35 "Nothing cheers me": LS/JD, April 4, 1877.
    "I can fancy": LS/JD, August 18, 1877.
    "I feel with my": LS/JD, February 8, 1885.
    "You look worn": LS/JD, May 19, 1892.
    "You know how": LS/JD, January 29, 1894.

36 "I hope it does": JD/LS, February 6, 1877.
    "You do not know": JD/LS, February 8, 1877.
    "My poor dear": JD/LS, March 31, 1877.
    "a very icy": JD/LS, April 6, 1877.
    "convent grating": LS/JD, April 4, 1877.
    "The better I know": LS/JD, April 6, 1877.

37 "Who are the people": JD/LS, April 12, 1877.
    "I don't think it": LS/JD, August 18, 1877.
    "I feel as if": JD/LS, July 31, 1877.
    "If you really": JD/LS, August 5, 1877.

38 "I did not mean": LS/JD, August 7, 1877.
    "I spoke of": *MB*, 56–57.

39 "well and good": LS/JD, December 27, 1877.
    "Be my wife": LS/JD, December 28, 1877.
    "I know that things": JD/LS, December 28, 1877.
    "We talked the matter": *MB*, 57.

40 "good and beautiful": Maitland, *Life and Letters*, 310–11.
    "I am engaged": Ibid., 311.
    "sweetness of temper": *MB*, 35–36.

"like all very": *MoB* (1985), 89.

41   "her hair grey": *TTL*, 16.

"under her protection": Ibid., 15.

"air of expectation": Ibid., 22.

"walking rather fast": Ibid., 309.

"torch of her": Ibid., 68.

"like some queen": Ibid., 128–29.

"outside world": *Henry James Letters*, Vol II (January 4, 1879), ed. Leon Edel (Cambridge, Mass.: Harvard University Press 1975), 209.

"consented to become": Ibid., 157.

42   "lived in the heart": *TTL*, 62.

"by her laugh": Ibid., 63.

"if his little": Ibid., 75.

"made herself out": Ibid., 153.

"she was not clever": Ibid., 187.

"wanted the thing": Ibid., 189–90.

"could not understand": Ibid., 130.

"pitying people": Ibid., 132.

"pitied men always": Ibid., 133.

43   "Never did anybody": Ibid., 49.

"It will end": Ibid., 101–2.

"some sealed vessel": Ibid., 103.

"a beam of light": *MoB* (1985), 89.

". . . that when he was": *TTL*, 107–8.

45   "to dip into privately": *MoB* (1985), 82.

"that she had": *TTL*, 154.

46   "so unhappy": *QB I*, 17.

"One is always": JD/LS, August 10, 1877; emphasis added.

47   "My darling was": *MB*, 81–83.

"It injured her": *TTL*, 68.

"Milly is alarming": JD/LS, August 11, 1877.

"You want me to": LS/JD, August 9, 1877.

48   "I am only unhappy": JD/LS, August 8, 1877.

"I get so puzzled": JD/LS, July 19, 1877.

"I don't know": JD/LS, December 31, 1877.

"You speak in some": LS/JD, December 30, 1877.

"a bothering old thing": JD/LS, January 23, 1878.

"no monotony of bliss": *TTL*, 305.

49   "I wish she could": LS/JD, December 17, 1881.

"She may not be": LS/JD, April 2, 1882.

"My darling Laura": LS/JD/LMS, April 7, 1882.

"I long to shake": LS/JD, April 9, 1882.

"mulishness": LS/JD, September 29, 1882.

"I tremble": LS/JD, October 11, 1882.

"I cannot see": LS/JD, March 24, 1884.

"She—Laura—told": LS/JD, October 11, 1884.

"Laura was in": LS/JD, July 17, 1885.

"When she is good": LS/JD, November 12, 1885.

"My poor Laura": *MB*, 103.

50   "On Saturday morning": in *QB I*, 32.

"the best beginning": *MoB* (1985), 128.

51   "Here is another": LS/JD, July 31, 1893.

"She sat on": LS/JD, October 10, 1883.

"Little 'Ginia is": LS/JD, April 13, 1884.

52   "those dependent on him": Annan, *Leslie Stephen*, 73.

"Victor Marshall": LS/JD, July 19, 1877.

"V. Marshall is": JD/LS, July 20, 1877.

53   "place of drudgery": LS/JD, January 26, 1885.

"attacks of horrors": LS/JD, November 12, 1882.

"bondage": LS/JD, October 13, 1886.

"it is hard work": LS/JD, January 22, 1883.

"Dictionary bothers": LS/JD, April 21, 1885.

"Certainly I will": *MB*, 93.

54   "I undertook to write": Ibid., 87.

55   "feeling stronger": LS/JD, January 21, 1887.

"She seems to be": LS/JD, January 22, 1887.

"get into the tantarums": LS/JD, February 4, 1887.

"It will . . . please": LS/JD, February 5, 1887.

"exile": LS/JD, February 7, 1887.

"I do not feel": LS/JD, April 5, 1887.

56   "Nobody seems to": LS/JD, April 6, 1887.

"Tell your mother": LS/JD, April 13, 1887.

" 'Ginia tells me": LS/JD, April 15, 1887.

" 'Ginia said she would": LS/JD, April 17, 1887.

"I thought, my darling": LS/JD, April 7, 1887.

vaguely benevolent: *QB I*, 20.

"sometimes three times": Ibid., 17.

57   "Dearest love": LS/JD, October 17, 1881.

"Dearest, as to our": LS/JD, April 3, 1884.

"I wish": LS/JD, March 31, 1884.

"I ought really": LS/JD, October 7, 1886.

57–58   "wished to come": JD/LS, October 31, 1877.

58   "treasuring": *MoB* (1985), 33.

"victims": *TTL*, 157.

59   "boobies": Ibid., 89.

"with immutable calm": Ibid., 81.

"For it was extraordinary": Ibid., 137.

"she was always": Ibid., 95.

63   "Hold yourself straight": *MoB* (1985), 84.
"I feel nothing": Ibid., 92.
"with his head bent": Ibid., 84.
"it was like kissing": Ibid., 92.

64   Even his notepaper: Ibid., 92–94.

65   "made her unreal": Ibid., 95.
"an unlovable phantom": Ibid., 45.
"nasty erotic": *QB I*, 43.

66   "a painful and embarrassing": Ibid., 43.
"and used to say": *VWL I*, July 25? 1911.
"I can remember": *MoB* (1985), 69.
"cowardice": *VWL IV*, June 26, 1930.
"I do not know": *QB I*, 44–45.

67   "dazzling parodies": Annan, *Leslie Stephen*, 113–14.

68   "I cannot shut": *MB*, 78.
"laid a claim": *QB I*, 46.

69   "We have just returned": *MB*, 100–1.

70   "over-sensitive": Ibid., 89–90.
"I was not as": *MoB* (1985), 41–42.
"canine devotion": Ibid., 96.
"conscious that she": Ibid., 45.
"part of herself": Ibid., 42.
reflecting moon: Ibid., 96.

71   "urgent, heartbreaking": *QB I*, 42.
"many young men": *MoB* (1985), 98.
"a commonplace little": Ibid., 101–4.

72   "He opened my eyes": Ibid., 103–4.
"We must all be": Ibid., 101.
"How could Stella": *QB I*, 48.
"smack of a whip": *MoB* (1985), 106.
"the condition of": *QB I*, 47.
"rooms, and habits": *MoB* (1985), 51.

73   "eyes shone": Ibid., 50.
"Here is a volume": *APA*, 134.

74   "This is written": Ibid., 43–44.

75   "poor Miss Jan": Ibid., 39.
"To bed very furious": Ibid., 69.
"I regret to say": Ibid., 73.
"Virginia has been": *MB*, 103.
"the greatest help": *APA*, 79.
"I suppose will be": LS/JD, July 27, 1893.
"Yesterday I discussed": LS/JD, July 29, 1893.
"She is certainly": LS/JD, January 25, 1891.

"devouring books": *MB*, 103.

"with discrimination": *QB I*, 51.

76   "Walked in the morning": *APA*, 24.

"It is a regular thaw": Ibid., 25 n. 107.

"A terrible idea": Ibid., 27.

"told him with great": Ibid., 28.

"Stella, Jack, Nessa": Ibid., 30.

77   "in mud and wet": Ibid., 33.

"stupid Bognor": Ibid., 35.

"a wonderful opal": Ibid., 47.

"going away dress": Ibid., 59.

"Today Stella was married": *MB*, 102–3.

78   "I am tired and excited": Ibid., xxvi.

"with a nice quiet": *APA*, 70–72.

"in bed with": Ibid., 77.

79   "midst of serious": *MoB* (1985), 52.

"Read Mr James": *APA*, 80.

"Finished the 5th": Ibid., 87.

"Finished the 3rd": Ibid., 105.

"Finished 1st vol": Ibid., 109.

"I slept with Nessa": Ibid., 78.

"most satisfactory": Ibid., 80.

"I was examined": Ibid., 83.

"made me so angry": Ibid., 88.

"certainly gives one": *QB I*, 56–57.

80   "My mother's death": *MoB* (1985), 124.

"It gave me a conception": Ibid., 105.

82   "soothe the first shock": Ibid., 58.

"Terrible long dinner": *APA*, 130.

"Everyone turned to her": *MoB* (1985), 53.

"victim": Ibid., 56.

"appreciated and shared": *QB I*, 63.

82–83   "uncompromising anger": *MoB* (1985), 56.

83   "not unwilling": *QB I*, 71.

"So you take": *MoB* (1985), 142.

84   "We reached Godmanchester": *APA*, 148–49.

85   "ancient tooled calf": Ibid., 159.

"too sacred to undergo": Ibid., 160.

86   "round about 1900...": *MoB* (1976), 127.

"ready with small talk": Ibid., 128.

87   "would unbend...": Ibid., 129.

"for we had to come": Ibid., 130.

89   "We ain't popular": *VWL I*, August 8, 1901.

"Providence inscrutably decreed": Ibid., December 27? 1902.

"simplicity itself": *MoB* (1985), 172–77.

90	"discoursing to his": Ibid., 176–77.
91	"It is enough to say": *MB*, 111.
	"breezy masculine": *QB I*, 83.
93	"a good hot letter": *VWL I*, October/November 1902.
	"I like them hot": Ibid.
	"I weep tears": *VWL I*, February? 1903.
	"Sparroy only flaps": Ibid., March 1903.
	"I feel myself curled up": Ibid., November 14, 1906.
	"It would draw tears": Ibid., June 30? 1903.
	"I would not write": Ibid., April 28, 1903.
	"You are the only sympathetic": Ibid., April 30, 1903.
	"He says that six months": Ibid., May 19? 1903.
	"Father has some inflammation": Ibid., autumn 1903.
	"Three mornings have I": Ibid., autumn 1903.
94	"George has been so": Ibid., early October, 1903.
	"He said he didn't": Ibid., October 11? 1903.
	"I shall write no more": *MB*, 112.
	"He does want": *VWL I*, December 25, 1903.
	"We should never get on": Ibid., December 31, 1903.
	"Father gave me": Ibid., January 25, 1904.
95	"Stupid fools": Ibid., March 4, 1904.
	"I don't find": Ibid., March 1904.
	"I find the country": Ibid., March 1904.
	"I keep thinking": *VWL I*, March 1904.
	"That vision came": *VWD II*, September 3, 1922.
96	"almost the only one": Ibid., March 1904.
	"... you can't think": Ibid., March 31, 1904.
	"three very dingy": Ibid., April 4, 1904.
	"a place to die": Ibid., April 25, 1904.
97	"the bad times": Ibid., May 6? 1904.
	"frantic intensity": *QB I*, 89.
	"all that summer": Ibid., 90.
	"all kinds of wild things": *VWL I*, September 22? 1904.
98	"Oh my Violet": Ibid., September 26, 1904.
	"I am longing": Ibid., September 30, 1904.
99	in complete chastity: *MoB* (1985), 169.
	"tranquil benevolence": *QB I*, 90.
	"in the arms": *VWL I*, October 22, 1904.
	"great authority": Ibid., October 24, 1904.
100	"I am getting through": Ibid., October 30, 1904.
	"As a matter of fact": Ibid., November 1904.
101	"took the exasperating": *QB I*, 91.
	"two more months": *VWL I*, October 30, 1904.
102	"Madge worshipped": *LW III*, 73.
	"to capture [Virginia's] heart": *QB I*, 60.

"Madge is here": Ibid., 61.
"knack": *VWL I*, November 11, 1904.
"seven unhappy years": *MoB* (1985), 136.
"I do enjoy flattery": *VWL I*, December 1, 1904.

THE VOYAGE OUT

107   "The gulf which we crossed": *VWD I*, October 23, 1918.
108   "family idol of old": *QB I*, 95.
       "£2.7.6. for Guardian articles": *APA*, 219.
       "delighted to accept": Ibid., 238.
       "wearing scarlet": *VWL I*, February 23, 1905.
109   "beautiful, and if": Ibid., February 28, 1905.
       "I am to start": *APA*, 217.
       "Morley college soirée": Ibid., 218.
       "whether there were fleas": Ibid., 225.
       "Tomorrow . . . is my": *VWL I*, May 1905.
110   "10 people: 4 men, 6 women": Ibid., November 9, 1905.
       "sat lightly upright": *APA*, 184.
       "general rejoicing": Ibid., 268.
111   "strikes one full": Ibid., 259.
       "We had the loveliest": *VWL I*, April 5, 1905.
       "much care for": *APA*, 262.
       "a serious criticism": *VWL I*, April 24, 1905.
       "3 fat books": Ibid., April 30, 1905.
112   "Sydney Turner and Strachey": *APA*, 245.
       "Sydney Turner and Gerald": Ibid., 253.
       "great trial": *VWL I*, October 1, 1905.
       "a sort of mixture": *MoB* (1985), 187–89.
113   "so charmed and domesticated": *QB I*, 103.
114   "I've no doubt": *MoB* (1985), 191.
       "proof of their superiority": Ibid., 192.
       "twitter of excitement": Ibid., 189–90.
115   "marriage was a very": Ibid., 191.
       "give up hunting": *VWL I*, August 27, 1905.
       "little corner of England": *APA*, 281.
       "Mrs. Pascoe was": Ibid., 288–89.
116   "these are rough notes": Ibid., 291.
       "I want to charge": *VWL I*, August 1905.
       "Do you think I shall": Ibid., October 1, 1905.
       "The Club flourishes": Ibid., December 3, 1905.
117   "I promise not to": Ibid., April 1906.
       "I lead the life": Ibid., April 16, 1906.
       "My only defence": Ibid., June? 1906.

"mostly alone": Ibid., April 21, 1906.

118   "I settle precisely": *APA*, 301.

"This is the largest": *VWL I*, July 22, 1906.

"rolling drunken sailors": Ibid., August 4, 1906.

"40 pages of manuscript": Ibid., August 24, 1906.

"It is one of the wilful": *APA*, 313.

119   "Unconsciousness, which means": "The Leaning Tower," *The Moment and Other Essays* (London: Hogarth Press, 1947), 109–10.

"across and above": *APA*, 319.

120   "in the evening": Ibid., 332–33.

"saluted each other": Ibid., 353.

"frail symbol": Ibid., 352.

121   "There was never a sight": Ibid., 331.

"it had been": *QB I*, 109.

"a profoundly untrustworthy": *VWL I*, August 25, 1907.

122   "through the discreet": *QB I*, 110.

"Thoby has a temp.": *VWL I*, November 7? 1906.

"Visitors come and use": Ibid., November 14, 1906.

"If you could put": Ibid., November 15, 1906.

"I must get out my pen": Ibid., November 20, 1906.

"Beloved Violet": Ibid., December 18, 1906.

123   "happier every day": Ibid., December 18, 1906.

"distinguished people": Ibid., December 10, 1906.

"a very simple": *MoB* (1976), 119–20.

124   "The thickness of this nib": *VWL I*, January 2, 1907.

"funny little creature": Ibid., December 30? 1906.

"but then old Nessa": Ibid., January 3, 1907.

125   "a book": Ibid., January 1907.

"I feel numb and dumb": Ibid., February 1907.

"I ought to be able to": *QB I*, 115 n.

"the most incompatible": *MoB* (1985), 193.

"should have no brother": *VWL I*, February 1907.

"15 years younger": Ibid., mid-April 1903.

"My Joy": *MoB* (1985), 83.

"he appeared no more": *QB I*, 116.

126   "literally sitting in an": *The Selected Letters of Vanessa Bell*, ed. Regina Marler (New York: Pantheon, 1993), March 8, 1909.

"Mrs Bell is struggling": *VWL I*, February 1907.

"They sound so happy": Ibid., February 15, 1907.

"I can't believe": Ibid., April 2, 1907.

"Write me a nice": Ibid., May 3, 1907.

"I wish I could play": Ibid., April 1907.

"very hastily polished": Ibid., August 1907.

127   "Leslie Stephen's children": *Henry James Letters* Vol. IV (September 11, 1907), 504 n. 1.

"the quite dreadful-looking": Ibid. (February 17, 1907), 437.

life of Vanessa: *MoB* (1985), "Reminiscences."

"at once, at some length": *VWL I*, September 1, 1907.

"not the stuff": Ibid., August 18, 1907.

" 'My dear Virginia' ": Ibid., August 25, 1907.

128   "her jealousies": *QB I*, 118.

"Why were the most gifted": *MoB* (1985), 194.

Virginia liked him: *QB I*, 118.

129   "It was a spring evening": *MoB* (1985), 195–96.

"in the *mores* of Bloomsbury": *QB I*, 125.

130   "I dreamt last night": *VWL I*, April 15, 1908.

"slipping from one agony": *QB I*, 129–30.

131   "A child is the very": *VWL I*, April 28, 1908.

132   "He quoted Shakespeare": *APA*, 384.

133   "You were the first person": *VWL II*, July 24, 1917.

"I have been reading": *VWL I*, May 6, 1908.

"cursed and burned": Ibid., July 1908.

135   "I shall work hard": Ibid., August 30, 1908.

"One old lady . . .": *APA*, 389.

136   "by means of infinite discords": Ibid., 393.

"discover real things": Ibid., 384.

137   "if that day ever comes": *VWL I*, February 7? 1909.

"How on earth": In *QB I*, Appendix D, 210.

"Our views about men": Ibid., 209.

"Of Helen": Ibid., 210.

138   "two most beautiful": In *LWL*, 139 n. 1.

"Wire me if she accepts": Ibid., February 19, 1909.

"Your letter has this": Ibid.

"I've had an éclaircissement": In *LWL*, February 20, 1909.

"We had Lytton last": *VWL I*, December 25, 1908.

"I was always sexually": *VWL IV*, June 22, 1930.

139   "Why should I excite": *VWL I*, April 13, 1909.

"Look at the conflict": *APA*, 397–98.

"who wrote devout books": Ibid., 400–1.

"I have an aunt": *VO*, 165.

"unloved, unwanted": *QB I*, 143.

"I think she would": Ibid., 144.

"I gather you": *VWL I*, August 10, 1908.

"Sally Duggan's *Life*": *JR*, 160.

140   "head of a Medusa": Ibid., May 1909.

"If you will have me": Ibid., January 16, 1909.

"with a thick golden": Ibid., May 13? 1909.

"marvellous female": in S. J. Darroch, *Ottoline: The Life of Lady Ottoline Morrell* (New York: Coward, McCann & Geoghegan, 1975), 66.

141   "wonderful": *MoB* (1985), 199.

"petticoats, frivolity": *QB I*, 145.

". . . her mind vapours": *VWL II*, February 27, 1919.

"He reminds me": *VWL I*, August 10, 1909.

"reading a dictionary": Ibid., August 24, 1909.

"I had to invent": Ibid., August 19, 1909.

142   "I can never quite": Ibid., August 16, 1909.

"substitute for Lytton": *QB I*, 152.

"and I have no": *VWL I*, December 25, 1909.

"old amethyst": Ibid., December 27, 1909.

"rock with delight": Ibid., December 26, 1909.

143   "one of the most": *APA*, 410.

"Dreadnought Hoax": *QB I*, Appendix E.

144   "masculine honour": Ibid., 160–61.

145   "a kind of polite": Ibid., 164.

"damnable": *VWL I*, June 24, 1910.

"I gather": Ibid., July 28, 1910.

146   "One is a very nice": Ibid., September 4, 1910.

"I lay awake till 5": Ibid., September 8, 1910.

147   "because that old Bitch": Ibid., December 29, 1910.

"who is so much": Ibid., January 1, 1911.

"read and write": Ibid., April 8, 1911.

"were no longer content": Frances Spalding, *Vanessa Bell* (New York: Ticknor & Fields, 1983), 91.

148   "a little more conscious": *QB I*, 168.

149   "diagrams of Ovaries": *VWL I*, May 25, 1911.

"transformation into a union": *QB I*, 169.

150   "all the devils": *VWL I*, June 8? 1911.

"utter despair": *MoB* (1985), 196.

"practically naked": Ibid., 201.

151   "It would be unpardonable": *VWL I*, December 9, 1911.

"a wilderness of monkeys": *QB I*, 178.

"Dear Mr Wolf": *VWL I*, July 8, 1911.

152   "inmates": Ibid., December 2, 1911.

"This is not": Ibid., August 31, 1911.

153   "a strange and beautiful": *QB I*, 176.

"spirited controversy": *VWL I*, October 21, 1911.

154   "There isn't anything": Ibid., January 13, 1912.

"You're the only person": Vanessa Bell, *Selected Letters*, January 14, 1912.

155   "wonderful stories": *VWL I*, March 5, 1912.

"A tepid lover": *QB I*, 183.

"bright, intelligent": *VWL I*, January 23, 1911.

156   ". . . I've read two": *LWL*, April 29, 1912.

157   "I've got a confession": *VWL I*, June 4, 1912.

"penniless Jew": Ibid., June 1912.

"Ha! Ha!": Ibid., June 6, 1912.

"At first I felt": Ibid., June 1912.

"Work and love": Ibid., June 1912.

INFINITE DISCORDS AND SHIVERING FRAGMENTS

161 "I began life": *VWL I*, March 1912.

162 "by rich, rapid scales": *MoB* (1985), 37.

 "contempt": LS/JD, August 29, 1893.

163 "the tyrant of inconceivable": *MoB* (1985), 56.

 "unlovable phantom": Ibid., 45.

 "tyrant father": Ibid., 116.

 "we were in league": Ibid., 111.

 "a mixture": Ibid., 90.

 "general presence": Ibid., 83.

 ". . . the scratch of": Ibid., 81.

164 "to concentrate": Ibid., 83.

 "towards death": Ibid., 36.

165 "hot to cold": *VWL I*, May 1, 1912.

 "I was suspended": *MoB* (1985), 78; also *VWD III*, September 30, 1926.

 "sprang up with": *MoB* (1985), 78.

 "ran naked": Ibid., 99.

165–66 "attacked with delirium": Martine Stemerick, "Virginia Woolf: The Distaff Side of History," in *Virginia Woolf: Centennial Essays*, ed. E. K. Ginsberg and L. M. Gottlieb (Troy, N.Y.: Whitson, 1983), 60.

166 "vacant-eyed girl": *MoB* (1985), 182.

 to commit suicide: Thomas C. Caramagno, *The Flight of the Mind: Virginia Woolf's Art and Manic-Depressive Illness* (Berkeley: University of California Press, 1992), 109.

 "augmented to absolute": Thackeray, *Letters and Private Papers*, Vol. I (September 17, 1840), 474.

 "devouring books": *MB*, 103.

 "I was a snob": *MoB* (1985), 111–12.

 "On the tow path": *VWD I*, January 9, 1915.

167 "Whether it be a benefit": *Julia Duckworth Stephen: Stories for Children, Essays for Adults*, ed. D. F. Gillespie and E. Steele (New York: Syracuse University Press, 1987), 245–46.

 "I feel a respect": LS/JD, January 25, 1891.

 "a maimed file": *MD*, 100.

 "human beings have neither": Ibid., 99.

168 "ill or in some": *MoB* (1985), 83.

 "brilliant and imaginative": *QB I*, 151.

 "Virginia since early": Vanessa Bell, *Selected Letters*, June 25, 1910.

169 "some real thing": *MoB* (1985), 72.

 "I feel that": Ibid., 72–73.

"I cannot remember": Vanessa Bell, *Notes on Virginia's Childhood* (New York: Frank Hallman, 1974), unpaginated.

170 "Soliloquies in back streets": *TW*, 83.

"was happy; triumphant": *Pointz Hall: The Earlier and Later Typescripts of Between the Acts*, ed. Mitchell Leaska (New York: University Publications, 1983), 175–76.

171 "I remember of these": *MoB* (1976), 134.

"felt herself surrounded": *VO*, 181.

"door opens and people": *TW*, 76.

"good friend": *MoB* (1976), 134.

"I could even": *MoB* (1985), 155–56.

"the one dependable": *TTL*, 232.

"Brooding": Ibid., 119.

172 "You dwell in": *VWL I*, February 1907.

"Why did he sit": *VO*, 260–61.

"Voices crying behind": Ibid., 346–47.

174 "to be taken and drowned": Reading based on Acton Griscom's translation of the *Historia* (London: Longmans, 1929), 254–56; for a discussion of story variants, see Mitchell Leaska, *The Novels of Virginia Woolf: From Beginning to End* (London: Weidenfeld and Nicolson, 1977), 31–32.

176 "Possibly my great age": *VWL II*, September 4, 1912.

"Virginia is very lazy": Ibid., September 28, 1912.

"a little exercised": Vanessa Bell, *Selected Letters*, November 27, 1912.

176–177 "intense misery": *VWL II*, October 29? 1912.

177 "incredibly ancient": *LW III*, 84.

"It's triumphant": *VWL II*, November 16, 1912.

"incorrigibly philistine": *LW III*, 94.

"abominable race": *VWL II*, December 24, 1912.

"for the tenth": *LW III*, 87.

178 "Do her a world": Ibid., 82.

"We aren't going": *VWL II*, April 11, 1913.

"that she immediately": *QB II*, 11.

179 "I begin to undress": *VWL II*, April 25, 1913.

"a mere pudding": Ibid., May 16, 1913.

180 "second line of defence": *LW III*, 152.

181 "blackest despair": Ibid., 156.

"The drive": Ibid., 156–57.

182 "every reason to believe": *LWL*, September 14, 1913.

"It is the novel": *QB II*, 16 n.

"made an order": *LW III*, 158.

183 "I am inclined to think": Janet Oppenheim, *"Shattered Nerves": Doctors, Patients, and Depression in Victorian England*, (New York and London: Oxford University Press, 1991), 109.

"People suffering": *LW III*, 161.

184 "be a devoted animal": *VWL II*, December? 1913.

"I'm afraid you're having": in *LWL*, September 26, 1913.

"was clothed": *QB II*, 18.

185   "I am not professionally": In *LWL*, October 25, 1913.

"My dear Leonard": Ibid., December 11, 1913.

186   "hugely": Ibid., March 12, 1914.

"jangled mind": *LW III*, 166.

"milk, green fields": *VWL II*, early April, 1914.

"It's quite clear": *LWL*, May 21, 1914.

187   "an extremely nice": *LW III*, 170.

"the wife of": *QB II*, 21.

"adorable": *VWL II*, December 10, 1914.

188   "three beautiful tunes": *VWD I*, January 17, 1915.

"very bad in parts": Ibid., January 31, 1915.

"crept": Ibid., January 25, 1915.

189   "rank with the smell": Ibid., January 2, 1915.

"I begin to loathe": Ibid., January 3, 1915.

"I do not like": Ibid., January 4, 1915.

"I can imagine": Ibid., January 5, 1915.

"the beginning": *LW III*, 172.

190   "I am now all right": *VWL II*, February 25, 1915.

"a little better": Ibid., March 2, 1915.

"The expenses": *LWL*, March 7, 1915.

191   "seemed to have reached": *QB II*, 26.

"everyone would jeer": J. Thomas/V. Dickinson, September 14, 1913 (Berg Collection of the New York Public Library).

192   "brilliantly drawn": *M&M*, 9, 49–63.

193   "Mr L. S. Woolf": *LW III*, 178–79.

"went before the military": *VWL II*, June 25, 1916.

194   "these pregnant women": *LWL*, September 1, 1918.

"just like other people": *VWD I*, August 27, 1918.

195   "an old creature of 50": *VWL II*, September 24, 1916.

"good wine and cigars": Ibid., September 30, 1916.

196   "so you won't be": Ibid., May 14, 1916.

"a trifle ramshackle": *QB II*, 35.

"family dragon": Ibid., 34.

197   "the book would be": *LW III*, 232–33.

"like two hungry children": Ibid., 234.

198   "would have little": Ibid., 236.

"editors, or publishers": *VWL II*, July 26, 1917.

199   "in rather a state": Ibid., July 26, 1917.

"I promise faithfully": Ibid., October 29, 1917.

"I have rested": Ibid., October 30, 1917.

"I am drinking": Ibid., October 31, 1917.

200   "civet cat": *VWD I*, October 11, 1917.

"not all to her credit" Ibid., January 18, 1918.

"marmoreal": Ibid., May 28, 1918.

"vapourish": Ibid., July 12, 1918.

"interesting mind": Ibid., August 7, 1918.

201   "curse": Ibid., November 3, 1918.

"Since I am back": Ibid., November 4, 1918.

"Another lapse": Ibid., October 23, 1917.

"awkward moment": Ibid., April 8, 1918.

"Now wait a minute": Ibid., April 18, 1918.

"Clive starts his": Ibid., December 7, 1917.

"On Sunday": Ibid., January 14, 1918.

202   "best man-of-the-world": Ibid., May 7, 1918.

"I did my best": Ibid., April 18, 1918.

203   "method": *VWL II*, April 23, 1918.

"well expressed": *VWD I*, November 15, 1918.

204   "What a queer fate": Ibid., November 30, 1918.

"so that here I sit": Ibid., December 3, 1918.

"It fills up the time": Ibid., December 7, 1918.

205   "I own that his verdict": Ibid., March 27, 1919.

"was intended to be": *QB II*, 42.

"Club man's view": *VWD I*, April 2, 1919.

"what, I wonder": Ibid., May 7, 1919.

206   "Murry, Eliot, and myself": Ibid., May 12, 1919.

"doubt the value": Ibid., June 9, 1919.

207   "purple in the cheeks": Ibid., July 3, 1919.

"work of the highest": Ibid., October 23, 1919.

"strictly formal": Ibid., November 6, 1919.

"A decorous elderly": Ibid., November 28, 1919.

"to discover what aims": Ibid., September 18, 1918.

208   "a ghastly affair": Ibid., November 10, 1917.

"It was certainly": *VWL II*, November 27, 1919.

AN ORDINARY MIND ON AN ORDINARY DAY

211   "ordinary mind": *Common Reader*, 189.

"grope and experiment": *VWD II*, January 26, 1920.

212   "about six inches": *The Complete Shorter Fiction of Virginia Woolf*, ed. Susan Dick (New York: Harcourt Brace Jovanovich, 1985), 84.

"Life's what you see": Ibid., 106.

"bare as bone": Ibid., 115.

213   "I shall never forget": *VWL IV*, October 16, 1930.

214   "future reference": *VWD II*, May 11, 1920.

"my heart in my mouth": Ibid., August 2, 1920.

"Yesterday broody": Ibid., August 19, 1920.

"It was this": Ibid., October 1, 1920.

"probably being better": Ibid., September 26, 1920.

"scientific observation": Ibid., September 20, 1920.

215   "We talked": Ibid., September 19, 1920.

"had I been": Ibid., September 20, 1920.

"It is at this moment": *VWD I*, February 18, 1919.

". . . I find with Katherine": Ibid., March 22, 1919.

"steady discomposing": *VWD II*, May 31, 1920.

216   "Do I feel this": Ibid., August 25, 1920.

"I was happy to hear": Ibid., December 12, 1920.

"plucked out": Ibid., December 19, 1920.

"is that Virginia lives": Vanessa Bell, *Selected Letters*, October 10, 1936.

217   "like a little strip": *VWD II*, October 25, 1920.

"Victoria Worms": *VWL II*, January 25, 1921.

"quite magnificent": Ibid., April 17, 1921.

"a damp firework": *VWD II*, April 8, 1921.

218   "And suppose": Ibid., April 10, 1921.

"the Daily Mail": Ibid., May 3, 1921.

"newly found chapters": *VWL II*, April 14, 1922.

219   "I have made up": *VWD II*, February 18, 1922.

"God knows what": *VWL II*, May 18, 1922.

"So I'm having": May 21, 1922.

"He sang it": *VWD II*, June 23, 1922.

220   "Oh if I could": *VWL II*, May 6, 1922.

"Never did I read": Ibid., August 24, 1922.

221   "season of doubts": *VWD II*, June 23, 1922.

"amazingly well written": Ibid., July 26, 1922.

"not a third": Ibid., August 16, 1922.

"thin and pointless": Ibid., September 6, 1922.

"intelligent review": Ibid., September 7, 1922.

"We think *Jacob's Room*": Ibid., October 4, 1922.

222   "I can't bear people": Ibid., October 14, 1922.

"I breathe more freely": *VWL II*, October 10? 1922.

"and now I look": Ibid., November 1, 1922.

"rambling, redundant affair": *M&M*, 110.

223   "Your novel gave me": Ibid., 15.

"character without realism": *VWL II*, October 20, 1922.

"not vitally survive": *M&M*, 113.

"muzzy headed": *VWD II*, December 15, 1922.

224   "connected with literature": *VWL III*, February 12, 1923.

"He had tried": Ibid., February 24, 1923.

"Do you think": Ibid., March 13, 1923.

"had more spunk": *VWD II*, February 19, 1923.

"one feel that he": Ibid., March 6, 1923.

225   "his tragedy": Ibid., May 12, 1923.

"in one of my moods": Ibid., January 2, 1923.

"Katherine has been dead": Ibid., January 16, 1923.

"Please read Katherine's": *VWL III*, July 30, 1923.

226 "Virginia seemed": Ibid., 23 headnote.

"Here we are with": Ibid., May 13, 1923.

"simultaneously": Ibid., July 8, 1923.

". . . now I'm writing fiction": *VWD II*, June 19, 1923.

227 "to bring in": Ibid., June 4, 1923.

"For the truth is": *MD*, 99.

"mind squint": *VWD II*, June 19, 1923.

"the 100th page": Ibid., October 15, 1923.

228 "mute and mitigated": Ibid., June 28, 1923.

229 "dirt and dust": *VWL III*, March 18, 1924.

"If so, what and when": Ibid., May 21, 1924.

"Knole crushed me": Ibid., July 6, 1924.

"chairs that Shakespeare": *VWD II*, July 5, 1924.

230 "I was 13": Ibid., May 5, 1924.

"with my childlike": *VWL III*, September 15, 1924.

"I enjoyed your intimate": Ibid., August 19, 1924.

"as copy": *VSW/VW*, July 16, 1924.

231 "Vita was here": *VWD II*, September 15, 1924.

"practice equanimity": *LW IV*, 51–57.

233 "foundation of good fiction": *M&M*, 113.

"at life, human nature": "Mr. Bennett and Mrs. Brown," *The Captain's Death Bed,* 94–119.

"The method of writing": *VWD III*, February 12, 1927.

234 "There are splashes": In *QB II*, 106–7.

"the falsity of the past": *VWL III*, October 3, 1924.

235 "on or about December 1910": "Mr. Bennett and Mrs. Brown," 96.

"a series of gig lamps": "Modern Fiction," *Common Reader*, 189.

"We must reflect": "Mr. Bennett and Mrs. Brown," 117.

236 "on page 259": In *QB II*, 106.

238 "on the lips": *MD*, 40.

"busy": Ibid., 30.

"('Septimus, do put . . . ')": Ibid., 98.

239 "using nothing but": *VWD II*, September 7, 1924.

"But how entirely": Ibid., September 29, 1924.

"galloping": Ibid., December 13, 1924.

"putting on a spurt": Ibid., December 21, 1924.

240 "monstrous, kicking": *VWL III*, July 25, 1924.

"some intensities": *VWD III*, April 20, 1925.

VITA

243 "I see already": *VWD II*, October 17, 1924.

"Here I conceive": *VWD III*, January 6, 1925.

"I can only note": Ibid., May 8, 1925.

"I can't write": *VWL III*, July 27, 1925.

"All that a man": A. B. Goldenveizer, *Talks with Tolstoi*, trans. S. S. Koteliansky and Virginia Woolf (London: Hogarth Press, 1923), 137.

"far the greatest": *VWL III*, April 21, 1927.

244   "Since I wrote": *VWD III*, April 8, 1925.

"I have at last": Ibid., April 20, 1925.

"lovely place full": Ibid., May 4, 1925.

"I'm now all on": Ibid., May 14, 1925.

"(how I begin to love)": Ibid., December 7, 1925.

245   "to grasp the whole": Ibid., May 17, 1925.

"Here I salute": Ibid., June 14, 1925.

"sober and sensible": Ibid., May 9, 1925.

"combination of brilliance": *M&M*, 151.

"old gentlemen": *VWL III*, May 31, 1925.

"but then has he": *VWD III*, January 6, 1925.

"without bursting": *VWL III*, May 1, 1925.

"bewildering jumble": *Western Mail*, May 14, 1925.

"None but the mentally fit": *The Scotsman*, May 14, 1925.

246   "proficient in the difficult": *The Independent*, June 20, 1925.

"I shan't answer your": *VWL III*, June 14, 1925.

"without seeing": *VWD III*, January 6, 1925.

"so much admired": Ibid., May 17, 1925.

"I'm the only woman": Ibid., September 22, 1925.

"I never ask a soul": Ibid., July 19, 1925.

247   "superstitious wish": Ibid., July 20, 1925.

"that odd amphibious": Ibid., September 5, 1925.

"tumbled into bed": Ibid., November 27, 1925.

"I could lie down": "Stanzas Written in Dejection near Naples."

248   "Most children": *VWD III*, December 7, 1925.

"A peaceful evening": *VWL III*, 223 headnote.

"These Sapphists *love*": *VWD III*, December 21, 1925.

249   "I have missed you": *VWL III*, January 26, 1926.

"virginal, savage": Ibid., December 26, 1924.

252   "father and mother": *VWD III*, July 20, 1925.

"... things are crowding": *VWL III*, February 3, 1926.

253   "Holy Ghost": Ibid., March 29, 1926.

"As for the *mot juste*": Ibid., March 16, 1926.

"I don't want to press": Ibid., May 22, 1926.

254   "I cannot make it out": *VWD III*, April 18, 1926.

"Oh my dear": In *VSW/VW*, Introduction, 26.

"How long ought we": *VWD III*, July 25, 1926.

255   "easily within sight": Ibid., September 3, 1926.

"I had meant to end": Ibid., September 5, 1926.

256   "shut up": Ibid., September 28, 1926.

"quicker, keener at 44": Ibid., November 23, 1926.

257   "but I tell you": *VWL III*, November 19, 1926.

"Damn the woman": In *VSW/VW*, Introduction, 28.

258   "I am glad that": Ibid., 177 n. 1.

"that putty faced": *VWD III*, November 23, 1926.

"I don't know how": *VSW/VW*, January 28, 1927.

259   "I shall work so hard": Ibid., January 29, 1927.

"We got slightly merry": *VWL III*, February 18, 1927.

"It's off": Ibid., February 16, 1927.

". . . I have bought a coil": Ibid., April 5, 1927.

260   "the chief coquette": Ibid., February 23, 1927.

"I've got to buy": Ibid., March 27, 1927.

261   "the Lord who had come": *MD*, 29.

"noticed my melancholy": *VWL III*, March 15, 1927.

"swollen, affable": Ibid., March 5, 1927.

"ever sells a picture": Ibid., February 17, 1926.

262   "Lawrence pierced": Ibid., April 9, 1927.

"I wonder how": Ibid., 365 n. 3.

"I should make": Ibid., April 21, 1927.

263   "We had a terrible": Vanessa Bell, *Selected Letters*, May 3, 1927.

"I could think": *VWL III*, May 8, 1927.

"Of course nothing": Ibid., May 1, 1927.

"I should be much": Ibid., May 8, 1927.

"Clive simply raved": Ibid., 370 n. 1.

264   "I can never believe": Ibid., May 25, 1927.

"how lovely some parts": *VWD III*, March 21, 1927.

265   "dazzled and bewitched": *VSW/VW*, May 12, 1927.

"Do you think it": *VWL III*, May 13, 1927.

"You're no longer": Ibid., 385 n. 2.

"I am immensely glad": Ibid., May 27, 1927.

"I'm sure that there's": In *QB II*, 129.

266   "I meant *nothing*": *VWL III*, May 27, 1927.

Implicit in the changed: See Leaska, *The Novels of Virginia Woolf*, 154–56.

267   "life did not consist": *TTL* 186.

"the best book": *M&M*, 200–1.

268   "when at last": Ibid., 207–8.

"On the backs": *VWD III*, July 23, 1927.

"24 hours": *VWL III*, July 22, 1927.

269   "I have been wobbling": Ibid., July 24, 1927.

"spent motoring": Ibid., July 23, 1927.

"the bloody thing": Ibid., August 3, 1927.

"Back from Long Barn": *VWD III*, July 4, 1927.

"Darling, it makes me": *VSW/VW*, May 12, 1927.

271   "rung on the ladder": *VWL V*, February 15, 1935.

"Do you know": *VSW/VW*, June 11, 1927.

272 "You see I was reading": *VWL III*, June 14, 1927.
  "gambolling": Ibid., July 4, 1927.
  "called Orlando": *VWD III*, October 5, 1927.
  "thrilled and terrified": *VSW/VW*, October 11, 1927.

273 "Never do I leave you": *VWL III*, October 13, 1927.
  "I would never break": *VSW/VW*, October 11, 1927.
  "If you've given": *VWL III*, October 13, 1927.

274 "I'm not afraid": Ibid., October 21, 1927.
  "You made me feel": Ibid., November 11, 1927.
  "Promiscuous you are": Ibid., July 25, 1928.
  "many years before": *VWD II*, 126 n. 2.

275 "I find it difficult": *VSW/VW*, January 30, 1928.
  "poor Tom Eliot": *VWL III*, February 11, 1928.
  "knocked about": Ibid., May 25, 1928.
  "He is in search": Ibid., March 25, 1928.
  "The futility of it all": *VWD III*, February 11, 1928.
  "not a drop came": Ibid., February 18, 1928.
  "begun 8th October": Ibid., March 18, 1928.

276 "frivolous": Ibid., March 22, 1928.
  "10 pages daily": Ibid., April 24, 1928.
  "Did you feel": *VWL III*, March 20? 1928.
  "smacked me in public": *VWD III*, April 17, 1928.
  "I sometimes wonder": *VWL III*, April 21, 1928.
  "I always said": Ibid., April 17, 1928.

277 "insulted Vita": Ibid., February 11, 1928.
  "Thief, liar": *VWD III*, April 21, 1928.
  "all their characters": *VWL III*, May 9, 1928.
  "So sick of Orlando": *VWD III*, June 20, 1928.

278 "You must take me": *VWL III*, June 7, 1928.
  "her dozen lives": *VWD III*, June 20, 1928.
  "my show dog prize": *VWL III*, May 2, 1928.
  "Mrs Nicolson and Mrs Woolf": Ibid., May 4, 1928.
  "I remember your mother": *VWD III*, May 4, 1928.

279 "galloped through": *VWL III*, November 19? 1927.
  "I am enough": Ibid., November 1927.
  "very superficial": *VWD III*, May 31, 1928.

280 "the mouthpiece of Sapphism": *VWL III*, September 8, 1928.
  "You see": Ibid., September 16, 1928.
  "This is written": *VWD III*, September 22, 1928.
  "had a small": *VWL III*, 533 n. 1.
  "Vita is a perfect": Ibid., September 28, 1928.
  "Virginia is very sweet": Ibid., 533 headnote.
  "In the middle": Ibid., 538 n. 1.
  "I have seen": Ibid., October 7, 1928.

A ROOM OF HER OWN

283	"a small cheque": *VWL III*, October 7, 1928.
	"My darling, I am in no fit": *VSW/VW*, October 11, 1928.
284	"Orlando has filled me": *VWL III*, 548 n. 1.
	"Orlando at the end": *M&M*, 232–33.
	"You have written some": *VWL III*, 548 n. 2.
	"You made me": *VSW/VW*, October 11, 1928.
	"exhibit the most": *VWL III*, March 6, 1928.
285	"to write one little book": *Orlando* (London: Hogarth Press, 1928), 77.
	"Desire for fame": Ibid., 76.
	"Darling, you are my anchor": *VSW/VW*, November 29, 1928.
286	"There seems no doubt": Roger Fry, *Letters* I, November 3, 1928.
	"Roger is the only": *VWL III*, December 27, 1928.
287	"agreeable luxurious": *VWD III*, December 18, 1928.
288	"let me have one line": *VWL III*, December 31, 1928.
	" 'Joy's life's in the doing' "*VWD III*, October 27, 1928.
	"How odd to think": Ibid., January 4, 1929.
	"You have the children": *VWL III*, June 2, 1926.
289	"We spent one of": In *QB II*, 142.
	"feelings to which": *VSW/VW*, January 25, 1929.
290	"The giddiness lasted": *LWL*, January 28, 1929.
	"It's odd how I want": *VWL IV*, January 29, 1929.
	"I'm afraid I shall be": Ibid., January 30, 1929.
	"I've had this sort": Ibid., February 4, 1929.
	"a state of nervous": Ibid., February 7, 1929.
291	"I can't believe": *VSW/VW*, February 6, 1929.
	"sitting up like a woman": *VWL IV*, February 19, 1929.
	"I am going to enter": *VWD III*, March 28, 1929.
292	"And 7 people": Ibid., April 13, 1929.
	"get some pull": Ibid., May 15, 1929.
	"Now about this book": Ibid., May 28, 1929.
	"where he has been": *VWL IV*, May 11, 1929.
	"asking me to lunch": Ibid., May 18, 1929.
293	"a delicious life": Ibid., May 6, 1929.
	"almost overpowering": *VWD III*, June 15, 1929.
294	"I daresay he'll give": *VWL IV*, April 24, 1929.
	"intimate things": *VWD III*, October 13, 1929.
	"Now if you sometimes": *VWL IV*, June 25, 1929.
	"I would rather fail": *VSW/VW*, August 21, 1928.
	"Whether it is the mere beauty": Ibid., February 5, 1929.
295	"Lord, how deep": *VWD III*, June 23, 1929.
	"I must grind on": Ibid., May 15, 1929.

296 "This is perhaps not": *VSW/VW*, July 24, 1929.
"that her story": *VWD III*, August 10, 1929.
"I've had to retire": *VWL IV*, August 12, 1929.

297 "was a trumpet call": Ibid., November 3, 1929.
"I'm not writing": *VWD III*, October 11, 1929.

298 ". . . you might like me": *VWL IV*, January 30, 1930.
"She has descended": Ibid., February 27, 1930.
"brisk tramp": *VWD III*, February 21, 1930.

299 "and I am only": *VWL IV*, April 6, 1930.
"What about marriage": Ibid., March 15, 1930.
"And I heard stories": Ibid., June 22, 1930.
"Oh you can't think": Ibid., February 17, 1930.
"about £3,020 last year": *VWD III*, January 26, 1930.

300 "Odd as it may seem": *VWL IV*, 163 n. 1.
"hauling in money": Ibid., June 8, 1930.
"And it is not": *VWD III*, June 16, 1930.
"We have passed": *VWL IV*, July 4, 1930.
"Lord! What a go!": Ibid., July 8, 1930.
"incredible ease": Ibid., July 27, 1930.
"I don't see any reason": Ibid., August 9, 1930.

301 "unnatural": *VWD III*, August 25, 1930.
"old fires of Sapphism": Ibid., June 6, 1930.
"the usual chaos": *VWL IV*, July 16, 1930.
"If I were ill": Ibid., August 15, 1930.

302 "I can't conceive": Ibid., September 19, 1930.
"and only a little": Ibid., July 1, 1930.
"If this don't stop": *VWD III*, September 2, 1930.
"like a mulish pony": *VWL IV*, September 1, 1930.
"valiant": *VWD III*, September 2, 1930.

303 "Tell me all you do": *VWL IV*, September 11, 1930.
"self-absorbed": In *QB II*, 151–52.
"most complex": *VWD III*, March 28, 1930.

304 "What I now think": Ibid., April 9, 1930.
"Rarely, rarely comest": Ibid., September 4, 1927.
"There is the puddle": *TW*, 113.

305 "dramatic soliloquies": *VWD III*, August 20, 1930.
"with a new picture": Ibid., September 8, 1930.
"It occurred to me": Ibid., December 22, 1930.
"old Ethel": *VWL IV*, November 2, 1930.

306 "This sounded ominous": Ibid., November 8, 1930.
"Was there ever such": *VWD III*, November 8, 1930.
"unmistakably": *VWL IV*, November 8, 1930.

307 "a sequel to": *VWD IV*, January 20, 1931.
"I was interested": In *Pargiters*, xxxiv–xxxv.
"I wrote the words": *VWD IV*, February 7, 1931.

309	"culminating point": *QB II*, 158.
	"chatter and clatter": *VWL IV*, March 11, 1931.
310	"I look at you": Ibid., April 1, 1931.
	"Arnold Bennett died": *VWD IV*, March 28, 1931.
	"Lord, how you'd laugh": *VWL IV*, April 24, 1931.
	"Almost enough castles": Ibid., April 27, 1931.
	"Rang at Castle door" *VWD IV*, April 25, 1931.
311	"Rusty toned": Ibid., April 27, 1931.
	"This requires some": Ibid., May 13, 1931.
	"stamping like a dragoon": *VWL IV*, May 23, 1931.
312	"flashes of light": *VWD IV*, May 28, 1931.
	"like pilchards": *VWL IV*, June 11, 1931.
	"Potto is dead": Ibid., July 25, 1931.
313	"remorseless fangs": *VWD IV*, March 9, 1931.
	"sordid and ridiculous": Ibid., June 30, 1931.
	"I had the sense": *VWL IV*, July 4, 1931.
	"which lasted 20 minutes": *VWD IV*, July 7, 1931.
	"Lord! how I like": *VWL IV*, July 7, 1931.
314	"Leonard will read it": *VWD IV*, July 17, 1931.
	"a masterpiece": Ibid., July 19, 1931.
	"never, never to be": Ibid., August 17, 1931.
	"—a whole flower": *TW*, 91.
	"Lord!": *VWL IV*, September 11, 1931.
315	"I mean John Lehmann": *VWD IV*, September 15, 1931.
	"I'm like a bee": Ibid., September 16, 1931.
	"What I want": Ibid., September 22, 1931.
	"as real an experience": Vanessa Bell, *Selected Letters*, October 15? 1931.
	"perpetual and universal": *M&M*, 271.
	"What you say": *VWL IV*, October 27, 1931.
316	"It's difficult to express": *VWD IV*, November 16, 1931.
	"the first 100 pages": Ibid., October 17, 1931.
	"perfectly fearful": Ibid., 53 n. 5.
	" 'received' than any": Ibid., October 9, 1931.
	"one accord, here is": Ibid., October 17, 1931.
	"Everybody's taken to": *VWL IV*, October 29, 1931.
	"belonged to an age": *Two Cheers for Democracy* (New York: Harcourt Brace & World, 1942), 253–54.
	"There is the puddle": *TW*, 113.
317	". . . Percival is dead": *Virginia Woolf, The Waves, the Two Holograph Drafts*, ed. John Graham, (Toronto: University of Toronto Press, 1976), 258–59 (draft 1).
	"another important": *QB II*, 130.
	"I had once said to her": *LW V*, 95.
318	"repetitive and tedious": *VWD IV*, June 23, 1931.
	"a masterpiece": *New Statesman & Nation*, October 17, 1931.
	"their orders from": *VWD IV*, October 23, 1931.

319 "I seem to have lived": *VWL IV*, December 23, 1931.
"whizz into extinction": *VWD IV*, December 29, 1931.
"glide into words": *VWL IV*, December 27, 1931.
"to laugh at": *VWD IV*, December 27, 1931.
"No . . . I think you": *VWL IV*, December 29, 1931.
"every grade of feeling": *VWD IV*, December 29, 1931.

320 "Oh but Lytton won't": *VWL IV*, January 31, 1932.
"burst into tears": *VWD IV*, March 12, 1932.

PARGETING

325 "Think of me": *VWD IV*, February 29, 1932.
"win the esteem": Ibid., March 3, 1932.

326 "Listen, long ears": *VWL V*, April 1, 1932.
"warm, scattered": Ibid., September 12, 1932.

327 "Yes, but what": *VWD IV*, April 21, 1932.
"shower bath of erudition": *VWL V*, May 1, 1932.
"intellectual and moral": Ibid., April 19, 1932.
"too many olives": Ibid., May 2, 1932.

328 "how we've been off": Ibid., May 8, 1932.
"in search of some herb": *VWD IV*, May 2, 1932.
"And I could love Greece": Ibid., May 8, 1932.
"You bring it directly": *APA*, 313.
"Already my mind": *VWD IV*, May 15, 1932.

329 "It is perhaps true": Ibid., May 17, 1932.
"by way of proving": Ibid., February 16, 1932.
"wonderful woe-receiver": John Lehmann, *Thrown to the Woolfs* (London: Weidenfeld and Nicolson, 1978), 37.
"the irascible Leonard": *VWD IV*, May 17, 1932.

330 "as if it were": John Lehmann, *Thrown to the Woolfs*, 33.
"The question of any": Ibid., 36.
"My advice is": *VWD IV*, June 18, 1932.

331 "highly respectable": *VWL V*, March 20, 1932.
"No, I've not read": Ibid., October 26, 1932.
"vain though I am": Ibid., November 10, 1932.
"I have not studied": Ibid., March 19, 1932.

332 "How can you learn": In *The Death of the Moth and Other Essays* (New York: Harcourt Brace Jovanovich, 1974), 223.
"I admit": *VWL V*, July 31, 1932.
". . . they say Julian's": *VWD IV*, February 26, 1932.
"I don't think it much": *VWL V*, March 14? 1932.
"screwed up into a ball": *VWD IV*, May 25, 1932.

333 "How my brain": Ibid., May 26, 1932.
"curious sensation": Ibid., July 8, 1932.

"no sense of glory": Ibid., July 11, 1932.

"Here I am in bed": *VWL V*, August 14, 1932.

"I was looking": Ibid., August 18, 1932.

"nerve exhaustion": Ibid., November 8, 1932.

"long-drawn-out": John Lehmann, *Thrown to the Woolfs*, 37.

334   "blessing": *VWD IV*, September 2, 1932.

"Pinka and I": *VWL V*, October 18, 1932.

"I've just bought": Ibid., October 13, 1932.

"Oh I was in such": Ibid., October 18, 1932.

335   "I feel that": *VWD IV*, September 16, 1932.

"a very small crumb": *VWL V*, July 7, 1932.

"this moment": *VWD IV*, January 20, 1931.

336   "THE PARGITERS: An Essay": *Pargiters*, Introduction, vii–xix.

338   "For though both truths": "The New Biography," *Granite and Rainbow* (New York: Harcourt Brace Jovanovich, 1975), 154.

"silly": *VWD IV*, April 29, 1933.

"torrent of fact": Ibid., December 19, 1932.

"Today I finished": Ibid., February 2, 1933.

339   "marriage of granite": *Granite and Rainbow*, 155.

340   "an unattractive land": *VWL V*, January 7, 1933.

"all those virgins": Ibid., March 18, 1933.

"being a snail": Ibid., February 19, 1933.

"an aggressive": Ibid., August 7, 1933.

"I hate it": Ibid., June 6, 1933.

"with uncomfortable": *VWD IV*, January 15, 1933.

"connive at all": Ibid., March 25, 1933.

"polite": Ibid., March 28, 1933.

341   "I've written myself": Ibid., April 6, 1933.

"a terrific affair": Ibid., April 25, 1933.

"write for 4 months": Ibid., May 31, 1933.

"By God's grace": Ibid., September 23, 1933.

342   "That old woman": Nigel Nicolson, *Portrait of a Marriage* (New York: Atheneum, 1973), 185.

"libel, wrongful dismissal": *VWL V*, 216 n. 2.

"Yes, Vivienne seems": Ibid., July 20, 1933.

"paying guest": *VWD IV*, 178 n. 8.

"remarkable letter": *VWL V*, December 31, 1933.

"I looked into your book": Ibid., July 8, 1933.

343   "made Max sick": *VWL II*, December 26, 1915.

"tempted, but alarmed": Ibid., August 1? 1918.

"lured": Ibid., June 20, 1921.

"honest": Ibid., June 25, 1921.

344   "once, swinging": *VWL IV*, May 10, 1930.

"persuade her not to": Ibid., February 16, 1931.

"making out that": Ibid., April 15, 1931.

"a man of genius": Ibid., April 20, 1931.

"a thin exaggerated affair": *VWL V*, November 3, 1932.

"I admit the genius": Ibid., November 8? 1932.

"the refusal of some part": *VWD IV*, August 12, 1933.

"Clearly the mind": *AROO*, 146.

345   "I have just killed": *VWD IV*, August 24, 1933.

"stared down into": *TY*, 92.

"how I laughed": *VWD II*, May 5, 1924.

"turning aside": *VWD IV*, September 12, 1934.

346   "full and calm": Ibid., October 29, 1933.

"I prefer where truth": *Pargiters*, 9.

"Fiction . . . is likely to contain" *AROO*, 7.

347   "Flush, I think": *VWD IV*, September 2, 1933.

"I only want walking": Ibid., August 12, 1933.

"Mary makes love": *VWL V*, September 30, 1933.

"a queer experience": *VWD IV*, October 5, 1933.

"I sat rather": *VWL V*, October 7, 1933.

348   "infinite weariness": *VWD IV*, October 5, 1933.

"charming": Ibid., October 2, 1933.

"entirely beautiful": *M&M*, 321.

"It sometimes produces": *Daily Telegraph*, October 6, 1933.

"coarse yellow feeble": *VWD IV*, October 9, 1933.

". . . the deadly facility": Ibid., 186 n. 16.

"plenty of money": Ibid., October 9, 1933.

"perpetual little": Ibid., October 29, 1933.

349   "rather vainly": Ibid., October 16, 1933.

"Oh such a pang": *VWL V*, November 1, 1933.

"What fun to see you": Ibid., December 13, 1933.

350   "strongly and quietly": *VWD IV*, February 18, 1934.

"a more sordid": *VWL V*, March 5, 1934.

351   "most disagreeable": Ibid., March 29, 1934.

"I cannot describe": *VWD IV*, March 19, 1934.

"so old, so cold": Ibid., March 19, 1934.

352   "Already I am feeling": Ibid., October 11, 1934.

"Is it true": *VWL III*, October 13 [14], 1927.

"I enjoyed your intimate letter": Ibid., August 19, 1924.

"snuff the stinking tallow": Ibid., December 22, 1925.

"Chuck me as often": *VSW/VW*, Introduction, 12.

"scapegoat, the eternal": *MD*, 25.

353   "very hard up": *VWD IV*, January 30, 1934.

"I am much better off": *VWL V*, May 4, 1934.

"Julian is rather": Ibid., March 8, 1934.

354   "ramshackle . . . empty": *VWD IV*, April 30, 1934.

"But why isn't Mrs. F.": Ibid., May 3, 1934.

" 'That was where' ": Ibid., May 9, 1934.

355   "usual incongruous": Ibid., May 1, 1934.

356   "was to turn away": *Pargiters*, 50–51; Woolf deleted the italicized matter.

"waistcoat was often unbuttoned": *MoB* (1985), 112.

"Papa . . . would be": *Pargiters*, 48.

357   ". . . love of father": *Pargiters*, Holograph, VII, dated August 5, 1934, Berg; see also M. Leaska, *The Novels of Virginia Woolf*, 216.

"Now, self-confidence": *VWD IV*, May 18, 1934.

"my cheeks burn": Ibid., September 2, 1934.

"a smash": Ibid., August 21, 1934.

358   "diffidence": *VWL V*, September 23, 1934.

"I feel dazed": *VWD IV*, September 12, 1934.

". . . you happen to have": [11 Oct 1928] in Frances Spalding, *Roger Fry: Art and Life* (Berkeley: University of California Press, 1980), 259.

"I remember turning": *VWD IV*, September 12, 1934.

359   "all very simple": Ibid., September 15, 1934.

"The dreadful thing": *VWL I*, February 28, 1904.

"I can't believe": Ibid., March 1904.

"I still find": *VWL V*, September 23, 1934.

". . . I have felt since": Ibid., September 1934.

359–60 "the exalted sense": *VWD IV*, September 20, 1934.

360   "no tears and exaltation": Ibid., September 30, 1934.

"the old rays": Ibid., October 20, 1934.

"I am publicly": Ibid., October 11, 1934.

"Praise or blame": dated October 9, 1818, to J. A. Hessey. "This is a mere": dated October 14 or 15, 1818, to George and Georgina Keats.

"Perhaps I feel": *VWD IV*, October 11, 1934.

361   "certain critics": *M&M*, 331.

"blackness": *VWD IV*, October 15, 1934.

"I was I remember": Ibid., October 17, 1934.

"an immense relief": Ibid., October 15, 1934.

"I'm so ugly": Ibid., October 17, 1934.

"This is a book": *M&M*, 340.

"I have Leonard": *VWD IV*, November 2, 1934.

"And am now, 10.30": Ibid., November 15, 1934.

362   "like a formidable hen": Ibid., November 27, 1934.

"All this he knows": Ibid., December 2, 1934.

"I am pained": *VWL V*, January 8, 1935.

363   "I'm longing for": Ibid., February 15, 1935.

"A religious soul": *VWD IV*, February 5, 1935.

"I forgot to ask": Ibid., March 31, 1935.

"vast sorrow": Ibid., February 5, 1935.

364   "theoreticians": *M&M*, 348–50.

"on the whole": Ibid., 356–57.

365   "blasts from the": *VWD IV*, March 18, 1935.

"severe swingeings": Ibid., March 16, 1935.

"Leonard's nose": *VWL V*, April 18, 1935.

"since our Jewishness": Ibid., April 26, 1935.

366   "all desire": *VWD IV*, April 27, 1935.

"his distinguished wife": *LW IV*, 186.

"wherever we went": Ibid., 189.

"When they saw Mitz": Ibid., 191–93.

367   "d _____ d nonsense": *VWL V*, June 2, 1935.

"how I'm disliked": *VWD IV*, May 26, 1935.

"How insipid life": Ibid., May 29, 1935.

"So that's what's": Ibid., May 31, 1935.

"I can't get into": Ibid., June 1, 1935.

"Every time I say": Ibid., June 5, 1935.

"incurable moods": *VWL V*, June 6, 1935.

"hard on people": *VWD IV*, June 25, 1935.

368   "touchy": Ibid., September 6, 1935.

"full grown mature": Ibid., July 17, 1935.

"child being covered": *VWL V*, June 21, 1935.

"please love me": Ibid., July 3, 1935.

"first wild retyping": *VWD IV*, July 17, 1935.

"reconciliation": Ibid., August 3, 1935.

"indignation": John Lehmann, *Thrown to the Woolfs*, 57.

"most stodgy": *VWL V*, July 17, 1935.

369   "a whole big life": Ibid., December 9, 1935.

"I've had to give up": *VWD IV*, September 5, 1935.

"never have I had": Ibid., September 12, 1935.

"I will broach": Ibid., September 15, 1935.

"admirable sedative": Ibid., October 22, 1935.

"like being harnessed": Ibid., October 27, 1935.

370   "can't concentrate": Ibid., November 1, 1935.

"almost extinct": Ibid., December 28, 1935.

"another creative mood": Ibid., December 29, 1935.

"I can't write": Ibid., December 30, 1935.

371   "hoard": *VWD V*, January 3, 1936.

"I could only": Ibid., January 16, 1936.

"when you've struck": Ibid., January 28, 1936.

"a kind of amplification": Ibid., February 29, 1936.

372   "Old greybearded": *VWL VI*, January 23, 1936.

"deluged in tears": Ibid., January 30, 1936.

"are at this moment": Ibid., February 8, 1936.

373   "all day, every day": Ibid., March 10, 1936.

"The horror is": *VWD V*, April 9, 1936.

"complete flop": *VWL VI*, March 11, 1936.

"befogged, utterly vacant": Ibid., April 14, 1936.

"cursed irritable": Ibid., May 2, 1936.

374   "intense suffering": *VWD V*, June 21, 1936.

"...we [the daughters of": *Three Guineas*, 233–34.

375   "one of those typical": *Pargiters*, 9.

376   "Miracles will never": *VWD V*, November 3, 1936.

"extraordinarily good": Ibid., November 4, 1936.

"Leonard put down": Ibid., November 5, 1936.

377   "not absolutely": *LW IV*, 155.

"from death": *VWD V*, November 24, 1936.

"bodily two enormous": *LW IV*, 156.

"There is no need": *VWD V*, November 30, 1936.

" 'Prince Edward speaking' ": Ibid., December 13, 1936.

378   "...all those scattered": *VWL VI*, December 6, 1936.

379   "...d'you think it's": Ibid., December 27, 1936.

"work, work, work": *VWD V*, January 10, 1937.

"dull cold torture": Ibid., March 2, 1937.

"I must face": Ibid., February 12, 1937.

"people looked at me": Ibid., February 15, 1937.

380   "very small, red cheeked": Ibid., February 21, 1937.

"fatal day": Ibid., March 10, 1937.

"I must dig myself": Ibid., January 29, 1937.

"a maker of films": Ibid., February 18, 1937.

"tired book ...": Ibid., February 20, 1937.

"Probably people": Holograph Vol. VII, Berg.

"I wish I could": *VWD V*, March 1, 1937.

381   "doomed, discarded": Ibid., March 10, 1937.

"I'm going to be": Ibid., March 2, 1937.

"damned with faint": Ibid., March 7, 1937.

382   "Oh the relief!": Ibid., March 12, 1937.

"in contact not only": *M&M*, 367.

"a brilliant fantasia": Ibid., 370.

"*not* nonsense": *VWD V*, March 12, 1937.

"I am in such a": Ibid., March 14, 1937.

384   " 'they' say almost": Ibid., March 19, 1937.

"Dead and disappointing": Ibid., April 2, 1937.

"That is the achievement": Ibid., April 9, 1937.

"family complex": Ibid., March 14, 1937.

385   "peppery and pithy": Ibid., April 15, 1937.

"only a vague literary": Ibid., May 4, 1937.

"So, a strain": Ibid., June 11, 1937.

"Spaniards flying": Ibid., June 23, 1937.

386   Bilbao fell on: Ibid., 97 n. 16.

"Today they are": Ibid., July 19, 1937.

389 "It has been an": *VWL VI*, July 26? 1937.
   "an accident": *VWD V*, August 6, 1937.

390 "every sort of gift": *VWL VI*, July 26? 1937.
   "I was hurt": In *QB II*, Appendix C, 258 n.

391 "I shall be cheerful": *VWD V*, August 6, 1937.
   "extraordinary extinction": Ibid., September 26, 1937.
   "in the brain": Ibid., August 17, 1937.
   "never force himself": Ibid., September 2, 1937.
   "I think it's *much*": Vanessa Bell, *Selected Letters*, November 1, 1935.

392 "I've found out": *Julian Bell: Essays, Poems and Letters* (London: Hogarth Press,
   1938), 114.
   Both letters: Ibid., 194–96.
   "rather fun . . .": Ibid.
   "the utmost openness": *VWL VI*, 192 n. 3.

394 "anxious to explain": *VWD V*, August 25, 1937.
   "Yes, I'll come": *VWL VI*, August 1937.
   "My love has always": Ibid., August 12, 1937.
   ". . . I'm more nearly": Ibid., August 17, 1937.
   "I wish my dolphin": Ibid., August 5, 1937.
   "is demonstrative": Ibid., xv.
   "I want to see you": Ibid., August 23, 1937.

395 "when you're not": Ibid., October 2, 1937.
   "Please don't exhaust": Vanessa Bell, *Selected Letters*, September 9, 1937.
   "Isn't it odd": *VWL VI*, October 1, 1937.
   a metaphoric hedge: M. Leaska, *Virginia Woolf's Lighthouse: A Study in Critical
   Method* (London: Hogarth Press, 1970), 116–20.
   "When Thoby died": *VWD V*, October 12, 1937.
   " 'You alone . . . ' ": R. L. Stevenson, "In Memoriam F.A.S.," verse 3.
   "Thank God": *VWL VI*, October 3, 1937.
   "querulous sometimes": *VWD V*, November 1, 1937.

396 "for a handful": Ibid., November 30, 1937.
   "Heaven above us": *VWL VI*, December 26? 1937.
   ". . . with this knife": Ibid., 195 n. 2.

397 "I'm so beside myself": Ibid., January 14, 1938.
   "incessant writing": *VWD V*, January 9, 1938.
   "gravely": Ibid., February 4, 1938.
   "ward off the old": Ibid., March 22, 1938.
   "I suspect": Ibid., April 12, 1938.
   "let alone that I": *VWL VI*, March 11, 1938.

398 "Leonard was very": John Lehmann, *Thrown to the Woolfs*, 59–60.
   "I'm full of": *VWL VI*, April 22, 1938.
   "I am sorry": in John Lehmann, *Thrown to the Woolfs*, 60.

399 "some short account": *VWD V*, 135 n. 6.

"Odd how the sense": Ibid., April 27, 1938.

"I was self-conscious": Ibid., May 25, 1938.

"the solid world": Ibid., May 20, 1938.

400 "like a spider's web": Ibid., April 29, 1938.

"How can one cut": Ibid., May 3, 1938.

"very angry reviews": Ibid., May 30, 1938.

"with rapture": Ibid., 147 n. 17.

"face the music": Ibid., May 31, 1938.

"the most brilliant": *Times Literary Supplement*, June 4, 1938.

"You are a tantalising": *VSW/VW*, June 15, 1938.

401 "You say you don't": *VWL VI*, June 19, 1938.

"Letters . . . from that": Ibid., August 29, 1938.

"vocal pacifism": Ibid., July 4, 1938.

"attempt to involve": *QB II*, 205.

402 On September 7: *VWD V*, 167 n. 5.

On September 15: *VWL VI*, 274 n. 1.

The conference met: Harold Nicolson, *Diaries and Letters: 1930–1939*, ed. Nigel Nicolson (New York: Atheneum, 1966), 356.

403 "They're telling us": *VWD V*, September 28, 1938.

"I suppose they were": *VWL VI*, October 1, 1938.

"We came back": Ibid., October 3, 1938.

404 "peace without honour": Ibid., October 1, 1938.

"All the morning": *VWD V*, August 29, 1938.

"not much in detail": *VWL VI*, August 31, 1938.

". . . what Roger Fry could": Virginia Woolf, *Roger Fry: A Biography* (London: Hogarth Press, 1940), 96.

"What am I to say": *VWL VI*, October 8, 1938.

405 "crowing over": Ibid., October 18, 1938.

"cursed biography": Ibid., October 13, 1938.

"euphemise 20 different": Ibid., January 20, 1937.

"the truth about": Ibid., September 18, 1937.

"It was very": Ibid., December 25, 1938.

406 "great silent solid": *VWD V*, January 30, 1939.

"Dr Freud gave me": Ibid., January 29, 1939.

406–7 "old fashioned way . . .": *LW IV*, 168–69.

407 "monologist": *VWD V*, March 22, 1939 and n. 15.

"very bad": Ibid., March 29, 1939.

"gave me a full": Ibid., March 30, 1939.

408 "I like some of": *VWL VI*, March 19, 1940.

"As to my book . . .": *VWD V*, March 26, 1940.

409 "innumerable doubts": Ibid., March 11, 1939.

in violation of: *VWL VI*, 326 n. 1.

"At the moment": Ibid., April 17, 1939.

"I'm afraid it's": Ibid., October 1, 1939.

"The thing is": Ibid., December 31, 1939.

410   "the worst of all": *VWD V*, September 6, 1939.

"terrible passive": Ibid., June 28, 1939.

"Virginia must write": Ibid., July 3, 1939.

"What was she like": Ibid., July 6, 1939.

411   "At least today": *VWL VI*, September 8, 1939.

"headache; guilt": *VWD V*, July 28, 1939.

"Which is going to be": Ibid., July 13, 1939.

"Why am I so": Ibid., March 11, 1939.

"keep off the settling": Ibid., April 11, 1939.

"The Poles vibrating": Ibid., July 11, 1939.

"Roger seems hopeless": Ibid., September 25, 1939.

412   Germany attacked: Ibid., 232 n. 1.

"There's no petrol": Ibid., September 23, 1939.

"I've been slipping": Ibid., October 6, 1939.

"humped with": Ibid., October 22, 1939.

"I'm dumb and chill": *VWL VI*, September 2, 1939.

"shut up quite alone": *VWD V*, December 8, 1939.

413   "Roger a failure": Ibid., November 30, 1939.

"wider scope...": Ibid., December 2, 1939.

"that exciting layer": Ibid., April 11, 1939.

414   "surplus of unused": Ibid., May 31, 1940.

"it'll have no interest": Ibid., January 3, 1940.

"endless objections": *VWL VI*, February 1, 1940.

415   "I mean, if a bomb": *VWD V*, February 2, 1940.

"iridescent man": Ibid., February 9, 1940.

"Since Julian died": Vanessa Bell, *Selected Letters*, March 13, 1940.

"very alive and interesting": *VWD V*, March 20, 1940.

416   "the whole of life did not": *TTL*, 186.

"poor Leonard...": *VWD V*, March 21, 1940.

"...how I long": *VWL VI*, March 12, 1940.

417   "very tiresome piece": *VWD V*, May 6, 1940.

"But though Leonard": Ibid., May 13, 1940.

"suicide if Hitler": Ibid., May 15, 1940.

"and thus have read": Ibid., June 10, 1940.

418   "crimson chair with gilt claws": See M. Leaska, *The Novels of Virginia Woolf*, 203–4.

"playing with words": *VWD V*, May 31, 1940.

"...you've made me feel": *BA*, 179.

419   "huge symbolical figure": *Pointz Hall*, Earlier Typescript, 190.

"I must put my head": *VWD V*, June 10, 1940.

420   "killed": *VWD IV*, August 24, 1933.

"This, I thought": *VWD V*, June 22, 1940.

"outer wall of security": Ibid., June 27, 1940.

"The veil will be": Ibid., July 24, 1940.

421   "What a curious relation": Ibid., July 25, 1940.

NOTES

"an experiment": *VWL VI*, December 31, 1940.

422 "We lay down": *VWD V*, August 16, 1940.
"I'd just put flowers": *VWL VI*, August 30, 1940.
"preserved unashamed": *BA*, 217.

423 "I sometimes think": *VWD V*, September 14, 1940.
"a scuffle": Ibid., September 11, 1940.
"Common History book": Ibid., September 12, 1940.
"grieving and tender": Ibid., May 30, 1940.

424 "And all the air": Ibid., October 2, 1940.
"It's odd to feel": *VWL VI*, September 11, 1940.
"It's difficult": Ibid., March 13, 1941.

427 "Oh my Violet": *VWL I*, May 6? 1904.
"I know I can write": Ibid., September 30, 1904.
"Haddock and sausage": *VWD V*, March 8, 1941.

428 "I'm in a rage": Ibid., September 21, 1940.
"spawn in the village": *VWL VI*, October 1, 1940.
"cold and distant": *VWD V*, September 25, 1940.
"A rather strained": Ibid., September 26, 1940.

429 "Last night a great": Ibid., October 2, 1940.
"If it were not": Ibid., October 12, 1940.
"with a sigh": Ibid., October 20, 1940.
"infinite delight": *VWL VI*, November 15, 1940.
"seep[ed] in": *VWD V*, November 15, 1940.

430 "Anyone with 500": Ibid., November 29, 1940.
"As you can see": *VWL VI*, December 24, 1940.
"I write in haste": Ibid., December 23, 1940.
"I detest the hardness": *VWD V*, December 29, 1940.

431 "calmer and happier": *LW V*, 74.

432 "birds syllabling": *BA*, 245.
"Look your last": *VWD V*, January 9, 1941.
"ground down harshly": *VWL VI*, December 6, 1936.
"a battle against": *VWD V*, January 26, 1941.
"By the time": *VWL VI*, February 1, 1941.

433 "Little donkey": *Pointz Hall*, Later Typescript, 374; *BA*, 182; *Pointz Hall*, 557.
"silly and trivial": *VWL VI*, March 27? 1941.
"But shall I ever": *VWD V*, February 26, 1941.
"Observe perpetually": Ibid., March 8, 1941.

433–34 "I shall lose my child's": Ibid., December 22, 1940.

434 "hidden thoughts": *Common Reader,* 93.
"She had been sorting": Octavia Wilberforce, *The Autobiography of a Pioneer Woman Doctor*, ed. Pat Jalland (London: Cassell, 1989), 166–84.
"without shame": *VWD I*, January 21, 1918.
"remained almost unspeakable": Notes to *The Complete Shorter Fiction of Virginia Woolf*, ed. Susan Dick, 305; see also Lyndall Gordon, *Virginia Woolf: A Writer's Life* (New York: Norton, 1984), 279.

436   "not well": *LW V*, 90–91.

       "take away the pain": *MoB* (1985), 72.

437   "somewhat better": *LW V*, 91.

438   "Will you promise": Octavia Wilberforce, *Autobiography*, 181.

       "We felt": *LW V*, 92–93.

       "I seem to be mentally": *LW III*, 157.

439   large stone: *QB II*, 226.

       "This letter was not": *VWL VI*, 486 n. 3.

SELECTED BIBLIOGRAPHY

Annan, Noel. *Leslie Stephen: The Godless Victorian*. New York: Random House, 1984.

Bell, Clive. *Old Friends: Personal Recollections*. New York: Harcourt, Brace and Company, 1956.

———. *Proust*. New York: Harcourt, Brace and Company, 1929.

Bell, Julian. *Julian Bell: Essays, Poems and Letters*. Ed. Quentin Bell. London: Hogarth Press, 1938.

Bell, Quentin. *Virginia Woolf: A Biography (Volume I: Virginia Stephen, 1882–1912; Volume II: Virginia Woolf, 1912–1941)*. New York: Harcourt Brace Jovanovich, 1972.

Bell, Vanessa. *Notes on Virginia's Childhood: A Memoir*. Ed. R. F. Schaubeck, Jr. New York: Frank Hallman, 1974.

———. *The Selected Letters of Vanessa Bell*. Ed. Regina Marler. New York: Pantheon, 1993.

Caramagno, Thomas C. *The Flight of the Mind: Virginia Woolf's Art and Manic-Depressive Illness*. Berkeley: University of California Press, 1992.

Darroch, Sandra Jobson. *Ottoline: The Life of Lady Ottoline Morrell*. New York: Coward, McCann & Geoghegan, 1975.

Delattre, Floris. "La Durée Bergsonienne dans le roman de Virginia Woolf." *Revue Anglo-Américaine* (December 1931), 97–108.

DeSalvo, Louise. *Virginia Woolf's First Voyage: A Novel in the Making*. Totowa, N.J.: Rowman & Littlefield, 1980.

Edel, Leon. *Stuff of Sleep and Dreams: Experiments in Literary Psychology*. New York: Harper and Row, 1982.

———. *Writing Lives: Principia Biographica*. New York: W. W. Norton, 1984.

Flügel, J. C. *The Psycho-Analytic Study of the Family*. London: Hogarth Press, 1921.

Forster, E. M. *Virginia Woolf* [The Rede Lecture, 1942]. New York: Harcourt, Brace and World, 1951.

Fry, Roger. *Cézanne: A Study of His Development*. New York: Noonday Press, 1958.

———. *The Letters of Roger Fry*. Ed. Denys Sutton. London: Chatto & Windus, 1972.

———. *Vision and Design*. New York: Brentano's, 1925.

Gérin, Winifred. *Anne Thackeray Ritchie: A Biography*. New York: Oxford University Press, 1981.

Ginsberg, Elaine K., and Laura M. Gottlieb, eds. *Virginia Woolf: Centennial Essays*. Troy, N.Y.: Whitson, 1983.

Glendinning, Victoria. *Vita: The Life of V. Sackville-West*. London: Weidenfeld & Nicolson, 1983.

Heilbrun, Carolyn G. *Toward a Recognition of Androgyny*. New York: Knopf, 1973.

Hill, Katherine. "Virginia Woolf and Leslie Stephen: History and Literary Revolution." *PMLA* 96 (May 1981): 351–62.

Holroyd, Michael. *Lytton Strachey: The New Biography*. New York: Farrar, Straus and Giroux, 1994.

Holtby, Winifred. *Virginia Woolf*. London: Wishart, 1932.

Horney, Karen. *Neurosis and Human Growth: The Struggle Toward Self-Realization*. New York: W. W. Norton, 1950.

Hungerford, Edward A. " 'My Tunnelling Process': The Method of *Mrs. Dalloway*." *Modern Fiction Studies* 3 (Summer 1957): 164–67.

Kennedy, Richard. *A Boy at the Hogarth Press*. Harmondsworth: Penguin Books, 1978.

Kirkpatrick, B. J. *A Bibliography of Virginia Woolf*. 3rd ed. Oxford: Clarendon Press, 1980.

Kumar, Shiv K. *Bergson and the Stream of Consciousness Novel*. New York: New York University Press, 1963.

Laffal, Julius. *Pathological and Normal Language*. New York: Atherton, 1965.

Leaska, Mitchell A. *The Novels of Virginia Woolf: From Beginning to End*. London: Weidenfeld and Nicolson, 1977.

————. *Virginia Woolf's Lighthouse: A Study in Critical Method*. London: Hogarth Press, 1970.

————. "Virginia Woolf's *The Voyage Out*: Character Deduction and the Function of Ambiguity." *Virginia Woolf Quarterly* I (Winter 1973): 18–41.

Lehmann, John. *Thrown to the Woolfs*. London: Weidenfeld and Nicolson, 1978.

Maitland, Frederic. *The Life and Letters of Leslie Stephen*. London: Duckworth & Company, 1906; pages 474–76 comprise the "Note" Virginia wrote for Maitland in 1904.

Majumdar, Robin, and Allen McLaurin, eds. *Virginia Woolf: The Critical Heritage*. London: Routledge & Kegan Paul, 1975.

Nicolson, Nigel. *Portrait of a Marriage*. New York: Atheneum, 1973.

Noble, Joan Russell, ed. *Recollections of Virginia Woolf*. New York: William Morrow, 1972.

Oppenheim, Janet. *"Shattered Nerves": Doctors, Patients, and Depression in Victorian England*. New York: Oxford University Press, 1991.

Pederson, Glenn. "Vision in *To the Lighthouse*." *PMLA* 78 (December 1958): 585–600.

Quick, Jonathan R. "Virginia Woolf, Roger Fry and Post-Impressionism." *Massachusetts Review* (Winter 1985), 547–570.

Roberts, John Hawley. " 'Vision and Design' in Virginia Woolf." *PMLA* XLIV (September 1946): 835–47.

Rose, Phyllis. *Woman of Letters: A Life of Virginia Woolf*. New York: Harcourt Brace Jovanovich, 1978.

Rosenbaum, S. P., ed. *The Bloomsbury Group: A Collection of Memoirs, Commentary and Criticism*. Toronto: University of Toronto Press, 1975.

Rosenblatt, Louise M. *Literature as Exploration*. New York: Publications of the Modern Language Association, 1996.

————. *The Reader, the Text, the Poem: The Transactional Theory of the Literary Work*. Carbondale, Ill.: Southern Illinois University Press, 1978.

Sackville-West, Vita. *The Letters of Vita Sackville-West to Virginia Woolf*. Ed. Louise DeSalvo and Mitchell A. Leaska. London: Virago Press, 1992.

Seymour, Miranda. *Ottoline Morrell: Life on the Grand Scale*. New York: Farrar, Straus and Giroux, 1992.

Spalding, Frances. *Roger Fry: Art and Life*. Berkeley: University of California Press, 1980.

———. *Vanessa Bell*. New York: Ticknor & Fields, 1983.

Spater, George, and Ian Parsons. *A Marriage of True Minds*. New York: Harcourt Brace Jovanovich, 1977.

Spilka, Mark. *Virginia Woolf's Quarrel with Grieving*. Lincoln: University of Nebraska Press, 1980.

Stansky, Peter, and William Abrahams. *Journey to the Frontier*. Chicago: University of Chicago Press, 1966.

Stemerick, Martine. "Virginia Woolf: The Distaff Side of History." *Virginia Woolf: Centennial Essays*. Ed. E. K. Ginsberg and L. M. Gottlieb. Troy, N.Y.: Whitson, 1983.

Stephen, Julia. *Julia Duckworth Stephen: Stories for Children and Essays for Adults*. Ed. D. F. Gillespie and E. Steele. Syracuse, N.Y.: Syracuse University Press, 1987.

Stephen, Karin. *The Wish to Fall Ill: A Study of Psychoanalysis and Medicine*. Cambridge: Cambridge University Press, 1933.

Stephen, Leslie. *The Life of Sir James Fitzjames Stephen*. London: Smith, Elder, 1895.

Selected Letters of Leslie Stephen. 2 vols. Ed. John W. Bicknell. Columbus: Ohio State University Press, 1996.

———. *Sir Leslie Stephen's Mausoleum Book*. Ed. Alan Bell. Oxford: Clarendon Press, 1977.

Storr, Anthony. *The Dynamics of Creation*. New York: Atheneum, 1972.

Tomlin, Claire. *Katherine Mansfield: A Secret Life*. New York: Knopf, 1988.

Wickes, Frances G. *The Inner World of Childhood*. New York: D. Appleton & Company, 1927.

Wilberforce, Octavia. *The Autobiography of a Pioneer Woman Doctor*. Ed. Pat Jalland. London: Cassell, 1989.

Woolf, Leonard. *Beginning Again: An Autobiography of the Years 1911–1918*. New York: Harcourt Brace Jovanovich, 1964.

———. *Downhill All the Way: An Autobiography of the Years 1919–1939*. New York: Harcourt Brace Jovanovich, 1967.

———. *The Journey Not the Arrival Matters: An Autobiography of the Years 1939–1969*. New York: Harcourt Brace Jovanovich, 1969.

———. *Letters of Leonard Woolf*. Ed. Frederic Spotts. New York: Harcourt Brace Jovanovich, 1989.

THE WORKS OF VIRGINIA WOOLF

———. *The Voyage Out*. London: Hogarth Press, 1915.

———. *Night and Day*. London: Hogarth Press, 1919.

———. *Jacob's Room*. London: Hogarth Press, 1922.

———. *Mrs. Dalloway*. London: Hogarth Press, 1925.

———. *The Common Reader (First Series)*. London: Hogarth Press, 1925.

———. *To the Lighthouse*. London: Hogarth Press, 1927.

————. *Orlando: A Biography*. London: Hogarth Press, 1928.

————. *A Room of One's Own*. London: Hogarth Press, 1929.

————. *The Waves*. London: Hogarth Press, 1931.

————. *The Common Reader (Second Series)*. London: Hogarth Press, 1932.

————. *The Years*. London: Hogarth Press, 1937.

————. *Three Guineas*. London: Hogarth Press, 1938.

————. *Roger Fry: A Biography*. London: Hogarth Press, 1940.

(Posthumously published; for the complete bibliography,
see B. J. Kirkpatrick)

————. *Between the Acts*. London: Hogarth Press, 1941.

————. *A Passionate Apprentice: The Early Journals, 1897–1909*. Ed. Mitchell A. Leaska. London: Hogarth Press; New York: Harcourt Brace Jovanovich, 1990.

————. *The Diary of Virginia Woolf*. Ed. Anne Olivier Bell, assisted by Andrew McNeillie. 5 vols. London: Hogarth Press; New York: Harcourt Brace Jovanovich, 1977–1984.

————. *The Letters of Virginia Woolf*. Ed. Nigel Nicolson and Joanne Trautmann. 6 vols. London: Hogarth Press; New York: Harcourt Brace Jovanovich, 1975–1980.

————. *Moments of Being*. Ed. Jeanne Schulkind. 2nd Ed. New York: Harcourt Brace Jovanovich, 1985.

————. *The Complete Shorter Fiction of Virginia Woolf*. Ed. Susan Dick. New York: Harcourt Brace Jovanovich, 1985.

————. *The Pargiters: The Novel-Essay Portion of* The Years. Ed. Mitchell A. Leaska. London: Hogarth Press; New York: Harcourt Brace Jovanovich, 1977.

————. *Pointz Hall: The Earlier and Later Typescripts of* Between the Acts. Ed. Mitchell A. Leaska. New York: University Publications, 1983.

————. *The Waves: The Two Holograph Drafts*. Ed. J. W. Graham. Toronto: University of Toronto Press, 1976.

————. *The Captain's Death Bed and Other Essays*. New York: Harcourt Brace Jovanovich, 1950.

————. *The Death of the Moth and Other Essays*. New York: Harcourt Brace Jovanovich, 1974.

————. *Granite and Rainbow: Essays*. New York: Harcourt Brace Jovanovich, 1958.

————. *The Moment and Other Essays*. London: Hogarth Press, 1947.

INDEX